Cultural Anthropology

Fourth Canadian Edition

Emily A. Schultz
Robert H. Lavenda
Roberta Robin Dods

OXFORD
UNIVERSITY PRESS

OXFORD
UNIVERSITY PRESS

Oxford University Press is a department of the University of Oxford.
It furthers the University's objective of excellence in research, scholarship,
and education by publishing worldwide. Oxford is a registered trade mark of
Oxford University Press in the UK and in certain other countries.

Published in Canada by
Oxford University Press
8 Sampson Mews, Suite 204,
Don Mills, Ontario M3C 0H5 Canada

www.oupcanada.com

Library and Archives Canada Cataloguing in Publication

Schultz, Emily A. (Emily Ann), 1949-, author
Cultural anthropology : a perspective on the human condition/
Emily A. Schultz, Robert H. Lavenda, Roberta Robin Dods. — Fourth Canadian edition.

Includes bibliographical references and index.
Issued in print and electronic formats.
ISBN 978-0-19-902852-8 (softcover).—ISBN 978-0-19-902374-5 (PDF)

1. Ethnology—Textbooks. 2. Ethnology—Canada—Textbooks.
3. Textbooks. I. Lavenda, Robert H., author II. Dods, Roberta Robin,
author III. Title.

GN316.S38 2018   306   C2017-906734-6
                    C2017-906735-4

Cover and interior design: Laurie McGregor

Oxford University Press is committed to our environment.
Wherever possible, our books are printed on paper which comes from
responsible sources.

Printed and bound in the United States of America

1 2 3 4 — 21 20 19 18

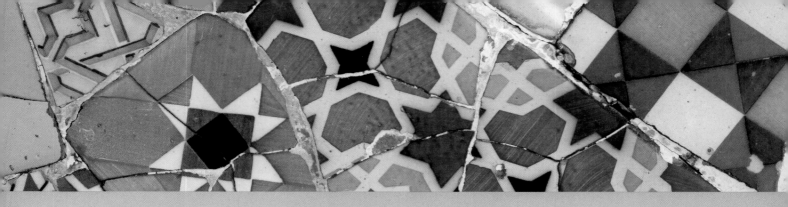

Brief Contents

Contents

PART I | The Tools of Cultural Anthropology I

The Anthropological Perspective on the Human Condition 2

Fieldwork: A Meeting of Cultural Traditions 26

Anthropology in History and the Explanation of Cultural Diversity   50

PART II | The Resources of Culture   75

Language   76

Culture, the Individual, and Identity   96

Inequality in the Contemporary World: Class, Caste, Race, Ethnicity, and Nationality   124

Social Relationships: Marriage, Family, Kinship, and Friendship 150

Making a Living 184

Play, Art, Myth, and Ritual 214

10   States of Being in Wellness and Illness   240

By Roberta Robin Dods

11   World View   274

PART III | Organization of Life: Local to Global   299

Maps

Map 2.1
Sidi Lahcen Lyussi   44

Map 5.4
Cairo   121

Map 8.1
Plains Cree   208

Map 12.3
Bolivian Tin Miners   317

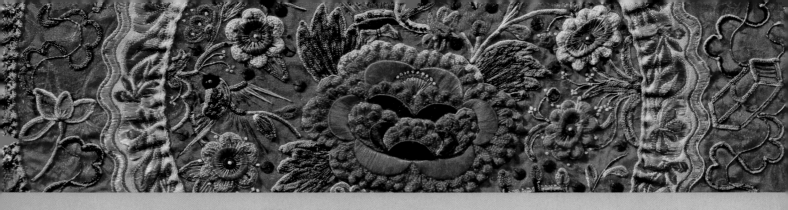

Preface to the Canadian Edition

Roberta Robin Dods

In this fourth Canadian edition of *Cultural Anthropology: A Perspective on the Human Condition*, we continue to situate students in a world view informed by a concern for social justice within a discussion of the discipline of anthropology—specifically, cultural anthropology. As globalization brings us into ever-closer relationships with peoples around the world, the anthropological perspective comes into sharper focus. We are challenged to find our better selves in times of change and upheaval as we consider the complications of living in a world of deep diversity. Of all the disciplines offered in our universities, anthropology is like no other in the opportunity to situate each of us in the better place of understanding ourselves and others.

Some chapters have been reorganized to add new materials but, as with the earlier Canadian editions, the conceptual integrity has been maintained. We continue with the 14-chapter structure, designed to fit the semester system of most Canadian universities. Each chapter begins with an outline and a set of learning objectives and concludes with a list of key terms, a chapter summary, critical thinking questions, and lists of suggested readings and related websites. These framing materials challenge students to integrate learned concepts while providing them with a window to a wider world of inquiry. This edition also contains a new "Living Anthropology" box at the end of most chapters that features insights on topical issues in the field from up-and-coming anthropologists in Canada.

In Chapter 1, the beginning of Part I: The Tools of Cultural Anthropology, we begin with a discussion of anthropology and its four traditional subfields—biological anthropology, archaeology, linguistic anthropology, and cultural anthropology—as well as what could effectively be considered its fifth subfield: applied anthropology. The theme of applied anthropology in its various forms echoes throughout this text. We continue with an introduction to cultural anthropology—its scope and its goals. Further, we explain the concept of culture and examine the critique of its use within a wider historical perspective, and we emerge with an understanding of the efficacy of a holistic approach to anthropological study. We also introduce the methodology of fieldwork and its resulting reportage—ethnography—and conclude with a discussion of ethnocentrism.

We examine ethnographic fieldwork in detail in Chapter 2, offering insight into forms of data collection, ways to prepare for "the field," professional ethics, and culture shock. We also compare three principal modes of ethnographic research: positivist, reflexive, and multi-sited. Our explanation of the dialectic of fieldwork considers the roles people play when acting as an anthropologist's guide in the field, the effects of fieldwork on all involved, and the value and open-ended nature of anthropological knowledge.

Our focus in Chapter 3 is on colonialism, capitalism, and modernity. Viewing historical developments through a critical lens, we examine the rise of political economies and place anthropology as a "player" in the colonial encounter. We then critique the development and use of various classification systems, including the culture areas classifications that evolved in North America. In conclusion, we reflect on post-colonial realities as a counterpoint and a challenge.

In Chapter 4, which begins Part II: The Resources of Culture, our objective is to understand the theoretical and practical aspects of language and its use. Here, we discuss the relationship between language and culture and the importance of symbolic representation. We introduce some of Charles Hockett's design features of language, and we overview the components of language (phonology, morphology, syntax, semantics, pragmatics, and ethnopragmatics). We also consider linguistic inequality and areas of negotiated meaning exemplified by pidgin languages. The chapter concludes with a brief statement on the dialectic between experience and language and the creation of ambiguity in symbolic systems.

Beginning from the observation that every individual views the world from a unique position, we investigate the nature of identity and the individual in Chapter 5. First, we explore how individual psychology is situated in the context of a symbolic, cultural world and how cultural schemas and prototypes shape the ways we perceive our experiences. We then outline interpretations of intelligence, cognitive (learning) styles, reasoning, and logic. Next, we examine emotion as the product of the dialectic between bodily arousal and cognitive interpretation mediated by, and embedded within, a cultural matrix. Finally, we discuss ranges of sexual and gender identities and how those identities are culturally informed. Norms and normative constructs are considered.

In Chapter 6, we delve into social inequality and explore the multi-dimensional nature of inequality in terms of class, caste, race, and ethnic divisions. We begin by considering the implications of class-stratified societies and class mobility. Next, we present examples of caste, focusing in particular on how divisions of caste impact peoples' way of living in India. We then survey the discredited concept of "race" and its manifestation in today's world, keeping in mind the ethical implications that often arise when "race" is perceived as a social division. Finally, we reflect upon definitions of *ethnicity* before concluding with an examination of what constitutes a *nation*, what a national identity is, and how national identity may manifest in *nationalism*.

In Chapter 7, we analyze the complexities of human social relationships, focusing on different interpretations of marriage, family, kinship, and friendship. Throughout the chapter, we investigate what determines relatedness and group membership, with an awareness of the role of sex and gender in systems of social organization. We discuss marriage as a social process in the context of economic exchange and family alliance. As we explore the dimensions of family life, we outline various family structures and note how families change over time and in response to new global circumstances. We also compare kin-based versus non–kin-based societies and conclude with an appreciation for the nuances of the dimensions of group life.

Making a living is our central focus in Chapter 8. We consider subsistence strategies before moving on to discuss the relationship between production, distribution, and consumption. Additionally, we note the differences between internal (needs) and external (resources) explanations of consumption patterns. We also explore the cultural and symbolic nature of consumption and then elucidate distribution and exchange at local and global levels by examining various forms of exchange—from reciprocity to redistribution to market exchange.

In Chapter 9, we discuss play, art, myth, and ritual. We begin with play, which is an open system that allows us to communicate about communicating (metacommunication) and provides an entrée to meaningful reflexivity. From play, we move on to discuss first sport as embedded in the prevailing social order and then art as play that produces significant transformation-representation. We also explore the relationships between myths, as charters for social action and providers of stories of truth, and ritual, a culturally defined schema that brings text and performance together and that can function as a powerful form of metacommunication.

Chapter 10 focuses on an applied discipline that has been gaining attention in recent years: medical anthropology. While a chapter is not enough to cover all the diverse topics of study that medical anthropologists investigate, we discuss many themes at the heart of the discipline and offer examples of how researchers have applied these themes to real-world situations. We emphasize holism, particularly in our discussion of the impact of physical, social, and cultural environments on the well-being of individuals. We also consider various culturally informed approaches to health care and ways of labelling and defining illness and disease. In addition, we revisit some ethical considerations as we explore the challenges involved in studying human health. Above all, we emphasize the importance of being open to traditional knowledge and non-Western ways of healing.

In Chapter 11, we consider the seemingly simple—yet actually very complex—subject of world view in the context of key metaphors. We explore the role of metaphor, metonymy, and symbolic thought and comment on the anthropological analysis of religion and secularism within the context of world view. As we come to understand world views as instruments of power, we also come to understand how key metaphors and world views are maintained and modified in a world of change.

We begin Part III: Organization of Life: Local to Global with a discussion of social organization and patterns of human interdependence in Chapter 12, noting that no single cause can explain the complexities of human social relations. We consider the human power to act, various forms of social power, and explanations of why human beings submit to institutionalized power. As we investigate how humans invest the world with meaning, we also discuss how people bargain for reality as they negotiate the meaning of history and tradition.

We explore the emergence of the *global world* in Chapter 13. In the context of the history of the development of political economies, we consider globalization and the pressures on nation-states as new cultural processes emerged and continue to emerge. A key issue is the challenge of human rights in a "globalized" world, and we discuss cultural imperialism, cultural hybridization, and cosmopolitanism as responses to this challenge.

In the concluding chapter, we present the idea that anthropology encompasses so much more than what students will learn in a classroom. Anthropology is about the lives and worlds of the people who gift us with their world views. It is a portal to effective global citizenship in a world of uncertainty. Finally, anthropology offers perspective and a way to develop awareness (reflexivity) in order to confront issues and challenge views on freedom and constraint.

A Final Note

Each new edition of *Cultural Anthropology* has moved forward in some small and/or large way to illuminate the trends of the discipline. Nonetheless, what has been constant is the book's core value: a respect for students. Like Emily Schultz and Robert Lavenda, I, too, have taken students seriously. I believe that they have the capacity to read and think as involved adults. It has been my experience using this book over the years that students are happy to be seen as capable of the reflexivity this book espouses. Readers may sometimes complain about or struggle with the content and the concepts, but I have found they can be charmed into learning as they come to appreciate that the text grounds them in an intellectual, emotional, and practical perspective that finds resonance in their—quite substantial—understanding of the world. What we offer are the tools for analysis. Inevitably, students appreciate this book and anthropology as a subject. This book situates them in a world of change and challenges them to engage the anthropological perspective as an increasingly important tool for effective global citizenship.

This edition is bittersweet for me as I retire from active participation in the classroom while continuing with some of my field research that I hope to complete in my final years. I speak to you from a life in anthropology and at a time when we are significantly challenged to hold on to our humanity and to our wonderful home in the stars. The gifts of understanding I have received from others have been magical. The generosities of many have enriched my professional and personal life and in some small way have come to you through my contribution to this book.

Sam Anderson, writing in *The New York Times Magazine* (1 October 2017) on the life and work of the writer John McPhee, comments, "Learning . . . is a way of loving the world, savoring it, before it is gone. In the grand cosmology . . . all the earth's facts touch one other—all its regions, creatures, and eras . . . Every part of time touches every other part of time" (33, 55).

We are all in this river of time—immersed in the waters of life. Swim!

Acknowledgements

Once again, I want to thank the people I met and worked with in the field who gifted me with their friendship and insights into their lives while teaching me to see their worlds and ways of being human. They have been my true teachers, and their kind involvement has been a sacred gift. As this book has always inferred, such generosity helps us face the world with humility, while the study of anthropology situates us in a place of analysis that fosters the development of humble concern and deep hope. None of this could be possible without the kindness of others.

I would like to thank, once more, Emily Schultz and Robert Lavenda for providing the foundation upon which the Canadian editions of *Cultural Anthropology* have been built and for their ongoing insightful comments on the progress made in the current edition.

In this edition we have included the voices of "new" academics in anthropology. Some recently have completed their PhDs, and one is in a post-doc position. Others are on the cusp of completion. They are representative of our future—their voices will keep us aware of our humanity as they continue to gather the sacred gifts others have to impart.

Alphonse Ndem Ahola, University of Alberta
David Cooney, Memorial University of Newfoundland
Joshua Friesen, McGill University
Jennifer Glassco, McGill University
Geoffrey Hobbis, University of British Columbia, Okanagan
Stephanie Ketterer Hobbis, University of British Columbia, Okanagan
Matt Husain, University of British Columbia, Okanagan

Sarah Jacobs, University of Calgary
Nancy Merrill, University of British Columbia, Okanagan
Nhi Ha Nguyen, Queen's University
Michael P. Oman-Reagan, Memorial University of Newfoundland
Maxime Polleri, York University
Judith van Roggen, University of British Columbia, Okanagan

Beyond my sincere thanks to those named above and below (and any I missed), I bid adieu. And to borrow from sci-fi, our portal to the imagining of future worlds, actual and metaphorical, some words of hope: "Live long and prosper" (Spock in *Star Trek)* and "May the force be with you" (Yoda in *Star Wars*). The emergent area of futurist anthropology will continue our legacy of supporting our humanity even onto changing times.

The work could not have proceeded without the exceedingly positive relationship that I developed with my first editors at Oxford University Press. Here, I note these editors from the years and editions specifically: Caroline Starr, senior acquisitions editor; Peter Chambers, developmental editor, higher education division; Amanda Maurice, assistant editor, higher education division; and, recently, Janice Evans, senior editor, higher education division; Rhiannon Wong, assistant editor; and Colleen Ste Marie, copy editor.

Peter worked with me in a sympathetic and supportive fashion on the first two Canadian editions. Without his input and the contribution of Amanda Maurice on the first Canadian edition, I could not have worked through the difficult process of making this book "Canadian" while keeping the tone of the original authors.

The second edition became what it was because of Janice Evans, and she continued to provide great assistance in working through the final processes for the third edition. To her and our new additions to the editorial team for this book, Tanuja Weerasooriya and Dani Pacey, fell the monumental task of smoothing out the tone of three voices, setting a better order for the material while reconciling the struggle of the reorganization of chapters and the adding of new and, at times, controversial materials. By this, the fourth edition, things had settled to reading the current literature and incorporating as much as possible in such an introductory text. Here Rhiannon Wong and Colleen Ste Marie became my go-to people—and thankfully so.

All the people thanked in previous editions have their place in this edition as well. I would like to join the publisher in thanking the following reviewers, as well as those who wish to remain anonymous, whose thoughtful comments and suggestions helped shape these, now four, Canadian editions:

Hugo De Burgos, University of British Columbia, Okanagan

Steven Ferzacca, University of Lethbridge

Diana French, University of British Columbia, Okanagan

David Geary, University of British Columbia, Okanagan

Dawn Grimes-MacLellan, Saint Mary's University

Nicole Hayes, University of Waterloo

Chris Holdsworth, University of Calgary

David Howes, Concordia University

Magdalena Kazubowski-Houston, Wilfrid Laurier University

Carlota McAllister, York University

Laurie Milne, Medicine Hat College

Charles R. Menzies, University of British Columbia

Timothy Panas, University of Saskatchewan

David Ryniker, University of British Columbia

Alan Smart, University of Calgary

Pamela Stern, Simon Fraser University

Douglass Drozdow-St Christian, Western University

Susan Walter, Saint Mary's University

Terry Webb, Western University

Marty Zelenietz, Saint Mary's University

Roberta Robin Dods

From the Publisher

Building on the solid foundation of past editions, this fourth Canadian edition of *Cultural Anthropology: A Perspective on the Human Condition* invites students to embark on a journey of cross-cultural comparison. Featuring ethnographic insight from the experiences of the authors' own fieldwork as well as from top researchers in Canada and around the world, *Cultural Anthropology* takes a contemporary and dynamic look at how human agency, cultural creativity, and the material conditions of everyday life interact to shape cultural practices. This thought-provoking text will inspire students to engage with the world beyond the classroom, a world that is stunningly diverse, surprisingly similar, and thoroughly human.

Key Features

Canadian focus. A host of Canadian examples, points of view, and issues offer insight into the many ways in which Canadians have contributed to the field. Students will also enjoy learning about the breadth and depth of anthropological research being carried out in this country today.

Expanded coverage of technology, gender and sexuality, health, globalization, and other essential topics.

New discussions of topics such as cyborg anthropology, virtual realities, transgender identities, Indigenous language revitalization, refugee mental health, and visual research methods offer students insight into important areas of study within anthropology.

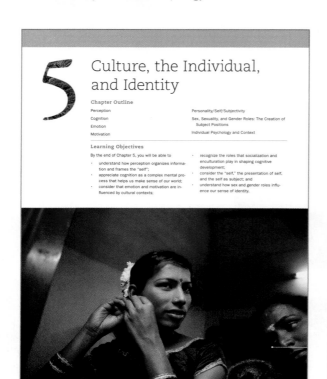

Broad theoretical coverage. The authors bring together traditional anthropological perspectives and cutting-edge theories to reflect the most recent trends in the discipline. The result is a comprehensive, holistic approach that sheds new light on standard topics.

Living Anthropology

New "Living Anthropology" boxes. New end-of-chapter boxes feature insights on topical issues in the field from up-and-coming anthropologists in Canada, highlighting for students critical research being conducted today.

EthnoProfile

"Ethnoprofile" boxes. Brief overviews of relevant geographic, linguistic, demographic, and organizational information offer students contextual information on various societies discussed in the text.

In Their Own Words

"In Their Own Words" boxes. Short commentaries from experts in the field provide students with personal insights and alternative perspectives on key issues.

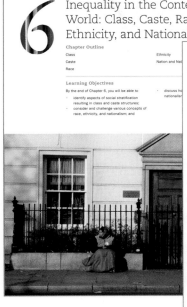

Vibrant four-colour design. A wide array of photos, illustrations, maps, tables, and graphs helps bring anthropology to life!

Engaging learning tools. Learning objectives, marginal definitions of key terms, critical thinking questions, annotated suggestions for further reading, lists of related websites, and an end-of-book glossary encourage students to actively engage with what they are reading and explore resources beyond the text to enhance their learning experience.

Extensive Ancillary Package. The fourth Canadian edition of *Cultural Anthropology* is supported by a wide range of supplementary resources for the student and the instructor, all designed to enhance and complete the learning experience. The companion websites for *Cultural Anthropology* are found at

 **www.oupcanada.com/Schultz4Ce**

For the Student

- **Student Study Guide.** An updated and expanded package of review material—including a list of relevant films, self-testing quizzes of multiple choice and true-or-false questions, essay topics and discussion questions, kinship diagrams, new video links, and weblinks to resources such as online ethnographies—is designed to reinforce student understanding of each chapter and provide direction for further research. The Student Study Guide also contains short commentaries for each chapter written by Roberta Robin Dods that challenge students to think critically about a variety of engaging and relevant cultural topics.

For the Instructor

The following instructors' resources are available online to qualifying adopters. Please contact your OUP Canada sales representative for more information.

- **Instructor's Manual.** This comprehensive package features chapter summaries, suggestions for discussion and debate, suggested lecture topics and teaching resources, and a sample syllabus and grading rubric.

- **PowerPoint Slides.** These dynamic lecture slides summarize key points from each chapter and incorporate figures and tables from the text.

- **Image Bank.** This expansive resource contains a wealth of full-colour figures, photographs, and tables that will make classroom lectures more engaging and relevant for students.

- **Test Generator.** This comprehensive bank of test questions provides hundreds of multiple choice, true-or-false, short answer, and mini essay questions along with suggested answers and page references guiding students to related in-text discussions.

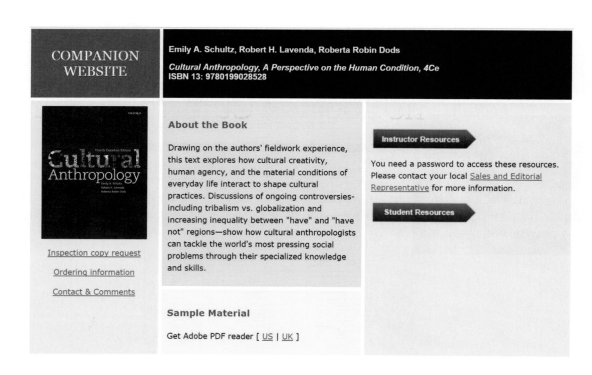

PART I | The Tools of Cultural Anthropology

In Part I, we introduce anthropology—specifically, cultural anthropology—as a way of exploring and gaining knowledge about our world and ourselves. We also consider the possibilities made available by fieldwork, cultural anthropologists' principal method of data collection. Finally, we discuss the historical context for how anthropologists have attempted to make sense of human cultural diversity.

1 The Anthropological Perspective on the Human Condition

Chapter Outline

Learning Objectives

By the end of Chapter 1, you will be able to

- define anthropology's aims and scope of study;
- explain culture as a concept within anthropology;
- distinguish cultural anthropology as a subfield of anthropology;
- articulate connections and relationships between the four major subfields of anthropology in North America;

- explain the world views of dualism and holism, and show ways that the conflict between them has shaped anthropology; and
- explain the relationship between cultural relativism and ethnocentrism, and give examples of both.

Explanations of the Human Condition

Dualistic, Idealistic, and Materialistic Explanations of Our World

What is the world like? And what is the human condition within the world? Indeed, does it make sense to speak of a *single condition* or even a shared *time*? Members of all societies pose questions such as these. And all societies develop their own answers. Bryonny Goodwin-Hawkins observes that we are, in effect, in "co-existent temporality" (2012: 22), a cultural/environmental construct, while at the same time experiencing a personal history: "Just as some anticipate an improved future, others look back to a preferred past" (25). Thus, there is great variation in the interpretation of *beingness*. We all struggle with finding our place and its meaning on a personal and a cultural level. If asked what is known about human nature, for example, many North Americans would answer that human nature has two parts: *mind* and *matter*, or *soul* and *body*, or *spirit* and *flesh*. The belief that human nature, or reality as a whole, is made up of two radically different yet equal forces is called dualism. The pair of forces is often referred to as a binary opposition.

For thousands of years, from the time of the Greek philosopher Plato (428–347 BCE) onward, people of the Western tradition have debated the importance of each half of human nature. They have understood each person as made up of a material (physical) body inhabited by an ethereal mind or spirit. According to Plato, the drama of human existence consists of the internal struggle between the body (drawn naturally to base, corruptible matter) and the mind or soul (drawn naturally to pure, unchanging forms). Christian theology later incorporated the view that each human being consists of a soul that seeks God and a physical body that is tempted by the material world. This view of earthly life as a struggle between spirit (good) and flesh (evil) is sometimes called *conflict dualism*.

Subsequently, Platonic and Christian theories of human nature came to emphasize that although human beings are equipped with physical bodies, their true nature is spiritual, not material; the body is a material obstacle that prevents the full development of the mind or spirit. This view is known as idealism. Conversely, others have argued that the activities of our physical bodies in the material world make us who we are. From this perspective, human existence becomes the struggle to exercise our physicality as fully as we can; to put spiritual values above bodily needs would "go against human nature." This view is known as materialism. In their most extreme forms, idealism and materialism pose competing forms of determinism: idealists claim that human nature is *determined by* the causal force of mind or spirit; materialists argue that human nature is *determined by* the causal force of physical matter.

Many idealists and materialists have sought to strip away our seemingly minor or unnecessary attributes in order to reveal an unchanging core or essence of human nature. Indeed, across the history of Western philosophy, various philosophers have assumed that our species has an essence but have disagreed about just what that essence is. Yet other thinkers have argued that human beings come into the world with *no fixed essence*. For them, people are shaped by various forces that they encounter throughout their lives. But what those forces might be, how many there are, and which of them is the most powerful remain part of the debate.

Some nineteenth-century thinkers argued that the most powerful material forces that shape human nature were to be found in the surrounding *natural environment*. Environmental factors thereby shaped past and present societies and, ultimately, their inhabitants' sense of self and society. German philosopher Karl Marx (1818–1883) and his followers, by contrast, argued that forces shaping human beings' self-understanding were rooted in social relations shaped by the mode of economic production that sustained a society (Figure 1.1). Because different groups, or *classes*, played different roles in that production process, members of each group would develop a different sense of what life was all about. An extreme idealist reaction against such materialist thinking, influential in cultural anthropology, has argued that human beings have no fixed essence when they come into the world but they

dualism The philosophical view that reality consists of two equal and irreducible forces.

binary opposition A pair of opposites used as an organizing principle (e.g., body–soul; yin–yang; male–female).

idealism The philosophical view that pure, incorruptible ideas—or the mind that produces such ideas—constitute the essence of human nature.

materialism The philosophical view that the activities of our physical bodies in the material world constitute the essence of human nature.

determinism The philosophical view that one simple force (or a few simple forces) causes (or determines) complex events.

essence An unchanging core of features unique to things of the same kind, making them what they are.

A crowd of around 12,000 people gathers to watch and take photos of sunrise at Stonehenge during the summer solstice. The prehistoric monument in Wiltshire, England became a popular site for pagan traditions during the twentieth century. How can an anthropological perspective inform our understanding of the relationship between cultural traditions and new forms of technology?

Canada, Dept. of National Defence/Library and Archives Canada

Figure 1.1 Factory workers in Woodstock, Ontario, during World War I. Karl Marx believed that modes of production shape social relations and, in turn, individuals' perceptions of themselves and their place in society. Can you identify some of the modes of production that impact your own life?

holism A perspective on the human condition that assumes that mind and body, individual and society, and individual and environment interpenetrate and even define one another.

become different kinds of human beings as a result of the particular *ideas, meanings, beliefs,* and *values* that they absorb as members of particular societies (see Benedict 1934).

As liberating as the proposition of being born without a fixed essence may sound, such accounts are not always optimistic. A number of scholars have adapted this basic assumption to portray humans as passive, pliable creatures who are *wholly* formed by environmental, sociohistorical, cultural, or other forces beyond their control. According to these scholars, the open possibilities with which we begin are inevitably closed down tight as human possibilities are overwhelmed by environmental determinism, sociohistorical determinism, or cultural determinism.

Holistic Explanations

Yet there is another approach to the human condition that is less distorting than dualism and less simplistic than idealism or materialism: **holism** (see Figure 1.2). Holism assumes that no sharp boundaries separate mind from body, body from environment, individual from society, my ideas from your ideas, or our traditions from the traditions of others. Rather, it proposes that mind and body, body and environment, and so on, interpenetrate and even define one another. Holism holds great appeal for those who seek a theory of human nature that is rich enough to do justice to its complex subject matter—namely, humans themselves.

Holism sees the whole as greater than the sum of its parts. Human beings are what they are

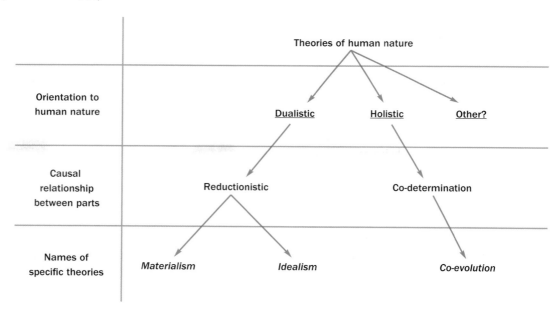

Figure 1.2 Perspectives on the human condition. While the dualistic approach reduces the human condition to the sum of its parts, the holistic approach considers the human condition to be co-determined through a complex interplay among many internal and external influences. Can you think of any other way(s) of looking at the human condition?

because the mutual shaping of genes and **culture** and experience has produced something new, something that cannot be reduced to the materials used to construct it. Similarly, a society is not just the sum of the behaviours of its individual members but a unique entity, and human beings living in groups are so deeply affected by shared cultural experiences that they become different from what they would have been had they matured in isolation. Cultural anthropologist Clifford Geertz notes that human beings raised in isolation would be neither failed apes nor "natural" people stripped of their veneer of culture; they would be "mental basket cases" (1973: 40). Social living and cultural sharing are necessary for individual human beings to develop what we recognize as a *human* nature—in all its wonderful diversity.

The Anthropological Perspective: The Cross-Disciplinary Discipline

From the optimistic promise of holism we can engage with the subject matter of **anthropology**, a scholarly discipline that aims to describe, in the broadest possible sense, what it means to be human. Anthropologists want to learn about different human ways of life. Essentially, the anthropological experience is a gift from teachers who live or lived in different social, economic, or geographical circumstances. Anthropologists are often treated to the sweet discovery of familiarity and the joy of making the unfamiliar familiar. They often face, as well, the experience of the familiar becoming unfamiliar; as frightening as this discovery can be, it is also a source of great insight and immense pleasure.

Anthropologists are not alone in focusing their attention on human beings and their creations. Human biology, literature, art, history, linguistics, sociology, political science, economics—all these disciplines and many more—concentrate on one aspect of human life or another. The **anthropological perspective**, unique in the social sciences, draws on the findings of these other disciplines and attempts to fit them together with its own findings in order to understand how different forces collectively shape human life. Anthropologists are convinced that explanations of human activities will inevitably be superficial unless they are holistic—that is, unless they acknowledge that human life is greater than the sum of its parts. Thus, the anthropological perspective recognizes that so long as

they are alive, individuals and societies always remain open to influences and opportunities that may take them beyond what they are at the present moment or what they have been in the past.

To generalize about humanity requires evidence from the widest possible range of human societies. Thus, in addition to being holistic, anthropology is **comparative**. Anthropologists understand that it is not enough, for example, to observe only the group with which they are working, discover that they do not eat insects, and conclude that all human beings do not eat insects. When anthropologists compare human diets in different societies, they discover that insect-eating is quite common and that the North American aversion to this practice is specific to North American society (Figure 1.3). In making such comparisons, anthropologists recognize that all social groups deserve equal treatment and respect, and they reject terms such as *exotic*, *primitive*, and *savage* to describe practices that differ from those of their own group. Thus, anthropological study involves (1) gathering data from many cultures, both past and present, (2) comparing those data to derive informed and testable hypotheses about what it means to be human, and (3) investigating what, if anything, can be said about the human condition that might be valid across space and over time.

This interest in change over time leads anthropologists to explore how individual humans, their societies, and their cultures have evolved.

culture Sets of learned behaviours and ideas that humans acquire as members of a society.

anthropology The integrated study of human nature, human society, and human history.

anthropological perspective An approach to the human condition that is holistic, comparative, and evolutionary.

comparative A characteristic of the anthropological perspective that requires anthropologists to consider similarities and differences in a wide range of human societies before generalizing about human nature, human society, or human history.

Figure 1.3 Fried scorpions being sold at a market in Beijing, China. Insects are commonly eaten as a source of protein in many regions of the world. Can you think of any Western dietary staples that might be considered unusual elsewhere?

biological evolution
Change (through mutation) in the genetic makeup (the DNA/RNA) of a population that is passed on through the generations.

cultural evolution Evolution of the beliefs and behaviours incorporated into human development through the experiences of teaching and learning.

evolutionary A characteristic of the anthropological perspective that requires anthropologists to place their observations about human nature, human society, or human history in a flexible framework that takes into consideration change over time.

biological (or physical) anthropology The specialty of anthropology that looks at humans as biological organisms and tries to discover what characteristics make humans different from and/or similar to other living things.

Consequently, some anthropologists study the **biological evolution** of the human species, paying attention not only to human origins but also to the patterns of biological variation in living human populations; others study **cultural evolution**, tracing how elements of culture have changed over time. In general, one of anthropology's most important contributions to the study of human evolution has been to demonstrate the critical differences that separate biological evolution, which is situated in environmental *circumstances*, from cultural evolution. This distinction remains important as a way of demonstrating the inadequacy of arguments that assert that everything people do or think can be explained biologically—for example, in terms of "race" or "sex." Because anthropologists are interested in documenting and explaining change, the anthropological perspective is **evolutionary** at its core. And today, as humans move into an era in which even our biological being can be altered through technology, anthropologists' interest in human evolution has taken on additional cross-disciplinary implications.

The diverse ways that people come to understand the meaning of being human through the anthropological perspective can be seen in Figure 1.4. This diagram shows the connections among the four traditional specialties, or subdisciplines, of anthropology and their combined linkage to applied anthropology. As this figure illustrates, at the most inclusive level anthropology is the holistic study of human nature, human society, and human history. The following subsections will explain each of the four major specialties—biological anthropology, archaeology, linguistic anthropology, and cultural anthropology—as well as applied and medical anthropology.

Biological Anthropology

Biological (or physical) anthropology focuses on human beings as living organisms and what makes the genus *Homo* different from or similar to other living things. This specialty of anthropology has its roots in the nineteenth-century interest in human physical variation, which was a by-product of centuries of exploration and encounters between people from geographically distant societies. At the time, variation in the physical appearance of peoples around the world was a matter of interest, and early physical anthropologists invented elaborate techniques to measure observable features of human populations, including skin colour, hair, and body type. This "scientific" evidence facilitated the classification of all peoples into supposedly unambiguous categories based on distinct sets of biological attributes. Such categories were called "*races*," and many nineteenth- and early twentieth-century physical anthropologists were convinced that their studies would reveal clear-cut criteria for racial classification.

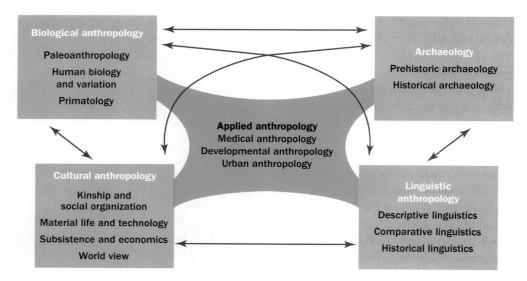

Figure 1.4 In North America, anthropology is traditionally divided into four specialties: biological anthropology, archaeology, linguistic anthropology, and cultural anthropology. Applied (action) anthropology draws on information provided by the other four specialties to facilitate and support change in those communities that seek advocacy-oriented help, which anthropologists can provide.

The peoples whom these early physical anthropologists were trying to assign to racial categories were, in most cases, non-European peoples, peoples coming under increasing political and economic domination by colonizing European (and European-ancestry) capitalist societies. These peoples differed from "white" Europeans in ways other than physical appearance—they had their own languages and customs, and they possessed technologies that were, in most cases, no match for the might of the industrialized West. As a result, racial categorization not only noted individuals' physical characteristics but also made judgments on people's mental and moral attributes, and races were ranked in terms of these attributes. Not surprisingly, "white" Europeans and their "white" descendants in power outside Europe were seen as superior, while other "races" were considered to represent varying grades of inferiority. In this way, the first physical anthropologists helped develop theories that would justify the social practice of racism (see Chapter 6). Indeed, racism influenced official social policies in many Western nations well into the twentieth century. In Canada, one of the most destructive of such policies was the government's implementation of mandatory residential schools for Indigenous children. Oneida scholar Roland Chrisjohn and his colleagues observe that these schools destroyed the circles of life and life-affirming metaphors of unity and wholeness, substituting instead Euro-Canadian "circle games" of the "empty non-existence of zero" (1997: 115).

Yet even as racist policies continued to affect the lives of individuals, many physical anthropologists in the early twentieth century began realizing the fallacy of racial categorization. New theories, many based on principles of holism, led these anthropologists to question past assumptions. In addition, new scientific advancements, such as the discovery of blood types, led them to add data on individuals' internal features to their calculations. The more they learned about the inner biological attributes of human beings, the more they realized that "races" with distinct and unique sets of such attributes simply did not exist. They concluded that the concept of "race" was not a reflection of fact but instead a cultural label invented to sort people into groups set in socioeconomic power hierarchies.

Support for non-racial understandings of human populations has a long history among anthropologists in North America. Pioneering anthropologist Franz Boas, for example, who in the early 1900s founded the first department of anthropology in North America (at Columbia University), had long been uncomfortable with racial classifications. Boas and his students devoted much energy to debunking racist stereotypes, using both their knowledge of biology and their understanding of culture. As the discipline of anthropology developed in the United States and then Canada, students continued to be trained in both human biology and human culture, to provide them with the tools to fight racial and ethnic stereotyping. Rejecting the racial thinking of the nineteenth century, many modern anthropologists who study human biology prefer to call themselves *biological anthropologists* and focus on patterns of variation within the human species as a whole.

Today, some biological anthropologists, such as Biruté Galdikas (Simon Fraser University), work in the subfield of **primatology**; others, such as Pamela Willoughby (University of Alberta), work in the field of **paleoanthropology**. Other specialties focus on human adaptability in different ecological settings, on human growth and development, or on the connections between a population's evolutionary history and its susceptibility to disease. Forensic anthropologists, as noted below in the applied anthropology discussion, use their knowledge of human skeletal anatomy to aid law enforcement and human rights investigators (see Figure 1.5). Molecular anthropologists trace

primatology The study of non-human primates, the closest living relatives of human beings.

paleoanthropology The study of the fossilized remains of human beings' earliest ancestors.

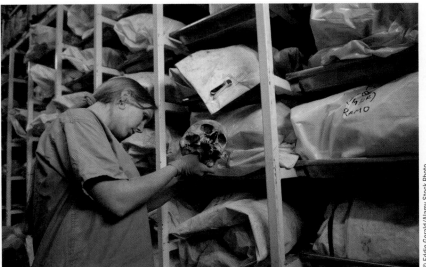

Figure 1.5 A forensic anthropologist examines a human skull at the mortuary facility of the International Commission on Missing Persons in Bosnia. Forensic anthropologists work with human remains to aid police investigations. How do you think the work of forensic anthropologists contributes to social justice and the discussion of cultural contexts?

chemical similarities and differences in cells, tissues, and organs; what they have learned about the immune system, for example, has enabled them to contribute actively to HIV/AIDS research. In all these ways, biological anthropologists can illuminate what makes human beings similar to (and different from) one another, from other primates, and from other living organisms.

Archaeology

archaeology The specialty of anthropology interested in what human beings can learn from material remains left behind by earlier human societies.

Archaeology is the study of the human past through the analysis of material remains (Figure 1.6). Archaeologists must also be knowledgeable about the history of the sites they investigate—they must be familiar with past technologies and environmental as well as economic indicators (e.g., plant and animal remains)—so they can recognize valuable details and situate their findings within the greater scientific landscape. Archaeologists frequently work in teams with other scientists who specialize in specific areas of research. Their findings complement those of paleoanthropologists and indeed sometimes become common interest. For example, archaeological information about the use of stone tools in a particular region may correlate with fossil evidence of prehistoric human occupations.

One such example of an archaeological research project involving experts from various fields is the Dakhleh Oasis Project in Egypt (see EthnoProfile 1.1).

Project director Anthony J. Mills, who initiated the project in 1978, describes it as

> a long-term regional study of the interaction between environmental changes and human activity in the closed area of the Dakhleh Oasis . . . since the first incursion of humans in the Middle Pleistocene, perhaps 400,000 years ago, down to the twenty-first century oasis farmers, and all the human activity and all the changing environmental conditions for which there is evidence within the time period. (Mills 2013)

Participants in the study include environmentalists, physical anthropologists, linguists, historians, and archaeologists specializing in various areas of study. The project has attracted researchers from around the globe, and several Canadians—including anthropologist Maxine Kleindienst—have signed on to contribute to the massive undertaking.

Scientific dating techniques allow archaeologists to make hypotheses about the age, territorial ranges, and patterns of sociocultural change in ancient societies, thus tracing the spread of cultural inventions over time and space. American archaeologist Jeremy Sabloff points out that archaeology is an "action" science in the modern world, as it "can play helpful roles in broad, critical issues facing the world today . . . inform[ing] us in general about lessons to be learned from the successes and failures of past cultures and provid[ing] policy-makers with useful contexts for future decision-making" (2008: 17). In such a context, archaeology becomes applied anthropology, which we discuss later in this chapter.

Linguistic Anthropology

Perhaps the most striking cultural feature of our species is language—symbolic communication (see Chapter 4). Anthropologists have long recognized the connections between language and human culture, and many early anthropologists were the first researchers to transcribe non-Western languages and to produce grammars and dictionaries of those languages. When investigating living cultures, linguistic anthropologists often connect with one or a few members of the culture who can act as guides to the language and customs of specific social groups (Figure 1.7). The loss of languages is also a concern, as each language is a unique way of understanding ourselves and our place in the universe. Contemporary linguistic anthropologists and their counterparts in sociology (called *sociolinguists*) study the

Figure 1.6 An archaeological dig at Qumran, the site where the Dead Sea Scrolls were discovered in 11 caves near the Dead Sea between 1947 and 1956. Excavation work and analysis of material remains are central to archaeologists' study of the human past. What sorts of insights can material remains offer about the ways that cultures change over time?

© Rafael Ben-Ari/123RF

EthnoProfile 1.1
Dakhleh

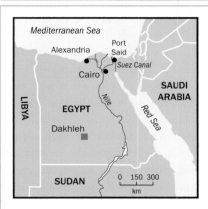

Region: Northeastern Africa

Nation: Egypt

Language: Nearly all of the 14 colonies that constitute the Dakhleh Oasis—including Mut, Al-Qasr, and Qalamoun—have their own dialect of Arabic.

Population: 75,000 (2002)

Environment: Desert oasis

Livelihood: Farming (dates, oranges, mangoes, wheat)

Political organization: Region in a modern nation-state

For more information: Chandler, Graham. 2006. "Before the Mummies: The Desert Origins of the Pharaohs," *Saudi Aramco World* 57, 5: 2–11; Mills, Anthony J. 2013. "Dakhleh Oasis Project," *Monash University Arts*, available at http://artsonline.monash.edu.au/ancient-cultures/excavations-in-dakhleh-oasis-egypt

linguistic anthropology
The specialty of anthropology concerned with the study of human languages.

cultural anthropology
The specialty of anthropology that studies how variation in beliefs and behaviours is shaped by culture and learned by different members of human groups.

way language differences frequently correlate with differences in gender, class, or ethnic identity.

Linguistic anthropology has become so highly specialized that modern linguistic anthropologists are deeply trained in both linguistic and cultural anthropology, and many cultural anthropologists receive linguistics training as part of their professional preparation. Linguistic anthropologists are applied anthropologists in some instances, working to maintain endangered languages and attempting to help us understand the nature of language and its links to our cultural identity.

Cultural Anthropology

Now we come to the central topic of this book: **cultural anthropology**, which is sometimes called *sociocultural anthropology*, *social anthropology*, or *ethnology*. In general, cultural anthropology focuses on sets of learned behaviours and ideas that human beings acquire as members of a society. Recognizing that people ordinarily take their culturally shaped beliefs and behaviours for granted, anthropologist Michael Herzfeld has suggested that cultural anthropology might be usefully defined as "the study of common sense," although "sense" as a concept is not *common* to all cultures, and what one group considers to be "common sense" may not seem *sensible* to anyone outside that group (2001: 1).

Because people everywhere use culture to adapt to and transform everything in their wider world, the field of cultural anthropology is vast. Cultural anthropologists tend to specialize in one domain of human cultural activity or another. Many cultural anthropologists, for example, study language, music, dance, art, poetry, philosophy, religion, or ritual. Some study the ways particular groups of human

Figure 1.7 Canadian linguistic anthropologist William Thurston with his friend Avel, a Lusi speaker, travelling in Papua New Guinea. During their travels, Avel acted as guide and introduced Thurston to the community, where he collected material on the Mouk language. How can understanding a group's language help anthropologists understand that group's culture?

beings organize themselves to carry out collective tasks, whether economic, political, or spiritual. This focus is in some ways similar to the discipline of sociology (the study of social behaviour or society, which, broadly, looks at the organization, institutions, and social interactions of large groups), and from it has come the identification of anthropology as one of the social sciences. In fact, sociology and anthropology developed during the same period of the late nineteenth and early twentieth centuries and thus share some similar interests in social organization. Sociology, however, is usually conducted within the society in which the researcher lives—in effect their "home" culture. Now this is not to say that anthropologists do not work in their "home" culture, but they do extend into other cultures for their cross-cultural directive. While both disciplines can address similar issues, it is the interest in *comparing* different forms of human social life that sets anthropology apart from sociology.

Anthropologists have worked diligently to come to

> . . . an honest accounting of anthropology's checkered history, [which] must recognize the role of colonial subsidy (van Willigen 2002; Willis 1974). Without it, there would be no discipline of anthropology. Ethnology played an important role in the colonial administrative experience of many countries [and the] British, in particular, made extensive use of anthropologists, most commonly as staff researchers. There is little evidence, however, that anthropologists served in positions with line authority or policy-making capacity. (Rylko-Bauer et al. 2006: 179–80)

As a result, modern cultural anthropologists have become concerned with studying *all* human societies, including their own, and they reject labels such as *civilized* and *primitive* for the same reason they reject the term *"race"*: these concepts all carry offensive connotations.

In recent years, many cultural anthropologists have researched contemporary issues of gender and sexuality, environmental change, transnational migration, urbanization, globalization, and the lasting impact of colonialism. One interesting area of research focuses on material culture. Like archaeologists, cultural anthropologists interested in material life describe the natural setting for which technologies have been developed, and they analyze the way technologies and environments shape each other. They also study the effects of foreign technologies on local populations using post-colonial perspectives. We will take a closer look at these topics in later sections of this chapter as well as in chapters to come.

Historically, colonialism brought many Western technologies (e.g., railroads, mechanical clocks, firearms) to non-Western peoples, often with enormous impact. With the age of globalization upon us, another area of interest is the spread and influence of electronic media and communications technologies. Studies have shown, for example, the creative and unanticipated ways that peoples use popular media and online communication tools (e.g., email, instant messaging) to make sense of their own local cultural context and situate it in a wider world. For example, consider the ways in which social media aided in the organization of women's marches in over 80 countries around the world on 21 January 2017 (including several in major Canadian cities) to advocate for a number of human rights issues, including women's rights, immigration reform, LGBTQIA rights, racial equality, and freedom of religion following Donald Trump's inauguration as president of the United States.

As cultural anthropologists have become increasingly aware of the many influences that stretch across space to affect local communities, they have also become sensitive to those that stretch across time. As a result, many contemporary cultural anthropologists make serious efforts to place themselves and their cultural analyses in detailed historical contexts and are open to engaging with archaeologists and historians with related interests.

Cultural anthropologists, no matter what their area of specialization, ordinarily collect their data during an extended period of fieldwork (the topic of Chapter 2). Fieldwork entails involvement in the everyday routine of those among whom they live and is a period when the anthropologist receives one of the most meaningful gifts that any human can receive—entry into the lives of others. This gift is part of an act of *reciprocity*: an exchange of mutual benefit. Researchers can enhance the reciprocal relationship by participating in social activities and negotiating the meaning of what they observe with the people they work with. Fieldwork is also a time of deep *reflexivity*: thinking about why and how one thinks about specific things.

People who share information about their lives have traditionally been called **informants**; however,

informants People in a particular culture who work with anthropologists and provide them with insights about local ways of life.

some anthropologists object to the use of this term because it suggests a role that is limited to supplying information for the benefit of the researcher. Therefore, many contemporary anthropologists choose to describe the people they encounter in the field as *partners*, *participants*, *consultants*, or simply *the people I work with* because these terms emphasize a relationship of equality based on mutual respect. Others prefer the term *teachers*, making it explicit that fieldwork is an active dialogue between the researcher (the student) and the people who are the experts on their own lives (the teachers). Of course, these experts, like all teachers, also learn and develop new perspectives as they interact with their students—reciprocity, again!

Researchers make written notes (documents) even when audio recordings are permitted. The essential written notes can be augmented significantly by the use of videos or photographs (Figure 1.8). Indeed, the use of "shadow catching" technologies—devices that capture a visual representation of life—in the discipline dates back to the earliest period of photography in the nineteenth century. Such photographs have been an invaluable record. In many cases, however, visual records say more about the photographer or videographer than about the image's content. This notion is well illustrated by some of Franz Boas's pictures taken for the US National Museum (see more on this in Chapter 13). Another historical example is photographer Edward Curtis's movie *In the Land of the War Canoes* (1914), which depicts a fictionalized account of the lives of the Kwakiutl (Kwakwaka'wakw) peoples (Northern Vancouver Island).

Two related terms for anthropological studies are *ethnography* and *ethnology*. An **ethnography** is a recorded description of a particular group of people's way of life; **ethnology** is the comparative study of two or more such groups. Thus, cultural anthropologists who write ethnographies are sometimes called *ethnographers*, and cultural anthropologists who compare ethnographic information on many different cultural practices are sometimes called *ethnologists*.

Emerging Approaches: Applied Anthropology

Applied anthropology could be termed *action anthropology*. In applied anthropology, anthropological information is put to practical use to propose solutions to important problems. You may be familiar with the practical applications of forensic anthropology—perhaps

Figure 1.8 Anthropologist Ryan Cook continues the anthropological tradition of the use of technology as he videotapes the spectators and ritual performers at the Popocatépetl volcano in Mexico. How do you think using technology impacts the research process?

you've even encountered media coverage of forensic anthropologists, such as Mark Skinner (Simon Fraser University), who have worked on highly publicized crime cases or genocide investigations. Although generally exposed to less public attention, other areas of application can also make important contributions to social life. For example, when working with a traditionally structured non-Western community, applied anthropologists could

- use the culture's ideas about illness and health to introduce useful public-health practices in a way that makes sense to, and will be accepted by, members of that culture;
- place emphasis on health hazards from environmental contamination (for an example, see more on Grassy Narrows in Chapter 10);
- draw on the knowledge of traditional social organization to ease the problems for refugees trying to settle in a new land; and
- integrate traditional and Western methods of cultivation to help farmers increase their crop yields.

Anthropologists use their professional training to seek social justice, eliminate discrimination, and support human and cultural rights. In Canada, applied anthropologists have frequently acted to

ethnography
An anthropologist's recorded description of a particular group of people's way of life.

ethnology The comparative study of two or more cultures.

applied anthropology
The use of information gathered from the other anthropological specialties to solve practical problems within and between cultures.

support First Nations land claims and resolve public policy issues (Hedican 2008).

While many anthropologists would argue that applied work can be done *within* any of the four traditional specialties, an increasing number of anthropologists have come to view applied anthropology as a separate field of professional specialization (see Figure 1.4). Thus, more universities in Canada and the United States have begun to develop courses and programs specifically in applied anthropology.

Emerging Approaches: Medical Anthropology

medical anthropology
An area of anthropological inquiry that focuses on issues of well-being, health, illness, and disease as they are situated in their wider cultural contexts.

Medical anthropology is one of the most rapidly growing branches of anthropology. Beginning half a century ago as a form of applied anthropology, it has developed into an important anthropological specialty that has offered new ways to link biological and cultural anthropology. Medical anthropology concerns itself with human health—the factors that contribute to disease or illness and the ways that human populations deal with disease or illness (Baer et al. 2003: 3). Medical anthropologists may consider the physiological variables that are involved with human health and disease, the environmental features that affect human well-being, and the way the human body adapts to various environments. Contemporary medical anthropologists engage in work that directly addresses the anthropological proposition that human beings must be understood as biological organisms.

Particularly significant has been the development of *critical medical anthropology*, which links questions of human health and illness in local settings to social, economic, and political processes operating on a national or global scale. Indeed, critical medical anthropologists have been among the most vocal in pointing out how various forms of suffering and disease cannot be explained only by the presence of microbes in a diseased body but may depend on—or be made worse by—the presence of social inequality and a lack of access to health care. According to anthropologist Merrill Singer, critical medical anthropology "is committed to the 'making social' and the 'making political' of health and medicine" (1998: 195). Thus, critical medical anthropologists pay attention to the way social divisions based on class, "race," gender, and ethnicity can block access to medical attention or make people more vulnerable to disease and suffering. They draw attention to the way traditional Western

biocultural organisms
Organisms whose defining features are co-determined by biological and cultural factors.

biomedicine "encourages people to fight disease rather than to make the changes necessary to prevent it," for example, by linking low birth weight in newborn babies to poor nutrition but failing to note that poor nutrition "may be a major health factor among impoverished social classes and oppressed ethnic groups in developed countries despite an abundance of food in society generally" (Singer 1998: 106, 109).

One of the most important insights of critical medical anthropologists has been to point out that "various practices that bioculturalist anthropologists have traditionally called 'adaptations' might better be analyzed as social adjustments to the consequences of oppressive sociopolitical relationships" (Singer 1998: 115). Gavin Smith and R. Brooke Thomas, for example, draw attention to situations where "social relations compromise people's opinions" for attaining biological well-being and cultural satisfaction but where people do not passively accept this situation and choose instead to "try to escape or change these relations"; Smith and Thomas call these practices "adaptations of resistance" (Smith and Thomas 1998: 466). We will examine medical anthropology in more detail in Chapter 10.

Anthropology and the Concept of Culture

Unquestionably, the emergence of culture has had a profound impact on the evolution of human nature and human society. Thus, it is not surprising that the idea of culture as a marker of our humanness has been central to anthropological thought since the early days of the discipline. Pioneering anthropologist Edward B. Tylor defined culture as "that complex whole which includes knowledge, belief, art, morals, law, customs, and any other capabilities and habits acquired . . . as a member of society" (1958 [1871]: 1). Most of the later definitions have built on this theme.

From the anthropological perspective, culture is central to explanations of why people are what they are and why they do what they do. Anthropologists have shown that members of a social group behave in a particular way *not* because the behaviour is an inevitable result of human biology but because it is *learned*—individuals observe and then copy certain actions performed by others. At the same time, no one would deny that biology plays a role in determining what people *can* learn. As such humans are **biocultural organisms**. Their biological makeup, formed by their genes and cellular chemistry, contributes to their capacity to create and use culture.

Of course, other living species learn, but humans' way of interacting with the wider world is distinct for two reasons:

1. Humans' large, complex brains are capable of extremely intricate open symbolic thought.
2. Their hands are capable of manipulating matter in both powerful and delicate ways.

Being capable of open symbolic thought means that people are able to make sense of their world through **symbols**. For example, consider alphabetic symbols, which are used to represent the sounds of spoken languages. On a deeper level, the sounds themselves are shared symbols for meanings that speakers try to express. The fact that human beings can translate from one language to another suggests that the same or similar meanings can be expressed by different symbols in different languages. However, people do not use symbols only to form language. Everything people do in society has a symbolic dimension, from how they conduct themselves at the dinner table to how they bury the dead.

To understand the power of culture, anthropologists are also paying increasing attention to the role played by **material culture** in the lives of biocultural human organisms—for example, worldwide variations in clothing, housing, tools, and techniques for getting and preparing food and making material goods (Figure 1.9). Many cultural anthropologists have traditionally emphasized the way that people's dealings with artifacts are shaped by the cultural meanings they attach to those artifacts. This emphasis has seemed particularly necessary in the face of the widespread assumptions in our own North American society that material objects have obvious functional meanings that are the same for everyone, everywhere. But cultural anthropologists have found repeatedly that the same object can mean different things to different people.

At the same time, innovative theories of materiality developed in the fields, called cyborg anthropology and science studies, have provided cultural anthropologists with new ways of conceptualizing relations between persons and things. Many examples centre on human experiences with new kinds of things—computers, cellphones, the Internet—that are increasingly central to the everyday lives of people all over the world. For instance, persons who play online video games seem to join

Figure 1.9 A Bedouin woman in Jordan makes bread on the top of an oil drum, which she has reshaped and placed on top of rocks; in the past, she would have used more traditional materials. What might this use of materials tell us about the environment in which this woman lives?

Figure 1.10 LAN parties allow people to establish a local area network (LAN) connection between their devices in order to play multi-player video games together. Here gamers participate in a LAN party at the gaming festival "DreamHack" in Leipzig, Germany. What could cultural anthropologists take away from these new relationships between persons and technology?

with the technology and the other players to form a seamless hybrid entity (Figure 1.10); similarly, the technology that links us to friends on Facebook or Instagram disappears from our awareness. This is a phenomenon that anthropologist Daniel Miller calls *the humility of things*: "objects are important, not because they are evident and physically constrain or enable, but quite the opposite. It is often

symbol Something that stands for something else.

material culture Objects created or shaped by human beings and given meaning by cultural practices.

precisely because we do not *see* them" (2010: 50). The merging of persons and things is sometimes a source of pleasure, as when people do their holiday shopping on the Internet; but it can also be troubling when they realize that their web-surfing activities are being tracked by commercial web bots. For these and other reasons, we agree with Daniel Miller that "the best way to understand, convey, and appreciate our humanity is through attention to our fundamental materiality" (2010: 4). And this means taking material culture seriously.

Culture's beginnings are deep in time. They can perhaps be glimpsed, in our modern world among Japanese macaques, who have invented a custom of washing sweet potatoes, and among wild chimpanzees, who have developed techniques to gain access to food or water (Figure 1.11). Humans' primate ancestors surely shared similar aptitudes when they started walking bipedally over 5 million years ago, possibly with tools of wood and bone. Two-and-a-half million years later, their descendants were making stone tools, conceptually from an imagination of a different order. We can follow this path to the silicon chip and beyond. Thus, as paleoanthropologist Richard Potts puts it, "an evolutionary bridge exists between the human and animal realms of behaviour" (1996: 197). Potts urges us to think of the modern human capacity for culture not as a uniform monolith but rather as a structure whose various pieces were added at different times in our evolutionary past (Figure 1.12). The foundation of culture, he proposes, contains five elements:

1. *Transmission*, the ability to copy behaviour by observation and/or instruction
2. *Memory*, the ability to remember new behaviours (which allowed traditions to develop)
3. *Reiteration*, the ability to reproduce or imitate behaviour or information that has been learned
4. *Innovation*, the ability to invent and modify behaviours
5. *Selection*, the ability to select which innovations to keep and which to discard

To the five basic elements, Potts adds three elements that evolved later and made *human* culture possible:

6. *Symbolic coding*, or *symbolic representation*, the ability to use symbols to represent elements of reality

Figure 1.11 A six-year-old western chimpanzee, Joya, uses rocks as tools to crack open palm oil nuts in Bossou Forest, Mont Nimba, Guinea.

7. *Complex symbolic representation*, the ability to communicate freely about the past, the future, and the invisible or imaginary
8. *Institutional development*, the ability to create complex and variable forms of social organizations unique to our species

Symbolic coding is something human beings share with other species, in particular the great apes. *Complex symbolic representation* distinguishes human language, however, from the simpler vocal communication systems of apes. Apes, and indeed other mammals, have limited abilities to remember complex symbolic structures and to hold information on things remote in time and space; human beings, on the other hand, can think about, invent, and discuss much more complex ideas in great detail and depth. Indeed, humans evolved to be far more capable than any other species of learning and manipulating symbolic representations. Moreover, as biological anthropologist Terrence

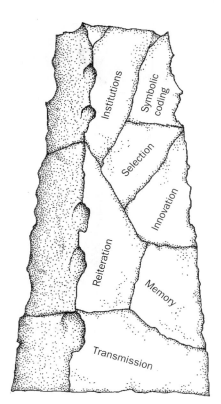

Institutions

Symbolic coding

Selection

Innovation

Reiteration

Memory

Transmission

Figure 1.12 The modern human capacity for culture did not appear all at once. Rather, the various pieces that make it up were added at different times in our evolutionary past.

Deacon suggests, the huge adaptive value of complex symbolic representation for our ancestors appears to have led to genetic changes that improved our brain's symbolic capacities. Put another way, culture and the human brain **co-evolved**, each shaping the development of the other (Deacon 1997). Yet it is the final element given by Potts—*institutional development*—that made it possible for human culture to develop in such elaborate ways. As a result of our ability to create complex social organizations, culture has become "the predominant manner in which human groups vary from one another . . . it *swamps* the biological differences among populations" (Marks 1995: 200). Humans are truly biocultural organisms.

Humanity has survived and prospered in often difficult situations because traditions are passed on to new generations and people can modify them to meet their changing needs. Many practical survival skills, such as what is good to eat and where it is safe to sleep, are never explicitly taught but are learned by contact with other members of our social group. Such learning is sometimes called **habitus** since it is rooted in habitual behaviour. In addition, because cultural traditions encompass the varied situational knowledges and skills of many different individuals, they allow the group to adapt and accomplish beyond any individual's limitations.

Looking at human cultures across time and space, anthropologists can see they are *patterned*; that is, related cultural beliefs and practices repeatedly show up within a cultural group. An example of a common **cultural pattern** is a particular group's language. (See the discussion of *schemas* in Chapter 5.) Some cultural patterns are rooted in specific historical events: that English and French are widely spoken in Canada is connected to the colonial conquest and domination of Canada by speakers of English and French. Many factors contribute to cultural pattern variation. The English of Newfoundland and Labrador, the English of southwestern Quebec, and the English of various First Nations communities differ in rhythm and vocabulary. Researchers have found that cultural constructs and language learning environments in Indigenous communities influence the acquisition of what are termed "heritage languages" as well as English (Bernhardt, Ball, and Deby 2007).

Because of this patterned cultural variation, anthropologists frequently distinguish different "cultural traditions" from one another. Although doing so can be useful as a kind of shorthand, we must remember that the boundaries between cultural traditions can be fuzzy, ultimately resting on someone's judgment about how different one set of customs is from another. Indeed, customs in one area of a culture may contradict customs in another area, as when religion tells people to share with others and economics tells them to look out for themselves. In addition, people have always borrowed cultural elements, so there may be much overlap between apparently distinct traditions.

With cultural traditions we must not assume conformity over time. Cultures constantly change, and many people refuse to be limited by cultural practices of the past. Yet there is also the question of *traditional culture*: What aspects of the past do specific peoples want to protect, maintain, or retrieve? (Note Regna Darnell's discussion in the "In Their Own Words" box that follows.) Worldwide, this is a fundamental dilemma for peoples who have been subjugated or forced to abandon elements of their traditional cultures (e.g., under colonization). In the Canadian context, this question is of

habitus Everyday, routine social activity rooted in habitual behaviour.

cultural pattern A behaviour or idea that members of a specific society repeatedly pass on to one another, across generations, and that is thus recognizable to all members of that society.

co-evolution The relationship between biological processes and symbolic cultural processes in which each makes up an important part of the environment to which the other must adapt.

In Their Own Words

Invisible Genealogies

Canadian anthropologist Regna Darnell speaks to the concepts of "tradition" and "traditional" culture.

"Traditional" culture is a moving target, always changing and adapting to new circumstances. It is located in the contemporary practices of the communities whose interests and concerns direct the work of anthropologists. The label "traditional" is used with considerable rhetorical force in contemporary Native American communities and in their interactions with non-Native institutions and individuals. "Tradition" does not imply returning to some idealized pure culture that existed before Columbus spearheaded the invasion of the "new" world. Native Americans recognize that their societies, like those of white people, whether in Europe or America, have changed in 500 years; all peoples have a history in which living traditions are continuously invented and reinvented.

. . . In my view, anthropologists, in the field and in their writing alike, must respect both the cultural heritage and the contemporary practice of the peoples with whom they work. "Tradition," in such a discourse, refers to that which is continuous with the past, in line with the practices and values of a moral community. Native people themselves can and should define what is traditional within their own communities. They do so in terms of innovations that serve to maintain the identity of the community and its members in relation to their collective histories and personal agencies. "Tradition," in Native American terms, holds much of the meaning that "culture" embodies for anthropologists. If it is invented, we must celebrate its creativity and adaptability under conditions of change. That anthropologists sometimes produce alternative interpretations for other purposes is, of course, another matter.

Source: Darnell, Regna. 2001. *Invisible Genealogies: A History of Americanist Anthropology* (Lincoln: University of Nebraska Press), 16–17.

---

particular concern to First Nations peoples. Ron Ignace, a member of a First Nations band in British Columbia, expressed such concerns in an interview with anthropologist Noel Dyck:

> They [some anthropologists and museums] don't seem to understand that we still exist as a people, that we adapt and change and we have that right to adapt and change, while still maintaining some of our principles that were tried and true over the years. Particularly principles that are necessary for survival as a people. (Ignace et al. 1993: 168–9)

As Ignace's comments suggest, the question of how anthropologists can best represent the cultures they study to an outside population is a matter that requires great consideration, sensitivity, and, most importantly, consultation.

Beyond Anthropology and Culture/Cultures

For many years, the concept of "culture" anchored the anthropological perspective and illuminated the human condition in powerful ways. Yet, over time,

the term *culture* came to mean somewhat different things to different people. In the 1990s and through the beginning of the twenty-first century, culture became the most contested concept of anthropology.

Essentially, the critique centred on the specific definition of *culture* (singular) and of *cultures* (plural). The former distinguishes the human characteristic of being able to create and imitate patterned, symbolically mediated ideas and activities that promote the survival of the species, while the latter indicates a particular, learned way of life belonging to a specific group of human beings. Of the two definitions, the second has elicited the most objections. Those who "write against culture" (Abu-Lughod 1991) defend the validity of *culture* as a concept, but they object to the use of the term *cultures* because it highlights the differences, rather than shared humanness, between groups of people. To some, this focus on differences suggests a lingering racism in the field of anthropology.

Sherry Ortner notes that the essence of the critique was that in the atmosphere of post-colonialism, "many ethnic groups, and many contemporary post-colonial intellectuals, react very strongly against being studied as specimens of cultural differences and otherness" (1999: 8). But Ortner also points out that it is not an issue of "banishing" the concept of cultures but rather of thinking on the process of "reconfiguring this enormously productive concept [*cultures*] for a changing world, . . . a changing landscape of theoretical possibilities" (8). What she calls for are three "imperatives":

1. "[E]xoticize and objectify the culture of the ethnographer, placing it in the same analytic framework" (8). This imperative would allow anthropologists to highlight differences between cultures without implying that their own culture is better or more "normal" than others.
2. "Emphasize the issue of meaning-*making*," an active process (8–9). This imperative would ensure that anthropologists represent cultures as dynamic rather than static and that they recognize individuals as active participants in making sense of their own lives.
3. "[S]ituate cultural analysis within . . . larger analyses of social and political events and processes" (9). This imperative would force anthropologists to work toward a greater purpose, rather than simply engaging in cultural analysis as an "end in itself." It would also force them to recognize the reality that no community exists in isolation.

In recent years this debate has receded to be replaced with an urgency to address specific important issues in a world of change. Applied approaches and advocacy have found prominence in the discussion of emerging global concerns, and anthropologists work to understand as well as offer expertise. An example of this can be found in the literature on children in war:

> The humanitarian definition of childhood and its expression in international law is embedded in transnational politics, is not cross-culturally grounded, and is extremely limiting. . . . A more complex and nuanced understanding, informed by ethnographic research and anthropological insight, can offer the possibility for finding appropriate and effective solutions in different sets of circumstances. . . . [and] a more nuanced view of both the vagaries of war and the contextual definition of childhood should deepen our ability to create more effective approaches that will protect the most vulnerable members of society and give

> victims of war a sense that justice has been achieved, whatever the cultural context. (Rosen 2007: 304–5)

So people are turning increasingly to issues of human rights in a multitude of specifics, such as personhood, loss of place through environment change, forced migration, development, and globalization. Goodale (2006) wants us to accept an *irreducible ethical pluralism*, arguing that it is "so valuable for a reconfigured anthropology . . . to shed light on how specific ethical theories reflect the interplay between important ideas and social practices . . ." (34). This is the response to the culture/cultures critique. Further, many anthropologists now work outside the academy. As Bierschenk notes, "a hitherto largely unused opportunity for greater self-reflection arises . . . in the entirely practical sense of the ethnographic research of the roles, practices and functions of . . . anthropologists who operate outside of academe" (2014: 90–1).

The Challenge of Cultural Differences

The same objects, actions, or events frequently mean different things to people within different cultures. In fact, what counts as an object or event in one culture may not be recognized as such in another. Even within a single cultural tradition, the meaning of an object or an action may differ depending on the context. Quoting philosopher Gilbert Ryle, anthropologist Clifford Geertz notes that "there is a world of difference between a wink and a blink, as anyone who has ever mistaken one for the other has undoubtedly learned" (1973: 6).

Thus, human experience is inherently ambiguous. To resolve the ambiguity, experience must be interpreted. Human beings turn to their own cultural traditions in search of an interpretation that makes sense and is coherent. They do this daily as they go about life among others with whom they share traditions. But this interpretive activity does not cease at the boundary of their specific place in their culture, and serious misunderstandings may arise when two individuals are unaware that their cultural traditions or cultural ground rules differ. Noting the potential for misunderstanding in such encounters, anthropologists are careful to distinguish between two approaches: *ethnocentrism* and *cultural relativism*.

Ethnocentrism

ethnocentrism The opinion that one's own way of life is the most natural, correct, or fully human way of life.

Ethnocentrism is the term anthropologists use to describe the opinion that one's own way of life is natural or correct—indeed, the only way of being fully human. Ethnocentrism is one response to the inevitable tension between individuals from different cultural backgrounds. Yet this "solution" is problematic because it reduces other ways of life to distorted versions of one's own.

The greatest problems with ethnocentrism arise when the members of one society go beyond merely interpreting another way of life in ethnocentric terms and decide to do something about the differences they observe. For example, if individuals from one group conclude that the other way of life is wrong, they might try to convert the members of the other group to their own way of doing things. If the others are unwilling to change their ways, the failed attempt at conversion may transform into an active dualism: *we* versus *they*, *civilization* versus *savagery*, *good* versus *evil*. The ultimate result may be war and *genocide*—the deliberate attempt to exterminate an entire group based on "race," religion, national origin, or other cultural features. Throughout history, such assumed differences have also been used as an excuse for economic and political gains by one group over another. Anthropologist and genocide specialist Alexander Laban Hinton goes so far as to call genocide "the Janus face"—the darker flip side—of the Western **metanarratives** of "civilization" and "progress" that drove the rise of the modern nation-state (2002: 1). Even in more recent times, ethnocentric justifications for war and genocide have persisted, playing a large part in such conflicts as the Rwandan and Bosnian genocides in the 1990s and the continuing tragedy in Darfur.

metanarrative A grand-scale story or theme that members of a given culture recognize and that often drives ideas and actions within that culture.

cultural relativism Approaching the cultures of other peoples with a sympathy such that applying your own beliefs, values, and practices does not become the standard for the basis of understanding.

Is it possible to avoid ethnocentric bias? A holistic approach to relationships between ourselves and others, both across and within cultural traditions, holds promise. So too does humans' lifelong ability to learn—if people honour this potential in themselves and in others. People with a cultural background very different from your own may help you see possibilities for belief and action that are drastically at odds with everything your tradition considers possible. By becoming aware of these unsuspected possibilities, you become a different person. In effect you may be gifted with an "Aha!" moment—a moment of sudden clarity and discovery. In addition, when you share elements of your own culture with people from another cultural background, those individuals are likely to be affected in a similar way.

Learning about other cultures opens us up to new possibilities. Once such learning occurs, people can no longer claim that any single culture has a monopoly on truth. Rather, they must recognize that the truth embodied in any cultural tradition is bound to be partial, approximate, and open to further insight and growth.

Cultural Relativism

Anthropologists must come to terms with the consequences of learning about cultural differences as they do their fieldwork. One result has been the formulation of the concept of **cultural relativism**. Boas taught that cultural relativism was the considered response to racism and prejudice. One of his students, Ruth Benedict, commented that all cultures are "equally valid patterns of life, which mankind has created for itself from the raw materials of existence" (1934: 279). Definitions of cultural relativism have varied over time as different anthropologists have tried to draw conclusions based on their own experiences with other ways of life. One definition that attempts a holistic approach states that cultural relativism involves "understanding another culture in its own terms sympathetically enough so that the culture appears to be a coherent and meaningful design for living" (Greenwood and Stini 1977: 182).

Taking a relativistic approach can help us understand what at first might seem incomprehensible from an outsider's perspective. For example, cultural relativism can help us understand how genocide could develop in a society. Consider the example of the Holocaust in Europe. The Holocaust was intimately related to certain cultural patterns and historical processes that were, and perhaps are yet, deeply rooted in German and European society (Figure 1.13). Answering questions on the causes of the Holocaust involves investigating the historical roots of anti-Semitism and nationalism in Germany.

Some people might be inclined to take a deterministic approach to explaining such an event, arguing that the killers cannot be blamed for their own actions because they had no choice but to do what their culture dictated. These same people might also argue that all members of the culture committing the genocide are responsible because it was their collectively constructed culture that led to the genocide. Yet to accept the argument that "their" culture made them do it is to accept a pessimistic version of cultural determinism that can offer only a simplified account of any complex phenomena. This sort of cultural determinism makes three major faulty assumptions about human nature and human society:

1. Cultures have neat boundaries between them and are sealed off from one another.
2. Every culture offers people only one way to interpret experience (cultures are uniform and permit no variety, harbour no contradictions, and allow no dissent).
3. People living in these closed cultural worlds are passively shaped by culture, helpless to resist indoctrination into a single world view, and incapable of inventing alternatives to that view.

Yet lived human experience undermines all three of these assumptions. To begin with, cultures are not sealed off from one another. Their boundaries are fuzzy, indeed porous, and people with different cultural backgrounds regularly exchange ideas and practices. Internally, they are not uniform. Even without the alternatives introduced from the outside, every culture offers a variety of ways to interpret experience, although not all may be officially sanctioned. In addition, cultures are constantly being redefined by their members. Finally, human beings are not passive lumps shaped unresistingly to fit a single cultural mould. After all, there is no such thing as a single cultural mould in a society acquainted with variety; and, in a society where options exist, choices must be made.

In contrast to the deterministic approach, a relativistic understanding of the Holocaust—and mass genocides in general—accomplishes several things. Such an understanding makes the events more comprehensible, even coherent. It reveals, to our horror, how the persecution and murder of human beings can appear perfectly acceptable when placed in a particular context of meaning, thus challenging our own views on violence. The one thing that this relativistic understanding does not do, however, is allow us to excuse mass killers for what they have done on the grounds that it was all due to their culture.

Understanding something is not the same as approving of or excusing it. When people grow to understand a cultural practice that they at first found repellent, they may arrive at a number of different conclusions. They may change their minds and decide that the practice is desirable, at least in some contexts. They may conclude that the practice in question is more suitable for the people who employ it than any of their own practices would be. They might even recommend that the practice be adopted in their own society. But the opposite may also be the case.

United States Holocaust Memorial Museum, courtesy of National Archives and Records Administration, College Park

Figure 1.13 A sign posted in Berlin, Germany, in 1933 assaults passersby: "Germans defend yourselves against jewish [sic] atrocity propaganda, buy only at German shops!" Such public displays of combined anti-Semitism and nationalism are evidence of the cultural preoccupations that led to the Holocaust. How can taking a relativistic approach to other cultures help us make sense of this sort of hateful display?

People may understand perfectly the cultural rationales—for example, those behind such practices as slavery, infanticide, headhunting, or genocide—and still refuse their approval. They may not be persuaded by the reasons offered to justify the practice, or they may be aware of alternative practices that could achieve the desired outcome using less drastic methods. Indeed, any cultural practice with far-reaching consequences for human life likely will have critics as well as supporters within the society where it is practised. This is certainly the case in North American societies, where such sensitive topics as abortion, capital punishment, gun laws, and same-sex marriage have been and continue to be discussed in many contexts.

Cultural relativism makes moral reasoning more complex and, often, less comfortable. It does not, however, require people to abandon every value their own society has taught them. Someone's culture, like every other culture, offers more than one way of evaluating experience. Exposure to the interpretations of an unfamiliar culture forces people to reconsider the possibilities their culture recognizes in light of new alternatives. It invites people to search for areas of intersection as well as areas of disagreement. What cultural relativism does discourage is the easy solution of refusing to consider alternatives from the outset. Also, it does not free humans from sometimes facing difficult choices between alternatives whose rightness or wrongness is less than clear-cut. In this sense, "cultural relativism is a 'tough-minded' philosophy" (Herskovits 1973: 37). As cultural anthropologist Renato Rosaldo (2008) comments,

> Relativism . . . argues for engagement, for dialogue between cultures. This is not the kind of easy cosmopolitanism that implies enormous privilege—the capacity, for example, to spend three days in the Bali Hilton. It's a deeper form of knowing that entails some recognition that I am one among others. I'm not the centre of the universe.

Thus, at its core, cultural relativism is an argument against ethnocentrism.

Culture, History, and Human Agency

The human condition is rooted in time and shaped by history. As part of the human condition, culture is also historical, worked out and reconstructed in every generation. As paleoanthropologists have shown, the human species is itself a product of millions of years of evolution. Hence, human history is an essential aspect of the human story.

Anthropologists sometimes disagree about how to approach human history. Nineteenth-century thinkers, such as Herbert Spencer, argued that examining the evolution of social structures over time was central to the study of the human condition. Other anthropologists, however, were not interested in change over time. In the 1930s, British anthropologist A.R. Radcliffe-Brown justified this lack of interest by pointing out that in societies without written records, knowledge about past life is non-existent; according to him, any attempt to reconstruct such past life would be an unfounded attempt at "conjectural history."

Approaches such as this, which ignore the significance of *oral* (as opposed to *written*) histories, lost support by the end of the twentieth century. Lyotard argues that traditional cultures or traditional segments of post-traditional societies— societies that do not have written records—work in worlds of *knowledge* ("savoir") as opposed to worlds of *learning* ("connaissance"). Dods elaborates further on this distinction:

> . . . The world of *savoir* can be reduced neither to science nor to learning, as we understand these terms in the world of Western science or the academy. In this context *savoir* is reminiscent of the Lévi-Strauss discussion of mythical thought as "an intellectual form of *bricolage*" (1966: 21). What has meaning in the world of *savoir* is not a form of knowledge located in a set of denotative statements but rather sets of knowing that include "notions of 'know-how,' *savoir-faire* 'knowing how to live,' *savoir-vivre* 'how to listen' *savoir-écouter*" (Lyotard 1987: 78–9). It is the way things are done, much like the Japanese concept of *do*. Knowledge becomes a question of competence, not merely the simple determination and application of the criterion of truth. (Dods 2004: 547)

In other words, anthropologists cannot conclude that knowledge shared orally, through storytelling, is any less meaningful than more rigidly recorded history. Different ways of transmitting knowledge from person to person, generation to generation, simply reflect the diversity of the human condition. No matter what the method of transmission, all societies choose what aspects of their history they want to remember, and the collective memory of a people is transmitted "in their historical, social, and political context" (Rodriguez and Fortier 2009: 7).

Other early anthropologists had no interest in history for a different reason. Western capitalist culture, with its eye on the future and its faith in progress—a theme from the Enlightenment—has had little use for the past. It is therefore no wonder that some anthropologists built clockwork models of social structures that could be trusted to run reliably without "losing time." In these models, human beings and societies are likened to machines. If a living organism is used as the model of society, and if organisms are nothing but machines, then a machine model of society, with individuals as robot-like moving parts, is not at all far-fetched (Figure 1.14).

A holistic approach—one that focuses on inclusive assessment of counter points of view—to human history, however, rejects these clockwork models. Our biocultural heritage has produced a living species that uses culture to overcome biological and individual limitations. The result has been the emergence of beings capable of studying themselves and their own biocultural evolution.

But just how free from limitations are humans? Opinion in Western societies often polarizes around one of two extremes: either people have *free will* and may do just as they please, or their behaviour is *completely determined* by biology or society. Many social scientists, however, are convinced that a more realistic description of human freedom was offered by Karl Marx, who wrote, "Men make their own history, but they do not make it just as they please; they do not make it under circumstances chosen by themselves but under circumstances directly encountered, given, and transmitted by the past" (1963 [1852]: 15). Humans regularly struggle, often against great odds, to exercise some control over their lives (Figure 1.15). People are *agents*, but agents who cannot escape from the cultural and historical contexts within which they act. People must frequently select a course of action when the "correct" choice is unclear and the outcome uncertain. Some anthropologists even liken humanity's existence to a minefield that people must painstakingly try to cross without blowing themselves up. In

Figure 1.14 In the 1927 film *Metropolis*, a lower class of labourers work within a machine-like power plant, which strictly limits what they can do, to supply the ruling classes. Does this technological metaphor speak to the issues of globalization and the place of workers in our changing world?

Shawn Goldberg/Shutterstock.com

Figure 1.15 The Women's March took place on 21 January 2017, with participation from several Canadian cities and an estimated five million people marching worldwide. The rallies were in opposition to the political positions of newly elected President Donald Trump and his administration. Besides protest, what other ways do humans demonstrate agency in their lives?

of **human agency**—the stuff of people's dreams and the realm of their potential for growth.

The Promise of the Anthropological Perspective

The anthropological perspective on the human condition is not easy to maintain. It forces people to question the common-sense assumptions with which they are most comfortable. It increases the difficulty they encounter when faced with moral and political decisions. It does not allow people an easy retreat to ethnocentrism when the going gets rough. Once human beings are exposed to the kinds of experiences that the anthropological undertaking makes possible, they are changed—for better or worse. They cannot easily pretend that these new experiences never happened to them. Once they have had a genuine glimpse of "the other" as human beings equal to themselves, there is no going back—except in bad faith.

So, anthropology is guaranteed to complicate your life. Nevertheless, the anthropological perspective can give you a broader understanding of human nature and the wider world—of society, culture, and history—and thus help you construct more realistic and authentic ways of coping with those complications.

human agency Human beings' ability to exercise at least some control over their lives.

such cultural contexts, with their ragged edges and fuzzy boundaries, human beings must make interpretations, formulate goals, and set out in pursuit of them. A holistic, dialectical approach to the human condition recognizes the existence and importance

Living Anthropology

Linguistic Belonging: Francophone Communities in Canada's Northwest Territories

by Joshua Friesen, PhD Candidate, Anthropology, McGill University

"Home is where the heart is." This proverb rings true for many people in Canada and elsewhere. But how is a home defined? And what about the heart? Does this proverb mean that you feel at home wherever you truly desire to be or that your heart is wedded to a particular landscape, a set of social relations, or a tradition? Is the home a social construct that affords security, entertainment, and economic opportunity, or is it a physical artifact with walls, a roof, and a door? Likewise, is the heart an embodied sense of attachment, a pumping organ, or the seat of human emotion? Cultural anthropologists investigate these questions all over the world by studying how people create and maintain a sense of belonging in a particular time and place. By asking what binds people

together and to their environment, cultural anthropology aims to understand more about a central feature of the human condition: community.

Anthropologists have studied belonging and community in a variety of ways. Research has been done on the difference between spaces and places or on how a physical environment is made over into a cultural landscape with particular meanings, resonances, and collectively significant markers (Low and Lawrence-Zúñiga 2003). Research has also been done on the definition and creation of social communities (Hobsbawm and Ranger 1992). How a community is represented, symbolized, and memorialized all has an effect on who feels included therein (Anderson 1991).

More recently, terms such *social-inclusion*, *belonging*, and *community* have become especially important for countries with large groups of new immigrants. Researchers have found that newcomers who feel included by their adoptive communities have better economic and social outcomes than those who feel excluded (Government of Canada 2006).

In Canada and elsewhere, domestic labour mobility is an important feature of the national economy. Global competition and international markets for goods and services create a constant flux in the profitability and competitiveness of Canadian commodities. In the domain of primary resource extraction this flux and change is especially noticeable, and large flows of Canadian labourers regularly move across the country—from Newfoundland to Alberta, from Quebec to the Northwest Territories, and so on—in order to find work (Ferguson 2011).

For these mobile workers, creating a sense of belonging can be difficult. In their ethnographic fieldwork on French-Canadian migrant workers in Canada's Northwest Territories (NWT), Lindsay Bell and Monica Heller examine how French speakers from francophone communities in Ontario, Quebec, and New Brunswick create and recreate a sense of belonging and community in the NWT (in Duchêne and Heller 2012). They highlight the essential role that language plays in the production and maintenance of community for these workers. In the predominantly anglophone economy of the NWT, francophone community institutions, such as French elementary and secondary schools, were identified as the primary means for French Canadians to maintain their ties to a francophone "home." The Canadian federal government funds these institutions as part of a nation-building project meant to create and project the image of Canada as a truly bilingual community. Despite the efforts of the federal government to support French schooling and francophone community organizations in the NWT and elsewhere, Bell and Heller find that, "francophone institutional spaces are . . . complicated sites of tensions between pride and profit" (2012: 178). They argue that while these institutions help to reproduce the pride a community feels in its language, identity, and belonging, they are also sites for non-francophone individuals to acquire the cultural capital that comes with being bilingual in a federal Canada (177). In this way, government-sponsored community-building institutions act as sites both for grounding a mobile francophone community in a linguistic heritage that is localized elsewhere, and for creating a new pan-Canadian bilingual identity, which is more sought-after on the domestic and global labour markets.

Ethnographies such as Bell and Heller's highlight the ways in which belonging and community are always connected to political and economic conditions. In the case of francophone migrants to the NWT, attempts by Canada's federal government to support and affirm the French language have also created the conditions for the erasure of French-Canadian distinctiveness. Marketing and promoting a bilingual Canadian population is at once both more inclusive and also at odds with original notions of French-Canadian belonging and community. This tension between, as Bell and Heller put it, "pride and profit" straddles a recurring theme in examinations of the human condition: that of the trade-offs between the prideful traditions of home and the incentives of work and profit. In short, sometimes the heart leads humans away from their homes.

Key Terms

anthropological perspective 5	cultural relativism 18	idealism 3
anthropology 5	culture 5	informants 10
applied anthropology 11	determinism 3	linguistic anthropology 9
archaeology 8	dualism 3	material culture 13
binary opposition 3	essence 3	materialism 3
biocultural organisms 12	ethnocentrism 18	medical anthropology 12
biological (or physical) anthropology 6	ethnography 11	metanarrative 18
biological evolution 6	ethnology 11	paleoanthropology 7
comparative 5	evolutionary 6	primatology 7
cultural anthropology 9	habitus 15	symbol 13
cultural evolution 6	holism 4	
cultural pattern 15	human agency 22	

Chapter Summary

1. Various models have been devised to explain humans and their cultures: dualism, idealism, and cultural determinism, for example. Since anthropology aims to describe, in the broadest sense, what it means to be human, anthropologists have developed a perspective on the human condition that is holistic, comparative, and evolutionary.

2. North American anthropology is usually considered to have four major specialties or subdisciplines: biological anthropology, archaeology, linguistic anthropology, and cultural anthropology. Some anthropologists consider a fifth to be applied anthropology, and some consider medical anthropology to be an emerging approach as well. Each of the four traditional subdisciplines can inform the others, and each can contribute to problem-solving within and between cultures.

3. Many anthropologists criticized the use of the term *cultures* to refer to particular, learned ways of life belonging to specific groups of human beings. Critics argue that the plural concept of *cultures* seems to endorse an oppressive kind of cultural determinism. This has somewhat lessened as time has moved on and anthropologists have turned increasingly to what could best be termed issues of human rights and the development of *irreducible ethical pluralism.*

4. Ethnocentrism is a form of reductionism. Anthropologists believe it can be countered by a commitment to cultural relativism, an attempt to understand the cultural underpinnings of behaviour. Cultural relativism makes moral decisions more difficult because it requires us to take into account many things before we make up our minds. Cultural relativism does not require us to abandon every value our society has taught us; however, it does not permit the easy solution of refusing to consider alternatives from the outset.

5. Through fieldwork, cultural anthropologists gain insight into another culture, both by participating with their informants in social activities and by observing those activities as outsiders. Ethnographies are published accounts of what an anthropologist learned during fieldwork. Ethnology involves comparing ethnographic information from two or more different cultures. Because human experience is often ambiguous, adaptation requires cultural interpretation, which is a constant, necessary process, whether it is an attempt to understand people or symbols within one's own culture or those of another culture.

Critical Thinking Questions

1. Using the concepts of *idealism* and *materialism*, how would you develop definitions of what it means to be human? How deterministic are your definitions?

2. What are the advantages of taking a holistic approach in anthropology? How does the concept of holism relate to the concept of cultural relativism? Can holism succeed in anthropology without cultural relativism?

3. How do the four original subdisciplines of anthropology—biological anthropology, archaeology, linguistic anthropology, and cultural anthropology—contribute to an understanding of humans? How does applied anthropology add to this anthropological perspective, and what would you consider to be its ethical position in anthropology?

4. Can we move from ethnocentrism to an *irreducible ethical pluralism*?

Suggested Readings

In Recent (and Relatively Recent) Publications

Benhabib, Seyla. 2002. *The Claims of Culture: Equality and Diversity in the Global Era* (Princeton, NJ: Princeton University Press). This book examines what we mean by "political membership" and what constitutes a "political community": How do we bring people we term "aliens"—strangers, immigrants, asylum seekers—into our political processes? What boundaries must be negotiated?

Borofsky, Robert, Fredrik Barth, Richard A. Shweder, Lars Rodseth, and Nomi Maya Stolzenberg. 2001. "When: A Conversation about Culture," *American Anthropologist,* New Series, 103, 2: 432–46. A discussion of what culture is and is not, as well as how and when anthropologists should use the culture concept.

Feder, Kenneth L. 2014. *Frauds, Myths, and Mysteries: Science and Pseudoscience in Archaeology*, 8th edn (New York: McGraw-Hill). An entertaining and informative exploration of fascinating frauds and genuine archaeological mysteries seen through an application of the scientific method.

Marks, Jonathan. 2002. *What It Means to Be 98% Chimpanzee: Apes, People, and Their Genes* (Berkeley: University of California Press). A lively and provocative text by a molecular anthropologist who explains what can and cannot be concluded from the fact that the genomes of chimpanzees and humans are nearly identical.

Ortner, Sherry. B. 2006. *Anthropology and Social Theory: Culture, Power, and the Acting Subject* **(Durham, NC: Duke University Press).** So you want to be an anthropologist? This is a must-read, either now or when you are in an advanced theory course!

Relethford, John. 2013. *The Human Species: An Introduction to Biological Anthropology*, **9th edn (New York: McGraw-Hill).** An excellent, clear introduction to biological anthropology.

Sahlins, Marshall. 1999. "Two or Three Things That I Know about Culture," *Journal of the Royal Anthropological Institute* **5, 3: 399–421.** A thoughtful consideration of the lasting importance of culture as an anthropological concept.

Skinner, Mark, and Kristina Bowie. 2009. "Forensic Anthropology: Canadian Content and Contributions," in *Handbook of Forensic Anthropology and Archaeology*, **ed. Soren Blau and Douglas H. Ubelaker (Walnut Creek, CA: Left Coast Press), 87–103.** A survey of forensic anthropology in Canada, Chapter 8 in an in-depth handbook for forensic anthropologists.

Smedley, Audrey. 1998. "'Race' and the Construction of Human Identity," *American Anthropologist*, **New Series, 100, 3: 690–702.** An examination of how "race" came to be associated with human identity, and the problems with this association.

Taylor, Christopher C. 2002. "The Cultural Face of Terror in the Rwandan Genocide of 1994," in *Annihilating Difference: The Anthropology of Genocide*, **ed. Alexander Laban Hinton (Berkeley: University of California Press), 138–78.** Exploring a topic central to Canadian discussions of participation in peacekeeping, this chapter from a book on genocide challenges us on the nature of culture.

Watson, Patty Jo. 1995. "Archaeology, Anthropology, and the Culture Concept," *American Anthropologist*, **New Series, 97, 4: 683–94.** This article relates how an anthropologist/archaeologist evolved in her thinking about the nature of the subject of her discipline and her specialty within that discipline.

Historical Perspective (1940s–1960s)

Boas, Franz. 1940. *Race, Language and Culture* **(New York: Macmillan).** A collection of Boas's most influential essays on anthropology.

Kroeber, Alfred L. 1948. "White's View of Culture," *American Anthropologist*, **New Series, 50, 3 (Part 1): 405–15.** American cultural anthropologist Alfred L. Kroeber, who studied under Boas, examines and clarifies a view of culture put forth by Leslie A. White (see below).

Montagu, Ashley. 1962. "The Concept of Race," *American Anthropologist*, **New Series, 64, 5 (Part 1): 919–28.** An examination of "the concepts of race as they are used with reference to man," written by a highly accomplished British-American anthropologist.

Stocking, George W., Jr. 1966. "Franz Boas and the Culture Concept in Historical Perspective," *American Anthropologist*, **New Series, 68, 4: 867–82.** German-American scholar George W. Stocking, Jr, takes a close look at Boas's view of culture, just over 20 years after Boas's death.

White, Leslie A. 1959. "The Concept of Culture," *American Anthropologist*, **New Series, 61, 2: 227–51.** Another classic analysis of the culture concept, this time from American anthropologist Leslie A. White, writing a decade after Kroeber (see above) published his comments on White's earlier view of culture.

Related Websites

Archaeology at Parks Canada
www.pc.gc.ca/eng/progs/arch/index.aspx

Canadian Anthropology Society
www.cas-sca.ca

CBC News: Residential Schools
www.cbc.ca/news/
canada/a-history-of-residential-schools-in-canada-1.702280

American Anthropological Association
www.aaanet.org

AnthroBase: Informant (Debated Terminology)
www.anthrobase.com/Dic/eng/def/informant.htm

Society for Applied Anthropology
www.sfaa.net

Online Videos

Cross-Cultural Comparisons of Mass Murder in the US and Canada (Lecture by Dr Kim MacInnis)
www.youtube.com/watch?v=XWv8sYCNUsc

National Geographic: Cultural Differences
video.nationalgeographic.com/video/movies/
cultural-differences-ggtu

Uncontacted Tribes: First Ever Aerial Footage of Uncontacted Amazon Tribe
www.uncontactedtribes.org/brazilfootage

2

Fieldwork: A Meeting of Cultural Traditions

Learning Objectives

By the end of Chapter 2, you will be able to
* understand the value of ethnographic fieldwork;
* describe how fieldwork is used in cultural anthropology;
* outline key stages in the process of preparing to do fieldwork;
* understand the importance of professional ethics;
* compare and contrast three modes of ethnographic research: positivist, reflexive (including phenomenological), and multi-sited;
* consider the effects of fieldwork on all involved; and
* appreciate the value and open-ended nature of anthropological knowledge.

Ethnographic fieldwork is challenging. This has remained so even as anthropologists' understanding of the world has changed with the ease of travel, their wider knowledge of cultures, their broader research interest even within their own communities, and the somewhat ubiquitous access to modern communications. If anthropologists consider all of this in a historical perspective of, say, Bronisław Malinowski in the "field," it all seems so very adventurous and somewhat romantic. And this view detracts from the seriousness of what anthropologists ask others to do and the seriousness of the work in which they engage.

Generally, "the anthropologist" is the person who shows up in a community with plans to be there for a year or more, claims to be interested in the community's way of life, interacts with the local peoples, and records observations (Figure 2.1). Here, the anthropologist is the recipient of a great gift. People in diverse communities give of themselves and their resources. They share their families and friendships, homes and food, as well as insights into their lives and culture. This was so in the past and remains so today. Receiving this gift can be a deeply humbling experience. Anthropologists know, too, that deep learning occurs on both sides of the cultural divide. The process of *reciprocal* action and influence in this space changes all in essential ways. Thus, **fieldwork** broadens understandings of cultural worlds and transforms the self-understandings of anthropologists and the people with whom they work.

There is a deep obligation on the part of the anthropologist to remember one essential thing: an anthropologist gets to go home, but the people of the community *are at home* and they stay there. Thus, transformations that occur during fieldwork may have a strong impact on their lives. There is, then, the profound responsibility of behaving ethically in seeking and accepting the gift of insight into other people's lives.

Methods of Collecting Information

Anthropologists conducting fieldwork collect data using various methods. They consult published

© Priscilla Magrath

Figure 2.1 Ethnographic fieldwork involves entering into a community and forming reciprocal relationships with the people of that community. What kinds of effects do you think fieldwork can have on the people whose lives are being observed? How might anthropologists be affected by the process?

literature and archives. **Structured interviews** are also important for, as Charles L. Briggs comments, they allow anthropologists to consider "science/anti-science debates, questions of scale, and explorations of similarities of methods between anthropology and other forms of 'expert' knowledge" (2007: 551), and these *experts* may well be our teachers in other cultures (Dods 2004). Sometimes questionnaires and psychological tests are used but never alone since the information they uncover may not have an appropriate context and therefore may be highly misleading. To mediate this, anthropologists use **participant-observation** (Figure 2.2). Participant-observation involves direct, face-to-face interaction between the researcher and his or her local research partners, as they go about their daily lives. The method was pioneered by cultural anthropologists and remains characteristic of anthropological work. It allows anthropologists to understand interactions in a wider context of social networks and cultural beliefs and values because it is embedded in the

fieldwork An extended period of close involvement with the people in whose way of life anthropologists are interested, during which anthropologists ordinarily collect most of their data.

structured interviews A method for gathering information whereby an anthropologist (or another researcher) asks a set of predetermined questions and records participants' responses.

participant-observation The method anthropologists use to gather information by living and working with the people whose culture they are studying while participating in their lives as much as possible.

Figure 2.2 Participant-observation has long been a hallmark of research in cultural anthropology, whether in the 1920s with pioneering cultural anthropologist Margaret Mead on the island of Samoa (left) or in the 1980s with Canadian anthropologist Naomi McPherson in Papua New Guinea (right). What could be some of the benefits and challenges of participant-observation over other information-gathering techniques (e.g., interviewing, handing out questionnaires)?

positivism The view that there is a single reality "out there" that can be detected through the senses and that there is a single, appropriate scientific method for investigating that reality.

day-to-day life of the community. However, as Nayar notes, "Going to the field raises questions about methodology as often the reality is not as straightforward as theory.... [since] relations are complex and messy. The consequence is that ... we need to keep some basic principles of research in mind and then adapt them accordingly" (2012: 36).

Modes of Ethnographic Fieldwork: A Short History

> Over the last century, ethnography as an imaginative analytical vehicle produced true knowledge about a great range of patterns of human relationship.... As much as we can recognize it as the product of a particular author, we can equally comprehend an ethnography as taking holistic shape at the tense intersection of ethnographic conversations and social scientific debates involving many differently placed voices. (Wardle and Blasco 2011: 124)

When anthropology began to take on its own identity as an intellectual discipline during the

nineteenth century, it aspired to be scientific. As a result, early anthropologists adopted **positivism**, the traditional philosophy of the physical sciences. Indeed, this perspective heavily influenced the pioneering ethnographers who established the fieldwork tradition—for example, Bronisław Malinowski, credited with "inventing" long-term participant-observation–based fieldwork; Franz Boas, who did much of his fieldwork on the Kwakwaka'wakw (Kwakiutl) in British Columbia; Margaret Mead, Boas's best-known student, who conducted extensive fieldwork in the South Pacific; and Frank G. Speck, with his extensive work with the Algonquians of eastern Canada.

Since the early twentieth century, anthropologists' approaches to fieldwork have changed. While anthropologists still aim to be scientific in their study of human nature, human society, and human history, they now understand "science" very differently, recognizing that there is not just one but a *variety* of scientific methods, each able to produce reliable knowledge about the world (e.g., Knorr Cetina 2000). Similarly, they recognize that this can produce diverse perspectives, thereby enriching our understanding of reality. Thus the *reflexive* approach and, increasingly, phenomenological analysis have emerged in recent decades. In the following discussion, we will examine in greater detail the positivist and the reflexive approach as well as phenomenology.

The Positivist Approach

The positivist approach has its roots in French philosopher Auguste Comte's (1798–1857) "positive philosophy." In the late nineteenth and early twentieth centuries, it was refined by a group of influential thinkers known as *positivists*. Today, *positivism* has become a label for a particular way of looking at and studying the world scientifically.

First, positivists want to explain the **material world** in terms of material causes and processes detected through our senses. Second, they are committed to a separation of facts from values. They justify this separation on the grounds that facts relate to the nature of physical, material reality—what *is*—whereas values are based on speculation about what *ought to be*. To positivists, scientific research is concerned only with the former. As a result, all valid scientific inquiry, no matter the focus, should be understood as different aspects of a single, disinterested quest for knowledge. In other words, the truth remains the truth whether people like it or not, whether it conforms to their idea of what is good and proper or not. Third, they are convinced that a single scientific method can be used to investigate any domain of reality, from planetary motion to chemical reactions to human life. The most ambitious positivists are convinced that all scientific knowledge will ultimately be unified in a "theory of everything"—Stephen Hawking aside. As a result, the goal of the positivist program has been to produce **objective knowledge**.

Applying Positivist Methods to Anthropology

For the positivist, the standard research scenario involves a scientist in a laboratory. This approach creates obstacles for those who study human life by means of participant-observation. Early cultural anthropologists were aware of these obstacles, and they tried to devise ways to get around them. Their first step was to approximate lab conditions by testing hypotheses in different cultural settings. These settings were carefully selected to display the same range of variation, naturally, that a laboratory scientist could create artificially. As a result, the field could be seen as a living laboratory. Each research setting would

correspond to a separate experimental situation, a method called *controlled comparison*. Margaret Mead used this method in the 1930s when she studied four different societies in an attempt to discover the range and causes of gender roles.

Anthropologists such as Mead were encouraged by the enormous successes that the physical scientists had attained through positivist approaches. From the mid-nineteenth to the mid-twentieth century, positivistically inclined anthropologists studied cultures their contemporaries had neither heard of nor cared to know. Rejecting the unstructured, impressionistic work of an earlier period, they attempted to produce accounts that were systematic and accurate. Overall, they were more or less successful, although they were sometimes accused of insensitivity.

Yet there remained a problem: in order to remain true to positivism, anthropologists had to record objective facts from the perspective of an invisible observer; yet in order to get closer to the truth, they had to admit that they were personally involved in the situation. In fact, they regularly developed close ties to the people among whom they worked, often defending their full humanity to outsiders and, at times, even intervening on their behalf with governments. Yet none of these efforts showed up in their ethnographies. To resolve these apparent conflicts, they needed to find a new approach.

Questioning the Positivist Approach

In the 1960s and 1970s many assumptions about the way the world worked were called into question, as was the nature of scientific inquiry. Anthropologist Derek Freeman's critique (1983, 1998) of Margaret Mead's early fieldwork in Samoa illustrates the tone of the debate (see Côté [2000] for a summary of the Mead–Freeman controversy and Shankman's [2009] critical discussion of the Freeman evaluation). Anthropologists began to show how different observers, working from different assumptions, often produce different ethnographies about the same society. At the same time, they noted that differently situated fieldworkers also came to many similar conclusions, and these conclusions allowed them to link their work in productive ways.

Consider the case of anthropologist Annette Weiner, who conducted fieldwork in the Trobriand Islands nearly 60 years after Bronisław Malinowski. Malinowski and Weiner were anthropologists of different nationalities and different genders working in different villages with different participants during

material world The physical world in all its manifestations. We experience this world through our senses of sight, hearing, smell, taste, touch, and movement.

objective knowledge Knowledge about reality that is absolute and true for all people, in all times and places.

different periods of time. Weiner made an important contribution to our understanding of Trobriand life by describing and explaining activities involving Trobriand women's "wealth" (Figure 2.3)—activities that were central to the continued healthy functioning of Trobriand life but about which Malinowski had written nothing. Weiner might have published her findings by declaring that Malinowski had got it wrong. But this route did not appeal to her, primarily because, as she alluded to, he got so very much right. Malinowski's own preoccupations led him to write about aspects of Trobriand life different from those that interested Weiner. As a result, he left behind a portrait of Trobriand society that Weiner later felt obliged to supplement. Nevertheless, much of Malinowski's work remained valid and insightful to Weiner. In tribute to him, she quoted long passages from his ethnographies (see Weiner 1976, 1988; see also the EthnoProfile on the Trobriand Islanders in Chapter 8).

Beginning in the 1960s, anthropologists also began to reconsider the ethics and politics of positivist science in general and of participant-observation in particular. They began to pay close attention to the nature of the relationships they developed with their participants, and they re-examined the laboratory model of fieldwork, noting the differences between anthropology and other more traditionally scientific disciplines. In the physical sciences, for example, it is fairly easy to justify a hierarchy elevating scientists over their subject matter. Indeed, it seems difficult to imagine the ethical or political obligations that a geologist might have to a rock. Matters are otherwise when human beings are the subject of inquiry. To approach human beings as objects, lacking the same inquisitive intelligence as the scientists who study them, is to mischaracterize the subject matter of anthropology. Anthropologists *do* have ethical obligations to other human beings; political factors *can* complicate the relationships ethnographers develop during fieldwork. Further, there *is* a mutual inquisitiveness that needs to be acknowledged in the fieldwork experience. It is *human interaction* that is central to cross-cultural understanding. Thus, by extension, anthropologists came to understand that they are *human beings* in relationships, not impersonal recording machines. In doing so, they become aware that observation "has a subjective component by virtue of the observer's . . . decision to recognize certain distinctions" (Allen and Hoekstra 1991: 49). In effect, anthropological observation cannot be entirely value free.

Figure 2.3 Trobriand women's wealth, consisting of dried, processed banana leaves, being collected at a funeral.

Questioning positivist science is not taken lightly. Those who do raise objections are often accused of abandoning scientific discipline entirely, allowing material facts to be obscured by the researcher's individual, *subjective* values and preferences. But does the rejection of positivism turn anthropological fieldwork into just one person's subjective impressions of other people? Most anthropologists would answer a firm *no* because fieldwork is a *dialogue*; ethnographers engage in real conversations with their local research partners. Such dialogues are often characterized by mutual patience and painstaking collaborative attempts to sort things out and to piece things together in mutually coherent pictures of reality. When successful, the outcome is a new understanding of the world that both anthropologist and participant can share. This means that field data have not subjective meaning but intersubjective meaning: field data are the product of long dialogues between researcher and participant. Through dialogue and negotiation, intersubjective meanings are achieved.

The Reflexive Approach

The intersubjective meanings on which participants rely are public, not private. Participants take them for granted, but they may not be obvious to an outsider. In order to make these meanings explicit, anthropologist and participants together must occasionally step back from the ordinary flow of daily life and examine them critically. They must think about the way members of the culture *normally* think about their lives. This thinking about thinking is known as reflexivity; thus, fieldwork in cultural anthropology is a reflexive experience.

Reflexive fieldwork retains a respect for detailed, accurate information-gathering, but it also takes into consideration a broader range of contextual information than does positivist fieldwork. It pays explicit attention to the ethical and political context of research, the background of researchers, and the full partnership with our in-culture teachers that produce collaborative relationships leading to anthropological knowledge. Ethnographic knowledge shaped by reflexivity becomes what science and technology scholar Donna Haraway (1991) has called situated knowledge and involves making explicit exactly who you are as an ethnographer—your gender, nationality, political preference, class/ethnic/educational backgrounds, and so forth. Once you have identified your own social location, you will be better able to understand your unique perspective—your *situated subjectivity*—that informs your research choices. You will also be better able to present who you are to the people with whom you will be working. Both these distinctions inform you as an ethnographer and shape the relationships you have in the field.

Being *aware* of who you are will help you identify the limits of what you can discover. For example, in some societies, being a female ethnographer may bar you from studying certain social activities that are central to the local culture. In such a case, your ethnographic account is bound to be partial and could be seen as weak under the test of "scientific objectivity." Nevertheless, a detailed, reflexive account of what you were able to learn may be far more reliable than a strictly "objective" account. After all, such an account would explicitly acknowledge the fact that you did not talk to everybody or see everything, and it would openly admit that your observations are partial and thus *situated*. This avoids suggesting sweeping generalizations about an entire social group. As such, it allows anthropologists to develop a fuller, truer account of aspects of people's lives.

Reflexive commitment means anthropologists are obligated to reveal to everyone involved how data are gathered. Additionally, anthropologists have argued that they must also share their conclusions with their participants and include their participants' reflections on those conclusions in their published ethnographies. For example, after conducting fieldwork in a poor neighbourhood in the US, cultural anthropologist Bettylou Valentine (1978) persuaded several of her participants to comment on her manuscript before publication. She visited them for lengthy discussions and found that, in general, they agreed with her conclusions. In the published volume, *Hustling and Other Hard Work: Life Styles in the Ghetto*, Valentine includes both her own conclusions and her participants' voices in the final chapter. Valentine's ethnography presents a vivid example of the open-endedness of the dialogue between anthropologist and participant: no single interpretation of human experience is final. This kind of mutual reflexivity is at the heart of anthropological knowledge, and it invites future anthropologists and others to continue the dialogue from their own uniquely situated position.

Anthropologists can also take what is known as a phenomenological approach. Robert Desjarlais and C. Jason Throop define phenomenology as "the study of phenoma as they appear to the consciousness of an individual or a group of people; the study

subjective meaning Meaning that seems true to a particular person, based on his or her personal values, beliefs, opinions, and assumptions.

intersubjective meaning Meaning rooted in the symbolic systems of a culture and shared by participants in that culture.

reflexivity Critically thinking about the way one thinks; reflecting on one's own experience.

situated knowledge Knowledge that is set within or specific to a precise context or situation.

phenomenology The study of first-person experience of consciousness in the material world, which is based on the conscious (intentional) framing of the meaning or content of the observed. In different conditions or situations, people come to recognize their responses to different conditions of intentionality. These include "embodiment, bodily skills, cultural context, language and other social practices, social background, and contextual aspects of intentional activities" (Stanford Encyclopedia of Philosophy, https://plato.stanford.edu/entries/phenomenology/#WhatPhen).

In Their Own Words

Phenomenological Approaches in Anthropology

Robert Desjarlais and C. Jason Throop speak to phenomenological approaches in anthropology.

Many anthropologists have found great utility in phenomenological methods in anthropological inquiry. The focus on "life as lived" and human consciousness in all of its lived realities . . . have enabled anthropologists to step beyond, on the one hand, anthropological considerations of cultural discourses, social relations, and political economy alone and, on the other, psychological considerations of selfhood, psychodynamics, and subjectivity (Abu-Lughod 1991; Biehl et al. 2007; Jackson 1998). At the same time, anthropologists have tended to shy away from the more general, categorical, culture-free pronouncements often sounded by phenomenological philosophers, preferring instead to couch their findings within specific cultural and historical settings (Jackson 1998, 2009b). Anthropologists have also rooted much of their research less in philosophical reasoning than in ethnographic research and so . . . anthropologists have worked to introduce more fully the historical, the cultural, the variable, and the relative into phenomenology. They have also given priority, at times, to people's own formulations of the world and their place within it as they have sought to detail the contours of "local phenomenoloies" (Halliburton 2002). . . .

Starting in the mid-1980s, several anthropologists . . . had come to focus unduly on questions of meaning, discourse, structural relations, and political economy to the neglect of the everyday experiences, contingencies, and dilemmas that weigh so heavily on people's lives (Desjarlais 1992; Jackson 2005; Kleinman 1995, 1999; Seeman 2009; Stoller 1997; Turner & Bruner 1986; Wikan 1990). Subsequent inquiries along these lines have offered reflections on the cultural, genealogical, ontological, and epistemological dimensions of the concept of "experience" itself, leading to the somewhat

paradoxical understanding that the category of experience is, at once, highly needed in anthropological thought and deeply charged, overdetermined, and culturally constituted (Desjarlais 1997; Mattingly 1998; Throop 2003, 2010c). Indeed, on the one hand, phenomenological anthropologists have often explicitly relied on the concept of experience as a way to orient their research generatively to the complexly temporal, at times ambiguous, and deeply ambivalent realities of human existence. On the other hand, when used in an unreflexive way, the category itself at times presumes and promotes unexamined cultural assumptions concerning articulations of self, subjectivity, and social action that may blind us to other possible forms of life and ways of being. Along with efforts toward an anthropology of experience, a number of orientations have emerged out of interest to map out how phenomenal processes take form in particular cultural and historical settings. . . . In undertaking inquiries along the lines of a "cultural phenomenology," anthropologists have examined how questions of selfhood, sociality, temporality, agency, pain, and morality, among others, tie into social and cultural formations in specific sociocultural settings and lifeworlds (Csordas 1990, 1994a, b; Geurts 2002; Pinto 2008; Throop 2009b, 2010a–c). Advocates of a critical phenomenology, in turn, have stressed the need to attend to the many, and often highly charged, political, social, and discursive forces that contribute to life in particular settings (Biehl et al. 2007; Good 1994; Desjarlais 1997; Scheper-Hughes 1993; Willen 2007b). . . . In general, this work, while attending to particular situations faced by people in specific sociopolitical settings, often inquires into ostensibly universal dimensions of human experience.

Source: Republished with permission of Annual Reviews. From Robert Desjarlais and C. Jason Throop, 2011. "Phenomenological Approaches in Anthropology." *Annual Review of Anthropology*, Vol. 40, pp. 87–102; permission conveyed via Copyright Clearance Center.

positionality A person's uniquely situated social position, which reflects his or her gender, nationality, political views, previous experiences, and so on. See *situated knowledge*.

of things as they appear in our lived experiences" (2011: 92). According to Desjarlais and Throop, anthropologists employing a phenomenological approach "focus on 'life as lived' and human consciousness in all of its lived realities" (2011: 92). The desire for an "anthropology of experience" started in the mid-1980s, when several anthropologists began to feel that anthropology had come to "neglect . . . the everyday experiences, contingencies, and dilemmas that weigh so heavily on people's lives" (Desjarlais

and Throop 2011: 92–3). From Desjarlais and Throop, anthropologists see that reflexivity and phenomenology go hand in hand. This is explored further in the "In Their Own Words" box above.

While the reflexive and phenomenological methods are accepted by many contemporary anthropologists, such acceptance is not without criticism, most of which centres on the reliability of anthropologists' self-reports on **positionality**. People's descriptions of themselves are not always reliable. Indeed, most people, when describing themselves, tend to overlook their own faults and embellish their better qualities (Salzman 2002). Yet even though the critics note such flaws, most would agree that the reflexive and phenomenological methods are far more useful than the positivist alternative. Indeed, we would argue that the best ethnographies have always been reflexive, whether or not this was realized at the time.

The Fieldwork Experience: A Brief Overview

Today, as in the past, ethnographic fieldwork continues to be the quintessential anthropological experience. Many students first experience fieldwork when they are in their undergraduate or early graduate studies, when they work on research projects or in field schools run by established anthropologists. An extended period of fieldwork is the final phase of formal anthropological training, and many anthropologists incorporate additional periods of field research into their subsequent careers. Beginning anthropologists usually decide during graduate school where they want to do their research and on what topic they wish to focus.

Many students who have never participated in fieldwork have an idealized image of the experience: at first, the disoriented fieldworker faces suspicious potential participants, but uncertainty soon moves to understanding and trust as the anthropologist's good intentions are made known and accepted. Soon, the fieldworker becomes so well loved and trusted and accepted as an equal that she or he is allowed access to the culture's secrets. Yet this is naive thinking. Fieldwork is entangled with the realities of diverse, complex relationships (Pack 2006). Gaining acceptance in the field takes time and effort, and there is no guarantee that the fieldworker will be accepted by everyone. In addition, as anthropologist Pierre Bettez Gravel (1976) notes, fieldwork can be rather dull: "The substantive part of fieldwork has no glamour. It is made up of . . . the same little administrative tasks [e.g., cleaning, filing, making notes] we try to get away from . . . the tedium of daily life with suddenly no one to share it with" (121).

Many novice researchers do not anticipate the amount of preplanning required. Something as seemingly simple as finding a place to live may be challenging. Sometimes, a researcher will simply move into a pre-existing residence in the research locale; but other times, particularly when the researcher will be working among remote peoples in a rainforest, desert, or tundra area, he or she may need to bring along materials to establish adequate living quarters.

Success depends on a number of things. Starting at home, preparing for the field is essential. Travel documents are needed and passports should be relatively new—being close to a renewal date could be problematic. Visas must be obtained from appropriate governmental agencies for travel in specific jurisdictions. Travel advisories have to be checked. Clothing and personal items need to be packed, and travel medical issues need to be sorted out as some medical preparations require more time—certain immunizations can occur over a series of weeks and, in some instances, several months. (The World Health Organization and the US Centers for Disease Control are excellent sources for information on specific areas.) Proof of sufficient funds may need to be provided. Most importantly, there needs to be support from the communities where the study will occur—they will need to know the anthropologist is coming and what the anthropologist is planning to do, and they will have to offer their permission. In the past, such acceptance was not always sought, and the people who were to be studied did not always know that an anthropologist was on the way. Arriving in Pond Inlet, on Baffin Island, in 1963, anthropologist John Matthiasson noted, "No one in the settlement knew of my impending arrival although I was equipped with an Explorer's and Scientist's licence properly signed by the appropriate officials in Ottawa—a bureaucratic prerequisite for research in the Northwest Territories" (1992: 13). Today this would never do! Researchers also need to seek funds to support their studies, and funding agencies have strict codes of ethics for research involving human participants. No ethics document, no research! The application needs to be detailed and include permission documents for the members of the study community that are accessible to them. In some situations, translations may need to be produced. All of this takes time.

Obtaining grants from private or government agencies involves, among other things, persuading them that (1) the work will focus on a topic of current interest within anthropology and (2) the work is connected to their funding priorities. As a result, "field sites . . . end up being defined by the cross-hatched intersection of visa and clearance procedures, the interests of funding agencies, and intellectual debates within the discipline and its subfields" (Gupta and Ferguson 1997: 11). Since funds are finite, not all topics of current interest can be funded; to get around this limitation, some anthropologists pay for their research themselves by finding a job in the area where they want to do fieldwork or by supplementing small grants out of their own pockets.

Anthropologists are accountable not only to the agencies or people who fund their projects but also to the communities and individuals who allow them entry into their lives (see, e.g., Carrithers 2005). To help researchers protect the rights and dignity of their participants, professional associations—such as the Canadian Anthropology Society/Société canadienne d'anthropologie (CASCA) and the American Anthropological Association (AAA)—provide networks through which researchers can connect with one another to discuss best practices. Some associations also offer guidelines for conducting ethical research. The AAA's *Code of Ethics*, for example, states that "Anthropological researchers have *primary ethical obligations* to the people, species, and materials they study and to the people with whom they work" and must "ensure that they do not harm the safety, dignity, or privacy of the people with whom they work, conduct research, or perform other professional activities" (2009: III, A.1, A.2; italics added). In Canada, the *Tri-Council Policy Statement* (*TCPS*), first published in 1998, sets ethical guidelines for researchers and informs the research ethics boards (REBs) of all federally funded institutions. It explicitly states that "researchers are expected, as a condition of funding, to adhere to the *TCPS*" (CIHR, NSERC, SSHRC 2010).

As you might expect, policies evolve from the problems, constraints, and considerations that arise from fieldwork, but no policy can suit every researcher or address every problem one might encounter. Mike Evans (2004), reflecting on his research into the Island Cache in British Columbia, has noted the problem of giving voice and representation to participants while also meeting the *TCPS* requirement of maintaining their confidentiality. Evans, like most anthropologists, feels strongly that participants have the right to protect their identities. Indeed, the need for protection is paramount when participants belong to marginal or powerless groups that might suffer retaliation from more powerful agencies. However, Evans emphasizes that in certain situations, such as community-centred research when participants wish to express their identities and ideas, anthropologists need to record people's stories without depriving individuals of their right to be acknowledged.

Once the anthropologist arrives on site, what is the experience of fieldwork like? Early in their stay, it is not uncommon for fieldworkers to feel overwhelmed. With time, however, they discover that the great process of human survival begins to assert itself: they begin to adapt. The rhythms of daily activity become familiar. Their use of the local language improves. Faces of the local inhabitants become the faces of neighbours. They are participating and observing—and doing a lot of writing as well. It seems as though fieldworkers always have a notebook somewhere handy and, whenever possible, jot down notes on what they are seeing, hearing, doing, or wondering. These days, laptops, digital cameras, video cameras, and digital recorders are usually considered essential to the accurate recording of field data. Anthropologists cannot really trust their memories to keep track of the extraordinary range of information that comes at them in the field. But note taking is not sufficient. The quickly jotted scrawls in notebooks must be turned into field notes; as a result, anthropologists spend a lot of their time in front of their computers, writing notes that are as complete and coherent as possible. Most ethnographers try to write up field notes on a daily basis, and they also try to code the information so that they can find it later. There are very useful field manuals for neophyte ethnographers to consult to assist them in developing workable and straightforward coding systems (e.g., Bernard 2011; DeWalt and DeWalt 2011). As fieldworkers type up their notes, places for further inquiry become clear, and a back-and-forth process begins. The ethnographer collects information, writes it down, thinks about it, analyzes it, and then takes new questions and interpretations back to the people with whom he or she is working to see if these questions and interpretations are more accurate than the previous ones.

Even the best field notes, however, are not ethnographies, published books or articles based on anthropological fieldwork. Writing about the cultural practices one has learned is not as straightforward as it may seem to non-anthropologists. Over the past century, anthropologists' ideas about what ethnographies ought to look like—how long they ought to be, how much and what kinds of details they should contain, whether they should be addressed to audiences of other professionals or to popular audiences or to members of the societies being studied—have undergone revision. Contemporary ethnographers try to be explicit about who they are and how they came to do their research and try to take into account who the various intended (and unintended) readers of their work might be.

Classic anthropological fieldwork emphasized working "abroad" but such an orientation bears clear traces of European colonialist attitudes although it can also draw attention to ways of life among peoples whom elite groups in powerful Western nations have traditionally dismissed or marginalized. It is here that cross-cultural understandings and links between different types of knowledges can be found (see Gupta and Ferguson 1997). Recently anthropological fieldwork has become engaged in working "at home." For example, studies of social inequality and marginalization provide insight from an insider's perspective. It is common for anthropologists working in their own societies to interpret and write about their experiences, both as observers and as members of those societies (see, e.g., Kumar 1992; Turgeon and Pastinelli 2002; Undie 2007) thereby producing auto-ethnographies. Fieldwork at home has long been the norm in Mexico, Brazil, India, and Russia. In the twenty-first century, developments such as these are helping create "decolonized anthropology in a deterritorialized world" (Gupta and Ferguson 1997: 35).

Furthermore, as virtual worlds—*World of Warcraft* or *Second Life*, for example—have become increasingly popular around the world, anthropologists have been trying to figure out ways to study them. One of the most successful studies is Tom Boellstorff's *Coming of Age in Second Life*. Boellstorff argues that *Second Life* (Figure 2.4), and virtual worlds in general, are sites of human culture and can be studied in the same way a cultural anthropologist may study any other cultural site: through participant-observation. As Boellstorff puts it,

> Not only did I create the avatar Tom Bukowski; I shopped for clothes for my avatar in the same stores as any Second Life resident. I bought land with the help of a real estate agent and learned how to use Second Life's building tools. I then created a home and office for my research named "Ethnographia," purchasing items like textures, furniture, and artwork. I learned games created and played inside Second Life, like "Tringo" (a combination of Tetris and Bingo) and "primtionary" (a variant of Pictionary). I wandered across the Second Life landscape, flying, teleporting, or floating along in my hot air balloon, stopping

Figure 2.4 An avatar visits a mosque in *Second Life*. What sort of things can cultural anthropologists learn by studying virtual worlds?

to investigate events, buildings, or people I happened to encounter. I also used the "events" list and notices in Second Life publications to learn of interesting places to visit. In turn, many people stumbled upon my house, either during leisurely explorations of their own or to attend an event I was hosting. I joined many Second Life groups and participated in a range of activities, from impromptu relationship counseling to large-scale events like a community fair. (Boellstorff 2008: 70).

One could hardly ask for a better description of participant-observation in any kind of world!

Interactions in the Field: Interpretation and Translation

Fieldwork is a risky business. Fieldworkers face the shock of the unfamiliar and their own vulnerability. Indeed, they must embrace this shock and cultivate this vulnerability if they are to achieve any kind of meaningful understandings. They resist ethnocentric impulses by recalling "that if what we observe appears to be odd or irrational, it is probably because we do not understand it and not because it is a product of a 'savage' culture in which such nonsense is to be expected" (Greenwood and Stini 1977: 185).

Anthropologist Michael Agar (1996) uses the expression "rich points" for unexpected moments when problems in cross-cultural understanding emerge. These moments occur when words or actions signal gaps between the anthropologist's and the local people's assumptions about how the world works. Such moments are "rich" because they offer opportunities for a great number of valuable insights. Rich points are the raw material of ethnography. As Agar says, "it is this distance between two worlds of experience that is exactly the problem that ethnographic research is designed to locate and resolve" (1996: 31). That the anthropologist doesn't understand what is going on is the anthropologist's problem, not the local people's; therefore, it is up to the anthropologist to identify rich points, to interpret these moments, and to investigate the accuracy of interpretations.

Interpreting Actions and Ideas

How does one go about interpreting the actions and ideas of other human beings? Any form of interpretation is based on reflexivity rather than objectivity.

dialectic of fieldwork The process of building a bridge of understanding between anthropologist and participant so that each can begin to understand the other.

In *Reflections on Fieldwork in Morocco* (1977), Rabinow addresses this problem:

> Following [French philosopher Paul] Ricoeur, I define the problem of [interpretation] . . . as "the comprehension of the self by the detour of the comprehension of the other." It is vital to stress that this is not psychology of any sort. . . . The self being discussed is perfectly public. . . . [It is] the culturally mediated and historically situated self which finds itself in a continuously changing world of meaning. (1977: 5–6)

In the field, then, interpretation becomes a task of coming to comprehend the *cultural self* by way of comprehending the *cultural other*. Such understanding of the cultural other is intersubjectively constructed, using elements drawn from the cultural systems of the anthropologist and participant alike. The gulf between self and other that seemed unbridgeable at first narrows as meaning is negotiated. Eventually, common—albeit at times partial—understandings emerge, and continued discussion eventually reveals areas of intersection for understanding and describing the same behaviour. Any intersection, however small, can form the foundation on which to build a new intersubjective symbolic language. This process is what Rabinow refers to as "the **dialectic of fieldwork**" (1977: 39). Indeed, it is the effort to arrive at a deeper cross-cultural understanding that sets anthropological work apart, as more than merely documenting a culture from an outsider's perspective (Figure 2.5). (See more on this in Anthony Seeger's work in the "In Their Own Words" box that follows.)

Let's take a look at how this process might unfold in a typical fieldwork situation. Traditional fieldwork often begins with collecting data on kinship relations (i.e., significant family and social ties) in the host society. As the fieldworker begins to ask participants questions about kinship, he or she may discover that they have no word in their language that accurately conveys the range of meaning carried by the term *kinship*. This does not mean that the anthropologist must give up. Rather, he or she must enter into the dialectic process of interpretation and translation. The process works something like this:

- The anthropologist poses a question about kinship using the term in the participants' language that seems to come closest in meaning to *kinship*.

© Anton_Ivanov/Shutterstock.com

Figure 2.5 Tourists take a ride on an elephant in Jaipur, India. What are some of the ways in which anthropologists' interactions with their participants differ from tourists' interactions with local people in a foreign land?

In Their Own Words

Who's Studying Whom?

Anthony Seeger is an anthropologist who has carried out multiyear research on music in Amazonian Brazil among the Suyá. Seeger, the nephew of legendary folk musician Pete Seeger, and his wife are both accomplished musicians who brought their instruments—guitar and banjo—to the field with them. This led Seeger to deep insight into the process of ethnographic research.

The first time we played and sang in an Indian village, my whole perception of our roles as fieldworkers in Xingu region was changed. We were invited to record some flute music in the village of the Yawalapiti, near Posto Leonardo Villas Boas. When we finished recording, the men asked us to return and play some of our own music. So the next day we went back with our instruments. The men were finishing an afternoon of singing themselves, and were covered with red body paint, brightly colored head ornaments, and feather arm bands. In the lengthening shadows we sat down by the flute house and tuned up our banjo and guitar. As we started to play, a Yawalapit man, painted and ornamented like the others but wearing dark glasses and carrying a Sony tape recorder, walked over to us and started recording our music!

Who was studying whom? What was a tape recorder doing in the middle of the jungle? Our astonishment quickly gave way to a clearer understanding of the situation in which we were working. In the Xingu, different societies were confronting each other with curiosity and some hostility. All of my research would be two-sided. We would be watched, studied, evaluated, and discussed just as I was watching, writing, and discussing.

The Indians in the Xingu expected to be treated as equals or superiors. The Suyá once threatened to kill a passing anthropologist who they believed had ordered them to do something. "Here, we tell people what to do," they affirmed. One woman told us the Suyá liked us because we never told them what to do or criticized the way they did something.

What I learned that first day when we were recorded in the Yawalapiti village, and in subsequent months, applies to anthropological research throughout the world. We are not dealing with passive objects, or "subjects." We live in a world in which realignment of power is occurring, and in which a solitary researcher inevitably has to accede to the will of the members of the society with which he or she works or find him or herself quickly removed. If this passage from colonialism to mutual respect and curiosity can be bridged, it will be better for both anthropology and ethnomusicology (to say nothing of the people themselves). But it takes some patience on the part of researchers unaccustomed to having their images of themselves questioned.

Increasingly anthropologists are being asked, "What can you do for us?" by the people whose societies they are doing research on. It is sometimes a disturbing question, but generally a healthy one, indicating an end to some forms of colonial domination. The Suyá never asked us this question, partly because they knew what they wanted us for: we could become "their Whites," bring them things they wanted, treat their sick, answer questions they had about our world, and sing for them.

Source: Seeger, Anthony. 2004. *Why Suya Sing: A Musical Ethnography of an Amazonian People* (Urbana, IL: University of Illinois Press), 22–3. Reprinted with permission of Anthony Seeger.

- The participants do their best to interpret the anthropologist's question in a way that makes sense to them. That is, each participant has to be reflexive, thinking about how people in his or her society think about a certain domain of experience.
- Having formulated an answer, the response to the anthropologist's question is made in terms they think the anthropologist will understand.
- The anthropologist interprets this response, deciding whether it carries the kind of information that he or she is looking for or whether it carries information that he or she can use to rephrase the initial question to get closer to an understanding.

As you can see, all are active agents in this process. Each party tries to figure out what the other is trying to say. If there is goodwill on the part of both, each party also tries to provide responses that make sense to the other. In many ways, anthropological fieldwork is *translation*. Translation is complicated and delicate, full of false starts and misunderstandings. As time passes and the partners in this effort learn from their mistakes and successes, their ability to communicate increases. The anthropologist learns to structure questions; the instructor learns how to provide answers that the anthropologist can understand. Gradually, these interactions build a new world of knowledge that is meaningful to both.

While participants/instructors are equally involved in this dialogue and may end up learning much about the anthropologist, remember that the dialogue is initiated by the anthropologists who have come to the field with their own sets of issues and concerns determined not by the field situation but by academics within the discipline of anthropology and others who are supporting the research project. This continues to be true even when anthropologists find that their project is changing direction in response to developments at the field site. Furthermore, when anthropologists are finished with a particular research project, they are free to break off the dialogue with the field community and resume discussions with fellow scholars. In many cases, the only link between these two sets of dialogues is the anthropologist who conducted the research in the field. This moves beyond situated knowledge to situated ethics (accountability) when conveying the learnings achieved. Here,

> the contested nature of authenticity, its temporal simultaneity, and its plural conceptualizations entail valuable lessons for those analysts who liberate themselves from the expectation of singular authenticity and embrace analytically more than one parallel claim of the authentic. In most everyday life situations, more than one type of authenticity is articulated simultaneously—directly or indirectly—and these types are compared to each other during this process. (Theodossopoulos 2013: 355)

This is so very important when academics have traditionally relied on fieldworkers to interpret and speak for participants, often assuming that participants would/could not speak for themselves. In recent years, however, scholars who began to question this assumption have continued the challenge, noting that many members of marginalized societies are perfectly willing and capable of self-representation. Additionally, members of Indigenous societies who began to speak powerfully on their own behalf on a much broader scale have become powerful political advocates for their people, as lawyers, as organizers, and as professional scholars. Language and other barriers may prevent participants from speaking directly to an audience of professional scholars, but such difficulties can be overcome in our increasingly wired world. Thus, some anthropologists have suggested replacing the traditional dialectic of fieldwork with a more inclusive model for generating anthropological knowledge that is situated beyond the Western-centric roots of the discipline in a more global community of colleagues—both academic and non-academic—who can work together to generate and spread anthropological knowledge. Arjun Appadurai, for example, has called for a global effort to encourage academics, researchers, and participants to become equal partners in an ongoing "conversation about research"—a conversation in which "scholars from other societies and traditions of inquiry" could discuss *their own* ideas of "what counts as new knowledge" and how to measure the researcher's *accountability* to those among whom they work (2002: 281).

An essential step toward creating a more inclusive approach to generating knowledge is identifying and moving beyond cultural biases that can distort a researcher's interpretation. Roberto DaMatta, a Brazilian anthropologist, has addressed problems associated with characterizing Indigenous peoples as "others." This issue resonates with Canadian researchers. As inheritors of the colonial concept of *terra nullius*, the "empty land," early Canadian anthropologists engaged with Indigenous peoples as the "mythical other" or the "noble savage." Even while approaching Indigenous cultures as "new," these anthropologists essentially saw them as representative of an earlier stage of human evolution. While echoes of such interpretations persist today, most contemporary anthropologists actively try to avoid suggesting that Indigenous cultures are any less "evolved" than non-Indigenous cultures (see, e.g., Liebersohn 1994; Darnell 2009).

In light of such concerns, researchers have re-evaluated the responsibilities they have toward the participants in the research. One question comes up often: Is it enough to build cross-cultural understandings and discuss field observations in academic contexts, or should anthropologists go so far as to act as advocates for the people they study? Anthropologists Kirsten Hastrup and Peter Elsass (1990), who have explored issues of advocacy in relation to their fieldwork with the Arhuacos of the Sierra Nevada of northern Colombia, note that this question is not easy to answer:

> There is a continuum of anthropological interest from [1] the countering of Western, colonial ethnocentrism by providing systematic knowledge about other cultures

to [2] the active pleading of the cause of a particular ethnic group vis-à-vis a government (Van Esterik 1985). In principle this continuum leaves no anthropologist untouched by the problem of advocacy . . . When anthropologists use their knowledge for a particular cause, they can be charged with furthering "the colonial processes still at work by stealing crucial decisions and political initiatives from Indigenous peoples" (Henriksen 1985: 124–5). . . . There is . . . an inherent dilemma in anthropological advocacy. Anthropology is concerned with context rather than interest, while advocacy means making a choice among interests within the context. (Hastrup and Elsass 1990: 302–7)

Anthropologists' sense of ethics, as well as their concern for preserving human decency, leads them to understand that some things require them to choose among interests within contexts. Indeed, anthropologists must sometimes choose to stand with others to achieve justice.

Examples from the Field

Fieldwork is, by definition, an active process that takes place in the real world, in the middle of the action. Therefore, let's turn to two examples of researchers' experiences in the field to help illustrate some of the interests and concerns at the heart of the dialectic of fieldwork.

Nita Kumar is an anthropologist from Delhi, India. She works in different regions within her home country. Kumar chose to do fieldwork in the Banaras (or Varanasi) region of India, a region very different from the one where she grew up:

> Banaras was such a mystery to me when I arrived there in 1981, ironically *because* I was an Indian and expected to have a privileged insight into it. In fact, from Banaras I was *thrice* removed: through my education and upbringing, than which there is no greater moulder of attitudes; by language and linguistic culture; and by region and regional culture. (1992: 15)

Although her social connections smoothed the way for her in official circles, she had no special advantage when trying to make contact with the artisans whose way of life interested her (Figure 2.6).

© kaetana/123RF

Figure 2.6 Prayer and worship on the Ganges River, Banaras, India. Indian anthropologist Nita Kumar found Banaras to be a mystery because of her background and her unfamiliarity with local cultures. In what ways might you feel similarly out of place studying in a region of Canada other than the one in which you live?

Establishing a good research relationship is a necessary first step in fieldwork, but there are no foolproof procedures that guarantee success. In *Friends, Brothers, and Informants* (1992), Kumar shares her four failed attempts—and her final successful effort—to contact weavers. In her first attempt, the weavers she approached turned out to have well-established ties to rickshaw pullers and taxi drivers, who regularly brought tourists to visit their shop and buy souvenirs. Not wishing to become just another business contact, she left. Her second attempt was with the owner of a weaving business whose suspicions of her motives caused her to turn elsewhere. Her third attempt was made through a sari salesman who took her to a market where silk weavers sold their wares. Unfortunately for her, he would periodically announce to all assembled who she was and invite weavers to come up and speak with her, a procedure she found deeply embarrassing. Her fourth attempt followed her accidental discovery of several members of a family who were weavers. When she was invited to see one brother's loom, however, she grew "uncomfortable with all the obvious evidence of bachelor existence and their readiness to welcome [her] into it" (99). On her fifth attempt, a silk-yarn merchant introduced her to weavers living in a government-subsidized housing project next to his house. In the home of a weaver named Shaukatullah, surrounded by members of Shaukatullah's family, she finally found a setting in which she felt welcome and able to do her work. A few weeks after meeting Shaukatullah and his family, she "was given the status of a daughter of Shaukatullah" (105). That status was not only important to Kumar's research, but it also made her feel comfortable in the local setting. Ultimately, she developed a unique perspective as both outsider and insider.

Jean Briggs is an anthropologist who was also adopted by a family of participants. Briggs worked among the Utkuhikhalingmiut (Utku, for short) in northern Canada (Figure 2.7; EthnoProfile 2.1). When she first arrived in their community, the Utku thought she was strange, entirely unlike them. Once she had been adopted by her new "father," Inuttiaq, and "mother," Allaq, however, the community began to see her as able to be educated in their ways of life:

> From the moment that the adoption was settled, I was "Inuttiaq's daughter" in the camp. Inuttiaq and his relatives, with much amusement, drilled me in the use of kin terms appropriate to my position, just as they drilled his three-year-old daughter, who was learning to speak. (1980: 46)

The context of their interactions changed as a result of the adoption, and Briggs's family had new expectations both of Briggs and of themselves:

> Allaq, and especially Inuttiaq . . . more and more attempted to assimilate me into a proper adult parent–daughter relationship. I was expected to help with the household work . . . and I was expected to obey unquestioningly when Inuttiaq told me to do something. . . . Inevitably, conflicts, covert but pervasive, developed. (47)

Briggs became increasingly uneasy in her situation. She began to realize that part of the problem had to do with differences between her ideas of how parents ought to relate to their daughters and Utku beliefs on this matter. She also experienced contradictions between her role as daughter and her role as anthropologist. Unlike Kumar, Briggs found that assuming the role of daughter was uncomfortable. While it initially provided her with an opportunity to "fit into" the community she was studying, it also posed challenges to the very continuation of her fieldwork.

One incident in particular marked a turning point. It arose in part out of differing ideas about acceptable behaviour and in part out of a misunderstanding. A few summers before Briggs's arrival, sportsmen from Canada and the United States had begun to fly into the inlet where the Utku lived. Once there, they borrowed canoes belonging to the Utku. Although there had at one time been several usable canoes in the community, only two remained when Briggs arrived. That summer some sportsmen borrowed one canoe but ran it onto a rock. They then asked if they could borrow the remaining canoe, which happened to belong to Inuttiaq.

Because the Utku used the canoes for getting food, the loss had serious economic consequences for her participants. When the outsiders asked to use the last good canoe, Briggs "exploded." She lectured the sportsmen about their carelessness and insensitivity, and she explained how important canoes were to the Utku. Then, remembering Inuttiaq's often-repeated warning never to lend his canoe, she told the sportsmen that the owner of the remaining canoe did not want to lend it. When Inuttiaq insisted that the canoe be lent, she was shocked.

But this was only the beginning. Briggs discovered that following her outburst, the people she worked with in the community seemed to turn against *her* rather than the sportsmen:

> I had spoken unbidden and in anger. . . . Punishment was a subtle form of ostracism. . . . I was isolated. It was as though I were not there. . . . But . . . I was still treated with [great care and concern]. (1980: 56–7)

Figure 2.7 Summer in the traditional lands of the Utku Inuit in Nunavut.

EthnoProfile 2.1
Utkuhikhalingmiut (Utku Inuit)

Region: North America
Nation: Canada (Nunavut); the area between Franklin Lake and Chantrey Inlet (Tariunnuaq) on the east side of Adelaide Peninsula
Language: Utkuhiksalingmiutitut, a dialect of Inuktitut
Population: 35 (1970)
Environment: Tundra
Livelihood: Seasonal fishing, hunting, and gathering
Political organization: Communal, with hunting territories
For more information: Briggs, Jean. 1970. *Never in Anger: Portrait of an Eskimo Family* (Cambridge, MA: Harvard University Press); 2000. "Emotions Have Many Faces: Inuit Lessons," *Anthropologica* 42, 2.

Prior to her outburst, Briggs had understood that anger was dangerous and must never be shown. She was also aware of the various ways to divert or diffuse angry feelings. Nevertheless, it wasn't until she had seriously violated the Utku value of avoiding angry displays that she understood its importance.

This breach might well have ended Briggs's fieldwork if a Westernized Utku friend, Ikayuqtuq, had not come to her rescue. She wrote to Ikayuqtuq to explain her version of the story, which was that she had been trying "to protect the Utku from the impositions of the *kaplunas* [white men]" (58). In her letter, she asked her friend for help explaining her position to the Utku. Ikayuqtuq agreed to help. Once Ikayuqtuq's letter arrived, everything changed. Briggs's friend had found a way to translate her intentions into terms that Allaq and Inuttiaq could understand. Indeed, "the effect was magical." Inuttiaq began to tell the others what a dangerous task Briggs had taken on to defend the Utkus against the white men. Briggs was no longer frozen out of Utku society. And she knew that relationships had been restored (and perhaps deepened) when Inuttiaq called her *daughter* once again.

The struggle that ensued when Briggs tried to be a good Utku daughter stems in part from what happens when ethnographers struggle to keep the full expression of their own cultural selves in check, in an effort to avoid offending. The situation is complicated by the fieldworker's imperfect awareness of the sort of behaviour that is likely to offend participants. As a result, fieldworkers have frequently felt that their motto ought to be "The informant is always right" (see Rabinow 1977). Many fieldworkers

therefore forbid themselves to express anger, disgust, or disagreement. But such self-imposed restrictions are likely to cause problems. After all, what sort of person is always smiling, never angry, without opinions? Anthropologists who refuse to challenge or be challenged by their participants dehumanize both themselves and their participants. Thus, anthropologists must be careful to find a balance between being authentic and avoiding offence.

These examples illustrate how a researcher's reflexive awareness can affect the ways in which the dialectic of fieldwork produces anthropological knowledge. They also show how reflexivity can enhance the ethnographies that anthropologists write. Unlike in earlier ethnographies committed to the positivist approach, in reflexive ethnographies and through the use of phenomenological perspectives the presence, personalities, and voices of ethnographers and participants alike become vivid elements.

Multi-sited Fieldwork

Changes in the world as a whole in recent decades have led many anthropologists to undertake fieldwork projects that include more than a single site. The push toward multi-sited fieldwork came from within anthropology and related social sciences as they responded to wider social and political changes. One spark for such changes came in 1974, when American sociologist Immanuel Wallerstein published *The Modern World System,* in which he argues that the rise and expansion of the European capitalist economy between 1450 and 1750 had incorporated vast regions of the globe into a world system held together by *the market*. This work had important implications for anthropologists, for Wallerstein argued that many parts of the world where anthropologists worked had been remade to occupy specialized niches within the capitalist world system (*the market economy*). Thus, anthropological attempts to account for the current beliefs and practices of small-scale societies in these parts of the world could not ignore the historical impact upon them of world-system influences, such as European colonialism.

Austrian-born anthropologist Eric Wolf's book *Europe and the People without History* (1982) became equally important. This ironically titled text opened our eyes to the histories of non-European people—people inaccurately described in colonialist parlance as being "without history." Wolf draws attention to how non-European groups changed and adapted over time, and how they became very much involved in the history of European expansion. Tracing some of the same world-system interconnections discussed by Wallerstein, Wolf regularly abandons the abstract view of the overall system in order to focus on the historical ethnographic details of specific societies. Thus, in Wolf's discussion, Indigenous peoples of North America appear as actors creatively coping with the challenge of the fur trade and European settlement, developing some of their now characteristic forms of social organization.

The influence of Wallerstein and Wolf on ethnographers was profound. American anthropologist George Marcus notes that single-site fieldwork continued, but from the perspective of the world system (1995: 96). Anthropologists began to supplement their own data-gathering with archival research that allowed them to historically situate their "field." Moreover, they began to rethink existing social arrangements and cultural understandings as the products of *active response* to outside pressures rather than as timeless practices. Such work reanimated their awareness of the *lack* of isolation of the societies they studied, both in the past and in the present, and it reinforced an awareness of their participants' *agency*. The result was that neat boundaries between particular societies and the larger world system began to dissolve as ethnographers contextualized their own field data in relation to places and processes that stretched far beyond their original field site. By the early 1990s—after such developments as the break-up of the Soviet Union, the somewhat piecemeal move of capitalism into China, and an extraordinary surge of migrants around the world—all traditional boundaries seemed on the verge of crumbling.

This is more the case today, as global processes—including global social movements, international trade, and climate change—increasingly link disparate groups of people. For example, think of the many ties between various fundamentalist activists—frequently described as "terrorists"—who are dedicated to promoting their individual causes by redefining political, ethnic, linguistic, economic, and religious boundaries. Think also of capitalists who promote continued economic growth at all costs, bringing the world together so they can gain access to dwindling resources and create markets for their products. (Note Benjamin R. Barber's discussion in the "In Their Own Words" box that follows.)

Ethnographic research focuses on cultural processes that are not contained by social, ethnic, religious, or national boundaries, in which the ethnographer follows the process from site to site. How do you proceed with fieldwork, then, when the study of any cultural group demands the mapping of various seemingly disconnected, fragmentary processes in a globalized world? For increasing numbers of anthropologists, the answer is **multi-sited ethnography**, which focuses on widespread cultural processes and leads the researcher from site to site as new considerations present themselves. As Marcus describes it, "Multi-sited research is designed around chains, paths, threads, conjunctions, or juxtapositions of locations" as researchers trace "a complex cultural phenomenon" that has many connections across the globe (1995: 105–6). Like all good investigators working on complex issues, multi-sited ethnographers follow *people, things, metaphors, plots,* and *lives* (107).

Marcus (1995) admits that multi-sited fieldwork may present certain limitations. Compared to single-sited fieldwork, it appears to dilute the intensity of involvement and the depth of understanding that fieldworkers develop with their participants in each situated study. Further, some activist anthropologists who use their ethnography to draw public attention to the plight of the people whose lives they study see multi-sited research as weakening their political commitments to their primary participants. Yet Marcus does not see these drawbacks as fatal. After all, he notes, multi-sited fieldwork is usually *based* in one primary site; its major innovation involves doing fieldwork in additional sites and bringing information from all these sites together in a single study. Additionally, multi-sited ethnography highlights the multi-centred, complex conflicts of the contemporary

multi-sited ethnography
A method of anthropological research focused on a specific topic followed through different field situations. These field situations can be within one culture but socially distinct (social class and caste, for example) or in different geographical locations (different cultures). Data collection relies on detailed methods of survey (objective) and interviews (subjective).

In Their Own Words

Jihad vs. McWorld

Writing in 1992, American political scientist Benjamin R. Barber describes the conflict between tribalism and globalism. In that year, a number of observers were concerned with these issues, although many anthropologists were dubious about claims of "retribalization." How much has changed since Barber made his argument?

Just beyond the horizon of current events lie two possible political futures—both bleak, neither democratic. The first is a retribalization of large swaths of humankind by war and bloodshed: a threatened Lebanonization of national states in which culture is pitted against culture, people against people, tribe against tribe—a Jihad in the name of a hundred narrowly conceived faiths against every kind of interdependence, every kind of artificial social co-operation and civic mutuality. The second is being borne in on us by the onrush of economic and ecological forces that demand integration and uniformity and that mesmerize the world with fast music, fast computers, and fast food—with MTV, Macintosh, and McDonald's pressing nations into one commercially homogenous global network: one McWorld tied together by technology, ecology, communications, and commerce. The planet is falling precipitately apart *and* coming reluctantly together at the very same moment.

These two tendencies are sometimes visible in the same countries at the same instant: thus Yugoslavia, clamouring just recently to join the New Europe, is exploding into fragments; India is trying to live up to its reputation as the world's largest integral democracy while powerful new fundamentalist parties like the Hindu nationalist Bharatiya Janata Party, along with nationalist assassins, are imperilling its hard-won unity. States are breaking up or joining up: the Soviet Union has disappeared almost overnight, its parts forming new unions with one another or with like-minded nationalities in neighbouring states. The old interwar national state based on territory and political sovereignty looks to be a mere transitional development.

The tendencies of what I am here calling the forces of Jihad and the forces of McWorld operate with equal strength in opposite directions, the one driven by parochial hatreds, the other by universalizing markets, the one recreating ancient sub-national and ethnic borders from within, the other making national borders porous from without. They have one thing in common: neither offers much hope to citizens looking for practical ways to govern themselves democratically. If the global future is to pit Jihad's centrifugal whirlwind against McWorld's centripetal black hole, the outcome is unlikely to be democratic.

Source: Republished with permission of The Atlantic Monthly Group, Inc. From Benjamin Barber, 1992. "Jihad vs McWorld," *Atlantic Monthly*, 269, 3: 53–65; permission conveyed via Copyright Clearance Center.

world in which clear-cut "good guys" and "bad guys" are increasingly hard to identify. By narrowly focusing on the needs of one group, a researcher may draw attention away from another group in equal—or even greater—need. For example, to defend the views of working-class women in a single site is to downplay or ignore the views of unemployed women. Or, such a focus may gloss over differences *among* those women based on class, "race," ethnicity, or religion. Further, it ignores entirely the points of view of all men. On a global scale, the spread of industrial capitalism across the globe means that the growth of an urban immigrant workforce in one place is probably connected to a lack of employment somewhere else—certainly a central point of contention in any free trade treaty. Multi-sited ethnography offers the possibility of juxtaposing more than one place, more than one time, and more than one point of view, thereby bringing to light connections among them that would otherwise remain unknown. Indeed, in a world where Skype, YouTube, Snapchat, and Instagram can connect people and places across the globe in an instant, multi-sited ethnographies will continue to become increasingly important.

The Effects of Fieldwork

The Effects on the Participants

Fieldwork changes all participants. What kinds of effects can fieldwork produce? Anthropologists have not always been able to report on this, as the effects may take many years to manifest. Yet in some cases, it becomes clear in the course of fieldwork that the anthropologist's presence and questions have made the participants aware of their own cultural selves in new ways that are surprising and perhaps even uncomfortable.

Upon reflecting on his work in Morocco, Paul Rabinow recalled some cases in which his participants' new reflexivity led to unanticipated consequences (Figure 2.8). One key participant, Malik, agreed to help Rabinow compile a list of landholdings and other possessions of the villagers of Sidi Lahcen Lyussi (see Map 2.1). As a first step in tracing economic statuses within the community, Rabinow suggested that Malik list his own possessions. Initially, Malik appeared to be neither rich nor poor, and he considered himself "not well-off."

> As we began to make a detailed list of his possessions, he became touchy and defensive. . . . It was clear that he was not as impoverished as he had portrayed himself. . . . This was confusing and troubling for him. . . . Malik began to see that there was a disparity between his self-image and my classification system. The emergence of this "hard" data before his eyes and through his own efforts was highly disconcerting for him. (1977: 117–18)

Malik's easy understanding of himself and his world had been disrupted, and he could not ignore the disruption. He would either have to change his self-image or find some way to integrate this new information about himself into his old self-image. In the end, Malik managed to reaffirm his conclusion that he was not well-off by arguing that wealth

culture shock The feeling of physical and mental dislocation/discomfort a person experiences when in a new or strange cultural setting.

lay not in material possessions alone. Although he might be rich in material goods, his son's health was bad, his own father was dead, he was responsible for his mother and unmarried brothers, and he had to be constantly vigilant in order to prevent his uncle from stealing his land (117–19).

The Effects on the Researcher

What are the consequences of the fieldwork experience for the fieldworker? While the experience is often exciting and enlightening, it is not uncommon for field researchers to feel overwhelmed by the unfamiliarity of the situation. They need to adjust to local water, food, and climate, and many encounter plants, animals, insects, and diseases with which they have had no previous experience (Figure 2.9). In addition, the cultural differences a researcher faces—the very reason the researcher has entered the field in the first place—can be a source of added stress. As a result, many field researchers experience **culture shock**. In fact, many anthropologists feel very anxious and isolated in the field, at least in the early stages of a project, as they find they have nothing familiar to turn to, no common sense on which to rely, and no relationships that can be taken for granted.

The researcher's sense of isolation may lead to the search for close contacts in the research setting. Interpersonal relationships can often help researchers adapt to local culture, but they can also make a researcher more vulnerable to feelings of hurt or betrayal. They might also re-emphasize the distance between researcher and participant. Rabinow provides an example of such a situation when he recalls the relationship he formed with his first Moroccan participant, a

Figure 2.8 Paul Rabinow's reflections on his fieldwork in a Moroccan village much like this one led him to reconceptualize the nature of anthropological fieldwork. At what point should anthropologists start thinking about the potential impacts of their work in the field?

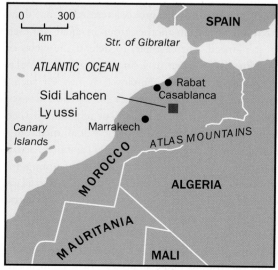

Map 2.1 Sidi Lahcen Lyussi

man called Ibrahim, whom he had hired to teach him Arabic. Rabinow and Ibrahim seemed to get along well together and, because of the language lessons, they saw each other a great deal, leading Rabinow to think of Ibrahim as a friend. When Rabinow planned a trip to another city, Ibrahim offered to go along as a guide and stay with relatives. This only confirmed Ibrahim's friendliness in Rabinow's eyes. But things changed once they arrived at their destination. Ibrahim told Rabinow that the relatives with whom he was to stay did not exist, that he had no money, and that he expected Rabinow to pay for his hotel room. When Rabinow was unable to do so, however, Ibrahim paid for it himself. Rabinow was shocked and hurt by this experience, and his relationship with Ibrahim was forever altered. Rabinow remarks,

> Basically, I had been conceiving of him as a friend because of the seeming personal relationship we had established. But Ibrahim, a lot less confusedly, had basically conceptualized me as a resource. He was not unjustly situating me with the other Europeans with whom he had dealings. (1977: 29)

Rabinow's experience illustrates what he calls the *shock of otherness*.

To some degree, researchers can prepare for the mental stress of entering an unfamiliar setting by anticipating as many potential circumstances as possible. Nancy Howell, a demographer involved with anthropological research in areas such as Botswana, has explored risk factors involved in fieldwork and has observed this:

> Anthropologists need to be mentally prepared to cope with . . . risks (diseases, criminal and political threats, vehicle accidents, etc. . . .) to their health and safety and to the health and safety of . . . others who accompany them on field trips. We don't need to write the kind of guidebook that systematically warns about sunburn, jet lag, and the inoculations needed in various countries. . . . What is needed for anthropology is the sensitizing to the hazards that are likely to be encountered, systematic sharing of experiences with hazards in the field, the best available advice on prevention and responses when they are encountered, and some mental rehearsals of what to do under those circumstances. (1988: 786–7)

Yet in most cases, the immensity of what they will encounter is difficult for researchers to fully

Figure 2.9 An Aldabra giant tortoise crosses the road in the Seychelles. Many anthropologists encounter unfamiliar plants, animals, and insects in the field. How do you think you would react if you found yourself living in a place entirely different from anywhere you have ever been before?

anticipate. Initially, just getting through the day—finding a place to stay and food to eat—may seem an enormous accomplishment. With time, however, researchers adapt, become more confident in their position, and feel more comfortable in their new surroundings. And then there is coming home—a whole new set of unexpected adjustments!

The Humanizing Effects

Anthropological knowledge is the product of the mutual attempts of anthropologists and participants to understand each other. Often, it can provide answers to questions about human nature, human society, and human history. Fieldwork offers extraordinary opportunities. Researchers are in privileged positions, positions that do not come easily or automatically. They must be cultivated with great care. Researchers will have made an important first step if they can come to recognize, as Rabinow did, that "there is no primitive. There are other [people] living other lives" (1977: 151). All human beings *live in their own modernity*—their own place—in this world they share (Figure 2.10).

Multi-sited ethnography can complicate the picture by simultaneously offering rich portraits of "other people living other lives" and by demonstrating that members of these groups share important cultural commitments. In the best ethnographic writing, readers can grasp the humanity—the generosity, greed, compassion, suffering, pleasure,

Figure 2.10 Unlike most Western commercial fishers, these men and women in Mozambique fish by pulling a fishing net from the water. All people experience their own modernity.

confusion, and ambivalence—of the people who have granted the anthropologist the privilege of living with them for an extended period of time. It may also become more natural to talk about cultural differences by saying "not 'they,' not 'we,' not 'you,' but 'some of us' are thus-and-so" (Smith 1982: 70).

The Production of Anthropological Knowledge

If anthropological knowledge is the intersubjective creation of fieldworker and participant together, so too are the **facts** that anthropologists collect. The dialectic of fieldwork, however, often involves extended discussions about just what counts as "the facts." Anthropologist David Hess defines fact as a widely accepted observation, a taken-for-granted item of common knowledge (1997: 101–2). Ethnographers' field notebooks will be full of facts collected from different participants, as well as facts based on their own cultural experiences and professional training. But what happens when facts from these various sources contradict one another?

Facts turn out to be complex phenomena. On the one hand, they assert that a particular state of affairs about the world is true. On the other hand, they do not speak for themselves. They speak only when they are interpreted and placed in a context of meaning that makes them intelligible. What constitutes a cultural fact is ambiguous. Anthropologists and participants can disagree; anthropologists can

fact A widely accepted observation that becomes intelligible only when it is interpreted and placed in a context of meaning.

disagree among themselves; participants can disagree among themselves. The facts of anthropology exist neither in the culture of the anthropologist nor in the culture of the participant: "Anthropological facts are cross-cultural because they are made across cultural boundaries" (Rabinow 1977: 152). In short, anthropological facts are not just out there waiting for someone to come along and pick them up. They are made and remade

- in the field,
- when fieldworkers re-examine field notes and reflect on the field experience,
- when fieldworkers write about their experiences or discuss them with other anthropologists, and
- when fieldwork is redone to mark the changes that have occurred.

For anthropologist Daniel Bradburd, fieldwork begins with "being there." But simply being there is not enough. As he puts it,

> my experiences among the Komachi [in Iran] shaped my understanding of them, and that part of field experience consists of a constant process of being brought up short, of having expectations confounded, of being forced to think very hard about what is happening, right now, with me and them, let alone the thinking and rethinking about those experiences when they have—sometimes mercifully—passed. (1998: 161–2; see Map 2.2)

After all, fieldwork is field*work*—there are notes to be taken, interviews to be carried out,

Map 2.2 Komachi

observations and interpretations to be made. There is also the transformation of the experience of being there into the beginnings of an understanding. According to Harry Wolcott, it is what ethnographers *do* with data that makes fieldwork experience different from just experience and turns it into ethnography. Indeed, ethnographers are concerned with

> making considered generalizations about how members of a group tend to speak and act, warranted generalizations appropriate for collectivities of people rather than the usual shoot-from-the-hip stereotyping adequate for allowing us to achieve our individual purposes. (Wolcott 1999: 262)

In multi-sited fieldwork, this experience is further complicated. As the researcher moves from site to site, new facts come into view, facts that would otherwise never be known. Such discoveries add a further layer to the thinking and rethinking that all fieldwork sets in motion.

Anthropological Knowledge as Open-Ended

Because anthropologists can never escape from their humanity, the knowledge they uncover can never be fully objective. Nor should objective knowledge be the goal. Rather, anthropologists must be *reflexive* rather than *objective* when seeking anthropological knowledge. Cultivating reflexivity allows them to produce less distorted views of human nature and the human condition. And reflexivity is a never-ending process—the more anthropologists experience, the more they have to reflect on.

In the field of anthropology, there will always be more to discover. After all, human beings are constantly learning and evolving, and human societies are constantly changing. Ultimately, then, the ethnographic record of anthropological knowledge is perhaps best understood as a vast, ongoing commentary on human possibility. As with all commentaries, it depends on an original text—in this case, the "text" of human experience. This experience is and always will be ambiguous, speaking with many voices, capable of supporting more than one interpretation. Growth of anthropological knowledge is essentially no different from the growth of human self-understanding in general—of where we have come from, and where we may be going.

This could be considered a sobering possibility, making it appear as though people can never succeed in understanding another culture. It also suggests that participants are equally condemned to never fully know their own way of life. Yet although people may never know everything, it does not follow that our efforts can teach us nothing. As Canadian philosopher Wilfred Cantwell Smith observes,

> Two of the fundamental qualities of humanity are the capacity to understand one another and the capacity to be understood. Not fully certainly. Yet not negligibly, certainly.... There is no person on earth that I can fully understand. There is and has been no person on earth that I cannot understand at all. (1982: 68–9)

Living Anthropology

Beyond a Place: Fieldwork as a Concept

by *Maxime Polleri, PhD Student, Social Anthropology,* York University

Margaret Mead is famous for her study conducted in Samoa, Clifford Geertz is inseparable from the island of Bali, and one of Lévi-Strauss's most poignant ethnographic works was born in Brazil. Fieldwork is often associated with the tropes of an exotic and remote location to be conquered by a fearless anthropologist aiming to objectively depict the reality that happens before his or her eyes. It remains an important rite of passage for every anthropologist, allowing one to explore counter narratives by focusing on the voices and experiences of local residents as a key analytical frame.

Yet, beyond prolonged stretches of time in a given place, fieldwork can also be thought of as a concept imbued with its own cultural traditions, which can affect both the ethnographer and its informants. More than a means to collect stories—or data, as the funding agency prefers—fieldwork is equally a state of mind and more importantly about making

Continued

connections with fellow human beings. As such, as a participant-observer, the anthropologist does not merely describe or report the reality of the field but invariably performs and intervenes in it, sometimes without even being aware of the consequences of his or her own presence. As "experts," anthropologists do not merely report sociocultural forms of knowledge; they also re-encode them in their own cultural tradition, through terms that might very well create their own hierarchical distinctions and potential categories of harms. In this case, one should question to what extent the anthropologist can and should take responsibility for the effects that his or her own translation has brought through the practice of fieldwork.

Along that line of thought, Canadian anthropologist Julie Cruikshank (2006) has demonstrated that ethnographic fieldworkers trained in the Boasian tradition have often re-rooted Indigenous discourses in a thoroughly modernist practice, that is, preservation and protection, while continuing to burnish them as authentic replications of the "native" point of view (2006: 59). These formulations subsequently "deny varieties of local knowledge their own histories," in which the expertise of knowledgeable people, such as First Nations, are taken out of their "evocative contexts" of relevance to be merely "taped, transcribed, codified, and labelled" (Cruikshank 2006: 256). While trying to understand specific knowledge forms by looking over the shoulder of the so-called "other," ethnographic practices can, in such manner, potentially construct knowledge in a selective and asymmetrical manner.

Furthermore, the effects of fieldwork are equally reverberated on anthropologists themselves. The different textures, dissents, pain, and wonderful moments utterly present while doing fieldwork—so lively that you can feel them across the shivering surface of your skin—can also appear as irrelevant to the stoic writing practices of academic tradition, leaving the ethnographer to trouble upon the task and role of his or her work. As the anthropologist Michael Taussig echoes, "the fieldwork diary is built upon a sense of failure—a foreboding sense that the writing is always inadequate to the experience it records" (2011: 100). Amidst such uncertainties, one of the most potent changes brought by fieldwork is ironically to be found in the anthropologist, or as Taussig argues, this quintessential "stranger in a foreign land asking for directions and, in the process, likely to be changed in some fundamental way" (2011: 144). By enabling one to understand and experience the "wisdom of others" (Stoller 2007: 179), fieldwork can permanently shift an individual's world view, permitting the appreciation of the cultural complexities and tensions found in an interconnected world, while fending off paradigmatic and stereotypical ways of thinking.

As opposed to his or her voice recorder, there is no "on and off" mental switch that enables the anthropologist to pass directly from the fieldwork to the writing. One of the oddest things about finally leaving your field site is realizing that fieldwork doesn't end per se, even while looking through the tiny windows of the jet carrier taking you to the place that you call home; you'll inevitably bring it with you. Like culture, fieldwork is not bound to a reified notion based on space, it remains a concept, a concept that has real effects both on the anthropologist and his or her informants.

Key Terms

culture shock   44
dialectic of fieldwork   36
fact   46
fieldwork   27
intersubjective meaning   31
material world   29

multi-sited ethnography   42
objective knowledge   29
participant-observation   27
phenomenology   31
positionality   32
positivism   28

reflexivity   31
situated knowledge   31
structured interviews   27
subjective meaning   31

Chapter Summary

1. Anthropological fieldwork traditionally involves extended periods of close contact with members of another society. This method of gathering information is known as *participant-observation*. This type of interaction in the field has the potential to change both researchers and participants in unpredictable ways.

2. In modern anthropology, researchers understand that they must recognize that participants are human beings and relate to them as such. Successful fieldwork involves anthropologists who are reflexive—who think about the way they think about other cultures. Participants must also reflect on the way they and others in

their society think and try to convey their insights to the anthropologist.

3. Multi-sited ethnography encourages anthropologists to acknowledge that societies are not isolated. It focuses on cultural processes that are not contained by social,

ethnic, religious, or national boundaries, and the ethnographer follows the process from site to site.

4. The ethnographic record of anthropological knowledge is perhaps best understood as a vast, unfinished commentary on human possibility. Anthropologists may never learn all there is to know, but they can always learn more.

Critical Thinking Questions

1. Why do many anthropologists consider participant-observation to be the central method for ethnographic data collection? What alternative methods could they use? What are some potential weaknesses of each method?

2. First, take a moment to reflect on how you see the world. Why do you think the way you do about certain people and things? How do you reach conclusions when you are trying to answer questions or solve problems? Next, answer the following question: How do these personal reflections inform your understanding of the

reflexivity discussed in this chapter and its use to the anthropologist?

3. Three modes of ethnographic fieldwork have been developed over the last hundred years or so: positivist, reflexive, and multi-sited. What are the benefits and drawbacks of each approach? Would you expect different results from each?

4. Anthropological professional organizations and government-funded granting agencies have codes of conduct. Why are carefully designed moral and ethical obligations a critical part of ethnographic fieldwork?

Suggested Readings

Bradburd, Daniel. 1998. *Being There: The Necessity of Fieldwork* **(Washington, DC: Smithsonian Institution Press).** An engaging personal study of how the many seemingly small details of experience during field research add up to anthropological understanding.

Godina, Vesna V. 2003. "Anthropological Fieldwork at the Beginning of the Twenty-First Century: Crisis and Location of Knowledge," *Anthropos*, 98: 473–87. A "where are we now?" discussion that contextualizes fieldwork experience.

Kumar, Nita. 1992. *Friends, Brothers, and Informants: Fieldwork Memoirs of Banaras* **(Berkeley: University of California Press).** A moving and thought-provoking reflection on the experience of fieldwork in the author's own country but in a culture quite different from her own.

Lévi-Strauss, Claude. 1974. *Tristes Tropiques* **(New York: Pocket Books).** A multi-faceted work about voyaging, fieldwork, self-knowledge, philosophy, and much more. Originally published in French in 1955, this work is considered by some to be the greatest book ever written by an anthropologist.

Liebersohn, Harry. 1994. "Discovering Indigenous Nobility: Tocqueville, Chamisso, and Romantic Travel Writing," *American Historical Review* 99, 3: 746–66. A discussion of the development of the construct of the "noble savage."

Nurse, Andrew. 2008. "'Their Ancient Customs Are Gone': Anthropology as Cultural Process," in *Around and about Marius Barbeau: Modelling Twentieth-Century Culture*, ed. Lynda Jessup, Andrew Nurse, and Gordon E. Smith **(Seattle: University of Washington Press).** An examination of the cultural significance of Canadian anthropologist Marius Barbeau's representation of First Nations in his ethnographic research.

Rabinow, Paul. 2007 [1977]. *Reflections on Fieldwork in Morocco, 30th Anniversary Edition* **(Berkeley: University of California Press).** An important, accessible, powerfully written reflection on the nature of fieldwork. The thirtieth anniversary edition contains a new preface in which the author reflects on his classic work from a contemporary perspective.

Related Websites

American Anthropological Association
www.aaanet.org
Government of Canada: Interagency Advisory Panel on Research Ethics
www.pre.ethics.gc.ca

Canadian Anthropology Society
www.cas-sca.ca

A woman walks by St Joseph's Cathedral in Hanoi, Vietnam. The church was built by the French colonial government, opening for the first time on Christmas Day in 1886, and remains a landmark for Vietnamese Catholics today.

3

Anthropology in History and the Explanation of Cultural Diversity

Chapter Outline

The Roots of Canadian Anthropology

Capitalism, Colonialism, and the Emergence of "The Field"

Anthropology and the Colonial Encounter

Toward Classifying Forms of Human Society

Studying Human Societies Today

Learning Objectives

By the end of Chapter 3, you will be able to

- situate North American anthropology in a historical perspective;
- describe in brief how colonialism and capitalism have transformed societies around the world;
- understand the influence of colonialism on early anthropological work;
- identify various typologies and classification systems that have been applied to human societies; and
- explain why many contemporary anthropologists reject attempts to apply categories to human societies.

Third-century BCE Chinese scientific thought focused on the five elements: wood, metal, fire, water, and earth. These elements fit into a circular relational structure where each "conquered" the preceding element (Ronan and Needham 1978: 151)—much like our rock, paper, scissors circle. The five elements gradually took on greater significance and "came to be associated with every conceivable category of things in the universe that it was possible to classify in fives" (153), such as the seasons, the points of the compass, tastes, smells, numbers, kinds of musical notes, and heavenly bodies. The typology eventually was associated with periods of dynastic history, styles of government, and social order in general; therefore, many saw the five elements typology as logical and useful for retrodiction (historical explanation) and for prediction (future planning). In effect it was what anthropologists call a *key metaphor*—a symbolic representation that is widely understood within a culture and central to that culture's world view (see Chapter 11). As with any apt metaphor or good scientific theory,

> these correlations met with criticism, sometimes severe, because they led to many absurdities.... Yet in spite of such criticisms, it seems that in the beginning these correlations were helpful to scientific thought in China.... [I]t was only when they became over-elaborate and fanciful, too far removed from the observation of Nature, that they were positively harmful. (156–7)

In the end, these criticisms resulted in a shift away from the traditional five-point classification system.

Like the Chinese sages, anthropologists in the nineteenth century first sorted human cultures into different categories based on what they believed to be their similarities and differences. Over time, the purposes and the categories have been modified in ways that reflect changes in the wider world, changing research interests and philosophical perspectives, as well as critical analyses of past approaches. In this chapter we situate the discipline of anthropology within contexts that have shaped its development and try to reach a clearer understanding of the kinds of situated knowledge anthropologists have developed.

The Roots of Canadian Anthropology

Before we delve into the history of anthropological study in general, you should understand a bit about the way anthropology became established in Canada. Canadian institutions were somewhat late to the game, although cultural research had been conducted in Canada since the nineteenth century. The work of Sir Daniel Wilson (1816–1892; Figure 3.1) is illustrative of this early period. He studied, as he would have called them, the Native peoples in Canada—Natives from the view that they were "important not in and for themselves but rather because they exemplified living, primitive cultures that had once existed in prehistoric Europe" (Berger 1990). Other materials of considerable ethnographic interest also remain from the pre–twentieth century, including, for example, the *Jesuit Relations*, the records of the Hudson's Bay Company, and the art of Paul Kane. In 1936, Thomas McIlwraith (1899–1964) (Figure 3.2) founded the first Canadian department of anthropology, at the University of Toronto. Like earlier ethnographers, McIlwraith was interested in "primitive peoples," but his Canadian experience

Library and Archives Canada/PA-123653

Figure 3.1 Sir Daniel Wilson (1816–1892) is considered by many to be the first professional scholar in Canadian archaeology and ethnography.

Scott, W.L./Library and Archives Canada/PA-066645

Figure 3.2 Thomas McIlwraith (1899–1964), like A.G. Bailey, was interested in ethnology and how Indigenous peoples in Canada were affected by change. This approach assumed that Indigenous peoples would survive the devastation of the past and remain part of the evolving Canadian reality.

capitalism An economic system dominated by a supply and demand market designed to create capital and profit.

colonialism The cultural domination of a people by larger, wealthier powers.

imperialism A system in which one country controls other, less powerful territories through colonization, often augmented by military force.

provides greater context for these peoples' lifeways. The later research of A.G. Bailey (1905–1997) on French–Indigenous contact (1969 [1937]) shows the mettle of what Canadian anthropology was to become. Bailey was influenced by his association with McIlwraith, his time at the University of Toronto (where he completed his PhD in ethnohistory and Indigenous culture), and his professional roles at both the University of New Brunswick and the New Brunswick Museum. Bailey became highly respected in Canada and abroad for his ethnographical work, and his research "prefigure[d] . . . the development of American Indian ethnohistory" in North America (Trigger 1975: 636).

Over time, three major anthropological schools of thought came to influence the development of Canadian anthropology: American, British, and French. Our proximity to the United States with the dominant position of Franz Boas and his fieldwork involvement on the West Coast of Canada, as well as our historical and intellectual ties to England and France,

helped to shape anthropological study in Canada. The result, a sometimes happy happenstance of time and place, was an integrative, flexible approach that has remained productive for Canadian researchers even as advances have continued in the discipline. Waldram from the University of Saskatchewan has characterized Canadian anthropologists as "engaged" anthropologists. He concludes by noting the following:

> "Militant" anthropology did not develop here for a reason. Canadian anthropologists . . . are rather nervous about adopting a Foucauldian activism to "speak truth to power" . . . Of course engaged anthropology puts us in the middle of controversies and, by definition, makes us targets. We must never turn a blind eye to this fact: there are always costs to engaged anthropology. (2010: 230)

But first there came a colonial prologue and its lessons as Canadians came to experience them.

Capitalism, Colonialism, and the Emergence of "The Field"

In *Europe and the People without History* (1982), Eric Wolf reflects on the ways in which **capitalism** and **colonialism** emerged as global forces. In his analysis, he finds the seeds of anthropology in **imperialist** Europeans' first meetings with other cultures as they "reached out to seize the resources and populations of the other continents" (1982: 18). He also finds in these encounters the beginnings of the problematic, "tacit anthropological supposition that [Indigenous] people . . . are people without history," a notion that disregards the changes and developments these people have experienced over time (18). If, as Wolf contends, anthropology was forged in the fire of change so central to European imperialist/capitalist endeavours, what is our legacy?

At the end of the nineteenth century, anthropology was assigned "the savage slot" as its "field" of inquiry in the social sciences. In North America, this meant that anthropology's primary task was to examine the Indigenous inhabitants of the Americas. They occupied what Europeans characterized as a wilderness—unimproved, unused, empty, "uncivilized" land. This wilderness became, in anthropologist Gaile McGregor's analysis, the "view from the fort" (1985: 5)—the "field" of emerging Canadian anthropology.

This field had emerged from the strong desire for westward European expansion dating to the reign of Queen Elizabeth I of England (r. 1558–1603). North America came to be thought of as a potential source of fresh resources and a distant place to effectively discard unwanted populations. In 1606 King James I granted the Virginia Company, essentially a group of gentlemen entrepreneurs, permission to establish a settlement in the New World. This settlement, known as "Jamestown," would become the first permanent British settlement in what is now the United States of America. In this and later settlements, the principle of *terra regis*—the belief that all newly discovered territories were the king's land by divine right—was assumed.

In 1670, King Charles II signed a royal charter establishing the Hudson's Bay Company (HBC). The HBC soon gained control of the area surrounding Hudson Bay, known as "Rupert's Land" (Figure 3.3). The objectives of the HBC were the exploitation of resources and exploration for the Northwest Passage (Rich 1961: 56). Of course, there were two vital differences between the Virginia and the Rupert's Land enterprises:

1. The HBC was *all* about commerce. Although its charter gave equal weight to trade and colonization, the HBC was almost solely interested in trade (55). In contrast, the Virginia Company's Jamestown, in an effort to graft upon the wild the tame, included colonization along with commerce.

2. The HBC project required the participation, albeit manipulated, of Indigenous peoples. The Jamestown enterprise, on the other hand, dealt with Indigenous peoples as troublesome and mostly expendable threats to the safety of colony property and colonist life.

In these and other instances of colonization, early settlers "knew virtually nothing of the Native languages of the Americas, even as they freely translated them" with seeming accuracy that was a mere fiction of power (Cheyfitz 1991: xv). Language can be a powerful tool to facilitate the process of colonization. As American studies scholar Eric Cheyfitz observes,

> [w]hat the English and Europeans could not achieve in actuality they achieved textually ... [through] early narratives: the translation of the Indians into proper English. ... [T]hese narratives became models

Charles A. Keefer/Library and Archives Canada/PA-073998

Figure 3.3 Commercial operations had an enduring presence in the lives of many Indigenous peoples in Canada. Here, a group of Dogrib people await a visit from the Fur Trade Commissioner in front of an HBC store in 1937. Aside from giving rise to a number of department stores across the country, what are some of the lasting effects of the HBC's domination of trade relations in the seventeenth and eighteenth centuries?

> of actuality, models for legal decisions in which the Indians were literally forced to speak proper English, to speak, that is, whether they could speak English or not, in the letter of a law that recognized only the terms of property. (10)

The ramifications of European colonial aspirations and ideas of progress have been felt across time and space, even into what we consider our modern era.

The Key Metaphor of Capitalism

On capitalism, Wolf comments that "The guiding fiction ... [and] one of the key tenets ... is that land, labour, and wealth are commodities, that is, goods produced not for use but for sale" (1969: 277). The world is a market, and everything within the world has, or should have, its price. For early colonialists, capitalism very much became a key metaphor. Today, the metaphor of capitalism persists, but it is no longer aligned with just a few cultural traditions; it permeates everyone's life. It is global.

The genius of capitalism is the way in which its supporters have been able to convert anything that exists into a commodity with a price tag: land becomes real estate; material objects become inventory. Price tags are attached to ideas (e.g., patented inventions). Even human beings have been treated as merchandise reducing all workers, even those who are not slaves, to objects; their value is in their labour power, which is worth whatever price the laws of supply and demand determine. The market system also restricts buyers' abilities to make decisions for themselves, forcing them to follow the fundamental rules of capitalism: buy low, sell high.

To be sure, complex commercial activity was not invented by Western capitalists. Stratified societies have always devised sophisticated socioeconomic systems. In the early days of capitalism, therefore, elite members of such societies around the globe were prepared to take advantage of new economic opportunities offered by Western entrepreneurs. These elites traded with Westerners, often helping to establish capitalist practices in their own societies and benefiting as a result. However, the consequences of capitalism were frequently negative for non-elite members of these societies, who lost many traditional socioeconomic supports.

Capitalism was even more devastating for those in a **small-scale society**. Members of these societies saw their land turned into a commodity for sale on the capitalist market. They experienced the devaluation of their traditional social identities based on kinship, descent, alliance, and residence. And they witnessed the erosion of traditional ways of life that protected them from destitution. In short, they experienced colonialism.

Colonial empires came in two historical phases. In the first phase, led by Spain, Portugal, and Holland, colonies were required to pay tribute to the ruling empire through trading companies. In the second phase, driven by England and France, colonies were treated as "plantations" and governed to meet the demands of industrial capitalism (Gledhill 1994: 74). To function within the capitalist world order, colonized peoples had to begin seeing the world as a storehouse of potential commodities. Much of recent world history can be usefully viewed as a narrative of non-Western responses to this new world view and the practical actions it encouraged and justified. Some people responded with enthusiasm, some were resentful but compliant, others were violent in rejection; through it all, displacement and destitution gutted what had been vibrant societies. However, it was European diseases with their high mortality rates that "devastated and decimated some groups, modifying social organizational features and ecological relationships" (Bishop 1981: 45).

Further, Canadian anthropologist Bruce Trigger notes that "failure to cope with epidemic diseases led to a spiritual crisis" (1981: 36). In general, settlements located close to active trade routes were most susceptible to infection. This problem continued into the twentieth century. During the Spanish flu pandemic (1918–19), Manitoba's Norway House Cree Nation lost 18 per cent of their adult population (ages 20 to 64) in the span of six weeks; the average loss among other Indigenous populations in that year was closer to 3 per cent (Herring 1994: 96). As Herring notes, "Its key position in the fur trade network and frequent contact with locations to the west, northwest, northeast, and south left it particularly vulnerable to imported micro-organisms" (97).

Responses to European Colonialism: The Fur Trade in North America

Like many Indigenous peoples worldwide, the First Nations populations of Canada have been through a journey of both immense tragedy and tremendous courage, and along the way they have made many compromises as they were forced to adapt to changed circumstances. Initially, one of the most invasive disturbances to Indigenous peoples' lives came from the fur trade.

The international fur trade's expansion into North America's new and untapped territory sent European profits skyrocketing (see Wolf 1982: 158ff.). The "winners" in all of this were the British, who overcame both the Dutch and the French for control of resources, mostly beavers. Beavers were not only a keystone species—a species on which the balance of an entire ecosystem depended—but also a feature of the key metaphor of many Algonquian peoples (Dods 2003, 2007; Overholt and Callicott 1982: 74–5). At contact, the animal seemed to be an inexhaustible resource; the estimate of the beaver population was 60 million to 400 million (Naiman et al. 1986: 1254). However, by the nineteenth century, the beaver populations in areas such as northern Ontario were reduced to the point of regional extinction. The capitalist response to declining resources was to open new territory—the fur traders moved on. Yet this response was not viable for Indigenous peoples who were and are deeply connected to the land. Many of them were forced to change food strategies. Canadian anthropologists Edward Rogers and Mary Black (1976: 13–14) recount an example of such a forced shift that occurred in northern Ontario between 1880 and 1920.

small-scale society
A community of several dozen to several hundred people usually held together by family (kinship) ties and often engaged in traditional subsistence activities.

In what has been referred to as the "fish and hare" period, the Anishinaabe (Ojibwe) were forced by starvation to turn to fishing and trapping of hare after the depletion of their primary food source—the caribou.

Resource depletion and the dietary changes that followed also caused many social issues to develop. For example, anthropologist Charles A. Bishop (1973) has identified the post-contact collapse of the food chain as the major factor contributing to a condition that has been labelled "the Wendigo complex"—a state in which a person is said to crave human flesh. This condition, first documented in the early nineteenth century (Bishop 1970: 8), has been interpreted by modern psychologists as a psychosis (see Chapter 10). However, Bishop (1973) considers the condition to be the direct result of protein starvation, and his interpretation is somewhat supported by work done with Arctic peoples in Lapland, Siberia, and northern North America. In a similar case, Norwegian physician and nutrition researcher Arne Høygaard (1941) examined reports of "hysterical fits" and "periodical madness" among Arctic peoples; he found the cause to be a lack of certain minerals and vitamins that are essential to the nervous system (Dods 1998).

The Slave and Commodities Trades

While the fur trade unfolded in the north, the slave trade and the trade in commodities, such as sugar and cotton, accompanied the rise of capitalist industry to the south (Figure 3.4). Humans and crops were exchanged in world markets as commodities. The slave trade, after a decline in available Europeans as slaves and indentured workers (Painter 2010), came to be dominated by commerce between Europeans and coastal Africans by the eighteenth century. This trade had a devastating effect on the societies of the African hinterland, whose members were captured and sold to meet European market demand. But the slave trade did not alter social relations in Africa alone. In the Americas, it profoundly reshaped the lives of both local Indigenous peoples and European colonists. The growth of plantation economies in areas that had been used for hunting, gathering, and small-scale farming altered local ecologies as well as local societies. And the wealth produced in these economies transformed both the local gentry and the European nations who claimed ownership of the land. As a result, Africa, the Americas, and Europe

© CORBIS/Corbis via Getty Images

Figure 3.4 Four generations of a family of slaves in Beaufort, South Carolina. The slave trade had a devastating effect on many Indigenous peoples around the world. What are the short- and long-term social impacts of treating human beings as commodities?

became inextricably intertwined. In many ways, this was the beginning of globalization.

"Modernity"

What is "modernity"? Its prototype was the European-style industrial city, so post-medieval and quite markedly different from the great Indigenous cities of pre-colonial times (e.g., the Aztec capital Tenochtitlan, over which the Spanish later built Mexico City). In colonial cities, colonial administrators, merchants, and local elites united to defend their joint interests against those they perceived as "outliers"—both the geographically removed "others" of the resource-rich hinterland and the socially removed "others" within the colonial cities. Elaborate systems for extracting raw materials and recruiting labour, sometimes by force, were devised. These and other capitalist-colonialist processes disrupted or destroyed existing Indigenous communities. At times, they also created new centres of population struggling to become communities, as was the case with the mining towns of southern Africa. Thus, little by little, in an effort to organize the systems of exploitation, society was restructured.

To some, the term *modern* reflects the modernization—both of technologies and of ideas—that came about in the Enlightenment, which began in the late seventeenth century. The spirit of the Enlightenment was humanist, based on the philosophy of **humanism**, and its primary goal was to come to an understanding of the "moral, genetic, and historical unity of mankind" (Mafeje 1976: 310). However, this intellectual environment also provided the justification behind the European notion of the "civilizing mission." This notion led to the "rationalization of more mundane things such as economic plunder, political imposition, and other inhuman practices" (311). Here, we see the dual forces of modernity at work: development and destruction.

In the colonial context, "modernity" has often been understood as nothing more than adopting the practices and world view of Western capitalism. As a result, the so-called backward rural peoples often turned out to be either those who escaped capitalism's embrace or those who actively opposed it. For many of them, the colonial city and the life it represented symbolized everything that was wrong with the colonial order. Not surprisingly, this perception persists today among peoples who feel invaded or ignored by Western capitalism.

The Colonial Political Economy

Because the colonial order focused on the extraction of material wealth, it came to link communities around the globe in a diverse market system. Yet this new economic order did not spring up painlessly by itself; it was imposed and maintained by force. For this reason, many anthropologists describe the colonial order as a **political economy** that created three kinds of connections:

1. Between conquered communities within a conquered territory
2. Between different conquered territories
3. Between conquered territories and the country of the colonizers

Wolf describes a particularly striking example of how some of these connections came together in the sixteenth century: silver mined in Spanish-American colonies was shipped to the Spanish-controlled Philippines, where it was used to buy textiles from the Chinese (1982: 153). If we take Wolf's example one step further and suggest that the profits from the sale of the Chinese textiles in the

European market were in turn used to fund colonialist projects in North America, we can see how the political economy might come full circle.

One way that colonial enterprises connected communities *within* a conquered territory was by drawing labour from neighbouring regions. For example, in Africa, mine owners recruited Africans from some distance; money earned in one area was thus sent away to support families in another area. These linkages did not come about spontaneously; rather, they were established and reinforced through political manipulation. In the early days of colonialism in Africa, Africans were still largely able to guarantee their own subsistence through traditional means, so they were unwilling to work for wages in the mines except on a short-term basis. Therefore, profitability in mining required that African self-sufficiency be eliminated so that Africans would have no choice but to work for whatever wages mine owners offered. The colonial government achieved this goal through two policies:

1. It imposed taxes on conquered African populations, insisting that the taxes could be paid only in cash.
2. It deliberately prevented the growth of a cash economy in African areas. Thus, the only way Africans could obtain the cash to pay their taxes was by working for wages in the mines.

As destructive as these policies were, they did not arise out of a desire to be cruel: colonial administrators were generally convinced that the work of the empire would benefit those they dominated—if not now, then in the future—a rudimentary version of the "trickle down" effect.

However, as the misguided efforts of past Canadian governments have taught us, policies that restrict the freedom of dominated people benefit no one. Consider the example of residential schools for Indigenous children (Figure 3.5). Such schools, first introduced in the first half of the nineteenth century, are seen by First Nations peoples as factories of cultural genocide designed by the Canadian government to eliminate the "Indian Problem" once and for all (Chrisjohn et al. 1997: 42). Like the colonial governments that implemented pro-mining policies in Africa, the authorities who set up the residential school system believed that they were doing good work. Consider the widespread ideal espoused by Canadian politician Alexander Morris in 1877: "let us have a wise and paternal Government . . . doing

humanism "... A philosophical and ethical stance that emphasizes the value and agency of human beings, individually and collectively, and generally prefers critical thinking and evidence (rationalism and empiricism) over acceptance of dogma or superstition" (*Wikipedia*).

political economy A social structure that is organized around material (economic) interests, in which these interests are protected and enhanced through the use of power (politics).

Public Archives Manitoba/n102264

Figure 3.5 Indigenous parents camp by a residential school to visit their children in Birtle, Manitoba, in 1904. How do the impacts of the residential school system continue to be felt in contemporary Canada?

its utmost to help and elevate the Indian population, who have been cast upon our care, . . . [and doing] its duty by the red man." Notice how Morris's sentiments echo the colonialist hubris of the **"white man's burden"**! Some First Nations peoples have argued that the actual agenda was much more selfish:

> the "problem" was (and is) that there were (and are) Aboriginal owners (and their legal descendants) inhabiting the land to which the Europeans wished to lay claim. . . . [The] genocide of Aboriginal peoples grew out of . . . [a] need to extinguish Aboriginal title to the land without violating the letter and spirit of established British policy. (Chrisjohn et al. 1997: 51–2)

Others have argued that the government's intent was cultural genocide—not the physical eradication of Indigenous peoples, but their death "spiritually, mentally, economically, and socially" (Waubageshig 1970: vi).

Women and Colonization

Ethnographic data show that colonial conquest did not affect all groups equally. Notably, Indigenous women's experience with colonialism was different from that of Indigenous men. In addition, colonialism did not treat all groups of women in all conquered territories in the same way. Trobriand women of New Guinea (see EthnoProfile 8.1), for example, were able to maintain status roles under colonial rule. Baule women of Ivory Coast in western Africa (see EthnoProfile 3.1) were less fortunate.

Before France colonized Baule society in 1893, production among the Baule centred on two products: yams and cloth (Etienne 1980). The traditional division of labour found men preparing farm plots for planting and women tending the crops. The women raised the cotton and spun it into thread, and the men did the actual weaving. The result was a highly egalitarian balance of power. But in 1923, the French built a textile factory that sold factory-spun thread for cash. Baule men with cash could therefore buy their own thread, and they, not their wives, would control any cloth woven from it. French colonial administrators also encouraged Baule farmers to plant new varieties of cotton as a cash crop. Baule women had traditionally practised crop rotation with the yams and cotton. Now the fields were devoted to growing only the new cotton. This industrial crop required new farming techniques, which the French taught only to Baule men. Consequently, women's roles in cotton production

"white man's burden" Europeans' sense that it was their duty to colonize, rule, and "civilize" all peoples they viewed as "savage."

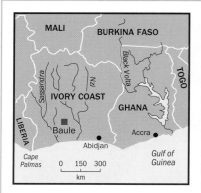

EthnoProfile 3.1
Baule

Region: Western Africa

Nation: Ivory Coast; originally from the area where the Koussou Dam was built (1971), the project resulted in the relocation of many Baule to the forests in the southwestern area of the country

Language: Fante-Akan

Population: 3,615,000 (2011 estimate)

Environment: Savannah

Livelihood: Farming (yams in particular); coffee, cocoa, and cloth production

Political organization: In the pre-colonial period, no state and no clear stratification; today, part of a modern nation-state

For more information: Vogel, Susan M. 1997. *Baule: African Art, Western Eyes* (New Haven: Yale University Press).

were reduced considerably. Now women had to work in their husbands' cash-crop fields and in the traditional yam plots. The agricultural work for women increased.

The colonial government required men to pay taxes in cash for themselves and for their wives, a move that seemed to justify the right of Baule men to control the production of crops that could be sold for cash. By the 1970s, many Baule women had become wage labourers in the textile factory in order to earn cash to buy their own cloth, which they could then control. They were aware of the loss of status and power they had suffered over the years, and their discontent had undermined traditional Baule marriage. Anthropologist Mona Etienne reported the following in 1980:

> The wife–husband production relationship has become a constant source of conflict. Because the production relationship has always been the foundation of marriage, and because cloth and cash now tend to be the measure of a husband's affection and respect, the whole personal relationship is also conflict-laden. Inevitably, many women prefer to remain unmarried and all seek to acquire their own cash. (1980: 231)

In this way, the traditional Baule mode of production was transformed by contact with the capitalist market. The previously egalitarian relations of production linking women and men (wives and husbands) were destroyed.

Anthropology and the Colonial Encounter

This section's title has been borrowed from the title of a book edited by anthropologist Talal Asad (Figure 3.6). Published in 1973, Asad's book was the first high-profile work by anthropologists to consider the connections between anthropology and

Figure 3.6 Anthropologist Talal Asad, who edited *Anthropology and the Colonial Encounter* (1973), has investigated the relationship between anthropology and colonialism.

colonialism. It constituted an important exercise in disciplinary self-scrutiny. Three decades after its publication, Asad (2002) revisited the questions raised in the earlier publication. In particular, he addressed the charge, made frequently from within and without the discipline, that anthropology was nothing more than a form of "applied colonialism." He concluded that the charge was false for two reasons:

1. Anthropological findings were too specialized to be used by colonial administrators, especially compared to the enormous amount of information supplied to them by merchants, missionaries, and other government functionaries.
2. Colonial governments were interested only in research that would help them rule with as little difficulty as possible; they did not share anthropologists' wider interest in conquered peoples' histories and cultures.

Anthropologists sometimes played ambiguous roles in the colonial and post-colonial settings since they were valued for the expert knowledge they could provide; those same administrators also viewed them with suspicion because their expert knowledge might easily work against administrative goals. Meanwhile, anthropologists felt they needed to avoid upsetting administrative officials so that they would be allowed to access colonial settings and further their own, hopefully altruistic, goals. Consequently, the impact of colonialism has always been a factor, but this does not mean that anthropologists worked to support colonialist interests.

One way of coping with colonial power was to address it indirectly, as part of a wider topic of study. For example, in the early to mid-twentieth century, a number of North American anthropologists promoted an impartial and scientific program of research that would, they hoped, discover the laws governing how cultures change. They considered situations encountered under colonialism, but they also considered situations where contact and change occurred in the absence of political conquest. The latter cases involved autonomous groups whose members could be freer about what they selected and rejected. The anthropologists did not see themselves as supporting any particular political position, but they were sympathetic to the plight of colonial subjects. Many openly defended the right of Indigenous peoples to control their own destinies.

In the years following World War II, colonized peoples increasingly rejected the role they had been forced to play as students of European civilization. The colonial order was no longer a given, and its ultimate benevolence was sharply questioned. This critical attitude persisted after what was termed **decolonization**. However, it soon became clear that formal political independence could not easily undo the profound social and economic entanglements linking the former colonial territories to the countries that had colonized them. The persistence of ties in the face of political sovereignty came to be called **neocolonialism**.

Studies of neocolonialism have created new awareness of just how strongly the fate of the colonized and the fate of the colonizers are interconnected. For example, the "underdevelopment" that now characterizes many Third World nations has developed in large part from conditions established under colonialist rule. The effects of colonialism also continue to impact once-subjugated Indigenous peoples living in more "developed" countries, such as Canada, Australia, and the United States. Canadians cannot deny the realities of the remains of the "colonial day." Consider the emerging debate on the naming of our schools and the use of Sir John A. MacDonald's name or the Halifax statue of Edward Cornwallis. One has only to read the newspaper or watch the evening news to know that the aspirations of the First Nations peoples of Canada have yet to be addressed in an adequate way (Figure 3.7).

decolonization The withdrawal of a colonial power from a territory that had been under its control.

neocolonialism The persistence of profound social and economic ties linking former colonial territories to their former colonial rulers despite political sovereignty.

Figure 3.7 An Indigenous community member leads a march with Dakota Access Pipeline protestors in Toronto to show support for the Standing Rock Sioux tribe. The pipeline project, which became operational on 1 June 2017, threatens the region's clean water and ancient burial grounds. What recent news stories have you seen that highlight the lasting impact of colonialism on Indigenous peoples in Canada today?

Today, through the efforts of organizations such as the Assembly of First Nations (AFN), Indigenous peoples have a greater voice than they did in the past, but there is much work ongoing and much that is yet to be addressed. Tellingly, the maxim is true: justice delayed is justice denied.

Toward Classifying Forms of Human Society

We can now consider several conclusions that have informed current anthropological approaches:

- First, all peoples live in their own modernity. Therefore, the peoples studied by anthropologists are not now—nor were they ever—leading timeless, unchanging ways of life unaffected by the presence of others.
- Second, *cultural patterns* have been affected everywhere by the arrival of Europeans and/or the transformations set in motion by the spread of European colonialism and capitalism.
- Third, many groups have shaped new identities and devised new **social forms** to deal with the effects of contact and conquest. These new social forms sometimes draw on very ancient traditions, reworked to meet the demands of new experiences.
- Fourth, ways of life that were invented long ago continue to prove their worth, and many ways that were lost as a result of colonialism are being reintroduced today—at times with the help of information gathered by anthropologists. Yet some time-tested modes of living continue to fall before the advance of Western technology and the rigours of market capitalism (see, e.g., Lee as discussed in Hitchcock 2012).
- Fifth, colonial empires have been replaced by the empires of transnational corporations. The reach of these corporations is vast, and their actions affect peoples in all regions of the world. Anthropologists must work to understand how these corporations influence everyday life and social relations; they must also devise new forms of recourse to challenge, where appropriate, the agents of such change.

As anthropologist Laura Nader (1972) has observed, modern anthropologists must "study up"—that is, they must investigate who has power, where power comes from, and how the powerful make decisions. When combined with more traditional approaches of examining the lives of the marginalized and powerless, this approach can give anthropologists a very detailed, accurate understanding of a society, indeed a holistic vision of reality.

Evolutionary Typologies: The Nineteenth Century

Early anthropologists, like all children of the Age of Enlightenment, liked to devise **typologies**. They believed that such classification systems would facilitate their study of similarities and differences among different cultures. Of course, every system of classification reflects the qualities believed to be most significant by its creator. Therefore, different assessments can lead to different classifications. In the nineteenth century, most Europeans described the differences they noticed in terms of *deficiencies*: lack of formal schools, lack of sophisticated technology, lack of organized religion, and so forth. For example, a colonial official eager to establish a trading post and to maximize profits would ask: How do you "pay" for beaver pelts when the "sellers" are not interested in money? Europeans faced with such practical problems frequently saw life outside Europe in terms of a series of insufficiencies compared to what they could count on "back home."

More contemplative nineteenth-century observers pondered why such deficiencies existed in the first place. As they sat in their libraries studying the reports of travellers and reading books about history, they learned that many of the aspects of daily life they took for granted had not always existed. By studying back in time beyond the Middle Ages, they discovered that their more distant ancestors had lived much the same way as many contemporary peoples around the world. Indeed, they found evidence to support their theories in the written accounts of Julius Caesar (100–15 BCE), who had painted a picture of Indigenous life in early Europe that resembled what Europeans thought they were discovering in the Americas and Africa, supported by archaeological discoveries of ancient artifacts in European soil.

The experience of social change in the Age of Enlightenment and through the Industrial Revolution, together with historical and archaeological evidence

social forms Culturally conforming collective ways of interacting with our surroundings and the people we encounter; these forms of interaction, often taken for granted, are encoded forms of behaviour that are enforced by the group.

typology A classification system based on systematic organization into types on the basis of shared qualities.

of past change, led these thinkers to a new idea: perhaps the ways of life of the non-Western peoples were not only similar to but repeats of the ways of life of Europeans of long ago; perhaps the West had already moved through *stages* of history the same as those of contemporary non-Western societies. Accordingly, these scholars thought that non-Western societies in their own time would make the same discoveries and social changes that European society had made in its distant past.

This way of thinking has been termed **unilineal cultural evolutionism** (Figure 3.8). It quickly gained in popularity as an explanation for the widespread cultural diversity that Europeans had been observing since their forays outward starting in the Age of Exploration in the fifteenth century. The theory accounted for this diversity by arguing that different kinds of societies represented different stages of societal evolution through which every human society either had passed or would pass. Proponents of the theory saw late nineteenth-century European capitalist industrial society as the most advanced stage of cultural evolution. Living societies that had not

already reached this level were seen as primitive relics of the stages the West had already left behind.

To understand how the stages involved in unilineal cultural evolutionism were conceptualized in the nineteenth century, we will consider two popular schemes:

1. The "three-age system" developed by Danish scholar C. J. Thomsen (1788–1865)
2. The "ethnical stages" of the American anthropologist and social theorist Lewis Henry Morgan (1818–1881)

Thomsen's "Three-Age System"

In 1836, around the time Charles Darwin was developing his theory of biological evolution, C. J. Thomsen published his ideas on cultural change in *A Guide to Northern Antiquities,* in which he outlines his three-age system developed on his systematic study of artifacts in the National Museum of Denmark. Thomsen noticed that the choice of raw materials to manufacture tools had changed over time. The oldest tools were made of stone; later tools, of bronze; and still later tools, of iron. Thomsen proposed that Europeans had passed through three technological stages or "ages":

1. The Stone Age
2. The Bronze Age
3. The Iron Age

Later, the Stone Age was subdivided into the *Paleo*lithic ("*Old*" Stone Age—itself divided into Lower, Middle, and Upper divisions), *Meso*lithic ("*Middle*" Stone Age), and *Neo*lithic ("*New*" Stone Age) on the basis of changes in manufacturing techniques and the resulting tool forms.

Morgan's "Ethnical Stages"

Subsequently more influential than Thomsen's typology were Lewis Henry Morgan's "ethnical stages" in *Ancient Society: or, Researches in the Lines of Human Progress from Savagery through Barbarism to Civilization* (1877). Morgan also divided ancient societies into three stages:

1. "Savagery"
2. "Barbarism"
3. "Civilization"

As in the Stone Age, lower, middle, and upper categories for savagery and barbarianism were

unilineal cultural evolutionism
A nineteenth-century theory that proposed a series of stages through which all societies must go (or had gone) in order to reach civilization.

Wikipedia

Figure 3.8 E.B. Tylor (1832–1917), one of the founders of anthropology in Great Britain, was convinced that societies moved through a series of unilineal stages. What advantages might there be to unilineal systems? What disadvantages?

defined by technological features, in particular food-acquisition technologies. One striking feature, however, effectively kept "Civilization" for Europeans alone—the use of the phonetic alphabet. *Ancient Society* was based in equal parts on Morgan's mid-nineteenth-century field observations of the Iroquois of the Finger Lakes District of New York, the emerging concepts of evolution (biological and cultural), and the ideas of progress from the Age of Enlightenment. In effect, the text was an attempt at "anthropological" synthesis of the unilineal evolution of human society.

Morgan's typology was immensely influential, most notably in *The Origin of the Family, Private Property and the State* (1884) by Friedrich Engels. Well into the twentieth century, Morgan's classification, because of its link through Engels to Marxism, was *popular* in some sectors of the academic world. For example, Morgan was the main authority cited in Chinese archaeological reports well into the 1970s. In the Americas, Morgan's typology gained renewed attention in the 1940s and 1950s with the unilineal evolutionary perspective of anthropologist Leslie White, whose approach differed markedly from that of his teacher, Franz Boas.

Morgan's typology was frequently used to justify racism, however. Under this typology, some people were considered to have "stagnated" or even "slid back" from a later to an earlier stage. Others were considered to be "eminently gifted" (de Gobineau 1967 [1915]: 27). Racial inferiority, French writer and theorist Arthur de Gobineau pronounced, "is shown, not only by defeat, but also by the lack of the attributes that may be seen in the conquerors" (31). He asks, if all men are brothers and the brain of the "Huron Indian" is the same as that of an Englishman or a Frenchman, "Why then, in the course of the ages, has [the Huron] not invented printing or steam power?" (37). Of course, de Gobineau neglected to note that printing was actually the invention of a group classified by Europeans as Upper Barbarians—namely, the Chinese! Such omissions are indicative of the ways in which Europeans assumed credit for all social and technological "advancements." Western "civilization" self-assigned the position of purveyors of modernity while in the emerging discipline of anthropology, anthropologists were assigned as interpreters of the "savage slot," the peoples who were considered living examples of a distant human past.

historical particularism
The study of cultures in their own historical contexts.

Reactions against Unilineal Evolutionism

As you might expect, contemporary anthropologists find labels such as *savage*, *barbaric*, and *civilized* to be not only inadequate but also misleading, and they avoid using such labels in their research and object to their use in less scientific contexts. In 2007, for example, the British-based Association of Social Anthropologists and the activist group Survival International initiated a campaign to "challenge racist descriptions . . . of tribal peoples in the media," citing the use of such terms as *Stone Age* and *primitive* as offensive (Kesterton 2007; Survival International 2014). Regardless, such classificatory schemes continue to resonate, seemingly, while falsely offering coherent frameworks.

What has replaced unilineal cultural evolutionism in modern anthropological thought is the realization that all cultures develop along their own paths. Boas told us this with his use of **historical particularism**, covered in more detail later in this chapter. These paths are shaped, not insignificantly, by circumstances situated in various forms of resources. For example, some researchers have noted that Europeans' seeming superiority is tied to their particular geographic location. A major advantage for early Europeans was their access to temperate environments, allowing for the diffusion from West Asia of domesticated crops and the adoption or domestication of animals, resulting in highly effective farming practices that spread with relative ease. As a result of these and other time-saving developments, some would argue that Europeans had more free time to explore new ideas and, thus, develop or adopt and innovate new technologies leading to new economies. The colonial advantage did not come from innate superiority but from control of technological development, which would not have been possible without the luck of physical geography.

For more objections to unilineal evolutionism of the nineteenth century, see the later discussion on Boas and his students (pp. 65–7).

Social Structural Typologies: The British Emphasis

Although unilineal cultural evolutionism may have self-justified Europe's global ambitions and made colonial rule appear inevitable and just, it was inadequate for meeting the practical needs of colonials once they were in power. By the end of the nineteenth century, most of Africa and much of Asia had

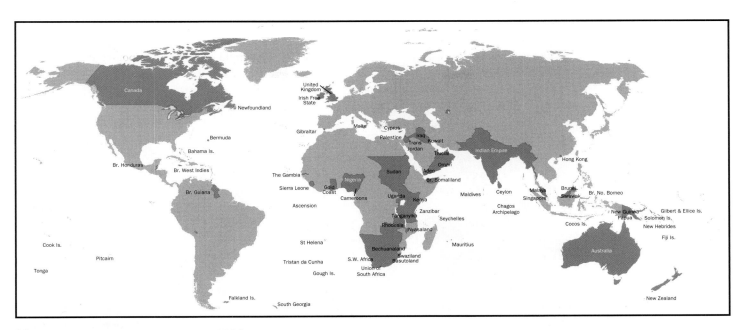

Map 3.1 The British Empire in the 1920s

Source: James Alcock

been divided up among European powers, although British imperialism dominated (Map 3.1). Meanwhile, Canada and the US adopted a colonial management style toward Indigenous peoples of North America.

In order to effectively oversee their subject peoples, administrators required accurate information about those peoples. For example, one goal of a colonial administrator in Africa was to keep peace among various groups. To achieve this goal, the administrator needed to know how those diverse peoples resolved disputes. This knowledge could then help the administrator develop a policy for dispute resolution that would be accepted by local peoples—sort of a mandated intersubjective space. Reaching other goals—for example, introducing elements of European law and political economy—without totally disrupting life in the colonies also required a deeper understanding of local practices. Since this would require Europeans to observe and interact with local peoples, colonial governments began supporting anthropological research. The changing relationships between the West and the rest of the world fostered the development of a new anthropological research model—one that grew out of a desire to gather detailed information while not overtly meaning to support colonialism. Anthropological sympathies often lay with the colonized peoples with whom anthropologists worked. For example, Edward Evans-Pritchard, who worked in central Africa for the British government in the

1920s and 1930s, saw himself as an educator of colonial administrators. He tried to convey to the British government the humanity and rationality of Africans. His goal was to combat the racism and oppression embedded in colonial rule. Not surprisingly, such criticisms of colonialism often caused colonial officials to be wary of anthropologists and distrustful of their motives.

Based on early observations, colonial officials quickly learned that administering their rule would be easier if they could rely on traditional leaders as intermediaries (Figure 3.9). Accordingly, the British policy of *indirect rule* was developed. The task of uncovering information on the traditional political structures of different groups frequently fell to anthropologists. As a result, British anthropologists developed a new way of classifying forms of human society. Their focus was on the **social structure**, especially the political structure, of groups under colonial rule. That British anthropologists came to call themselves *social anthropologists* reflects these developments and came to influence many anthropologists in the early twentieth century. For example, in 1940, in a classic work on African political systems, Fortes and Evans-Pritchard distinguished between *state* and *stateless* societies. This distinction had some similarity to Morgan's ethnical stages, and it described stateless societies in negative terms (i.e., what they lacked in comparison to state societies), but notably did not refer to "progress" in relation to either

social structure The enduring aspects of the social forms in a society, including its political and kinship systems.

Figure 3.9 Colonial officers often relied on traditional rulers to keep the peace among their subjects. This 1895 photograph shows the British governor of the Gold Coast (seated on the right) together with a contingent of Native police. What are the advantages—both for the foreign officers and for the locals—of this sort of arrangement? What might be the disadvantages? How does historical terminology indicate issues around colonial governance and behaviour?

band A form of social organization that consists of a small group of foragers (usually fewer than 50 people), in which labour is divided according to age and sex, and social relations are highly egalitarian.

tribe A form of social organization generally larger than a band, in which members usually farm or herd for a living; social relations are relatively egalitarian, although there may be a chief who speaks for the group.

chiefdom A form of social organization in which the leader (a chief) and the leader's close relatives are set apart from the rest of society and allowed privileged access to wealth, power, and prestige.

system. An emphasis on social structures emerged, and questions of evolution and social change faded to be replaced by concerns about the enduring traditional structures. Anthropologists came to believe that having a detailed knowledge of social structures would allow them to identify the social type of any particular society. Similarities and differences were researched, and there emerged a new classification, a typology, of social forms.

The Classification of Political Structures

An example of a typical social structural classification is shown in Figure 3.10. In this system, outlined by anthropologist Ted Lewellen in 1983, the major distinction is between *centralized* and *uncentralized* (*egalitarian*) political systems. Lewellen's system is similar to that established by Fortes and Evans-Pritchard in 1940; however, note that uncentralized societies are now distinguished in positive terms, not in terms of what they lack. A major difference between the two political systems is that centralized systems have distinct, permanent public decision-making institutions (e.g., a chief, a king or a queen, a formal government), while in uncentralized systems groups and individuals enjoy relative autonomy and equal status.

Within Lewellen's classification, uncentralized political systems can be further subdivided into two types:

1. **Band:** a small social group whose members neither farm nor herd but depend on wild food sources. Lewellen refers to three subtypes of a band, including the *family band*.
2. **Tribe:** a group that lies somewhere between a band and a centralized political system. A tribe is generally larger than a band and has domesticated plants and animals, but its political organization remains largely egalitarian. Lewellen identifies five subtypes of a tribe but comments that there are likely others (1983: 26).

Centralized political systems have a central, institutionalized focus of authority, such as a chief or a king. Some members of centralized societies have greater wealth, power, or prestige than other members; hierarchy is evident. Centralized systems are divided into two types:

1. **Chiefdom:** usually only the chief and the chief's family are set above the rest of society, which remains fairly egalitarian

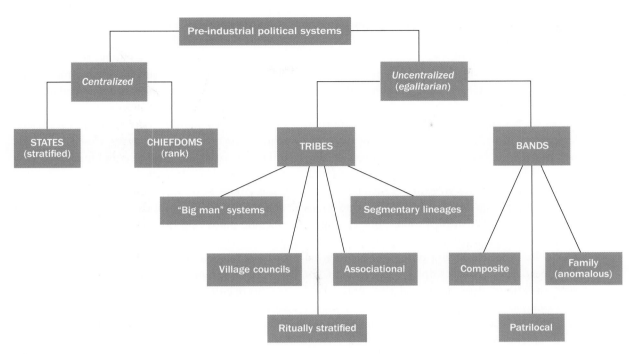

Figure 3.10 A typical classification of forms of human society.

Source: Adapted from Lewellen 1983: 16.

2. **State**: different groups suffer permanent inequality of access to wealth, power, and prestige; this signals the presence of social stratification

The major advantage of Lewellen's typology is that it does not attempt to make any hypotheses about evolutionary, **diachronic** relationships. Tracing change over time is not its purpose. Instead, the focus is on structural similarities and differences observed at one point in time—a **synchronic** analysis. Yet we can see in this approach the lasting influence of colonialism on anthropology, as classifications of this kind were originally made to help colonial authorities rule local peoples. By asking, "How do African political systems work today?" these officials were trying to answer the more practical question, "What do we need to know about these systems to make them work for us?"

Structural-Functional Theory

The theories of British social anthropologists dealt with how particular social forms function from day to day in order to reproduce their traditional structures. Such **structural-functional theory** was perhaps most highly developed by British social anthropologist A.R. Radcliffe-Brown in the 1930s and 1940s. Around this time, many social anthropologists were beginning to ask questions, such as the following, about why things did or did not change:

- Why do some social structures last for centuries (e.g., the Roman Catholic Church) and others disappear quickly (e.g., the Shakers of nineteenth-century United States)?
- Why did some societies abandon foraging for agriculture thousands of years ago, while others are still hunting and gathering today?

A balanced approach in anthropology involves equal consideration of reasons for change and reasons for stability, i.e., the *status quo*. This approach recognizes that an emphasis on one tends to downplay or ignore questions about the other.

In the first half of the twentieth century, the structural-functional focus in British social anthropology produced a variety of non-evolutionary social structure classifications with myriad diverse subtypes. Not surprisingly, many contemporary anthropologists question the point of developing such typologies at all.

Attempting to Do without Typologies: Culture Area Studies in North America

In the late nineteenth and early twentieth centuries, most American anthropologists were becoming increasingly dissatisfied with unilineal

state A stratified society, controlled by a formal government, that possesses a territory that is defended from outside enemies with an army and from internal disorder with police.

diachronic Considering one entity through its timeline.

synchronic Considering a number of entities in the same timeframe.

structural-functional theory A position that explores how particular social forms function from day to day in order to reproduce the traditional structure of the society.

evolutionism. The most significant figure in the attempt to move away from this approach was Franz Boas. Boas and his students worked primarily among American Indigenous peoples, including West Coast First Nations. They collected data about these societies, especially relating to the histories of individual groups and their languages. They found that these societies did not pass through uniform, shared stages as they changed over time. For example, they found that two societies with similar forms of social organization might have arrived at their current positions through different historical routes: one through a process of simplification (i.e., becoming less complex), the other through a process of elaboration (i.e., becoming more complex). To account for such situations, Boas developed the approach of *historical particularism* (defined earlier).

Boas emphasized that many seemingly new cultural forms were actually borrowed (diffused) from neighbouring societies (Figure 3.11). He and his followers were quick to note that if cultural borrowing, rather than independent invention, played an important role in culture change, then any unilineal evolutionary scheme was doomed. In addition, their focus on cultural borrowing emphasized the porous

boundaries around individual societies that made such borrowing possible.

As a result of such observations, the view of society that became dominant in North America was quite different from the one that dominated in Great Britain. Most of Boas's followers rejected the unilineal cultural evolutionists' view of societies as isolated representatives of universal stages, closed to outside influences. Critical of the structural-functional view of societies as bounded, *timeless* social types, they saw social groups as fundamentally open to the outside world. Change was considered more a result of idiosyncratic borrowing from neighbours than a result of inevitable, law-governed *progress*. Therefore, the Boasians focused their attention on a form of research called *cultural area studies*. They began by developing lists of **culture traits**, such as particular rituals or styles of housing. They then determined how widely those cultural traits had spread into neighbouring societies. A **culture area** was defined by the limits of borrowing, or the *diffusion* of, a particular trait or set of traits (see Map 3.2).

North American anthropologists, most famously Alfred Kroeber (1939), were able to discuss social groups without evoking "timeless" classification schemes. Yet new difficulties arose, as they found

culture traits Particular features or parts of a cultural tradition, such as a dance, ritual, or style of pottery.

culture area A geographical region in which cultural traditions share similar culture traits.

Figure 3.11 Franz Boas observed that the culture of the Zuni people of New Mexico seemed to be deeply influenced by Spanish culture, which the Zuni would have encountered under colonialism.

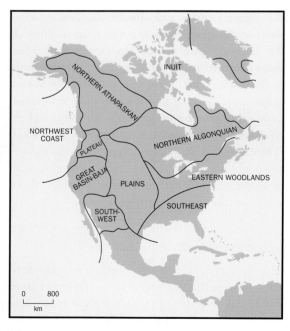

Map 3.2 The Indigenous American culture areas for North America, north of Mexico

it impossible to discuss, in unambiguous terms, societies perpetually open to cultural borrowing. These new orderings were either broader than an individual society (culture areas) or narrower than an individual society (culture traits). Rather than finding a typology-free methodology, these anthropologists had simply arrived at a new system of classification, albeit one in which societal boundaries were ignored.

Post-colonial Realities

Around the middle of the twentieth century, the world changed again. World War II was closely followed by the break-up of European colonial empires in Africa and Asia. Former colonies were now classified as independent states (whose boundaries were negotiated by competing colonial powers), and their citizens rejected the traditional Western view of them as "primitives." A deepening global awareness developed of the need to promote human rights and principles of equality. Changing realities thus created, for Westerners, new views that made the pretensions of unilineal evolutionism completely unacceptable. Decolonization forced anthropologists to pay direct attention to colonialism as a form of political domination—one that eliminated the autonomy of Indigenous social groups and forcibly restructured them into subordinate positions within a larger entity.

Concurrently, anthropologists with roots in the non-Western world began to add their voices to those of Western anthropologists (Figure 3.12) becoming highly critical of unilineal evolutionist

and structural-functionalist approaches, noting that these approaches helped to spread cultural stereotypes. They have also been critical of the fact that "ranking" typologies have not disappeared altogether in contemporary cultural and social anthropology. (See the "In Their Own Words" box that follows on the lasting impact of the stereotype that Africans did not practise same-sex sexuality.)

Figure 3.12 Sri Lankan anthropologist Arjun Guneratne converses with some of his informants in Nepal. In what ways can researchers from the non-Western world help us gain broader perspectives on the human condition?

In Their Own Words

"Bisexuality" and the Politics of Normal in African Ethnography

Marc Epprecht is head of the Department of Global Development Studies at Queen's University. In the following discussion, he examines the lasting impact of the common stereotype, created and spread by Europeans in colonialist times, that Africans did not practise same-sex sexuality.

Anthropologists have played a central role in documenting the diversity of human sexuality as it is understood and expressed in different cultures around the world. . . . However . . . anthropologists at times "conscripted" select evidence and even

fabricated "facts" about the people they studied in order to advance ideals and preferences around sexuality in their own societies. By conjuring idealized or exoticized Others, they helped to create an understanding of "normal" and "modern" by way of contrast. This has resulted in a body of purportedly empirical or scientific data that in retrospect we can see as deeply flawed, morally normative, and sometimes actually complicit in the construction and maintenance of racist colonialist structures. . . .

[Consider] the commonplace assumption or assertion as an unqualified fact that Africans south of the Sahara either

Continued

did not practice same-sex sexuality in their traditional societies, or that they only did so so rarely that it was inconsequential. . . . [More recently,] a growing body of research, activism, and art has comprehensively demonstrated the falseness of the "fact" of Africans' exclusive heterosexuality. . . . A growing, pan-African network of lesbian, gay, bisexual, transgender, and intersex (LGBTI) associations also attests to diverse, indigenous, same-sex, and bisexual cultures and practices in Africa. A range of images written or produced by Africans in fiction, theatre, and film further destabilizes the stereotype of the "pure" African heterosexual.

These sources on the whole do not propose a timeless, archetypal African gay or lesbian in opposition to that older stereotype. Rather, the women and men who have same-sex sexual relations most often also continue to marry, to have children, and to engage in heterosexual relationships. Whether this should properly be termed "bisexual" is a matter of debate. However, whether men who sometimes have sex with men but do not identify as homo- or bisexual (MSM), and whether women who sometimes have sex with women but do not identify as lesbian or bisexual (WSW) exist in Africa in greater numbers than commonly assumed or asserted cannot in good scholarship be disputed. That it *does* continue to be disputed is a cause for far greater concern than academic quibbling over numbers. Indeed, scholars, activists, and community leaders who deny the existence of MSM and WSW in Africa, who rationalize it as imported or recent, or who simply disregard the evidence, may be fuelling unhelpful or even dangerous homophobic and xenophobic rhetoric. Such rhetoric stigmatizes already vulnerable groups and self-evidently impedes HIV/AIDS awareness and prevention campaigns. . . .

Clearly, many factors contribute to the tenacity of the no same-sex sexuality in Africa argument. The ethnography, however, is unquestionably foundational in that it provides a scientific-sounding canon that gives authority to contemporary claims about what is normal and traditional, and what is deviant, non-existent, or modern. But how trustworthy is that canon? [There are] key discrepancies in the documentary record dating as far back as the eighteenth century . . . [that]

offer insight into the complex relationship between colonial rulers and subjects, and can help us to understand why some Africans today still remain attracted to and defensive of colonial notions of normal. Awareness of this history could also move us toward more pointed research about sexuality in the present that could, in turn, improve our ability to design more effective interventions against HIV/AIDS. A queer analysis of African ethnography could also sharpen the postcolonial critique of anthropology more generally by alerting us to hitherto unsuspected essentialist, "Westocentric" terms and concepts. . . .

[This] new anthropology . . . represents the kind of bold challenges to mainstream scholarship predicted by Kath Weston in her reflections on queer ethnographic research (1998). These would include:

First, establishing beyond reasonable objection that most African societies had normative ways of dealing with sexual difference that were discreetly hidden within the dominant hetero-patriarchal norms. Sweeping claims about non-existence . . . [of] same-sex sexuality are thus empirically unfounded. Expressions of same-sex sexuality, moreover, changed over time in response to many factors, almost certainly including interventions by Western anthropologists.

Second, the research raises compelling questions on a number of contemporary issues. Are men who sometimes have sex with men but do not admit it and do not consider themselves homosexual or bisexual a more significant vector for HIV than has previously been considered? Do women who have sex with women yet consider themselves straight or normal engage in practices that would more accurately be termed bisexual or lesbian-like? It seems likely.

The new anthropology also causes us to reflect on whether the attitudes and political agendas that obscured MSM and WSW from the view of earlier anthropologists and other researchers had a bigger role in shaping heteronormative gender roles and identities in the majority population than has thus far been investigated.

Source: Epprecht, Marc. "'Bisexuality' and the Politics of Normal in African Ethnography," *Anthropologica* 48, 2: 187–201. Reprinted with permission of University of Toronto Press.

Locating Cultural Processes in History

The research of many anthropologists has revealed the destructive consequences of colonialism, the uneven spread of capitalism, and the enduring inequalities that resulted. Many authors stressed that the development of the rich world had actually *produced* the so-called underdevelopment of poor countries by colonizing their lands, exploiting their peoples, and expropriating their wealth (Frank

1967; Rodney 1972). Anthropologists inspired by Immanuel Wallerstein and Eric Wolf became increasingly conscious of the distortions of ethnographies written in ways that seemed to locate the societies they described in a timeless bubble, unaffected by history.

Anthropologists John and Jean Comaroff drew on these insights to craft an influential theoretical orientation they called "neomodern anthropology."

Neomodern anthropology grew out of their efforts to write a historical ethnography of the encounter between the Tswana of southern Africa and the West, beginning with the arrival of Scottish Nonconformist Christian missionaries in the early nineteenth century. The Comaroffs' neomodern anthropology draws attention to "the reality of power and constraint" in human affairs (1992: x), while also insisting that power and constraint are never total, always leaving gaps within which human actors might develop new interpretations or new forms of actions. At any given point, these new interpretations or actions may seem insignificant; however, the accumulation of many such changes over decades or centuries can produce wide-ranging and unanticipated changes in a society's cultural practices, for good and for ill. This effort to set ethnography in historical context can be found in the work of many contemporary cultural anthropologists.

Furthermore, other anthropologists have also noted a shift to more experimental postmodern forms, with many "tak[ing] up the challenge to incorporate politics and poetics into the ethnographic enterprise" (Darnell 2011). This, however, has not occurred without tension and contradiction, as Regna Darnell notes:

> Ethnographies look different these days: we put words in quotation marks to problematize the absence of shared meaning underlying their usage; we invent new words or hyphenate old ones to emphasize their etymologies or simultaneous but alternative senses... Moreover, anthropologists wander further astray than we used to from the boundaries of our own discipline in search for theorists who can speak alongside our ethnographic insights. Under the influence of postmodernism, anthropologists began to cite French theorists in preference to their own disciplinary ancestors...

> Postmodernism has been accused of denying the continuities and decisive conclusions of history... As an historian of anthropology, I argue to the contrary that there are multiple histories of anthropology, that they move in diverse ways into the anthropological present, and that it matters how we got to where we are now. (2011: 328; reprinted with permission of University of Toronto Press)

Studying Human Societies Today

Some contemporary anthropologists, especially those interested in political and economic issues, continue to find typologies useful. Others reject typologies altogether, arguing that such categorizations are too limited to be of any use. Still, most would agree that the points of comparison on which any anthropologists choose to focus are closely related to the type of questions that they ask and the theoretical approaches they apply. Defining different domains of relevance always results in different typologies.

One domain that became of great interest to Western countries during the mid-twentieth century was *political ideology*. In particular, people were concerned with the divide between *capitalist* and *communist* societies. During the Cold War (1948–91), a new set of categories came into existence that ordered states into the First World (capitalist democratic countries that supported the United States), the Second World (communist countries that supported the Soviet Union), and the Third World (countries that remained neutral). After the Cold War ended, a nation's political ideology became of less general significance than its economic development, and these categories shifted to reflect these changing interests: the label *"First World"* came to signify the "developed" world, *"Second World"* came to signify "developing" countries (in particular those that had supported or continue to support communism), and *"Third World"* came to signify "underdeveloped" countries. In addition, a fourth category—*"Fourth World"*—was added to signify the "neocolonial" world (e.g., pockets of Indigenous peoples living within First World countries).

As these categories came to redefine how modern nations were viewed, anthropologists were forced to adjust to this altered context. Yet many of them eventually became highly critical of the way "development" and "underdevelopment" were understood and addressed by scholars and government officials alike. These distinctions have become even more problematic in recent decades, as anthropologists face complex divisions in a globalized world economy and as they confront increasing tensions between capitalist and fundamentalist-religious ideologies.

Globalization suggests a world full of movement and mixture, contracts and linkages, and persistent cultural interaction and exchange (Inda

globalization Reshaping of local conditions by powerful global forces on an ever-intensifying scale.

and Rosaldo 2002: 2). Globalization is seen in the growth of transnational corporations that relocate their manufacturing operations to low-wage countries or that appropriate local cultural forms and turn them into images and commodities to be marketed throughout the world (Figure 3.13). It is seen in tourism, which has grown into the world's largest industry, and in migration of people from peripheral parts of the globe to the industrialized core. Globalization has created new opportunities for Indigenous peoples to build worldwide organizations to defend their interests (Kearney 1995; Niezen 2003). At the same time, global processes can reinforce

© teodoral/123RF

Figure 3.13 One dimension of globalization involves the appropriation of local cultural forms and their use on a variety of widely sold commodities. Dream catchers were part of Ojibwe (Anishinaabe) spiritual practice to prevent bad dreams and had distinct ways of being made. They spread to other Indigenous peoples in the United States and Canada who share some of the same beliefs and practices. Dream catchers are now manufactured and sold on a massive scale, marketed as everything from ornamental objects, such as earrings, to objects for New Age spiritual practice. Can you think of other examples of local cultural forms that have been appropriated and turned into commodities? What are the effects of such appropriation?

old constraints as poor people in many parts of the world encounter new forms of economic or political exclusion that reinforce previous marginality. Based on evidence of this kind, anthropologists have long argued that the effects of globalization are *uneven*: Some people have clearly benefited from globalization whereas others have suffered, and people everywhere struggle to respond to effects of globalization that seem impossible to manage.

In a globalized world, it is no longer possible to presume that peoples and cultures are firmly attached to specific geographical locations. Not only that: People who "deterritorialize" from one location always "reterritorialize" in a new location. Such reterritorialization regularly sparks social conflicts and generates new forms of cultural identity as nation-states try to retain control over citizens living beyond their borders and as relocated populations struggle both for recognition in their new homes and for influence in their places of origin. Globalization has drawn the attention of many anthropologists to regions such as the borderland between northern Mexico and the southwestern United States, where struggles with contradictory social practices and ambiguous identities have long been the rule, rather than the exception. Because borderland conditions worldwide display diverse and complex fracture lines, they undermine views of culture that depend upon settled peoples with distinct cultural attributes. Such heterogeneous and unstable cultural spaces also call into question views, such as that of Wallerstein, that portray global processes as part of a world *system*. Anthropologist Arjun Appadurai (1990) has argued, to the contrary, that global flows that can be traced across the world today are highly contradictory, generating global processes that are fundamentally disorganized and unpredictable.

In recent years, global flows of technology and commodities in particular have pushed ethnographers to expand their ethnographic focus to topics and settings that are unprecedented from the perspective of ethnographic research undertaken during most of the twentieth century. Especially striking has been the move of cultural anthropologists to fields like computer engineering or into ethnographic settings, such as scientific laboratories or the Internet. But these are growing areas of ethnographic interest that intersect productively with ethnographic work on processes of cultural reorganization and hybridization produced by globalization.

An important early contributor to such revised anthropological thinking was Donna Haraway, a biologist and radical feminist, who first published

"A Cyborg Manifesto" in 1984. The image of the cyborg—an organism–machine hybrid—was drawn from the science (and science fiction) of cybernetics. Haraway pointed out that, for good or for ill, such hybrids were all around us, from cybernetically enhanced weapons systems to laboratory rats with implanted cyber-control devices to our own increasingly diverse everyday engagements with computer technology (Figure 3.14).

Haraway's work attracted the attention of a wide range of scholars in many disciplines. Anthropologists influenced by her approach are sometimes said to do **cyborg anthropology**. Cyborg anthropology opened the way for new forms of political analysis but also required rethinking standard ways in which ethnographers understood the connections between organisms and material objects. As Gray, Mentor, and Figueroa-Sarriera put it, cyborg anthropology "attempts to understand the broader implications of human-machine coevolution" (1995: 6). Ethnographic work in this area investigates these implications in fields such as science and engineering, art, technology, and politics.

Another area of influence has been what is referred to as **science studies**—research exploring the interconnections among the sociocultural, political, economic, and historic conditions that make scientific research both possible and successful. One innovation of science studies that is important for anthropology was *laboratory ethnography*. One of the first laboratory ethnographers was Latour, who carried out fieldwork at the Salk Institute in Southern California in the 1970s (Latour and Woolgar 1986). Laboratory fieldwork involves following scientists as they go about their everyday laboratory activities and brings to light the range of embodied skills that scientists in certain fields must master if they are to effectively operate the often elaborate technological apparatuses that make research possible.

The legacy of science studies in anthropology extends well beyond laboratory ethnography. For instance, scholars including Latour and others drew ethnographic and theoretical attention to the role of material technology in scientific research, which provided theoretical inspiration for anthropologists interested in all kinds of material culture, from clothing and computers to art objects and archaeological artifacts (e.g., Miller 2005).

Taken together, the recent theoretical developments we have just reviewed show how today's cultural anthropologists have extended the anthropological perspective beyond its original focus on small-scale, non-Western societies. Furthermore, virtually all of the familiar anthropological classifications are dropping away as anthropologists explore the continuing cultural creativity of all human beings in all societies, particularly as these societies face challenging changing conditions. Contemporary anthropologists have had to develop/adopt new and innovative approaches as they continue to study the meaning of being human.

cyborg anthropology A form of anthropological analysis, based on the notion of organism–machine hybrids, or cyborgs; it offers a new model for challenging rigid social, political, and economic boundaries that have been used to separate people by gender, sexuality, class, and "race"—boundaries proclaimed by their defenders as "natural."

science studies Research that explores the interconnections among the sociocultural, political, economic, and historic conditions that make scientific research both possible and successful.

Figure 3.14 An ophthalmologist examining a mouse with a retinal implant. How will cyborg anthropology allow us to rethink the connections between organisms and material objects?

Living Anthropology

Testimonies of Endurance: Anthropology as History and Witness

by Judith van Roggen, PhD, Paleoethnobotanical and Ethnoarchaeological Consultant, Sessional Instructor, University of British Columbia (Okanagan) and Okanagan College, Kelowna, BC.

In his 1939 novel, *The Grapes of Wrath*, author John Steinbeck poses the question, "How will we know it's us without our past?" It is a question well worth asking. We carry residuals of our pasts—our cultural histories—in our understandings of the

Continued

world and the people around us. These qualities we call "culture" reflect a kind of DNA of values that informs our present whether we are aware or not. Regardless of who our ancestors were, we share an original history—a common trajectory of our species and one where our first ideas about life, death, and the cosmos were originally conceived. Culture is like a garment we wear, a tapestry of interwoven ideas, both old and new, of what we value and how we think of ourselves as part of a specific group.

An example of culture is traditional costuming, one of many expressions that encode an evolution of group-specific ideas. These garments are artifacts of thought and expressions of diversity, artistry, creativity, and values. In our contemporary world of globalization, immigration, emigration, conflict, and misinterpretations, it is important that we understand and appreciate difference, thinking about diversity as if admiring a traditional garment. Through this kind of lens, anthropology offers an array of opportunities to understand, embrace, and champion diversity as a reflection of a trajectory of history and tradition. Diversity's greatest potential is its reflection of unique knowledge of the world and what anthropologist Clifford Geertz described as "webs of significance" and symbolism, in which we, as a diverse and creative species, exist. Diversity is, quite literally, a celebration of creativity and the boundless imagination of the human mind.

Anthropologists of all specialties are not simply voyeurs of "difference" but witnesses. We testify to the diversity of the human condition. We can be allies to the disaffected. We can mediate between peoples by demonstrating the wisdom of difference. While it is true that anthropology has a deeply flawed and checkered past, this reflects an age of cultural ignorance and arrogance. It is also clear that many historical anthropologists became friends with their consultants, were pained by their experiences, and ultimately mourned the dehumanizing acts by others. Importantly, they preserved the words of others—elders, knowledge holders, and specialists in many communities under threat of continued abuse. Early female anthropologists opened up the discipline to the previously "invisible" lives of women and children. It is also true that revisiting historic records can be a shame-inducing experience for both researcher and "researched," but this is part of the social context that continues to cast a shadow on our relationships with each other. We need to come to grips with the fact that we are all tribal by nature, often judgmental, ultimately vulnerable, and

fundamentally in need of each other. Diversity is, in reality, a safety net. It is wise to revisit the voices of *all* our ancestral "others," not by re-writing history but through understanding, empathy, our capacity for welcome, and our ability to change.

As an environmental anthropologist studying archaeological plant remains, I rely heavily on historic ethnobotanies and ethnographies for my "first" impressions and hypotheses of plant use by people in the past. The historic language and traditional practice recorded in these resources provide a glimpse of a past in place—local for often longer that we can conceive. They hold clues of ancestor experts in a wide variety of sciences, not just botany, but astronomy, chemistry, physics, biology, geography, geology, medicine, health, and disease. Underlying this diverse array of knowledge is evidence of a cosmology that is coherent, cohesive, and comprehensive. A core strength of anthropology is demonstrating that indigeneity over depths of time is an original cultural context that resonates in the minutia of the present. We can learn endurance and resilience from these ancestors who persisted into the present through artifacts: strong social systems, personal bonds, shared values, and diverse responses to life's challenges.

Two quite remarkable examples of ethnographic work with historic Indigenous specialists are Matilda Coxe Stevenson's *Ethnobotany of the Zuñi Indians* (1915) and Elsie Clews Parsons' *Pueblo Indian Religion* (1939). Best read together, these sources are a collection of information about plant use, medicine, and social organization that can illuminate the divides between what we call "the Western" perspective and the intricate and holistic ways that the Pueblo peoples of the now American Southwest have lived in the world, thrived, and endured. Viewed within the Pueblo cosmological system, plants are connected in a web of relationships of clans, leaders, people, and practice. Even the colour of a plant can indicate something of its deeper meaning within the system. We would do well to heed the "difference," not simply asking ourselves which cultures have persisted longer, but *why* and *how*? We have much to learn from first peoples, through our shared ancestral and historic histories and our diverse ways of knowing. In today's global culture of value through wealth and objects, all of us can stop and revisit the ethnographic past for the deeper meanings and the awesome knowledge it holds. Just think of the tapestry and appreciate its wonder.

Key Terms

Chapter Summary

1. Modern Western history has been characterized by the rise of capitalism. To function under capitalism, colonized peoples had to learn to view everything—including land, objects, ideas, and human beings—as a potential commodity. As colonialists imposed this new world order and increased their control over colonized regions, Indigenous peoples lost much of their autonomy.

2. The context of colonialism has been an ever-present reality for anthropologists. Today, formerly colonized peoples remain tied to their former rulers in many ways. These ties have, in some cases, persisted for over 100 years and are called *neocolonialism*.

3. Anthropologists have considered various ways of classifying societies. The earliest important anthropological typologies were based on ideas that different kinds of societies represented different stages along a single path of cultural evolution. Following Boas, North American anthropologists rejected such ideas on the grounds that societies could easily borrow from one another, thus skipping supposedly universal evolutionary stages. Consequently, the aim of much research shifted to making lists of culture traits and mapping the culture areas through which they had spread as a result of cultural borrowing.

4. Although some anthropologists still find some typologies useful for investigating particular kinds of issues, classifying forms of human society is not an ultimate goal for most anthropologists today. The fuzziness of category boundaries reminds us that classification systems are human constructions, not pure reflections of objective reality.

Critical Thinking Questions

1. What were the three major schools of anthropological thought that influenced the development of anthropology in Canada? Why do you suppose these schools were so influential in Canada?

2. What were the crucial differences between the British colonial enterprise in Virginia and that in Rupert's Land? How might these early encounters have affected later relationships between Indigenous peoples and Europeans?

3. What are some of the criticisms that anthropologists faced for the roles they played under colonial rule?

4. What are some advantages to being able to classify societies into different types? What are some difficulties anthropologists have faced when trying to develop new systems of classification?

Suggested Readings

Barnard, Alan. 2000. *History and Theory in Anthropology* **(Cambridge: Cambridge University Press).** A concise overview of the history of anthropological ideas, tying together developments on both sides of the Atlantic.

Driver, Harold E. 1961. *Indians of North America* **(Chicago: University of Chicago Press).** A comprehensive overview of Indigenous traditional life in North America.

Kroeber, Alfred. 1939. *Cultural and Natural Areas of Native North America* **(Berkeley: University of California Press).** This popular work explores the relationship between environment and culture. It has influenced work in cultural diffusion, cultural sharing, and analysis of cultural responses to environmental settings.

Lewellen, Ted C. 2003. *Political Anthropology,* **3rd edn (Westport, CT: Praeger Publishers).** Contains much useful information about the different kinds of societies that scholars have identified.

Quimby, George I. 1954. "Cultural and Natural Areas before Kroeber," *American Antiquity* XIX, 4: 317–31. An overview of the development of the culture area concept.

Weatherford, Jack. 1988. *Indian Givers: How the Indians of the Americas Transformed the World* **(New York: Fawcett**

Columbine). An engaging account of the consequences of contact between the Old World and the New World. Also worth reading are Weatherford's *Native Roots: How the Indians Enriched America* (1991) and *Savages and Civilization: Who Will Survive* (1994), which explore similar themes.

Wolf, Eric. 1982. *Europe and the People without History* **(Berkeley: University of California Press).** A classic text about European expansion and the impact this expansion had on European societies and the rest of the world. This work also discusses the effect of European contact on Indigenous societies.

————. **1999.** *Envisioning Power: Ideologies of Dominance and Crisis* **(Berkeley: University of California Press).** An analysis of the historical relationship of ideas, power, and culture in which Wolf argues that power is central to shaping the circumstances and form of cultural production.

Related Websites

A Brief History of Anthropology at the University of Toronto
http://anthropology.utoronto.ca/home/about/history

Assembly of First Nations (AFN)
www.afn.ca

Association of Social Anthropologists of the UK and Commonwealth (ASA)
www.theasa.org

Survival, the Global Movement for Tribal Peoples' Rights
www.survival-international.org

Truth and Reconciliation Commission of Canada
www.trc.ca/websites/trcinstitution/index.php?p=4

PART II | The Resources of Culture

The chapters in Part II focus on a range of human capacities that lie at the centre of human cultural creativity, flexibility, and diversity. We all live in a material world. We make our way through this world by assigning meaning to the things—objects, places, ideas, ourselves, other people, and so on—that we encounter. As a result, our contact with the material world is always mediated by a web of meanings of our own creation. Cultural meaning is perhaps most directly encountered in language, but it is also revealed in habitual patterns of thought and action as well as in social relationships, and it is at its most elaborate in those creations that Westerners traditionally call art, myth, ritual, and world view. Through created meaning, we fashion our individual and group identities. Because we depend on culture for survival, a proper awareness of the depth, breadth, and complexity of human cultural resources is, from the anthropological perspective, indispensable for an adequate understanding of the human condition in all its guises.

Language

Chapter Outline

Language and Culture

Design Features of Human Language

Language and Context

Linguistic Relativity

Components of Language

Non-verbal Communication

Pidgin Languages: Negotiated Meaning

Linguistic Inequality and Oppression

Language and Gender

The Flexibility of Language

Language and Change

Learning Objectives

By the end of Chapter 4, you will be able to

- explain why cultural anthropologists are interested in language;
- outline the design features and components of language;
- describe why language must be examined in context;

- understand the concept of linguistic relativity;
- recognize the role inequality plays in shaping language use;
- appreciate the flexibility of language; and
- consider how language can change over time.

Language provides us with basic tools for diverse forms of creativity. It allows us to name and consider the various aspects of our world and to communicate with one another. Yet language also creates barriers to communication. One major barrier is linguistic diversity (Figure 4.1). The number of languages spoken in the world today is difficult to determine. According to David Crystal, author of *The Cambridge Encyclopedia of Language,* estimates range between 3,000 and 10,000, although he believes that it is unlikely that there are fewer than 4,000. Yet these estimates are problematic because new languages are regularly being identified while old languages continue to disappear (1987: 284–5). This chapter will help you understand why so many languages exist, and it will reveal to you the power of human language in forming individual and group identity.

Language and Culture

Humans are cultural organisms: a human raised in isolation or by non-cultural animals will be as deficient as a bird prevented from flying or a mole prevented from digging. A human child comes into the world with a capacity (and a hunger) to absorb its caregivers' language, music, ethical norms, clothing styles, and myriad other systems, and will do so nearly effortlessly and without conscious thought or explicit tuition. . . . Because of the human reliance on socially shared information and norms, with language playing a central role, we are able to a large degree shape our own selective environment. (Fitch 2011: 323–4)

Anthropological Interest in Language

Language is of primary interest to anthropologists for at least four reasons:

1. Fieldwork proceeds through oral communication. Often, anthropologists must learn a new language to do fieldwork among people whose language is different from their own.

2. Language is the best tool anthropologists have to access informants' perceptions and interpretations. In this they may gain unsuspected insights into the nature of their own language and culture.

3. Grammatical and conceptual complexities provide insights into a culture. Indeed, some schools of anthropological theory have based their theories of culture explicitly on ideas taken from linguistics.

4. Applied anthropologists work to support and maintain the diverse languages spoken in the world.

As anthropologists came to recognize that there is no such thing as a "primitive" human culture, so, too, they came to recognize that all human groups possess fully developed *languages.* They also came to realize that problems could arise when they think of specific *languages* as being entirely separate from one another. Indeed, the difficulties associated with marking the boundaries between one language and another, or with distinguishing between dialects and languages, become particularly obvious in studies of pidgins and creoles, as we will see.

language The system of symbols we use to encode our experiences of the world and of one another.

linguistics The scientific study of language.

Figure 4.1 The phrase "I love you" is written over a thousand times in more than 300 different languages on The Wall of Love in Paris, France. What are some of the ways in which linguistic diversity creates opportunities for communication? What are some of the ways in which it can create barriers? How can commonly understood symbols help to transmit information across linguistic barriers?

A schoolteacher in Rabat, Morocco, instructs a class on Amazigh, the language of the Berber people, a group indigenous to North Africa. The Amazigh language was brought to elementary classes in 2004 following Moroccan King Mohammed VI's establishment of the Royal Institute of the Amazigh Culture to promote Berber language and culture. How can anthropologists work with communities to help people retain their language?

It is useful, however, to distinguish *language* from *speech* and from *communication*. People usually think of spoken language (speech) when the term *language* is used, but language can also be transmitted by various non-spoken media, such as written words, Morse code, or gestures (as is the case in sign languages). And, as we move deeper into digital communication, computer language (CL) code (see below) could be added to our forms of transmission of complex ideas and instructions. Indeed, since the advent of the computer age, CLs have been diverse and evolving in a Darwinian fashion (Valverde and Solé 2015). And, finally, *human communication* can be defined as the transfer of information from one person to another, either verbally or non-verbally (e.g., through facial expressions, body language, mannerisms, and technology).

Native speakers of a language share not just **vocabulary** and **grammar** but also a number of assumptions about how to use the language. Students learning a new language discover early on that translation from one language to another does not always work. Sometimes there are no equivalent forms in another language; and, even when there are, the translation may not carry over the original meaning.

Interestingly, with children now being taught computer coding, there is emerging an ever-expanding group of people who communicate in

and through CLs. This communication system currently is based in a binary code of 0s and 1s (bits) that represent text through patterned arrangement of the bits. There are other binary information systems. For example, consider DNA and with it adenine/thymine and cytosine/guanine nucleotides. These binary systems transmit information for reproduction, growth, and repair of biological organisms.

Learning a second language is often frustrating and even unsettling, and the experience can result in a sense of culture shock that is as disorienting as being physically immersed in another culture. Often, it is less a matter of learning new labels for old objects than it is of learning how to use the components of the new language to convey the intended meaning in any given situation. Therefore, in order to increase fluency in a language, the student must move beyond abstract understandings and situate that particular language in its cultural context.

Talking about Experience

Language, like the rest of culture, is a product of our attempt to come to terms with experience. Naturally, people tend to develop larger vocabularies to discuss those aspects of life that are important to them. For this reason, it may be easier to talk about the Polynesian concept of **mana** in Polynesian languages (e.g., Hawaiian) than in English. In addition, different languages have developed to be more or less complex in different ways. For example, some languages require their speakers to master a larger (or narrower) range of sounds than other languages do; some have more complex (or less complex) sentence structures than others have; and the range of meanings associated with a particular expression in one language may be hard to map onto a single expression in another language (Figure 4.2). Nonetheless, all languages appear to be equal in their open potential to communicate experiences.

Languages specifically associated with groups of people are called *speech communities*. All speech communities display a tension between diversity and commonality since identical knowledge about the language is not shared by all. Individuals and subgroups make use of linguistic resources in different ways as they create personal and unique voices. This is offset by the pressure to negotiate a common code for communication within the larger social group. In this way, language is produced and reproduced through the activity of its speakers.

native speaker A person who has spoken a particular language since early childhood.

vocabulary The words used in a particular language or by members of a particular speech community.

grammar A set of rules that describe the patterns of linguistic usage observed by members of a particular speech community.

mana From Austronesian languages; it denotes a supernatural power or force that can be embodied in a person or an object (e.g., "May the force be with you").

©Patryk Ko?mider/123RF

Figure 4.2 The Fushimi Inari Taisha Shrine in Kyoto, Japan. The path is lined with thousands of *torii*, a traditional Japanese gate commonly found in shrines. These gates were donated by Japanese businesses and have words of thanks and hopes for the future written on them. How might the meanings associated with these prayers be difficult to translate? In what ways is something always lost in translation?

Design Features of Human Language

Charles Hockett (1966) listed 16 **design features** that he considered set human language apart from other forms of animal communication. Six of these design features seem especially useful for our discussion: openness, displacement, prevarication, arbitrariness, duality of patterning, and semanticity.

Openness

Openness, probably the most important feature, is the ability to conceptualize, label, and discuss the same experiences using different words and various grammatical constructions. To understand how truly significant *openness* is to communication, compare our spoken language to the vocal communication systems (or *call systems*) of monkeys and apes. Whereas our language allows us to endlessly combine and recombine elements of our experiences in new and various ways, the possibilities of meaning are much more limited when it comes to call systems. Primates have several calls, all of which are contextually appropriate: when the animal is in the presence of food, when it is in danger or pain, when it wants to show friendly interest, when it wants to mark its location, and so on. Each call is appropriate in only one situation; as a result, the call systems of primates are said to be *closed* when compared to *open* human languages.

Modern human beings, however, do still possess a set of six calls: laughing, sobbing, screaming, crying, groaning, and sighing (Deacon 1997). These calls, together with gestures and speech rhythm, volume, and tonality, all appear to have co-evolved alongside our use of spoken language. Deacon emphasizes, however, that closed primate call systems—which contain between 15 and 40 calls, depending on species—do *not* map onto any of the elements of human language and are even controlled by different parts of the brain.

Displacement

Closed call systems also lack *displacement*, people's ability to talk about absent or nonexistent objects and past or future events as easily as they discuss their immediate situations. Although non-human primates have good memories, and some species, such as chimpanzees, seem to be able to plan social action in advance (as when hunting for meat), their call systems do not appear to be involved in these activities.

Prevarication

Perhaps the most striking design feature of language, however, is *prevarication*. Hockett's remarks here deserve particular attention: "Linguistic messages can be false, and they can be meaningless in the logician's sense" (1966). Not only can people use language to lie, but they can also use it to form statements that are grammatically correct but semantically nonsensical. Consider linguist Noam Chomsky's example: "Colourless green ideas sleep furiously" (1957: 15). This is grammatically correct on one level—the right kinds of words are used in the right places—but does it make sense? The ability of language users to prevaricate—to speak falsely or to make statements that violate convention (e.g., by speaking nonsense, or by writing poetry, or by developing testable scientific hypotheses)—is a major consequence of open symbolic systems.

Arbitrariness and Duality of Patterning

Also notably absent from closed call systems is *arbitrariness*, the lack of an inherent connection between a symbol (e.g., a word) and its function or meaning. As Shakespeare's Juliet says, "What's in a name? That which we call a rose by any other name would smell as sweet."

Arbitrariness is evident in *duality of patterning*. Language is patterned on two different levels: *sound* and *meaning*. On the first level, each language has a set of sounds called **phonemes**. In combination, phonemes compose **morphemes**, the shortest *meaningful* units of speech. On the second level, morphemes combine in grammatical ways to form meaningful clusters and, ultimately, sentences. Essentially, phonemes are patterned to create morphemes, or units of meaning, and these units of meaning are patterned to create sentences and, thus, discourse.

Semanticity

Arbitrariness shows up again in the design feature of *semanticity*: the association of linguistic signals with aspects of the social, cultural, and physical world of a speech community. People use language to refer to and make sense of objects and processes in the world. However, linguistic descriptions of reality are always selective, highlighting some features, downplaying others.

design features of language The characteristics of a language that, when taken together, differentiate it from other known animal communication systems.

phonemes Basic units of distinct sound that are characteristic of a language and that come together to form words (e.g., /b/ and /ɔɪ/ in *boy*).

morphemes The shortest meaning-bearing units in any language (e.g., /bɔɪ/ refers to a young male).

Language and Context

Anthropologists are powerfully aware of the influence of context on what people choose to say. Linguists have noted that social and cultural context has a strong impact on how children develop **linguistic competence** as well as **communicative competence** (Figure 4.3):

> From an early age they appear to communicate very fluently, producing utterances which *are not just remarkably well-formed according to the linguist's standards but also* appropriate to the social context in which the speakers find themselves. Children are thus learning far more about language than rules of grammar. [They are] acquiring communicative competence. (Elliot 1981: 13, emphasis added)

The term *communicative competence* was coined by anthropological linguist Dell Hymes (1972). Hymes objected to Noam Chomsky's (1965) suggestion that competent language use consists only of being able to use correct grammar. Hymes observed that competent adult speakers do more than follow grammatical rules when they speak: they also choose words and topics of conversation appropriate to (1) their social position, (2) the social position of the person they are addressing, and (3) the social context of interaction.

linguistic competence Mastery of adult grammar.

communicative competence Mastery of adult rules for socially and culturally appropriate speech.

linguistic relativity principle The assertion that language has the power to shape the way people see the world.

Linguistic Relativity

The **linguistic relativity principle**, or the Sapir–Whorf hypothesis, posited in the first half of the twentieth century, noted that the grammars of different languages often described the same situation in different ways. Edward Sapir and Benjamin Whorf concluded that language has the power to shape the cognitive representations of the experienced world and thus habitual thought. Although this hypothesis has been highly controversial, it has maintained an important position in diverse disciplines, such as anthropological linguistics, psychology, cognitive science, and philosophy of language to name but a few.

Some consider the Sapir–Whorf hypothesis to be *linguistic determinism* and a rather inflexible view of language that holds that the patterns of our thoughts and our culture are *determined by* the patterns of the language we speak. If a grammar classifies nouns and/or pronouns in gender categories, for example, linguistic determinism concludes that speakers of that language are *forced* to think of males and females as radically different kinds of beings. In contrast, a language that makes no grammatical distinctions on the basis of gender presumably trains its speakers to think of males and females as exactly the same. If linguistic determinism is correct, then a change in grammar should change thought patterns: if English speakers replaced *he* and *she* with a new, gender-neutral pronoun such as *te*, then, linguistic determinists predict, English speakers would begin to treat men and women as equals. However, consider the language Fulfulde (spoken in West Africa): Fulfulde has only one third-person pronoun, *o*, used for males and females, yet Fulfulde speakers tend to follow male-dominant social patterns. We as Canadians now can be the test case. Canada's federal Bill C-16 proposes to add the legal protection of "gender identity" and "gender expression" to the Canadian Human Rights Act. As well, Bill C-210 proposes to change a line in O Canada from "True patriot love in all thy sons command" to "True patriot love in all of us command." What kind of effect, if any, do you think these proposed changes could have on Canadian society if enacted?

There are other problems with linguistic determinism. If language determines thought in an absolute way, it would be impossible to translate

Figure 4.3 The contexts in which children learn to communicate impact the ways in which they master the rules of grammar and the rules for using language in different settings. How might the process of learning socially and culturally appropriate table behaviours, for example, also impact what children learn about language?

© Christopher Futcher/Thinkstock

from one language to another or even to learn another language with a different grammatical structure. Additionally, in most of the world's societies, people grow up speaking more than one language, yet they do not also grow up struggling to reconcile two different views of reality (Figure 4.4). Indeed, bilingual children ordinarily benefit from knowing two languages; they do not confuse them, they can switch readily between them, and they even appear to demonstrate greater creativity and cognitive flexibility than do monolingual children (e.g., Adesope et al. 2010; Elliot 1981; Leikin 2012). Thus, many researchers offer an alternative or "weak" version of the Sapir–Whorf hypothesis that rejects linguistic determinism but continues to claim that language shapes thought and culture. This actually fits with Sapir's view that language's importance lies in the way it directs our attention to some aspects of experience rather than others. Sapir was impressed by the fact that "it is generally difficult to make a complete divorce between objective reality and our linguistic symbols of reference to it" (1966 [1933]: 9, 15).

Whorf's discussions of linguistic relativity are more complex, and, in recent years, scholars have recognized that there are several different ways to ask about the relationship of language to thought. For instance, linguist Dan Slobin has proposed a "thinking for speaking" hypothesis, suggesting that the influence of linguistic forms on thought may be greatest when people prepare to speak to others on a specific topic in a specific setting: "One fits one's thoughts into available linguistic forms. . . . 'Thinking for speaking' involves picking those characteristics that (a) fit some conceptualization of the event, and (b) are readily encodable in the language" (Slobin 1987: 435). For example, an English speaker who is trying to say "I like fast food" in Spanish will have to use a passive encoding—*me gusta la comida rápida* ("fast food pleases me"). This encoding is not easy for many English speakers to learn, precisely because it is not the standard English way to encode the thought.

Dedre Gentner and Susan Goldin-Meadow (2003) point out that some researchers still take a traditional Whorfian approach, viewing language as a lens through which people view the world. Still others think of language as a category-maker that influences the way people classify experiences and objects in the world. Gentner and Goldin-Meadow note that research producing the most consistent evidence of the influence of language on thought

comes from those who view language as a toolkit— that is, as a set of resources that speakers make use of for conceptual or communicative purposes (10). Nevertheless, they emphasize that defining the research question in such variable ways means that "we are unlikely to get a yes-or-no answer to the whole of Whorf's thesis. But if we have delineated a set of more specific questions for which the answer is *no* to some and *yes* to others, we will have achieved our goal" (12).

Figure 4.4 Bilingual children can switch from one language to the other with relative ease. What benefits can there be for children who grow up learning more than one language?

Components of Language

Linguistic study involves a search for patterns described through a set of rules called a *grammar*. Over time, linguists came to recognize a number of components that form part of the grammar of any language. The most widely acknowledged components of language are phonology, morphology, syntax, semantics, and pragmatics.

Phonology: Sounds

phonology The study of the sounds (phones and phonemes) of a language.

morphology The study of the smallest units of meaning (morphemes) in a language.

The study of the sounds of language is called **phonology**. The sounds of language are special because they are produced by a set of organs—the speech organs (Figure 4.5)—that belong only to the human species. The actual sounds that come out of our mouths are called *phones*, and speakers of a particular language recognize phones that are very similar to one another as functionally the same. These functional groups of phones are known as *phonemes*, the characteristic speech sounds in the language.

Part of the phonologist's job is to map out how speech sounds are produced and interpreted. Another part is to examine individual languages to discover the particular sound combinations they contain and the patterns into which those sound combinations are organized. Phonologists have found that no language makes use of all the many sounds the human speech organs can produce, and no two languages use exactly the same set of sounds. Canadian English uses only 38 sounds (more or less, depending on the dialect). Speakers of the same language often differ in the way they pattern their phonemes, producing "accents," which constitute one kind of variety within a language. This variety is not random; the speech sounds characteristic of any particular accent follow a pattern. Speakers with different accents are usually able to understand one another, but their distinctive articulation is a clue to their ethnic, regional, or social class origins.

Morphology: Word Structure

Morphology is the study of the smallest units of meaning in a language, known as *morphemes*. In English, some words consist of a single morpheme (e.g., *dog, top, up*), while others consist of two or more morphemes (e.g., *dog/s [2], up/root/ed [3]*). Many languages—but not all of them—are made up of words that are formed in this way. Consider Shawnee, a language spoken by some Indigenous peoples in North America. A sample utterance in Shawnee is *nikookitepeena*, which translates into English as "I dipped his head in the water" (Whorf 1956: 172). Although the Shawnee utterance is composed of parts, the parts do not possess the characteristics we attribute to words in, say, English or French (Table 4.1). As this example illustrates, describing the smallest units of meaning as *morphemes* rather than *words* allows us to compare the morphology of different languages.

Morphemic patterning in languages such as Shawnee may seem complex, yet the patterning of morphemes in English is no less so if we consider that some English morphemes can stand alone as words while others (e.g., *-s, -ing, -ed*) cannot.

Syntax: Sentence Structure

syntax The study of sentence structure.

A third component of language is **syntax**, or sentence structure. While sentence structure helps us fit meanings together, it also leaves space for possible confusion. In languages, such as English, rules governing word order cannot explain what is puzzling about the following sentence: "Smoking grass means trouble." For many native English speakers, this sentence exhibits what linguists call *structural ambiguity*. We must ask ourselves what kind of *trouble* is involved: the consequences of smoking an illegal substance or the danger of a prairie fire? In the first reading, *smoking* is a noun derived from a verb (in grammar, termed as a gerund) that conveys an action (the act of smoking); in the second, it is an adjective that describes the grass (grass that is smoking). Structural ambiguity can result when it

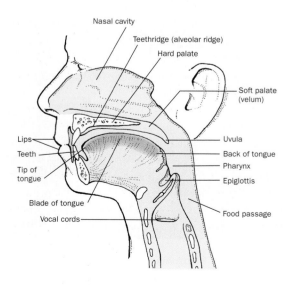

Figure 4.5 The speech organs.

Table 4.1 Morphemes of Shawnee Utterance and Their Glosses

ni	kooki	tepe	en	a
I	immersed in water	point of action at head	by hand action	cause to him

is unclear how a word is functioning within a sentence: as a noun, a verb, an adjective, an adverb, and so on. Linguists have discovered numerous other features of sentence structure that are difficult to explain, leading to a growth of interest in the study of syntactic patterns in different languages.

Semantics: Meaning

Semantics, the study of meaning, can be a particularly tricky area of study, as *meaning* is a highly ambiguous term. What do we mean when we say that a word or a sentence means something? We may be asking what each individual word in the sentence means, or what the sentence as a whole means, or what I mean when I utter the sentence, which may differ from what someone else would mean if he or she uttered the same sentence.

Semanticists examine how words link to each other within a language. They explore relations such as *synonymy*, or "same meaning" (*old* and *aged*); *homophony*, or "same sound, different meaning" (*would* and *wood*); and *antonymy*, or "opposite meaning" (*tall* and *short*). They look closely at words' **denotative meanings**, and they also consider **connotative meanings**. The denotative or dictionary meaning of the word *pig*, for example, might be "an omnivorous, domesticated animal with short legs, a broad flat nose, sparse hair, and a curly tail." In contrast, the connotative meanings associated with the word *pig* might be "dirty," "fat," "offensive,"

and "greedy." To complicate matters further, words often have informal or slang definitions that may or may not be listed in a dictionary, and of which not all English speakers may be aware. For example, an informal meaning of the word *pig* is "police officer." From a denotative point of view, to call police officers *pigs* is to create ambiguity, because a police officer is not a farm animal. This sort of ambiguous reference is an example of *metaphor*—a form of thought and language that asserts a meaningful link between two expressions from different semantic domains (see Chapter 11). In this case, the metaphor links the unrelated semantic domains of *law enforcement* and *livestock* (Figure 4.6). To understand what this metaphor means, we must understand that some people see police officers (particularly when the police are considered to be corrupt) as greedy and offensive—characteristics also attributed to pigs. Our ability to use the same words in different ways (and different words in the same way) is a hallmark of the openness of language. Thus, to understand what words or sentences mean, we must always be aware of the context in which they are used.

Pragmatics: Language in Contexts of Use

Pragmatics can be defined as the study of language in the context of its use. Each context offers limitations and opportunities concerning what we may say and how we may say it. An understanding of context is particularly important for determining the referential meaning of language. We must consider two kinds of context here: linguistic and non-linguistic. *Linguistic context* consists of the other words, expressions, and sentences that surround the expression whose meaning we are trying to determine. We cannot, for example, determine the meaning of *it* in the sentence "I really enjoyed it" by considering the sentence on its own. However, if we know that the previous sentence was "My aunt gave me this book for my birthday," we have a linguistic context that allows us to deduce that *it* refers to "this book." *Non-linguistic context* consists of objects and activities that are present in the situation of speech at the same time we are speaking. Consider the sentence "What is that on the door?" To give referential

semantics The study of meaning.

denotative meaning The formal meaning(s) of a word, as given in a dictionary.

connotative meaning Additional meanings of a word that derive from the typical contexts in which they are used and rely on personal and cultural associations.

pragmatics The study of language in the context of its use.

Figure 4.6 The phrase "police are pigs" is a metaphor. What metaphors do you use in everyday speech? What do you mean when you use them?

meaning to the word *that*, we need to inspect the actual door and whatever is on it. Furthermore, even if we know what a door is in a formal sense, we need the non-linguistic context to clarify what counts as a door in this instance (e.g., it could be a rough opening in the wall).

By forcing analysts to go beyond syntax and semantics, pragmatics directs our attention to **discourse**. Linguistic discourse includes a spoken one-word greeting, a series of sentences uttered by a single individual, a conversation among two or more speakers, or an extended narrative. Many linguistic anthropologists accept the arguments of linguistic theorists Mikhail Bakhtin and Valentin Voloshinov (see, e.g., Voloshinov 1986 [1929]) that the series of replies in conversation is the primary form of discourse. In this view, the speech of any single individual, whether a simple "yes" or a book-length dissertation, is only one reply in an ongoing dialogue.

In recent years, linguistic anthropologists have challenged us to consider **metalanguage**, a specific system used to describe or analyze another language or symbolic system (see, e.g., Mertz and Yovel 2010). Examples of metalanguage include direct references to words (e.g., "Words are symbols," "The word *cat* has three letters") as well as comments on our communication (e.g., "I told you," "I can't understand what he's saying," "Does that explanation make sense to you?"). Metalanguage directs attention to the language we are using as words or as structure in discourse.

Ethnopragmatics

Linguistic anthropologists analyze the way discourse is produced when people talk to one another. But they go far beyond formal pragmatics, paying attention not only to the immediate contexts but also to broader cultural contexts, which are shaped by unequal social relationships and rooted in history (Brenneis and Macauley 1996; Hill and Irvine 1992). Anthropologist Alessandro Duranti calls this **ethnopragmatics**: "a study of language use that relies on ethnography to illuminate the ways in which speech is both constituted by and constitutive of social interaction" (1994: 11). Such a study focuses on how language is used in *practice*—in commonplace situations in which the rules of grammar, cultural values, and physical action are all conjoined (Hanks 1996). This perspective locates the source of meaning in everyday, routine social activity, or

habitus, rather than in grammar alone. As a result, phonemes, morphemes, syntax, and semantics are viewed as linguistic resources people can make use of (or not), rather than factors that impose strict rules on how we use language.

If mutual understanding (intersubjectivity) is shaped by shared routine activity and not solely by grammar, then communication is possible even if the people interacting with one another speak mutually unintelligible languages. All they need is a shared sense of "what is going on here" and the ability to negotiate who will do what. Such mutually co-engaged people shape *communicative practices* that involve spoken language but also include values and shared habitual knowledge that may never be put into words even when abstract ideas are imparted.

Most people regularly engage in a wide range of practical activities with different subgroups within a population, each with distinctive communication practices and linguistic habits. For example, you may eat dinner with your family, attend class with other students, live in an apartment with roommates, attend religious services with fellow worshippers, and work at a part-time job with other employees. Because you simultaneously know which linguistic habits to use in each of these social situations, your overall linguistic knowledge is characterized by what linguist Mikhail Bakhtin (1981 [1975]) calls **heteroglossia**. This is a normal linguistic knowledge in any society with internal divisions—a multiplicity of coexisting linguistic norms and forms, many of which are anchored in more than one social subgroup. This makes our language use complex, even when we know only one language.

The context in which we communicate heavily influences the words we choose. In his work in a small Samoan village, Duranti (1994) learned just how important a sense of audience is to the professional orators who argue cases before the titled people, called *matai*, in the village council, or *fono* (Figure 4.7) (see EthnoProfile 4.1). Orators use a form of language midway in formality between everyday speech and ceremonial speech. Because the *fono* renders judgments that assign praise and blame, the main struggle between orators for different sides is "often centred on the ability to frame the reason for the meeting as involving or not involving certain key social actors" (Duranti 1994: 3). Of all the grammatical resources used by orators, the form called the *ergative agent* most attracted Duranti's attention. The ergative agent is a "wilful initiator of an event" (Duranti 1994: 125). In Samoan, ergative

discourse In speech, a meaningful utterance or series of utterances united by a common theme.

metalanguage Language used to talk about language.

ethnopragmatics The study of language use in a specific culture, grounded in an ethnographic approach, with close attention to the relationships among language, communication, and social interaction.

heteroglossia The coexistence of multiple varieties of a specific language.

Figure 4.7 Although nominal power rests with Samoan chiefs, when village elders meet in the *fono*, titled orators such as this man from the island of Tutuila tend to direct its proceedings. These orators carefully tailor their words for their audience.

agents are marked by the preposition *e*, to distinguish them grammatically. Other forms of agency are marked by different prepositions: for example, *i* or *ia* frames the human agent as the source of the transaction rather than as its willful initiator. Framing agency in grammatical terms is common in the *fono*, as disputants argue over who should be held accountable for some act. Possible agents include God, particular individuals, or groups. In all cases, final judgments are the outcome of talk that is influenced by both the immediate context and the broader cultural context.

Non-verbal Communication

So far, we have focused mainly on how people communicate through spoken language. But human beings can also communicate quite effectively through non-verbal means. In some instances, non-verbal communication is necessary because of hearing loss or damage to vocal chords. In other cases, we may want to communicate silently for some strategic purpose. For example, Aboriginal hunting parties in Australia communicate through "hand talk" to avoid startling their prey. Simple hand gestures, movements, and facial expressions can also help people who speak different languages overcome linguistic barriers.

For people who are unable to hear and/or speak, sign languages offer a way of conveying complex messages. Similar to the way in which spoken languages use words as symbols, sign languages use hand gestures, facial expressions, and bodily movement to represent objects and ideas. Globally, there are many different types of sign language. In North America, the most commonly used type is American Sign

EthnoProfile 4.1
Samoans

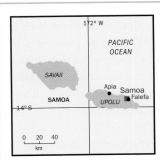

Region: Oceania

Nation: Independent State of Samoa

Language: Samoan, a language of the Malayo-Polynesian family, part of the Austronesian languages

Population: 182,080 (2014 estimate; approximately 92.6 per cent of the total population of Samoa), most living on the main island of Upolu

Environment: Tropical

Livelihood: Farming (tropical and subtropical crops), fishing, wage labour

Political organization: Ranked, with linguistic markers for high- and low-status people; now part of a modern nation-state

For more information: Duranti, Alessandro. 1994. *From Grammar to Politics: Linguistic Anthropology in a Western Samoan Village* (Berkeley: University of California Press); Mead, Margaret. 1928. *Coming of Age in Samoa* (New York: Morrow).

Language (ASL). Studies show that deaf children learn sign language in much the same way that hearing children learn spoken language, simply by being exposed to the language. One difference, however, is that infants may be able to use sign language much earlier than they can produce speech because hand–eye coordination develops sooner than the ability to speak. For this reason, some parents have begun to teach their hearing babies to use a simplified version of ASL known as "baby sign language" to communicate their needs and wants at a very early age.

We also communicate non-verbally in more subtle ways. Think of how much we "say" through gestures, movements, facial expressions, and gaze. We communicate, through our facial expressions, whether we are happy or sad, friendly or unfriendly, interested or bored. By touching or avoiding touch, moreover, we communicate affection or dislike. By holding out our hand in a certain way we either welcome others or warn them to stay away. We even communicate our gender, age, class, and ethnicity through our physical appearance: our body shape, clothing, hairstyle, and so on. We also construct much of our public identity through body language and gestures, habits we learn based on the cultural norms we see around us. Indeed, body language and gestures are often culturally specific—a fact that anthropologists must be aware of when interacting with people from different cultures.

Non-verbal messages can interact with or relate to verbal messages in a variety of ways (see, e.g., Ekman 1965; Knapp et al. 2013). For example, non-verbal behaviours can be used to do the following:

1. *Complement* what is being said (e.g., raising eyebrows while asking a question)
2. *Accent* what is being said (e.g., pounding a table while making an important point)
3. *Contradict* what is being said (e.g., nodding while saying "no")
4. *Repeat* what has been said (e.g., nodding after saying "yes")
5. *Substitute* for something that might have been said (e.g., pointing at someone and gesturing to the door instead of asking that person to leave)
6. *Regulate* a discussion (e.g., looking at another person in anticipation to encourage her or him to speak)

In many cases, non-verbal behaviours help people understand verbal messages. Difficulties arise, however, when a non-verbal message conflicts with a verbal message, resulting in a *mixed message*. Mixed messages can lead to breakdowns in communication as well as feelings of distrust, as the confused listener begins to doubt the truthfulness of the speaker's verbal message.

American anthropologist Edward T. Hall (1959) has also found that people communicate non-verbally through their uses of *time* and *space*. In Euro–North American societies, people tend to treat time as a commodity that can be "bought, sold, saved, spent, wasted, lost, made up, and measured," and they use it to structure their daily lives (137). They similarly treat space as a commodity, and measure and divide it to suit their needs. These approaches to time and space communicate three fundamental aspects of the Western outlook: (1) everything has an economic value, (2) everything can and should be broken down into component parts in order to be better understood, and (3) humans have the right to use everything in the natural world for their own purposes. Recall from Chapter 3 that it was this sort of thinking that drove colonialism, particularly the view that territories were "empty" until they had been mapped and named (see, e.g., Dods 2002). As you might expect, other cultures treat time and space differently, and their approaches reflect different world views. For many North American Indigenous peoples, for example, time is much more flexible, and there is a sense that things will happen when they happen. Similarly, many Indigenous peoples understand space in spiritual rather than material terms, seeing themselves as guardians rather than owners of the land.

Hall (1959) further notes that our use of *personal space* communicates a great deal about our feelings toward other people. When we stand close to a friend or family member, we may communicate goodwill and affection; when we stand close to a casual acquaintance or a stranger, on the other hand, we may communicate hostility. But *close* is a relative term. What people consider to be *close* in North America may seem to be an uncomfortably great distance to someone from a culture in which standing very close is the norm. As Hall observes,

> In Latin America, the interaction distance is much less than it is in [North America]. Indeed, [Latin American] people cannot talk comfortably with one another unless they are very close to the distance that evokes either sexual or hostile feelings in the North American. The result is that

when they move close, we withdraw and back away. As a consequence, they think we are distant and cold, withdrawn and unfriendly. We, on the other hand, are constantly accusing them of breathing down our necks, crowding us, and spraying our faces. (163–4)

Of course, anthropologists must overcome these sorts of ethnocentric impulses and must avoid judging other peoples' behaviours based on their own cultural norms.

Pidgin Languages: Negotiated Meaning

When members of communities with radically different language traditions are forced to communicate, they must work together to negotiate new meanings. These sorts of situations may arise when one community is conquered by another (e.g., through war or colonization) or when groups that speak different languages want to initiate trade relationships. While there is no way to predict the outcome of such contact on either speech community, it is likely that new forms of communication—including a new form of language, **pidgin**—may develop.

A pidgin language is different from the languages that gave birth to it. Its shape reflects the context in which it arises (e.g., colonial conquest, commercial exchanges). Vocabulary is usually taken from the language of the dominant group, making it easy for that group to learn the new language. Syntax and phonology may be similar to the subordinate language (or languages), however, making it easier for subordinated speakers to learn the new language. Morphemes that mark the gender or number of nouns or the tenses of verbs tend to disappear (Holm 1988). Accordingly, pidgins are traditionally defined as reduced languages that develop in a single generation. When speakers of a pidgin language pass that language on to a new generation, linguists usually refer to the language of the new generation as a **creole**. The creolization of pidgins involves increased complexity in phonology, morphology, syntax, semantics, and pragmatics, such that the pidgin comes to resemble a conventional language.

Linguist Derek Bickerton (1981) has suggested that the way in which pidgins form could shed light on the universal biological bases of language. He notes that Hawaiian Pidgin English differs in many ways from Hawaiian Creole, which descended from it. Because, in his view, none of these differences can be connected to the languages available to those who invented Hawaiian Creole, Bickerton concludes that they were produced by the innate linguistic "bio-program" of the creole creators. He further claims that these same "bio-program" forms can be found in other creoles.

Other students of pidgins and creoles have tried to test Bickerton's hypothesis. While their work has not confirmed his views, it has revealed that the distinction between pidgins and creoles is more complex than previously thought. For example, linguists have found that creolization can take place at any time after a pidgin forms, creoles can exist without having been preceded by pidgins, pidgins can remain pidgins for long periods and undergo linguistic change without acquiring native speakers, and pidgin and creole varieties of the same language can coexist in the same society (Jourdan 1991: 192ff.). In fact, it looks as if heteroglossia is as widespread among speakers of pidgins and creoles as it is among speakers of other languages.

Awareness of heteroglossia in pidgin/creole speech communities has led to the redefinition of a pidgin as a *shared secondary language* in a speech community in which speakers also use some other main language, and a creole as a *main language* in a speech community, whether or not it has native speakers. According to this view, creolization is likely when pidgin speakers find themselves in new social contexts requiring a new language for *all* the practical activities of everyday life. Without such a context, it is unlikely that creoles will emerge (Jourdan 1991: 196).

Contemporary linguistic anthropologists view pidgin creation as an active form of communicative practice, and they have explored the role of pidgin creators as agents in the process. It appears that as people negotiate meaning across language barriers, they have intuitions about which parts of their speech carry the most meaning and which parts can be safely dropped. Neither party to the negotiation, moreover, may be trying to learn the other's language; rather, "speakers in the course of negotiating communication use whatever linguistic and socio-linguistic resources they have at their disposal until the shared meaning is established and conventionalized" (Jourdan 1991: 200). Such analysis can be extended to other spheres of creative co-communication, such as popular music. The musical

pidgin A fairly simple language with no native speakers that develops in a single generation between members of communities that possess distinct native languages.

creole A complex language with native speakers that has developed over one or more past generations from two or more distinct languages.

styles and lyrics used in the modern music genres of hip-hop (Petchauer 2011) and grime (Barron 2013), for example, bring together elements from different cultures and different music genres to create new ways of communicating through music.

Linguistic Inequality and Oppression

Pidgins and creoles are far more complex—and the result of far more active human input—than previously thought, which is why they are so attractive to linguists and linguistic anthropologists as objects of study. Where they coexist, however, alongside the language of a dominant group (e.g., Hawaiian Pidgin English and English in Hawaii), they are ordinarily viewed by members of society as defective and inferior languages. Such views frequently stem from the situation that led to the formation of most pidgins: systems of race, gender, and class discrimination that are usually tied to colonial domination.

In such settings, the language of the powerful is often considered to be superior to all others. Colonizers and their descendants generally look down on "other" languages (frequently Indigenous) as lesser forms of communication, and they characterize pidgins and creoles as broken, imperfect versions of their own language. The situation only worsens for dominated populations when formal education is carried out in the "correct" language. Consider the lasting impact of the residential school system in Canada, where administrators firmly and sometimes violently discouraged Indigenous children from using their original languages. In addition, speakers of a pidgin, a creole, or an Indigenous language who do not master the language of the powerful may find themselves effectively barred from participating in the civic life of mainstream society.

To take one language variety as the standard against which all others are measured is linguistic ethnocentrism. It involves making value judgments about other people's speech in a context of dominance and subordination. Thus, it contributes to linguistic inequality.

We can find a powerful example of the effects of linguistic inequality in the history and controversies surrounding African American English (AAE) in the United States. In the 1960s, some psychologists claimed that African American children living in urban areas of the northern United States

suffered from linguistic deprivation. They argued that these children started school with a limited vocabulary and no grammar. As a result, they continued, these children could not perform as well as Euro-American children in the classroom. In short, the psychologists claimed that these children's language was unequal to the challenges of communication. Some sociolinguists, including William Labov and his colleagues, found such claims incredible and undertook research of their own. They proved that the form of English spoken in the inner city was not a defective "lesser" language (Labov 1972). Further, they showed how a change in research context permitted inner-city African American children to display a level of linguistic sophistication that the psychologists had never dreamed these children possessed.

When African American children were in the classroom (a Euro-American dominated context) being interrogated by Euro-American adults about topics of no interest to them, they said little. This did not necessarily mean, Labov argued, that they had no language. Rather, their minimal responses were better understood as defensive attempts to keep threatening Euro-American questioners from learning anything about them. For the African American children, the classroom was part of a broader racist culture. The psychologists, due to their ethnocentrism, had been oblivious to the effect this context might have on their research. Reasoning that reliable samples of African American speech had to be collected in contexts where the racist threat was lessened, Labov and his colleagues conducted fieldwork in the children's homes and on the streets of the inner city. They recorded enormous amounts of speech in AAE produced by the same children who had had nothing to say in the classroom. Labov's analysis demonstrated that AAE was a variety of English that had certain rules not found in standard English. These rules do not make it "defective"; they simply make it distinct.

Linguistic differences exist between most social subgroups in a society that is characterized by heteroglossia. These differences mark a speaker's membership in a particular speech community. Since Labov's time, AAE has gone through stages of invention, borrowing, and evolution—stages common to all "living" languages (Childs and Mallinson 2004). Indeed, many elements from AAE have entered into more mainstream usage, both in North America and in other English-speaking regions of the world.

The situation is quite different for Indigenous peoples in Canada. Today, many Indigenous communities are struggling to retain original languages that have been pushed to extinction or near-extinction by the consequences of colonialism (Figure 4.8). In many communities, English continues to be thought of as the language of domination. In contrast, original languages are thought of as tools that can preserve the collective memories of the culture: "Memory needs a place, a context. Its place, if it finds one that lives beyond a single generation, is to be found in the stories that we tell" (Kenny 1999: 421). Further, learning original languages becomes one route to healing the injured individuals and groups who have suffered loss through the colonial process. Thus, many First Nations communities are engaged in programs of **language revitalization** to retain and/or recall and teach their languages. (See the "In Their Own Words" box that follows.)

A number of languages around the world are facing the threat of extinction. Attempts to implement language revitalization have been met with mixed success. Maintaining or reviving endangered languages faces many obstacles, not the least of which is the concern of many parents who care less about preserving their dying language than they do about making sure their children become literate in a world language that will offer them a chance at economic and social mobility (Figure 4.9). Some Indigenous groups in the world are concerned that loss of language will mean loss of access to traditional sources of religious power, which can only be addressed in the traditional tongue. Yet other Indigenous speakers would not like to see what was once a fully functioning mode of communication reduced to nothing but ceremonial use. Clearly, language endangerment is a delicate topic of discussion. This is unfortunate, in Walsh's view, since practical solutions require "frank and forthright discussions of the issues . . . and good clear statements of advice" (2005: 308). But Walsh also believes that concerned people who want to save their languages ought to try to do what they can and not wait until scholarly experts arrive at consensus.

The various perceptions of languages and of their speakers we have discussed in this section lead us to consider the study of **language ideology**: the intersection "between social forms and forms of talk" (Woolard 1998: 3). The study of language ideology reveals speakers' basic understandings of their world and highlights how our speech is

Figure 4.8 The Haida language is a highly endangered Indigenous language. Jordan Lachler, a Haida language apprentice and linguist, writes Haida for a language class in Ketchikan, Alaska. The extinction or near-extinction of languages is one of the many consequences of colonialism. How can anthropologists work with communities to help people retain endangered languages?

Figure 4.9 Schoolchildren in Rankin Inlet, Nunavut, reading aloud in the Inuktitut language. The inclusion of threatened languages as a method of instruction in schools can play a vital role in producing more Indigenous language speakers in Indigenous communities. What barriers do language revitalization programs face?

always embedded in a social world of power differences. It also uncovers struggles between social groups with different interests, as these struggles are often revealed in what people say and how they say it. The way people monitor their speech to bring it into line with a particular language ideology illustrates that language ideologies are "active and effective . . . they transform the material reality they comment on" (11). In settings with a history of colonization, where groups with different power

language revitalization
Attempts by linguists and activists to preserve or revive languages with few native speakers that appear to be on the verge of extinction.

language ideology A system of beliefs about how language features relate to social features and what they reveal about the people who use them.

In Their Own Words

Programs for Revitalizing Indigenous Languages in Canada

In this excerpt from research conducted by Esther Usborne, Josephine Peck, Donna-Lee Smith, and Donald M. Taylor on Mi'kmaq language programs in Cape Breton, Nova Scotia, the researchers discuss the importance of Indigenous language programs in Canada.

The celebrated Canadian anthropologist Wade Davis compared the extinction of a language to the extinction of a species. Davis (2009) argued that "language is an old-growth forest of the mind," and that the death of a language is equivalent to the death of a fertile, intricate, and incredibly valuable way of being (3). In Canada, Aboriginal languages, once complex vehicles for communicating rich and unique cultures, are under severe threat. Of the 53 Aboriginal languages that are currently spoken in Canada, only three are thought to have a good chance of survival: Inuktitut, Cree, and Ojibway (Norris 2007). Furthermore, only one in four Aboriginal people in Canada currently speak an Aboriginal language (Norris 2007). The Aboriginal languages that have survived a destructive colonization process are now increasingly threatened by the rising power and prevalence of English information technologies and by the general dominance of English and French in modern Canadian society. According to Davis (2009) and others (e.g., Berger 2006; Simon 2010), the revitalization of Aboriginal languages is currently one of Canada's most important challenges.

Aboriginal communities in Canada have responded to this challenge and are working towards revitalizing—and in some cases, re-learning—their Aboriginal tongue. One of the most promising methods of language revitalization is through the inclusion of the Aboriginal language as a language of instruction in schools. In the case of a threatened language, teaching young students in this language has been shown to be an effective method of producing more language speakers (Baker 2003, 2006). Research has repeatedly demonstrated that the education children receive in school can play a vital role in developing a language and in teaching young students to speak, understand, and use a language that is under threat from a more dominant mainstream language and culture (Baker 2003, 2006; Cummins 1983, 1986; Fishman 1991, 2001). . . .

For Aboriginal communities in Canada who want to revitalize and/or preserve their language, while at the same time prepare their students for success in mainstream society, having the Aboriginal language as the principal language of instruction appears to be a very promising course of action. Even in communities where the Aboriginal language is not used as the primary means of communication, our research has demonstrated the benefits of a strong immersion program. These results speak to concerns that educators and parents have about the Mi'kmaq immersion classroom: learning Mi'kmaq does not have a negative impact on learning English.

In addition, the results speak to the importance of revitalizing an Aboriginal language for connecting with one's culture and identity. Beyond the transfer of specific language skills, researchers argue that education in a heritage language may be particularly important for students' cultural identity (Cummins 1983, 1986). Wright and Taylor (1995) found that Aboriginal students educated in their heritage language actually showed increased self- and collective-esteem compared to those educated in a second language (English or French). This is consistent with other research showing that understanding one's cultural identity is important for psychological well-being (Usborne & Taylor 2010), and that language learning is an excellent tool for connecting with one's Indigenous cultural identity through education (Battiste 2002).

Source: Esther Usborne, Josephine Peck, Donna-Lee Smith, and Donald M. Taylor, "Learning through an Aboriginal Language: The Impact on Students' English and Aboriginal Language Skills." *Canadian Society for the Study of Education*, Vol. 34, No. 4 (2011), 597–601. Reprinted with permission from the Canadian Journal of Education.

statuses and different languages coexist in tension, the study of language ideologies has long been significant (16). Linguistic anthropologists are particularly well suited to study language ideologies because (1) their linguistic training allows them to describe linguistic features (e.g., phonemes, morphemes, syntax) in detail and (2) their training in cultural analysis allows them to explain how those linguistic features come to be used symbolically by a particular social group.

Anthropologists are also concerned with how certain forms of communication have come to be ideologically privileged over others, specifically speech and writing. This has led scholars to investigate other forms of human communication. For example, Eric Hoenes del Pinal, working with the Q'eqchi' Maya peoples, has investigated gesture as another ideological dimension. Gesture, "like speech, is influenced by cultural values and historical tradition, and its usage is adjusted according to the setting, social circumstances, and micro organization of any given occasion of interaction" (Kendon 1997:117, quoted in Hoenes del Pinal 2011: 599). With respect to the benefits of studying other forms of communication, Hoenes del Pinal notes:

> By analyzing discourses about the nature of language in general and specific languages in particular, we are able to gain greater insight into a variety of social and cultural phenomena, such as people's social and moral identities, political relations, epistemologies, and the aesthetics of their expressive culture. . . . Of course, speech and writing are not the only forms of human communication. A number of scholars have argued that human communication needs to be understood as something that happens when co-present actors coordinate their actions to co-construct or jointly produce the terms of their interaction (Goffman 1981, Clark 1996), and that although verbal language is an important component of this (perhaps even a privileged one), interactions are fundamentally multimodal in nature, encompassing a wide range of embodied semiotic practices (e.g., Goodwin 2000, Norris 2004). In addition to speech, one might consider the role of gaze (Kendon 1990, Goodwin 1981), kinesics or body movement (Birdwhistell 1970), proxemics or spatial arrangement (Hall 1968), and gesture (Goodwin 200, Kendon 2004) in shaping human communicative behavior and social interaction. Understanding how these practices are themselves ideologically regimented can give us new insights that previous work on the ideological dimensions of spoken and written language may have obscured. (598–9)

Language and Gender

Language habits differ not only among ethnic groups but also between culturally identified genders. Indeed, one of the early objections to work on African American English was that it focused only on the ways African American men use language. Since the 1970s, the language habits of African American women and girls have figured in numerous studies (see, e.g., Lanehart 2009; Morgan 1995: 336ff.; Washington and Craig 1998).

Sociolinguist Deborah Tannen has written several popular books based on her studies of speech patterns of men and women. Tannen focuses on typical male and female styles of discourse, arguing that men and women use language for different reasons: men tend to use language as a competitive weapon in public settings, whereas women tend to use language as a way of building closeness in private settings (e.g., Tannen 1990). Tannen has found examples of how miscommunications can occur when men and women assume that members of the other gender understand language use in the same way they do. For example, when a husband and a wife get home from work at the end of the day, the wife may be eager to talk while the husband is just as eager to remain silent. She may interpret his silence as a sign of distance or coldness and may be hurt, while he may interpret her eagerness to talk as pressure to perform and may be irritated.

Some researchers have suggested that differences in the ways men and women use the right and left sides of their brains may be the cause of differences in communication styles. However, after analyzing a number of studies on the topic, psychiatrist Iris Sommer and colleagues (2004) found little evidence for this interpretation. It seems that the reasons for the observed differences may be based more in learned behaviours— that is, in cultural factors—than in biology.

Researchers have also looked at the ways women and men communicate online. Because the Internet allows for a certain degree of anonymity, meaning that people can communicate online without clearly stating their gender, some researchers have suspected that gender differences in language use would be eliminated or at least greatly reduced in online forums. Similarly, some have suggested that male-dominated power dynamics would break down online. Yet neither appears to be the case (see, e.g., Herring and Stoerger 2014; Sussman and Tyson 2000). Indeed, men and women often choose different words and use different language patterns when communicating online. In addition, men tend to write longer entries, while women tend to post more frequently (Sussman and Tyson 2000). Such findings suggest that gendered differences in language use are rooted very deeply in our communication habits.

Beyond differences in language use based on gender there is the use of language to denigrate others. We can see this in Twitter use and in the "naming" of "others" in sexist, racist, ageist language. Linguist and philosopher Croom discusses derogatory words and phrases, noting that they "are frequently picked up and appropriated by the very in-group members that the slur was originally intended to target, . . . for instance, as a means for like speakers to strengthen in-group solidarity" (2013: 177). The feminist Mary Daly (1978, 1984, 2001) was an early advocate of re-examining and reclaiming derogatory terms in order to reclaim aspects of ourselves. She used the example of *spinster*, meaning a woman who spins thread—an essential task necessary for the production of cloth, as a powerful example. *Spinster* became a derogatory term for an unmarried woman of a certain age. Thus, a word that once referred to a highly valued creation/economic role was twisted to convey a sexist, ageist view of single women. By reclaiming the term *spinster* and defining it in a more positive light, women once shamed by the term can reclaim a more positive identity as esteemed creators.

The Flexibility of Language

As you have seen throughout this chapter, language is a flexible and versatile tool that allows us to describe and make sense of our world in various ways. To some degree, it even shapes our understanding of reality. After all, it is language that connects our thoughts to the world beyond our mind. Therefore, it is difficult—if not impossible—for us to think of something as "real" if we cannot describe it with words.

Language is also a living system, capable of shifting and evolving as our experiences and observations change. Every time biologists discover a new species, for example, they must create a new word to describe it—a taxonomic term. Similarly, every time researchers develop a new technology, they must name it—sometimes by creating a new word, such as *telephone*. Often, words are combined or repurposed to take on new meanings. Today, for example, when we hear words such as *tablet*, *smartphone*, or *laptop*, we immediately think of the objects these words name. However, these same words would have meant something very different to people living 50 years ago. The term smartphone would likely have seemed nonsensical—how can a *phone* be *smart*? Other terms are added to describe new concepts. A relatively recent example is the word *wackadoodle*, meaning "an eccentric or fanatical person," which was added to the *Oxford English Dictionary* in 2014.

Language's capability for shifting and evolving highlights its essential quality of ambiguity. We saw examples of this quality when we considered *structural ambiguity* and *metaphor*. Of course, such ambiguities are not experienced only by people in Western societies. Anthropologist Edward Evans-Pritchard (1963) describes the use of metaphor among the Azande of central Africa (see EthnoProfile 11.1). The Azande people are well aware of the ambiguity inherent in language, and they exploit it by using metaphor (what they call *sanza*) to disguise speech that might be received badly if uttered directly. For example,

> A man says, in the presence of his wife, to his friend, "Friend, those swallows, how they flit about in there." He is speaking about the flightiness of his wife and in case she should understand the allusion, he covers himself by looking up at the swallows as he makes his seemingly innocent remark. (1963: 211)

Evans-Pritchard later observes that *sanza* adds greatly to the difficulties of anthropological inquiry. Despite learning to speak the local language, anthropologists may be unaware of the nuances embedded in that language. Even if they suspect that a word or phrase has more than one meaning, it is difficult for them to be sure. Indeed, even locals can sometimes be unaware or unsure of what a speaker means (228).

However much we learn about language, we will never be able to exhaust its meanings or circumscribe its rules once and for all. Human language is an open system, and as long as human history continues, new forms will be created and old forms will continue to be put to new uses.

Language and Change

Change can be both a negative and a positive process with language—we gain some and we lose some. Yet the losses of entire languages are hard to take, even if we never were a speaker of those languages. Linguist Anthony Woodbury (2012), writing on behalf of the Linguistic Society of America, estimates that about 5,000 to 6,000 languages are spoken in the world today (although, as we noted earlier, this number is difficult to determine). Woodbury predicts that several thousands of these languages will be lost over the next century. As he notes, "the pressure on languages can be economic, social, cultural, religious, political, military, or any combination of these. The peoples directly affected are minorities almost by definition, yet they are the bearers of most of the linguistic diversity that has developed over the course of human history."

So much of who we were, who we are, and how we pronounce our place in the cosmos and in our cultures is the creation of language. Voice marks our identity in relation to place and time. For those languages on the brink of silence, anthropologists and native speakers struggle with maintenance and revitalization in a world where the languages of the powerful dominate. Linguist Christine Sims notes that "revitalization at its heart involves re-establishing traditional functions of language use in the context of everyday speaker interactions" (2005: 104). However, as linguistic anthropologist Michael Walsh warns us, "it remains unclear why some attempts at language revitalization succeed, whereas others fail. What is clear is that the process is profoundly political" (2005: 293, 313).

Survival and modernity may go hand in hand. A language may not survive completely, but it may survive in a form that contains the essentials of identity. An example of this sort of survival can be seen in the history of the English language. As anyone who has ever tried to read a text written in Old or Middle English knows, the English language has changed considerably over time. Indeed, these earlier forms of the language are almost entirely unintelligible to modern English speakers. Over time, obsolete words such as *brabble* (meaning "to quarrel noisily") were dropped, while new words were added to meet changing needs. Many of the greatest changes occurred around the time of the Norman invasion in the eleventh century. Following their conquest by Norman French–speaking invaders, the people of England gradually adapted their Indigenous language to reflect their changed social and cultural circumstances. In particular, they incorporated aspects of Norman French into the language. Essentially, they adjusted their language to ensure it would survive in the new modernity of the day.

Similar processes have occurred—and continue to occur—throughout the world. The many regional variations of English that exist around the world are evidence of such changes. Linguist Jamie Shinhee Lee (2006) has identified an ongoing example of language mixing in South Korea. Drawing on observations from Korean television commercials, Lee argues that "mixing English with Korean is a linguistic mechanism for the construction of modernity in contemporary South Korea" (59, 90–1). Just as mixing English with Norman French was a sign of modernity for eleventh-century inhabitants of England, mixing Korean with English appears to be a sign of modernity for contemporary South Koreans. These examples once again highlight the openness and flexibility of language and the endless adaptability of human culture.

Living Anthropology

A Case of Thinking Like a Cultural Anthropologist about Digital Literacy

by Nancy Merrill, PhD Candidate, University of British Columbia (Okanagan)

Pedagogical researchers around the world have adopted a cultural imaginary, created by North American scholars in 1990, of the ideal critical thinker as someone who is

> habitually inquisitive, well-informed, trustful of reason, open-minded, flexible, fair-minded in evaluation, honest in facing personal biases, prudent in making judgments, willing to reconsider, clear about issues, orderly in complex matters, diligent in seeking relevant information, reasonable in the selection of criteria, focused in inquiry, and persistent in seeking results which are as precise as the subject and the circumstances of inquiry permit. (APA 1990)

I suggest typing "critical thinking dispositions" into Google Scholar (GS) to see the global reach of this conceptual construct. I have been doing this in various ways for five years to investigate how my constant interaction with GS may be impacting my body's neural networking processes that produce these dispositions.

I was sitting in an armchair in the living room in my home in Peachland, British Columbia, caught up in my usual research routine of gathering data with GS from texts written by other researchers to compare with the data in the thick descriptions I write about my own experiences. I was engrossed in reading another doctoral student's dissertation about his experiences of discovering factors that affect

Continued

his critical thinking dispositions. His authentic voice elicited a strong feeling of being engaged with a cognitive presence enacting a critical thinking routine in this intersubjective space of the text. I felt a sense of being with someone who thinks about these things the same way as I do, who has learned (which gives me hope that I can, too) how to understand, think, speak, and write with the academic lingo that a particular group of critical thinking scholars use. My hand was reaching for MS Word to draft a question for him.

But I did not follow through. Instead my attention was diverted by the sound my computer makes when an email is arriving.

The email conveyed an invitation to write a commentary about digital literacy from my program supervisor, R.R. Dods, one of the authors of this textbook. I accepted before realizing I could not actually use the term to make sense of my online meaning-making practices. This would be an opportunity, I thought, to learn how to understand ways that my digital practices and my critical meaning-making practices were related. I called Dr Dods and asked, "How does a cultural anthropologist think about digital literacy?"

The priority, she answered, is reflexive practice. She later described, in an email, "the adoption of reflexivity as the process whereby each of us can come to a deeper understanding of how/what/why we think of things the way we do . . ." which I quote with her permission (Dods 2017).

The takeaway from reflecting on my notes from that morning research session indicates three things about my digital reading and writing literacy practices. It indicates that sensing another human cognitive presence and the authenticity of the storytelling helps me to grasp an abstract concept, in this case, a cognitive presence, and to integrate the concept the words stand for into my situated knowledge (Haraway 1988). Reading words written in the author's own voice, not the voice from nowhere, helped me to internalize the concept (see Vygotsky elsewhere in this book), which in turn gave me confidence—one of the dispositions—to check on the validity of my belief—another of the dispositions—to ask if we were making sense of a phenomenon (cognitive presence) in the same way.

On the other hand, the beeping noise the computer makes to signal that an email is coming does not support critical disposition emergence. It disrupted my follow-through, when the body forms and enacts dispositions to remain focused, to persist, to put the question into words, and to send it.

Instead I observed my body changing its mind when it heard the email beep. As soon as I saw that the email was from my program supervisor, instead of thinking about what I was thinking, which takes time and effort, my index finger was already heading toward the email icon to open up the invitation and away from the word-composing program. The body went for the quick fix, of enjoying the rush of pleasure-giving hormones that comes with being contacted by someone of importance to me. I wrote this note: "Here's a tell-tale sign of the body acting and making up the mind before the self, who is supposed to be in charge of deciding and knows what the body is doing."

The laptop hard drive, my extended memory, shows that after accepting the invitation my first impulse was to type the words *digital literacy* into the GS search form and to let this trusted research companion find a definition. In less than a second, it found 49,700 instances of texts. *Digital Literacy* by Paul Gilster (1997) gets the top-ranked position. He coined the term and it is the most frequently cited data source about the concept. A more recent literature review and analysis by the anthropologist Kathy Mills, however, is a text I recommend.

Key Terms

communicative competence 80

connotative meaning 83

creole 87

denotative meaning 83

design features of language 79

discourse 84

ethnopragmatics 84

grammar 78

heteroglossia 84

language 77

language ideology 89

language revitalization 89

linguistic competence 80

linguistic relativity principle 80

linguistics 77

mana 78

metalanguage 84

morphemes 79

morphology 82

native speaker 78

phonemes 79

phonology 82

pidgin 87

pragmatics 83

semantics 83

syntax 82

vocabulary 78

Chapter Summary

1. Language is a uniquely human faculty that people use to encode their experiences, to structure their understanding of the world and of themselves, and to engage with one another. It is a fundamental part of culture. In addition to communicating verbally, we also communicate non-verbally, through formal sign languages as well as through our body language, facial expressions, and behaviours.
2. In anthropological investigations of language, the most significant design features of language are openness, displacement, prevarication, arbitrariness, duality of patterning, and semanticity. Also important is Edward Sapir and Benjamin Whorf's hypothesis, known as the *linguistic relativity principle*, that language has the power to shape the way people see the world.
3. Formal linguistic analysis is usually divided into five specialties: phonology, the study of the sounds of a language; morphology, the study of the smallest units of meaning in a language; syntax, the study of sentence structure; semantics, the study of meaning; and pragmatics, the study of language in the context of its use. Ethnopragmatics pays attention both to the immediate context of speech and to the broader cultural contexts that are rooted in history and shaped by everyday social interactions. Different social groups generate different communicative practices, contributing to heteroglossia.
4. Pidgin languages display the radical negotiation of new meaning. These languages are actively constructed, and they often develop into complex languages known as *creoles*. Against the backdrop of colonialism, members of more powerful groups tend to look down on the languages of less powerful groups, resulting in linguistic inequality and oppression.

Critical Thinking Questions

1. What is language? What is communication? What is conversation? How do these concepts relate to and differ from one another?
2. What are the design features of language? How do these features separate human language from communication systems used by other animals?
3. Why do speakers of a particular language have different "accents"? What factors—historical and current—might contribute to the variety of accents across Canada today?
4. How many friends do you interact with in person? How many do you interact with online? Does the way you use language in face-to-face conversations differ from how you use it online? Do your feelings of connection with other people change depending on the medium of communication?
5. In what ways does language change over time? How has language evolved in your lifetime?

Suggested Readings

Akmajian, Adrian, et al. 2010. *Linguistics: An Introduction to Language and Communication,* 6th edn (Cambridge, MA: MIT Press). A fine introduction to the study of language as a formal system.

Lakoff, George, and Mark Johnson. 2003 [1980]. *Metaphors We Live By,* rev. edn (Chicago: University of Chicago Press). An important, clear, and accessible book that presents a radical and persuasive view of metaphor. The revised edition contains a new afterword that places the text in a more contemporary context.

Salzmann, Zdenek, James Stanlaw, and Nobuko Adachi. 2014. *Language, Culture, and Society: An Introduction to Linguistic Anthropology,* 6th edn (Boulder, CO: Westview Press). An up-to-date and thorough text on linguistic anthropology.

Turkle, Sherry. 21 April 2012. "The Flight from Conversation." *New York Times.* Available at www.nytimes.com. An insightful opinion piece on how modern communications technologies have impacted the ways in which we connect and converse with other people.

Related Websites

Franglais
www.yrad.com/franglais
Newfoundland Word Game
www.nfld.com/nfld/other/words/word.html

New Words in English
www.learn-english-today.com/new-words/new-words-in-english1.html
Tok Pisin–English Dictionary
www.tok-pisin.com

5 Culture, the Individual, and Identity

Chapter Outline

Perception

Cognition

Emotion

Motivation

Personality/Self/Subjectivity

Sex, Sexuality, and Gender Roles: The Creation of Subject Positions

Individual Psychology and Context

Learning Objectives

By the end of Chapter 5, you will be able to

- understand how perception organizes information and frames the "self";
- appreciate cognition as a complex mental process that helps us make sense of our world;
- consider that emotion and motivation are influenced by cultural contexts;

- recognize the roles that socialization and enculturation play in shaping cognitive development;
- consider the "self," the presentation of self, and the self as subject; and
- understand how sex and gender roles influence our sense of identity.

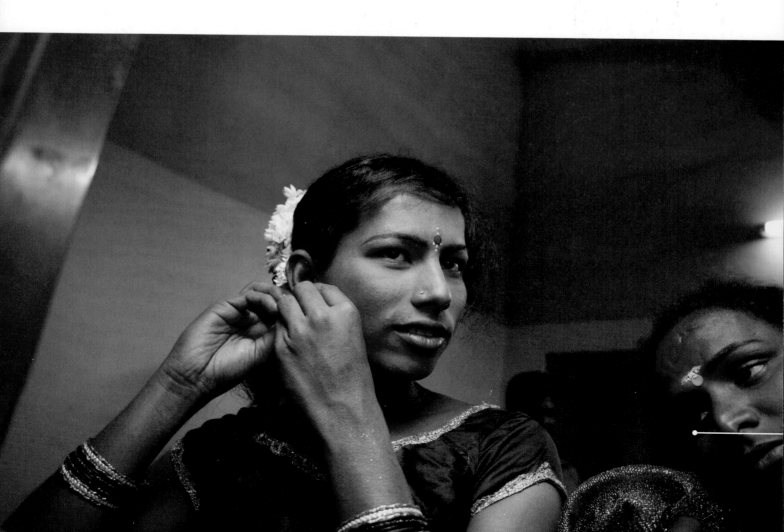

We do not all learn the same things, even if we live in the same society. Our learning is socially and culturally shaped by differences in status and experience. Anthropologists are interested in the patterns and variations in patterns of how individuals engage in cultural learning—how people learn from one another within a culture. Historically, anthropology addressed this phenomenon by seeking answers for a series of persistent questions: "What characteristics of our species are found in all times and places? What features are limited to specific groups of humans? How can we best take account of individual uniqueness?" (Bock 1994: ix).

Anthropologists who want to understand how individuals perceive and make sense of their world have incorporated psychological theories into their studies. Some of the first to do so were Margaret Mead and Ruth Benedict, whose early studies initiated a pattern of analysis that remained central to much psychological anthropology: that of critically examining Western researchers' claims about human nature. This critical role is especially important in situations where researchers make extreme claims about all members of the human species. When faced with such claims, anthropologists must ask, "Is this claim universal in all human groups, or is it relevant only to certain people in certain times and places?" In Western societies, claims about universal human psychology compete with assertions of individual uniqueness. This competition is clear in ongoing "nature versus nurture" debates, in which one side claims that biology (nature) is responsible for some aspect of human behaviour, while the other side claims that culture (nurture) is responsible. Relying on "either/or" rather than the "both/and" approaches of humans as *biocultural* can cause anthropologists to miss the variation and complexity they encounter in their fieldwork experiences.

One of the more promising approaches has come from recent work in developmental biology: developmental systems theory (DST), which focuses on genetic as well as environmental contributions to an organism's development (Oyama et al. 2001). This approach recognizes that socially constructed environments—along with their social, economic, and political resources—get passed on to subsequent generations as faithfully as genes. This social transmission influences how individuals develop. Sahlins (2011) emphasizes the immediacy of this process during infancy by exploring the work of Tomasello in the following passage:

> Even before they acquire linguistic competence, according to Tomasello, human infants engage in similar collaborative relations with others: "At around 9 months of age, infants begin displaying a whole new suite of social behaviors, based on their ability to understand others as intentional and rational agents like the self and in their ability to participate with others in interactions involving joint goals, intentions and attention (shared intentionality)" (2008: 139). This shared intentionality, explains Tomasello, entails an interchange of standpoints and roles in which each person, knowing the other as an intentional being like oneself, assumes the perspective of the other, while aware also that the other is doing the same. (229–30)

In this chapter, we will consider the human experience of perception, cognition, emotion, and motivation, resulting in what we call our *subject position*, from which each of us views "... the world from the vantage point of that position and in terms of [its] particular images, metaphors, storylines, and concepts" (Davies and Harré 1990: 46). In turn, these images, metaphors, storylines, and concepts become a conceptual repertoire for future use. As with language, this repertoire is an *open* system shaped by the cultural factors we encounter. Additionally, our ways of thinking and feeling develop in the context of culturally shaped activities that draw our attention to some parts of the world while leading us to ignore others. What we think or feel about something depends greatly on what we have learned to pay attention to in the past and on the associated values (Figure 5.1). As a result, different groups in a society—with different histories and experiences—are likely to develop different subject positions.

Backstage preparations for a hijra beauty contest in Chennai, India. In 2014 the Supreme Court of India finally awarded hijras legal recognition as a third gender. Gender identity is one of many factors—including ethnicity, occupation, class, and socioeconomic status—that shape the subject positions through which we view and engage with the world around us.

© Sergei Bachlakov/Shutterstock.com

Figure 5.1 People spread positive messages while attending the annual Pride Parade in Vancouver, Canada. How are these messages shaped by cultural factors and values in Canada?

perception The act of becoming aware of the world through what we have termed the five traditional senses: taste, touch, sight, hearing, smell. To this could be added the sensing of movement, balance, gravity, temperature, and pain.

cultural synaesthesia A culturally shared response to a sense other than the one being stimulated (e.g., hearing a sound and seeing it as a colour).

schemas Patterned, repetitive experiences that are shared and easily understood by members of a particular culture.

prototypes Examples of a typical instance, element, relation, or experience within a culture.

It may be useful to keep in mind the design features of language (see Chapter 4). Besides openness, the features of displacement and prevarication can be informative. Consider that when we learn from culturally shaped experience, we can use pre-existing categories to help us interpret new experiences. This is a version of *displacement*. Moreover, all our senses can play tricks on us, and we can mistakenly perceive something that "does not exist." Thus, *prevarication* is a built-in feature of human psychological processes.

Heavily influenced by symbols, the meaning of what we see, touch, smell, taste, or hear depends on context. Two contexts are normally invoked: the *immediate* context of the perception itself and the broader *displaced* context of culturally shaped memory. The "same" object or symbol can mean different things in different contexts.

Perception

Perception is the "processes by which people organize and experience information that is primarily of sensory origin" (Cole and Scribner 1974: 61). Traditionally, people have tried to deal with perceptions in two principal ways: (1) through intellect (rationality, logic) and (2) through emotion (passion, intuition). Although some tend to emphasize one approach, experience shows that both our rational thoughts and our emotions help us

to make sense of our perceptions. Culture affects perception, influencing *what* we perceive and how we *respond* (intellectually and emotionally) to those perceptions. Diana Young's (2005) study of **cultural synaesthesia** with Aboriginal people of the Western Desert of Australia (see EthnoProfile 5.1) provides us with an excellent example of the link between perception and culture. Young found that the odour of wet earth after a rainfall elicits a sense of "greenness" in these people. Smell and colour become one as they perceive in the odour of wet soil the new green growth that is to come (61). Psychological anthropologist Anton Sidoroff-Dorso (2014) has also examined cultural synaesthesia. He finds in this phenomenon evidence that

1. we perceive what our culture tells us to perceive, and
2. we frame our sensing through cultural constructs.

Further, he sees synaesthesia as reflecting "both biology and culture" since the "brain is shaped by exposure and experience" and "human experience comes from . . . shared practices, beliefs, [and] ecology [i.e., physical surroundings]."

Within a given culture, certain chunks of perceptual experience appear to hang together. These patterned collections of perceptions are called **schemas**. As children grow up, they gradually become aware of and recognize their cultural schemas. Such schemas are often embedded in practical activities and labelled linguistically, and they may serve as a focus for discourse. People living in North America, for example, cannot avoid a schema called *Christmas*, a chunk of experience that recurs yearly. This schema can include features such as snowy weather, images of Santa Claus and mistletoe, colourful decorations on a Christmas tree, as well as activities such as baking cookies, singing carols, going to church, and exchanging gifts (Figure 5.2). However, not everyone will interpret a schema in the same way. For example, in North America, devout Christians may struggle to accept the secularization of what was originally a religious holiday, while non-Christians might question why they must be subjected to the Christmas schema every year.

Most of the schemas that a culture recognizes become rote as simplified interpretive frameworks for judging new experiences (D'Andrade 1992: 48). Schemas thus become **prototypes** that help us navigate routine cultural practices. However, when we organize sensory information on the basis of prototypes, the categories can have fuzzy (open) boundaries because our experiences do not always neatly fit our prototypes. Does a "library" that contains fewer books than DVDs, videotapes, and electronic databases fit the prototypical idea of a library? Linguist R.A. Hudson (1980) suggests that a person must simply recognize the openness of language and apply linguistic labels creatively. Similarly, when confronted with novel perceptions—that is, experiences for which no ready-made cultural interpretation is available—we must extrapolate creatively to make sense of what is going on.

Inevitably, observers situated in different subject positions will draw on different background knowledge and different prototypes. As a result, the same sensory information may be interpreted in different ways, which may be influenced by *context*. For example, psychologists Michael Cole and Sylvia Scribner (1974) recount a study in which researchers tested non-literate South African miners using two-dimensional line drawings of three-dimensional objects (Figure 5.3). The test results indicated that the miners consistently interpreted the drawings in two dimensions. For example, when asked which animal the man was pointing his spear at on Card 1, subjects would usually respond "the elephant." The elephant is, in fact, directly in line with and closest to the spear point in the drawing. However, the researchers thought

Figure 5.2 A Christmas-themed Coca-Cola advertisement featuring Santa Claus in Beijing, China. The figure of Santa Claus has become ubiquitous with Coca-Cola holiday ads and is now considered part of the Christmas schema worldwide.

that the subjects should interpret the elephant as standing on top of the distant hill. Did the subjects' responses mean that they could not perceive in three dimensions?

To address this question, researchers devised the following test. First, they presented different African subjects with the same drawings and asked them to describe what they saw. Again, the subjects

© ZUMA Press, Inc./Alamy Stock Photo

EthnoProfile 5.1
Pitjantjatjara (Anangu)

Region: Central Australia, which includes the Western Desert area

Nation: Australia; area around Alice Springs extending to the west

Language: Pitjantjatjara

Population: 4,000 (2014 estimate)

Environment: Arid desert of interior Australia—the Outback

Livelihood: Farming, hunting, gathering; originally nomadic but now more settled in small communities

Political organization: Since 1981, under the management of a central political authority

For more information: Young, Diana. 2005. "The Smell of Greenness: Cultural Synaesthesia in the Western Desert (Australia)," *Etnofoor* 18, 1: 61–77.

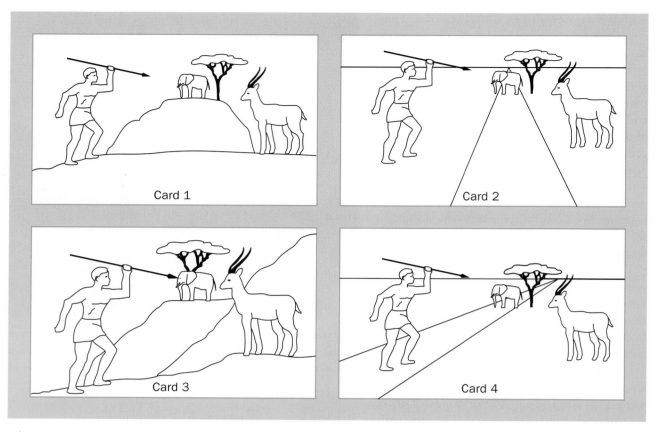

Figure 5.3 Line drawings used to elicit verbal responses in the depth-perception test in Africa.

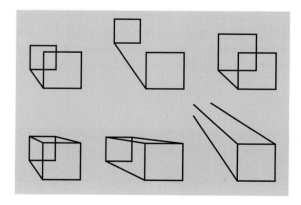

Figure 5.4 Line drawings used for the construction of models in the depth-perception test in Africa.

responded with two-dimensional verbal reports. Next, the researchers presented the same subjects with the line drawings in Figure 5.4. This time, they asked the subjects to construct models based on the drawings. The subjects had no difficulty producing three-dimensional models.

In these tests, the "correct" solution depended on the subject's mastery of a Western convention for interpreting two-dimensional images. For the drawings in Figure 5.3, the Western convention includes assumptions about perspective that relate the size of objects to their distance from the observer. Without such a convention in mind, it is not obvious that the size of an object has any connection with distance. Thus, far from providing insights about Africans' perceptual abilities, the tests highlight the assumptions behind Western perceptual conventions. As Cole and Scribner (1974) point out, the images make sense to us only once we accept certain rules for interpreting them. And we need to remember that *perspective* in Western drawing is a relatively recent "invention" dating to the fifteenth-century Italian Renaissance—through our capacity for openness, our conventions changed.

Illusion

If you examine Figure 5.5, you will see that marks on a piece of paper can be ambiguous. The signals we receive from the outside world—be they shapes, smells, tastes, sounds, or words—tend to be open to more than one interpretation. The contrast between

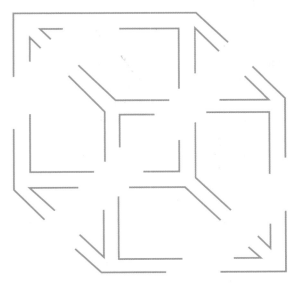

Figure 5.5 Ambiguous marks.

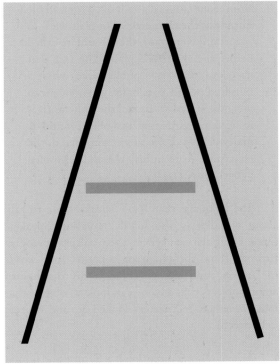

Figure 5.6 An example of distortion: the Ponzo illusion.

literal and metaphorical language is not unlike the contrast between reality and illusion as it relates to perception. In both cases, knowledge of context permits us to distinguish between the literal and the metaphorical, the real and the illusory. Richard Gregory (1983), a cognitive psychologist, argued that visual illusions are produced when the wrong cognitive processes are selected and applied to a particular set of visual signals. Consider *distortion*, in which what you see appears larger or smaller, longer or shorter, and so on, than it really is. Look at the Ponzo illusion in Figure 5.6. Typically, the upper parallel line appears to be longer than the lower one when in fact they are equal. The illusion occurs because we interpret the two-dimensional drawing as if it were three-dimensional. The Africans discussed by Cole and Scribner (1974) did not attempt to interpret the Ponzo-like lines on Card 2 of Figure 5.3 as representations of three-dimensional reality but seemed to keep the relationships between objects on the card in two dimensions, regardless of the apparent distortion. When we compare the Western interpretation of the Ponzo illusion with the African interpretation, we discover something important: the ways in which people interpret ambiguous drawings depend on pre-existing experiences and cultural conventions.

Visuality: Learning to Look

Anthropologist Susan Vogel has studied the sculpture of the Baule people of Ivory Coast (see EthnoProfile 3.1) since the early 1970s, and her research has taught her that looking and seeing are culturally learned modes of sensory perception (1997: 108–11). She terms this interpretive process **visuality**. Vogel notes that, for the Baule, objects are powerful and spiritually significant. Westerners would call them *sculptures*—thus, "art." But for the Baule, such objects are potentially dangerous: "Even an inadvertent glimpse of a forbidden object can make a person sick, can expose them to huge fines or sacrifices, or can even be fatal" (110). For the Baule, looking is the most important of all perceptual activities: seeing something may be more significant and more dangerous than touching, eating, or drinking something. An explicit etiquette governs how one ought to look at things, and staring is highly inappropriate. It is, therefore, disrespectful for younger people to look directly at their elders. In many cases, the rules for looking actually limit the "visibility" of spiritually significant objects. Western worshippers might feel free to gaze intently at the adorned altar of a medieval Christian cathedral; the Baule would consider analogous behaviour to be highly improper:

visuality The ways that individuals from different societies learn to interpret what they see and to construct mental pictures using the visual practices that their own cultural system favours.

cognition (1) The mental process by which human beings gain knowledge, and (2) the "nexus of relations between the mind at work and the world in which it works" (Lave 1988: 1).

taxonomies Hierarchical systems that sort groups of things that share at least one quality (e.g., dogs) into subgroups that share a greater number of qualities (e.g., poodles, collies, boxers).

If someone stopped and looked for a whole minute at the altar erected in plain view in [a certain] courtyard, they would be called before the chief to explain. The fact that the altar stands in a public place, where a hundred people pass daily, does not mean it can be stared at. In fact the only motives for looking hard at such an object would be malevolent: a desire to kill someone in the courtyard, or to nullify the altar's powers. (Vogel 1997: 111)

The language that Baule speakers use to talk about visuality is also highly revealing. Speakers shape vocabulary to reflect their cultural preoccupations; thus, the language contains four words for *looking* and *seeing*. These terms distinguish among objects that anyone can look at, objects that must never be deliberately looked at, and degrees in between:

1. *Nian* connotes intentional watching and is used for watching mask dances intended for entertainment and for watching television.
2. *Nyin* means "a stare" or "a good hard look." The phrase *nyin kpa*, "a real stare," is used to describe looking at objects with no sacred meaning.
3. *Kanngle* means "evil looks from the corner of the eye."
4. *Nian klekle* means "to look secretly," to "cast a rapid glance" (Vogel 1997: 91).

The most awesome objects and events—the men's sacred masks, divination dances, and funerals—are not spoken of with any of these words: "One never says one has seen or looked at these potent things; one merely says *N'wo se bo*, 'I went to the funeral,' or *N'su ko awebo*, 'I went to the divination dance'" (Vogel 1997: 92).

For the Baule, life is lived knowing that powerful objects are present but cannot be examined, cannot be looked at closely. However, even incompletely seen, these objects make an extraordinary impression and impact on their world view.

Cognition

The study of illusion demonstrates that there can be a gulf, but no sharp boundary, between what we perceive and what we conceive. Usually these differences seem to be manageable: there is coherence between perceptions and conceptions. Not only can new perceptions lead us to modify our conceptions (i.e., we learn), but new conceptions can also lead us to perceive aspects of the world around us that we didn't pay attention to before. We are active meaning-makers, internally negotiating our experiences. As a result, **cognition** is perhaps best understood as "a nexus of relations between the mind at work and the world in which it works" (Lave 1988: 1).

Anthropologists began to study cognition in the 1960s, when there was a growing interest in the ways different people classified cultural knowledge. These anthropologists used folk **taxonomies** and generic terms to lump things into categories. Over recent decades, anthropologists have expanded their investigations to incorporate the links between language and culture, focusing on the many ways of "labelling" the social and cultural worlds of their informants. Today, cognitive anthropologists look closely at the mental processes people use to label and make sense of their experiences. (See Gelman and Legare 2011 for folk theories, Young 2011 for post-colonial meaning of colour, and Aikhenvald 2012 for gender classification.)

Cognitive Capacities and Intelligence

A "scientific" approach to measuring human potential has emerged based on personal genetic testing. This is available because of the commercialization of the Human Genome Project (HGP), and some researchers consider it to yield "a powerful framing of DNA as biological potential, encoding a life force that awaits release to fulfill its promise..." (Lee 2013: 585). Anthropologists also look to the environment in which this "potential" develops and consider what makes it possible for people to receive signals from the outside world (or from within their own bodies) and then interpret those signals in a way that makes appropriate action possible. It has been traditionally thought that every person either possesses at birth or develops over time certain basic *cognitive capacities*. At one time the goal of psychological testing was to measure how much of each cognitive capacity an individual had. Consequently, intelligence was "measured" using "intelligence tests," and the results were the assignment of a number called the "intelligence quotient," or IQ. Some researchers equated differences in *performance on intelligence tests* with differences in *intelligence*. Today, psychologists and others take a more nuanced approach.

For example, in the work of psychologist Lev Vygotsky, Cole and Scribner (1974) found an approach that distinguishes between **elementary cognitive processes** and **functional cognitive systems**. Elementary cognitive processes include the ability to make abstractions, to categorize, to reason inferentially, and so forth. Different cultures, however, organize these elementary processes into different functional cognitive systems that govern how people respond to different tasks, which means that individuals from different cultures may have different routine responses for tackling equivalent tasks. More recently, Canadian psychological researchers Christopher Mushquash and Dana Bova (2007) have taken a closer look at the problems with using intelligence tests in cross-cultural settings. As they note, "culture influences many aspects of an individual's life; thus measurement of various psychological constructs is also likely to be influenced by cultural characteristics" (54). They point out that every facet of this sort of testing is impacted by culture:

- The content of the test
- The materials used to administer the test
- The wording of the test
- The way the directions and conditions are organized
- The way the test is scored
- The behaviour of the test administrator
- The behaviour of the participants (Mushquash and Bova 2007: 56)

They conclude that researchers need to be very "cautious when interpreting standardized test scores of intelligence from culturally diverse clients" (62).

Cognitive Style

Cultures provide people with a *range* of **cognitive styles** that are appropriate for different cognitive tasks in different contexts. Psychological anthropologists have attempted to compare cognitive styles cross-culturally. Some have argued that the styles of individuals and of groups can be located on a continuum between a **global style** and an **articulated style**. People who use a global style tend to view the world holistically: they first see a

bundle of relationships and only later see the bits and pieces that are related. They are said to be *field dependent* because they consider everything in relation to its context. In contrast, people who use an articulated style tend to break up the world into smaller and smaller pieces, which they can then organize into larger chunks. They also tend to see a sharp boundary between their own bodies and the outside world. People using an articulated style are said to be *field independent* because they are able to consider whatever they happen to be paying attention to apart from its context (Cole and Scribner 1974: 82).

Originally, most people in Western societies were thought to be field independent, whereas most people in non-Western cultures were thought to be field dependent. However, more detailed research shows that these generalizations are misleading. For instance, the preferred cognitive style of an individual often varies from task to task and from context to context. People who use articulated styles for some tasks also use global styles for other tasks. In fact, they may bring a range of different styles to bear on a single task—that is, they may look at a task or a problem in more than one way.

Indeed, research by social anthropologist Jean Lave (1988) demonstrated that North Americans are not field independent in all contexts, even when the task involves mathematics, which would seem to be the most field independent of all cognitive activities. The researchers wanted to test the widespread assumption that cognitive style does not vary across contexts. In particular, they wanted to find out whether ordinary people use the same mathematical skills in the supermarket that they use in the classroom. As part of the research, subjects were given a pencil-and-paper math test to determine how well they could solve mathematical problems in a school-like context. Then, the same subjects were observed while using mathematics to make buying decisions at a grocery store. Finally, the subjects were presented with paired grocery items and asked to calculate the best buy.

Surprisingly, the subjects averaged only 59 per cent correct in the school-like context but achieved averages of 98 per cent correct in the supermarket experiment and 93 per cent correct in the best-buy experiment. The high scores were achieved with very little reliance on mathematics taught in school—shoppers were better able to make wise economic decisions using informal calculation

elementary cognitive processes Mental tasks common to all humans without cognitive impairment.

functional cognitive systems Culturally linked sets of cognitive processes that guide perception, conception, reason, and emotion.

cognitive style Recurring patterns of cognitive activity that characterize an individual's perceptual and intellectual activities.

global style A field-dependent way of viewing the world that first sees it as a bundle of relationships and only later sees the smaller pieces involved in these relationships.

articulated style A field-independent way of viewing the world that breaks it up into small pieces, which can then be organized into larger chunks.

strategies. The three most common informal strategies were:

- *inspection* (recognizing that an item was lower in price and/or larger in volume),
- *best-buy calculations* (comparing quantities and prices, and then choosing the better value), and
- *a difference strategy* (deciding whether a marginal difference in quantity was worth the marginal difference in price) (Lave 1988: 107ff.).

To conclude from these results that there was something primitive or illogical about the informal strategies—and, by extension, about the people who used them—would contradict the evidence showing that the shoppers' informal strategies were exceptionally accurate (see Lave 1988: 79ff., 107ff.).

These observations point to a major difference between "school" math and "grocery store" math. In school, the only purpose of solving a mathematical problem is to obtain a single correct answer. However, shoppers do not visit supermarkets to practise formal mathematics; they go to buy food. Consequently, the choices they make are influenced not merely by unit–price ratios but by their family's food preferences, the amount of storage space at home, the amount of time they can spend shopping, and so on (Figure 5.7). The supermarket "problems' are dilemmas to be resolved, rarely problems to be solved" (Lave 1988: 20). Formal mathematical calculations

may help resolve some dilemmas, but in other cases they may be irrelevant or too troublesome to bother with. Shoppers are free to use means other than formal mathematics to resolve a dilemma (58).

One feature that all of Lave's subjects shared was the knowledge that school-like tests required a specific problem-solving style—an articulated style. In non-Western societies, individuals who have been educated in the Western system also tend to reserve articulated cognitive styles for the classroom, preferring a variety of more global strategies to resolve the dilemmas of everyday life. So it seems that human beings can choose to employ a range of cognitive styles, depending on the situation. Further, they are able to adopt new cognitive styles as they have new experiences. Studies have shown, for example, that individuals can acquire cognitive styles through social interaction (see, e.g., Levinson 1998). When studying cognitive styles, then, anthropologists must be careful to give their informants the freedom to express a wide variety of global and articulated styles.

In moving beyond cognitive studies, anthropologists are now reintroducing phenomenology as well as adding "practice theory," which adds a new dimension that directs anthropologists to study intension and motives and how they can explain the ways human beings transform their world. Anthropologists now study the dynamic between how people have been enculturated (their norms and values) and their agency. Do you ever act on gut feelings? Or respond in certain ways because of what others may think? In his review, Marchand emphasizes embodied knowledge, noting it is more than merely

> skilled practice and performance, [since] the body plays a key role in the making and recall of a wide spectrum of knowledge, including the conceptual kind. If this is so, the need for an analytic framework that accounts for the complex relations of interdependence between minds, bodies, and environment is all the more necessary to our studies of society and culture. (2010: 518)

Reason and the Reasoning Process: Thinking

In the context of Western colonialism, the debate regarding *reasoning ability* and the lack of literacy was rarely disinterested, for Europeans often justified their position of dominance on the grounds that those dominated were irrational. Faced with

Figure 5.7 Shoppers often rely on informal mathematical strategies to calculate the best buy because numbers for quantity and price are not often easy to transform into unit–price ratios. What sorts of strategies do you use to find the best values when you shop?

this problematic history, how might anthropologists study rational thinking?

Most cognitive psychologists have adopted psychologist Jerome Bruner's (1957) famous definition of **thinking** as "going beyond the information given." This distinction suggests that thinking is different from only remembering (which involves referring to information already given) and also from learning (which involves acquiring new information being given). Going beyond the *information given* thus implies a complex interrelationship between *remembering* and *learning* in a *cognitive process* that integrates information. This definition also reminds us of the nature of cognition as the "nexus of relations between the mind at work and the world in which it works" (Lave 1988: 1; quoted above). Thinking is open and active, and it has no predetermined outcome.

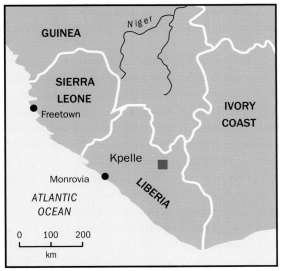

thinking The active cognitive process of "going beyond the information given" (Bruner 1957).

Map 5.1 Kpelle

Culture and Logic

One set of cognitive tests has to do with verbal reasoning ability. These tests present subjects with three statements in the form of a **syllogism**. Here is an example:

1. All men are mortal.
2. Socrates is a man.
3. Therefore, Socrates is mortal.

In a syllogism, the first two statements are the *premises*, and the third statement is the *conclusion*. For a syllogism to be sound, the conclusion must follow from the premises. In Western culture, **syllogistic reasoning** is considered to be a perfect example of rational thought. In the past, some researchers suggested that the rational capacities of non-Western peoples could be tested using logical problems in syllogistic form—the assumption being that rationality would be confirmed if they could correctly deduce when the conclusion followed logically from the premises and when it did not. This was tested on the Kpelle of Liberia (see Map 5.1). The logical problem was embedded in a folktale-like story and read to the "subjects," who were then asked a series of questions designed to reveal whether they could draw a "correct" conclusion from the premises given (Cole and Scribner 1974).

Here is one test story that Cole and Scribner prepared:

Spider went to a feast. He was told to answer this question before he could eat any of the food. The question is: Spider and

Black Deer always eat together. Spider is eating. Is Black Deer eating? (1974: 162)

Given the two premises, the conclusion should be that *Black Deer is eating*. Now consider a typical Kpelle response to hearing this story:

Subject: Were they in the bush?

Experimenter: Yes.

Subject: Were they eating together?

Experimenter: Spider and Black Deer always eat together. Spider is eating. Is Black Deer eating?

Subject: But I was not there. How can I answer such a question?

Experimenter: Can't you answer it? Even if you were not there, you can answer it. (Repeats the question.)

Subject: Oh, oh, Black Deer is eating.

Experimenter: What is your reason for saying that Black Deer was eating?

Subject: The reason is that Black Deer always walks about all day eating green leaves in the bush. Then he rests for a while and gets up again to eat. (162)

syllogism A series of three statements in which the final statement (the conclusion) must follow logically from the first two statements (the premises).

syllogistic reasoning A form of reasoning based on the syllogism.

The subject's answer and justification seemed to have nothing to do with the logical problem presented.

The researchers devised this story the same way schoolteachers devise mathematical word problems. That is, the contextual material is nothing more than a kind of window dressing. Schoolchildren quickly learn to disregard the window dressing and seek out the mathematical problem it hides. In the research setting, the Kpelle, however, did not understand that they were supposed to disregard the window dressing. Cole and Scribner interpreted their subject's response to this problem as being due not to irrationality but to a "failure to accept the logical task" (1974: 162). In a follow-up study, the Kpelle children who were studying at a Western-style high school responded "correctly" to the logical problems 90 per cent of the time. This finding suggests a strong correlation between Western-style schooling and a willingness to accept context-free analytic tasks in testing situations (164).

But this is not all. David Lancy, one of Cole and Scribner's colleagues, discovered that Western-style syllogisms are very similar to certain forms of Kpelle riddles. Unlike syllogisms, however, those riddles have no single "logically correct" answer: "Rather, as the riddle is posed to a group, the right answer is the one among many offered that seems most illuminating, resourceful, and convincing as determined by consensus and circumstance" (Lancy, cited in Fernandez 1980: 47–8). The "right" answer, then, is the one that seems most enlightening and informative to the particular audience in the particular setting where the riddle is posed. This approach to identifying the correct answer also reinforces the concept of consensus, thus making problem-solving a group activity.

There is no question that all humans come equipped with the same elementary cognitive processes—for example, the ability to make abstractions, the ability to create conceptual categories, and the ability to reason inferentially. The difficulty is to understand how these elementary cognitive processes are put to work within culturally shared schemas to produce different **reasoning styles**.

Emotion

Psychological anthropologists who try to define **emotion** in cross-cultural terms run into a familiar problem: they discover that not all languages possess a term that might be translated as *emotion*. To get out of this tangle, they have tried to develop a theory of cognitive functioning that accounts for the experiences that some cultures recognize as emotional.

In Western culture, emotion has been somewhat genderized and associated with the body (feminine) and generally separated from rational thought (masculine), which is typically associated with the mind. However, any attempt to explain emotion must deal with the nature of bodily arousal, and such arousal is contextually *interpreted*. Thus, cognitive activity (mind) influences our emotional experience (see Mandler 1975: 97). Conversely, a particular interpretation of our experience can trigger bodily arousal.

Approaching emotion from this perspective accomplishes three things:

1. It integrates mind and body in a holistic fashion.
2. It acknowledges ambiguity as a central feature of emotional experience (recall that ambiguity is also central to linguistic, perceptual, and conceptual experience).
3. It suggests how different cultural interpretations might shape what we feel (because cultural interpretations shape our thoughts).

We experience bodily arousal when our familiar world is somehow interrupted. Such arousal may either fade away or develop into an emotional experience, depending on the meaning we assign to it. Possible meanings arise out of cultural interpretations of recurring experiential schemas. We should not be surprised to find some overlap in the categories of feeling recognized by different cultures. After all, certain experiential schemas that interrupt the familiar world—birth and death, for example—are human universals. At the same time, the wider cultural context will, in each case, modify the perspective from which such experiences are understood and, thus, the categories of feeling associated with them. Generations of new spouses, new parents, and anthropological fieldworkers can testify to the overwhelming truth of this statement (Figure 5.8).

Emotion in an Eastern African Culture

David Parkin (1984) studied the cultural construction of emotion among the Giriama of coastal

reasoning style Culture- and context-dependent ways in which we appraise, come to understand, and think about a cognitive task.

emotion The product of entanglements connecting bodily arousal and cognitive interpretation.

Kenya (see Map 5.2). Their theory of human nature does not recognize a mind–body dualism of the Western sort. They are unwilling to set up sharp, mutually exclusive oppositions of any kind when discussing human nature. Therefore, such behaviour as spirit possession, madness, hysteria, witchcraft, persistent violence, drunkenness, and thieving are explained

> as the result of what we might call imbalances in human nature.... [T]he Giriama do not believe that a person can be intrinsically or irredeemably evil: at some stage, usually remarkably quickly, he will be brought back into the fold, even if he subsequently leaves it again. A large number of terms, roughly translatable as greed, lust, envy, jealousy, malice, resentment, anger, are used to refer to these imbalances of character and the accompanying behaviour. (Parkin 1984: 14)

As with Westerners, the Giriama associate different feelings with different parts of the body. In the West, people conventionally connect the brain with reason and the heart with emotion. For the Giriama, however, the heart, liver, kidneys, and eyes are the seat of reason *and* emotion. They may distinguish thinking from feeling in discussing the actual behaviour of real people, but they nevertheless presume a common origin for both (Parkin 1984: 17). What about particular emotions? Although the categories of feeling recognized by the

Figure 5.8 A Congolese mother holds her newborn baby with a midwife in a refugee camp in Rwanda. New parents must learn through whole-body experience how to care for their newborns.

© Friedrich Stark/Alamy Stock Photo

Giriama overlap in some respects with the experiences labelled by English terms, Parkin suggests that there are important differences that stem from the nature of recognized Giriama schemas and from the prototypical thoughts and feelings that are appropriate to those schemas. Consider the term *utsungu*:

> *Utsungu* means poison, bitterness, resentment, and anger, on the one hand, but also grief on the other. It is the feeling experienced at a funeral of a loved or respected relative or friend. A man or woman is grieved at the loss but also bitter that it has happened at all, and angry with the witch who caused the death. Since the witch will be made to pay, the sentiment carried with it both the consequences of the loss of a dear one and the intention to avenge his or her death. (118)

In Western societies, people also feel "grief." But the prototypical Western experience of grief does not contain the additional meaning involving anger at witchcraft. In some cases, however, a person who has lost a loved one may associate grief with a desire for vengeance—for example, if the loved one was murdered. Thus, although we may not believe in witchcraft, we can begin to understand the Giriama people's association of grief with vengeance.

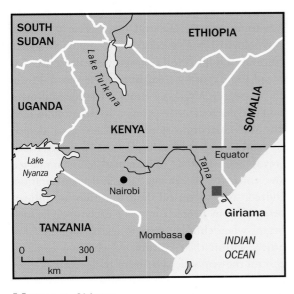

Map 5.2 Giriama

Motivation

Perception and cognition acquaint us with the inner and outer "worlds" of our experiences and assist us in making sense of those worlds. Human life also involves activity, agency: we set goals and pursue them, driven by **motivation**. Where does this motivation come from? Some assume it comes from "instinct." However, many anthropologists think the term *instinct* is unhelpful and misleading because different societies establish different culturally defined goals to motivate their members.

In the 1930s and 1940s, pioneering anthropologist Ruth Benedict argued that each culture has its own set of motives reflecting culturally specific models of ideal behaviour. Identifying peoples' cultural motivations is an important part of the anthropological task, as it can help anthropologists to understand where the people with whom they work are "coming from" (see, e.g., Rosenblatt 2004). As Catherine Lutz (1988) has observed, gaining an understanding of people's cultural motivations requires anthropologists to do the following:

1.   Pay close attention to social and cultural contexts.
2.   Learn to understand local discourse about vice and virtue.
3.   Come to terms with local practices and values in the framework of agency.

In short, anthropologists can uncover the mainsprings of motivation by studying **socialization** and **enculturation**.

Socialization and Enculturation

Children use their own bodies and brains to explore their world. Their exploration of the world is not merely trial and error: the path is cleared by others who shape their experiences—and their interpretations of their experiences—for them. Two terms in the social sciences refer to this process of culturally and socially shaped cognitive development: *socialization* and *enculturation*. For children, becoming human involves both of these processes as they learn how to act, think, feel, and speak at the same time that they participate in the joint activities of social groups to which they belong (Figure 5.9). Enculturation and socialization are thus intimately connected. (For more on the socialization of young children, see the "In Their Own Words" box that follows.)

motivation The inner impulse to set (or accept) and accomplish goals.

socialization The process by which human beings learn to become members of a group, both by interacting appropriately with others and by coping with the behavioural rules established by the group.

enculturation The process by which human beings living with one another must learn to come to terms with the ways of thinking and feeling that are considered appropriate in their respective cultures.

Figure 5.9 A woman teaching young children to read in Myanmar. In what ways are we culturally and socially shaped by our environments, starting from a very young age?

Anthropologists seek a holistic theory of cognitive development. Therefore, the ideas of philosopher George Herbert Mead (micro approach: face-to-face interaction) and, more recently, those of psychologist Lev Vygotsky (macro approach: social, cultural, and historical context) were attractive. For Mead and Vygotsky alike, human life is social from the outset. As Vygotsky wrote, "The social dimension of consciousness is primary in time and in fact. The individual dimension of consciousness is derivative and secondary" (1978: 30). Like Vygotsky, Mead (1934) believed that human nature is completed and enhanced by socialization and enculturation. Indeed, the successful humanization of human beings lies in people's mastery of symbols, which begins when children start to learn language from others within their culture. As children come to control the symbolic systems of their cultures, they gain the ability to distinguish objects and relationships in the world, and they come to see themselves as objects as well as subjects.

In Their Own Words

The Sociality of Children

Karen Fog Olwig discusses kindergarten life and the extent to which children may be seen as important actors in this adult-constructed institution.

Of particular salience in the accounts of kindergarten life were the relationships made with other children: some of the young adults stated that they continue to maintain friendships that had begun at that time (Rasmussen and Smidt 2001, 26, 61–2). This suggests that the kindergarten in many ways figures as a house of positive memories. Central to this experience of the kindergarten, Rasmussen and Smidt suggest, is children's feel for "circumventing, softening, reinterpreting, and resisting the established order and the established rules" of the institution (ibid.: 26). The authors also point to children's "symbolic creativity," based on their ability to "create meaning or add a layer of meaning on top of already given meanings" (ibid.: 65). These independent activities, according to Rasmussen and Smidt, "compose one of the constitutive traits of these institutions for children," making children important actors in the daily construction and reconstruction of the institution (ibid.: 85). Identifying children's basic social and creative capacities as the key to understanding their ability to renegotiate the established order of the kindergarten, and with reference to Erving Goffman's work on institutions, Rasmussen and Smidt (2001: 170) argue that the drive to test and explore the structure of an institution is a general human characteristic. However, it is one thing to suggest the existence of general human capacities for self-assertion, but quite another to account for the ways in which children become able to exercise these capacities as children within the institutional order of the kindergarten. [I argue] that children's ability to use their capacity for reinterpretation and creativity inheres, to a great extent, in their status in the adult-constructed order of the kindergarten as not-yet civilized human beings who cannot be expected to master appropriate forms of emotional and bodily expression.

. . . Elias (1997: 190) argues that the concept of childhood entails setting aside a certain category of humans as creatures who need to be civilized before they can become proper members of society (see also Elias [1939] 2000: xi). This understanding of children emerged with the development of modern middle-class culture, in which specific manners and moral values are regarded as marks of social worth and societal acceptance (Elias 1997). The notion of civilization differs from the concept of socialization, which is often used to refer to the general process of imparting to children the skills necessary to become members of a particular society (Hojlund 2009a). Thus, while children may be socialized to become members of different segments of the population, only those who are taught the manners of the dominant class will be recognized as civilized, leaving the rest to be considered uncivilized. A key element in the civilizing of children in modern society is the ability to control bodily functions, exercise emotional self-control, and master social conventions and manners identified with the middle class (Frykman and Lofgren 1987).

Source: Olwig, Karen Fog. 2011. "Children's Sociality: The Civilizing Project in the Danish Kindergarten," *Social Analysis: The International Journal of Social and Cultural Practice* 55, 2: 121–41. Reproduced by permission of Berghahn Books Inc.

Vygotsky argued that this learning process creates in the child a new plane of consciousness resting on the dialogue-based, question-and-answer format of social interaction. From this, he inferred that our internal thought processes would also take the format of a dialogue. Mead suggested something similar when he spoke of every person as being able to carry on internal conversations between the *I* (the unsocialized self) and the *me* (the socially conditioned self). Only on this basis can an individual's sense of identity develop as the **self** comes to distinguish itself from the conversational other. Vygotsky also developed the related concept of the **zone of proximal development (ZPD)**, which is the distance between a child's "actual development level as determined by independent problem solving" and the level of "potential development as determined through problem solving under adult guidance or in collaboration with more capable peers" (Vygotsky 1978: 86). Psychologists everywhere have long been aware that children can often achieve more when they are coached than when they work alone. Vygotsky and his followers see this difference in achievement as demonstrating how growth is rooted in social interaction, especially in educational settings (Moll 1990). The concept of the zone of proximal development enables anthropologists and comparative psychologists to link cognitive development to

self The result of the process of socialization and enculturation for an individual.

zone of proximal development (ZPD) The difference between what individuals can achieve on their own and what they can achieve under the guidance of more experienced individuals.

society, culture, and history because practices of coaching or formal instruction are shaped by social, cultural, and historical factors. To the extent that these factors can vary, we can expect cognitive development to vary as well.

The question that arose was this: Is cognitive development the same for everyone? Most theories portray cognitive development as a progression through a series of stages and posit that the stages are the same for all human beings or at least all human beings in a particular society. However, anthropological observations suggest that this is not always the case. A Vygotskian perspective helps us explain not only cross-cultural differences in development but also differences in the cognitive development of different subgroups in a single society.

Psychologist Carol Gilligan's (1982) comparative study on the moral development of women and men in North American society offers an example. Gilligan argued that middle-class boys and girls begin their moral development in different sociocultural contexts. Boys are encouraged from an early age to break away from their mothers and families and make it on their own. In this context, they learn that independence is good, that dependency is weakness, and that their first duty is to themselves and what they stand for. In contrast, girls mature in a sociocultural context in which their bond with their mothers and families is never sharply broken. They learn that connection to others is good, that the destruction of relationships is damaging, and that their first responsibility in any difficult situation is to ensure that nobody gets hurt.

The zone of proximal development provides a useful tool for describing Gilligan's results. Thus, in Vygotskian terms, the moral development of boys and girls proceeds in different directions because boys and girls are coached differently by more mature members of society. In this way, each gender category builds up a different set of schemas as to what constitutes the "good." Gilligan (1982) argued that men are able to present their moral perspective as universally correct because men as a group hold power over women as a group in North American society. She predicted, however, that as women continue to gain social power and status, their "different voice" will acquire ever more legitimacy, and the culturally embedded paths of moral development may themselves eventually be altered.

personality The relative integration of an individual's perceptions, motives, cognitions, and behaviour within a sociocultural matrix.

More recently, Roy Ellen situates cognitive anthropology in a wider perspective that examines the intersection of biology and culture:

> One major theoretical focus that satisfies conditions of distinctively anthropological theory is the new cognitive anthropology, or cultural cognition. To understand how this potential can translate under particular ecological conditions requires us to look to theories that address the interface between biology and culture, brain structure and evolutionary explanations (e.g., Reyna 2002; Samuel 1990), and to explore an embodied notion of cognition and the difficult area where the Cartesian distinction between material and psychological begins no longer to hold (Varela, Thompson & Rosch 1993). . . . Our major concern as anthropologists is to explain how objects, practices, ideas, patterns of interaction, and relationships continue to be transmitted sufficiently accurately to allow for the reproductive continuity, not of each unit of "Culture" or "society," but of each locally or virtually delineated population. (2010: 393–4)

Personality/Self/Subjectivity

Early psychological anthropologists often spoke of individual **personality** rather than the *self* when discussing an individual's sense of identity and personal place in the world. Many Western psychologists and psychological anthropologists also assumed that the mature self or personality was a bounded, independent, self-contained entity with a clear and non-contradictory sense of identity that persisted through time. According to this interpretation of the self, individuals would naturally strive to be self-sufficient and work to further their own individual interests, whether or not those interests benefited others. Anthropologists working in non-Western societies, however, have found that the development of such an independent entity was not always the goal of socialization and enculturation. In many cases, the objective was to shape selves that were motivated to look out for others and to work for the well-being of the family, the lineage, or the community. As African psychologist Augustine Nwoye

(2006) points out, "the Western notion of the self is largely incompatible with the African view. The Western model is based on the notion of the self as a demarcated entity set off against the world, whereas the African views the self as an entity in close interaction with the multi-faceted aspects of the world" (119).

Psychological anthropologists, such as Philip K. Bock (1994), have looked very closely at the relationship between culture and the individual in different cultural contexts. What they have found is that an individual's personality is not merely a reflection of a culturally ideal type; it is also shaped by "quasi-universal" factors, such as "the individual's position in the social structure, including his or her social class, gender, occupational role, and even birth order" (Bock 1994: xiv). Thus, it seems that different dimensions of one's personality or self can be activated or de-activated in different contexts and over time as contexts change. What, then, does this mean for our understanding of "the self" or "personality" as a constant, unchanging entity?

Aware that conceptions of the self as unchanging do not fully encompass our continually shifting sense of identity and place in the world, contemporary psychological anthropologists are more likely to speak of individual **subjectivity** than of individual personality or the self. *Individual subjectivity* has been described as "the felt interior experience of the person that includes his or her positions in a field of relational power" (Das and Kleinman 2000: 1). Thinking of individuals as *subjects* who occupy various positions within society has two major advantages. First, it highlights individual **agency**, as each of us is the initiating subject of our actions. Second, it acknowledges that our power to act is limited by our circumstances. After all, individual agency is not absolute; it is circumscribed by various limitations that result from the distribution of social, economic, and political power in the societies in which we live. These limitations may be greater or lesser, depending on social variables such as class, gender, occupation, or birth order. That is, we are *subject to* the workings of institutionalized power in the various **subject positions** we occupy.

Our subject positions are formed in and through our cultural context; consequently, they reflect certain social, economic, and political circumstances, both past and present. People in all societies occupy a variety of different subject positions: a particular individual may, in different contexts, be differently positioned in terms of gender, ethnicity, occupation, class, or some combination of these positions. At the same time, however, all of us can potentially play the insights gained from each subject position against the others and thus gain a measure of reflexive awareness and understanding of our own situations.

The Presentation of Self

Whenever we interact with others, we present a version of our "self." Our conventions of grooming and clothing as well as the ways we move and speak all create an image of self. Specific presentation is context defined. Think of the Catholic pope, who must wear specific liturgical vestments and assume a specific public demeanour to set himself apart from those he leads (cardinals, archbishops, bishops, priests, the Catholic congregationals). In Western Pueblo culture, ceremonial dancers present themselves as *katsinim* (singular: *katsina* [Hopi]) (immortal spirit beings of the natural world) by wearing specific masks and clothes and performing specific activities not appropriate outside the ceremonial space/time context. A non-religious example, but perhaps more familiar to North Americans, may be the "red carpet" phenomenon, in which celebrities (mostly female) are expected to don "designer" clothes and jewellery in a highly formalized presentation of self.

On a more general level, we are expected to present a self that reflects the **norms** and the **values** of our culture. Youth and independence are valued ideals in North America; thus, North Americans strive to present themselves as young, strong, and self-sufficient. Western cultural norms have expanded in recent decades to be more inclusive; our presentation of self has become more open as well (Van Wolputte 2004: 264). Naturally, other cultures have different ideals, and those ideals shape expectations of self-presentation differently. It has also become easier to achieve our ideal individualism, whatever it may be, "through tattoos, piercings, branding, liposuction, or cosmetic surgery"—a purchased commodification of the "dominant ideology" (264).

In presenting the self, individuals sometimes draw on what cultural anthropologist Mark Edberg (2004) calls a **cultural persona**: "a type of personified cultural model that appears to serve as a distinct nexus between representation and practice" (258).

subjectivity An individual's awareness of his or her own agency and position as a subject.

agency An individual's ability to make choices and to effect change through her or his actions.

subject position An individual's unique position in the world, which is shaped by social variables, such as class, gender, and socioeconomic status.

norms Rules (usually unwritten) for behaviour assumed to be typical within a specific social or cultural group.

values Specific culturally defined principles of behaviour.

cultural persona The presentation of self in compliance with specific cultural models (patterns) of values and meanings.

Consider the tough-guy persona of the US–Mexican narcotics trafficker. As Edberg describes them, "cultural personas are recycled and may surface in a particular setting as a 'type,' ... which represents a cluster of values and meanings that are expressed through a particular pattern of action that is many steps removed from the persona in its original or 'pure' form" (273). To the insider who is familiar with the cultural meanings on which a particular persona is built, that persona makes sense. Taken out of context, or from a cultural outsider's perspective, a cultural persona can easily be misunderstood or manipulated for specific ends.

In recent years, anthropologists have increasingly turned their attention to the presentation of self in technology-mediated social environments. Electronic media—first telegraph, telephone, and radio; then TV; and now the Internet—broaden the reach of the presented self. In our ever-expanding world of various forms of online sharing of selfies, text, and videos (Facebook, Twitter, Snapchat, etc.), it is relatively easy to present whatever self we like to a great number of people. Politicians and other personalities in the public eye are very aware of the power of selective self-presentation on social networking sites. American president Donald Trump, for example, during the election campaign of 2016, had, famously, a very active Twitter account that he has continued to use into his presidency. As social anthropologist Steffen Dalsgaard (2008) argues, the presentation of self via social networking services may even be "a new form of presentation of self ... that focuses on the social relations of the person rather than the person as an individual" (8). (For more on the presentation of the self and social media's effects on social relations, see the "In Their Own Words" box that follows.)

In Their Own Words

Media and Romantic Relationships in Industrial China

In this excerpt, Xinyuan Wang presents an ethnographic account of the effects social media has on romantic relationships in a small factory town in southeast China. QQ is a Facebook-like social media platform that offers users a multitude of services, including instant messaging, emailing, video sharing, TV streaming, and online shopping.

The very action of men and women adding each other on QQ can easily be interpreted as romance, since, in the words of one girl, "QQ is not used for talking business or other things; QQ is for you to fall in love (*tan lian ai*)." It has become almost a consensus among young people that one of the major functions of social media is to develop and maintain romantic relationships. Xiao Lin, a 20-year-old factory worker, sent me QQ messages explaining how QQ helped him to become a better lover:

> I am much more bold and romantic on QQ . . . you just wouldn't say those sweet words face to face . . . And I used lots of cute stickers when we were chatting on QQ, which made her find me really funny.

Many young migrant workers, like Xiao Lin, think they can be a better lover on social media. Vivid stickers and emojis enrich people's expression; an element of time delay allows more scope for strategic communication. Behind the screens of their smartphones, people feel more empowered and confident. Rather than a diminished form of intimate interaction, romantic relationships on social media have become an efficient modality combining elements of voice, image, and text, as well as emojis and stickers. There is another reason why social media is regarded as a place for romantic love: a public display of love offline is usually frowned upon in Goodpath. Walking hand in hand was the most intimate interaction that one could spot on the street. When Xiao Yu, a 21-year-old hairdresser's apprentice, posted photos of herself kissing her boyfriend on QQ, she perceived QQ to be a romantic and liberating place where one can feel free to display intimacy as the "public" was different:

> In big cities people won't make a fuss [about kissing in public]. But here some traditional people would dislike it . . . but the good thing is they are not on my QQ!

Source: Wang, Xinyuan. 2016. *Social Media in Industrial China* (London: UCL Press), 109–10.

Sex, Sexuality, and Gender Roles: The Creation of Subject Positions

Our "selves" or "subject positions" are shaped by our **sex** and our adoption of a **gender role** or roles (see, e.g., Peletz 2006). In most Western societies, concepts of sex and **gender** have traditionally been closely linked. As philosopher of science Sarah S. Richardson (2012) observes,

> there is a broad popular, scientific, and medical conception of the X chromosome as the mediator of the differences between males and females. . . . The still very contemporary view is that the double X makes females unpredictable, mysterious, chimeric, and conservative, while the single X allows men to learn, evolve, and have bigger brains but also makes them the more risk taking. . . . [This] shows how conceptions of X chromosome structure and function often reflect and support traditional gender stereotypes. (927)

To truly understand the roles that sex and gender—not to mention **sexuality**—play in our lives, we need to differentiate the three fundamental terms of *sex*, *gender*, and *sexuality*. Conventionally, *sex* refers to anatomy (biology), *gender* refers to sociocultural beliefs and practices, and *sexuality* refers to the way that sexual desire is experienced, including an individual's preferences in sexual partners and practices.

Sex, sexuality, and gender identities define subject positions, sorting each of us into categories—and often hierarchies—defined by our cultures. This type of sorting is not an inconsequential matter. Consider how narrow and limiting the traditional categories of "male" and "female" or "heterosexual" and "non-heterosexual" are. In contrast, consider the openness of the identity categories suggested by the acronym LGBTQIA (lesbian, gay, bisexual, transgender, queer or questioning, intersex, asexual or ally), which is now commonly used to draw attention to a range of possible identities. Undoubtedly, this inclusive conception of human gender and sexuality is much better equipped to describe our diversity of identities and attractions. From an anthropological linguistic point of view, Aikhenvald supports this perspective, noting "the multifaceted notion of gender pervades every aspect of life and of living. The way gender is articulated shapes the world of individuals, and of the societies they live in. But gender is not a unitary concept" (2012: 32). He suggests that gender has three "faces" (see Table 5.1). As you read about these "faces" you may recall some of the themes we explored in Chapter 4, on language.

Despite progressive human rights developments in many cultures, **heteronormativity**—which separates sexuality and gender into fixed, hierarchically defined categories based on strict definitions of "male"

sex The conventional biological distinction between male and female based on *morphological sex* (observable sex characteristics), *gonadal sex* (ovaries in females; testes in males), and chromosomal sex (XX or XY chromosomes).

gender roles Sets of behaviours that are commonly perceived as masculine or feminine within a specific culture.

gender The culturally constructed beliefs and behaviours considered appropriate for each sex.

sexuality An individual's sense of his or her own sexual desires, orientation, and preferences.

heteronormativity An ideology that promotes heterosexuality as the social ideal, supported by the cultural definition of "appropriate" behaviour based on culturally defined categories of "male" and "female," "masculine" and "feminine."

Table 5.1 The Three "Faces" of Gender

Natural gender/N-gender	Social gender/S-gender	Linguistic gender/L-gender
Until recently simply called "sex"—male versus female. A female is able to bear children, a male is not. N-gender entails anatomical and hormonal differences, linked to concomitant physiological and psychological traits.	The social implications of being a man or a woman (or perhaps something in between). In Simone de Beauvoir's adage, "One is not born a woman but becomes a woman" (1949: 267). In many traditional societies of New Guinea, social manhood is achieved, and defined, through male initiation (see, e.g., Schieffelin 1977: 121–8; Silverman 2001); social womanhood used to be achieved through female initiation (see, e.g., Roscoe 1995). S-gender relates to contrasting social roles of the sexes, and how these are embodied in cultural practices and public ritualized behaviour, including gender etiquette (in the spirit of Parker 1988), traditional knowledge, and social stereotypes.	The original sense of the term "gender." Nouns are divided into classes associated with different morphological marking. The class that includes most words referring to females is called "feminine"; similarly for males and "masculine." Gender classes are typically defined by their male and female members, but may extend beyond these. The ways in which animals, birds, insects, plants, and natural phenomena (such as thunder and wind) are assigned to genders may reflect roles in legend and reveal folk taxonomies (see Aikhenvald 2000, 2004, 2006; Corbett 1991; Dixon 1982).

Source: Aikhenvald 2012: 32–3.

and "female" and of "masculine" and "feminine"—persists. Many people today live in heteronormative cultures where we can find evidence of heteronormalizing boundaries in the differential use of public and private space, and in approved forms of dress.

Supporters of the heteronormative view often employ **naturalizing discourses** to reinforce their position (see, e.g., Sullivan-Blum 2006), with claims that presume what is *natural* can be meaningfully distinguished from what has been *culturally constructed*. Anthropologist Pamela L. Geller (2009) observes that this sort of confusion arises even in scientific research settings. She notes that many biological anthropologists, through their reliance on Western biomedical ideas about the human body, "unwittingly naturalize cultural values that are in fact modern constructs" (504). For example, the biomedical approach tends to see the male body as "standard" and the female body as notable primarily for its reproductive capabilities, a view that disempowers women. Further, it regards sex as "dichotomous, immutable, and interchangeable with gender" (505), clearly blurring the lines between what is "natural" and what is socially constructed.

Anthropologists, in their holistic approach, tend to view sexuality and gender in a context that includes local, national, and global views on sexuality and gender roles (see Boellstorff 2007). This is a refreshing development if we consider that "colonial-era

anthropologists tended to suppress, minimize, or exoticize evidence of [non-heterosexual] practices in conformity with colonial ideologies, practices, and prevailing debates around gender and sexuality in Europe and America" (Epprecht 2006:187).

Further, biological determiners of sex are not always obvious, and physical sex differences do not always help us to predict the roles that an individual will play in any particular society. For example, sometimes genetic or hormonal factors produce variations in sex characteristics (both internal and external) that blur the line between what we typically think of as "male" or "female." Individuals with these sorts of variations are often referred to as *intersex*. Steroid 5-alpha-reductase deficiency (5-ARD), a rare hormonal condition, is an example where genetic males are born with ambiguous genitalia and at puberty display male morphological changes. Cultural anthropologist Gilbert Herdt (1994) investigated 5-ARD in the Dominican Republic and New Guinea. In both places, the sexually anomalous individuals were assigned to a locally recognized third sex. This third sex was called *guevedoces* ("testicles at twelve") in the Dominican Republic and *kwolu-aatmwol* ("changing into a male thing") among the Sambia of New Guinea.

Also, we have records dating to late antiquity that show phenotypic differences were deliberately created in the case of eunuchs, whose testicles were removed or destroyed, often before puberty (Ringrose 1994). With the *hijras* of Gujarat, India, adult males deliberately cut off both penis and testicles in order to dedicate themselves to the mother goddess Bahuchara Mata (Nanda 1994) (Figure 5.10). In both cases, members of the wider society understand these third gender roles to be distinct from feminine and masculine gender roles.

Perhaps the most famous anthropological example of supernumerary sexes and genders without morphological sex anomalies is that of individuals called *berdache,* a contested appellation somewhat supplanted by the use of the term *two spirit*. Perhaps no single term is adequate; after all, two-spirited males have been described in almost 150 Indigenous North American societies, and two-spirited females in perhaps half that number. For a deeper understanding, see the work of Canadian anthropologist Goulet (1996), who discusses personhood and gender, arguing that "anthropologists have conceptualized gender variance among Native North Americans without paying attention to the ways in which Indigenous practices construct members of a community 'as' woman or 'as' man (or member of other gender category)" (683).

naturalizing discourses The deliberate representation of particular identities (e.g., caste, class, race, ethnicity, and nationality) as if they were a result of biology or nature rather than history or culture, making them appear eternal and unchanging.

Figure 5.10 Hijras celebrate the Urs festival near Kolkata, India. In hijra communities, third gender roles—distinct from traditional masculine and feminine gender roles—are considered appropriate for third-sex individuals. How can other cultures' ideas about sex and gender help us see our own culture's ideas about sex and gender in a new way?

© PACIFIC PRESS/Alamy Stock Photo

Cultural scholar Roscoe points out that the role can be marked by cross-dressing (1994). Individuals in such a role are accepted and respected members of their communities, and their economic and religious pursuits are frequently more culturally significant than their sexual practices:

> [T]he key features of male and female *ber-dache* roles were, in order of importance, *productive specialization* (crafts and domestic work for male berdaches, and warfare, hunting, and leadership roles for female berdaches), *supernatural sanction* (in the form of an authorization and/or bestowal of powers from extra-societal sources), and *gender variation* (in relation to normative cultural expectations for male and female genders). (332)

In Canada, sex and gender are now evident in public discourse although some Canadians still hold traditional views of the existence of only two sexes, each with its own gender role as both natural and obvious. Yet American historian Thomas Laqueur (1990) notes that the "two-sex model" took root only after the Renaissance. Prior to that, the bodies of all humans were of a "one-sex model" based on the Platonic notion that there was one ideal human form, male. In this the female was defined as lacking aspects of the ideal form.

Sexuality, Gender, and Identity

The range of sexual practices in the world is vast. It is vast even across our own continent, as suggested by the *Kinsey Reports* (1948 on males and 1953 on females) and more recently in various large-scale studies on sexuality. Contemporary anthropologists recognize that sexual activity is an essential part of social behaviour and that a desire for sex is a strong motivation in most individuals. As such, they have made observations on how sexual practices, as situated within the sexual norms of a culture, influence an individual's identity and social position.

Currently, one of the most productive fields of inquiry is the postmodern body of research called *queer theory*. Queer theory challenges and rejects "defined categories of male/female, man/woman, heterosexual/homosexual" (Hatzfeldt 2011). It avoids placing fixed boundaries around ideas of sexuality. If we return to the *Kinsey Reports* (Kinsey et al. 1948, 1953), we could note that these reports supported the conclusion that human sexuality exhibits a wide range of behaviours. And although the Kinsey Scale (Figure 5.11) assigned categories to sexual orientation, these categories were not seen to be impermeable. The scale actually "showed people did not fit into neat and exclusive heterosexual or homosexual categories" (Kinsey Institute 2014). Subsequently, other organizational systems, such as the Klein Sexual Orientation Grid (Figure 5.12) (Klein 1978) were devised.

Queer politics moves to facilitate change in our general ideas about sex, gender, sexuality, and social tendencies (Sullivan 2003: 81). The terminology for sexual orientation and sexual identity used today—for example, androphilia (sexual attraction to men/males), gynephilia (sexual attraction to women/females), pansexuality and polysexuality (sexual attraction to men/males and women/females), third

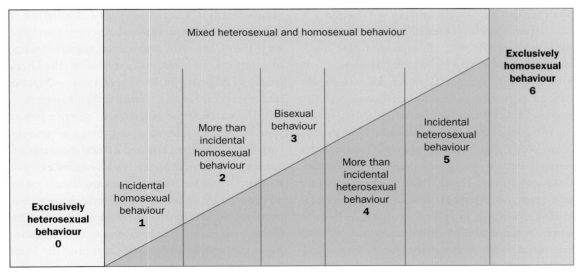

Figure 5.11 The Kinsey Scale, developed by pioneering sex researcher Alfred Kinsey and his colleagues in the late 1940s, attempts to describe a person's sexual orientation based on her or his behaviours.

Variable	Past	Present	Ideal
Sexual Attraction			
Sexual Behaviour			
Sexual Fantasies			
Emotional Preference			
Social Preference			
Self-Identification			
Heterosexual/Homosexual Lifestyle			

Please rate the first five variables in the above table according to the following scale:

1	2	3	4	5	6	7
Other sex only	Other sex mostly	Other sex somewhat more	Both sexes equally	Same sex some-what more	Same sex mostly	Same sex only

Please rate the final two variables in the above table according to the following scale:

1	2	3	4	5	6	7
Heterosexual only	Heterosexual mostly	Heterosexual somewhat more	Heterosexual/ homosexual equally	Homosexual somewhat more	Homosexual mostly	Homosexual only

Figure 5.12 The Klein Sexual Orientation Grid, developed by psychiatrist Fritz Klein in the late 1970s, attempts to "measure" a person's sexual orientation based on her or his thoughts and behaviours.

homosexuality The heteronormative opposite of heterosexuality; that is sexual relations involving two men or two women (i.e., same-sex sexuality).

gay An affirmative and empowering self-designation for individuals medically classified as homosexual, which became widespread over the course of the twentieth century.

lesbian A term used around the turn of the twentieth century to describe female same-sex sexuality; based on the name of the Greek island of Lesbos, the home of the female poet Sappho, who was reputed to love women rather than men.

bisexuality Sexual attraction to both males and females.

gender, two spirit—somewhat reflects the serious consideration of our sexual and gendered selves. But these terms are subject to change as we move to deeper and more nuanced interpretations of identity (or identities). As anthropologist Ana Mariella Bacigalupo comments, "selfhood is gendered dynamically by individual desire and competing cultural and religious norms" (2004: 440). We are challenged by conventional notions—the "rules" of "the norm"—to seek the experiential realities of our own identities.

In fact, historians of sexuality have demonstrated the recent introduction of heteronormative thinking, and heteronormative sexual classifications, in Euro-American societies. Consider, for example, the concept of heterosexuality and its routine opposite, homosexuality—that is, sexual relations involving two men or two women (i.e., same-sex sexuality). Many people assume that these terms identify stable forms of sexuality going back deep into the past, but this is not the case. David Halperin observes that the first appearance in print of the word *homosexuality* was in 1869, in German, in a pamphlet urging the German government not to criminalize "homosexual" relations between men; paradoxically, therefore, "'homosexuality' began life as a progay, politically activist coinage" (2014: 481). Before long, however, the term was appropriated by medical specialists called "sexologists," who

turned it into a clinical term designating a particular variety of sexual deviance. By the end of the nineteenth century, however, individuals classified as homosexual by the medical authorities began to use the term **gay** to refer to themselves, an affirmative and empowering self-designation that became widespread over the course of the twentieth century.

Although the term *gay* may be applied to any person who is sexually attracted to someone of the same sex, it is more commonly used in reference to gay men and the cultures and practices associated with them. The term **lesbian** did actually emerge in antiquity, but it originally referred to the Greek island of Lesbos, the home of the female poet Sappho, who was reputed to love women rather than men.

The standard use of *lesbian* to describe female same-sex sexuality, however, only began around the turn of the twentieth century. In fact, the terms *homosexuality*, *heterosexuality*, and **bisexuality** (that is, sexual attraction to both males and females) were all invented by Euro-American medical researchers in the late nineteenth and early twentieth centuries, and *heterosexuality* did not assume its current meaning as the opposite of *homosexuality* until the 1930s (see Halperin 2014: 458–61). The term **transgender** is even more recent, proposed in the 1960s in an attempt by medical researchers to clarify differences among individuals who, in one way or another, seemed dissatisfied with the sex and gender assignments they had received at birth.

Physicians now recognize *gender identity disorder* or *gender dysphoria* as a formal medical diagnosis, but many individuals who claim a transgender identity deny validity of this diagnosis, arguing that is based on heteronormative bias. Like individuals diagnosed as "homosexual" in earlier decades, many individuals diagnosed with gender dysphoria insist that their sexuality is not a medical condition to be treated but a valid form of gender variation that requires recognition and support.

In the 1990s, some persons whose gender identities or sexual practices fell outside the range defined by the "heterosexual–homosexual continuum" began to refer to themselves as **queer**, taking back as a badge of pride a term once used to insult non-heterosexuals.

Debates about how to distinguish and label proliferating varieties of sexuality are ongoing. For example, on 9 June 2015, following the highly publicized transition of former male Olympic athlete Bruce Jenner into a woman called Caitlyn, *The New York Times* published an article describing the difficulty of determining statistically the proportion of the US population who might be classified as transgender (Miller 2015) (Figure 5.13). Being able to quantify more accurately the proportion of transgender individuals in the US population would have wide-ranging biopolitical effects, for good or for ill: as Miller notes, "knowing more about this population is important for policymaking in health, education, criminal justice, social services, sports, the military, and more" (2015: A3). However, the US Census Bureau does not ask about gender identity, and many transgender persons hide their gender identity in order to avoid discrimination. At the same time, Miller also notes that "gender identity can be hard to define in a multiple-choice list. There are now more than 50 gender options on Facebook, for instance" (Miller 2015: A3). Similarly, a basic Internet search yields several definitions of *transgender*. In part, the struggle over terminology reflects the desire of some transgender persons to gain public recognition of an identity label of their own choice, as a claim to dignity; at the same time, the proliferation of labels reveals deep disagreements about what that identity might be.

Cross-Cultural Approaches to Sexuality

Many societies insist that a woman must be a virgin until she is married. In some Arab societies, a couple must produce bloodstained sheets the morning after

transgender A term proposed in the 1960s by medical researchers to classify individuals who, in one way or another, seemed dissatisfied with the sex and gender assignments they had received at birth.

queer A self-identification claimed by some persons whose gender identities or sexual practices fall outside the range defined by "the heterosexual–homosexual continuum."

© JStone/Shutterstock.com

Figure 5.13 Caitlyn Jenner promoting her autobiography. While she is a high-profile figure, many transgender persons hide their gender identity in order to avoid discrimination.

the consummation of their marriage to demonstrate that the bride was indeed a virgin. Other cultures take a relatively open approach to sexuality. For example, consider the Ju/'hoansi, of northeastern Namibia and the Northwest District of Botswana, who begin sexual activity at an early age (Lee 1992). As a result of this early sexual openness, the social and sexual constraints of marriage represent quite a shock at first, especially for young women. Some Ju/'hoansi are strictly faithful to one another, but a significant minority of both men and women take lovers. However, discretion is necessary when taking a lover because both husbands and wives can become very jealous and start fights. Sexual satisfaction is important to the Ju/'hoansi; female orgasm is known, and women expect both husbands and lovers to satisfy them sexually. Yet not all societies are as accepting of female expressions of sexuality. For the Mundurucu of the Brazilian Amazon, for example, female orgasm is more accidental than expected (Murphy and Murphy 1974).

Many cultures place taboos on certain types of sexual activity, and individuals are expected to respect these taboos. For example, anthropologist Karl Heider (1979) observed a strict postpartum sex taboo among the Dani, a people of highland New Guinea (see Map 5.3). For five years after the birth of a child, Dani parents do not have sexual intercourse with each other. While such taboos are found in all cultures, they generally last for only a few weeks to months. (In North America, people say that the mother needs time to heal; other societies have other justifications.) Yet to most Westerners, the Dani's five-year wait would seem to be exceptional. What could explain this difference in opinion? Heider points out that Westerners assume that the sex drive is perhaps the most powerful biological drive of all; the Dani do not share this assumption. The Dani are not celibate, yet they do not seem very interested in sex (78–81). It seems that the Dani represent an extreme in the cultural construction of sexuality.

Not all sexual practices map onto the Western heterosexual model. Indeed, the fact that people in almost every society have developed complex ideological and ritual structures to encourage heterosexual practices, ostensibly to promote procreation, suggests that human sexual expression would resist such confinement if it were not under strict and sometimes life-threatening control. Anthropological information about supernumerary sexes and genders undermines the "two-sex model" that is dominant in Euro-American cultures. Anthropologists Evelyn Blackwood and Saskia Wieringa (1999) have similarly undermined Western heterosexual assumptions in their exploration of how culture shapes female desires. These researchers concluded that focusing on the ways that female bodies are assigned cultural meanings in different historical and ethnographic settings, and on how those meanings affect the way that females constitute their relations with other females, reveals a wide range of "varied and rich cultural identities and same-sex practices between those with female bodies" (1999: ix). Significantly, they note that this sort of research does not assume that having a male body or a female body necessarily determines any individual's traits, feelings, or experiences (x). As a result, this research provides a vital comparative context that can illuminate our understanding of sexual practices that Euro-Americans term, perhaps from an ethnocentric perspective, *homosexuality* and *bisexuality*.

Consider the Nicaraguan concept of *cochónes* within the greater social construct of *machismo* (aggressive masculinity). As anthropologist Roger Lancaster learned while he was doing fieldwork in Nicaragua in the 1980s, working-class Nicaraguans admire *machistas*—"real men"—who are active, violent, and dominant. They see the penis as a weapon that can dominate a sexual partner—male or female—who is thereby rendered passive, abused, and subordinate. A "passive" male who allows a "manly man" to have sexual intercourse with him is called a *cochón*. The identity and social position of a *cochón* differs greatly from that of a man who is perceived as sexually dominant. While the "passive" *cochón* is stigmatized, the male who takes the "active" role in sexual intercourse with other males and with females is seen as "normal." These distinctions pervade social interactions, as public challenges for dominance are a constant of male–male interaction in Nicaragua, even when sexual intercourse is not involved. *Cochón* may be used as an epithet not only for a man who yields publicly to another man but also for cats that don't catch mice or indeed anything that somehow fails to perform its proper function. As Lancaster notes, *cochónes* are made, not born:

> Those who consistently lose out in the competition for male status . . . discover pleasure in the passive sexual role or its social status: these men are made into *cochónes*. And those who master the rules of conventional masculinity . . . are made into *machistas*. (1992: 249)

The position of the *cochón* is thus a social construct.

A more recent example is the work of Afsaneh Najmabadi, who returned to Iran to carry out ethnographic fieldwork after being intrigued by a burst of attention in the Iranian and international press in 2003 concerning what was being called "the 'trans' phenomenon" (2014: 1). Najmabadi knew that in the decade prior to the 1979 revolution, Iranian physicians had become involved in hormonal and surgical treatments for persons wishing to change their sex.

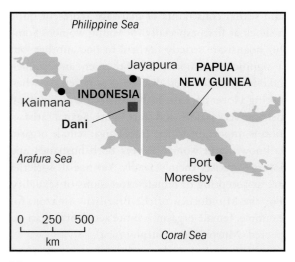

Map 5.3 Dani

By 2003, however, journalists seemed both surprised and puzzled that this sort of "progressive" treatment could be possible in an Islamic state, the same state that had ruled same-sex sexual relations to be illegal, often equating them with "sodomy," which was punished with the death penalty (2014: 1).

Najmabadi discovered that the distinctions between sex, gender, and sexuality, developed by Western scholars, did not easily map onto Iranian categories: most Iranians she spoke to did not recognize a distinction between sex and gender, and most also presumed a more or less direct causal link between an individual's sex/gender and the focus of her or his sexual desire: "The indistinction between gender/sex/sexuality . . . regularly disrupts attempts to separate the homosexual from the trans, even as that distinction is regularly invoked" (2014: 8). Iranians had also developed their own version of heteronormativity as a consequence of the "modernization" of Iranian family life: even Muslim theologians she spoke with seemed to take the existence of a heteronormative gender binary for granted (2014: 91). However, Iranian historical and cultural attitudes toward sex/gender/sexuality meant that the status of "trans" persons in contemporary Iranian society did not easily map onto "trans" identities recognized in the West. In Iran, she found that physicians linked "trans" identity with that of "intersex," which itself was associated historically with the category of "hermaphrodite" recognized in Islamic law. Just like infants born with ambiguous external genitalia, therefore, persons who believed that their inner soul or psyche was mismatched with their outer anatomy were considered to be entitled to hormonal and surgical interventions that would "clarify" their "true" sex/gender. This conclusion had been proclaimed lawful in a *fatwa* (or Islamic religious opinion) first issued in the 1960s by Ayatollah Khomeini, leader of the Islamic Revolution in Iran and the highest-ranking Shi'a Muslim religious authority in recent Iranian history, whose authority remains unchallenged (2014; see Chapter 5).

Najmabadi undertook participant-observation in order to learn exactly how trans activists engaged psychological, medical, religious, and governmental authorities on an everyday basis; she also interviewed key figures in these different institutions. Although she expected to encounter rigid attitudes in officials, especially religious authorities, she describes herself as surprised and humbled by how many of them were not interested in denouncing sexual nonconformity, but who in their own ways were working to find human solutions for affected individuals. The religious endorsement of treatment for "gender dysphoria" has made it possible for Muslim clerics, psychologists, physicians, and government bureaucrats to find some common ground, but it had taken the determined lobbying efforts of trans activists to persuade these officials to make needed changes.

At first Najmabadi was surprised when trans activists told her that they did not want to "politicize" their cause. What they meant, she found, was that they did not want to turn their activism into a human rights issue that would involve the Iranian parliament passing legislation. Rather, they wanted to make sure that civil servants and others knew who they were and would continue to work with them, regardless of which political faction was in power. Their activism was intended to gain official awareness of the "needs" of trans people; to remove a series of medical, legal, and religious barriers; and to get support and protection from harassment in order to make "livable lives" for themselves (2014: 12). By such methods, trans activists eventually gained official recognition as members of a "vulnerable" population deserving of state protection (2014: 214). Nevertheless, to become entitled to such protection, they had to pass a series of medical, psychological, and legal examinations designed to prove that they were indeed what they said they were. Once they obtained official certification as trans, they could have their name and sex/gender changed on their national identity papers, complete their sex change treatments, and, if they wished, disappear into the Iranian population.

The high barrier to gaining formal trans certification in Iran points to another difference between Western and Iranian notions about sex, gender, and sexuality. The "filtering" process leading to trans certification was so intense because Iranian authorities wanted to make sure that the applicants they certified were *genuinely* "trans;" put another way, their goal was to *detect and exclude* candidates for trans status who did *not* experience "gender dysphoria" but who, in their view, were trying to mask their sexual attraction to members of their own sex/gender. Indeed, male-to-female trans persons in Iran were constantly suspected of trying to use sex change to hide what was interpreted as their shameful desire to be the passive male partner in sexual relations between males. Nevertheless, Najmabadi "never saw the commission exercise the option of turning down an application altogether . . . there seemed to be a general attitude . . . that . . . it was their job to find a socially acceptable 'solution for the problem'" (2014: 8).

As noted, relationships between couples whom a Western perspective might classify as "gay" or "lesbian" are condemned as immoral and illegal in Iran; such "same-sex players" (as they are called in Persian) are forced to keep their relationships hidden from family and society, which causes them considerable hardship, especially when faced with what Najmabadi calls the Iranian *marriage imperative:* "The adulthood of everyone is bound to marriage. It is almost incomprehensible that someone would wish to not marry" (2014: 124). The pressure of the marriage imperative sometimes led non-heteronormative Iranians, who usually described themselves as "gay" or "lesbian," to wonder if they might be "trans" and ought to consider changing sex. Such thoughts were often prompted by their partners, who wanted to regularize their relationship, and who might threaten to leave them if they did not agree to undergo sex change. Indeed, Najmabadi found attitudes amounting to homophobia among some non-heteronormative couples who insisted that they were not "same-sex players," and who strove to interpret their relationships with their partners in ways that did not violate hegemonic Iranian understandings of sex/gender/sexuality (2014: 248).

At the same time, some persons who obtained trans certification did not always go on to complete their transition. This might be because they could not afford to pay for the surgery right away. But it might also be because, even though they believed that they truly were trans, they also knew that their families and neighbours would never accept them as such. One post-operative male-to-female trans person she knew "still lives as a man at home; it is very critical for her to remain a man with her family and in the neighbourhood everyone knew her as a man.... When she is at her boyfriend's house, she explains, she goes into female clothes" (2014: 281). Najmabadi concluded that

> [w]hat seemed to matter for trans subjecthood was articulated in terms of figuring out how to live livable lives—with families, with partners, in terms of employment, of getting medical and legal changes they wanted, and of what made them comfortable in different spaces of life . . . living livable lives, for some, called for flexibility and the ability to switch back and forth when necessary. (2014: 286)

These examples reveal that the physical activity referred to as *sexual intercourse* is not just doing what comes naturally and that Western notions of sex, gender, and sexuality are not always transferable across cultures. Like many things in human life, sex does not speak for itself nor does it have only one meaning. Sexual practices can be used to give concrete form to more abstract notions we have about the place of men and women in the world. They may serve as a metaphor for expressing differential power within a society. That is, sexual practices can be used as an excuse to enact, in unmistakable physical terms, the reality of differential power. Anthropologists must remember that sexual practices never occur in a vacuum. They are entrenched in other social practices, such as food production, political organization, legal protection, and kinship, all of which act to shape who people are, how they see themselves, and how they are perceived by others.

Individual Psychology and Context

Cross-cultural studies of human psychological functioning all stress the vital importance of *context*—not just the immediate context but also the displaced context of culture and history that may be invisible in local settings but present in people's habits of thought and feeling. Sometimes researchers can identify contextual factors with little effort. When administering a psychological test on visual illusions to the Fang in Gabon, for example, anthropologist James Fernandez (1980) discovered that many questioned his explanation of the "real" reason behind such a bizarre activity as psychological testing. He deduced that years of colonial domination and exploitation at the hands of outsiders made these people suspicious of his research motives.

Contextual factors shape human experiences in subtle ways, contributing to nuanced, holistic ethnographic understandings of other ways of making meaning. An excellent description of this kind of holistic experience is given by anthropologist Michael Gilsenan (1982), who worked for a time among urban Muslims in Cairo, Egypt (see Map 5.4). He spent many hours with his informants, observing their prayers in the local mosque. Along the inside wall of the mosque were verses from the Quran shaped out of bright green neon tubing. Green is the colour of the prophet Muhammad, so finding that colour used prominently in mosque decoration is not surprising. However, Gilsenan's experiences in Western culture did not include schemas in which neon lights and serious worship went together, and for several months the neon interfered with his attempts to assume a properly reverential attitude. Then one day, Gilsenan reports, "I turned unthinkingly away from the swaying bodies and the rhythms of the remembrance of God and saw, not neon, but simply

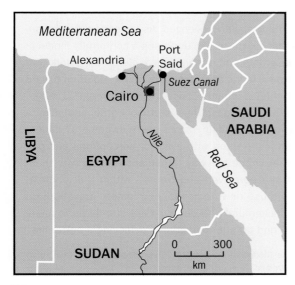

Map 5.4 Cairo

greenness.... No gaps existed between colour, shape, light, and form. From that unreflecting and unsuspecting moment, I ceased to see neon at all" (1982: 266).

Nothing had happened to Gilsenan's eyes or his other senses, which continued to receive the same signals they had always received, but the meaning of the signals had been altered. The experience in the mosque situated neon light within a new schema, and his growing familiarity with that schema made the neon seem more and more natural. Eventually, Gilsenan was noticing only the colour green. He was still able to report, of course, that the green light was produced by green neon tubing; however, that fact seemed irrelevant given the new schema he used to interpret his experience.

These sorts of transformations of perception and understanding remain mysterious, but they seem to occur whenever we have an insight of any kind. Insights, like good metaphors, reshape the world for us, throwing new aspects into sharp focus and casting other aspects into the background. Our ability to achieve insights, like our ability to create good metaphors, remains a central and highly mysterious aspect of human psychological processes.

Living Anthropology

The Invisible Culture

by Alphonse Ndem Ahola, PhD Student, Anthropology, University of Alberta

Travellers' attention seems to be caught much more by differences than similarities. In normal circumstances, travellers notice new things, learn new ways, and meet new people. When Clifford James (1997) talks about travel and translation, he describes a world that reveals itself en route: in the airports, marketplaces and museums. Edmonton's Servus Heritage Festival is one of these places where being en route is like being in a wonderworld. The colourful and diverse cultural performances visitors enjoy are remarkable.

The first time I visited the Heritage Festival, I contemplated cultural performances from all around the world. Pondering the richness and the beauty of these exhibitions, it came to me suddenly that I had not stood in front of the Canadian tent. Despite a large variety of cultural performances, one could witness, something was missing. I remember noticing the Canadian flag waving on top of all the tents I visited. Yet, there was not a Canadian tent. As a newcomer, I wrestled with the question "What does it mean to be Canadian?" All the performances at the Heritage Festival, except for the First Nations, appeared to be from foreign countries, and the question of what Canadian culture looks like remained

unanswered. What I had anticipated Canadian culture to be, on coming to Canada, did not have a stage at the Heritage Festival; it was missing altogether and therefore invisible. Why on such an occasion does Canada not perform any act of self-presentation? Goffman studied social interaction and focused on the presentation of self in everyday life (Goffman 1973). Goffman's perspective can be broadened to apply to Canada. In fact, Canada presents itself in many documents, targeting skilled immigrants all over the world. Why is it that these extensive campaigns advertising the country's features abroad have no replica inside the country?

Here lies the problem surrounding the understanding of culture. Mainstream Canadians do not see themselves as having a "culture." The notion of culture in this context refers to those picturesque things that are part of one's ethnic group, such as food, clothing, and dance, as opposed to less materially identifiable attitudes and social relationships that affect how one engages with society. This makes Canadian multiculturalism misleading because it suggests that all cultural backgrounds are welcome and celebrated in Canada when in fact this is not the case. The dilemma for newcomers is to determine to what extent and how

Continued

to maintain ethnically specific behavioural standards and to what extent and how to conform to Canadian standards.

Canada's multicultural system tells newcomers that their culture is something to be proud of and contributes to Canada's valuable cultural diversity, to the point that festivals like Servus Heritage Festival are devoted to displaying such cultures. Nevertheless, these same newcomers become aware that they have no choice but to comply with policies related to important aspects of their life, such as their relations with their spouse and children (Himani 2000). While trying to abide by these policies, they feel they are bound to give up valuable aspects of their individual and family life. They are forced by compelling experiences to negotiate multiple identities and relations.[1] They might not be aware of cultural challenges on coming to Canada because their priorities are finding a job and making money. However, they will soon realize that cultural challenges are as compelling

as economic and financial challenges. As Li points out, "the analysis shows that the discourse endorses a conformity model in assessing immigrants and a monolithic cultural framework that preaches tolerance in the abstract but remains intolerant toward cultural specificities deemed outside the mainstream" (1998).

The narrative around cultures is ethnocentric, assuming a clear superiority of Canadian values over newcomers' values. Newcomers are confronted with a set of perceptions and categorizations that shape the way Canadians engage with them and how they are perceived and treated within that context. In adjusting to these new demands, newcomers draw both on their cultural background and on dominant standards to maintain family ties and pursue their goal of achieving a better life.

1. See for instance Theophilus Ejorh, 2012, "The African Diasporic Community in Contemporary Ireland: Intersection of Ascriptive and Circumstantial Identities," in Ethnicities 12, 1: 67–85.

Key Terms

agency 111
articulated style 103
bisexuality 116
cognition 102
cognitive style 103
cultural persona 112
cultural synaesthesia 98
elementary cognitive processes 103
emotion 106
enculturation 108
functional cognitive systems 103
gay 116
gender 113
gender roles 113

global style 103
heteronormativity 113
homosexuality 116
lesbian 116
motivation 108
naturalizing discourses 114
norms 111
perception 98
personality 110
prototypes 98
queer 117
reasoning style 106
schemas 98
self 110

sex 113
sexuality 113
socialization 108
subject position 111
subjectivity 111
syllogism 105
syllogistic reasoning 105
taxonomies 103
thinking 105
transgender 117
values 111
visuality 101
zone of proximal development (ZPD) 110

Chapter Summary

1. Psychological anthropology can be grouped into four basic areas of human experience: perception, cognition, emotion, and motivation. Research overwhelmingly sustains the view that human psychological processes are open to a wide variety of influences.
2. Human psychological perception always takes place in a cultural context. Alternative understandings of a situation are possible because of the ambiguity of many perceptual signals. Both looking and seeing are culturally learned modes of sensory perception.
3. Some anthropologists argue that people in different cultures have different cognitive styles that range from global (field dependent) to articulated (field independent).

Research suggests that the same individual may use a global style for some tasks and an articulated style for others.
4. Our emotions, like our thoughts, are culturally constructed. Different cultures conceptualize emotions differently. For this reason, it is often difficult to translate the language of emotion from one culture to another.
5. The mainsprings of motivation develop through socialization and enculturation. Humans must learn to pattern and adapt behaviour and ways of thinking and feeling to the standards considered appropriate in their respective cultures. Cognitive development results from a dialogue with others and the coaching received from others.

6. The forming of self and persona is discussed and situated in the context of values and norms.
7. Different cultures conceptualize sex roles and gender roles differently. These roles greatly influence how individuals see themselves, how they define their place with a social group, and how they are perceived by others. Individuals' sexual practices vary greatly—both within a single culture and between different cultures.

Critical Thinking Questions

1. Human psychology, like language, is an open system. How can the design features of language, in particular *displacement* and *prevarication,* help us to better understand human psychology?
2. Why is it sometimes difficult for individuals from different cultures to discuss specific emotions? Which aspects of emotion seem universal to the human experience? Which are defined by the culture in which a person lives?
3. How would you distinguish among sex, gender, and sexuality? How is gender culturally defined? What role do legislative decisions play in defining the boundaries of what the general population perceives as "normal" sexual behaviour?
4. In what ways have your cultural experiences shaped your sense of identity? Do you share a similar world view to that of your peers from similar backgrounds? Does your world view differ from theirs in any major ways?

Suggested Readings

Berlin, Brent, and David G. Casagrande. 2000. "Cognitive Prototypes in Tzeltal Maya Medicinal Plant Selection," available at http://gravlee.org/ang5091/proposals/casagrande_nsf.pdf. This article, an example of applied anthropology, discusses bridging the gap between traditional medicinal plant knowledge and Western biomedical knowledge, an important example of coming to understand taxonomies.

Bock, Philip K. 1999. *Rethinking Psychological Anthropology: Continuity and Change in the Study of Human Action*, 2nd edn (Prospect Heights, IL: Waveland Press). A thorough introduction to psychological anthropology, tracing developments from the early twentieth century to current directions in the field.

Cole, Michael, and Sylvia Scribner. 1974. *Culture and Thought: A Psychological Introduction* (New York: Wiley). A clear, readable survey of the literature and case studies on the cultural shaping of cognition.

D'Andrade, Roy G. 1995. *The Development of Cognitive Anthropology* (Cambridge: Cambridge University Press). An interesting and comprehensive review of the early application of theories of cognition. Chapter 5, which is on folk taxonomies, gives insight into shared salient cognitive features; of particular use here are the early studies of ethnobotany and ethnozoology.

Dods, Roberta Robin. 2004. "Knowing Ways/Ways of Knowing: Reconciling Science and Tradition," *World Archaeology* **36, 4: 547–57.** This paper distinguishes two ways of knowing, traditional and scientific, suggesting their compatibility and utility for the development of a wider perspective in both anthropology and archaeology.

Harland, Robert, and Gerard Hutchinson. 2004. "Phenomenology, Science, and the Anthropology of the Self: A New Model for the Aetiology of Psychosis," *British Journal of Psychiatry* **185: 361–2,** available at http://bjp.rcpsych.org/cgi/content/full/185/5/361. An examination of the links between psychoses, such as schizophrenia, and socioenvironmental factors.

Jansen, Willy. 1987. *Women without Men: Gender and Marginality in an Algerian Town* (The Netherlands: E.J. Brill). An excellent examination of the lives of North African women, with deep comment on gender roles and social restrictions.

Lyons, Andrew P., and Harriet D. Lyons. 2006. "The New Anthropology of Sexuality," *Anthropologica* **48, 2: 153–7.** A good review of the history of anthropological studies of sexuality and a discussion of current work.

Schwartz, Theodore, Geoffrey M. White, and Catherine A. Lutz, eds. 1992. *New Directions in Psychological Anthropology* (Cambridge: Cambridge University Press). A survey of psychological anthropology, with articles by experts in the fields of cognition, human development, bio-psychological studies, and psychiatric and psychoanalytic anthropology.

Related Websites

Department of Anthropology, University of Alabama: Anthropological Theories (Cognitive Anthropology)
http://anthropology.ua.edu/cultures/cultures.php
Encyclopedia.com: Culture and Personality School
www.encyclopedia.com/doc/1088-CultureandPersonality Schl.html

American Psychological Association: Definition of Terms: *Sex, Gender, Gender Identity, Sexual Orientation*
www.apa.org/pi/lgbt/resources/sexuality-definitions.pdf
AllPsych: Optical Illusions
http://allpsych.com/opticalillusions/index.html

6 Inequality in the Contemporary World: Class, Caste, Race, Ethnicity, and Nationality

Chapter Outline

Class

Caste

Race

Ethnicity

Nation and Nationalism

Learning Objectives

By the end of Chapter 6, you will be able to

- identify aspects of social stratification resulting in class and caste structures;
- consider and challenge various concepts of race, ethnicity, and nationalism; and

- discuss how issues of inequality relate to nationalism.

While anthropologists have documented some distinctive forms of social organization that are relatively egalitarian, in today's increasingly globalized world they most often find **stratified societies**. In stratified societies, higher-ranking groups have a disproportionate access to wealth, power, and prestige. At times, stratification is minimal—for example, in societies that anthropologists call *chiefdoms* (see Chapter 3), the chief may be the only person with a permanently superior status while social and economic relations among other members of the group may remain relatively egalitarian. More elaborate social stratification is found in societies classified as *states*, which not only are much larger than chiefdoms but also employ a variety of mechanisms to bind different subgroups together into a hierarchy that regulates each group's access to wealth, power, and prestige.

All people in the world today, including the stateless and refugees, must deal with the authority of one or many nation-states or even transnational authorities. All nation-states are socially stratified and this holds true for many transnational supra-state bureaucracies as well. But the inequality that exists in any given nation-state may be constructed out of multiple categories arranged in different hierarchies of stratification. In this chapter we confine our discussion to five categories of inequality but stress that other topics, such as sexism and ageism, would also apply. The five categories we will focus on are as follows:

1. **Class**
2. **Caste**
3. **Race**
4. **Ethnicity**
5. **Nationality**

Note that *every one* of these categories is a cultural invention designed to create boundaries around one imagined community or another. *None* of these categories maps onto permanent biological subdivisions within the human species, although members of societies that employ these categories often will invoke "nature" to support their legitimacy.

Some patterns of inequality appear to reach back through deep historic time while others seem to have gained currency far more recently and are closely associated with the spread of colonialism and capitalism.

In many cases, capitalist and colonialist forces introduced new forms of stratification to formerly independent, egalitarian societies; in others, these forces reshaped forms of stratification that predated European contact. Social scientists have argued with one another about how the categories of inequality should be defined, and they have asked whether these categories can be usefully applied cross-culturally. We will look at some of their arguments.

Class

In general, classes are hierarchically arranged social groups defined on economic grounds. That is, members of higher-ranked social classes have disproportionate access to resources and sources of wealth, whereas members of lower-ranked classes have much more limited access to wealth and most resources (Figure 6.1).

Figure 6.1 Social classes often live within easy sight of one another. Here, luxury apartments and squatter settlements rub shoulders in Caracas, Venezuela. Where in your own life do you see social classes coming together?

stratified societies Societies in which there is a permanent hierarchy that accords some members privileged access to wealth, power, and prestige.

class A ranked group within a hierarchically stratified society whose membership is defined primarily in terms of wealth, occupation, and/or access to power.

caste A ranked group within a socially stratified society that is closed, prohibiting individuals from moving from one caste into another.

race A broad human population category that allegedly corresponds to distinct, heritable sets of biological attributes and often conflates geographic ancestry and physical type.

ethnicity A social classification based on a common cultural heritage and selected cultural features, such as language, religion, or dress.

nationality A sense of identification with and loyalty to a nation-state; membership, defined by citizenship, in a geopolitical sovereign state.

A Roma woman begs for money on a street in Dublin, Ireland. People like the Roma who face widespread discrimination tend to be forced to the margins of society, where they have little access to wealth, power, or prestige.

The concept of class has a double heritage in modern anthropology, one stemming from Europe, the other from North America. European social scientists lived in states with a long history of social-class divisions, reaching back to ancient times. In their experience, entrenched social classes were relatively closed groups. Ideas of progress were articulated during the Enlightenment, and the French Revolution and the Industrial Revolution promised to end the oppressive privileges of the ruling class and to equalize everyone's access to wealth. However, class divisions did not wither away in Europe during the nineteenth century; they just changed their contours. Karl Marx and, subsequently, his adherents judged that feudal aristocrats had been replaced by bourgeois capitalists. The lowest level in European societies—rural peasants—were partially displaced as well with the appearance of the urban working class. Many of the displaced rural and urban poor were shipped to the emerging overseas European colonial holdings. For Canadians, the two European powers that effectively carved up the northern half of North America were the British and the French. Initially, the barriers separating those at the top of the class hierarchy from those at the bottom seemed just as rigid as ever. However, the "New World" did provide a sense that class mobility was a possibility, however remote.

Significantly, Marx defines classes in terms of their members' different relations to the means of production. As long as a particular set of unequal productive relations flourishes in a society, the classes defined by these unequal roles will also persist. The French Revolution had triggered the displacement of aristocrats and peasants, who had played the key roles in European feudalism, only to replace them with new key classes—industrial entrepreneurs and the industrial working class—that were linked together within the capitalist mode of production. In time, Marx predicted, these industrial workers would become the new "leading class," rising up to oust capitalists when the socialist revolution came.

As Marx was well aware, all those who are linked to the means of production in the same way (e.g., as workers) do not often recognize what they have in common and may therefore fail to develop the kind of solidarity—the "class consciousness"—that could, in Marx's view, lead to revolution. Indeed, the possibility of peasant- or working-class solidarity in many of the stratified societies studied by anthropologists is actively undercut by institutions of **clientage**, which describes relationships between individuals—**patrons** and **clients**—rather than

groups. Stratified societies united by links of clientage can be very stable. Low-status clients believe their security depends on finding a high-status individual who can protect them. (For example, see discussion of *compadrazgo* relationships in Chapter 7.)

Marx's view of class is clearly different from the traditional view of class in North America. As mentioned, North Americans have long assumed that individuals may pursue wealth, power, and prestige unhampered by the unyielding class barriers characteristic of "Old World" societies. This assumption is the basis for what is commonly referred to as the "American Dream," but this "dream" of equal opportunity for upward class mobility has more than a little currency here in Canada as well. As a result, many social scientists trained in North America have tended to define social classes primarily in terms of income level and to argue that such social classes are open, porous, and permeable rather than rigid and exclusionary. Yet the promise of equal opportunity for upward class mobility has not been fully realized.

In the early twentieth century, social scientists began to investigate "race" as a limiting factor to class mobility in North America. In the United States, black and white social scientists concluded that an unyielding "colour bar" prevented upward class mobility. First applied to citizens with African ancestry, the analysis could also be extended to Indigenous peoples and other non-white racial groups. One participant in these early studies, an anthropologist named W. Lloyd Warner (1936), argued that the colour bar looked more like the rigid barrier reported to exist between castes in India than the supposedly permeable boundary separating social classes. In Warner's interpretation, membership in a caste is ascribed at birth, and individuals are not allowed to move from one caste into another. While membership in a social class is also ascribed at birth, individual social mobility between classes is possible. Warner's distinction between *caste* and *class* became standard for decades in North American cultural anthropology.

Is this a plausible contrast? The aspect of caste that impressed Warner was the reported rigidity of the barrier between castes, which seemed much like the barrier separating blacks and whites in the racially divided United States. But in 1948, a black Trinidadian American sociologist named Oliver Cromwell Cox rejected an equation between caste and race. Cox pointed out that many authorities on caste in India claimed that Hindu castes were harmoniously integrated within a *caste system* shaped by Hindu religious beliefs about purity and pollution. Most

clientage Institution linking individuals from upper and lower levels in a stratified society.

patron The party of higher status in a clientage.

client The party of lower status in a clientage.

importantly, it appeared that members of low-ranked "impure" castes did not challenge the caste system even though it oppressed them. If this were true, Cox concluded, caste relations were *unlike* race relations in the United States, and by extension Canada, because whites had imposed the colour bar and only by force had they been able to repress black resistance to this injustice. Social scientist Ursula Sharma (1999) points out, however, that both Warner and Cox were relying on an understanding of Hindu castes that, today, is considered highly misleading. Indeed, more recently, both *race* and *caste* have been considered as metaphorical constructs that have been employed to various ends in sociopolitical struggles (Reddy 2005).

Caste

The word *caste* comes from the Portuguese word *casta*, meaning "chaste." Portuguese explorers applied the term to the stratification systems they encountered in South Asia in the sixteenth century. They understood that these societies were divided into a hierarchy of ranked subgroups, each of which was "chaste" in the sense that sexual and marital links across group boundaries were forbidden. It should also be noted that differences can manifest themselves within a caste as well, particularly in terms of relative wealth. Most Western scholars have taken the stratification system of India as the prototype of caste stratification, and some insist that caste cannot properly be said to exist outside India. Others, however, do find value in applying the term to forms of social stratification, developed elsewhere, that bear a certain resemblance to the Indian pattern.

Caste in India

The term *caste*, as most Western observers use it, collapses two different South Asian concepts:

1. **Varna**, which refers to the widespread notion that Indian society is ideally divided into four functional subdivisions: priests, nobility (rulers and warriors), commoners (farmers and merchants), and labourers or servants
2. **Jāti**, which refers to localized, named, endogamous groups

Although *jāti* names are frequently the names of occupations (e.g., farmer, saltmaker), there is no conventional way to group the many local *jātis* within one of the four varnas, which is why *jāti* members

can disagree with others about where their own *jāti* ought to belong. In any case, varna divisions are more theoretical in nature, whereas *jāti* divisions are more significant in most of the local village settings where anthropologists have traditionally conducted fieldwork.

Villagers in the southern Indian town of Gopalpur (see Map 6.1) defined a *jāti* for anthropologist Alan Beals while he was working among them in the 1950s. They described it as "a category of men thought to be related, to occupy a particular position within a hierarchy of jātis, to marry among themselves, and to follow particular practices and occupations" (Beals 1962: 25). They also compared the relationship between *jātis* of different rank to the relationship between brothers. Ideally, they said, members of low-ranking *jātis* respect and obey members of high-ranking *jātis*, just as younger brothers respect and obey older brothers. The villagers were aware of at least 50 different *jātis*, although not all were represented in their village. Because *jātis* have different occupational specialties that they alone can perform, these villagers were sometimes dependent on the services of outsiders. It is often in the context of ritual that *jāti* interdependence is most clear:

> To arrange a marriage, to set up the doorway of a new house, to stage a drama, or to hold an entertainment, the householder must call on a wide range of jātis. The entertainment of even a modest number of guests requires the presence of the Singer. The Potter must provide new pots in which to cook the food; the Boin from the Farmer

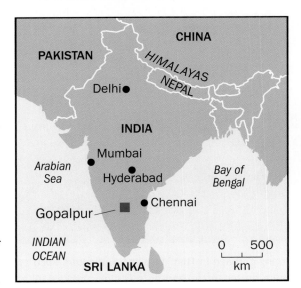

Map 6.1 Gopalpur

varna Traditional social ranks that divide Indian society into four functional subdivisions: priests, nobility (rulers and warriors), commoners (farmers and merchants), and labourers or servants.

jāti A localized, named, endogamous group.

jāti must carry the pot; the Shepherd must sacrifice the goat; the Crier, a Saltmaker, must invite the guests. To survive, one requires the co-operation of only a few *jātis*; to enjoy life and do things in the proper manner requires the co-operation of many. (Beals 1962: 41)

Traditionally, food taboos have a ritual significance that affects interactions between members of different *jātis*. In Hindu belief, certain foods and occupations are classed as pure and others as polluting. And, in theory, all *jātis* are ranked on a scale from purest to most polluted. Highest are the vegetarian Brahmins (priests), who are pure enough to approach the gods. Carpenters and blacksmiths, who also eat a vegetarian diet, are also assigned a high rank. Below the vegetarians are those who eat "clean," or "pure," meat, such as sheep, goats, chicken, and fish but not pork or beef (e.g., saltmakers, farmers, and shepherds). The lowest-ranking and "unclean" are meat-eaters who eat pork as well as beef (e.g., leatherworkers). Occupations that involve slaughtering animals or touching polluted things are themselves polluting (Figure 6.2). Hindu dietary rules also deal with the circumstances in which members of one *jāti* may accept food prepared by members of another. Members of a lower-ranking *jāti* may accept any food prepared by members of a higher-ranking *jāti*. Members of a higher-ranking *jāti*, however, may accept only certain foods prepared by a lower-ranking *jāti*.

In addition, members of different *jātis* should not eat together. In practice, these rules may not be as confining as they appear since "eating together" means "eating from the same dish or sitting on the same line" (Beals 1962: 41); generally, strict observance of the rules is saved for ceremonial occasions.

Certain non-Hindus could be loosely incorporated into the *jāti* system. In Gopalpur, Muslims, for example, were given a place based on the characteristics locals attributed to them as a group. Muslims had long held political power in parts of India (see the emerging states of Pakistan and subsequently Bangladesh after Indian independence in 1947), so political powerfulness was considered to be an important attribute of Muslim identity. In addition, Muslims do not eat pork or the meat of animals that have not been ritually slaughtered. Such characteristics allowed Muslims to be ranked above those who ate pork. However, they were still considered to be eaters of unclean meat as consumers of beef.

There is no direct correlation between the status of a *jāti* on the scale of purity and pollution and the class status of members of that *jāti*. For example, the high status of Brahmins meant that "there are a relatively large number of ways in which a poor Brahmin may become wealthy" (Beals 1962: 37). Similarly, members of low-status *jātis* may find their attempts to amass wealth curtailed by the opposition of their status superiors. A person who wishes to advance economically "must be prepared to defend his gains against jealous neighbours. Anyone who buys land is limiting his neighbour's opportunities to buy land. Most people safeguard themselves by tying themselves through indebtedness to a powerful landlord who will give them support when difficulties are encountered" (39).

Aspects of Beals's study of caste relations that remain particularly relevant to our understanding of caste in India include firstly the fact that *jāti* membership mattered most on ritual occasions. But in recent years many village rituals that were once associated with caste have become less widely practised, mostly due to the increasing numbers of Indians that have moved to large cities, where they are surrounded by strangers whose caste membership they do not know (Sharma 1999: 37). City dwellers still use the idiom of purity and pollution in debates on castes and status although rituals are not the main theme.

Second, Beals described members of middle-ranking *jātis* who treated one another as equals outside of ritual contexts. Political scientist Subrata Mitra points out that "by the 1960s, electoral mobilization had led to a new phenomenon called

© dbimages/Alamy Stock Photo

Figure 6.2 Workers collecting garbage in Thanjavur, India. Workers such as these men, whose occupations are characterized as polluting, are ranked at the bottom of the Hindu caste society.

horizontal mobilization, whereby people situated at comparable levels within the local caste hierarchy came together in caste associations," forming new political parties to support their own interests (1994: 61). Increased involvement of Indians in capitalist markets led to "a proliferation of modern associations that use traditional ties of jāti and varna to promote collective economic well-being" (65). These interests "often turn out to be class interests. . . . This does not mean that caste and class are the same. . . Rather it tells us that class and caste are not . . . antithetical" (Sharma 1999: 68).

The third aspect of Beals's study relevant to our understanding of caste showed that members of middle-ranking *jātis* were willing to use violence to block the upward economic mobility of members of a low-ranking *jāti*. Gerald Berreman's work in the late 1950s supports this. He observed that members of higher-ranking castes "rely heavily on threats of economic and physical sanctions to keep their subordinates in line" (1962: 15–16).

In recent years, a number of low-caste groups in urban India have undertaken collective efforts to lift themselves off the bottom of society, either by imitating the practices of higher castes (a process called *Sanskritization*) or by converting to a non-Hindu religion (such as Buddhism or Christianity) in which caste plays no role. Typically, however, these moves have had no effect in changing the negative stereotypes of so-called "untouchables" held by the so-called "clean" castes. The constitution of India prohibits the practice of untouchability, and the national government has acted to improve the lot of the low castes by regularly passing legislation designed to improve their economic and educational opportunities. In some cases, these measures seem to have succeeded, but caste-related violence continues to be a serious problem in both rural and urban settings. However, violence between those designated as belonging to specific socioeconomic or religiously bounded groups is not confined to societies with caste systems. More recent work also illustrates that changing socioeconomic aspects are shifting traditional patterns, resulting in economic relationships and political systems that are not founded on caste alone. These changes indicate the growing importance of class along with caste (Béteille 2010).

Caste in Other Societies

Over the years, anthropologists have applied the concept of caste to systems of social stratifications outside India as well. For example, Jacques Maquet (1970) used it to describe the closed, endogamous ranked strata of the Tutsi, Hutu, and Twa peoples in the central African kingdom of Rwanda prior to 1959. Pierre van den Berghe (1970) documented caste-like relationships in southern Africa, beginning with white settlement in the area and culminating in the twentieth-century "colour caste" system that was enforced in apartheid South Africa. George De Vos and Hiroshi Wagatsuma (1966) used the term *caste* to describe the Burakumin of Japan: low-ranking endogamous groups, traditionally associated with polluting occupations, who have been subject to dehumanizing stereotypes and residential segregation from other Japanese people. Similarly low-ranking "caste" groups include the Cagots in Spain and France and the Al-Akhdam in Yemen. Ursula Sharma (1999) has also suggested that the concept of caste might be fruitfully used to characterize the relations between the Roma people of Europe and their non-Roma neighbours, who for centuries have subjected the Roma to stigmatization, social segregation, and economic exclusion (1999: 85–6) (Figure 6.3).

A key element recognized by most researchers who use the concept of caste is the endogamy that is forced, at least in theory, on the members of each ranked group. As van den Berghe puts it,

© Sean Gallup/Getty Images

Figure 6.3 Social and economic segregation of the Roma people continues to this day. The problem is particularly problematic in western Europe, where longstanding prejudices against the Roma influence political decisions in many countries, and Roma people must often participate in alternative economies to support themselves.

membership in such groups is "determined by birth and for life" (1970: 351). Sharma highlights the significance of the link between descent and caste, observing that "in societies where descent is regarded as a crucial and persistent principle (however reckoned, and whatever ideological value it is given), almost any social cleavage can become stabilized in a caste-like form" (1999: 85).

But the principle of descent has also played a central role in the identification and persistence of race, ethnicity, and nationality. These three categories are all closely bound with historical developments over the past 500 years that have built the modern world. Indeed, these categories are particularly significant in nation-states, and many contemporary nation-states are of very recent, post-colonial origin. Clearly, to make sense of contemporary post-colonial forms of social stratification, we will also need some understanding of the categories of race, ethnicity, and nationality.

Race

The concept of "race" developed, expanded, and was formalized in the context of European exploration and conquest beginning in the fifteenth century. Europeans conquered Indigenous peoples in the Americas and established colonial political economies that soon depended on the labour of Africans imported as slaves. (See the "In Their Own Words" box that follows.) By the end of the nineteenth century, light-skinned Europeans had established colonial rule over large territories inhabited by darker-skinned peoples, marking the beginnings of a global racial order (see Painter 2010; Smedley 1998). Both as a way of explaining the existence of the human diversity they had encountered, and as a way of justifying their domination over Indigenous peoples and enslavement of Africans, European intellectuals argued that the human species was subdivided into "natural kinds" of human beings called *races* that could be sharply distinguished from one another on the basis of outward physical (or **phenotypic**) appearance. All individuals assigned to the same "race" were assumed to share many features other than just clearly visible physical characteristics.

Belief in the existence of biologically distinct "races" (sometimes called **racialism**) was then joined to an ancient Western notion called the "Great Chain of Being," which proposed that all "natural kinds" could be ranked in a hierarchy. In

Figure 6.4 Racism has been common in countries that were colonized by Europeans. In South Africa, for example, apartheid policies forced the majority population of non-whites into positions of subordination under the ruling white minority. What types of power do policies such as these give to those implementing them?

the latter half of the nineteenth century, European thinkers, including many anthropologists, devised schemes for ranking the "races of mankind" from lowest to highest. Not surprisingly, the "white" Europeans at the apex of imperial power were placed at the top of this global hierarchy. Darker-skinned peoples, such as the Indigenous inhabitants of the Americas or of Asia, were ranked somewhere in the middle. But Africans, whom Europeans had bought and sold as slaves, ranked lowest of all. In this way, the identification of races was transformed into **racism** (Figure 6.4).

However, it is important to emphasize that races are *imagined communities* that *do not correspond to major biological differences* within the human species.

The Biology of Human Variation

Contemporary biologists and biological anthropologists distinguish between macroevolution and microevolution. *Macroevolution* focuses on long-term evolutionary changes, especially the origins of new species and their diversification across space and over millions of years. Macroevolutionary changes revealed in the fossil record of human ancestors were of primary interest to paleoanthropologists. *Microevolution*, by contrast, concentrates on short-term evolutionary changes that occur within a given species over relatively few generations. Microevolutionary studies in evolutionary biology were made possible by *modern*

phenotype Observable, measurable outward characteristics of an organism.

racialism Belief in the existence of biologically distinct races.

racism The systemic oppression of members of one or more socially defined "races" by members of another socially defined "race" that is justified within the ruling society by the rulers' faulty belief in their own biological superiority.

In Their Own Words

The Slave Narrative in Life History and Myth

Anthropologist Susan J. Rasmussen draws on her experiences with the Tuareg people of Niger as she speaks to us on the slave "story" and identity.

Anthropologists and narrators may become mutually implicated with one another in a variety of ways. As a researcher among the Tuareg, I stood in a relationship of friendship, but also of marginality, to the community. In effect, I became a sign facilitating the storytellers in making their points. The act of constructing a life narrative can expand historical and ethnographic consciousness by compelling the author to move from accounts of discrete experiences to an account of why and how his or her life took the shape it did, at a given time, and why this was revealed from a particular viewpoint. The Personal Narratives Group (1989: 4–5) observes that the dynamics of gender emerge more clearly in personal narratives of women than in those of men. Likewise, it would seem to follow that the dynamics of social differentiation, inequality and domination, negotiation and resistance, would also emerge more clearly in slave narratives than in non-slave narratives. Or do they? Former slave and noble both used the experience of marginality and interdependence as a device by which to express their sense of how they have been treated in the post-colonial era. The tales of Tama the noble woman, as

a discourse on servitude, in effect complement the narrative of the former slave man although they are not mirror images of each other. Gender and age were shown to be significant in both of them, in historical memory as well as social practice. Women and former slaves were also revealed as united in certain contexts, rather than always competing or opposed.

Discourse about past servitude offers an expressive vocabulary that provides not only reflection about social stratification and gender but also meaning for suffering from any basis of declared social difference. Additionally, these slave narratives—both in life history and myth—empower, each in their own manner. They enable an inversion of deprivation and effect a recasting of roles and relationships in a way that does not merely recreate social difference or redirect oppression but that reconciles the interests of all the parties to the narratives. There emerges from them an expanded consciousness, on the part of local residents of diverse origins and outside anthropologists in the audiences. The personal slave narrative/life history and the mythology about slavery constitute a counterpoint through which Atakor and other Tuareg remember, but also recast, their social and political history.

Source: Rasmussen, Susan J. 1999. "The Slave Narrative in Life History and Myth, and Problems of Ethnographic Representation of the Tuareg Cultural Predicament," *Ethnohistory* 46, 1: 67–108.

---

evolutionary synthesis, a major theoretical innovation accomplished in the 1930s and 1940s that integrated genetics and Darwinian natural selection into the expanded framework of *population genetics*. As we saw in Chapter 1, biological anthropologists began to use concepts and methods drawn from popular genetics in the 1950s to address questions about *patterns of biological variation within the species as a whole*.

The modern synthesis defined a **species** as "a reproductive community of populations (reproductively isolated from others) that occupies a specific niche in nature" (Mayr 1982: 273). The ability of human beings from anywhere in the world to interbreed successfully is one measure of our membership in a single species. In addition, geneticists had demonstrated that most genes come in a variety of forms, called *alleles*. Population genetics has shown that genetic variation in human populations is mostly a

matter of differences in the relative proportions of the same set of alleles and that the distribution of particular phenotypes shifts gradually from place to place across populations, as the frequencies of some alleles increase while others decrease or stay the same. These observations lead to an inescapable conclusion: "Humankind . . . is not divided into a series of genetically distinct units" (Jones 1986: 324). Put another way, the boundaries said to define human "races" have been culturally imposed on shifting and unstable clusters of alleles (Marks 1995: 117). In addition, the distributions of some traits (such as skin colour) do not match the distributions of other traits (such as hair type). The pattern of gradually shifting geographic frequency of a phenotypic trait across human populations is called a **cline**. Clines can be represented on maps, such as Figure 6.5, which shows the per cent of the population that has the O blood type.

species A reproductive community of populations (reproductively isolated from others) that occupies a specific niche in nature.

cline The gradual intergradation of genetic variation from population to population.

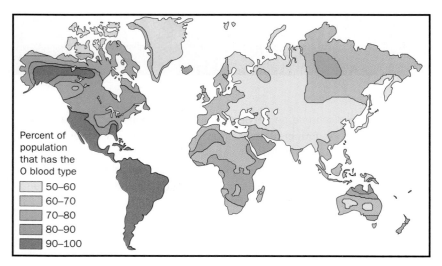

Figure 6.5 Clines can be represented on maps such as this one, which shows the percent of the population that has the O blood type.

Source: Wikipedia

Evolutionary biologists argue that skin pigmentation is distributed as a consequence of natural selection: individuals in tropical populations with darker skin pigmentation had a selective advantage in equatorial habitats over individuals with light pigmentation. By contrast, populations farther away from the equator faced less intense selection pressure for darkly pigmented skin and perhaps even selective pressures in favour of lighter skin. But *different* selection pressures would have been at work on other traits, such as stature and hair type, within the same population, which is why the geographical distributions of these traits do *not* match up neatly with the distribution of skin pigmentation. To make things even more complex, different genes may be involved in the production of similar phenotypic traits in different populations. For example, although different ancestral populations of humans living near the equator all have dark skin, the identity and the number of alleles involved in the production of this phenotypic trait may be different in different populations. At the same time, because people have always migrated, different populations vary in the number of generations exposed to the selective pressures of any single regime of solar radiation. The interbreeding of human populations with different selective histories would further mix any genes contributing to skin pigmentation. Finally, human cultural practices (wearing clothes, using sunblock, staying indoors) have also shaped the level of pigmentation in particular individuals and populations.

Evidence of intergradation in human phenotypes led biological anthropologist Frank Livingstone to declare 50 years ago, "There are no races, there are only clines" (1964: 279). Clinal variation explains why people trying to find biological races have never been able to agree on how many there are or how they can be identified. *Clines are not groups.* Each cline is a map of the distribution of a *single* trait. Biologists might compare the clinal maps of trait A and trait B to see if they overlap and, if so, by how much. But the more clines they superimpose, the more obvious it becomes that the trait distributions they map *do not coincide* in ways that neatly subdivide into distinct human subpopulations. Since the biological concept of "race" predicts exactly such overlap, the biological concept of "race" cannot be correct. In other words, *clinal analysis tests the biological concept of race and finds nothing in nature to match it.* And if biological races cannot be found, then the so-called races identified over the years can only be symbolic constructs, based on cultural elaboration of a few superficial phenotypic differences: skin colour, hair type and quantity, skin folds, lip shape, and the like. In short, early race theorists "weren't extracting races from their set of data, they were imposing races upon it" (Marks 1995: 132).

Many anthropologists hoped that the cultural category of "race" would disappear once its supposed biological underpinnings were exposed as false. However, it has become clear that genetic and other biological evidence alone cannot dismantle oppressive sociopolitical structures, even if it can provide an important component in the struggle to eliminate racist practices from our societies. Of course, to deny the existence of biological "race" is not to deny the existence of human biological or genetic diversity. It is, rather, to deny that the patterns of human diversity can be usefully sorted into a handful of mutually exclusive biological categories.

Race as a Social Category

Even though the concept of "race" is biologically meaningless, however, racial thinking persists in the twenty-first century, and the concept continues to be used as a culturally constructed social category. The end result is a highly distorted, but seemingly coherent, set of criteria that members of a society can use to assign people to one culturally defined racial category or another. Once this happens, members of a society can treat racial categories *as if* they reflect biological reality, using them to build institutions that include or exclude particular "races." In this way, "race" can become "real" in its consequences, even if it has no reality in biology.

Since the days of colonialism, white domination of Euro-American and Euro-Canadian racial hierarchies has been a constant (Figure 6.6). However, some researchers who study the cultural construction of whiteness point out that, even in North America, "whiteness" is not monolithic and that the cultural attributes supposedly shared by "white people" have varied in different times and places. Some members of white ruling groups in the southern United States, for example, have traditionally distanced themselves from lower-class whites, whom they call "white trash." And in South Africa, the meaning of "whiteness" has been complicated by differences of class and culture separating British South Africans from Afrikaners (Hartigan 1997). Moreover, the sharp "caste-like" racial divide between blacks and whites in North America has become complicated by increasing numbers of citizens who identify with so-called "brown" (Latin American/Hispanic or South Asian) and "yellow" (Asian) racial categories. Diverse researchers recognize that racial categorization and repression take different forms in different places. As we shall see, those working in Latin America describe racial practices that do not match those characteristic of the United States and Canada.

Race in Colonial Oaxaca

Anthropologist John Chance studied the development of ideas about "race" and class in the city of Oaxaca, Mexico (see EthnoProfile 6.1). Oaxaca (known as *Antequera* during the period of Spanish colonial domination) is a highland city founded in an area that was densely populated, prior to the Spanish conquest, by Indigenous people. Chance (1978) examined how social stratification changed from the period of Spanish conquest, in 1521, to the early years of the Mexican War of Independence, in 1812. He used an anthropological perspective to interpret census records, wills, and other archival materials preserved in Mexico and Spain. As a result, he was able to show that changes occurred both in the categories used to describe social groups and in the meanings attached to those categories, with associated changes in the dynamics of social stratification itself.

When the Spanish arrived in Mexico in 1521, they found a number of Indigenous societies

© Marc Bruxelle/Alamy Stock Photo

Figure 6.6 The Black Lives Matter movement in downtown Toronto, Canada. #BlackLivesMatter was created in 2012 after Trayvon Martin was shot and killed by George Zimmerman, who was later acquitted of the crime. The movement is a call to action against anti-black racism and, largely through social media, has been able to draw attention to a number of racial issues that continue today in the United States and Canada. In what ways do racial inequalities continue to be prevalent in Canadian society today?

organized into stratified states. The Aztecs, for example, were divided into an upper ruling stratum of nobles and a lower, commoner stratum. The Spanish conquerors also came from a society stratified into a system of *estates*, which were legally recognized social categories entitled to a voice in government. European estates prototypically included the nobility, the clergy, and the common people. By 1529, African slaves had been brought to New Spain. The colonizers in colonial Oaxaca reworked the European notion of estates to accommodate these new arrivals by assigning people membership into one or another estate on the basis of their observable physical traits, including skin colour.

In general, the "white" Spanish formed the nobility and the clergy; Indigenous groups were merged together to form the common people, and "black" African slaves formed a final layer at the bottom of the colonial hierarchy. There were exceptions to this system, however. Indigenous nobles were given special status in post-conquest society and were used by the colonial administration to control the common people. Moreover, the conquistadors, who brought no Spanish women with them, soon established sexual relationships with

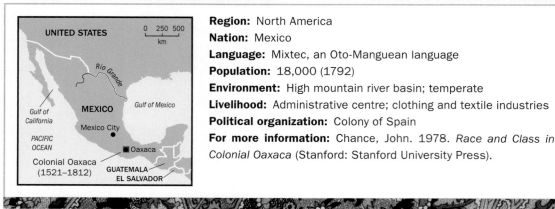

EthnoProfile 6.1
Colonial Oaxaca (1521–1812)

Region: North America
Nation: Mexico
Language: Mixtec, an Oto-Manguean language
Population: 18,000 (1792)
Environment: High mountain river basin; temperate
Livelihood: Administrative centre; clothing and textile industries
Political organization: Colony of Spain
For more information: Chance, John. 1978. *Race and Class in Colonial Oaxaca* (Stanford: Stanford University Press).

local Indigenous women. In the early years, if these unions involved marriage, the offspring were usually considered Spanish, but if they were casual or clandestine, the offspring were more likely to be considered Indigenous. Over the years, sexual relations between Europeans, Indigenous peoples, and Africans created a population of mixed descent. According to the system of estates, people of mixed ancestry were not supposed to exist. By the mid-sixteenth century, however, their numbers and their economic importance made them impossible to ignore. As a result, the rulers of New Spain developed the *sistema de castas* to classify all people of mixed racial heritage (Figure 6.7). The first *castas* recognized were *mestizos* (people of mixed Spanish and Indigenous descent) and *mulattos* (people who showed evidence of African ancestry).

As soon as there were enough *mestizos* and *mulattos* to attract attention, the colonial government tried to limit their social mobility by legal means. Yet their status was ambiguous. *Mestizos* were ranked above *mulattos* because they had no African ancestry, but they were ranked below the Spanish because of their "illegitimacy." In cases where Indigenous and Spanish people were legally married, their children were called *españoles* (Spaniards). They were distinguished from *españoles europeos* (Spaniards born in Spain). In later years, the term *creole* (*criollo*) was also used to refer to people of mixed Indigenous and Spanish ancestry. Some *mestizos* managed to obtain elite privileges, such as the right to carry arms. Most *mulattos* were classed with Africans and could be enslaved. Yet free *mulattos* could also apply for the right to carry arms, which shows that even their status was ambiguous.

Figure 6.7 By the late eighteenth century, the number of *castas* recognized in Mexico had proliferated. This painting displays 16 different outcomes of various cross-*casta* matings. Note that the child of a *castizo* (who has three Spanish grandparents) and an *española* (who has four Spanish grandparents) would be an *español*. The painting attempts to represent not only the phenotypes of different *castas* but also the relative social statuses their members might occupy, as suggested by the clothing they wear (note especially the presence or absence of shoes).

During the seventeenth century, the *castas* were acknowledged as legitimate strata in the system of colonial stratification. A number of new *castas* were recognized: *castizo* (a person of mixed Spanish and *mestizo* descent), *mulatto libre* ("free mulatto"), *mulatto esclavo* ("mulato slave"), *negro libre* ("free black"), and *negro esclavo* ("black slave"). Perhaps most striking is the *castizo* category. This seems to have been designed by the colonial elite to stem the tide of ever "whiter" *mestizos* who might be mistaken for genuine Spaniards. Chance points out that racial mixing was primarily an urban phenomenon and that individuals of Spanish–Indigenous descent perceived themselves, and were perceived by the elite, as belonging to Hispanic rather than Indigenous society (1978: 126). It is perhaps not surprising that lighter-skinned *castas* became increasingly indistinguishable from middle-class and lower-class creoles. In fact, census records in Oaxaca list creoles as the largest segment of the city's population throughout the entire colonial period.

Other Stratification Systems

As if the *sistema de castas* were not enough, colonial society in Oaxaca recognized three additional systems of classification that cut across the *castas*. One distinguished groups required to pay tribute to the Spanish crown (Indigenous groups, Africans, and *mulattos*) from everyone else. The second distinguished *gente de razon* ("rational people," who practised the Hispanic culture of the city) from *indios* (the rural, culturally distinct Indigenous population). And a third distinguished *gente decente* ("respectable people") from *la plebe* (the "common people"). Chance suggests that the last distinction, which made the most sense in the urban setting, represented the beginning of socioeconomic classes (1978: 127).

Mobility in the Casta System

Throughout the colonial period, the boundaries of the stratification system in Oaxaca were most rigid for those of "unmixed" Indigenous, African, and European descent. Those of mixed background had the most ambiguous status and therefore the greatest opportunity to improve it. For example, when a couple married, the priest decided the *casta* membership of the bride and groom. The strategy for upward mobility called for choosing a marriage partner who was light-skinned enough for the priest to decide

that both spouses belonged in a high-ranking *casta*. Over time, such manoeuvring swelled the ranks of the creoles.

The growth of the population coincided with the transformation of the colonial economy from one based on tribute and mining to one based on commercial capitalism. The prosperity this transformation brought to Oaxaca was greatest in the eighteenth century, when the city became the centre of an important textile and dye-manufacturing industry. People from lower *castas* were able to accumulate wealth, which together with light skin and adoption of the urban culture made it possible for them to achieve the status of creole.

Chance argued that during the late colonial period, racial status had become an achieved, rather than an ascribed, status. By that time, the increasing rate of legitimacy in all *castas* meant that descent lost its importance as a criterion of group membership. Creole status could be claimed by anyone who was able to show that his or her ancestors had not paid tribute. At the same time, people's idea of what high-status people looked like had changed. As people with Indigenous and African ancestry moved up the social scale, their phenotypes widened the range of phenotypes considered prototypical for creoles.

Chance concludes that the *sistema de castas* is best understood as "a cognitive and legal system of ranked socio-racial statuses" (1978: viii). Anthropologists have called this sort of status **social race**. The stratification system in Oaxaca was a hybrid, beginning with closed, caste-like racial categories whose "purity" could not be maintained and ending up with open, class-like categories with racial labels.

social race An achieved status with a racial label in a system of stratification that is composed of open, class-like categories to which racial labels are assigned.

Colourism in Nicaragua

Some observers might expect that once "race" becomes an achieved status, racism has disappeared. But the situation is not so simple. Let us compare the case of Oaxaca, Mexico, with that of Managua, Nicaragua. Anthropologist Roger Lancaster argues that, in Nicaragua, racism exists, but it is "not as absolute and encompassing a racism as that which one encounters in the United States" (1992: 215). One dimension of Nicaraguan racism contrasts the Spanish-speaking *mestizo* majority of the highlands with the Indigenous Miskitos and African Caribbeans along the Atlantic coast. Highland *mestizos* tend to regard these coastal groups as backward, inferior, and dangerous—notions overlain with political suspicions deriving from the fact that some

Miskito factions had fought with the contras against the Sandinistas.

Lancaster came to see racism toward the coastal peoples as an extension of the pattern of race relations internal to highland *mestizo* culture. He calls this **colourism**, where no fixed "racial" boundaries exist. Instead, individuals negotiate their colour identity anew in every social situation they enter. Thus, in this system, the colour a person might claim or be accorded changes from situation to situation.

Lancaster identified three different systems of colour classification at work among the *mestizos* of Nicaragua, all of which presupposed white superiority and black inferiority:

1. A *phenotypic* system composed of three categories: (1) *blanco* (white), (2) *moreno* (brown, the category into which most *mestizos* fell), and (3) *negro* (black)
2. A *polite* system composed of three categories that roughly correspond to the categories in the phenotypic system: (1) *chele* ("blue," as in "blue eyes," used for Europeans), (2) *blanco* (used for *morenos*), and (3) *moreno* (used for *negroes*)
3. A *pejorative/affectionate* system composed of only two terms: (1) *chele* (lighter skin and hair) and (2) *negro* (darker skin and hair)

Each system was considered appropriate to different contexts. The phenotypic system was appropriate for discussing colour distinctions generally. The polite system was appropriate for use in the presence of the person about whom one was speaking. As Lancaster noted, it was "a grave and violent offence to refer to a black-skinned person as *negro*" (1992: 217). Finally, the *pejorative/affectionate* system was appropriate in two situations: when a less powerful person wanted to express her or his displeasure toward a more powerful person, and, somewhat paradoxically, when family members wanted to express affection for one another. In both cases, this system was appropriate because it was relatively "informal" and violated the rules of "polite" discourse (218).

Lancaster discovered that "whiteness is a desired quality, and polite discourse inflates its descriptions of people" (1992: 219). People compete in different settings to claim whiteness. In some settings, individuals may be addressed as *blanco* if everyone else has darker skin; in other settings, they may be addressed as *moreno* if someone else has lighter skin. Because it allows people some freedom

to negotiate their colour status, Nicaraguan colourism may seem less repressive than the more rigid forms of racism found in other countries. Yet, in Lancaster's opinion, it still represented "a significant social problem" (215).

Lancaster is not optimistic about the possibility of successfully overturning this system in Nicaragua any time soon. Similarly, anthropologist Faye Harrison argues that racial solidarity and rebellion are hard to achieve or sustain in societies where social race is present, and she is not optimistic that similar systems would have the same effect in other countries. For example, considering race relations in the United States, she fears that a "more multi-shaded discourse" would be more likely to contribute to "an enduring stigmatization of blackness" than to "democratization and the dismantling of race" (1998: 618–19).

Ethnicity

For anthropologists, **ethnic groups** are social groups whose members distinguish themselves (and/or are distinguished by others) in terms of *ethnicity*—that is, in terms of distinctive cultural features, such as language, religion, or dress (Figure 6.8). Ethnicity, like race, is a culturally constructed concept. Many anthropologists today would agree with anthropologists John Comaroff and Jean Comaroff that ethnicity is created by historical processes that incorporate distinct social groups into a single political structure under conditions of inequality (1992: 55–7). Comaroff and Comaroff point out that ethnic consciousness existed in pre-colonial and pre-capitalist societies; however, they and most contemporary anthropologists have been more interested in forms of ethnic consciousness that were generated under capitalist colonial domination.

Ethnicity develops as members of different groups try to make sense of the struggle between *self-ascription* (i.e., insiders' efforts to define their own identity) and *other-ascription* (i.e., outsiders' efforts to define the identities of other groups). In Comaroff and Comaroff's view, furthermore, the ruling group turns both itself and the subordinated groups into *classes* because all subordinated social groupings lose independent control "over the means of production and/or reproduction" (1992: 56).

One outcome of this struggle is the appearance of new ethnic groups and identities that are not continuous with any single earlier cultural group (Comaroff and Comaroff 1992: 56). In northern Cameroon, for

colourism A system of social identities negotiated, based on the situation, along a continuum of skin colours between white and black.

ethnic groups Social groups that are distinguished from one another on the basis of ethnicity.

example, Emily Schultz (1984) found that successive German, French, and British colonial officials relied on local Muslim chiefs to identify significant local social divisions for them, and they adopted the Muslim practice of lumping together all the myriad non-Muslim peoples of the hills and plains and calling them *Haabe* or *Kirdi*—that is, "pagans." To the extent, therefore, that Guidar, Daba, Fali, Ndjegn, Guiziga, and other non-Muslim peoples were treated the same by colonial authorities and came to share a common set of interests, they developed a new, more inclusive level of ethnic identity. This new, postcolonial identity, like many others, cannot be linked to any single pre-colonial cultural reality but has been constructed out of cultural materials borrowed from a variety of non-Muslim Indigenous groups who were incorporated as "pagans" within the colonial political order. (See the "In Their Own Words" box about a people's name that follows.)

Comaroff and Comaroff (1992) argue that a particular structure of *nesting identities* was quite common throughout European colonies in Africa. The lowest and least inclusive consisted of local groups, often called *tribes*, who struggled to

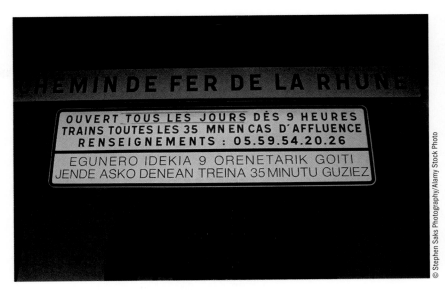

Figure 6.8 A train station sign in French and Euskara (Basque) languages advises that the station will be open at 9:00 a.m. every morning, with trains departing every 35 minutes during peak times. The Euskara language, which has at various periods in history been suppressed by governments, is a key element of ethnic identity and continuing trend towards nationalism in the Basque region, which crosses the border between France and Spain. Why is language important to a people's sense of ethnicity?

In Their Own Words

The Emergence of a New Political Paradigm

Anthropologist John Matthiasson first went to Baffin Island, in the Canadian Arctic, to do fieldwork among the Inuit in 1963. He returned a decade later to carry out additional fieldwork and has kept up with events in the Canadian Arctic since then. Here, he writes about a people's name.

The names by which we refer to ourselves or others can also be used to manipulate our identity and to align with or isolate ourselves from others, as well as to rationalize our treatment of others. When I lived with the Aullativikmiut in the 1960s they referred to themselves as Eskimos, as did all of the Tununermiut. By the 1970s many of them had ceased to use the term, which was now considered pejorative. (Its etymological origins have always been murky, although many sources claim that it means "eaters of raw meat.") It was, of course, replaced in both singular and plural by Inuk and Inuit, for "a person" and "the people." The change in terminology of self-reference had, I am convinced, enormous political significance.

Not everyone accepted the change readily, and in some instances it was never adopted. One elderly man who had lived virtually all of his life in the camps told me in 1973, "I was born an Eskimo and I will die an Eskimo." However, his was to become a minority position. Others—even of his generation—soon saw the political significance of rejecting the term, and certainly that man's children and grandchildren did. This change, which was so important in the construction of new individual and group identities, was the work of the Inuit Tapirisat of Canada (ITC), or Inuit Brotherhood, a new organization that sought to create a pan-Inuit consciousness. The ITC was external to the Tununermiut, but when it offered them a new political agenda, they responded and, in the process, took further steps toward a renewed sense of self-determination.

Source: Matthiasson, John S. 1992. "The Emergence of a New Political Paradigm," in *Living on the Land: Northern Baffin Inuit Respond to Change* (Peterborough, ON: Broadview Press), 161–2.

dominate one another within separate colonial states. The middle levels consisted of a variety of entities that crossed local boundaries, sometimes called *supertribes* or *nations*. For example, the British administered the settler colony of Southern Rhodesia (later to become Zimbabwe) according to the policy of "indirect rule," which used Indigenous "tribal" authorities to maintain order on the local level. The effect of indirect rule was thus both to reinforce "tribal" identities where they existed and to create them where they had been absent in pre-colonial times. Two such tribal identities, those of the Shona and the Ndebele, became pre-eminent, and each gave rise to its own "(supratribal) nationalist movement."

Both movements joined together in a "patriotic front" to win a war of independence against white settlers. This confrontation took place at the highest level of the ethnic hierarchy where "Europeans" and "Africans" opposed one another, and each group developed its own encompassing ethnic identity with "race" as a defining feature. Africans regularly dealing with Europeans began to conceive of such a thing as "African culture" (as opposed to European culture) and "pan-African solidarity" (to counter the hegemony of the European colonizers). Conversely, in the British settler colonies of southern and eastern Africa, European immigrants defined themselves in opposition to Africans by developing their own "settler–colonial order" based on a caricature of aristocratic Victorian English society (Comaroff and Comaroff 1992: 58).

Because ethnic groups are incorporated into the colony on unequal terms, it is not surprising to discover that many individuals in colonies attempted to achieve upward mobility by manipulating ethnicity. For example, Schultz (1984) investigated ethnic mobility in Guider, Cameroon, in 1976 (Figure 6.9). Guider began as a small settlement of non-Muslim Guidar people. In 1830, it was brought

into the Muslim Fulbe empire of Yola and remained a Fulbe stronghold under subsequent colonial rule. The Fulbe remained numerically dominant in town until after World War II; by 1958, individuals from over a dozen non-Fulbe groups had migrated to town, primarily from the neighbouring countryside. By 1976, 83 per cent of household heads in town were recent migrants, and 74 per cent did not claim Fulbe origins.

In Comaroff and Comaroff's terms, all these groups, including the Fulbe, had lost political and economic independence with the coming of colonial rule and, under conditions of inequality, were incorporated as ethnic groups into first the German and later the French colony of Cameroon. The colonizers uniformly admired the political, cultural, and religious accomplishments of the Muslim Fulbe. In their own version of indirect rule, they allowed Fulbe chiefs to administer territories they had controlled prior to colonization and, in some cases, handed over additional territories, whose residents had successfully resisted Fulbe domination in pre-colonial times.

In 1976, the local ethnic hierarchy in Guider placed Fulbe at the top; and recent non-Muslim, non-Fulfulde-speaking migrants from rural areas, at the bottom. But in the middle were numerous individuals and families of Fulfulde-speaking Muslims who could claim, and in some cases be accorded, recognition as Fulbe by others in the town. These people's narrower identity as Ndjegn or Fali, for example, nested within the broader identity of Fulbe (see Figure 6.9). Depending on the situation, they would emphasize one ethnic identity over the other. When with family, they emphasized their narrower ethnic identity; in urban public settings, they emphasized their Fulbe identity.

Indeed, by 1976, Fulbe identity had become an achieved status; it was the ethnicity claimed by the

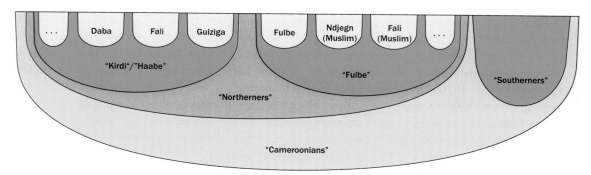

Figure 6.9 Nesting identities in northern Cameroon in 1976.

Source: Adapted from Schultz 1984.

upwardly mobile in Guider. People born outside the dominant Fulbe ethnic group could achieve Fulbe status in their lifetimes (Schultz 1984). To do this, they had to be successful in three tasks: (1) they had to learn the Fulbe language (Fulfulde), (2) they had to practise the Fulbe religion (Islam), and (3) they had to adopt the Fulbe "way of life," which was identified with urban customs and the traditional high culture of western Sudan. Many Fulbe claimed that descent from one Fulbe lineage or another was needed in order to claim Fulbe identity. Nevertheless, they seemed willing to accept "Fulbeized pagans" as Fulbe (e.g., by giving their daughters to them as brides) because those people were committed defenders of the urban Fulbe way of life. Those who were "Fulbeizing," however, came from societies in which descent had never been an important criterion of group membership. For those people, ethnic identity depended on territorial affiliation of the group to which they were currently committed. In becoming Fulbe, they had simply chosen to commit themselves to Fulfulde, Islam, and life in "Fulbe territory"—the town.

This example illustrates some of the key attributes often associated with ethnicity: ethnicity is fluid, malleable, and something that can be voluntarily embraced or successfully ignored in different situations. Ambitious individuals and groups in an ethnically stratified society can manipulate ethnicity as a resource in order to pursue their interests. When nesting identities are present, people may regularly alternate between different identities in different contexts. Ethnic "Fulbeization" in northern Cameroon might be described as the formation of a "supertribe." Like the formation of caste alliances in India, it involves the expansion of group boundaries, allowing for the creation of stronger solidarity linkages among more people of different backgrounds. When such expanded alliances actually achieve increased success in political, economic, and social struggles, they may affect the very structures that gave rise to them (as the Shona–Ndebele alliance did in Zimbabwe) (Comaroff and Comaroff 1992: 61).

For dominant groups, however, defence of ethnic identity can be a way of defending privilege. Members of the dominant ethnic group may stress their cultural superiority and question the eligibility (and even the humanity) of subordinate groups who challenge them. It is at this point that Faye Harrison would argue that ethnicity becomes *racialized*. In her view, "race" differs from ethnicity precisely because it is used to "mark and stigmatize certain peoples as essentially and irreconcilably different, while treating the privileges of others as normative. This quality of difference, whether constructed through a bio-determinist or culturalist idiom, is what constitutes the social category and material phenomenon of 'race'" (Harrison 1998: 613). Racialization in Western societies would thus bear a family resemblance to castification in South Asian societies.

Harrison argues that by the middle of the nineteenth century, white northern Europeans, connecting their growing colonial power with their whiteness, began to racialize ethnic, religious, and class stereotypes associated with other Europeans (e.g., Irish, Jews, Italians, Poles, Slavs), viewing them as less human or, at any rate, differently human from themselves and attributing this difference to biologically inherited factors (1995: 52). Conversely, some racialized ethnic groups, such as the Irish, were able to reverse this process once they moved to Canada or the United States, shedding their stigma and *ethnicizing* into just another Canadian or American ethnic group. Some social scientists might argue, or at any rate hope, that all racialized groups should be able to ethnicize sooner or later. But such a perspective risks ignoring the plight of racialized groups whose status never seems to change. Historians argue, for example, that the Irish were able to ethnicize in the United States precisely because they accepted the racialization of black Americans (Allen 1994–7). With the presupposition of white privilege, non-white races in the United States "historically have defined layers of the social bottom" (Harrison 1995: 49). For these reasons, Harrison argues that attempts to interpret race relations in the United States as ethnic relations "euphemize if not deny race" by failing to address the social, political, and economic factors responsible for keeping groups like African Americans excluded and stigmatized at the bottom of society (1995: 48).

As we have seen, anthropologists have argued about which technical terms ought to be used to describe which forms of identity under which circumstances. We would agree with Ursula Sharma that social scientists should use a particular term only if it highlights a dimension of social relationships that would otherwise go unnoticed (1999: 93). Thus, ethnicity probably needs to be supplemented by the discredited but yet used notion of "race" in order to distinguish the dehumanizing confinement of certain social groups to the bottom layers of society, and caste's emphasis on endogamy and hierarchical ranking highlights features of social organization that elude the usual scope of race, class, or ethnicity. Anthropologist Pnina Werbner (1997) further builds on these distinctions when she argues that in order to make progress in analyzing ethnic violence as a social force, practices of "everyday" ethnic identification need to be distinguished from racism. Therefore, ethnicity's "form and substance must be related to other social phenomena and to historical changes that contextualize ethnic identification" (Lindgren 2005).

Research on multicultural social relations distinguishes two different social processes at work in multicultural societies: **objectification** and **reification** (Werbner 1997). *Objectification* refers to the intentional construction of a collective public identity; it is the process that produces "everyday" or "normal" ethnicity. Ethnic identities are distinguished by the fact that they are "evoked situationally[,] . . . highlighted pragmatically, and objectified relationally and contingently" (Werbner 1997: 241). They are also distinguished by the fact that they focus on two key issues: "a demand for ethnic rights, including religious rights, and a demand for protection against racism" (241). Social relations between objectified ethnic groups are based on a "rightful performance" of multiple shifting, highly valued forms of collective identification based on religion, dress, food, language, and politics. Interaction between groups that differentiate themselves along such lines ordinarily do not lead to violent confrontations (229). *Reification*, in contrast, is a form of negative racial or ethnic absolutism that encourages the violent elimination of targeted groups and is central to the practice of racism. Reification "distorts and silences"; it is "essentialist in the pernicious sense" (229). Violence differentiates racism from everyday ethnicity, and if ethnic confrontation becomes violent, then it turns into a form of racism (234–5). Making this distinction is crucial in multi-ethnic situations because when people fail to distinguish non-violent forms of everyday ethnicity from racism, they are, in effect, criminalizing valid ethnic sentiments and letting racists off the hook (233).

Nation and Nationalism

As we saw earlier, state societies are not new social forms. **Nation-states**, however, are a far more recent invention. For Europeans, prior to the French Revolution, states were ruled by kings and emperors whose access to the throne was officially believed to have been ordained by God. After the French Revolution in 1789, which thoroughly discredited the divine right of kings, rulers needed to find a new basis on which to found legitimate state authority. The solution that was eventually adopted rooted political authority in **nations**: groups of people believed to share the same history, culture, language, and even physical substance. Nations were associated with territories, as were states, and a nation-state came to be viewed as an ideal political unit in which national identity and political territory coincided.

The building of the first nation-states is closely associated with the rise and spread of capitalism and its related cultural institutions during the nineteenth century. Following the demise of European colonial empires and the end of the Cold War, the final decades of the twentieth century witnessed a scramble in which former colonies or newly independent states struggled to turn themselves into nation-states capable of competing successfully in a "transnational culture of nationalism" (Malkki 1992).

On the one hand, the ideology of the nation-state implies that every nation is entitled to its own state. (Here we could consider the aspirations of the Kurds to establish their own nation-state in West Asia.) On the other hand, it also suggests that a state containing heterogeneous populations *might be made into a nation* if all peoples within its borders could somehow be made to adopt a common nationality: a sense of identification with and loyalty to the nation-state. The attempt made by government officials and state institutions to instill this sense of nationality into the citizens of a state has been called *nation-building*, or **nationalism**.

States are the very political structures that generate ethnic identities among the various cultural groupings unequally incorporated within them. Thus, anthropologists studying state formation often find themselves studying ethnicity as well as nationalism. However, groups with different forms of identity that continue to persist within the boundaries of the nation-state are often viewed as obstacles to nationalism. If such groups successfully resist assimilation into the nationality that the state is supposed to represent, their very existence calls into question the legitimacy of the state. Indeed, if their numbers are sufficient, they might well claim that they are a separate nation, entitled to a state of their own. Canadians have seen this sort of separatist impulse arise over the years among French-speaking

objectification The intentional construction of a collective public identity; the process that produces what we commonly think of as ethnicity.

reification A form of negative racial or ethnic absolutism that encourages the violent elimination of targeted groups and is central to the practice of racism.

nation-state An ideal political unit in which national identity and political territory coincide.

nation A group of people believed to share the same history, culture, language, and even physical substance.

nationalism The attempt made by government officials to instill a sense of nationality into the citizens of a state.

people in Quebec. This impulse led to two provincial referendums on the topic, one in 1980 and one in 1995; in both cases, the proposal for separation was rejected by the voters of Quebec. Today, the separatist movement continues to find favour among some, particularly older, French-speaking Quebecers, but overall support for the movement has dwindled over time (Patriquin 2014) (Figure 6.10).

To decrease the likelihood that an ethnically distinct group will separate to form its own nation-state, nationalist ideologies typically include some cultural features of subordinate cultural groups. In Canada, the strongest example of this sort of inclusion is the promotion of French as well as English as an official language. Such inclusion is possible because nationalist traditions are often carefully thought out. A national identity is usually based on cultural attributes of the dominant group, but it also integrates specially chosen cultural elements of other, subordinated groups. Those who control the nation-state try to define nationality in ways that "identify and ensure loyalty among citizens," with the goal of creating "criteria of inclusion and exclusion to control and delimit the group" (Williams 1989: 407). The hope seems to be that if at least some aspects of their ways of life are acknowledged as essential to national identity, subordinated groups will identify with and be loyal to the nation. Following Italian political theorist Antonio Gramsci (see Chapter 12), Williams calls this process a **transformist hegemony** in which nationalist ideologues are attempting to "create purity out of impurity" (429, 435).

National leaders will measure the trustworthiness and loyalty of citizens by how closely they copy (or refuse to copy) the cultural practices that define national identity (Williams 1989: 407). Unfortunately, the practices of subordinated groups that do not get incorporated into nationalist ideology are regularly marginalized and devalued, and continued adherence to such practices may be viewed as subversive. Some groups, moreover, may be totally ignored. Anthropologist Ana María Alonso (1994) points out, for example, that Mexican nationalism is "*mestizo* nationalism" rooted in the official doctrine that the Mexican people are a hybrid of European whites and the Indigenous people they conquered. As we saw in colonial Oaxaca, African slaves were also a part of early colonial Mexican society. Nationalist ideology, however, erases their presence entirely (Alonso 1994: 396).

© meunierd/Shutterstock.com

Figure 6.10 Although Quebecers did not ultimately separate from Canada following the 1995 referendum on the question of separation, the preservation of a distinct national identity remains important to many people in the province. One reminder of this identity is Saint-Jean-Baptiste Day, officially known in Quebec as *la fête nationale* ("the national holiday"), celebrated annually on 24 June. *Je me souviens* on Quebec licence plates also reinforces the Québécois identity.

Australian Nationalism

Australia began its existence as a penal then settler colony of Great Britain. Early settlers laid claim to the land and other resources under the doctrine of *terra nullius*: the idea that before the arrival of the Europeans, the land had been owned by nobody. Of course, this position ignored the fact that the land was being used by the Aboriginal peoples who lived there. In European capitalist terms, "ownership" meant permanent settlement and "improvement" of the land by clearing it and planting crops or grazing animals. Since the Aboriginal peoples were foragers who did not depend on domesticated plants or animals, European settlers felt justified in displacing them and "improving" the land as they saw fit. In general, Aboriginal peoples were viewed as a "dying race," and white settler domination was taken as a

transformist hegemony A nationalist program to define nationality in a way that preserves the cultural domination of the ruling group while including enough cultural features from subordinated groups to ensure their loyalty.

foregone conclusion. This was not so different from what happened in North America.

It was against this backdrop that the Australian national identity developed. Not surprisingly, this identity was based primarily on the racial and cultural features of the British colonialists. Until relatively recently, non-Aboriginal Australians did not recognize the need to incorporate aspects of Aboriginal culture into this identity.

But times change and, for the past few decades, Australians have been rethinking the nature of Australian national identity. Indeed, according to anthropologist Robert Tonkinson (1998), two kinds of nation-building are going on at the same time. First, an intense national debate has developed over the possibility of creating a new nation-state whose constitution would affirm the existence and rights of the country's Indigenous peoples. For that to happen, however, "the nation as a whole must re-imagine itself via a myth-making process, in which the search for distinctively Australian national symbols may well include elements drawn from Indigenous cultures" (Tonkinson 1998: 287–8). This will not be easy because such a myth-making process (or transformist hegemony) immediately

runs up against a second, alternative myth-making process generated by Australia's Indigenous minorities, who have, for decades, struggled to construct a sense of identity that is inclusive of all Aboriginal Australians. Since the 1970s, a central theme in this struggle has been the demand for land rights, which was given an enormous boost in 1992 by the court decision in the case of *Eddie Mabo and Others v. The State of Queensland*. The *Mabo* decision rejected the doctrine of *terra nullius*, proclaiming that the Native title of Australia's Indigenous people was part of Australian common law.

The symbolic significance of the *Mabo* decision has been enormous. The Australian federal government has made reconciliation with Indigenous minorities a major policy goal, well aware that "unless Australia achieves a formal and lasting reconciliation with its Indigenous people, its self-image as a fair and just land will continue to be mocked by the history of its oppression of them" (Tonkinson 1998: 291). Many white Australians and the national government are seeking ways of incorporating Aboriginality into Australian national identity. A measure of success is indicated by increasing interest on the national level in the artistic, literary, and athletic accomplishments of Aboriginal people.

However, many problems remain (Figure 6.11). Some come from white Australians who reject a multicultural national identity or who see their economic interests threatened by the *Mabo* decision. But even Aboriginal people criticize the *Mabo* decision, which was supposed to help them, because of its limitations and unresolved complexities. For example, the only lands eligible for Indigenous claims turn out to be those that have demonstrable historical connection to contemporary Aboriginal groups who continue to practise "traditional" Aboriginal customs. This not only exempts most of Australia from Indigenous land claims, it also bars most of Australia's Aboriginal people from making land claims because they live in large towns and cities and have, for generations, been separated from the lands of their ancestors.

Since the *Mabo* decision, however, expressions of Aboriginality seem to be moving toward "a more culture-centred—and to non-Aboriginal Australians more easily accommodated—emphasis on Aboriginal commonalities, continuity, and survival" (Tonkinson 1998: 289). The *Mabo* decision has recognized the legitimacy not only of Aboriginal land rights but also of Aboriginal customs. This

Figure 6.11 The Sydney Invasion Day March took place on 26 January 2017 in Sydney, Australia, and brought together Indigenous people and supporters in protest of "Australia Day." Australia Day is celebrated on the same day and marks the arrival of the first fleet of British ships at Port Jackson, Sydney, Australia. Many Indigenous people and supporters have advocated that the date for Australia Day be changed to be more inclusive and recognize the issues that Indigenous people of Australia continue to face.

has stimulated the explosion of Aboriginal cultural expression that white Australians have come to appreciate, as well as numerous programs that have brought urban Aboriginals into remote areas to work, to learn about rural Aboriginal traditions, and to contribute to the growth of biculturalism among rural Aboriginal people. Even in a multicultural Australia, however, many Aboriginal people would insist that they must not be lumped together with other "ethnic minorities," given their special status as descendants of the original inhabitants and victims of centuries of exploitation. Tonkinson concludes that "despite the limitations of *Mabo* . . . its symbolic force is such that it may provide the basis for reconciliation between Indigenous and other Australians" (300). Australian legal scholar Janice Gray likewise recognizes the mixed effect of the *Mabo* decision:

> The fact that the *Native Title Act* ([Cth] 1993), which was a response to the [*Mabo*] decision, has generated no successful Native title claims leads one to conclude that the decision has not had very radical consequences. That, however, does not mean . . . that the decision is undeserving of praise. What the decision has done is put Aboriginal issues on the national agenda and paved a path for reconciliation. (1997: 67)

And it is reconciliation that is the most promising outcome of the Aboriginal civil rights movement in Australia and the *Mabo* case of 1992. At the same time, in the early twenty-first century, the struggle for Aboriginal rights is far from over in Australia, and it has experienced reversals as well as advances.

Naturalizing Discourses

We have emphasized that all the social categories under discussion—class, caste, "race," ethnicity, and nationality—are culturally created and cannot be justified with reference to biology or nature. Yet many people around the world argue just the opposite, employing what some anthropologists call *naturalizing discourses*—the deliberate representation of particular identities (e.g., caste, class, race, ethnicity, and nationality) as if they were a result of biology or nature rather than history or culture, making them appear eternal and unchanging.

Naturalizing discourses rely on the imaginary reduction or conflation of identities to achieve persuasive power (Williams 1989). For example, every one of the forms of identity we have discussed in this chapter has been described or justified by someone, at some time, in terms of *shared bodily substance*. Thus, living within the same borders is conflated with having the same ancestors and inheriting the same culture, which is conflated with sharing the same blood or the same genes. Culture is reduced to blood, and "the magic of forgetfulness and selectivity, both deliberate and inadvertent, allows the once recognizably arbitrary classifications of one generation to become the given inherent properties of reality several generations later" (Williams 1989: 431).

Nation-states frequently use trees as national symbols, rooting the nation in the soil of its territory (Figure 6.12). Sometimes they use kinship imagery, referring to the nation-state as a "motherland" or "fatherland"; sometimes the territory of a nation-state itself can be a unifying image, especially when portrayed on a map (Alonso 1994). The case of Australia shows, however, that doctrines like *terra nullius* enable newcomers to deny Indigenous inhabitants' "natural" links to the land in order to make way for their own "natural" links to the land through "improvement."

Figure 6.12 The tree-like symbol at the centre of the Mexican coat of arms (the cactus on which the eagle stands) is a pre-Conquest Aztec symbol. It symbolizes the connection between the nation-state of Mexico and the land on which this nation-state exists. Does Canada have any national symbols that connect the nation-state to the land on which it exists?

The Paradox of Essentialized Identities

The struggle of Aboriginal people to defend themselves and claim their rights after centuries of exploitation and neglect was extraordinarily important in making the *Mabo* decision possible in Australia. In response to dominant groups that attempted to conflate their humanity with a narrow, unflattering stereotype, these people chose to accept their racial designation but to view it as a positive *essence*, an "inner something or distinctive 'spirituality' possessed by everyone who is Aboriginal" (Tonkinson 1998: 294–5). Similar kinds of essentialist rhetoric have helped many stigmatized groups build a positive self-image and unite politically.

Many observers would argue that the essentialist rhetoric of Aboriginal activists does not, in fact, reflect what those activists believe about Aboriginality at all. They would describe what the activists are promoting as **strategic essentialism**, a term coined by social theorist Gayatri Chakravorty Spivak (1987). Most activists are perfectly aware that essentialized racial or ethnic identities have no scientific validity. Nevertheless, they press their claims, hoping that by stressing their difference they may be able to extract concessions that the national government cannot refuse without violating its own laws and sense of justice. The concessions may be substantial, as in the case of the *Mabo* decision. At the same time, strategic essentialism is troubling to many observers and participants in these struggles, for those who promote it as a political strategy risk "reproducing the same logic that once oppressed them" (Hale 1997: 547). Thus, rather than bringing about a more just society, it may simply "serve to perpetuate an ethnically ordered world" (Comaroff and Comaroff 1992: 62).

Over the years, the concept of *strategic essentialism* has gained ground in the analysis of political action in various human-rights areas and has also been extended into other areas of application. In the realm of environmental sustainability, for example, environmental groups with different agendas have come together as a single political force to add weight to the environmental movement as a whole (Dourish 2008). In our increasingly globalized world, forming this sort of alliance may prove to be an effective strategy for relatively small or marginalized "action" groups to get their message heard.

Nation-Building in a Post-colonial World: The Example of Fiji

While the citizens of nation-states need to construct a shared public identity, they also need to establish concrete legal mechanisms for taking group action to influence the state. As anthropologists John Kelly and Martha Kaplan (2001) argue, nation-states are more than imagined communities; they are also *represented* communities. For this reason, nation-building involves more than constructing an image of national unity; it also requires institutions of political representation that channel the efforts of citizens into effective state support. But what happens when citizens of a nation-state do not agree about what nation they are building or what kinds of legal and political structures are necessary to bring it about? One answer to this question can be seen in the South Pacific island nation of Fiji, which became independent from Britain in 1970 and experienced four political coups in twenty years (between 1987 and 2006).

At independence, the image of the Fijian nation was that of a "three-legged stool," with each "leg" representing a separate category of voters:

1. "General electors" (a minority of the population that includes Europeans)
2. "Fijians" (ethnic Fijians, descended from the original inhabitants of the island)
3. "Indians" (or Indo-Fijians, descendants of indentured labourers brought to Fiji by the British from Mumbai [Bombay] and Kolkata [Calcutta] in the nineteenth century)

Kelly and Kaplan show that these three categories have deep roots in the colonial period, where they were said to correspond to separate "races." In the British Empire, "race" was an accepted way to categorize subordinated peoples, even though in many cases—as in the case of the Indo-Fijians—the people so labelled had shared no common identity prior to their arrival in their new home.

These distinctions were recognized in colonial law, and the legal status of ethnic Fijians was different from the legal status of Indo-Fijians. The status of ethnic Fijians was determined by the Deed of Cession, a document signed by some Fijian chiefs

strategic essentialism
The use of essentialist rhetoric as a conscious political strategy to create a temporary solidarity to facilitate a specific social action.

with the British in 1874, which linked ethnic Fijians to the colonial government through their hierarchy of chiefs. The status of Indo-Fijians, however, was determined by the contracts of indenture that each individual labourer had signed in order to come to Fiji. Thus, ethnic Fijians were accorded a hierarchical, collective legal identity, whereas Indo-Fijians had the status of legal individuals, with no legally recognized ties to any collectivity.

Inspired by the freedom movement in India in the early twentieth century, Indo-Fijians began to resist racial oppression and struggle for equal rights in Fiji, but their efforts were repeatedly blocked by the British. When it became possible for them to vote after 1929, for example, Indo-Fijians lobbied for equal citizenship and the abolition of separate racial voting rolls, and they lost: the voting rolls were divided by race in order to limit representation for Indo-Fijians in government. At the time of World War II, Indo-Fijians agreed to serve in the armed forces but only if they were treated as equal with white soldiers. These efforts were resisted: they spent the war serving in a labour battalion for very low wages while ethnic Fijians joined a Fijian Defence Force. It was primarily Indo-Fijians who pushed for independence in the late 1960s, and once again they engaged in difficult negotiations for equal citizenship and a common voting roll; they eventually had to consent to separate race-based voting rolls in order to obtain independence.

> Thus, when Fiji's independence became real in 1970, the constitution insisted that races still existed in Fiji and had to vote separately. Since then parties have generally and increasingly followed racial lines, and the army has remained an enclave of Indigenous Fijians. When political parties, backed mostly by Indo-Fijian voters, won Fiji's 1987 election, this army took over the country within a month. The constitution that was then installed in 1990 returned to even more naked discrimination against Indo-Fijians in regard to voting rights. (Kelly and Kaplan 2001: 77)

The constitution was revised yet again, in a manner that favoured ethnic Fijian interests and seemed guaranteed to prevent parties backed by Indo-Fijian voters from winning control of the government in the 1999 election. To everyone's surprise,

parties backed by ethnic Fijians lost this election as well. Another coup came on 19 May 2000. Finally, after new elections in 2001, ethnic Fijians won control of the government. The military coup of 2006 was a direct result of the continuing consequences of the coup of 2000. It focused primarily on the Reconciliation, Tolerance, and Unity Bill that proposed amnesty legislation for those involved in the 2000 coup. The coup of 2006 resulted in the military effectively taking control of the country (Figure 6.13). In October 2008, the Fijian High Court ruled that the resulting government was the legal government.

What lessons does this history suggest about nation-building in post-colonial states? The issues are many and complex. But one key factor is that the image of a united Fijian nation projected at independence was severely undermined by legal mechanisms of political representation carried over from the colonial period, particularly the race-based voting rolls. What became apparent in the years after independence was the fact that Indo-Fijians and ethnic Fijians had imagined very different national communities. Indo-Fijians had supported the image of a Fijian nation in which all citizens, Indo-Fijian or ethnic Fijian or other, would have equal status, voting on a single roll, working together to build a constitutional democracy. However, "few among the ethnic Fijians have yet come to see themselves as partners with immigrants" (2001: 41). Ever since independence, and particularly after each coup,

Figure 6.13 A Fijian citizen reads a newspaper on 2 December 2006, as tensions rise between Prime Minister Laisenia Qarase and the Fijian military. The military took control of the government on 6 December 2006.

ethnic Fijians worked to construct an image of the Fijian nation based solely on their own traditions—traditions in which Indo-Fijians had no meaningful place. Thus, Kelly and Kaplan conclude, in Fiji (and in many other parts of the world) "'the nation' is a contested idea, not an experienced reality" (142).

Nationalism and Its Dangers

The most horrifying consequence of nation-building movements in the twentieth century has been the discovery of just how far the ruling groups of some nation-states are willing to go in order to enforce their version of national identity.

After World War II, the world was shocked to learn about Nazi programs to "liquidate" Jews, Roma, and other groups that failed to conform to Nazi ideals of Aryan purity. Many people hoped that the Nazi Holocaust was exceptional, but subsequent developments suggest that it may have been the most dramatic example of an exterminationist temptation that accompanies all drives to nationalism. Sociologist Zygmunt Bauman argued in his book *Modernity and the Holocaust* (1989) that modern nation-states with rationalized bureaucracies and industrial technology were the first societies in history to make efficient mass extermination of deviants technically possible. In a transnational culture of nationalism, not to belong to a nation-state made up of loyal, ambitious, like-minded citizens is a severe, possibly fatal, handicap. Using violence against all citizens who undermine claims of national homogeneity and common purpose may thus be a peculiarly modern way for insecure rulers of embattled nation-states to try to bring about solidarity and stability. In the late twentieth century, warring nationalities in the former Yugoslavia used selective assassinations and forced migration to rid their fledgling nation-states of unwanted *others*, a policy known as *ethnic cleansing* (Figure 6.14). And reports of ethnic cleansing have continued into the first decades of the twenty-first centuries; many of these reports come from Congo, Libya, South Sudan, and other chronically war-torn regions of Africa and the Middle East. Additionally, in 2014 the people of the world were challenged for a response to the ethnic murders (as well as the murders not directly related to ethnicity) of men, women, and children in Syria and Iraq by the Islamic State of Iraq and al-Sham (ISIS). Thus, rather than relics of a barbarian past, ethnic cleansing, *ethnocide* (the destruction of a culture), and *genocide* (the extermination of an entire people) may constitute a series of related practices that are all signs of things to come. All are measures of the high stakes for which rulers of these nation-states see themselves competing.

Figure 6.14 The Srebrenica–Potočari Memorial and Cemetery for the Victims of the 1995 Genocide.

Living Anthropology

Construction of Poverty and Wealth Inequality in the Twenty-First Century

by Matt Husain, PhD Candidate, Anthropology of Development, and Adjunct Faculty, University of British Columbia (Okanagan)

The OXFAM 2017 report on global wealth inequality states that only "eight men own the same amount of wealth as the poorest half of the world" (Hardoon et al. 2017). Earlier in 2014 during an interview by *The Economist*, Bill Gates, who tops the list of the richest persons, responded on the increasing global wealth gap:

. . . the human values are the children should survive, kids should have enough nutrition, people should be educated, and we'd like average lifespans to be 80 plus years for every country. If you are achieving those goals and at the same time few people are getting ridiculous amounts of money, I'd rather have that than some sort of communistic idea of equality. (*The Economist* 2014)

In this section, we will critically interpret the OXFAM findings in conjunction with the remarks of Bill Gates. Historical evidence indicates poverty has all along been part of every civilization, but in the first quarter of the twenty-first century, while remaining connected with others more than ever before, we face the most adverse form of wealth inequality.

These outcomes have been largely generated by various profit-driven factors, including excessive privatization and globalization that put a premium on individual or corporate ownership of public or government resources. Before the nineteenth century, the human economy was always embedded in society. Here the term *embeddedness* expresses the idea that the economy is not autonomous but subordinated to politics, religion, and social relations (Polanyi 1964: 23). However, economics secured importance above all else in various political philosophies, facilitating the industrial revolution and having deep roots in colonial history. This construct became deeper with the advancements in technology, deregulation in finance, increasing role of media, movement of people, and popularizing of universal values, such as democracy and human rights. While our world became modern, as a result, this progress came at a cost—extreme wealth inequality.

Learning about poverty is an essential part of understanding inequality. Poverty is about not having enough resources to meet basic needs, such as food, clothing, and shelter (World Bank 2016). Poverty is also relative because feeling impoverished in a developing country, such as Bangladesh, is different from feeling poor in a developed country, such as Canada. Considering poverty as more than just not having enough money, social scientists, such as David Harvey (2005), David Mosse (2010), and Amartya Sen (1982), respectively, argue that poverty is a human-made construct.

Harvey (2005) considers capitalist factors, such as exploiting weak governance and high interest loans, as leading causes of poverty. Mosse (2010) highlights non-capitalist forms of exclusion based on gender, religion, social class, and education as paving paths for poverty (1157). Finally, Sen (1982) conclusively proves that famines are caused not by a lack of food but due to mismanagement and corruption within distribution systems and fixing of prices for basic necessities (160–6).

As resources on this planet are finite, most peoples have no choice but to live with less because only a handful of people own most of our resources. Realizing the depth of this issue on the surface is challenging because we mainly measure the economic growth of a country through gross domestic product (GDP), which is a basic percentage calculation and is calculated as an aggregate measure of all production and gross values divided by the total number of people in a country (OECD 2015). Critically speaking, GDP at face value can mask reality on the ground by portraying a generalized image of an economy. For example, although Canada's 2015 per person GDP was $50,000, that does not mean every Canadian owned assets worth $50,000. In comparison, while India's per capita GDP in 2015 was $1751, there are many billionaires in India. The flaw of GDP algorithms is as the rich get richer, the average GDP increases and that mistakenly infers that the poor are doing better as well. This disjuncture in fact masks the unequal relation between the rich and the poor.

Overall, for as long as the liberal economy (or capitalism) thrives, there will always be inequality because this system keeps maximizing profit, avoids paying tax by cutting government interference, relies on cheaper labour, and creates new markets for profit maximization.

While we applaud the accomplishments of successful entrepreneurs such as Bill Gates, economists such as Muhammad Yunus (2011) and Manfred Max-Neef (2010) identify the bottomless pit of human greed as the major problem behind economic inequality. Thus, the first logical step toward fixing this human-made issue is to create collective awareness of the factors and causes that generate wealth inequality.

Key Terms

caste   125
class   125
client   126
clientage   126
cline   131

colourism   136
ethnic groups   136
ethnicity   125
jāti   127
nation   140

nationalism   140
nationality   125
nation-state   140
objectification   140
patron   126

Chapter Summary

1. All people in the world today must deal with the authority of one nation-state or another, each of which contains multiple hierarchies of stratification. Every one of these hierarchies is a cultural invention designed to create boundaries around imagined communities. Some patterns of stratification reach back thousands of years, but others are closely associated with the rise of European capitalism and colonialism.

2. The concept of class in anthropology has a double heritage: Europeans tended to view class boundaries as closed and rigid, whereas North Americans tended to view them as open and permeable. Class solidarity may be undercut by clientage relations that bind individuals to one another across class boundaries.

3. India has been used as the prototype of caste stratification, although anthropologists have applied the concept to social hierarchies encountered elsewhere in the world. Contemporary anthropologists reject views of caste in India that portray it as internally harmonious and uncontested by those at the bottom of the caste hierarchy.

4. The contemporary concept of "race" developed in the context of European colonialism beginning in the fifteenth century, as lighter-skinned Europeans came to rule over darker-skinned peoples in different parts of the world. In many regions today, a hierarchy persists in which whiteness symbolizes high status; and blackness, low status.

5. Although ethnic consciousness existed in pre-colonial and pre-capitalist societies, contemporary anthropologists have been most interested in forms of ethnicity that were generated under capitalist colonial domination, when different groups were subordinated within a single political structure under conditions of inequality. This process frequently creates "nesting identities" that individuals often manipulate in order to achieve upward mobility. When dominant ethnic groups feel threatened, they may attempt to stigmatize subordinate groups by "racializing" them.

6. Nation-states were invented in nineteenth-century Europe, but they have spread throughout the world. Nationalist thinking aims to create a political unit in which national identity and political territory coincide, which has led to various practices designed to force subordinate social groups to adopt a national identity defined primarily in terms of the culture of the dominant group. If the creation of such an imagined hybrid identity is not accompanied by legal and political changes that support it, however, the end result may be political turmoil.

Critical Thinking Questions

1. How has the "American Dream" been realized in the Canadian context? Does our interpretation of class mobility differ from that of our neighbour to the south?

2. Which aspects of social stratification do you consider to be associated with capitalism?

3. Discuss open and closed stratification systems. Beyond their permeable or non-permeable boundaries, what would you consider to be their main differences?

Suggested Readings

Domhoff, G. William. 2013. *Who Rules America? Challenges to Corporate and Class Dominance*, **7th edn (New York: McGraw-Hill).** This book has become a classic in sociology, and it is also relevant to the anthropologist interested in theory on elites, as it discusses how power and politics operate in the United States.

Magat, Ilan N. 1999. "**Israeli and Japanese Immigrants to Canada: Home, Belonging, and the Territorialization of Identity,**" *Ethos* **27, 2: 119–44.** This article investigates identity formation, management, and change, and the interrelationship of the personal, the cultural, and the national for immigrants to Canada from Israel and Japan.

Nash, Manning. 1989. *The Cauldron of Ethnicity in the Modern World* **(Chicago: University of Chicago Press).** Nash looks at ethnicity in the post-colonial world and sees more of a seething cauldron than a melting pot. He examines the relations between Ladinos and Maya in Guatemala, Chinese and Malays in Malaysia, and Jews and non-Jews in the United States.

Painter, Nell Irvin. 2010. *The History of White People* **(New York: W. W. Norton and Company).** A great book that looks at the development of the concept of "whiteness" and what it has led to in recent times.

Razack, Sherene. 2000. "From the 'Clean Snows of Petawawa': The Violence of Canadian Peacekeepers in Somalia," *Cultural Anthropology* **15, 1: 127–63.** This article discusses the violence of Canadian peacekeepers in the context of gender roles and racist responses.

Schryer, Frans J. 2001. "Multiple Hierarchies and the Duplex Nature of Groups," *Journal of the Royal Anthropological Institute* **7, 4: 705–21.** This article examines the links between multiple hierarchies and broad-based groups to create a theoretical framework for integrating group phenomena, social identities, and political mobilization.

Sharma, Ursula. 1999. *Caste* **(Philadelphia: Open University Press).** A brief survey of anthropological scholarship dealing with caste in South Asia.

Smedley, Audrey, and Brian Smedley. 2011. *Race in North America: Origin and Evolution of a World View*, **4th edn (Boulder, CO: Westview Press).** This book offers a comprehensive historical overview of the development of the concept of "race" in North America, beginning in the late eighteenth century. The authors show how the concept of "race" is a cultural construct that has been used in different ways, for different purposes.

Related Websites

Historica: French Canadian Nationalism
www.thecanadianencyclopedia.com/en/article/french-canadian-nationalism
Immigration and Refugee Board of Canada
www.irb-cisr.gc.ca

Politics of Racism
www.japanesecanadianhistory.ca
Australian Government: Reconciliation (Australia)
http://australia.gov.au/about-australia/australian-story/reconciliation

7 Social Relationships: Marriage, Family, Kinship, and Friendship

Learning Objectives

By the end of Chapter 7, you will be able to

- understand "marriage" as a social process;
- identify variations in family structure;
- consider how families change over time and in response to new circumstances;
- appreciate kinship patterns of descent;

- see kinship terminology as statements of rights and obligations;
- situate marriage and kinship in an economic world; and
- understand the value of friendship and voluntary alliances.

Human beings are highly social creatures endeavouring to establish and maintain relationships with others. Our need for companionship is well explored in Kurt Vonnegut Jr's science fiction novel *Slapstick, or Lonesome No More!* (1976). In the novel, Dr Wilbur Daffodil-11 Swain presents a plan to end loneliness with a new system of interrelatedness, one in which every person has a large number of relatives on whom they can depend. Swain proposes that everyone will be given a new middle name composed of a noun and a number (e.g., Daffodil-11). Everyone with the same noun will be cousins and everyone with the same noun and number will be siblings. A side effect is the development of clubs based on shared characteristics. While the setting is a fictional re-imagining of America, the author's comments on loneliness resonate beyond the American context, illustrating that **relatedness** is a central concern for most of us. We all want to belong. Our primary *positionality* (see Chapter 2) begins with familial relatedness before we become situated in a wider community.

We start life physically and emotionally tied to our mothers. To survive on our own, we must bind ourselves to others through alliances of **marriage**, **family**, **kinship**, and **friendship**. We become enmeshed in a changing web of relatives and friends—a web of rights and obligations. In this chapter, we focus on relatedness and how relatedness is selectively understood and culturally formed in our deeply layered social practices.

Marriage

Different cultures have different criteria for defining marriage. Some cultures recognize only heterosexual alliances, while others include same-sex partnerships. Some allow individuals only one spouse at a time, while others permit individuals to have multiple spouses at the same time. Some treat marriage as a prerequisite for sexual activity (especially for females), while others do not. Some insist on a ceremony and/or a legal document to formalize a marriage, while others accept long-term cohabitation as a marker of such unions. In some cultures, the definition of marriage has evolved. Today, more and more Western couples are choosing less rigidly defined forms of marriage (see tables 7.1 and 7.2).

Marriage always creates new *relationships*—between the individuals marrying one another, among their relatives, and among members of the wider society. Frequently, the community recognizes the new union by participating in the rites of marriage. On the familial level, marriages affect **affinal** relationships (relationships created via marriage, therefore based on *affinity*) as well as **consanguineal** relationships (relationships of descent, regardless of whether the child is related by birth, adoption, sperm/ovum donation, or surrogacy, therefore based on "blood," either genetically or socially defined). If the couple has children, these children will go on to form relationships of their own. Thus, many anthropologists choose to think of marriage as a social process.

relatedness The socially recognized ties that connect people in a variety of ways.

marriage An institution that prototypically (1) involves a man and a woman, (2) transforms the status of the participants, (3) carries implications about sexual access, (4) gives offspring a position in society, and (5) establishes connections between the kin of a husband and the kin of a wife.

family At minimum, a woman or a man and her or his dependent children.

kinship Social relationships that are prototypically derived from the universal human experiences of mating, birth, and nurturance.

friendship The relatively unofficial bonds that people construct with one another that tend to be personal, affective, and a matter of choice.

affinal Related through marriage.

consanguineal Relationships of descent, regardless of whether the child is related by birth, adoption, sperm/ovum donation, or surrogacy, therefore based on "blood" either genetically or socially defined.

Table 7.1 Marital Status of Individuals 15 Years of Age and Older, Canada, 2016

	Not Living Common Law	Living Common Law
Single (never legally married)	8,254,340	2,583,350
Married (and not separated)	13,383,455	0
Separated (but still legally married)	718,295	129,680
Divorced	1,816,005	713,465
Widowed	1,629,800	83,765
Total	25,801,900	3,510,265

Note: *Common law* refers to two people living together as a couple but not legally married to each other.

Source: Adapted from Statistics Canada, 2016 Census of Population, Statistics Canada Catalogue no. 98-400-X2016031.

A traditional wedding ceremony in Meiji Jingu Shrine, a Shinto shrine in Tokyo, Japan. While some weddings are still held according to Shinto traditions, Christian wedding ceremonies have largely been the ceremony of choice in Japan since the 1990s.

Table 7.2 Opposite-Sex and Same-Sex Couples, with and without Children, Canada, 2011

	Opposite-Sex Couples	Female Couples	Male Couples
Without children	3,694,400	24,305	33,855
With children	4,102,880	5,075	1,340
Total	7,797,280	29,380	35,195

Source: Adapted from Statistics Canada. 2013. "2011 Census of Canada."

Marriage as a Social Process

We use the term *marriage* to define the alliances and essential social roles that establish and reinforce rights and obligations at the core of social life. Looking at the variety of alliances that we subsume under the term *marriage* allows us to see such alliances as a social process. Our frames of reference now expand beyond traditional Western definitions (Lamphere 2005) (Figure 7.1). Roles evolve as societal norms change with changing times. For example, before Bill 16 was passed in 1964, a woman who entered marriage in Quebec lost her status as an independent adult unless she had a previously arranged legal contract, similar to what we would call a "prenup" (i.e., a prenuptial agreement) today. A married woman under Quebec's Civil Code could not inherit property, open a bank account, or sign her children into hospital for treatment; these "rights" were reserved for her husband. Since 1964, due in large part to social changes supporting women's equality, women in Quebec have shared these rights with their husbands. In 2005, Canada saw further changes to the definition of marriage with the passing of the Civil

> **bridewealth** The transfer of certain symbolically important goods from the family of the groom to the family of the bride, representing compensation to the wife's lineage for the loss of her labour and for child-bearing capacities.

Marriage Act, which legally recognized same-sex marriage. More recently, in 2015 the United States legalized same-sex marriage in all states although it remains a somewhat contested issue.

Post-marital living arrangements may reflect the role each partner is expected to adopt in familial and social relationships (see Table 7.3). In many societies, the partners are expected to live with a specific set of family members. Such arrangements, traditionally called "residence rules" by anthropologists, suggest how that culture understands family bonds. This may take on alternative meanings for those living in transnational situations, such as those living in refugee camps and forced to leave the place defined as "home." Here "... notions of continuity and belonging are continuously negotiated in relation to processes of change" (Pedersen 2011: 15). Living away from the daily activities, routines, and institutions of "home" is very difficult and requires physical and psychological resources, without which maintaining social bonds may be nearly impossible (16–17).

Some cultures use forms of creative marriage to develop specifically needed social relationships. Evans-Pritchard (1951) described two such forms among the Nuer of East Africa in the early twentieth century. In the first form, a woman could marry another woman and become the "father" of the wife's children. To understand this sort of arrangement, we must distinguish between *pater* (social father role) and *genitor* (biological father or sperm provider role). To establish the marriage, the female husband (the *pater*) gave the bride's lineage cattle as **bridewealth** payments. Then, a male kinsman, friend, or neighbour (the *genitor*) impregnated the wife and contributed labour by performing tasks considered to be men's work. The female husband played the social role of a man. She could marry several women if her wealth permitted, and she could demand damage payment if any wife engaged in sexual activity (adultery) without her consent. She was the *pater* of her wives' children, who were of her patrilineage and called her "father." She administered her compound and her herds as any male head of household

Figure 7.1 Couples wait for their turn during a mass wedding ceremony (an event in which many couples are married at the same time) in Navi Mumbai, India.

© Dinodia Photos/Alamy Stock Photo

Table 7.3 **Patterns of Residence after Marriage**

Pattern Name	Residence	Comments	Example
Neolocal (major pattern)	In a place of the couple's own choosing	Found in societies that are more or less individualistic in their social organization	Most Western nations, including Canada and the United States
Patrilocal (major pattern)	With (or near) the husband's father's family	Most common in herding and farming societies; observed by more societies in the contemporary world than any other residence pattern	China (villages and traditional communities); Turkey (villages and traditional communities)
Matrilocal (major pattern)	With (or near) the family in which the wife was raised	Most common in horticultural groups; the core of the social group consists of a woman, her sisters, and their daughters, together with their husbands	Iroquois (NE North America); Hopi (SW North America); Tlingit (NW Coast North America)
Avunculocal (major pattern)	With (or near) the husband's mother's brother	Found in matrilineal societies in which a boy inherits from his mother's brother	Chamorros (Mariana Islands); Taíno (Turks and Caicos Islands)
Ambilocal (minor pattern)	First with the family of one spouse and later with the family of the other	Eventually the couple chooses which family they want to affiliate with permanently	SE Porno and E Porno (California); Mbuti (NE Democratic Republic of the Congo)
Duolocal (minor pattern)	Each partner lives with members of his or her own lineage even after marriage	Seen where lineage membership is the most important societal aspect	Nayar (NE India); Minangkabau (Indonesia)

would, she was treated by her wives and children with the same deference shown to a male husband and father, and she fulfilled all her duties to her relatives through her role as a man.

The second form, *ghost marriage*, was more common. Since a basic obligation of Nuer kinship was for a man to be remembered through and by his sons, a man who died without male heirs became an unhappy, angry spirit. To appease this ghost, the man's kinsman—a brother or a brother's son—would marry a woman "to his name." Bridewealth cattle were paid in the ghost's name. From the marriage ceremony onward, the kinsman acted as husband and the children were commonly referred to as his—but legally they were the children of the ghost husband. The kinsman was *genitor*, but the ghost husband was *pater*, and

the ghost husband's name would be remembered in the history of the lineage. Marrying a woman "to his kinsman's name" before the man himself married presented difficulties in subsequently contracting a marriage in his own right as his relatives would want to allocate cattle for bridewealth to the unmarried brothers. Even if he eventually accumulated enough cattle to afford to marry for himself, he would feel that those cattle should provide the bridewealth for the sons he had raised for his dead kinsman. He then died without any sons of his own, thus becoming an angry spirit in his own turn. Someone else (in fact, one of the sons he had raised for the ghost) had to marry a woman to *his* name and so the pattern continued.

This practice is similar to the more widely documented practice of *levirate* (discussed in the Bible in

Deuteronomy 25:1–5), in which a widow marries her deceased husband's brother. When it is a widower who marries a sister (or sometimes a specific cousin) of his deceased wife, the practice is known as *sororate*. There are advantages to such systems when considerable resources are invested in the marriage. Another advantage of sororate is that the stepmother is a kinswoman of any existing children from the first marriage, meaning that she is very likely to feel protective of those children. The "Cinderella Effect," as discussed in sociobiology (Daly and Wilson 1985), continues to be debated regarding the data surrounding better outcomes for stepchildren in the care of biologically related caregivers.

Endogamy is the term for marrying within a particular social group while **exogamy** is the term for marrying outside a particular group. In all societies, some close kin are off limits as spouses or sexual partners, specifically members of the nuclear family, which is known as the *incest taboo*. Pressure to marry specific partners can be formally defined or covertly manoeuvred. Collective identities of ethnicity, religion, language, class, and caste may be bounded by law or custom (see, e.g., Connolly 2009). In some cases, marrying outside the prescribed group can lead to social exclusion or even formal disenfranchisement (removal of rights). This was certainly true for Canadian First Nations women under the Indian Act (1876). They were denied certain rights, including residency rights, if they married non-Native men. When the act was amended, the great Mohawk activist Mary Two-Axe Earley (Figure 7.2) observed, "After all these years, I'll be legally entitled to live on the reserve, to own property, die and be buried with my own people" (Brown 2003).

In December 1993, then 83, and as a witness for the Native Council of Canada, she rolled her wheelchair into the Federal Court of Canada to testify about the hardships of women expelled from their home reserves. One of her most striking points was that the Kahnawake reserve had three graveyards: one for Catholics, one for Protestants, and one for dogs. While dogs could be buried on the reserve, "if you were a Mohawk woman who married a non-Indian, you had to be buried outside the community." . . . Most significantly, she was buried in the Catholic cemetery that lies on a small hill in the heart of the reserve. That was possible only because of the 1985

endogamy Marriage within a defined social group.

exogamy Marriage outside a defined social group.

monogamy A marriage pattern in which a person may be married to only one person at a time.

polygamy A marriage pattern in which a person may be married to more than one person at a time.

CP PICTURE ARCHIVE/Toronto Star

Figure 7.2 Mohawk activist Mary Two-Axe Earley, from Kahnawake, Quebec, was a catalyst for the establishment of Bill C-31, which led to the reinstatement of treaty status for First Nations women married to non-Native men.

legislative changes for which she had fought so many years. (Brown 2003)

Monogamy and Polygamy

The number of spouses a person may have varies cross-culturally. **Monogamy** signifies one spouse at a time. This is the form of marriage that predominates in Canada. Before the twentieth century, divorce was rare, and people in European-style societies generally married only once unless they were widowed. Today, as some observers have noted, North Americans practise *serial monogamy*—that is, they marry several different people throughout their lives, but they are married to only one person at a time.

Polygamy allows a person to have more than one spouse, and has two subcategories: *polygyny* (multiple wives; see Figure 7.3) and *polyandry* (multiple husbands). Some polygynous societies have no limit on the number of wives because not every man can afford to be polygynous and there are simply not enough women. Some societies, however, do limit the number of wives. Traditionally, a Muslim man may have four wives but only on the condition that he can support them equally. Some Islamic theorists today argue that equal support must be emotional, not just financial. Convinced that no man can feel exactly the same toward each of his wives, these theorists have concluded that monogamy must be the rule. Many Western countries now have significant Muslim populations and there has arisen concern in some sectors for faith-based arbitration in the context of Sharia (Islamic) laws around marriage. This has reached the courts in Ontario where women's rights have been considered and have resulted in the ruling that "...until and unless minority religious laws...can stand the test of constitutionality and gender equality principles, Canadian Family Law provides the best safeguard for women from minority and immigrant communities" (Philips 2011: 284).

Polyandry is much rarer than polygyny. Polyandrous societies tend to separate a woman's sexuality from her reproductive capacity, and some researchers have suggested that polyandry is uncommon because, unlike polygyny or even monogamy, it is not as concerned with controlling women's sexuality (see, e.g., Levine and Sangree 1980). Anthropologists generally recognize three forms of polyandry: fraternal, associated, and secondary marriage.

Most anthropologists consider fraternal polyandry—particularly that found in Nepal and Tibet—to be the prototype for other forms of polyandry. Here the oldest brother serves as the groom, but all brothers, even those yet unborn, are married to the same woman in a publicly recognized wedding. The wife and her husbands live together patrilocally (see Table 7.3). All brothers have equal sexual access to the wife, and all act as fathers (*pater*) to the children without distinguishing the identity of the *genitor*. A notable exception is found with the Nyinba of Nepal (see Map 7.1), where each child is recognized as having one particular *genitor* (Levine 1980, 1988). Sexual jealousy is rare, and the brothers have a strong sense of solidarity with one another (Levine 1988). If the wife proves sterile, the brothers may marry another woman. Solidarity of brothers is a central kinship ideal in societies that practise fraternal polyandry, and it helps to keep the household and the landholdings unified. Fraternal polyandry, by its essential structure, diminishes fragmentation of landholdings while limiting population growth (Mishra et al. 2003). Land and resources are limited, so the concentration of resources increases a household's political position and economic viability.

Associated polyandry is open to men who are not brothers (Levine and Sangree 1980). There is evidence it was an acceptable marriage variant with some peoples of the Pacific and North and South America.

Figure 7.3 Portrait of a man with his children and three wives in Iraq. How might polygynous family structures affect the structure of a society?

But it is best described with the Sinhalese of past generations, where marriage began monogamously and a second husband was brought into the union later. The first husband was the principal husband in terms of authority, while each man looked after his own economic resources. Both husbands were considered fathers to any children the wife bore. Once the primary polyandrous relationship was established, the three spouses could decide to take another woman into the

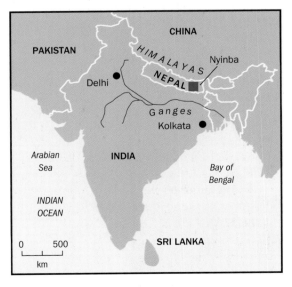

Map 7.1 Nyinba

marriage—often the sister of the wife—creating a marriage pattern called *polygynandry*. Depending on relative wealth and the availability of economic opportunity, a traditional Sinhalese household may be monogamous, polyandrous, or polygynandrous.

With *secondary marriage*—as practised, for example, in northern Nigeria and northern Cameroon—a woman marries one or more *secondary* husbands while staying married to her first husband (Levine and Sangree 1980: 400). She lives with only one husband at a time, but she retains the right to return to a previous husband and to have legitimate children by him at a later date. There is no divorce; marriage is for life. However, men are as polygynous as women are polyandrous. A man marries a series of women and lives with one or more of them at his homestead, while the women independently pursue their own marital careers. Technically, secondary marriage is a combination of polyandry and polygyny, resulting from the overlap of men seeking several wives and women seeking several husbands. Thus, it can build extensive networks of marriage-based ties throughout a region (Levine and Sangree 1980).

Flexibility and Negotiation in Marriage

At this point, it may seem as though the rules that govern marriage are often rigid, compelling people to adhere to social norms and, at times, do things they do not want to do. Marriage rules, however, are always subject to some negotiation. For example, the Iteso (Map 7.2) take the marriage ritual very seriously, using it as the basis for the physical and social reproduction of Iteso patrilineages. Anthropologist

Ivan Karp (1978) analyzed the meaning of the Iteso marriage ritual from two perspectives: that of the men and that of the women. He found that the men's perspective presents the "official" view, which emphasizes how marriage brings the bride's sexuality and reproductive capacity under the control of her husband's lineage. By contrast, the women's "unofficial" view in a sense celebrates the fact that although men control women's bodies for reproduction, these bodies belong to outsider women. These same outsiders direct the two ritual events crucial to lineage reproduction—marriage and birth—and men of the lineage are not allowed to attend either ritual. Thus, women control the continued existence of patrilineages whose male members are supposed to control them! Iteso women see the irony in this: they are at once controlled and controlling. In the marriage ritual this paradox is displayed through laughter that subverts, at least momentarily, men's sense of control.

Further flexibility in marriage can also be seen in new data that are emerging on the development of relationships with respect to love, intimacy, and sexuality (Spronk 2011). Spronk, in her work in urban Kenya, notes that "sexuality is crucial in the development of contemporary notions of selfhood among young adults" (148) and that these views are reinforced by current forms of media on what it means to be in a modern relationship. Thus the once popular idea that "sex is a marital duty," which is interpreted as "enforcing the sexual subordination of women," has been replaced with the idea that the "'modern' duty is the fulfilment of a mutual orgasm" (154).

It is also important to consider how (and why) ideas of relationships are perpetuated and negotiated. For example, Jankowiak and Gerth (2012) discuss the American media–supported ideal of love as "essentially a dyadic bond between two and only two individuals [arising from] feelings of eroticism, passion, and companionship that somehow merge together to form a unified conceptual whole" (2012: 95), which is only one way of viewing love out of many. What are some of the consequences this image of a relationship could have on a globalized world?

Marriage and Economic Exchange

Many societies transfer specific categories of symbolically important goods at marriage through *bridewealth* and/or **dowry** (Huber, Danaher, and Breedlove 2011). Bridewealth, briefly noted earlier with Nuer practices, is most common in

dowry The transfer of wealth from parents to their child (usually a daughter) at the time of the child's marriage.

Map 7.2 Iteso

patrilineal, patrilocal societies and, sometimes, in matrilineal societies with avunculocal residence rules (see Table 7.3). The goods exchanged may include shell ornaments, ivory tusks, brass gongs, bird feathers, fabrics, and animals. Bridewealth in animals is prevalent in eastern and southern Africa, where cattle have the most profound symbolic and economic value. In these societies, a man's father, and often his entire patrilineage, gives a specified number of cattle (often in instalments) to the patrilineage of the bride. Bridewealth formalizes the new affinal link. The bride's relatives, in turn, often use the bridewealth to find a bride for the woman's brother in yet another kinship group. In many such societies a woman gains power and influence over her brother when her marriage brings the cattle that will allow him to marry and continue their lineage; "Cattle beget children," according to the southern Bantu (Kuper 1982: 3)! And children can be used to consolidate a woman's position in the various linkages of blood and affinity. Bridewealth has been described as "a societal fund, a circulating pool of resources, the movement of which corresponds to the movement of rights over spouses, usually women" (Goody and Tambiah 1973: 17).

Dowry, on the other hand, is a transfer of family wealth, usually from parents to their daughter, at the time of marriage, and is found primarily in the agricultural societies of Europe and Asia and some parts of Africa now under Islamic sharia law. In societies where both women and men are seen as potential heirs, dowry is sometimes regarded as the buyout of the inheritance. Dowries are often considered the wife's contribution to the establishment of a new household, to which the husband may bring other forms of wealth. In stratified societies, a woman's dowry may ensure that she will continue to enjoy her accustomed lifestyle. Dowry resources vary in different societies and may or may not include land (Goody and Tambiah 1973) (Figure 7.4).

Anthropologist and psychologist Leigh Minturn (1993) has examined dowry practices among the Khalapur Rajputs of northern India (see Map 7.3). Here all land is held by a group of brothers with their wives and children living as a joint family. Daughters' dowries consist of transportable items (chattels, such as money, jewellery, clothing, and household decorations. Rajput marriages are village exogamous and *hypergamous*: that is, women normally marry into lineages of higher status than the ones into which they were born (recall the caste system mentioned in Chapter 6), living as low-ranking

Figure 7.4 Dowry can take many forms, such as these wedding gifts at a celebration in Ratchaburi, Thailand.

outsiders in the households and villages of their husbands. How well they marry and how well they are treated by their in-laws depends on the size of their dowries. In the 1950s, when Minturn first visited Khalapur, new Rajput wives were under the strict control of their mothers-in-law, who assigned tasks, limited their contact with their husbands, and controlled their dowries. Every time a wife visited her parents, moreover, she was expected to return with more gifts for her husband's family.

Dowry practices can cause considerable financial strain on the family providing the dowry. As many Rajputs believe, "It is best to have two

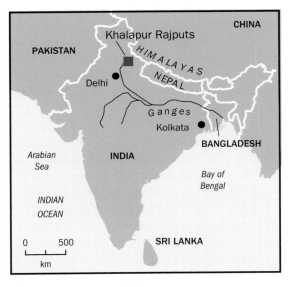

Map 7.3 Khalapur Rajputs

In Their Own Words

Dowry Too High: Lose Bride and Go to Jail

In some parts of the world, discussions of bridewealth or dowry seem so divorced from reality as to appear "academic." But elsewhere, these topics remain significant indeed. In May 2003, news media all over the world reported the story of a bride in India who called the police when a battle erupted over demands for additional dowry payments at her wedding. ***The New York Times* reports.**

Noida, India, May 16—The musicians were playing, the 2,000 guests were dining, the Hindu priest was preparing the ceremony and the bride was dressed in red, her hands and feet festively painted with henna.

Then, the bride's family says, the groom's family moved in for the kill. The dowry of two televisions, two home theater sets, two refrigerators, two air-conditioners and one car was too cheap. They wanted $25,000 in rupees, now, under the wedding tent.

As a free-for-all erupted between the two families, the bartered bride put her hennaed foot down. She reached for the royal blue cellphone and dialed 100. By calling the police, Nisha Sharma, a 21-year-old computer student, saw her potential groom land in jail and herself land in the national spotlight as Indian's new overnight sensation.

"Are they marrying with money, or marrying with me?" Ms. Sharma asked today, her dark eyes glaring under arched eyebrows. In the next room a fresh wave of reporters waited to interview her, sitting next to the unopened boxes of her wedding trousseau.

After fielding a call from a comic-book artist who wanted to bring her act of defiance last Sunday night to a mass market, she said, "I'm feeling proud of myself."

"It Takes Guts to Send Your Groom Packing," a headline in *The Times of India* read.

Rashtriya Sahara, a major Hindi daily, said in a salute, "Bravo: We're Proud of You."

"She is being hailed as a New Age woman and seen as a role model to many," the newspaper *Asian Age* wrote next to a front-page drawing of Ms. Sharma standing in front of red and green wedding pennants while flashing a V sign to cameras and wearing a sash over her blue sari with the words *Miss Anti-Dowry*.

"This was a brave thing for a girl dressed in all her wedding finery to do," said Vandana Sharma, president of the Women's Protection League, one of many women's rights leaders and

---

sons and one daughter, because then you will receive two dowries, but give only one" (Minturn 1993: 130). Poor people whose sons cannot attract women with dowries often engage in a practice called *buying a wife*, in which the husband's family gives money to the bride's family to purchase her dowry goods.

In 1961, the government of India passed a law prohibiting dowries, but it has proven impossible to enforce. (See the "In Their Own Words" box above.) Dowry violence and death occur with alarming frequency in India:

> Dowry violence takes a characteristic form. Following marriage and the requisite giving of dowry, the family of the groom makes additional demands for the payment of more cash or the provision of more goods . . . expressed in unremitting harassment of the bride . . . [and] culminating in the murder of the woman by members of her husband's family or by her

> suicide. The woman is typically burned to death with kerosene . . . hence the use of the term *bride-burning* in public discourse. . . . Police records do not match hospital records [and] far more violence occurs than the crime reports indicate. (van Willigen and Channa 1991: 369)

The murder of widows to keep them from withdrawing their husband's portion of the land from traditional joint holdings is not infrequent. Additionally widespread "selective female abortion" avoids having to pay dowries in the future (van Willigen and Channa 1991: 370).

Family Structure

What is a family? At minimum, we have the **non-conjugal family**: a parent (usually a woman) and dependent children. The second parent (usually the father) may be occasionally present or completely absent. Cross-culturally, non-conjugal families are

non-conjugal family
A woman (or, less commonly, a man) and her (or his) children, with or without a second parent.

politicians to make a pilgrimage this week to this eastern suburb of Delhi. "This girl has taken a very dynamic step." Indian's new 24-hour news stations have propelled Nisha Sharma to Hindi stardom. One television station set up a service allowing viewers to "send a message to Nisha." In the first two days, 1,500 messages came in.

Illegal for many decades in India, dowries are now often disguised by families as gifts to give the newlyweds a start in life. More than a media creation, Ms. Sharma and her dowry defiance struck a chord in this nation, whose expanding middle class is rebelling against a dowry tradition that is being overfed by a new commercialism.

"Advertisements now show parents giving things to make their daughters happy in life," Brinda Karat, general secretary of the All India Democratic Women's Association, a private group, said, referring to television commercials for products commonly given in dowries.

"It is the most modern aspects of information technology married to the most backward concepts of subordination of women," Ms. Karat continued in a telephone interview. Last year, she said, her group surveyed 10,000 people in 18 of India's 26 states. "We found an across-the-board increase in dowry demand," she said.

Much of the dowry greed is new, Ms. Karat added. In a survey 40 years ago, she noted, almost two-thirds of Indian communities reported that the local custom was for the groom to pay the bride's family, the reverse of the present dominant custom. According to government statistics, husbands and in-laws angry over small dowry payments killed nearly 7,000 women in 2001.

When Ms. Sharma's parents were married in 1970, "my father-in-law did not demand anything," her mother, Hem Lata Sharma, said while serving hot milk tea and cookies to guests.

For the Sharma family, the demands went far beyond giving the young couple a helping hand.

Dev Dutt Sharma, Nisha's father, said his potential in-laws were so demanding that they had stipulated brands. "She specified a Sony home theater, not a Philips," Mr. Sharma, an owner of car battery factories, said of Vidya Dalal, the mother of the groom, Munish Dalal, 25.

Sharma Jaikumar, a telecommunications engineer and friend of the Sharma family, said as the press mob ebbed and flowed through the house: "My daughter was married recently and there was no dowry. But anyone can turn greedy. What can be more easy money than a dowry? All you have to do is ask."

Source: Brooke, James. 2003. "Dowry Too High: Lose Bride and Go to Jail," *New York Times* (17 May).

---

usually rather infrequent, but in some large-scale industrial societies, including Canada, they have become increasingly common.

Many families are **conjugal families** with members all living together. However, in some matrilineal societies, the husband lives with his matrilineage (i.e., members of his mother's kinship line) while his wife and children live with theirs; the husband usually visits his wife and children on a regular basis. Families in Canada today come in many forms (Figure 7.5). We will explore some of these family structures in the sections to come.

The Nuclear Family

Familiar to North Americans is the neolocal monogamous family, or **nuclear family**. This type of arrangement remains the prototype for many North Americans although only about 25 per cent of us currently live in such families. Each family member has a series of evolving relationships with every other member, which frequently involve feelings of

affection, jealousy, competition, and controversy. Sibling rivalry, for example, is a form of competition characteristic of nuclear families; it is shaped by the relationships between siblings and between siblings and their parents and is often debated in the context of birth order.

The Polygynous Family

Fairly common is the polygynous family where co-wives, individually and collectively, interact with each other and with the husband (Figure 7.6). Important distinctions are made between children with the same mother and children with a different mother. Children also have different kinds of relationships with their own mothers and with their fathers' other wives. In some polygynous cultures, a close connection with a particular brother or sister is emphasized by saying that he or she is "same father, same mother." Where there is a significant inheritance, these relationships can result in jealousy and conflict. The children compete with one another for

conjugal family A family based on marriage; at minimum, a spousal pair and their children.

nuclear family A family made up of two generations: parents and their unmarried children.

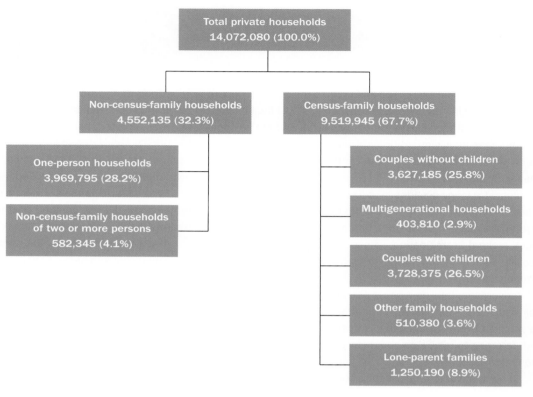

Figure 7.5 Overview of Household Types, Canada, 2016.

Source: Statistics Canada. 2017. Infographic 1. Overview of Household Types, Canada, 2016. Ottawa: Statistics Canada, available from www.statcan.gc.ca/daily-quotidien/170802/g-a001-eng.htm

extended family
A family pattern made up of three generations living together: parents, married children, and grandchildren.

joint family A family pattern made up of brothers and their wives (or sisters and their husbands) along with their children and sometimes their parents living together.

blended family A family created when previously divorced or widowed people marry, bringing with them children from their previous marriages.

their father's favour, and each mother tries to protect the interests of her own children, sometimes at the expense of her co-wives' children.

Among the Mende of Sierra Leone (see Map 7.4), co-wives come to compete with each other. Bledsoe (1993) explains that this competition is often focused on how many children each wife has and how likely it is that each child will obtain things of value, especially education. Mothers depend on the income that a child may earn to support her. Education often requires a significant cash outlay, and a man may be able to send only one child to school, or he may be able to send one child to a prestigious private school only if he sends another to a trade apprenticeship. These economic realities can lead to bitter feuds—and even divorce—as co-wives blame the husband for disparities in the accomplishments of their children. To avoid these problems, children are frequently sent to live with relatives who will send them to school. Also important are the rights to inherit property and positions of leadership from the father. Husbands try to avoid overt signs of favouritism, but wives are ranked by order of marriage and by the status of their natal (birth) families, and such rankings lay the groundwork for rivalries.

Extended, Joint, and Blended Families

Some societies have expanded definitions of the central family unit. Two traditional examples are the **extended family** and the **joint family**. In an extended family, the role each member plays in the family dynamic is tied to his or her position as child, parent, and/or grandparent. In a joint family, the dynamic is less constant since it is composed of, for example, a father and his married sons, as well as the sons' wives and children. Upon the death of the father, the eldest son inherits the position as household head. His younger brothers may not accept his authority as readily as they did their father's, and they may decide to establish separate households with the hope of starting their own joint families. Something similar happens among the polyandrous Nyinba discussed earlier. A group of brothers may take a second wife. At first, all brothers have equal sexual access to both wives, but in time they tend to form groups around each wife, eventually choosing to split the household in two.

In recent decades in North America, anthropologists have become more interested in the increase in the **blended family**. From a historical perspective, such families can be recognized in European folk tales, now termed fairy tales—consider *Cinderella*

Figure 7.6 Co-wives in polygynous households frequently co-operate in daily tasks, such as food preparation. What might be some of the advantages and disadvantages to this sort of family arrangement?

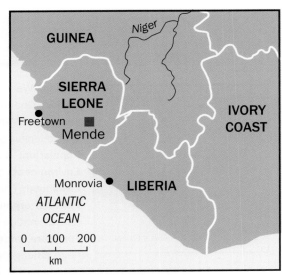

Map 7.4 Mende

or *Snow White* as examples. The internal dynamics of such a family—which can come to include one or both parents' children from previous unions, as well as children the couple have together—may resemble the dynamics of polygynous families, with complex relations among the children and between each child and each parent.

Brother–Sister Relationships

In North America, the relationship of the spousal pair ordinarily takes precedence over the brother–sister relationship. Yet in some societies, the most important adult relationships a man or a woman can have are those with his or her opposite-sex siblings. Anthropologist Meyer Fortes (1950) gave us the classic illustration from the Ashanti (EthnoProfile 7.1; Figure 7.7), where the central legal relationship is the tie between brother and sister. Legal power is vested in males, and brothers have power over the children of their sisters since all belong to a common matrilineage. A sister has claims on her brother because she is his closest female relative and

represents the only source of the continuity of his lineage. "Men find it difficult to decide which is more important to them, to have children or for their sisters to have children. But after discussion most men conclude that sad as it may be to die childless, a good citizen's first anxiety is for his lineage to survive" (1950: 274–5). More than this, the Ashanti brother and sister are close confidants on matters ranging from property and financial management to matrimonial difficulties (275). This closeness is reinforced by the Ashanti residence pattern: people live in their matrilineage's neighbourhoods, and, often, husbands and wives do not live together.

According to anthropologist Gracia Clark (1994), the status of women within Ashanti matrilineages has eroded since the 1940s. Based on fieldwork in Kumasi, Ghana, in the 1980s, Clark did observe that the women could still turn to their matrilineages for support against the risks of divorce, illness, or bankruptcy, but support beyond subsistence level is not automatic and must be negotiated between a woman and her kin. Clark concludes that Ashanti girls and women "unfortunately seem to be increasingly marginalized within their lineages, in leadership, residence, and inheritance" (335).

In patrilineal societies, the strength of the brother–sister relationship depends on kinship group organization. Where sisters do not move too far from home upon marriage and where they are not incorporated into their husbands' lineages, a group of brothers and sisters may control the lineage and its economic, political, social, and religious aspects. The senior members of the lineage—males and females alike—exercise control over the junior members, although the brothers generally have more control than do the sisters.

> **EthnoProfile 7.1**
> Ashanti
>
> **Region:** Western Africa
> **Nation:** Ghana
> **Language:** Various dialects of Twi (Akan), a member of the Niger-Congo language group
> **Population:** 3.7 million (2011 estimate)
> **Environment:** Slightly inland, partly mountainous
> **Livelihood:** Farming, fishing, market trading (women)
> **Political organization:** Traditionally, a kingdom; today, part of a modern nation-state
> **For more information:** Fortes, Meyer. 1950. "Kinship and Marriage among the Ashanti," in *African Systems of Kinship and Marriage*, ed. Alfred Reginald Radcliffe-Brown and Daryll Forde (Oxford: Oxford University Press); Clark, Gracia. 1994. *Onions Are My Husband* (Chicago: University of Chicago Press).

Families of Choice

family of choice A family created over time by new kin ties as friends and lovers demonstrate their genuine commitment to one another.

Not everyone defines a "family" as created by marriage or genetics (or adoption). For example, anthropologist Kath Weston (1991) looked at family forms among gay and lesbian individuals in the San Francisco Bay Area during the 1980s. A lesbian herself, Weston knew that a turning point in the lives of many gay and lesbian individuals was the decision to announce their sexual orientation to their parents and siblings. Sadly, this announcement sometimes resulted in parents' turning their child away, thus rejecting the bonds of blood. Living through—or even contemplating—such an experience has been enough to force many gay and lesbian individuals to think seriously about the sources of family ties. By the 1980s, some North American gay and lesbian individuals had reached two conclusions:

1. That blood ties *cannot* guarantee solidarity
2. That new kin ties *can* be created over time as friends and lovers demonstrate their genuine commitment to one another by creating **families of choice**

"Like their heterosexual counterparts, most gay men and lesbians insisted that family members are people who are 'there for you,' people you can count on emotionally and materially" (Weston 1991: 113). Some gay kinship ideologies now argue that "whatever endures is real" as a way of claiming legitimacy for chosen families. Such a definition of family is compatible with understandings of kinship based on nurturance.

Families and Change

Families change over time. Families can take on different forms and provide different opportunities for the interaction of family members at different points in time. Existing households commonly change through death, divorce, remarriage, the departure of

Figure 7.7 The men and women living in the Ashanti's matrilineal society are close confidants, often siding with their opposite-sex siblings over their spouses.

© Victor Englebert

or return of adult children, the addition of grand-children, and the break-up of extended families.

Individuals' sense of family belonging changes over time as well. Evans-Pritchard noted that for Nuer women, affinal ties gradually became kinship ties: *ruagh* (in-law relationships) became *mar* (kinship) (1951: 96). The birth of a child gave the wife kinship with her husband's relatives, and it gave the husband kinship with his wife's relatives. In many patrilineal societies, a woman begins to identify with and become more interested in the affairs of her husband's lineage, partly because she comes to be more intimate with the details of the lineage over the years. More significantly, however, what had been her *husband's* lineage becomes her *children's* lineage, a link to the lineage independent of her husband.

Divorce and Remarriage

Many societies now recognize divorce. In almost all societies childlessness is grounds for marriage dissolution while "incompatible differences" covers various issues ranging from quarrelling to cruelty to adultery. In some societies, the process can be drawn out, and difficult, especially when some or all of the bridewealth must be returned. For the wife's family to give back the bridewealth, a whole chain of marriages may be in jeopardy since her brothers may have to divorce to get back enough bridewealth from their in-laws to cover the debt. Sometimes a new husband will repay the bridewealth to the former husband's line, thus letting the bride's relatives off the hook.

In other societies, divorce is easier. With the Fulbe of Guider, Cameroon, a man frequently marries his father's brother's daughter (parallel cousin). In many cases, such marriages are contracted simply to oblige the families involved; after a few months, the couple splits up. In general, there is enough dissatisfaction with marriage in Guider to make household transformation through divorce quite common. Among Muslims in Guider, divorce is controlled by men; women are not legally allowed to initiate divorces. If a husband wants a divorce, he need only follow the simple procedure laid down in the Quran and sanctioned by long practice: he appears before two witnesses and pronounces the formula "I divorce you" three times. He is then divorced, and his wife must leave his household. She may take an infant with her, but any children at the toddler stage or older stay with the father. If she takes an infant, she must return the child to the father's household by the time the child is six to eight years old. Yet the wife is not entirely powerless. Although a woman cannot ask for a divorce directly, she can facilitate an escape from an unsatisfactory marriage by neglecting her household duties or by going to live in the compound of her father or brother.

For the Ju/'hoansi of the Kalahari Desert (see EthnoProfile 7.2), most divorces are initiated by women. The most common reasons for divorce among the Ju/'hoansi are a woman's displeasure with her husband and her desire to no longer be married (Lee 1992; Shostak 1981). After what is often a considerable debate, the couple simply separates. There is no bridewealth to return, no legal contract to be renegotiated. The children go with the mother. Ju/'hoansi divorces are generally cordial: ex-spouses may continue to joke with each other and even live next to each other with their new spouses (Lee 1992).

Traditional northwestern Inuit kin relationships, including marital ones, are viewed as permanent (Burch 1970). A husband and wife who stop having sexual relations and stop living with each other are considered to be separated and ready for another marriage. If each member of a separated couple remarries, then the two husbands of the wife become co-husbands, the two wives of the husband become co-wives, and the children of the first and second marriages become co-siblings. In such cases, a "divorce" results in more, not fewer, connections. Not all contemporary Inuit, especially those who are Christians, continue to follow this practice.

International Migration and the Family

Families also change their structure in response to globalization, environmental conditions, civil unrest, and war. Here we see migration to find work or refuge becoming increasingly common. The effects on those who go (Pedersen 2011) and those who stay (Archambault 2010) are increasingly explored by anthropologists, as Caroline S. Archambault notes in the following Tanzanian example:

> Migration has long been a ubiquitous phenomenon in Ugweno. Most older Ugweno men have lived migrant lives, while many women have spent most of their married lives in the rural environment. And although there is much movement back and forth by both wives and husbands, many of these couples have lived apart for a significant portion of their married lives. (2010: 926)

EthnoProfile 7.2
Ju/'hoansi (!Kung)

Region: Southern Africa

Nations: Botswana and Namibia

Language: Ju/'hoan, part of the Ju language family

Population: 50,000 (1996 estimate)

Environment: Desert

Livelihood: Hunting and gathering

Political organization: Traditionally, egalitarian bands; today, part of modern nation-states

For more information: Lee, Richard B. 2013. *The Dobe Ju/'hoansi*, 4th edn (New York: Holt, Rinehart, & Winston); Hitchcock, Robert K. 2003. "Land, Livestock, and Leadership among the Ju/'hoansi San of North Western Botswana," *Anthropologica* 45, 1: 89–94.

Earlier, anthropologist Eugenia Georges (1990) examined such effects of migration to the United States from Los Pinos, Dominican Republic (see Map 7.5). Families were divided, with some members moving to New York. Sometimes spouses separated, with the husband migrating and the wife staying home. Consequently, many households in Los Pinos were headed by women. In most cases, the husband worked to help his wife and children migrate. But relocating an entire family across an international border takes a significant amount of time and money. Children who were close to working age migrated, frequently with their mother, and younger children were sent for as they approached working age. After several years in the United States, the couple who started the migration cycle would often take their savings and return to the Dominican Republic while their children stayed in the United States and continued to send money home. Even when the husband was geographically separated from his family, he maintained an active role as the breadwinner and the main decision-maker in the household through visits, letters, and occasional telephone calls. Georges found that the divorce rate was slightly lower than average in migrant families, likely because dense and frequent exchange of information between Los Pinos and New York maintained strong ties of spousal affection.

Heather A. Horst (2011) also investigated the effects of migration, discussing the return from the United Kingdom for Jamaican migrants of the 1950s and 1960s and the reclaiming of place and sense of origin. In some sense this theme of "home" is central to the work of Pedersen (2011) as well. More recently,

with the resettlement of 46,700 refugees in Canada in 2016 (the majority being Syrian), we see the ways in which families continue to change, sometimes by force and in response to external social pressures.

The Internet is very important in the lives of families that are separated by migration, education, work, and so on (Pedersen 2011). The social landscape has been altered in the shape of linkages and connections (de Bruijn and van Dijk 2012) in ways that even recent generations could not have imagined. Anthropologist Daniel Miller and sociologist Don Slater (2000) studied Internet use in Trinidad, finding that email and instant messaging have strengthened considerably both nuclear and extended families, allowing closer relations between distant relatives. They remark on the experiences of a widow they

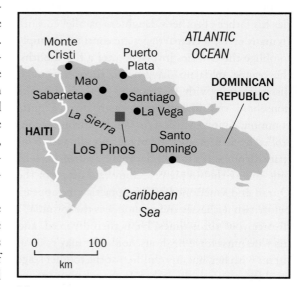

Map 7.5 Los Pinos

knew who, depressed after her husband's death, was convinced by relatives to learn to use email to contact a beloved grandchild who had gone abroad. This experience was so valuable to her that she began to contact other relatives, and younger members of her family "swear it has given [her a] 'new lease of life'" (2000: 61). Anthropologist Katy Gardner (2008) also observes, in her work on Bangladeshi people settled in British communities, that online communication can help migrants overcome "the political insecurity and social exclusion" they commonly experience in their new countries (277). Overall, the Internet offers a variety of tools that can help people feel connected to one another over great distances.

Kinship and Systems of Relatedness: Ways of Organizing Human Interdependence

Forms of relatedness are diverse and rich from a cross-cultural perspective. So far, we have discussed systems of relatedness in terms of *marriage* and *family*. But there are other forms of relatedness as well—for example, those based on *nurturance* or *invited kinship*. As you might expect, these sorts of relationships are sometimes difficult to define precisely. Early anthropologists focused mainly on relations of biology, believing that Western understandings of "real" relatives—mothers, fathers, sisters, brothers, sons, daughters, and so on—were universally valid. They searched for organizational patterns along genealogical (descent) lines and tried to define the formal "rules" that would be characteristic of, say, all patrilineal societies. This work did illuminate some patterns, but ethnographic evidence indicated that sometimes genealogical principles were at odds with concepts of relatedness. In some cases, relatedness based on *birth* was only one of several ways in which people created strong and enduring ties.

Today, anthropologists tend to take a broader approach to relatedness in a particular culture even though they still look at relationships stemming from mating, birth, and nurturance. Anthropologists also recognize that definitions of these experiences are not the same in every culture. Many people distinguish between *mating* and *marriage*. In some cultures, children whose parents are not married to each other are seen as illegitimate. Descent can be very complicated in cases of adoption, surrogacy, and conception through sperm and/or egg donation. Even nurturance

is not necessarily a sign of enduring relatedness—consider, for example, foster parents in Canada: custody of foster children is officially temporary.

Forms of relatedness are thus selective. One society may emphasize women as the "bearers" of children and base its kinship system on this fact, while men in another culture may emphasize the paternal role in conception. Another society may encourage the adoption of children as well as adult siblings, blurring the link between biological reproduction and family creation. These examples can be justified with reference to pan-human experiences of relatedness.

Consider the English-language kinship term *aunt*. This term most often refers to a woman occupying a unique position in one of four different ways:

1. Father's sister
2. Mother's sister
3. Father's sibling's wife
4. Mother's sibling's wife

The women in these positions in your life have something in common: they are sisters or sisters-in-law of your parents. But we may also refer to our mother's best friend as an *aunt*, thereby choosing to recognize her as a family member. In Chile, this concept is applied more broadly: children regularly use *tía* (Spanish for "aunt") to refer to female friends of their parents. Indeed, well into early adulthood, Chileans continue to use the term to refer to women who take on the role of "mother" but with whom they are not as intimate as they are with their own mothers.

Because understandings of relatedness differ cross-culturally, anthropologists tend to understand *kinship* as resulting from a selective interpretation of common human experiences and the assigning of individuals to certain groups of relatedness. The principles of kinship typically cover significant issues, including the following:

1. How to carry out the "recruiting" of legitimate group members (marriage, birthing, or adoption)
2. Where group members should live (residence rules)
3. How to establish intergenerational links (descent)
4. How to pass on social positions (succession) or material goods (inheritance)

In this way, people are located within social groups in relation to one another both in space and over time.

Patterns of Descent in Kinship

A central aspect of kinship is descent. Defined by ancestry, descent involves the transmission of group membership through parent–child links. Globally, there are two major patterns of descent: **bilateral descent** and the more common **unilineal descent**.

Bilateral Kindreds

Most Canadians are familiar with the bilateral kindred, a kinship group that includes all the people linked to an individual through kin of both sexes— what people conventionally call *relatives* in English (Figure 7.8). These people form a group only because of their connection to the central person, known in kinship terminology as **ego** (Latin for "I" or "the self"). Each person within Ego's bilateral kindred has his or her own separate kindred. For example, Ego's father's sister's daughter (what we term Ego's "cousin") has kindred through her father and his siblings—people to whom Ego is not related. The major strength of bilateral kindred is that it can form broad networks; its major weakness is that it does not endure beyond the lifetime of the Ego at its centre.

A classic bilateral kindred is found among the Ju/'hoansi (see Figure 7.9; see also EthnoProfile 7.2). Canadian anthropologist Richard B. Lee points out that every individual in Ju/'hoansi society can be linked to every other individual by a kinship term, either through male or female relatives:

> In essence, a Ju/'hoansi camp consists of relatives, friends, and in-laws who have found that they can live and work well together. Under this flexible principle a Ju/'hoansi, during his or her lifetime, may live at many water holes with many different groups but always in the presence of kin. (1992: 62)

A wide range of kin-people makes flexibility possible. However, such social flexibility can become problematic in at least four kinds of circumstances:

1. Where clear-cut membership in a particular social group must be determined
2. Where social action requires the formation of groups that are larger than individual families
3. Where conflicting claims to land and labour must be resolved
4. Where people want to maintain a particular social order over time

Unilineal Descent Groups

Unilineal descent groups, found all over the world, are based on the principle that certain kinds of parent–child relationships are more important than others. In a patrilineal society, women and men

bilateral descent A pattern of descent in which a descent group is formed based on connections of relatedness made through *both* a mother *and* a father.

unilineal descent A pattern of descent in which a descent group is formed based on connections of relatedness made through *either* a father (patrilineal descent) *or* a mother (matrilineal descent).

ego The person from whose perspective the kinship associations are being mapped and/or discussed. (Note that the term is capitalized when used to designate real, specific people.)

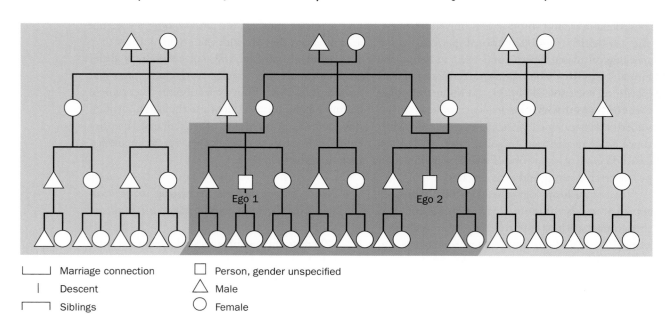

⌐‾‾⌐ Marriage connection	☐ Person, gender unspecified	
│ Descent	△ Male	
⌐‾‾⌐ Siblings	○ Female	

Figure 7.8 A bilateral kindred includes all recognized relatives on Ego's father's and mother's sides. The dark area in the centre indicates where the kindreds of Ego 1 and Ego 2 overlap.

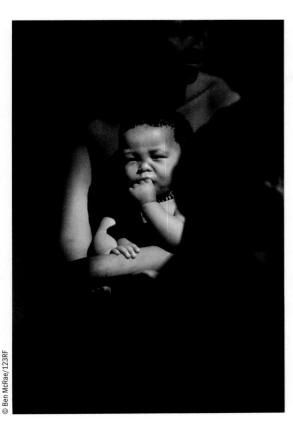

Figure 7.9 This Ju/'hoansi baby and his caregiver are members of a bilateral kinship group.

belong to a patrilineage formed by father–child links (Figure 7.10); in a matrilineal society, men and women belong to a matrilineage formed by mother–child connections (Figure 7.11). Membership, on the face of it, is unambiguous. Individuals belong to only one lineage although, as ethnologist Martine Segalen observes, a pattern of unilineal descent is "no more than a kind of external framework" that can support a wide range of cultural variations (1986: 51–2).

Lineages

Lineages vary in size, ranging from 20 or 30 members to several hundred or more. They can endure as long as people remember the descent lines, usually about five generations (grandparents, parents, Ego, children, and grandchildren). A lineage is a *corporate* organization—that is, it has a single legal character. As the Ashanti (see EthnoProfile 7.1) put it, a lineage is "one person" (Fortes 1953). To outsiders, all members of a lineage are equal *in law* to all others. Lineages are also corporate units as they control property, especially land and water.

When members of a group believe that they are related but can no longer specify ancient descent links, they arrange themselves in a **clan**, linked by the belief in a distant common ancestor. This ancestor may be a culture bearer or a powerful shape shifter/animal from the beginning of time. Raven is one such ancestor as recognized among many original North American cultures. Often, clans transmit beliefs about their common ancestry across generations through stories or legends that offer mythical justifications for the arrangements of the society. Many clans apply the incest taboo within their group; among the Nuer of East Africa, for example, clan members recognize that they cannot marry each other, and they consider sexual relations within the group to be incestuous. In addition, as with lineage, clan membership often brings with it certain political and legal statuses.

Patrilineages

Patrilineage is the most common form of lineage organization. Central is the father–son relationship. Women normally leave their childhood homes when they marry, although they may continue to have active roles in their own patrilineages for many years.

An assumption of hierarchy exists in patrilineal societies: men believe that they are superior to women, and many women seem to agree. However, there is an irony at the heart of these societies, as we suggested earlier in relation to the Iteso—the future of the patrilineage depends on people (women) who do not belong to it! A second irony is that women must leave their own lineages to produce the next generation of somebody else's lineage. Women in patrilineal societies are often torn between conflicting interests and loyalties. Should they support their own children, or should they support their fathers and brothers?

A classic patrilineal system was found among the Nuer of East Africa. In the 1930s, Evans-Pritchard noted 20 clans that were each segmented into separate lineages (see Figure 7.12 for an illustration of this sort of segmentation). The most basic segment constituted the *minimal lineage*, which consisted of three to five generations. Members of one minimal lineage could consider themselves related to another minimal lineage through ancient family connections—for example, if the founder of the first minimal lineage had been the brother of the founder of the second minimal lineage. Two

lineage A descent group composed of blood relatives who believe they can trace their descent from known ancestors.

clan A descent group formed by members who believe they have a common ancestor, even if they cannot specify the genealogical links.

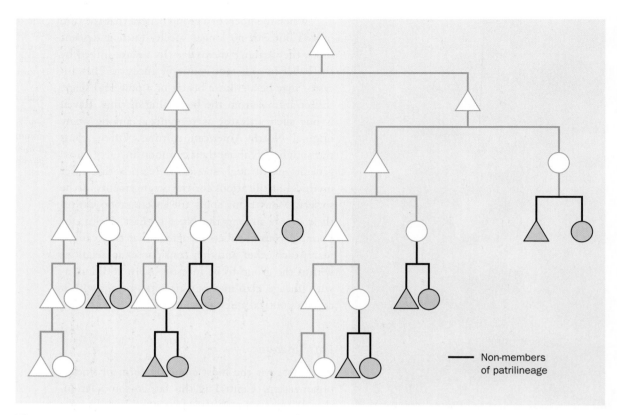

Figure 7.10 Patrilineal descent: all those who trace descent through males to a common male ancestor are indicated in white.

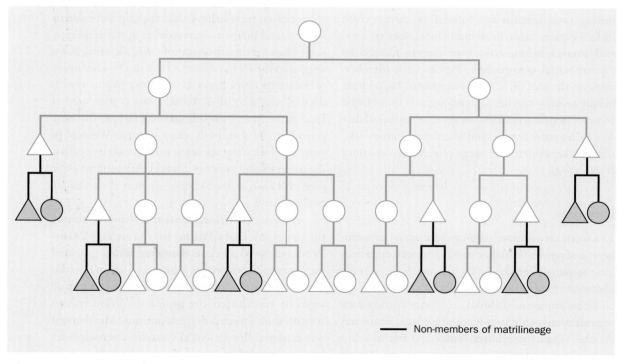

Figure 7.11 Matrilineal descent: all those who trace descent through females to a common female ancestor are indicated in white.

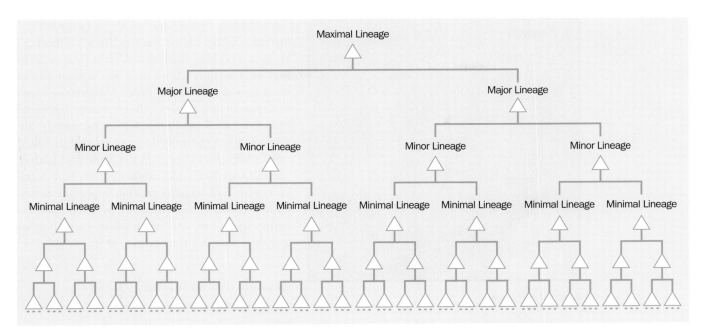

Figure 7.12 From a founder recognized by all descendants, lineages develop through *segmentation* across generations. The complexity of this segmentation is determined by the number and gender of the members of each generation.

minimal lineages related in such a way formed a *minor lineage*, which was composed of all those descended from the common father of the two founders. Minor lineages connected to other minor lineages by yet another presumed common male ancestor, forming *major lineages*. These major lineages were also believed to share a common male ancestor and thus formed a *maximal lineage*. The members of two maximal lineages believed their founders had been the sons of the clan's founding ancestor; thus, all members of the clan are believed to be patrilineally related. If a quarrel erupted between two men whose minimal lineages were in different minor lineages, each would be joined by men who belonged to his minor lineage. The dispute would be resolved when the quarrelling minor lineages recognized that they were all part of the same major lineage. Similarly, the minor lineages of one major lineage would ally if a dispute with an opposed major lineage broke out. This common social process of dispute resolution, expressed in kinship terms, is called **segmentary opposition**.

Nuer lineages are politically significant because members share rights over territory and property (cattle). Thus, individual status (positionality) is situated in their lineage. Lineages support marriages by providing the bridewealth cattle. If a man is killed, members of his lineage avenge his death.

Lineages also hold funeral ceremonies. This is not to say that tensions do not develop when individual interests conflict with lineage interests (see Evans-Pritchard 1951). Additionally, relationships can be stressed by societal conflict, such as the civil war and the separation of South Sudan in 2011. With deaths from war, drought, and famine, kinship became very fragmented for the Nuer.

Matrilineages

Matrilineages are not just mirror images of patrilineages. They are difficult to generalize, and ethnographic evidence suggests a case-by-case approach. Helpfully, there are a few common features:

- First, the central relationship is the sister–brother pair; a matrilineage may be thought of as a group of brothers and sisters connected through links made by women. Brothers marry out and often live with the family of their wives, but they maintain essential interest in the affairs of their birth lineage.
- Second, a matrilineage is not the same thing as a *matriarchy* (a society in which women rule); brothers often retain controlling interest in the lineage, and inheritances are generally passed to a man from his mother's brother.

segmentary opposition An approach to dispute resolution and social organization in which groups beyond the most basic emerge only in opposition to other groups on the same hierarchical level.

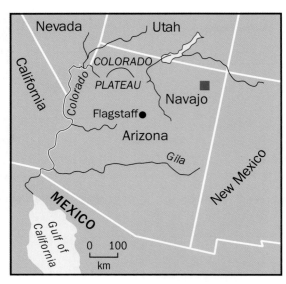

Map 7.6 Navajo

A representative example of a matrilineal society comes from the Navajo (Map 7.6). For the Navajo, the traditional basic unit of social organization is composed of a head mother, her husband, some of their children, and these children's spouses and children (Witherspoon 1975: 82). The visible leader of the unit is normally a man, usually the husband of the head mother. He directs livestock and agricultural operations, deals with the outside world, and generally seems to be in charge. In actuality, it is the head mother around whom the unit is organized, as she

> is identified with the land, the herd, and the agricultural fields. All residence rights can be traced back to her, and her opinions and wishes are always given the greatest consideration and usually prevail. In a sense, however, she delegates much of her role and prestige to the leader of the unit. If we think of the unit as a corporation, and the leader as its president, the head mother will be the chairman of the board.... When there is a divorce between the leader and the head, it is always the leader who leaves and the head mother who returns, even if the land originally belonged to the mother of the leader. (82–3)

In most matrilineal societies, there are some domains of experience in which men and women are equal, some in which men are in control, and some in which women are in control.

Men living in a matrilineal society may have conflicted feelings surrounding the rules of inheritance.

A man may feel great affection for his father but not his father's heir. He will inherit from his mother's brother, who lives elsewhere. A father may wish to have his son inherit from him, but he must give to his sister's son (Richards 1954). Malinowski found evidence of such mixed feelings among Trobriand Islanders (see EthnoProfile 8.1). Subsequently, anthropologist Annette Weiner argued that to understand matrilineal kinship in the Trobriand Islands, one must see the sister–brother pair as an integral unit, with each member making important contributions to the continuation of the lineage: a boy's mother gives him life, while his mother's brother gives him material inheritance (1980: 286–7).

Kinship Terminologies and Classification

We use somewhat culturally specific terms to refer to people we recognize as relatives. Table 7.4 shows the terms in general use in English. Thus, as you might expect, kinship terms do not always retain the same meanings and associations as they are translated across cultures and languages. Anthropologists David Greenwood and William Stini offer an example: "Just as the word *father* in English means a great deal more than lineal male ancestor of the first ascending generation, *aita* in Basque has many local connotations irreducible to *father*, as we understand the term" (1977: 333). Despite cross-cultural differences, anthropologists have been able to identify a variety of kinship roles and patterns that appear in multiple societies. Table 7.5 lists the main criteria that anthropologists have found people use to classify kinship relationships. By examining how individuals apply these criteria within their societies, anthropologists can begin to understand the logic people use to classify and attach importance to their relatives.

Kinship and Alliance

Societies based on kinship often attempt to resolve the difficulties of intergroup relations by connecting kinship and marriage. Unilineal societies frequently promote or *prescribe* certain kinds of marriage to

1. ensure reproduction of their own memberships and
2. maintain long-term alliances with other groups.

Table 7.4 **English Kinship Terms**

	Position and Kinship Chart Abbreviation	
Nuclear family	mother	son
	father	sister
	daughter	brother
Extended family	aunt	grandfather
	uncle	granddaughter
	niece	grandson
	nephew	great-grandmother
	cousin	great-grandfather
	grandmother	
Affines (marriage)	wife	brother-in-law
	husband	mother-in-law
	sister-in-law	father-in-law

Table 7.5 **Criteria of Relatedness**

Criterion	Distinction	Example
Generation	Place in descent group	*Cousin* conventionally refers to someone who is of the same generation as Ego but who is not considered a sibling.
Sex/gender	Male or female	*Uncle* and *aunt* are distinguished on the basis of both generation and sex/gender.
Affinity	Connection through marriage	*Mother* is distinguished from *mother-in-law*.
Collaterality	Direct (linking) or indirect (linked) relative	*Mother* and *father* denote direct connections; *aunt* and *uncle* denote relations "off to one side," linked through the mother or the father.
Sex/gender of linking relative	Linking relative is male or female	Not applied in English; some cultures distinguish parallel cousins (Ego's father's brother's children or Ego's mother's sister's children) from cross-cousins (Ego's mother's brother's children or Ego's father's sister's children). (See Figure 7.13.)
Bifurcation	Relation on mother's or father's side	Not applied in English; some cultures distinguish the mother's brother from the father's brother.
Relative age	Relatives of the same category who are older or younger than Ego	Not applied in English; Ju/'hoansi separate "older brother" (*!ko*) from "younger brother" (*tsin*).

Two major types of prescriptive marriage patterns facilitate both these needs: one in which a man must marry his father's sister's daughter, and one in which a man must marry his mother's brother's daughter; each forms an alliance between two cross-cousins (see Figure 7.13).

In patrilineal systems, the father's sister's daughter pattern sets up a *direct exchange marriage* where a line that has received a wife from another line in one generation gives a wife back in the next generation. In this system, a man's *father's sister's daughter* is the prototypical spouse, but any woman of the appropriate line can be chosen if both lines agree. In contrast, the mother's brother's daughter system (which is more common) sets up a pattern of *asymmetrical exchange marriage*; this pattern does not balance out over the generations, as men always find wives in the line their mother came from. However it provides a permanent alliance between two lines. While a man's mother's brother's daughter is the prototypical wife in this system, all is not lost if Ego's mother's brother does not have a daughter because another woman of his generation, who is a member of his mother's patrilineage, would be acceptable. Rarely, cross-cousin marriage is found in matrilineal systems and men marry out of their lineages, thus creating direct or asymmetrical exchange alliances.

Intergroup relations can also be strengthened by members of the younger generation working to maintain the established alliances they inherit from their kin. Anthropologist Naomi McPherson (2007) notes such inherited alliances in her discussion of trade networks and trade friendships among the Bariai in Northwest New Britain, Papua New Guinea. (See the "In Their Own Words" box that follows.) In her analysis, McPherson notes the links between economics, trade networks, friendships (trade partners), and kinship affiliation (particularly that between parents and their first-born child). For example, the ceremonial dress for the first-born becomes a display of trade friendship, as it is constructed out of both locally available raw materials (e.g., red ochre and obsidian) and traded "craft" materials (e.g., armbands woven by trade partners). In effect, the items used in the ceremonial dress of the first-born advertise the extent of the trade-friendship and the family's access to the network. In the Bariai trade system, first-borns inherit their parents' trade roles; they are exemplars of parental achievement and facilitate the trade partnerships and networks for their younger siblings.

Kinship and Practice

Kinship systems may appear to be fairly rigid sets of rules that use the accident of birth to thrust people into social positions laden with rights and obligations they cannot escape. Yet in practice, people encounter a flexible series of opportunities to choose how to deal with others. Everyday lived experiences provide opportunities for individuals to *create*

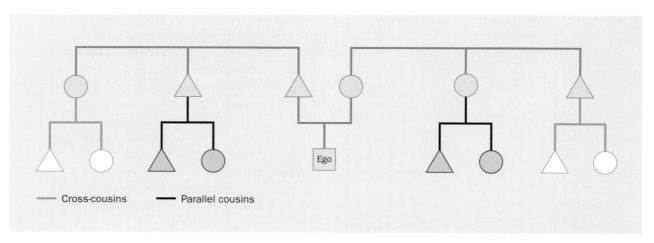

Figure 7.13 Cross-cousins and parallel cousins: Ego's cross-cousins are the children of Ego's father's sister and of Ego's mother's brother. Ego's parallel cousins are the children of Ego's father's brother and of Ego's mother's sister.

meaningful relationships in many different ways and for many different reasons. The following sections offer some examples.

Adoption

The accident of birth thrusts people into **ascribed statuses**. In contrast, individual or group efforts can lead to **achieved statuses**. Both statuses have rights and obligations. Adoption blurs the distinction between ascribed and achieved, however, because it allows people to transform relationships based on nurturance into relations of kinship.

Nurturance is the central theme in Barbara Bodenhorn's (2000) discussion of adoption among the Iñupiat of northern Alaska. (Similar adoption patterns are also found among the Yupik of southwestern Alaska, the Inuit of northern Canada, and the Kalaallit of Greenland.) Most adult Iñupiat have been adopted or have lived in a household with adopted children. The reasons that the Iñupiat gave for adoption included that they "wanted to" adopt, that they had too many boys and wanted a girl (or vice versa), or that all of their "brothers and sisters [had] adopted." Often, adoption occurred because the child wanted to be adopted. In many cases, adoption was to everyone's satisfaction, but when it was not, the question of where the child should end up was never based on the argument that he or she belonged with his or her biological parents. The degree to which a relationship is maintained between the birth parents and the adopted child becomes a matter of choice—there is no social stigma involved if a child ignores his or her biological parents. However, people do disapprove if the child does not act like a son or daughter to his or her adoptive parents. Here, parenting creates parents, for, as Bodenhorn notes,

> because [relatedness] is disconnected from anything permanent, it must be constantly reconstructed: shared tools, food, labour, political alliance, ceremonial participation, and simply company. . . . It is *this* labour— the work of being related—rather than the labour of giving birth or the "fact" of shared substance that marks out the kinship sphere from the potentially infinite universe of relatives who may or may not belong. (143)

This is kinship based on *active nurturance*; biology does not create parents, but actions do.

Negotiation of Kin Ties among the Ju/'hoansi

In his analysis of kinship among the Ju/'hoansi, anthropologist Lee (1992) notes that "the principles of kinship constitute not an invariant code of laws written in stone, but instead a whole series of codes consistent enough to provide structure but open enough to be flexible" (62). For the Ju/'hoansi, kin terms have behavioural correlates, which Lee calls *joking* and *avoidance* (Table 7.6). Joking relationships can be relaxed and affectionate, while avoidance relationships require respect and reserve. Many avoidance relationships may be warm and friendly if the relatives show one another proper respect in public; however, people in an avoidance relationship may not marry one another.

The Ju/'hoansi naming system is complex and contains 36 male names and 32 female names. A first-born son gets his father's father's name; a first-born daughter gets her father's mother's name. Second-born children are supposed to be named after the mother's father or mother. Later children are named after the father's brothers and sisters and the mother's brothers and sisters. Having the same name constitutes relatedness. A man older than Ego who shares his or her name is called *!kun!a* ("old name"), thus *grandfather*. A man younger than Ego who shares his or her name is called *!kuna* ("young name"), thus *grandson*. Ego would call anyone with her or his father's name *father* and anyone with her or his mother's name *mother*. Names restrict potential marriage partners: "a woman may not marry a man with her father's or brother's name, and a man

ascribed statuses Social positions people are assigned at birth.

achieved statuses Social positions people may attain later in life, often as the result of their own (or other people's) effort.

Table 7.6 Generation and Behaviour with the Ju/'hoansi

Generation	Behaviour
Grandparents'	Joking
Parents'	Avoidance
Ego's	Joking*
Children's	Avoidance
Grandchildren's	Joking

*Opposite-gender siblings of Ego's own generation are in the avoidance category.

In Their Own Words

Myth Primogeniture and Long-Distance Trade-Friends in Northwest New Britain, Papua New Guinea

Trade-friendships form important "official" bonds, as seen in the trade-friendships of the Bariai of Northwest New Britain, Papua New Guinea. Naomi McPherson examines how trade-friendships, kinship, and economics are intimately intertwined. Note how such integrated analysis offers deep insight into the workings of a society, illustrating our dedication to holism in anthropology.

Bariai trade-friendships are, in fact, relations between individual women and men (and their spouses) rather than kin groups or communities. Although couched in an idiom of kinship, trade-friendships entail different, albeit parallel, sets of rights, obligations, and motivations from those operating among consanguineal [blood] and affinal [marriage] exchange partners. . . .

Rules for conduct between trade-friends in the Vitiaz Strait include offering one another hospitality and protection, and both parties are under obligation to proffer, to accept, and to reciprocate pre-stations of all sorts. One ought not to lure away the trade-friends of others and, as a trade-friend host, one should act as intermediary for any exchanges between community members and one's trade-friend visitor (Harding 1967: 166–7). Harding characterizes the trade-friend relationship as "an expression of the social ethic of kinship" (166), an ethic that entails "generosity and mutual aid" (182). Rather than being the substrate out of which trade-friendships develop, "kin-like bonds develop partly as a consequence of [these] socially conducive relations" (176). The difference is that a trade-friendship depends on the two parties meeting their obligations; that is, they have a special performance of duty (Harding 1967). Kinship relations, on the other hand, are composed of a variety of acquired obligations and interests, and default in trade specifically does not sever the acquired ties. One can take advantage of kinspeople and get away with it. "Trading with relatives, therefore, may be burdensome for either side. . . . It is good to have kinsmen in faraway places, but it is better to have good trade-friends" (153). . . .

The analytical conflation of kinship and trade-friendship (prevalent in alliance theories of kinship) has made it difficult to fully appreciate trade-friendships as something other than kinship relations. For example, the idiom of kinship characterizes the Bariai concept of the trade-friend as an affine—indeed, some trade-friends are affinal kin based on contemporary intermarriages—and the trade-friend relationship is also subject to the rights and moral obligations that inform human relations in kinship-based societies. However, the majority of Bariai adults are hard pressed to trace definitive kinship connections with their trade-friends. Rather, a first-born formally inherits his or her mother's and father's trade-friendships within the context of the *mata pau* first-born ceremony. None of the first-born's subsequent siblings is the focus of a *mata pau*, but, as head of the sibling set, the first-born is expected to oversee and facilitate younger siblings' access to inherited trade-friendships. This provides a means for younger siblings to participate in the established trade-friendships while presenting them an opportunity to develop their own trade-friendships through these connections. Not unlike a system of descent reckoning, trade-friendships remain intact over generations while the origin of the relationship, which is of little immediate concern relative to the continuity, substance, and meaning of the relationship itself, is lost in the mists of antiquity. That trade-friendships resemble kinship relations should come as no surprise in societies where human relationships generally are founded on the moral obligations inherent in kinship relations. For the Bariai, trade-friendships can be distinguished from kinship in three important ways. First, the Bariai use the unique, non-kin term *sobo* to encompass the trade-friend relationship. Second, participation in trade-friendships is a household, rather than a descent group or lineage, activity (cf. Harding 1967: 182). Within the framework of day-to-day household activities, it is the spousal partners who, working as a team, produce or procure items of trade and who undertake the transactions involved in trade-friend activities, and it is their first-born who inherits the fruits and friendships of their joint labours. Finally, as noted above, the trade-friendship can be curtailed whereas the kinship relationship cannot. Bariai

may not marry a woman with his mother's or sister's name" (Lee 1992: 74). Further, an individual may not marry anyone with the name of one of her or his avoidance kin. It does not matter how people are "really" related to others with the same name; the name relationship takes precedence. To help resolve

any confusion that might arise, the Ju/'hoansi have a third component to their kinship system: *wi*. The older party chooses the term to be used in any relationship that can be described by more than one kin term. For example, a man may get married only to discover that his wife's aunt's husband has the same

can and do bring pressure to bear on trade-friends and may even sever a relationship if it is exploitative, an outcome that is next to impossible in the entangled world of affinal and consanguineal relations of kinship. . . .

Exchange relationships with kin and trade-friendships depend upon an ability to manipulate competently the complicated system of debits and credits of the prestige economy and an ability to balance one's own self-interests and the interests of others according to the principles of morality which structure human relations. The locus of trade (and renown) is the wife/husband team. Transactions between spouses and their kin/affines and between spouses and their trade-friends occur constantly and rather inconspicuously within the context of the household. Similarly, first-born ceremonies are not group efforts but are carried out individually by parents and their *baulo* for their first-born child, when and as they have the wherewithal to do so. These public events effectively deflect individual endeavours onto the person of the first-born who exemplifies parental abilities in forging and maintaining bonds beyond the household. Without a first-born and performance of first-born ceremonies, no one can hope to achieve a reputation for renown.

The Bariai distinguish between first-born ceremonies that require "small work" (K: *ololo kaukau*) and those that require "big work" (*ololo kapei*). The difference between the two types is one of relative scale. "Small work," or minor ceremonies, usually does not require the exchange of pigs, pork, or shell money, and there is no large assembly of witnesses/kin from other villages. Minor ceremonies are contingent upon circumstances and available resources, and none of the key participants (mother and child) is dressed in ceremonial finery. Minor ceremonies celebrate "firsts" in two senses: they mark the first occasion that others receive a particular food or consumable in the name of the child, and some minor ceremonies confirm phases in the child's physical development (first tooth, first haircut, first fish, first clothing). For these ceremonies, young, inexperienced, first-time parents depend on the resources provided for them by their parents and grandparents who, for example, planned for their descendants by planting stands of sago, coconut, and areca (betel nut) palms

for them. Accomplishing certain of the minor ceremonials also serves to release the parents from various taboos on food, mobility, personal hygiene, and appearance that were imposed upon them when their child was born. Ideally, the minor ceremonies are accomplished by the time the child is four to six years of age. (I have calculated that, in an ideal world, it can take a married couple 15 to 20 years to complete the 17 first-born ceremonies; some parents never do complete them all.)

While the expenditure of energy and wealth required for the performance of minor ceremonials is anything but small, it is only a fraction of that required for major ceremonials. For their proper performance, these ceremonies require vast quantities of one or more of the following: raw/cooked foods (especially taro, sago flour, and coconuts); pigs and/or pork; shell money; and other forms of material wealth such as clay pots, carved bowls, mats, and more. In contrast to the minor ceremonials where the wealth distributed in the child's name was acquired in large part from the child's grandparents and ancestors, the wealth in the major ceremonies is produced and acquired by the child's parents. Parents use their "strength" to produce more and larger gardens, to acquire and husband numerous pigs, and to access other wealth items by actively developing and engaging in an ever-widening network of social obligations, especially trade networks. Some of the major ceremonies are also concerned with "firsts," such as the child's first trip to the reef or first wearing of clothes, first excursion to another village. Others focus on a particular item of decorative finery (such as sago fringe, arm bands, red and yellow paint), items that parents and first-born are forbidden to display as personal adornment until the appropriate ceremony is complete. Many of these objects of value are only obtainable through trade; thus, when the first-born is elaborately decorated and paraded through the village to display the item of wealth, the child publicly demonstrates parental ability to forge and maintain relations of trade and exchange.

Source: Republished with permission of Wiley, from McPherson, Naomi. 2007. "Myth, Primogeniture and Long Distance Trade-Friends in Northwest New Britain, Papua New Guinea," *Oceania* 77, 2: 129–57; permission conveyed through Copyright Clearance Center, Inc.

name he has. What terms will he and his wife's aunt use for each other? According to the principle of *wi*, the aunt decides because she is older. If she calls him *nephew* (rather than *husband*), he knows to call her *aunt*. This means that a person's involvement with the kinship system is continually changing over the

course of his or her lifetime. In youth and young adulthood, people must accept the kin terms their elders choose. After midlife, however, they begin to impose *wi* on their juniors. Thus for the Ju/'hoansi, kinship connections are open to manipulation and negotiation.

Compadrazgo in Latin America

An important set of kinship practices in Roman Catholic Latin America is *compadrazgo*, or ritual co-parenthood (Figure 7.14). The baptism of a child requires the presence of a godmother and a godfather as sponsors who are expected to take an active interest in their godchildren. Importantly, the godparents and the parents become *compadres* ("co-parents"), and they are expected to behave toward each other in new ways. A couple often chooses godparents whose social standing is higher than their own. Participating together in the baptism changes these unequal strangers into ritual kin whose relationship, although still unequal, is now personalized, friendlier, and more open. *Compadres* help one another: the parents will support the godparents when that support is needed (e.g., politically), and the godparents will do favours for the parents.

Figure 7.14 In Latin America, when a child is baptized according to Roman Catholic traditions, the child's godparents become *compadres*, or ritual co-parents, with the child's birth parents. Do you or anyone you know have godparents? How does the concept of *compadrazgo* differ from the concept of godparenthood?

Anthropologist Catherine Allen notes that the bonds of *compadrazgo*, in combination with marriage alliances and kinship,

> form constellations of mutual obligation and dependence that shift with time as new *compadrazgo* relationships are formed, young relatives come of age, and old bonds fall into disuse through death or quarrelling. Like kin ties, bonds of *compadrazgo* can become as much a burden as an asset, and like kin ties they can be ignored or honoured in the breach. (1988: 90)

Euro-American Kinship and Reproductive Technologies

Euro-Americans tend to recognize kin related by blood and kin related by marriage; they also tend to believe that procreation—the process that brings kin into existence—is part of nature. Ties of kinship are supposed to stand for what is unalterable in a person's social world, in contrast to what is open to change. Yet reproductive technologies, such as in vitro fertilization and surrogate motherhood, reveal that even the world of "natural facts" is subject to social intervention.

Contemporary ambiguities surrounding kinship in the United States and Canada have put pressure on the courts to decide what constitutes biological parenthood and how it is related to legal parenthood. Consider, for example, the case of "Baby M" in America (see Dolgin 1995). The case began as a traditional surrogacy arrangement with Mary Beth Whitehead being impregnated with the sperm of the husband of the couple who intended to become the legal parents of the child she bore. Whitehead was supposed to terminate all parental rights when the child was born, but she refused to do so. The court faced a dilemma. Existing law backed Whitehead's maternal rights, but the parties had signed a legal contract. Focusing on Whitehead's attempt to break the surrogacy contract, the court terminated her legal rights as biological mother, although they awarded her visitation rights.

More complicated than traditional surrogacy, *gestational surrogacy*—a process in which the surrogate mother is implanted with an embryo formed from the intended mother's egg and the intended father's sperm—deconstructs the role of biological mother into two roles that can be performed by two different women. In another fairly early legal case exploring issues of surrogacy, the Calverts, a childless married couple, provided egg and sperm that were used in a laboratory to create an embryo, which was then implanted in Anna Johnson's uterus. But when Johnson gave birth to the baby, she refused to give it up. As anthropologist and legal scholar Dolgin points out, this case "provided a context in which to measure the generality of the assumption that the gestational role both produces and constitutes maternity" (1995: 58). While several previous court cases had emphasized the role of gestation in forming an indissoluble bond between mother and child, in this case the court referred to Anna Johnson "as a 'gestational carrier,' a 'genetic hereditary stranger' to the child, who acted like a 'foster parent'" (59). The court declared the Calverts and the child a family unit on genetic grounds and ruled that the Calverts were the baby's "natural" and legal parents.

Further, Dolgin noted the courts awarded legal custody to those parties whose living arrangements most closely approximated the traditional heteronormative two-parent family. In recent years, however, popular and legal views have been shifting away from the assumption that a child should be raised by a heterosexual couple—a shift closely tied to what sociologist Berkowitz (2013) terms the "emerging trend of reproductive outsourcing" among gay men and gay couples who want to become parents through surrogacy. Such parents "are at the cutting edge of pushing society to reassess its assumptions and constructions about sex, reproduction, and parenthood" (Berkowitz 2013: 71) and, thus, kinship. So it seems that some of our traditional ideas about kinship may not be so clear-cut after all.

Beyond Kinship

All people form significant links with individuals beyond their kin group. To fully understand how human beings relate to one another in any society, we must consider the importance of non-kin relationships in composing social worlds.

Initially we need to recognize that the line between "kin" and "non-kin" is not always clear; often, it is a matter of interpretation. In general, non-kin social relationships are less rigidly defined, and they generally involve fewer inherent obligations although kin terms are frequently used and roles in the relationship can be similar to those with kin. Such non-kin relationships can occur at both individual and institutional levels. At the individual level, for example, ritual co-parents refer to themselves as co-parents (*compadres*) and take on the formal role obligations of family members. At the institutional level, members of organizations, such as Catholic monastic orders, refer to one another as *brother*, *sister*, *father*, and *mother* and model their interactions on those of a family. Schneider (1968) argues that the emotion of North American kinship is the feeling of "enduring diffuse solidarity." This might just as well apply to friendship or to any other form of close companionship. Perhaps enduring diffuse solidarity is something that human beings regularly seek to establish in their relations with other people—kin or not.

Friendship

A common definition of *friend* is "one joined to another in intimacy and mutual benevolence independent of sexual or family love" (Brain 1976: 15). Yet the Western belief that friendship and kinship are separate phenomena often breaks down in practice. Some husbands and wives in Western societies consider each other "best friends," and we may be friends with some relatives while treating others as distant acquaintances. *Friendship* also differs cross-culturally and might best be understood more generally, as a relatively "unofficial" bond that is personal, affective (i.e., involving feelings), and—to a varying extent from society to society—a matter of choice (Bell and Coleman 1999) (Figure 7.15).

With globalization and widespread social change, ideas about friendship may be changing. In some contexts, the importance of friendship seems to be increasing: "In many shifting social contexts, ties of kinship tend to be transformed and often weakened [while] new forms of friendship are emerging" (Bell and Coleman 1999: 5). Anthropologist Claudia Barcellos Rezende (1999) has observed an example of such a relatively new form of friendship: in Rio de Janeiro, some middle-class women and their maids refer to each other as "friends" in "friendships" of affection, care, and consideration. Both sets of women value these relationships, which establish mutual trust and an "affinity that brings these people together as parts of the same social world" regardless of class distinctions (1999: 93). More recently, the rise of digital communication technologies has challenged us to consider what *friend* means in an increasingly connected world. As anthropologist Levent Soysal (2010) comments, these technologies allow us to experience intimate relationships "in virtual worlds where privacy proper . . . [is] no longer operational" (373). As

Figure 7.15 Friendships are based on the "unofficial" bonds that people create with one another, which vary from society to society. These two young men in Cameroon are the best of friends. What qualities do you consider necessary in a relationship in order to call someone a friend?

age sets Non-kin social groups composed of young men born within a specified time span.

sodalities Non-kin social groups that may be organized on the basis of age, sex, economic role, and/or personal interest.

friendship becomes more public in online environments, in many ways it has also become less personal.

Some cultures extend their interpretation of the bonds of friendship to apply to entire groups. We can find this perspective in the network that the National Association of Friendship Centres (NAFC) has established across Canada. The NAFC focuses on providing support to First Nations peoples in urban settings, helping them overcome problems, such as isolation

and alienation. NAFC offers individuals the sort of emotional and practical support commonly provided by friends or even family. Here we find a contemporary example of the importance of alliances for survival.

Sodalities

Sodalities offer members a more formal organization of non-kin bonds. Such organizations can have various functions,

> among them police, military, medical, initiation, religious, economic, and recreation. Some sodalities conduct their business in secret, others in public [Figure 7.16]. Membership may be ascribed or it may be obtained via inheritance, purchase, attainment, performance, or contract. Men's sodalities are more numerous and highly organized than women's and, generally, are also more secretive and seclusive in their activities. (Hunter and Whitten 1976: 362)

Sodalities create enduring diffuse solidarity among members of a larger society. A common example of this sort of group in Western societies is the labour union—an affiliation of workers who seek certain economic and workplace conditions from employers with negotiations highlighting issues of human rights, such as pay parity, safe working conditions, protection from harassment in the workplace, or enforcement of child labour laws.

Age Sets in Eastern Africa

Some groups establish sodalities based on generational distinctions. A number of east African societies assign men from different kinship groups to sodalities composed of **age sets**. These age sets "are part of the formal social order blessed by tradition, and membership is usually ascribed and is always obligatory" (Baxter and Almagor 1978: 4). These societies do not establish age-set systems for women, possibly because women are involved in domestic matters from an early age and marry shortly after puberty (11).

In a classic study, anthropologist Monica Wilson (1951) examined the role of age sets among the Nyakyusa (see Map 7.7). At the time of her fieldwork, the Nyakyusa were patrilineal and patrilocal with many independent chiefdoms. Each Nyakyusa age set began as a group of boys about 10 to 15 years of age. When the members of this junior set were about 33 to 35 years old, an elaborate series of rituals were held to mark their "coming out." At that time,

Figure 7.16 Diablada dancers wear costumes and dance in the Carnival parade through the city of Oruro, Bolivia. Can you think of other examples of sodalities in your own society? How do members show their affiliation?

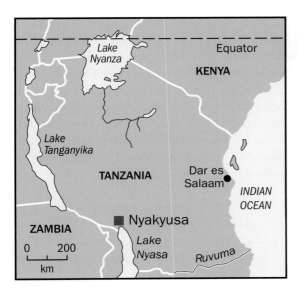

Map 7.7 Nyakyusa

Map 7.8 Boran

the reigning senior generation "handed the country over to them." At any point in time, there were three strata in the Nyakyusa age-set system:

1. Retired elders
2. Active adult men who carried political and military responsibilities for the entire society
3. Immature juniors

A somewhat more complex age-set system exists among the Boran of Kenya and Ethiopia (see Map 7.8; also see Baxter 1978). In this system, which the Boran call *gada,* there are five generation sets, which succeed one another over a 40-year period. Every eight years, a new generation set is formed and the oldest set retires. In many ways, *gada* is part of the Boran's traditional system of governance. Each age set has a specific role to play in social and political life, and each man has a place within his assigned age set.

Secret Societies in Western Africa

Several neighbouring peoples in western Africa use **secret societies** as a way of drawing members of different kinship groups into cross-cutting associations. The most famous secret societies are the Poro and the Sande among the Mende, Sherbro, Kpelle, and other neighbouring peoples of Sierra Leone, Ivory Coast, Liberia, and Guinea.

Poro is a secret society for men, and Sande is a secret society for women; both are hierarchically organized. Secrecy is vested in certain knowledge that can be revealed only to initiates. The higher a person's status within the sodality, the greater the secret

knowledge revealed. To carry out their regulatory responsibilities, high-status sodality members often impersonate important supernatural figures by donning masks and performing in public. Initiation of members brings them into social adulthood. These societies also supervise and regulate the sexual, social, and political conduct of all members of the wider society. Each community has its own Poro and Sande congregations, and a person initiated in one community is eligible to participate in the congregations of other communities. Various stages of initiation require fees. In any community where Poro and Sande are strong, authority in society is divided between a sodality of mature men and one of mature women. Together, these men and women work to keep society on the correct path in a relationship that is highly egalitarian.

The Sherbro (see Map 7.9) have a third secret society, called *Thoma,* which initiates both men and women. As with Poro and Sande initiations, Thoma initiations involve elaborate rituals that create kin-like bonds between co-initiates and transform the uninitiated into initiated, fully social adult human beings. Anthropologist Carol MacCormack (1980) describes the Thoma as "a microcosm of the whole": "Its local congregations or chapters are headed by a man and a woman, co-equal leaders who are 'husband and wife' in a ritual context" (97). The Sherbro are concerned with the reproduction of their society—not just the production of children but also the continuation of the division of labour between men and women. The Sherbro say that the ritual function of the Thoma sodality is "to cleanse the land and the village from evil and restore its fertility and well-being" (98).

secret societies Non-kin social groups that initiate young men or women into social adulthood and reveal "secret" knowledge to initiated members.

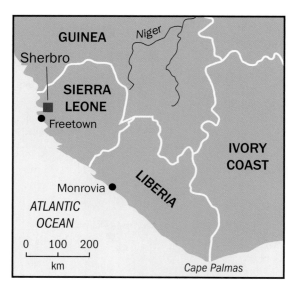

Map 7.9 Sherbro

So what is the secret? Beryl Bellman (1984) argues that initiation rituals are primarily concerned with teaching discretion—knowing when, how, and even whether to speak about various topics. This is a valued attribute of the social adult.

Theories of Relatedness: Kin-Based and Non–Kin-Based Societies

In the Western world, kinship has long been relegated to the realm of personal and family relations. For this reason, early Western anthropologists were struck by the ways in which the elaborate kinship systems they found in non-Western societies could regulate social life and organize behavioural patterns. Yet nineteenth-century scholars of classical antiquity recognized that kinship groups had played comparable roles in ancient European societies as well. Somehow, over time, those kin-ordered forms of social life had been displaced by the large-scale, impersonal, bureaucratically ordered forms of social life typical of a modern nation-state.

Sir Henry Maine, an English jurist who studied the roots of Roman law, described the shift as one from *status* to *contract*. Ancient societies organized people's relationships by the particular position, or status, that each person held within the group. Each status carried with it certain rights and obligations, or *roles*. Statuses and their roles complemented one another: holders of each status were responsible for particular tasks and could rely on other members of the system to perform different tasks. Ideally, these roles fit together like pieces of a puzzle, ensuring that all tasks needed for group survival were carried out. For Maine, the crucial feature of kinship-based societies was that people were not free to choose their own statuses, nor could they modify the rights and responsibilities associated with those statuses. Status and role were *ascribed*. Status-based societies contrasted with contract-based societies in four major ways:

1. Ideally, the parties to contractual relationships enter into them freely.
2. The contracting parties are equally free to specify the rights and obligations between them for the duration of the contract.
3. The range of possible statuses and roles is limitless, bound only by the imagination and interests of the contracting parties.
4. Once the terms of the contract are met, the parties may choose to terminate their relationship with one another.

In another interpretation, Émile Durkheim described the process as a shift from *mechanical solidarity* to *organic solidarity*. In his view, "primitive" societies (ancient and contemporary) were held together on the basis of mechanical solidarity that assigned the same social tasks to everybody who occupied the same kinship status. Tasks were based on age and sex, with each kinship group containing the full range of roles necessary for survival. Keeping kin groups together as parts of a larger whole was problematic, as nothing bound these groups together except "mechanical" similarities in language, mode of livelihood, and so on. Mechanical solidarity, therefore, was brittle, seriously affecting the group's ability to survive.

Conversely, "modern" societies were held together by organic solidarity, which depended on a highly developed *division of labour* rather than established kinship roles. In the "modern" system, each non-kin group specialized in a particular task needed for the survival of the larger whole. With organic solidarity, the division of labour became more elaborate, with some people specializing in food production and others in trade, government, and so on. Full-time specialization meant that each group had to depend on other groups to provide it with things it could not provide for itself, and if any one specialized group were to disappear, the society as a whole would suffer.

Essentially, Maine and Durkheim both asked this: What is the social glue that ensures social co-operation? Anthropologists as well as sociologists have suggested many answers to this question over the years. Sociologist Zygmunt Bauman argues that all human groups of a significant size "are first and foremost processes of collectivization of friends and enemies . . . [in which] individuals sharing a common group or category of enemies treat each other as friends" (1990: 152). Political scientist Benedict Anderson (1983) suggests that the bonds of nationalism that hold citizens of nation-states together are "imagined," as they have not existed for all time but are, rather, social constructions arising from historical circumstances. How will this hold as globalization moves forward? In this chapter, we have discussed a number of cohesive forces, notably Schneider's (1968) interpretation that it is our need for "enduring diffuse solidarity"—between kin and non-kin—that holds society together. Whatever the glue, it is clear that all people have developed patterned social relationships that aim to bind them for the long term.

Living Anthropology

Virtual Spaces for Youth Sociality

by Jennifer Glassco, PhD Candidate, McGill University

Like radio, television, and mobile phones did when they were first introduced, the Internet and associated digital technologies are having a profound impact on both human sociality and the discipline of anthropology itself. The global spread of access to social networking platforms, such as Facebook and Twitter, has forced anthropologists to reconsider the very nature of relationship-building and identity formation. Geographically distant individuals from different linguistic, cultural, and ethnic backgrounds are increasingly coming into contact, interacting and influencing each other on an unprecedented scale (Danet and Herring 2007).

Recently there has been a "technological turn" (Nardi 2015) in the anthropological literature, which takes technologies themselves as first-order subjects of study. Scholars such as anthropologists Whitehead and Wesch push us to pay attention to the diversity of features of online platforms and how they shape the possibilities of relationality:

Facebook and other platforms require persistent and mostly verifiable identities, whereas others allow for more identity play, pseudonymity, or anonymity. Some connect people around the world; others emphasize local connections. Some are text-only, others audio-only; some use video and some mix all three. Some are synchronous whereas others are asynchronous. Some are open, others closed . . . Every feature shapes the possibilities for sociality. (2012: 6)

Online platforms are of particular significance to youth. In countries such as Canada, social media is part of the coming-of-age process and represents a space in which young people can build relationships and assert their identities (Horst 2012). It is important to recognize, however, that not all youth can participate in online forms of sociality. As Hillewaert (2015) notes in her research in Lamu, Kenya, for instance, one must have sufficient literacy, knowledge of how to use a keypad, and the financial capacity to purchase a "smart" phone in order to use social networking platforms (198).

The Internet and social media platforms house vast and complex forums within which youth today can socialize. For example, Bonnie Nardi, in her study of the online game *World of Warcraft*, finds that players are not just interacting when they play the game, they also interact through "a dense online network of blogs, YouTube videos, gaming guides, player forums, Internet relay chat (IRC) channels, voice chat conversations," and many other mediums (2015: 15). Further, new forms of socializing have emerged that would be impossible offline, such as memorial Facebook pages allowing friends and family from around the world to post messages to a friend or loved one who has passed away and to support each other through the grieving process (Ryan 2012).

Youth today select which elements of their identities to emphasize and/or reveal online. In Abidjan, Ivory Coast, unemployed young men use social networking platforms and online dating sites to earn an income through "grazing," an illicit practice whereby they create fake online dating profiles, posing as young women looking for love. They carry on multiple long-term, online relationships periodically asking their partners for money using a number of different pretexts: to

Continued

buy a plane ticket to meet in Europe, to help them with daily living expenses, or even to get out of an abusive relationship (Koenig 2014: 10). These fraudulent relationships provide significant financial benefits, allowing these youth to gain a social status they would never otherwise be able to access. Online platforms offer a method of working around the economic barriers of a highly unequal and gerontocratic society.

It becomes clear when we look at these examples that the distinction between "virtual" relationships and real life is not clear-cut. Relationships built online articulate with offline life in complex and fascinating ways. A case in point is the Facebook groups used by youth in southern Kenya to expose corruption, express their frustration, and organize large protests (Archambault and Glassco forthcoming). Anthropologists must continue to refine our tools and concepts for analyzing these interactions.

In undertaking research into online social relationships, new anthropological methods are being developed and require continuing scrutiny. Online ethnography, digital anthropology, or "netnography" (Kozinets 2015) are all terms referring to the practice of using individuals' online activities and writings as a data source, often in combination with in-person discussions or interviews. These methods open up myriad new ethical and practical concerns around consent, privacy, and access. (For example, how does one ethically use posts made by a Facebook friend in academic work if their posts are only visible to "friends"?) Looking to the future, virtual spaces will continue to be the site of a large portion of youth social interaction. Digital or online ethnographies thus have a vital role to play in fulfilling the core anthropological mission of understanding human sociality.

Key Terms

achieved statuses   173

affinal   151

age sets   178

ascribed statuses   173

bilateral descent   166

blended family   160

bridewealth   152

clan   167

conjugal family   159

consanguineal   151

dowry   156

ego   166

endogamy   154

exogamy   154

extended family   160

family   151

family of choice   162

friendship   151

joint family   160

kinship   151

lineage   167

marriage   151

monogamy   154

non-conjugal family   158

nuclear family   159

polygamy   154

relatedness   151

secret societies   179

segmentary opposition   169

sodalities   178

unilineal descent   166

Chapter Summary

1. Human life is group life organized through relationships of marriage, family, kinship, and friendship.

2. Marriage is a social process that transforms the status of the participants, positions children, and creates relationships between the kin of the partners. Marriage patterns differ across the globe. A number of modern societies recognize same-sex marriages, while others do not. Some cultures promote monogamy, while others promote polygamy.

3. Different family structures produce different internal patterns and tensions. Families may change from one type to another over time and with the birth, growth, and marriage of children.

4. Kinship principles are based on the universal experiences of mating, birth, and nurturance.

5. Patrilineages and matrilineages are corporate groups that collectively control important property. By prescribing certain kinds of marriage, lineages establish long-term alliances with one another.

6. Kinship systems are governed by many rules, but they also offer flexibility. In some cultures, kin ties are open to negotiation; they can also be formed through relationships other than those of blood or marriage.

7. Every society provides ways of establishing links with non-kin. Close relationships—such as those between friends or co-members of a sodality—cultivate a sentiment of enduring diffuse solidarity.

Critical Thinking Questions

1. What is a "prototypical" marriage? Is the prototype the same in all cultures?
2. Distinguish between *pater* and *genitor*. Are they always the same person? Similarly, are gestational, biological, and social mothers always the same person? Do adopted children struggle with such categories?
3. How are joint, extended, and blended families different from nuclear families?
4. What criteria do people use to indicate relatedness? How do you distinguish between relationships of family, kinship, and friendship in your own life?

Suggested Readings

Chute, Janet E. 1999. "Frank G. Speck's Contributions to the Understanding of Mi'kmaq Land Use, Leadership, and Land Management," *Ethnohistory* 46, 3: 481–540. An interesting article on an early Canadian ethnographer's work with an Algonquian group.

Clarke, Morgan. 2007. "Closeness in the Age of Mechanical Reproduction: Debating Kinship and Biomedicine in Lebanon and the Middle East," *Anthropological Quarterly,* 80, 2: 379–402. A relatively recent article exploring the impact of assisted reproductive technologies from an anthropological perspective.

Ginsburg, Faye D., and Rayna Rapp, eds. 1995. *Conceiving the New World Order: The Global Politics of Reproduction* (Berkeley: University of California Press). An important collection of articles by anthropologists who address the ways human reproduction is structured across social and cultural boundaries.

Jamieson, Kathleen. 1986. "Sex Discrimination and the Indian Act," in *Arduous Journey: Canadian Indians and De-colonization,* ed. J. Rick Ponting (Toronto: McClelland & Stewart), 112–36. A discussion of the discrimination toward First Nations women found in the Indian Act and government policies associated with this act.

Letkemann, Paul G. 2009. "Resisting Marginalization: Social Networks and 'Communication Communities' of Urban Blackfoot Teenage Girls," *Anthropologica* 51, 1: 239–50. This article examines how urban Indigenous teens in Lethbridge, Alberta, use social networks to establish a sense of community. It reveals how social networks "serve to mitigate various forms of marginalization by creating and maintaining a sense of place in a community."

Smith, Mary F. 1981 [1954]. *Baba of Karo* (New Haven: Yale University Press). A remarkable document: the autobiography of a Hausa woman born in 1877. This text provides much information about Hausa patterns of friendship, adoption, kinship, marriage, and other intimate relationships.

Stone, Linda, ed. 2001. *New Directions in Anthropological Kinship* (Lanham, MD: Rowman & Littlefield). An excellent collection of relatively recent articles on kinship.

Related Websites

Parliament of Canada: Bill C-38: The Civil Marriage Act
www.parl.gc.ca/common/bills_ls.asp?Parl=38&Ses=1&ls=c38

National Association of Friendship Centres
http://NAFC.ca/about

Surrogacy Options for Gay Couples: In Search of a Womb of One's Own, It's Conceivable
http://itsconceivablenow.com/surrogacy

Timeline of Canadian Milestones in Marriage, Equal Marriage
www.samesexmarriage.ca/evolution/timeline.htm

Making a Living

Chapter Outline

Nature, Culture, and Landscape

Culture and Livelihood

Subsistence Strategies

Phases of Economic Activity

A Dialectic between the Meaningful and the Material

Learning Objectives

By the end of Chapter 8, you will be able to

- recognize how humans have devised a variety of subsistence strategies;
- understand the relationship between production, distribution, and consumption;
- consider economic theories as they relate to anthropological concerns;

- identify various forms of exchange;
- compare and contrast different explanations for consumption patterns; and
- consider change in relation to how people make a living, in local and global settings.

Nature, Culture, and Landscape

In recent years, anthropologists have taken an increasingly holistic view on issues of livelihood, recognizing the interrelationships among the physical, biological, environmental, economic, and cultural aspects of human existence. Foundational to this view is the understanding that this planet and its diversity sustain the living systems on which all life depends. The seminal guru for an impassioned, cogent and fact-based discussion of this view is James Lovelock and his work on the Gaia theory, a holistic look at our planet named for the personification of the earth as a primordial deity. In recommending such readings we are drawn to the fact that as we strive to understand our place on this planet anthropologists are already engaged in the integration of data and interpretations from many seemingly disparate disciplines, which will be all the more important as climate change continues to alter all aspects of the natural world. As Crate (2011) further notes, "anthropology's roles have expanded to engage local to global contexts."

Central is the fact that cross-disciplinary research encourages us to recognize that human culture is not *apart from* the natural world—rather, it is *a part of* this world and is contextualized by and interdependent with ecological processes. It is our cultural and adaptive responses and our capacity for reflexivity that have allowed for the development of diverse ways of "making and living" and that now need to direct us in diverse ways of survival.

Human beings have become and remain the dominant shapers of what we call the "natural" world. So much so that there is not a place on this planet where our presence is not felt. We now speak of both natural and cultural landscapes but even the natural is affected by our wants and needs (consider, for example, the disintegration of the ice field of Antarctica; see Figure 8.1). Thus, we may even go so far as to state that the concept of a natural world, as it is applied to the habitat of humans, is a *cultural construct* and, as such, has a definition that is in each case culturally specific. The landscapes of specific cultures are so very different from those of another culture (though these differences can be subtle). These differences are not fully founded in the actual environment or in particular parameters—such as the geology, hydrology, latitude, altitude, or even biotic communities that are specific to a certain tract of land—but on how these parameters are turned to the marking and making of human space. Therefore, the environment can be seen as a landscape symbolic of culture. An excellent example of this can be found in the Zuni Atlas (Ferguson et al. 1985). Although pre-GIS (geographic information system), it is nonetheless significantly informative on the definition of various culturally defined landscapes. For example, consider the Zuni waffle gardens in the flood plain of the Zuni River in 1919 (Figure 8.2). Traditionally these gardens were part of the matrilineal clan-based land tenure system held in both symbolic and metaphorical constructs engaged in both physical and transcendental worlds. This form of gardening remains today and sustains its ancient essential meanings.

Anthropologists have made observations on the diverse ways of making a living at various times and in various places, taking into consideration the roles of women and men in shaping these cultural realities.

© Carlos Mora/Alamy Stock Photo

Figure 8.1 Melting ice in the Weddell Sea, Antarctica. Ice in this area has been melting and breaking off at an alarming rate.

A family hand making rugs in rural Rajasthan, India. Our cultures suggest a wide range of options for making a living, many of which are becoming increasingly tied to the global economy through the forces of globalization.

A classic example comes from the work of Canadian anthropologist Richard B. Lee's 1963 study of the Ju/'hoansi (see EthnoProfile 7.2; Figure 8.3) of the Kalahari. When Lee arrived in the Kalahari Desert, he was asked by a man named N!eishi to drive him and his neighbours out to collect mongongo nuts—a staple of their diet and a great favourite. Lee agreed, and the men and women spent two hours gathering an impressive amount of food. Lee later weighed the food collected and calculated that "each woman had gathered enough to feed a person for ten days and each man enough for five days." The Ju/'hoansi were well nourished and had balanced diets, and they were choosy about what they ate, unwilling to settle for

unfree labour An all-encompassing term for the formalized coercion of men, women, and children (through need or violence) to provide their labour. Such labour can range from migrant farm work to sex slavery to the use of children as soldiers.

food they disliked. Thus, Lee found strong evidence to counter the Western stereotype of human beings who forage for a living as leading lives that are, in Thomas Hobbes's famous words, "nasty, brutish, and short."

It is imperative that anthropologists place such ethnographic information within the time-framed context of a people adapting to their emerging circumstances. As a further example, much has changed in southern Africa since the 1960s, and the Ju/'hoansi no longer forage as they once did. Until relatively recently, however, the cultural knowledge of the Ju/'hoansi enabled them to live rather well in what many see as a marginal environment. This can be seen in Robert Hitchcock's (2003) comments on Ju/'hoansi activism in northwestern Botswana with respect to land claims issues and herding. (For more, see the "In Their Own Words" box that follows.) Their innovative response includes community-based natural mapping to gain greater control of land, water, and wildlife resources. So even as things are changing, traditional cultural knowledge continues to frame their relationship to the natural environment and cultural landscape around them.

Anthropologists also consider who does the work, as well as the range of human rights issues surrounding itinerant and migrant workers and the use of child labour. Berlan (2013) analyzes the debate on **unfree labour** and challenges existing categorizations, which results in "a reconfiguration of the terminology of unfree labour" (1088) with respect to children and family. As Berlan further notes, "Labels can hinder the deconstruction of the processes inherent to unfree labour, and the literature on this makes a compelling case for them to come under greater scrutiny . . . it is an evolving landscape where exploitation and vulnerability feed off ever more complex and rapidly expanding commercial networks" (1098).

To uncover, discover, and recreate the worlds and roles that sustain all human beings is a journey in self-discovery as well as a journey into the diverse worlds of other cultures, times, and places. This can involve looking into various records from which anthropologists can construct an understanding of how a living was made. These records consist of ethnographic writings, ethno-historical and historical documents and writings, environmental materials and observations, supporting items of the material culture dating from deep time to today, and data from the earth and ecological sciences. For example, we could follow the history of wheat farming on the Prairies of Canada by seeking the out-of-date agricultural equipment dotting the rural landscape (Figure 8.4).

Figure 8.2 The Zuni waffle gardens in the flood plain of the Zuni River in 1919.

Figure 8.3 Richard B. Lee gathers mongongo nuts with the Ju/'hoansi.

In Their Own Words

Land, Livestock, and Leadership among the Ju/'hoansi San of North Western Botswana

In this excerpt anthropologist Robert K. Hitchcock discusses the strategies the Ju/'hoansi of north-western Botswana employed to gain control over land and natural resource rights, elaborating on the relationship between the natural environment and the cultural landscape for the Ju/'hoansi.

In the latter part of the 20th century, the Ju/'hoansi of north-western Botswana employed a multi-pronged set of strategies in their efforts to gain control over land and natural resource rights. They have used their traditional system of land use and management, the *n!ore* system, as a foundation for managing their land. At the same time, they have been quick to seize on opportunities offered by new Botswana government policies involving land and natural resource management, engaging in well-digging efforts and making formal claims to government land management institutions for land and water allocations. Unlike some other San groups in Botswana, they have not tied their claims to indigenous identity but rather have co-operated closely with non-San groups in seeking land and resource rights. They have built coalitions and formed alliances with Ju/'hoan groups and other San groups in neighbouring countries.

The Ju/'hoansi of north western Botswana have been careful about the ways in which they have asserted their collective identity. On the one hand, they have proclaimed their identity as Ju/'hoansi in struggles for recognition and rights at the community level, but they have been careful not to make such claims at the national level in Botswana, realizing full well that the idea of indigenousness does not sit well with government officials in the country (Hitchcock, 2002a; Saugestad, 2001; Sylvain, 2002). The Ju/'hoansi have accepted the government's classification of them as Remote Area Dwellers in order to access government programs and they have utilized other government programs to their advantage such as those aimed at providing livestock and agricultural inputs. As one Ju/'hoan woman at Dobe put it, "We know that the government wants us to have livestock and crops and to live like other people, so that is why we get these things whenever the Ministry of Agriculture offers them."

The Ju/'hoansi of Botswana have learned a great deal from their interactions with other groups involved in the larger world indigenous rights movement. They have learned about new ways to negotiate with nationstates, and they have put this knowledge to use at the local level, the national and in the international arena. They have also benefited from collaboration with international NGOs, donors and researchers.

Finally, the Ju/'hoansi and their neighbours in north western Botswana have purposely linked their systems of governance with conservation and development efforts. They have established multiethnic community-based institutions that have sought and received government recognition. These community-based bodies have been able to generate income for their members, sometimes in substantial amounts, as was the case with the XaiXai Tlhabololo Trust who in 2001–02 made some $200,000 and were able to generate over a dozen jobs for local people (Bernard Horton, Charlie Motshubi, personal communications, 2002). Without having participated in Botswana's community-based natural resource management program and the work of the various non-government organizations engaged in integrated conservation and development programs, the Ju/'hoansi would not have been able to obtain the rights to land and resources around communities in northwestern Botswana, and they would still be marginalized minorities, living in, as one Ju/'hoan woman put it, "a sea of poverty."

Source: Robert K. Hitchcock, 2003. "Land, Livestock and Leadership among the Ju/'hoansi San of North Western Botswana," *Anthropologica 45*: 89–94. Reprinted with permission of University of Toronto Press

---

Wheat farming speaks of the "domestication" of the Prairies by European immigrants as wheat, originally from the Neolithic of West Asia, was introduced on immigrant family farms. It was then superseded by the growing of diverse crops (corn, canola, flax, etc.) and the raising of animals (cattle, hogs, chickens, etc.) and by large industrial (factory) farms controlled by transnational corporations. There is now a dissonance between what could be considered "traditional" food production and the industrial, globalized production of food found worldwide today. Barlett's (1987) work captures this dissonance with respect to the family farm in the following passage:

The farm operator is the local-level actor who mediates among the imperatives of farm, family, industry, and state. Though increasingly constrained, the farm family determines the use of resources, the adoption of technology, and the response to changing societal values. Maladaptive decisions on the part of regulators may hurt the larger

© tbob/iStock

Figure 8.4 A rusted antique tractor covered with snow in Alberta. It is common to find abandoned agricultural equipment throughout the Prairies. How can the examination of old equipment, such as this tractor, provide new insights into how people make a living today?

system but usually will not challenge the regulators' elite status or economic security. Farmers must face a situation in which the long-term impacts of each decision are unknowable, but the immediate consequences of farm loss are often too visible. (148)

Markus von Glasenapp and Thomas F. Thornton (2011) discuss the smallholder-householder theory of adaptation, which argues that a household amid environmental change is the most resilient unit because of its flexible organization of labour and intimate local environmental knowledge. For larger corporations, survival is mediated by the resources available for production and distribution, as well as the current demands of the market (which can be manipulated).

Socioecological Data

Before anthropologists can engage in any serious debate on the relationship that human beings have to their natural and culture environments—their landscapes—they first need data. The advent of the digital age has given us powerful tools (and newly emerging methods) to develop more precise sets of information. The ability to efficiently collect, sort, and analyze information has always been the goal of the anthropologist. But many have moved from their notebooks and pencils to increasingly powerful and sophisticated tools. For example, this transition is

shown in moving from Kroeber's work on the cultural and natural areas of Indigenous America in 1939 to Steward's work in cultural ecology in 1968 to Lansing's work in Bali in 1988, in which he used a computer to model rice production and water management.

In recent decades, researchers have refined many approaches for gathering and situating data in meaningful and accessible discussions. For example, consider GIS (geographic information system), a software-based system that collects, organizes, downloads, and retrieves files for analysis and displays spatial/digital geographical data. Another example is human ecology mapping (HEM), which has become important in the management of natural resources and is now seen as significant in the discussion of human/land relationships. Some approaches to human ecology mapping include tenure and resource use (TRU), local ecological knowledge (LEK), and sense of place (SOP) (McLain et al. 2013). (See Table 8.1 for further details.)

Rebecca McLain and her co-authors note that agency is also an important component of these approaches; we come to see how the *emic* (from the perspective of the subject) and the *etic* (from the perspective of the observer) emerge from the ethnographers' interpretive process. McLain and co-authors note:

> Both TRU and LEK mapping emerged from efforts by indigenous and local communities to gain greater influence or control over land and resources and are theoretically and methodologically informed by the subfields of cultural ecology, political ecology, and international development in the disciplines of cultural geography and anthropology. TRU and LEK mapping draw heavily from the ethnographer's toolkit to translate individual and collective cognitive maps into "standard" maps adhering to western cartographic conventions. Both approaches emphasize the use of qualitative methods combined with field-based or remotely sensed measurements of boundaries, culturally important locations, or resource conditions. Additionally, many TRU and LEK mapping projects are driven by an empowerment model that seeks to maximize participants' control over the mapping process—and increasingly over the data and maps produced through those processes. In contrast, SOP mapping is informed theoretically and methodologically by the disciplines of behavioral geography, environmental psychology, and environmental planning. (2013: 661)

Table 8.1 Comparison of Human Ecology Mapping Approaches

	Tenure and Resource Use (TRU)	Local Ecological Knowledge (LEK)	Sense of Place (SOP)
Participation model	Empowerment	Empowerment/co-creation of knowledge	Variable: Mostly contributory but some studies are collaborative and others involve co-creation of planting knowledge or political empowerment
Major applications	• Advancement of claims for land and resources previously appropriated by nation-states • Land and resource conflict resolution and mitigation • Development of community management plans • Building relationships of trust between communities and external groups	• Integration with scientific data to produce predictive models (i.e., impacts of climate change on habitats) • Integration with scientific data to select locations for marine protected areas • Development of community management plans • Building relationships of trust between communities, scientists, and resource management agencies	• Identification of areas where values or place meanings conflict or mesh with proposed natural resource management actions • Identification of areas where values or place meanings conflict with each other • Building relationships of trust (collaborative mapping) • Improved understanding of the combination of environmental and social factors that provide a "feeling" of wilderness
Primary data collection methods	Wide range of methods • Focus groups • Semi-structured interviews • Oral histories • Land management histories • Transect walks • Surveys • Map biographies • Photo narratives • Trip diaries • Grounded diaries	Wide range of methods • Focus groups • Semi-structured interviews • Oral histories • Land management histories • Transect walks • Surveys • Map biographies • Photo narratives • Trip diaries • Grounded diaries	Values mapping • Surveys Place attachment • Semi-structured interviews • Focus groups for feedback Wilderness perceptions mapping • Surveys Collaborative mapping • Workshops or focus groups to develop consensual maps • Key informant interviews Hybrids • Mixed methods
Major challenges	• Mapping boundaries can have the unintended consequence of nursing fluid boundaries into rigid boundaries, reducing the capacity for communities to adapt to socioecological changes. • Communities are heterogeneous, and more powerful members may seek to dominate the mapping process, depriving less powerful community members of access to resources.	• Essential qualitative details, such as cultural meanings and histories, are not easily captured in LEK mapping, resulting in maps that are only partial representations of LEK. • Managers are often skeptical of the validity of LEK data and resist incorporating it into planning. • Communities often lack capacity to implement LEK mapping and outsiders may control the process. They may lead to misinterpretation or misuse of LEK data and undermine empowerment goals.	• Most SOP mapping does not include a ground-truthing component, making SOP maps highly susceptible to locational errors and ambiguities in spatial representations. • Boundaries of values and special places are fuzzy and challenging to depict in hand-drawn or computerized maps. • Certain subgroups are less likely to participate in surveys, interviews, and focus groups, resulting in a gap in the range of values, perceptions, or place attachments collected.

Continued

Table 8.1 Continued

Tenure and Resource Use (TRU)	Local Ecological Knowledge (LEK)	Sense of Place (SOP)
• Communities often lack capacity to map and analyze mapped data with the result that outsiders may end up controlling the process. This may lead to misrepresentations of boundaries or conflicts and undermine empowerment goals. • The process of defining boundaries can spark latent claims to resources leading to conflicts where there previously were none.	• LEK mapping projects typically have not included provisions for long-term data storage, maintenance, and updating. As a result, data from LEK mapping done several years ago may not reflect changes in socioecological conditions or understandings of the environment.	• Managers have tended to be resistant to using data from values mapping projects; they have been more open to incorporating data from place attachment projects. • The qualitative data generated by place attachment mapping and some hybrid SOP mapping projects are challenging to integrate into GIS databases and analyses.

Source: McLain 2013: 665. Reproduced with permission of Springer.

Culture and Livelihood

Although our physical survival depends on our making adequate use of the material resources around us, the resources themselves do not determine how they must be used. Rather, our cultures suggest a range of options for making a living and for furnishing the tools to pursue those options. Thus, each culture has its own **economy**. Anthropologist Richard Wilk has defined **economic anthropology** as "the part of the discipline that debates issues of *human nature* that relate directly to the decisions of daily life and making a living" (1996: xv).

Self-Interest, Institutions, and Morals

Richard Wilk and Lisa Cliggett (2007) argue that it is possible to identify three theoretical camps in economic anthropology, each of which depends on a different set of assumptions about human nature. Further, they note that the "real heat and argument in economic anthropology comes from underlying disagreement over these starting assumptions" (2007: 40). They discuss these assumptions by highlighting three models of human nature that correspond to the three theoretical camps.

The first model that Wilk and Cliggett identify is the *self-interested model*. This model of human nature originated during the Enlightenment and is based on the assumption that individuals are first and foremost interested in their own well-being, that selfishness is natural. Economists since Adam Smith (1723–1790) have argued that people's resources (e.g., money) are not and never will be great enough for them to obtain all the goods they want. This view of economy also assumes that economic analysis should focus on *individuals* who must maximize their *utility* (or satisfaction) under conditions of **scarcity**. Such economizing individuals set priorities and allocate resources rationally according to those priorities. Economic anthropologists who accept the self-interested model should therefore investigate the different priorities set by different societies and study how these priorities affect the maximizing decisions of individuals.

Other economic anthropologists, however, are committed to the *social model* of human nature. These anthropologists pay attention to "the way people form groups and exercise power" (Wilk and Cliggett 2007: 42). This view of human nature assumes that people ordinarily identify with the groups to which they belong and, in many cases, cannot even conceive of having a self with interests that diverge from the interests of the group. This view of human nature suggests that economics ought to focus on **institutions** rather than on individuals. From an institutional point of view, a

economy The culturally specific processes used by members of a society to provide themselves with material resources.

economic anthropology "The part of the discipline [of anthropology] that debates issues of *human nature* that relate directly to the decisions of daily life and making a living" (Wilk 1996: xv).

scarcity A condition under which it is assumed that resources (e.g., money) will never be plentiful enough for people to obtain all the goods or services they desire.

institutions Stable and enduring cultural practices that organize social life.

society's economy consists of the culturally specific processes its members use to provide themselves with material resources. Therefore, economic processes cannot be considered apart from the cultural institutions in which they are embedded (Halperin 1994).

Wilk and Cliggett's third model of human nature is the *moral model*. Economic anthropologists committed to a moral model of human nature assume that people's motivations "are shaped by culturally specific belief systems and values ... guided by a culturally patterned view of the universe and the human place within it" (2007: 43). People are socialized and enculturated into these values and practices over a lifetime, such that they will experience distress and conflict if tempted to make decisions—including economic decisions—that are contrary to their internalized morality. From the point of view of the moral model, "modern society ... has lost the morality and ethics that guided behaviour in traditional cultures, replacing them with amoral selfishness" (2007: 44). Wilk and Cliggett are unwilling to take any one model as a fact and are more interested in paying close ethnographic attention to the particularities of real human beings in real sociocultural settings:

> The problem is explaining why people are guided sometimes by one set of motivations and at other times by others.... By suspending our preconceptions about human nature, we can give more direct attention to this fundamental question, which forms the basis of each culture's practical ethics and its distinction between moral and immoral. (2007: 46)

Subsistence Strategies

Subsistence is linked to basic material survival needs: food, clothing, and shelter. The different ways to go about meeting these needs are called **subsistence strategies**. Anthropologists have devised a typology of subsistence strategies that has gained wide acceptance (Figure 8.5). The basic division has been between **food collectors** and **food producers**. Yet, although this typology suggests a clear distinction,

subsistence strategies The patterns of production, distribution, and consumption that members of a society use to meet their basic material survival needs.

food collectors People who gather wild plant materials, fish, and/or hunt for food.

food producers People who depend on domesticated plants and/or animals for food.

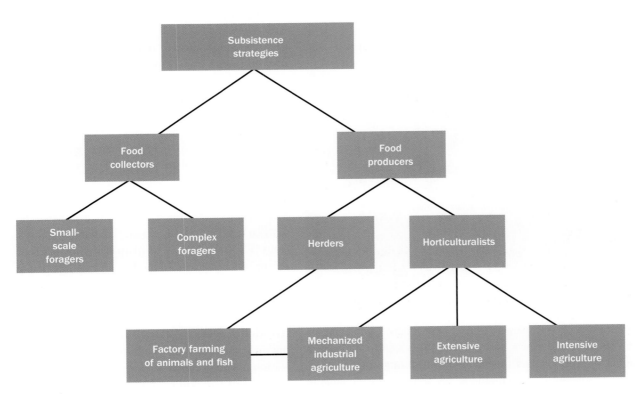

Figure 8.5 Subsistence strategies.

the two systems are not always separated in practice. For example, archaeological evidence shows that some of the first food producers in the world continued food collection for many generations, raising a few crops on the side and occasionally abandoning food production to return to full-time foraging. Additionally, the expansion of the urbanized, industrialized, globalized world is increasingly being considered for ways of making a living beyond food acquisition and food production. This is seen in particular when considering the industrialization of food acquisition and food production. The elaboration of craft specialization was first considered by Childe, who defined the *Neolithic Revolution*—a wide-scale transition from hunter-gatherer economies to economies based on agriculture with the domestication of plants and animals thousands of years ago. Through the history of our genus *Homo* we see the artifacts of making a living—the tools of survival.

The strategies followed by *food collectors* depend on the availability of resources in their environments. Small-scale food collectors, such as traditional Ju/'hoansi, live in environments with resources that are sufficient but patchy and frequently only seasonally available. Thus, small-scale food collectors are likely to change residence often. In contrast, complex food collectors live in environments where many foods are available at all times. As a result, complex food collectors may

even, like the Indigenous peoples of the northwest coast of North America, build permanent settlements.

Food producers may farm or herd, or both. Herders are often nomadic, moving their herds from place to place in search of fresh pasture. Today, nomadic herders are often in conflict with settled farmers who own the lands—and often the water—that they traditionally used to sustain their herds. Among those who farm, there are three major distinctions:

1. **Extensive agriculture**
2. **Intensive agriculture**
3. **Mechanized industrial agriculture**

In *extensive agriculture*, farmers clear plots of uncultivated land, burn the brush, and plant their crops in the ash-enriched soil. This is commonly called "*slash and burn.*" Eventually, these techniques exhaust the soil, and the plot must lie fallow as a new plot is cleared and the process repeated. The length of this cycle may range from two years to twenty or thirty years, depending on the region. In *intensive agriculture*, farmers use more complex tools and technologies (e.g., crop rotation, irrigation, and fertilizers) to work on the same plot of land for a longer period of time (see Figure 8.6). In *mechanized industrial agriculture*, farming is organized along industrial lines. Most often, this type of crop production is found alongside the factory farming of animals.

Today, most of us are very familiar with the processes involved in mechanized industrial agriculture. Huge agribusinesses ("factories in the field") and animal feedlots have transformed food production into a large-scale, technology-dependent industry. Within the context of our globalized economy, food is commonly transformed into a "commodity" that is produced and distributed by transnational corporate institutions (Phillips 2006). Unfortunately, our relatively recent "scientization" of food production has led to the loss of many traditional systems of production as well as the loss of traditional knowledge worked out over millennia (Brodt 2001). Although many traditional ways of making a living are disappearing under the forces of modernization and globalization, some do remain. (See the "In Their Own Words" box that follows on swidden cultivation in Calakmul, Mexico.)

extensive agriculture
A form of cultivation that depends on slash-and-burn (swidden) techniques, rainwater, human muscle power, and a few simple tools, such as digging sticks, hoes, and/or machetes.

intensive agriculture
A form of cultivation that employs plows, draft animals, irrigation, and fertilizer to bring a large amount of land under cultivation at one time.

mechanized industrial agriculture Large-scale farming that is highly dependent on industrial methods of technology and production.

Figure 8.6 Farmers use oxen to plow the fields near Mount Elgon National Park, Kenya. Some farmers use plows and animals for intensive agriculture to reduce the amount of time it takes them to cultivate a large plot of land. What might a culture's dominant farming methods say about its relationship to the world?

In Their Own Words

Persistence of Swidden Cultivation in the Face of Globalization:
A Case Study from Communities in Calakmul, Mexico

The problems being addressed here focus on the recent ef-ficacy of swidden systems of food production in the face of globalization and environmental changes. The questions are being addressed through the analysis on both subjective and objective data (interviews and timeline-based data on produc-tion). The results show that this longstanding traditional system has always evolved and responded to the contingencies of the times in which people live, thus supporting and maintaining not only subsistence but cultural reproduction.

Many farmers in the Global South rely on traditional farming practices, including swidden cultivation, as these traditional techniques have co-evolved over time as adaptations to par-ticular environmental, social, economic, and political circum-stances and pressures (Chambers 1988; Denevan 1995). While yields in traditional agricultural systems may be lower than those of more intensive production systems, they offer the advantages of a low level of monetary investment, includ-ing minimal agrochemical inputs. They also generate a rela-tively reliable harvest and, therefore, facilitate household food security in unpredictable agro-environments with highly variable soils and rainfall (Tuxill et al. 2010). The high crop diversity in some traditional systems constitutes an adaptive mechanism in these difficult agro-ecological environments (Altieri 1999). Farmers' strategy of minimizing risk by plant-ing several species and varieties of crops stabilizes yields over the long term, promotes dietary diversity, and maximizes returns under low levels of technology and limited resources (Chang 1977; Clawson 1985; Harwood 1996; Thrupp 1998). Livestock are kept, either as a primary agricultural enterprise or linked to crop production. The roles of livestock are mani-fold: the production of milk, meat, hides, manure, draft power, among others, as well as the accumulation of wealth, secur-ity against contingencies, and display of status (Moll 2005). Access to forest resources is often key in traditional systems as it provides farmers with building materials, fire wood, bush meat, and edible plants, and buffers farm families against market fluctuations and failed crop harvests (Alcom 1984; Chambers and Leach 1989; Barham et al. 1999).

In Central America and particularly in Mexico, the *milpa*, a traditional Maya swidden system, exemplifies these di-verse subsistence and livelihood security benefits. Ancient in origin, the Mexican *milpa* system refers to a complex combination of agronomic practices, crop associations, and rotation sequences that vary with cultural context and agro-environment. Traditional *milpa* cultivation involves cutting an area of forest, burning, and planting . . . annual, bi-annual and perennial cultivars with up to 87 different crops and tree crops within a single village (Terân and Rasmussen 1994). [R]ecently many farmers have turned their *milpas* into maize monocrops, as they increasingly use herbicides (Prebisch et al. 2002) that are incompatible with, for example, beans.

Slashing and burning clears the soil for planting, releases nutrients from slashed vegetation for crop growth, and reduces the population of weed seeds. Steggerda (1941) hypothesized that without the availability of draft animals, swidden cultiva-tion was the only method available to people farming in such a densely forested landscape. Extremely rocky soils and distinct wet and dry seasons are additional factors that contribute to the prevalence of the *milpa* systems. Each year, approximately two million farming households across Mexico continue to cul-tivate *milpas* on around six million hectares of land; and most of these households depend on *milpa* production for food se-curity (Bellon and Berthaud 2004).

Milpa, according to Alcorn and Toledo (2000) is both an institution and a process. It is a "cultural script"—an in-ternalized plan consisting of a series of routine steps with alternative subroutines, decision nodes, and room for experi-mentation, rather than simply a patch in space (Berkes et al. 2000). Culture plays a significant role in *milpa* management. Researchers have often commented on the integral role *milpa* plays in Mesoamerican life. For example, Nigh (1976), in a study of Maya agriculture in highland Chiapas, states that "the making of *milpa* is the central, most sacred act, one which binds together the family, the community, the universe." Hostettler (1998) notes that above all, identity is rooted in *milpa*, and that "maize is both the most important element of Maya diet and the 'stuff of life' in the wider sense of religious practice and identity." According to Mayan mythology, the *milpa* is the sacred place in which the raw material of humans was created, and maize is the holy substance from which the Maya emerged, and as such is considered to be sacred and life-giving (De Frece and Poole 2008).

There is evidence suggesting that, while the basic structure of the swidden system has persevered since pre-Columbian days (Terân and Rasmussen 1995), *milpas* in Mexico's Yucatan Peninsula have been largely transformed or replaced by more intensive or commercial production systems,

Continued

such as pasture or chili cultivation (Klepeis et al. 2004; Keys 2005). Global processes such as market integration, liberalization of national policies, international labor migration, climate change, and conservation measures have largely contributed to the reduction or modification of swidden in the Yucatan Peninsula (Toulmin and Guèye 2005).

Our aim is to understand the reasons for the persistence of maize swidden systems despite the large increase in intensive or commercial production. These reasons might include changing climate conditions and the incorporation of new economic activities like off-farm work and national and international migration by family members.

Source: Republished with permission from Springer Nature. Excerpt from Birgit Schmook, et al., 2013. "Persistence of Swidden Cultivation in the Face of Globalization: A Case Study from Communities in Calakmul, Mexico," *Human Ecology* 41, 1: 93–107; permission conveyed via Copyright Clearance Center.

Phases of Economic Activity

Economic activity has traditionally been subdivided into three distinct phases:

1.   **Production**
2.   **Distribution**
3.   **Consumption**

production The transformation of nature's raw materials into a form suitable for human use.

distribution The allocation of goods and services.

consumption Using up material goods necessary for human survival.

Anthropologists differ in the importance they attach to each phase. Most would agree that *exchange* is central to capitalist free enterprise. However, some anthropologists argue that exchange cannot be properly understood without first studying the nature of *production* as it shapes the context in which exchange can occur, determining the kind and quantity of goods to exchange. Other anthropologists have suggested that neither production nor exchange patterns make any sense without first specifying the *consumption* priorities of the people who are producing and exchanging. Consumption priorities, they argue, are designed to satisfy material needs. But the recognition of needs, and the recognition of appropriate ways to satisfy them, is shaped by arbitrary cultural patterns. Still others argue that patterns of production, exchange, and consumption are all seriously affected by the kind of *storage* used in a particular society (Figure 8.7).

Distribution and Exchange

Neoclassical Economic Theory and the Rise of Capitalism

neoclassical economic theory A formal attempt to explain the workings of capitalist enterprise, with particular attention to distribution.

In the eighteenth century, as capitalist enterprises continued to rise across Western Europe, thinkers such as Adam Smith and his disciples struggled to devise theories to explain the profound changes in European economic and social life. Their work became the foundation for **neoclassical economic** theory, a theory that some economic anthropologists continue to support today.

Capitalism differed in many ways from the preceding feudal economic system, particularly in distribution. Feudal economic relations allotted goods and services to individuals on the basis of their position in society, or their *status*. Because lords had high status, they had a right to more goods and services. Peasants, who had low status, were allowed far less. This time-honoured system was not open to modification. New capitalist economic relations, in contrast, were negotiated between buyers and sellers in the "market."

In Smith's ideal market, everyone has something to sell (if only his or her willingness to work), and everyone is also a potential buyer of the goods or services brought to the market. There is economic exchange with none of the old traditional restrictions governing who should get how much of what. Prices fluctuate depending on levels of supply and demand, and distribution is carried out in line with the preferences of individuals (needs, which are required, and wants, which are desired). High demand for certain items raises the price for those items, as many buyers bargain to obtain few goods. This high demand, in turn, entices more people to produce those goods to take advantage of their higher returns. As competition among suppliers increases, however, prices go down, as each supplier attempts to obtain a greater share of the market. Ideally, prices stabilize as suppliers begin offering "desired" goods at a cost sufficiently high to allow a profit but sufficiently low for buyers to afford.

Capitalist market exchange of goods and services (including labour) for other goods, services, or cash was an important development in Western economic history. It is not surprising, therefore, that eighteenth-century Western economic theory was preoccupied with explaining how the capitalist market worked. This preoccupation grew as it

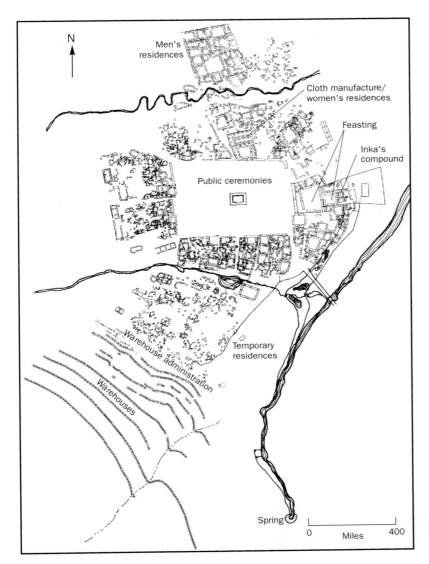

Figure 8.7 Above: A seventeenth-century drawing of storage warehouses built at the height of the Inca (Tawantinsuyu) Empire. Left: The plan of Huánuco Pampa, an Inca administration centre, which shows the location of these storage warehouses. Some anthropologists argue that food storage practices buffer a population from ecological fluctuations, making considerable cultural manipulation of the economic relations of consumption possible.

became clear that markets had a new central importance in society's functioning. Western neoclassical economics is based on the assumption that market forces are the central forces determining levels of both production and consumption in society. Thus, neoclassical economic analysis focuses on markets, scarcity hypotheses, and "laws" of supply and demand. In such a system, everything has a price.

Modes of Exchange

Some anthropologists have argued, however, that to take self-interested, materialistic decision-making in the capitalist market as the prototype of human decision-making is both overly simplistic and ethnocentric. Further, such analyses frequently encourage the use of unilineal evolutionary models of organization and interaction in the discussion of cultures defined as "other." Thus, Lewis Henry Morgan's ethnical stages of savagery, barbarism, and civilization (discussed in Chapter 3) become embedded, overtly or covertly, in the categories used in such discussions.

At this point in the discussion, we should take a moment to remember that capitalist markets and neoclassical economic theory are relatively recent cultural inventions. We should also remember that they were developed in specific societies with certain basic values, institutions, and assumptions about the human condition—to peoples with a certain shared world view. Non-Western, non-capitalist societies also have devised modes of exchange that distribute material goods in ways that are in accordance with their basic values, institutions, and assumptions about the human condition—their world views.

Characteristic of the Western-centric analysis of non-Western cultures is the work of anthropologist Marcel Mauss (2000 [1950]). Mauss contrasted non-capitalist *gift exchanges* with impersonal *commodity exchanges* typical of the capitalist market (Figure 8.8). Gift exchange is deeply embedded in social relations of kinship, partnerships, and acquaintanceships, always requiring a return "gift." In contrast, commodity exchange links the participants by cash—the cost of and payment for an item or labour. While Mauss associated gift exchanges with non-Western cultures, he associated commodity exchange with Western cultures. (Recall here Morgan's division between "savage" or "barbaric" non-Western societies and "civilized" European societies.) Consequently, Mauss did not fully address the fact that cultures may engage in *both* forms of exchange.

The work of American anthropologist Marshall Sahlins (1972) has a similarly ancient–modern directional tone. Sahlins drew on the writings of economic historian Karl Polanyi (1886–1964) to propose three **modes of exchange**: reciprocity, redistribution, and market exchange. Polanyi argued that these modes could be identified historically in many cultures. He also recognized that different modes of exchange often coexist within a single society—a recognition that makes his ideas very useful in an anthropological context.

Reciprocity

Reciprocity, the most ancient mode of exchange, is characteristic of egalitarian societies. Sahlins identified three kinds of reciprocity:

1. Generalized
2. Balanced
3. Negative

Generalized reciprocity is found when those who exchange do so without expecting an immediate return and without specifying the value of

Figure 8.8 In his book *The Gift* (1950), Marcel Mauss examines the Kula exchange ceremony of the Trobriand Islanders. Here, men dance at a modern Kula exchange celebration in the Trobriand Islands, Papua New Guinea. What advantages might this sort of exchange system have in comparison to the typical Western exchange system involving the exchange of money for goods?

the return. Everyone assumes that the exchanges will eventually balance out. *Balanced reciprocity* is found when those who exchange expect a return of equal value within a specified time limit. For example, Richard B. Lee noted that the Ju/'hoansi distinguish between barter, which requires an immediate return of an equivalent value, and *hxaro*, which is a kind of generalized reciprocity that encourages social obligations to be extended into the future (1992b: 103). *Negative reciprocity* is an exchange of goods and services in which at least one party attempts to get something for nothing without suffering any penalties. These attempts can range from haggling over prices to outright seizure.

Redistribution

The second mode of exchange, **redistribution**, requires some form of centralized social organization. Those who occupy the central position receive material contributions from all members of the group. It is then their responsibility to redistribute the goods they receive in a way that provides for every member of the group. A well-known Canadian institution of redistribution is the Canada Revenue Agency.

The potlatch (Ýaqʷqʷa) (Figure 8.9), or gift-giving ceremony, of First Nations peoples of Canada's West Coast has frequently been used erroneously to illustrate redistribution. While there are elements of exchange involved, reducing the event to a venue for redistribution of wealth ignores the complexity of the social interactions the potlatch represents: members of a community coming together to bear witness to specific culturally significant events, such as births, marriages, deaths, and remembrances. Further, as anthropologist Kenneth Tollefson observes, politics plays a very large part in the potlatch:

> [C]ertain clan goals could only be fulfilled through potlatching. These include (1) installation of clan leaders, (2) evaluation and verification of clan titles to resources, (3) bestowal of clan titles, (4) resolution of inter-clan disputes, (5) establishing or reaffirming clan alliances, (6) investment and diversification of clan wealth, (7) social removal of shame, and (8) maintenance of regional stability. (1995: 71)

There are interconnections among power, politics, cultural priorities, social interaction, and economic

Figure 8.9 The potlatch of the Kwakiutl (Kwakwaka'wakw) was a highly complex social event that held deep cultural importance for all involved in the gathering. The ceremony was banned by the Canadian government from 1884 to 1951, although it continued in the villages even in the face of arrests and punishment through the Canadian courts.

exchange; these ties should remind us of the necessity of looking at cultural processes through the anthropological lens of holism. (Note Daisy Sewid-Smith's discussion of the potlatch in the "In Their Own Words" box that follows.)

Market Exchange

Invented in capitalist society, **market exchange** is the most recent mode of exchange, according to Polanyi. Polanyi was well aware that trade, money, and market institutions had developed independently of one another. He also knew that they could be found in societies outside the West. The uniqueness of capitalism was how all three institutions were linked to one another in the societies of early modern Europe.

Production

Some economic anthropologists see production as the driving force behind economic activity. Production creates supplies of goods to which demand must respond, and it determines levels of possible consumption. Anthropologists who stress the centrality of production borrow their perspective on economic activity, as well as many key concepts, from the works of German philosopher Karl Marx (1818–1883). They argue that this perspective is far more insightful than the one taken by neoclassical theorists of market exchange.

redistribution A mode of exchange in which a centralized social organization receives contributions from all members of the group and redistributes them in a way that provides for every member.

market exchange A mode of exchange in which the exchange of goods (trade) is calculated in terms of a multi-purpose medium of exchange and standard of value (money) and carried on by means of a supply–demand–price mechanism (the market).

In Their Own Words

The Continuing Reshaping of Our Ritual World by Academic Adjuncts

Daisy Sewid-Smith, a daughter of the late Chief James Sewid, is a member of the Mamaliliqala tribe of Village Island, British Columbia. Here she discusses the "grossly misunderstood" economic system known as Pᴅssa, which is commonly confused with the gift-giving ceremony known as Ýaqwqwa (Ýaqwqwa), or potlatch. She also identifies problems with traditionally academic approaches to studying and writing about Indigenous peoples through the misuse or non-use of protocol—problems that have too often led to misunderstandings about culturally significant processes, such as the potlatch.

My great uncle joined with the other nobility to lament the loss of the great economic institutions of the past when he stated . . . "It's no use giving a potlatch any more. The old people don't do it; so nobody pays you back, and the young people don't even understand what it's all about." He was referring to the grossly misunderstood economic system we called Pᴅssa. This was the investing institution of the Kʷakʷakᴅwakaʷ and Liǧʷidaxʷ League of Nations. This institution charged interest, called in debts, gave credit, and kept records of all transactions for future generations. Both my father and my great uncle held hereditary positions in this complex system. It was to this institution that my great uncle was referring when he spoke of the young not understanding and the investment not being repaid.

Most of our people today have only seen what was known as Ýaqwqwa, meaning *gift-giving*. That is the reason the term *potlatch*, a Chinook word meaning *to give*, was assigned to this system by the Chinook speakers of our old trade world. The Ýaqwqwa, or potlatch, was a system that paid witnesses to validate such events as marriage, memorials, and the succession of ancestral names. The Ýaqwqwa, or potlatch system, did not have the same principles, purpose, laws, or membership as the Pᴅssa.

Unfortunately, my great uncle understood too well the changing landscape of his ritual world. He and the nobility he came from had struggled so hard to keep the culture alive despite the institutionalized oppression of our beliefs by the state and by religious zealots; the loss of their sacred land and resources by the encroachment and laws of the newcomers; the loss of life due to disease, social breakdown, and the very personal identity struggles of the younger generation; and the diminished use of our precious language that holds the keys to our past, our values, and our religion. Today, our struggle is not just of legal or religious prosecution. Today our struggle is sadly the reshaping of our ritual world by academic interpretations.

The academic world must, in its need to publish accounts of my Nation, begin to subscribe to rules that are consistent with our ritual structure. They must begin to identify the trained specialists who are working within our culture and use the same rules we have of validation and authority to ensure an accurate view of our ritual world. It is not enough to read and cite from previous misinterpretations to make a theory right. When a house is built on a foundation of sand, its structure is weak and unstable. So is it for our ritual world within academic rendering. We have sorrily witnessed the reshaping of the foundations of our old institutions, the validation of those within our Nation unschooled in our complexes, and the loss of our precious rights and privileges so embedded in our history.

The last words belong to one of our chiefs addressing the first academic to come among us, Franz Boas, when he said in 1894, "It is a strict law that bids us dance. It is a strict law that bids us distribute our property among our friends and neighbours. It is a good law. Let the white man observe his law, we shall observe ours."

Source: Sewid-Smith, Daisy. 1997. "The Continuing Reshaping of Our Ritual World by Academic Adjuncts," *Anthropology and Education Quarterly* 28, 4: 594–602.

Labour

labour The activity linking human social groups to the material world around them.

Labour is perhaps the most central Marxian concept these anthropologists have adopted. Through labour, human beings actively struggle together to transform natural substances into forms they can use. This is most clear in the case of food production but includes the production of clothing, shelter, and tools (Figure 8.10). Marx emphasized the importance of human physical labour in the material world, but he also recognized the importance of mental or cognitive labour. Human intelligence allows us to reflect on and organize productive activities. Mentally and physically, human social groups struggle together to ensure their material survival. In struggling, they reproduce patterns of social organization, production, and thought.

Modes, Means, and Relations of Production

Marx attempted to classify the ways that different human groups carry out production. Each way is called a **mode of production**. Wolf defined a mode of production as "a specific, historically occurring set of social relations through which labour is deployed to wrest energy from nature by means of tools, skills, organization, and knowledge" (1982: 75). Tools, skills, organization, and knowledge constitute what Marx called the **means of production**. The social relations linking human beings who use a given means of production within a particular mode of production are called the **relations of production**. That is, different productive tasks (clearing the bush, planting, harvesting, and so on) are assigned to different social groups, all of which must work together for production to be successful.

The concept of mode of production is holistic, highlighting recurring patterns of human activity in which certain forms of social organization, production practices, and cultural knowledge co-determine one another. While Wolf notes that Marx speaks of at least eight different modes of production in his own writings, Wolf focuses on three modes of production that he believes have been particularly important in human history:

1. A *kin-ordered mode* in which social labour is performed on the basis of kinship relations (e.g., husbands/fathers/brothers/sons clear the fields, the whole family plants, mothers/wives/sisters/daughters weed, small children keep animals out of the field)
2. A *tributary mode* in which labourers control the means of production but must provide payment (money, a percentage of the crop, or labour) to some figure of authority (e.g., a lord or ruler, as in the feudal peasant system of Europe)
3. The *capitalist mode*

The capitalist mode has three main features:

1. The means of production is property owned by the capitalists.
2. Workers are denied access to such ownership and must sell their labour to the capitalists in order to survive.
3. This labour produces for capitalists surpluses of wealth that capitalists may retain or plow back into production to increase output and generate further surpluses.

Figure 8.10 Women weave rope out of coir, a fibre extracted from coconut husks, in Kerala, India. Human beings continuously labour to turn natural substances into useful products. Which activities do you undertake that link you to your material world?

An overlap exists between this classification of modes of production and the traditional anthropological classification of subsistence strategies (see Figure 8.5). The kin-ordered mode of production is found among foragers and those farmers and herders whose political organization does not involve domination by one group. The tributary mode is found among farmers and herders living in a social system that is divided into classes of rulers and subjects. Subjects produce both for themselves and for their rulers, who take a certain proportion of their subjects' product as tribute. The capitalist mode, the most recent to develop, is found in industrial societies around the world but particularly those of North America and Western Europe.

Thus, in some ways the "mode of production" concept simply recognizes the same variation in the arts of subsistence that Lewis Henry Morgan recognized in the nineteenth century (see Chapter 3). Yet the concept of mode of production also highlights certain attributes of subsistence strategies that Morgan's approach tended to downplay. For example, modes of production are as much to do with forms of social and political organization as with material productive activities. That is, the kin-ordered mode of production is distinctive as much for its use of the kinship system to allocate labour to production as for the kind of production undertaken. In a

mode of production "A specific, historically occurring set of social relations through which labour is deployed to wrest energy from nature by means of tools, skills, organization, and knowledge" (Wolf 1982: 75).

means of production The tools, skills, organization, and knowledge used to extract energy from nature.

relations of production The social relations linking the people who use a given means of production within a particular mode of production.

kin-ordered mode of production, the *relations of kinship* serve as the *relations of production* that enable a particular *mode of production* to be carried out.

The Role of Conflict in Material Life

Traditionally, anthropologists have emphasized the important links between a society's social organization (kinship groups, chiefdom, or state) and the way that society meets its subsistence needs, either to demonstrate the stages of cultural evolution or to display the functional interrelationships between parts of a particular society. In both cases, however, the emphasis of the analysis was on the harmonious fashion in which societies either changed or stayed the same. This focus implied that social stability should not be tampered with. Social change was possible, but it would take place in an orderly fashion, in the fullness of time, according to laws of development beyond the control of individual members of society.

Many anthropologists have not been persuaded that social change is orderly or that social organization is by nature harmonious. They find the Marxian approach useful because it treats conflict as a natural part of the human condition. The concept of mode of production makes a major contribution to economic anthropology precisely because of the very different interpretation it gives to conflict, imbalance, and disharmony in social life.

Marx pointed out, for example, that the capitalist mode of production incorporates the workers and the owners in different and contradictory ways. These groups, which he called *classes*, have different interests, and what is good for one class may not be good for all classes. The workers' economic desires (higher wages to purchase more goods) are inevitably opposed to the owners' economic desires (lower wages to increase their profits or to reinvest in tools and raw materials).

This does not mean that warfare is constant between the different classes engaged in a particular mode of production; however, it does mean that the potential for conflict is built into the mode of production. The more complex and unequal the involvement of different classes in a mode of production, the more intense the struggle between them is likely to be. Such struggle may not always lead to outright rebellion, but minor forms of resistance—from sluggish efforts at work to intentional disruption of the status quo—are not uncommon. Marx was one of the first social analysts to document the high level of

human suffering generated by certain modes of production, particularly the capitalist mode.

Wolf's three modes of production (kin-ordered, tributary, and capitalist) describe not only a society's subsistence strategy but also that society's social organization. As a result, they accent the lines along which tension and conflict may develop between different segments of the society: between, say, parents and children or husbands and wives in the kin-ordered mode; between lords and peasants in the tributary mode; and between capitalists and workers in the capitalist mode.

Applying Production Theory to Social and Cultural Life

Economic anthropologists who focus on production as the main force in economic life tend to apply the metaphor of production to other areas of social life as well. They see production as involving far more than short-term satisfaction of material survival needs. If a given *mode* of production is to persist over time, the *means* and *relations* of production must also persist.

For example, farmers produce grain and leave behind harvested fields. They exchange some grain with cattle herders for milk and meat, and they permit the herders' cattle to graze in the harvested fields in exchange for the manure they need to fertilize their fields. Consequently, farmers and herders alike end up with a mix of foodstuffs to sustain human life. In addition, each group has what it needs in the coming season to renew its means of production. Both groups will want to ensure that similar exchanges are carried out by successive generations, who will consist of farmers and cattle herders producing the same goods and willing to exchange them. Therefore, not only must the means of production continue but so must the relations of production. The result, then, is the reproduction of society from generation to generation (Figure 8.11).

People also produce and reproduce *interpretations* of the production process and their roles in that process. Marx used the term **ideology** to refer to the cultural products of conscious reflection. As used in Marxian analysis, *ideology* refers to those beliefs that explain and justify the relations of production. Therefore, ideology was not independent of the production process since the act of taking part in a production process alters the way participants *think*. As a result, Marxian economic anthropologists are also interested in the kinds of ideas, beliefs,

ideology Those products of consciousness—such as morality, religion, and metaphysics—that purport to explain to people who they are and to justify the kinds of lives they lead.

and values that are produced and reproduced in societies with different modes of production. Members of the class in power usually hold to an ideology that justifies their domination. Those who are dominated may assent publicly to the ideology of the rulers, but in private they are likely to be highly critical and to offer alternative interpretations.

Unlike exchange theorists, production theorists tend to be interested in *why* the different parties to an exchange have different quantities of resources with which to bargain. They believe that access to resources is determined *before* exchange by the relations of production, which decide who is entitled to how much of what. They reject the assumption that access to valued resources is open to anyone with gumption and the spirit of enterprise. Different modes of production stack the deck in favour of some classes and against others. This is most clear in the capitalist mode, where owners have disproportionate access to wealth, power, and prestige and where workers' access to these goods is sharply restricted. Thus, the classes who fare poorly do so not because of any inherent inferiority, laziness, or carelessness; they fail to get ahead because the rules of the game (i.e., of the mode of production) were set up in a way that keeps them from winning.

Production theory also provides a perspective on cultural persistence and cultural change. It relates peoples' preferences for different goods to the interests and opportunities of the different classes to which they belong. People buy and sell as they do not out of idiosyncratic whimsy but because the choices open to them are shaped by the relations of production. From this perspective, poor people purchase cheap goods not because they have poor taste but because their position within the mode of production provides them with very limited income, and they must make do with the goods they can afford.

Finally, production theory views human beings as active social agents in the construction and reconstruction of human society through time. Traditions persist but only because people labour to reproduce them from one day to the next. Linking production (and reproduction), social relations, and ideologies highlights the contingent nature of social life, even as it suggests how traditions are carried on.

Consumption

Consumption usually refers to using up material goods necessary for human survival. These goods

Figure 8.11 Producers must find ways to pass their relations of production from one generation to the next. Here, children help harvest rice alongside adults in Chattrakarn Phitsanulok, Thailand. By participating, they are being taught to take on a role in the production process. What are some of the other ways in which the relations and means of production are reproduced from generation to generation?

include—at a minimum—food, drink, clothing, and shelter; they can, and often do, include much more. The study of consumption by economists and others was, until relatively recently, much neglected. To some extent, this is because many observers assumed that there were no interesting questions to ask about consumption. That is, it seemed clear that people either consume goods for obvious reasons, such as survival, or as a result of personal preferences. Today, consumption is often a central focus in studies of economic practices.

Explanations for Consumption Patterns

Anthropologists who make cross-cultural comparisons have always noticed striking differences in consumption patterns in different societies. Historically, they have taken three basic approaches to account for these patterns:

1. The internal explanation
2. The external explanation
3. The cultural explanation

The Internal Explanation

The internal explanation for human consumption patterns comes from the work of pioneering anthropologist Bronisław Malinowski. His theories explain certain social practices by relating them to basic human needs (biological or psychological). If these needs go unmet, the society might not survive. Malinowski proposed a list of basic human needs, which includes nourishment, reproduction, bodily comforts, safety, movement, growth, and health. Every culture responds in its own way to these needs with some form of the corresponding institutions: food-collecting techniques, kinship, shelter, protection, activities, training, and hygiene (Malinowski 1944: 91).

Malinowski's approach was useful because it emphasized human beings' dependence on the physical world. Further, Malinowski showed that many customs that appear bizarre to Western observers are in fact "rational" because they help people satisfy their basic human needs. Nonetheless, Malinowski's approach fell short of explaining why all societies do not share the same consumption patterns.

The External Explanation

Later anthropologists looked at consumption patterns from the perspective of **cultural ecology**—that is, in terms of the ways in which people adapt in response to our physical environment. From this perspective, human consumption patterns are a response to what people can obtain in a given environment. In order to survive, people must learn to make use of the available resources. This perspective draws on the field of **ecology**, making note of how different **ecozones** and **ecotones** (Figure 8.12) influence the range of **econiches** available to human beings. It also draws on the findings of socioecologists, who investigate why a particular animal population—say, a troop of baboons—organizes itself the way it does in a particular environment.

The term *cultural ecology* comes to us from American anthropologist Julian Steward (1972), who was influenced by the earlier work of Franz Boas and Alfred Kroeber. Steward did fieldwork among the Shoshone in the highly inhospitable Great Basin region of the United States. In conducting his research, he developed an approach that involved the following:

1. Outlining the subsistence technologies and methods of environmental exploitation used locally
2. Seeking patterned strategies tied to such exploitations
3. Investigating how these strategies (with associated technologies) affect other areas of the culture

Steward's approach continues to be of use in many disciplines. Consider the work of economic anthropologist Rhoda Halperin (1994) on the relationship between ecological anthropology (an extension of the cultural ecology perspective) and economic anthropology. Borrowing concepts from Karl Polanyi, Halperin argued that every economic system can be analyzed in terms of two kinds of movements:

1. *Locational movements*, or "changes of place"
2. *Appropriational movements*, or "changes of hands"

In her view, ecological relationships are properly understood as *changes of place*, as when people must move into the grasslands, gather mongongo nuts, and transport them back to camp. Economic relationships, in contrast, are more properly understood as *changes of hands*, as when mongongo nuts are distributed to all members of the camp, whether or not they helped to gather them. Thus, ecological (locational) movements involve transfers of energy (i.e., physical movement); economic (appropriational) movements, in contrast, involve transfers of rights (1994: 59).

Another way of seeing the difference between ecological and economic arrangements is to pay attention to the connection between food storage and food sharing. A socioecologist might argue that those who gather mongongo nuts are obliged to share them and consume them immediately because they have no way to store them. Ecological anthropologist Tim Ingold (1983) agrees that the obligation to share makes storage unnecessary, but he also points out that sharing with others today ordinarily obligates them to share with you tomorrow (reciprocity). Put another way, sharing food can be seen not only as a way of avoiding spoilage but also as a way of storing IOUs for the future!

Once societies develop ways to preserve and store food and other material goods, however, new possibilities open up (Figure 8.13). Archaeological evidence indicates that the more food there is to store, the more people invest in storage facilities, and the more quickly they become sedentary. Large-scale food-storage techniques involve a series of "changes of place" that buffer a population from ecological fluctuations for long periods of time. But techniques of food storage alone predict nothing about the "changes of hands" that food will undergo once it has been stored. Food storage techniques have been associated with all subsistence strategies, including that of complex food collectors. These findings suggest that economic relations of consumption, involving the transfer of rights

---

cultural ecology The study of the ways in which human beings relate to one another and to their natural environment.

ecology The study of the ways in which living species relate to one another and to their natural environment.

ecozone The particular mixture of plant and animal species occupying any particular region of the earth.

ecotone A transition area between two different ecozones that displays characteristics of both ecozones.

econiche The sum total of relations between a species and the plants and animals on which it relies for survival; these relations define those places where a species is "at home."

in stored food, have long been open to considerable cultural manipulation (Halperin 1994: 178).

From these examples, we can see that both ecological and economic relationships affect human consumption patterns. However, economic transfers of rights to material resources cannot be separated from wider political forces that impinge on those rights. Thus, according to anthropologist Elliot Fratkin, "a shift in theoretical understanding from *cultural* ecology to *political* ecology" is necessary (1997: 236). For example, the current adaptations of eastern African herders and their animals to the semi-arid environment in which they live is strongly affected by political pressures coming from the nation-states of eastern Africa. As a result, Fratkin says, contemporary anthropological studies of herders explain human–livestock interactions "less in terms of 'carrying capacity' or 'desertification' and more in terms of loss of common property rights (land and water commons), increased economic differentiation and social stratification, and incorporation and domination of tribal pastoral groups by larger state systems" (236).

The Cultural Explanation

From the perspective of cultural anthropology, the explanations for human consumption patterns that we have discussed so far have definite limitations. Consider how each would respond to the following question: Why do people X raise peanuts and sorghum? The internal, Malinowskian explanation would be "to meet their basic human need for food." The external, socioecological explanation would be "because peanuts and sorghum are the only food crops available in their ecozone." Both these answers are suggestive, but they remain incomplete. We might ask whether the local food sources that people X choose to exploit are the *only* local food sources available to them. Ethnographic data show that no society exploits every locally available food source to meet its consumption needs. Quite the contrary, consumption needs are selective; in other words, they are *culturally shaped*.

Here is the major shortcoming of both internal and external explanations for human consumption patterns—they ignore the possibility of *human agency*. Malinowski, and many cultural ecologists, assumed that patterns of consumption were dictated by environmental necessity that did not allow for alternatives. From such a perspective, individuals in most non-Western societies have little to no control over what they consume; they simply have no choice. Yet to rob people of choice is to dehumanize them. In contrast, by acknowledging that all people have at least some

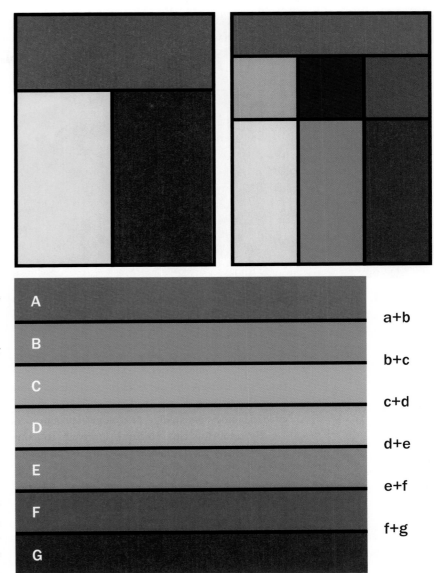

Figure 8.12 The composition of ecozones and ecotones is highly variable. The top left diagram represents three ecozones (red, blue, and yellow). The top right diagram adds ecotones (orange, purple, green, and brown) into the mix. Of the ecotones, the brown square has the most potential, as it has resources from all three ecozones. The lower diagram illustrates more specifically the many "tones" of transition between ecozones—for example, the forest (green) through to the coast line (orange) into the depths of a river, a lake, or an ocean (blue).

Source: Dods 1998, 249-50.

control over what they consume, and by recognizing that cultural forces influence these choices, we highlight human agency as central to the human experience.

The Cultural Construction of Needs

Needs is a vague concept. Hunger can be satisfied by beans and rice or steak and lobster. Thirst can be

© Dani Daniar/123RF

Figure 8.13 Traditional barns used for storing rice in Indonesia. How could the introduction of food storage change a culture's lifestyle? How about long-term food storage?

quenched by water or beer or soda pop. In effect, culture defines needs and provides for their satisfaction according to its own logic. And cultural logic is irreducible to biology, psychology, or ecological pressure.

By adopting this cultural approach to consumption, the distinctions between *needs* and *wants*, or between *necessities* and *luxuries*, disappear. Anthropologist Mary Douglas and economist Baron Isherwood propose the following:

> Let us put an end to the widespread and misleading distinction between goods that sustain life and health and others that service the mind and heart—spiritual goods…. The counter-argument proposed here is that all goods carry meaning…. The meaning is in the relations between all the goods, just as music is in the relations marked out by the sounds and not in any one note. (1979: 72–3)

For instance, a good's meaning may have to do with its edibility, but edibility is often culturally determined. Furthermore, the meaning of any individual item of food cannot be explained in isolation. That meaning becomes clear only when the item is compared with other items that are also marked by the culture as edible or inedible.

Dietary Laws
Consider the prohibition against eating pork. For Jews and Muslims, pork is inedible, culturally speaking. According to Mary Douglas (1966),

this restriction has nothing to do with ecological problems associated with pigs or with defects in the digestive systems of Jews or Muslims. Douglas analyzed the Jewish dietary prohibitions detailed in the biblical Book of Leviticus. She argued that certain animals were prohibited as food because something about them violated the prototypes for edibility recognized in ancient Hebrew culture (Table 8.2). Prototypically "clean" (and therefore edible) land animals were supposed to have four legs and cloven (i.e., split) hooves and to chew the cud; pigs were an "abomination" because they were cloven-hoofed four-legged beasts that did not chew the cud. "Clean" beasts of the air were supposed to have feathers and to fly with wings; therefore, hopping insects were "unclean" because they had six legs, neither walked nor flew, and lacked feathers. "Clean" water animals were supposed to have fins and scales; shrimp were forbidden because they lacked fins and scales.

By itself, Douglas argued, a prohibition against eating pork is meaningless and appears irrational. However, when this prohibition is taken together with other dietary prohibitions in Leviticus, and when these are compared with the foods that were permitted, a pattern emerges. Douglas and Isherwood write, "Goods assembled together in ownership make physical, visible statements about the hierarchy of values to which their chooser subscribes" (1979: 5). Thus, Jews who consume only "clean" foods are doing more than satisfying their hunger; they are also making a social declaration of solidarity with their religious community. Their need for food is being met, but selectively, and the selection they make carries a social message.

Dietary laws deal with food and drink and so might still be explained in biological or ecological terms. Such explanations are more difficult to construct, however, when we consider the role of banana leaves in the Trobriand Islands.

Banana Leaves in the Trobriand Islands
Anthropologist Annette Weiner travelled to the Trobriand Islands more than half a century after Malinowski carried out his classic research there (see EthnoProfile 8.1). To her surprise, she discovered a highly respected local tradition involving the accumulation and exchange of banana leaves, known locally as women's wealth (Figure 8.14) (Weiner 1980). Malinowski had never described this tradition, even though there

Table 8.2 **Jewish Dietary Prohibitions**

Realm	Class Prototype	Clean Examples	Unclean Examples	Reason Prohibited
Earth	Four-legged animals that hop, jump, or walk	Cattle, camels, sheep, goats (all cloven-hoofed and cud-chewing animals)	Hare, hyrax	Cud-chewing but not cloven-hoofed
			Pig	Cloven-hoofed but not cud-chewing
			Weasel, mouse, crocodile, shrew, chameleon, mole	Two legs, two hands, but go about on all fours
Air	Two-legged fowl that fly with wings	Chickens	Grasshoppers	Six legs, cannot walk or fly, lacks feathers
Water	Scaly fish that swim with fins	Carp, whitefish	Shrimp, clams	Possess neither fins nor scales

Source: Adapted from Douglas 1966: 41–57.

is evidence from photographs and writing that it was in force at the time of his fieldwork. There are probably two reasons Malinowski overlooked these transactions:

1. They are carried out by women, and he did not view women as important actors in the economy.

2. He labelled only activities that satisfied biological survival needs as "economic," and banana leaves are inedible.

However, explaining transactions involving women's wealth turns out to be crucial for understanding Trobriand kinship obligations.

EthnoProfile 8.1
Trobriand Islanders

Region: Oceania
Nation: Papua New Guinea
Language: Kilivila, part of the Kilivila-Louisiades language family
Population: 40,000 (2009 estimate)
Environment: Tropical rainforest on main islands of Kiriwina, Kaileuna, Vakuta, and Kitava
Livelihood: Subsistence horticulturalists (yams as main crop)
Political organization: Traditionally, chiefs and others of rank in matriclans; today, part of a modern nation-state
For more information: Malinowski, Bronisław. 1984 [1922]. *Argonauts of the Western Pacific* (Long Grove, IL: Waveland Press); Weiner, Annette. 1988. *The Trobrianders of Papua New Guinea* (New York: Holt, Rinehart, and Winston).

© WoodyStock/Alamy

Figure 8.14 In the Trobriand Islands, banana leaves, like the ones this woman is shaping, are recognized as women's wealth, a marker of economic, political, and social status.

Banana leaves might be said to have a "practical" use in that women make highly valued skirts out of them. But the bundles of leaves themselves are considered to be valuable. Why bother to exchange great amounts of money or other goods to obtain bundles of banana leaves? To an outsider, this would seem to be irrational consumption. And yet, as Weiner demonstrates, bundles of banana leaves are significant in that they are a "representation of the most fundamental relationships in the social system"—namely, kinship (Weiner 1980: 289).

Trobrianders are matrilineal, and men traditionally prepare yam gardens for their sisters. After the harvest, yams from these gardens are distributed by a woman's brother to her husband. Weiner's research suggests that what Malinowski took to be the *redistribution* of yams, from a wife's kin to her husband, could be better understood as a *reciprocal exchange* of yams for women's wealth. The parties central to this exchange are a woman, her brother, and her husband. The woman is the person through whom yams are passed from her own kin to her husband; she is also the person through whom women's wealth is passed from her husband to her own kin.

Transactions involving women's wealth occur when someone in the woman's kinship group dies. Surviving relatives must "buy back," metaphorically speaking, all the yams or other goods that

the deceased person gave to others during his or her lifetime. Each payment marks a social link between the deceased and the recipient, and the size of the payment marks the importance of their relationship. All the payments must be made in women's wealth.

The dead person's status, as well as the status of her or his family, depends on the size and number of the payments made, and the people who must be paid can number into the hundreds. Women make women's wealth themselves and exchange trade goods to obtain it from other women, but when someone in their matrilineage dies, they collect it from their husbands. Indeed, a woman's value is measured by the amount of women's wealth her husband provides. Furthermore,

> if a man does not work hard enough for his wife in accumulating wealth for her, then her brother will not increase his labour in the yam garden.... The production in yams and women's wealth is always being evaluated and calculated in terms of effort and energy expended on both sides of production. The value of a husband is read by a woman's kin as the value of his productive support in securing women's wealth for his wife. (Weiner 1980: 282)

Weiner argues that women's wealth upholds the kinship arrangements of Trobriand society. It balances out exchange relationships between lineages linked by marriage; it reinforces the pivotal role of women; and it publicly proclaims, during every funeral, the social relationships that make up the fabric of Trobriand society. Weiner suggests that this long-term stable system could collapse if cash ever became widely substitutable for yams. If this were to happen, then men might buy food and other items in the market; they would no longer be dependent on yams from their wives' kin, and they could therefore refuse to supply their wives' kin with women's wealth. This had not yet happened at the time of Weiner's research, but she saw it as a possible future development.

The Original Affluent Society

As the previous example suggests, Western definitions of wealth are not universal. Richard B. Lee came to a similar conclusion in his research with the Ju/'hoansi in the 1960s (see EthnoProfile 7.2). Many

Westerners believe that foraging peoples lead miserable lives, spending all of their waking hours searching for enough food to survive. Yet, as you may recall from the beginning of this chapter, Lee and other ethnographers have shown that the Ju/'hoansi were able, until relatively recently, to maintain a lifestyle that was very rich according to their own culturally informed definition of **affluence** (see Lee 1992a, 1992b; Solway and Lee 1990). Ju/'hoansi bands periodically suffered from shortages of their preferred foods and were forced to resort to less desired items; most of the time, however, their diet was balanced and adequate and consisted of foods of preference (56ff.).

Marshall Sahlins (1972) coined the expression "the original affluent society" to refer to the Ju/'hoansi and other foragers like them. Affluence, he argued, is having more than enough of whatever is required to satisfy consumption needs. There are two ways to create affluence:

1. By *producing much* (the path taken by Western capitalist society)
2. By *desiring little* (the option, Sahlins argues, that foragers have taken)

The wants of foraging peoples are few compared to those of most Westerners, but they are abundantly met by nature. Moreover, foragers do not suppress their natural greed; rather, their society simply does not institutionalize greed or reward the greedy. As a result, foragers cannot be considered poor, even though their material standard of living is low by Western standards. Poverty is not an absolute condition, nor is it a relationship between means and ends; it is a relationship between people and a cultural definition of *needs* and *wants*.

The Cultural Construction of Utility

Just as culture shapes needs so, too, does it offer standardized ways of satisfying them. No social exchange can occur unless all parties are able to assess the value of the items to be exchanged. Because of the openness of culture and the ambiguity inherent in many social situations, values and exchange rates may well be negotiated. Such exchanges ultimately rest on cultural principles for assessing value and fairness.

By understanding consumption as the use of goods and services to communicate cultural values,

we can arrive at a new understanding of wealth and poverty. We have noted Sahlins's comment that foragers with simple needs and ample means of satisfying those needs are affluent—not poor. Douglas and Isherwood also refuse to use the sheer amount of material possessions as a universal measure of wealth or poverty:

> Many of the countries that anthropologists study are poor on such material criteria—no wall-to-wall carpets, no air conditioning—but they do not regard themselves as poor. The Nuer of the Sudan in the 1930s would not trade with the Arabs because the only things they had to sell were their herds of cattle, and the only things they could possibly want from trade were more cattle. (1979: 17–18)

For the Nuer, to have few or no cattle constituted poverty because cattle mattered as much for their use as markers of social relations as for their use as food: "To be rich means to be well integrated in a rich community.... To be poor is to be isolated" (160).

Institutionalized Sharing

Capitalist societies have passed laws and created social institutions that reward individuals for accumulating wealth. The economic practices of some non-capitalist societies, in contrast, prevent individual accumulation of wealth; the goal is to spread any wealth that exists throughout the community. This pattern is called *institutionalized sharing*.

People accustomed to capitalist practices are often either incredulous or cynical when it is suggested that institutionalized sharing can be the backbone of economic life. They assume that such widespread "generosity" can be expected only of saintly altruists, not of ordinary human beings. Nevertheless, people in societies with institutionalized sharing are not saints who never experience greed any more than people in capitalist societies are devils who never experience compassion. Both societies support the stability of established social arrangements.

Institutionalized sharing can be found among the Plains Cree of North America (see Map 8.1), studied by Swedish anthropologist Niels Braroe (1975: 143ff.). At the time of Braroe's fieldwork, the Cree still practised their tradition-based institutionalized sharing of consumption items, such as food and clothing. They further practised generosity

affluence The condition of having more than enough of whatever is required to satisfy consumption needs.

Map 8.1 Plains Cree (across Alberta and Saskatchewan)

in ceremonies known as *giveaway dances*. In these ceremonies, participants danced around a room and gave away material goods, such as clothing, to other guests. Dancers aimed to give away more than they received.

The Cree ideal is that generosity should be spontaneous; and contempt for material goods, genuine. Nevertheless, Braroe observed that band members sometimes possessed consumption goods or money that they clearly wanted to keep for themselves. Individuals could enjoy such goods in private but only if they kept the existence of those goods secret. Men sometimes hid beer to avoid having to share it with others. A woman once asked Braroe's wife to keep a sizable amount of cash for her so others would not know she had it and demand some. The rule seemed to be that "any visible resource may legitimately be requested by another" (146), and Braroe reported that direct refusals of such requests were rare.

For the Cree, institutionalized sharing is supposed to ensure that consumption goods are not hoarded but spread out and enjoyed by all in the band. This consumption pattern clashes with that of the capitalist, who views accumulation and consumption by individuals in a positive light. Some individual Cree earned money off the reserve and tried to save it in order to get ahead—by capitalist standards. Those people were considered stingy by other Cree and were resented; they could not hope to gain a position of leadership in the band.

Consumption Studies in the Age of Globalization

The foregoing examples focus attention on distinctive consumption practices in different societies and remind us forcefully not to take the Western market as the measure of all things. They also encourage respect for alternative practices that, in different times and places, have worked as well as or better than capitalist markets to define needs and provide goods to satisfy those needs. Anthropologist B. Lynne Milgram (2008) gives us some insight into such markets in her analysis of Filipina entrepreneurs in Baguio City and their development of a trade in second-hand clothing between Hong Kong and the Philippines.

Examples such as these also draw attention to the way in which the arrival of capitalism, usually in the context of colonialism, has regularly undermined such alternatives, attempting to replace them with new needs and goods defined by the market. In many situations, local peoples tried to resist the influx of market commodities, perhaps because they were aware of these commodities' capacity to destroy (Miller 1995: 144–5). In our current era of globalization, however, the consumption of market commodities occurs everywhere in the world. Moreover, the evidence is mounting that not only are Western commodities sometimes embraced by those who might have been expected to reject them (e.g., video technology by Indigenous peoples of the Amazon), but this embrace frequently involves making use of these commodities for local purposes to defend or to enrich local culture rather than to replace it (e.g., the increasing popularity of sushi in North America).

Daniel Miller (1995), a pioneer in this kind of consumption study, has therefore urged anthropologists to recognize that these new circumstances require that they move beyond a narrow focus on the destructive potential of mass-produced commodities to a broader recognition of the role that commodities play in a globalizing world: "Desire for goods is not assumed to be natural nor goods per se as either positive or negative. Poverty is regarded as a relative lack of resources rather than the preservation of authenticity" (143). But this shift does not mean that concern about the negative consequences of capitalist practices disappears.

In a global world in which everyone everywhere increasingly relies on commodities provided by a capitalist market, Miller believes that critical attention needs to refocus on "inequalities of access and the deleterious impact of contemporary economic institutions on much of the world's population" (143).

The Anthropology of Food and Nutrition

One of the most recent areas of anthropological specialization centres on studies of food and nutrition. For some time, biological anthropologists have carried out cross-cultural comparisons of nutrition and growth in different societies, and cultural anthropologists, such as Miller, have written detailed studies of particular local or ethnic food habits. Today, however, the anthropology of food and nutrition is increasingly concerned with the way the global capitalist food market works, favouring the food security of some consumers over others. At the same time, exploring links between food and culture in a globally complex world exposes changing understandings of fatness and thinness and reveals the many ways different kinds of food and cooking can be embraced by different groups in society to bolster their gender, sexual, racial, ethnic, or national identities.

Carole Counihan is a pioneering anthropologist of food and nutrition whose work was initially inspired by a feminist desire to give an ethnographic voice to women. She found that food was an aspect of culture that many women used to express themselves when other avenues were blocked. Beginning in 1970, she lived and worked in Italy for 14 years. She initially began collecting food-centred life histories from women, but eventually collected them from men as well. Because these life histories came from individuals from different generations, they reflected historical changes in the political economy of food that had shaped the lives of her interview subjects over time. For example, situating the food memories of the oldest members of her sample required reconstructing the traditional *mezzadria* sharecropping system in Tuscany. This system was based on large landholdings worked by peasant labourers whose households were characterized by a strict division of labour by gender: the patriarch managed the food production in the fields and his wife supervised food preparation for the large extended family. The *mezzadria* system would disappear in the early twentieth century, but it constituted the foundation of Tuscan food practices that would follow.

Counihan's interviewees ate a so-called "Mediterranean" diet consisting of "pasta, fresh vegetables, legumes, olive oil, bread, and a little meat and fish" (2004: 74). Food was scarce in the first part of the twentieth century but more abundant after World War II: "This diet, however, was already being modified by the postmodern, ever-larger agro-food industry that continued to grow in 2003, but which Florentines and other Italians shaped by alternative food practices" (4).

The postwar capitalist market also drew younger Florentines into new kinds of paid occupations, which led to modifications of the earlier gendered division of labour, without eliminating it entirely. Counihan describes the struggle of Florentines of her generation, especially women, who needed to work for wages but who were still expected to maintain a household and a paying job at the same time and often could not count on assistance from their husbands with domestic chores, including cooking. She also describes men who cook on a regular basis, but who often do not take on the tasks of shopping for ingredients or cleaning up and who tend to dismiss cooking as easy, thereby diminishing the status of work that has long been central to Florentine women's sense of self-worth.

Food-centred life histories from Counihan's oldest interviewees traced nearly a century of changing Tuscan food practices and revealed, surprisingly, older people's nostalgia for the more constrained patterns of food consumption in their youth:

> When my older subjects were young before and during the Second World War, consumption was highly valued because it was scarce and precarious. Yet their children, born after the war in the context of the Italian economic miracle, grew up in a world where consumption was obligatory, taken for granted, and essential to a full personhood—a transformation lamented by older people. (2004: 5)

Even as Counihan's research documents continuities in Tuscan diet and cuisine, it also demonstrates the way deeply rooted consumption practices were upended by the Italian state under Mussolini in the 1920s and 1930s and by the international cataclysm of World War II. Anthropologists have long argued that economic life cannot be considered apart from political relations in any society.

A Dialectic between the Meaningful and the Material

As we have seen in this chapter, material goods carry culturally defined meanings, and what is viewed as meaningful (as stipulated by culture) can have material consequences. It is out of this dialectic between the meaningful and the material that the modes of livelihood followed by human beings everywhere emerge.

Living Anthropology

Making a Living on Bonavista's Past: Material Culture as Resource

by David S. Cooney, PhD Candidate, Memorial University

Situated atop Newfoundland's northeastern coast lies Bonavista, a historic fishing town whose past is inextricably linked to the cod fishery. European-based migratory fishers first arrived some 400 years ago, attracted to the area's flat terrain, accessible shoreline and abundance of cod. Early expeditions were seasonal in nature and migrants soon overwintered, establishing a British settlement in the mid–seventeenth century. As an island-based system of merchant capitalism increasingly mobilized the fishery, Bonavista's population started to grow. Younger generations and newcomers settled further inland, competing for favourable access to the sea and sufficient space to "make" or preserve their catch. This led to an asymmetrical settlement pattern and meandering network of lanes and roads, a "medieval geography" increasingly marked by saltbox homes, merchant premises, and other institutions that held sway, including the Catholic and Methodist churches, Loyal Orange Lodge, and harbourside courthouse.

Around the mid–twentieth century the family-based, merchant-capital fishery transitioned to a capitalist-intensive model. As productive relations changed, new technologies (boat types, nets, and fish-finding equipment) facilitated the commercial exploitation of cod like never before. While the expansion provided extensive employment and decent wages throughout the countryside, the environmental impact became too severe. By the time Federal Fisheries minister John Crosbie announced the cod moratorium in 1992, the northern cod stocks had collapsed. Across the island tens of thousands of fishery workers lost their jobs, and a meaningful way of life precious to many Newfoundlanders was destroyed. While a number of residents retrained and found work abroad, a segment of the population was left behind. Without the employment needed to sustain Bonavista's surplus population of labour, local authorities along with prominent citizens started to promote a heritage-based tourism sector. From the town's colourful array of architecture to its winding lanes and centuries-old cemeteries, Bonavista's material culture would be transformed into an economic resource that could generate benefits and employment.

Local organizations played an active role in the development of the tourism sector. For example, the Bonavista Historic Townscape Foundation (BHTF) is a nonprofit that designs improvement plans, solicits government funding, and manages the personnel who conduct the work. Projects range from general beautification, such as planting gardens and painting fences, to heritage restoration and the staffing of tourism sites. Second only to St John's in number of heritage structures accorded, make-work projects have already transformed the Ryan merchant premises into a National Historic Site, restored the exterior of the Orange Hall, retrofitted the Garrick Theatre, and built a floating replica of John Cabot's ship, *The Matthew*. In these and other ways, former fishery workers are building, maintaining, and servicing Bonavista's tourism sector—making a living today by curating the material culture of their ancestors' past.

While tourism has brought economic relief to the countryside, certain drawbacks exist. Due to the low pay, lack of benefits, and temporary nature of the employment at hand, residents have become dependent on this type of work to make a living, forced to move from project to project to survive. Given the seasonality of the tourism sector,

Bonavista now resembles a bustling vacation spot throughout the summer months and a slumbering fishing town in the winter. This trend is bolstered by visitors who decide to buy-in and stay, usually through the purchase of summer homes. As demand buoys property values, issues relating to housing affordability have been raised. Other residents worry that new developments may restrict beachfront access and/or compromise the waterfront's character and charm. In one case, however, outsiders have contributed positively to Bonavista's heritage appeal. Founded by a Toronto couple who visited the town and decided to invest, the newly-built luxury accommodations resemble steep gable roof and salt-box styles of architecture. Residents welcome the wealthier clientele (and vacation dollars) that the cottages attract; however, they lament that an old waterfront home was destroyed to make way for the contemporary "historic" designs. Short on historicity, the cottages demonstrate that the tourism/heritage sector can spur the *fabrication* as well as restoration of heritage structures.

Through the development of their material culture, Bonavistans are making a living today while actively shaping the future of their town. Although the sector provides relief in the form of basic remuneration, it maintains a cycle of economic dependence as workers must continuously secure temporary, low-pay work arrangements to survive. Bonavistans' labour has altered the local physical geography in a way that attracts tourists and visitors, who in turn impress their own changes upon the town's social and geographic landscape. As a result, Bonavista's character has taken on a dichotomous tone, oscillating between the *destination* that is encountered by tourists and *desperation* experienced by the workforce who builds and maintains the tertiary sector.

Key Terms

affluence 207
consumption 194
cultural ecology 202
distribution 194
ecology 202
econiche 202
economic anthropology 190
economy 190
ecotone 202
ecozone 202

extensive agriculture 192
food collectors 191
food producers 191
ideology 200
institutions 190
intensive agriculture 192
labour 198
market exchange 197
means of production 199
mechanized industrial agriculture 192

mode of production 199
modes of exchange 196
neoclassical economic theory 194
production 194
reciprocity 196
redistribution 197
relations of production 199
scarcity 190
subsistence strategies 191
unfree labour 186

Chapter Summary

1. Our cultures suggest a range of options for making a living. Human beings have devised a variety of subsistence strategies to satisfy their material survival needs.
2. Human economic activity is usefully divided into three phases: production, distribution, and consumption.
3. Formal neoclassical economic theory attempts to explain how capitalism works. Building on the emphasis that this theory gives to market exchange, economic anthropologists showed that non-capitalist societies regularly relied on non-market modes of exchange, such as reciprocity and redistribution, which still play restricted roles in societies dominated by the capitalist market.
4. Marxian economic anthropologists view production as more important than exchange in determining the patterns of economic life. They argue that societies can be classified in terms of their modes of production. Each mode of production contains within it the potential for conflict between classes of people who receive differential benefits and losses from the production process.

5. Consumption patterns are influenced by internal factors (e.g., basic human needs) as well as external factors (e.g., the availability of particular resources). In addition, our culture influences these patterns as it defines our needs and provides for their satisfaction according to its own logic—a logic that cannot be reduced to biology, psychology, or ecological pressures.

6. In our era of globalization, the consumption of Western market commodities is often embraced by non-Western peoples. Moreover, this embrace frequently involves making use of market commodities for local purposes to defend or enrich local culture rather than to replace it. In a global world in which everyone everywhere increasingly relies on market commodities, we need to pay critical attention to inequalities of access and the negative impact of contemporary economic institutions on most of the world's population.

Critical Thinking Questions

1. Anthropologists distinguish between *food collectors* and *food producers*. How does this division hearken back to the ethnical stages proposed by Lewis Henry Morgan in the nineteenth century (see Chapter 3)?

2. Is reciprocity in all its forms an efficient way of distributing material goods for consumption? Why or why not?

3. What are some examples of human beings' abilities to adapt to a wide variety of environments? What types of environments might provide the best prospects for humans to make a living? What types of environment might threaten human survival?

Suggested Readings

Douglas, Mary, and Baron Isherwood. 1996. *The World of Goods: Towards an Anthropology of Consumption*, rev. edn (New York: Routledge). A discussion of consumption, economic theories about consumption, and what anthropologists can contribute to the study of consumption.

Lee, Richard B. 2013. *The Dobe Ju/'hoansi*, 4th edn (Belmont, CA: Wadsworth). This highly readable ethnography contains important discussions about foraging as a way of making a living.

McIntosh, Roderick J. 1996. "History of Archaeology, Intellectual" in *The Oxford Companion to Archaeology*, ed. Brian M. Fagan (Oxford: Oxford University Press), 280–5. A brief but comprehensive look at how we consider the act of "knowing" in the Western tradition and how we have wrestled with the problem of what we can never come to know.

Sahlins, Marshall. 1972. *Stone Age Economics* (Chicago: Aldine). A series of classic essays on economic life; the collection includes "The Original Affluent Society."

Steward, Julian H. 1972. *Theory of Culture Change: The Methodology of Multilinear Evolution* (Urbana: University of Illinois Press). A collection of papers in which Steward presents culture change as a complex, ongoing process.

Wilk, Richard, and Lisa C. Cliggett. 2007. *Economies and Cultures: Foundations of Economic Anthropology*, 2nd edn (Boulder, CO: Westview). A relatively current, accessible guide to the conflicting views of human nature that underlie disputes in economic anthropology.

Related Websites

Cultural Ecology, Environment
www.environment.gen.tr/ecology-writings/484-cultural-ecology.html

absolutearts.com: Gifting and Feasting in the Northwest Coast Potlatch
https://www.absolutearts.com/artsnews/1999/07/07/25565.html

Financial Times: The Lessons that Flow from Bali's Water Temple
https://www.ft.com/content/83df61cc-caf2-11e1-8872-00144feabdc0?mhq5j=e5

The University of Alabama, Department of Anthropology: Marxist Anthropology
http://anthropology.ua.edu/cultures/cultures.php?culture=Marxist%20Anthropology

Balinese Rice Production, Regime Shifts Database
www.regimeshifts.org/item/60-balinese-rice-production
The Natural Food Hub: The Mongongo Nut
www.naturalhub.com/natural_food_guide_nuts_uncommon_
Ricinodendron_rautanenii.htm

**Global Forest Atlas: Traditional Land Use and
Shifting Cultivation**
http://globalforestatlas.yale.edu/amazon/land-use/
traditional-land-use-and-shifting-cultivation

9 Play, Art, Myth, and Ritual

Chapter Outline

Play

Art

Myth

Ritual

Combining Play, Art, Myth, and Ritual

Learning Objectives

By the end of Chapter 9, you will be able to

- perceive play as an open system that relates to cognition;
- consider sport and satire as forms of play that can have strong significance for adults;
- understand the significance of art;

- recognize myths as conceptual tools that explain certain aspects of social organization;
- perceive ritual as a form of metacommunication that brings text and performance together; and
- see the connections among play, art, myth, and ritual.

During her fieldwork in Botswana in the late 1970s, Roberta Robin Dods had a chance encounter with a group of children—three boys and eight girls about nine years of age—who were gathered at the side of the road. One boy was drawing shapes in the dusty red earth with a long stick. He had inscribed nine small circles inside a large circle. The boy stood in the middle of the large circle and pointed his stick at each girl, saying, "You will be the mommy." He concluded, "I will be the daddy." Each of the girls went to one of the smaller circles, and two of the boys retired to the remaining circle. And so, the game of "playing house" was inscribed in the dust and described by the children playing what all children play—family.

These children were members of a culture where polygyny is practised and where adult sons may live in separate quarters in a family compound. Children at play tell us so much about how play is culturally defined and defining. Childhood is a time when adult roles can be tried on with little or no consequences. Think of the role-playing games you may have engaged in as a child—"let's pretend" school, house, doctor, and so on. These sorts of games often involve working through specific aspects of potential adult roles. Play can be fun, but for the observer it is more than fun—it is a window into many aspects of cultural identity. Children's play can reflect the changing realities of the society in which the children live—the emerging new realities in a culture. **Play** is one of four elements (along with **art**, **myth**, and **ritual**) in which the interplay of openness and creativity with rules and constraints enables people to produce powerful and moving phenomena.

As anthropologists study these sensitive aspects of culture, they must be careful not to force their own cultural interpretations on other people's cultural practices. Indeed, anthropologist Robin Ridington (1998) cautions that theorizing occurs as a genre of Western academic expression and is not necessarily founded on the constructs of the peoples who provided the data (345). So, anthropologists must keep in mind what he describes as "shared ethnographic authority":

> The reasons for sharing authority are more than political and aesthetic. An ethnography that places the ethnographer's monologue above the voices of people being represented risks sacrificing effective engagement with its subject. . . . Its claim to objectivity may actually disguise the subjectivity of its singular isolated author. . . . A. Irving Hallowell [Anishinaabe (Ojibwe)], for instance, wrote that "a higher order of objectivity" may be obtained by "adopting a perspective which includes an analysis of the outlook of the people themselves as a complementary procedure." (1998: 344–5)

It is the "voices" of those living in and through their engagement with play, art, myth, and ritual that resonate with meaning.

Play

For the anthropologist, play has the characteristic of *openness* that we first discussed in relation to language in Chapter 4. In this case, such openness involves the ability to not only think and talk about but also *act out* or *portray* (1) the same things in different ways and (2) different things in the same way. Thus, play is a generalized form of *behavioural openness*.

Many species play, but we believe that humans play the most throughout their lives. Anthropologist Robert Fagen sees animal play as the product of natural selection that gives young animals (including young human beings) needed exercise, preparing them for the rigours of adulthood, which might include fighting, hunting, or fleeing when pursued. During early childhood, peak brain developments associated with motor skills and peak periods of play occur at the same time, suggesting that the development of cognitive and motor skills may be affected by play behaviour. Indeed, playful exploration of the environment aids learning and allows for the development of behavioural versatility (see Fagen 1981: 350–5). Play also seems to have a connection with the repair of certain types of brain damage caused either by injury or by trauma. All of these functions of play may help individuals survive.

play A framing (or orienting) context that (1) is consciously adopted by the players; (2) is pleasurable; and (3) alludes to the non-play world by transforming the objects, roles, actions, and relations of ends and means characteristic of the non-play world.

art A representation that relates to an object, an experience, or some other component of the world and that evokes a felt response.

myth A representative story that embodies a culture's assumptions about the way that society, or the world in general, must operate.

ritual A repetitive social practice set off from everyday routine and composed of a sequence of symbolic activities that adhere to a culturally defined ritual schema and are closely connected to a specific set of ideas significant to the culture.

First Nations artists work on a totem pole in the village of Old Massett, British Columbia.

© Ben Nelms/Bloomberg via Getty Images

Fagen proposes an additional, social function of play: to communicate the message "all's well" (1992: 48–9): "It seems likely that a frequent consequence and possible biological function of play is to convey information about short-term and long-term health, general well-being, and biological fitness to parents, littermates, or other social companions" (51).

Thinking about Play

Joking to Ease Tensions

Joking, which can be verbal or physical (e.g., practical jokes, pranks, horseplay), is a good example of how play operates within its cultural context. American anthropologist Andrew Miracle discusses joking behaviour among Aymara people in Bolivia (see EthnoProfile 9.1). He notes that the Aymara do not laugh in the presence of strangers because it is considered disrespectful. They laugh and joke only within a circle of acquaintances and friends; this kind of joking reinforces existing social bonds (1991: 151).

Much of the joking that Miracle observed took place on the crowded buses or trucks that transport rural people around the country. Ordinarily, Aymara personal space extends about one arm's length. Where there is any choice, people do not get any closer to one another. They also show respect and honour other people's privacy by not staring. Miracle notes that in everyday situations, "when stared at, the Aymara may yell at the one staring and become quite rude" (146). On buses or trucks, however, the context changes, and people who are strangers to one another are forced into artificial intimacy. They must sit or stand very close to one another for long periods of time, frequently looking right at one another. Their response is often to joke and laugh, behaviour normally reserved for intimates. Put another way, they choose to do "different things" (i.e., passing time with close friends and passing time with strangers in unusually close quarters) in the same way—by joking. This altered definition of context gives joking among strangers a new meaning: it temporarily changes strangers into friends, thus making a socially unpleasant situation more tolerable.

This type of work on the intimacies of interpersonal interaction was greatly facilitated by the research of Edward T. Hall from the 1950s onward. Hall introduced us to an understanding of the cross-cultural differences in how we sense and use space and time. He put forth a number of new concepts that take context into account when looking at human communication, including different use and structuring of time (monochromic and polychromic time), different ways of communicating in various cultures (low-context cultures and high-context cultures), and a "theory of proxemics," which identifies four specific distances "each reflecting a different way we feel toward others at a given time" (Adler et al. 2016). It is in Hall's second book, *The Hidden Dimension* (1966), that he explores the theory of proxemics and the ways in which we are surrounded by culturally specific temporal and spatial dimensions. How we sense space and time can be seen as a symbolic syncopation of our lives that we come to represent in play, art, myth, and ritual.

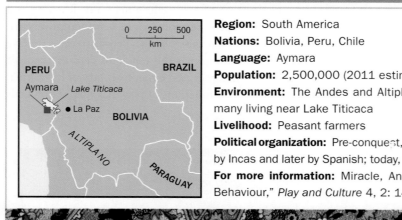

EthnoProfile 9.1
Aymara

Region: South America
Nations: Bolivia, Peru, Chile
Language: Aymara
Population: 2,500,000 (2011 estimate)
Environment: The Andes and Altiplano lake basin regions, with many living near Lake Titicaca
Livelihood: Peasant farmers
Political organization: Pre-conquest, state societies conquered first by Incas and later by Spanish; today, part of modern nation-states
For more information: Miracle, Andrew. 1991. "Aymara Joking Behaviour," *Play and Culture* 4, 2: 144–52.

Metacommunication and Play

Moving from everyday reality to play reality requires a radical transformation of perspective. To an outside observer, the switch may go undetected. However, when there is potential for the switch to have serious consequences for other people and their activities, play and non-play must be signalled clearly so that one is not mistaken for the other. According to anthropologist Gregory Bateson (1972), this shift requires a level of communication called **metacommunication**, which provides information about the relationship between those who are communicating. In play, there are two kinds of metacommunication: **framing** and *reflexivity*.

Framing is a cognitive boundary that marks certain behaviours as "play" or as "ordinary life." Dogs, for example, have a *play face*, a signal understood by other dogs indicating a willingness to play. If dogs agree to play, they bare their fangs and one animal attacks the other. But the bite is not a true bite; it is merely a nip. Both dogs have agreed to enter the *play frame*, an imaginative world in which bites don't mean bites. Human beings have many ways of marking the play frame: a smile, a particular tone of voice, a referee's whistle, or the words "Let's play" or "Let's pretend." The marker says that "everything from now until we end this activity is set apart from everyday life."

Reflexivity is the process of thinking about the social and cultural dimensions of the world in which we find ourselves. Because play tells us that ordinary life can be understood in more than one way, play can be a commentary on the nature of ordinary life (Handelman 1977: 186). Play communicates about what *can be* rather than about what *should be* or what *is* (186). For example, jokes keep us from taking ourselves too seriously by showing us that there are alternative, even ridiculous, explanations for our experience.

Some Effects of Children's Play

Some scholars view children's play as a simple imitation of adult activities. Others see play as rehearsal for the "real world" (Figure 9.1). According to this view, play can validate the adult role that the child is trying on, demonstrating the "rightness" of being a mommy or a daddy or the "rightness" of preparing meals to eat. Play can also give children the opportunity to try on a number of roles and ways of being that may come close to their reality later in

life. In North America, various forms of children's "edutainment"—cultural materials with the dual purpose of entertaining and educating—expose children to circumstances that may be beyond their first-hand experiences. For example, the children's book *The White Swan Express* (2002) gives young children a fictionalized window into international adoption practices and the situations of several nontraditional families as it tells the story of four Chinese baby girls who await adoption by four different families from across North American: a lesbian couple, a single woman, and two heterosexual married couples.

Some scholars have suggested that children's play (especially make-believe play) encourages creative interpretations of reality. In addition, it allows children to

metacommunication Communicating about the process of communication.

framing An understood boundary that marks certain behaviours as "play" or as "ordinary life."

Figure 9.1 Play enables this girl in Guider, Cameroon, to incorporate her European doll into the world she knows. What effects could play have on the person playing when the image is not representative of the lived reality?

overcome the limitations of their age, experience, and maturity, thus allowing them to have a richer experience of adult life (Schwartzman 1978: 116). Further, play may allow children to comment on and criticize the world of adults by sanctioning insults of authority figures and inversions of social status (232–45).

On another note, adult forms of play such as satire (e.g., satirical plays and novels, political cartoons) also act as commentary on the "real world." While children's play is generally viewed as harmless, this sort of adult play can threaten social norms by pointing out the folly of *what is* and suggesting better options for *what might be*. Most often, societies tend to undermine or contain this threat simply by defining play as "unserious," "untrue," "pretend," "make-believe," or "unreal" (Handelman 1977: 189). Repressive political regimes, however, frequently attempt to censor humour critical of their rulers, with the result that such humour becomes recognized as a form of political resistance.

Play and Alternative Views of Reality

We can easily see how humour shows an alternative view of reality, but what about non-joking play? For example, what about adults who climb mountains? "Is climbing a vertical face of rock at the risk of one's life play, or is it done in earnest?" (Csikszentmihalyi 1981: 16). On the one hand, it fits our definition of *play*—it is consciously adopted by the player, it is somehow pleasurable, and it transforms the relations of ends and means characteristic of the non-play world. On the other hand, it is a serious activity, as a rock climber risks bodily injury and is at all times "as immersed in reality as anyone can be" (17). The choice to climb a mountain, then, requires the climber to adopt an alternative view of reality—one that sees the possibility of bodily harm as an acceptable risk within the parameters of the play activity. Thus, non-joking forms of play show us that people do not always submit to the generally accepted rules of reality that govern everyday life. Indeed, it allows us to recognize that *no referential perspective is absolute*. As a result, play creates the awareness of alternatives and demonstrates the openness in human experience.

In the contemporary world, one increasingly popular type of play requires participants to adopt what are often highly creative alternative views of reality—that is, electronic gaming. Electronic games offer players the chance to engage with elaborate simulated worlds in which many of our everyday rules of reality do not apply. Cultural scholar Derek

Van Rheenen (2012) has examined the shift toward digital play in the North American landscape. He notes that "perhaps no single change in the game preferences of American children has been as dramatic as the introduction and widespread popularity of electronic games within the latter half of the twentieth century" (420). Indeed, national surveys have found that 83 per cent of teens in Canada and 87 per cent of teens in the United States have at least one gaming system in their home (CBC 2013; Rideout et al. 2010). Overall, the evidence suggests that playing electronic games may have some positive effects on overall learning, literacy, inventive problem-solving, achievement motivation, and visuospatial skills (Van Rheenen 2012: 422). Although more research is required, it is likely that at least some of these benefits are connected to the creative task of fully accepting and working within an alternative view of reality.

Sport

According to a well-accepted definition, **sport** is

> a physically exertive activity that is aggressively competitive within constraints imposed by definitions and rules. A component of culture, it is ritually patterned, game-like, and of varying amounts of play, work, and leisure. In addition, sport can be viewed as having both athletic and non-athletic variations, *athletic* referring to those activities requiring the greater amount of physical exertion. (Blanchard and Cheska 1985: 60)

Sport is play embedded in the prevailing social order. Sports reflect the basic values of the cultural setting in which they are performed.

Beyond play, sport can be work for the players and an investment for the owners of professional teams. It also offers a form of personal and social identification for fans, who are invited into a make-believe world in which they may playfully identify with their heroes, rage at the opponents, imagine coaching the team, suffer the team's losses, and rejoice in the team's victories. Sport is framed as play, but conflict in games and sports is different from conflict in ordinary life. Competitors agree "to strive for an incompatible goal—only one opponent can win—within the constraints of understood rules" (Lever 1995: 3). As with all forms of play, the relationships of ends and means in sport are altered. Sport is struggle for the sake of struggle.

sport An aggressively competitive, often physically exertive activity governed by game-like rules that are ritually patterned and agreed upon by all participants.

Because they can reflect a culture's values, some sports change form when they transfer from one cultural setting to another. Cricket in the Trobriand Islands (see EthnoProfile 8.1) offers us an excellent example of this transformation. An English missionary introduced the sport of cricket to the Trobrianders in the early twentieth century. By the 1970s, in the more rural parts of the islands, it had become a different game. Played between two villages, it became a substitute for warfare and a way of establishing political alliances. If the hosts had 40 men ready to play and the visitors had 36, then there were 36 to a side instead of the conventional 11. The game was always won by the home team—but not by too many runs because that would shame the visitors. War magic was employed to aid batsmen and bowlers. Teams had dances and chants for taking the field, leaving it, and celebrating outs. These dances and chants were used to comment on current events, and they became fertile ground for additional competition beyond that of the sporting event itself. The bat was redesigned for greater accuracy, and the entire activity was associated with the ceremonial exchange of food and other goods. Cricket, the sport of the British Empire, was radically transformed.

From the perspective of some Trobrianders, in fact, their version of cricket was a way of taking the English colonizers' favourite game—a game that was supposed to teach Trobrianders how to become "civilized"—and using it to express their rejection of the colonial world. As one Trobriand leader says in the film *Trobriand Cricket* (1974), "we rubbished the white man's game; now it's our game." Here is the "openness" of play: sport can transcend its function as an enjoyable way to pass the time and become a venue for social commentary and even collective rebellion against oppression.

Sport in the Nation-State

As international sporting events reveal, sport can be a source of national pride. Moreover, it can bring citizens of a nation-state together. Indeed, the most important and universal feature of sport in the nation-state today is that it helps complex modern societies cohere (Lever 1995: 3).

Consider how the sport of hockey gives Canadians from diverse backgrounds a common interest through which they can connect with one another. Interestingly, ethnologist Michael A. Robidoux suggests that hockey may appeal to Canadians because it embodies qualities that run counter to our

self-perception as unreasonably polite international peacekeepers (2002: 209) (see Figure 9.2). Yet historically,

> hockey enabled Canadians to display qualities that have been valued in patriarchal relations: stoicism, courage, perseverance, and proficiency. The singularity of the game and the manner in which it was played were critical for a young and disparate nation to have as its own as it faced encroaching social, political, and cultural interests from Europe and the United States. At a more pedestrian level, hockey was accessible to men of various ethnic and class backgrounds, and thus . . . it became a game of the people. (222)

Of course, in this historical context, *people* refers only to men. Indeed, even today women are often left out of the mass culture of sport. There are places in the world where cultural, and specifically religious, norms exclude women from all forms of sports. Any gendered separation that remains in more inclusive cultures often begins in childhood, when boys are more likely than girls to be encouraged to participate in team sports. In adulthood, the effects continue, as men and women cannot relate to one another through shared childhood experiences with sport. Thus, there is a fundamental ambiguity

Figure 9.2 A fight breaks out between the Toronto Marlies and the Hamilton Bulldogs at an American Hockey League (AHL) hockey game. Hockey gives Canadians the chance to value qualities, such as violence and aggression, that run counter to our national identity in realms outside sport. How else might hockey impact Canadian identity?

in the relation of sports and integration: as sports bring people together in one domain, they separate them in another. Sports can maintain and sharpen distinctions that are already significant in many other areas of a culture.

Sport as Metaphor

In his examination of the national importance of soccer in various European and South American countries, French anthropologist Christian Bromberger (1995) observes that sport is significant because "it lays bare the major symbolic horizon of our societies: the course of a match, of a competition, resembles the uncertain fate of people in the contemporary world. Further, the combination of rules that mold the genre give this uncertainty an *acceptable* feel" (197). In this interpretation, which could apply equally well to hockey, the game becomes a metaphor for our daily struggles. The complexity and sudden changes of a single game offer what Bromberger calls "a shortcut to the joys and dramas that make up a life" (197). A game features not only achievement on the basis of merit but also uncertainties introduced by strategy, luck, law, (in)justice (in the form of the referee), trickery, and unfairness. It offers the fan the opportunity to compare players, to reflect, to plan, to strategize, and to be surprised. And, as in life, the most innovative strategies don't always work, and the best team doesn't always win.

Art

Art is rooted in playful creativity, a birthright of all human beings. And yet, like sport, those activities defined as "art" differ from free play because they are circumscribed by rules. Artistic rules direct particular attention to, and provide standards for evaluating, the *form* of the activities or objects that artists produce.

A Definition

Anthropologist Alexander Alland defines *art* as "play with form producing some aesthetically successful transformation-representation" (1977: 39). *Form* refers to the rules of the art game: the culturally appropriate restrictions on the way this kind of play may be organized in time and space, and the culturally acceptable style and media. A painting is a form: it is two-dimensional; it is done with paint; it is intentionally made; it represents or symbolizes something in the world outside the canvas, paper, or wood on which it is created; it can be displayed. There are different kinds of paintings, as well. For example, there is the painting form called *portrait*, which depicts a person in some culturally appropriate way. By *aesthetic*, Alland means appreciative of, or responsive to, form (xii). "Aesthetically successful" means that the creator of the piece of art (and possibly its audience as well) experiences a positive or negative response. Indifference is the sign of something that is aesthetically unsuccessful. It is probably the case that the aesthetic response is a universal feature in all cultures and, as with play, may be part of the human condition.

Aesthetic response is holistic, involving all our faculties, including emotion, especially as these are shaped by our social and cultural experience. Linguistic theorist Valentin Voloshinov (1986 [1929]) argues that aesthetic response to form in a work of art is based largely on a culturally shaped evaluation of the appropriateness of *form* to *content*. Evaluations of appropriateness and of technical perfection involve a broad range of intellectual, emotional, and moral judgments on the part of the viewer.

Aesthetic value judgments guide the artist's choice of form, material, and presentation as she or he creates a piece of art; they also guide the observers' evaluations. This implies that art involves more than just the end product of an artist's labour. As Voloshinov notes, art is a creative "event of living communication" involving the work, the artist, and the artist's audience (107). Artists create their works with an audience in mind, and audiences respond to these works as though the works were addressed to them. Sometimes the response is enthusiastic; other times, it is highly critical. In either case, the aesthetic event does not leave its participants indifferent.

Art also involves the *process* through which some product is made. In a practical way, archaeologists can tell us about this process by studying material culture. In the making of things there is an order that archaeologists term the *chaîne opératoire* (French for "operational chain"); when followed, this order produces a specific repeatable result, such as a Clovis point (Figure 9.3). Of course, there is a certain amount of variability and creativity involved even within the constraints of artistic convention; creators of art follow a series of steps, but they do so with artistic licence.

Transformation-Representation

Symbols represent something other than themselves. They are arbitrary in that they have no necessary connection with what they represent. This means that they can be separated from the object or idea they represent and appreciated for their own sake. They may also be used to represent more than one object or idea. When a Javanese leather puppet maker makes a puppet of the mythic hero Bhima, for example, he is representing the traditional form of the hero in his work, but he is also *transforming* a three-dimensional human form into a two-dimensional flat puppet made of buffalo hide, in which the colours, style, inclination of the head, and adornment stand for the internal state of the hero at a specific moment (Figure 9.4). At the same time, the puppet maker is carrying out this work more or less skilfully and is embodying the meanings that Bhima has for the Javanese.

Because transformation and representation depend on each other, Alland (1977: 35) refers to them as **transformation-representations**; they are *metaphors*. A drawing, for example, is a metaphoric transformation of experience into visible marks on a two-dimensional surface. Similarly, a poem metaphorically transforms experience into concentrated and tightened language. This transformation-representation process is one place where the technical skill of the artist is involved.

But Is It Art?

In the Western view of art, there is a distinction between art and non-art. Some paintings, songs, stories, carvings, dances, and the like are considered art; some are not. People who accept this perspective might argue, for example, that the *Mona Lisa* is art but that paintings of Elvis Presley on black velvet are not. Why? Part of the answer may have to do with how aesthetically successfully the painting is—that is, the degree to which it elicits a positive or negative response from viewers. But part of the answer also involves the high degree of specialization in Western societies, which has led to the emergence of an "art establishment" that includes art critics, art historians, art teachers, journalists, schools, and museums—as well as professional artists. These people define what art is and what it is not; they distinguish between art and craft. That a painter may in fact have created an image of Elvis that is meaningful to at least some viewers does not change the opinion of members of the art

Figure 9.3 A Clovis point is an artifact associated with the Clovis culture, which existed approximately 13,000 years ago in what is now the southwestern United States.

establishment. To them, Elvis on velvet is not art because it does not address problems in art theory, because it does not refer to the beautiful or the true, because it does not portray the artist's struggle to produce a new expressive style, or because the artist seems ignorant or disdainful of the stylistic experimentation that makes up Western art history.

Nevertheless, many people—anthropologists included—have resisted the notion that art is only what a group of Western experts define as art. On the one hand, convinced that all humans have a

transformation-representation The process in which experience is transformed as it is represented symbolically in a different medium.

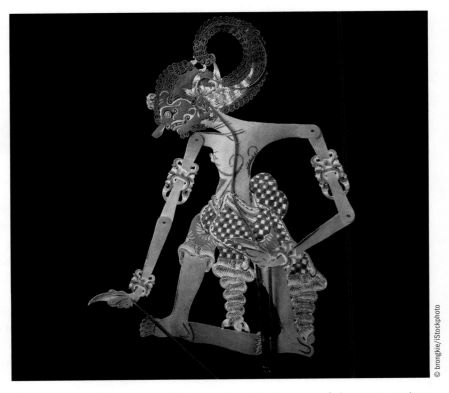

Figure 9.4 Bhima, one of the great mythic heroes of Javanese *wajang* (shadowpuppet theatre) is represented in this leather puppet. In what ways are the puppet maker's choices and skill as an artist evident in this creation?

capacity for art and aesthetic response, many anthropologists have attempted to redefine the concept of art broadly enough to include, on an equal basis, aesthetic products and activities that Western art experts would describe, at best, as "primitive," "ethnic," or "folk" art. On the other hand, anthropologists also recognize that not all cultures have a distinct category that corresponds to the Western notion of "art." Indeed, in many cultures, the products that Westerners might call "art" play a role in various cultural activities.

In recent decades, anthropologists have become increasingly interested in the way certain kinds of material objects made by tribal peoples flow into a global art market, where they are transformed into "primitive" or "ethnic" art. Cultural anthropologist Shelly Errington (1998) points out that even in the West many of the objects in fine art museums today, no matter where they came from, were not intended by their makers to be "art." They were intended to be masks for ritual use; paintings for religious contemplation; containers for holding the relics of saints, ancestor figures, furniture, jewellery boxes, architectural details, and so on. (See the "In Their Own Words" box that follows, as well as Figure 9.5.) They are in fine art museums today because at some point they were designated as "art" by an outsider "other" with the authority to put them in a museum.

© steve estvanik/123RF

Figure 9.5 A First Nations wood carving mask of a human face on display in Prince Rupert, British Columbia. Despite being featured in fine art museums today, masks were originally intended for ritual use by their makers.

In Their Own Words

The Mask as "Art"? And as Artifact in a Composed National Identity

One of the authors of this book (Dods) inserts a short observation on the meaning of "things."

The mask—a component of a specific configuration of cultural/social/oral tradition of record-keeping constructs founded both in the mundane and the metaphysical/metaphorical—became displayed essentially as an art piece. Usually, a brief description was provided of place and time of collection, with one or two short sentences of the meaning of the symbols used. I want to linger briefly on the mask as a metaphor and exemplar of the differences between culture as a performance art in the enacted lives of [a] culture and the presentation of the past of those *others* defined by us for our consumption. This is quite a

different process than having the story told, if it is appropriate to do so for strangers, by those whose only truncation from their past is effected by the interpretation of them by their *others, namely the transported from elsewhere* [the colonizer immigrant]. For a mask—such as those of international fame from the Northwest Coast of North America—is a physical representation of a multiplicity of cultural meanings found in a number of questions not exhausted in the list below:

- Who made the mask?
- From what materials?
- What is the mode of manufacture?
- How was it decorated?

For these reasons, Errington distinguishes "art by intention" from "art by appropriation." Art by intention includes objects that were made to be art, such as Impressionist paintings. Art by appropriation, however, consists of all the other objects that "became art" because, at a certain moment, certain people—usually those in powerful positions in colonial settings, or members of the art establishment from the countries they represented—decided that they belonged in the category of art. Because museums, art dealers, and art collectors are found everywhere in the world, it is now the case that potentially any material object crafted by human hands can be appropriated by these institutions as "art." For an example of such conflicting ideas about the nature of a specific piece of "art," consider the Haisla Nation's G'psgolox totem pole (Figure 9.6). In 1929 a government official cut it down and sold it to Sweden's Museum of Ethnography, where it was preserved as a piece of art. For members of the Haisla Nation, however, the pole was a reminder of a significant event in their culture's history. They understood the pole to be situated in a specific time and place, with a "life" that had a beginning and an end—essentially, it was meant to decay over time and thus move into the realm of the ancestors.

To be transformed into art, Errington argues, an object must have *exhibition value*—someone must be willing to display it. Objects that somehow fit into the Western definition of art tend to be selected for the art market. Looking at the collection of objects that have been defined as "art" over the years, Errington sees some common features: the objects are "portable (paintings preferred to murals), durable (bronze preferred to basketry), useless for practical purposes in the secular West (ancestral effigies and Byzantine icons preferred to hoes and grain grinders), representational (human and animal figures preferred to, say, heavily decorated ritual bowls)" (1998: 116–17). Errington further notes that the objects people make and "imbue with meaning" are "worthy of deep study," but they are not art until someone who carries around a particular definition of art says they are (103).

Redefining an object as art often strips it of much of its cultural significance. In their original contexts, most meaningful symbolic forms involve more than one sense: an audience watches masked dancers while hearing drumming, feeling a warm breeze, and smelling palm oil. But as masks and other objects are moved into the international art market, "they slough off their ... performance contexts, ... retaining only the durable part that can be set aside in a frame or on a pedestal" (84).

Traditionally, the cultural role of art was similar to that of play: it presented its creators and participants

- · What are the meanings of the symbols used?
- · How do these meanings encode specific information of both transcendental and mundane?
- · Who wears the mask?
- · In what context is it worn?
- · What do the ceremonies mean?
- · What is the *performance*?
- · Does it include song, dance, rhetoric that are part of a wider meaning?
- · How is the mask marked as belonging and how is it inherited?
- · Are these questions that we should ask at all?

And then when we are done we still do not really know that much, for the mask has a life in the wearing by a specific

individual in the performance art of a specific ceremony in a specific context within his or her culture. To this we are most likely denied entree. So, there is a configuration that causes the mask only to have meaning in specific contexts that it is impossible to display in the essentially static constructs of the museum. Making such as the mask into an *exotic* for our consumption marks it as outside the boundaries of the national identity being composed by those whose identity is still based on categories formed elsewhere, categories that support the institutionalization of *things* in support of the development of centralized concepts of self.

Source: Dods, R. Robin. 2010. "Nation/First Nations: Conflicts in Identity and the Role of Archaeology," in *Unquiet Pasts: Risk Society, Lived Cultural Heritage, Redesigning Reflexivity*, ed. Stephanie Koerner and Ian Russell (Ashgate: Aldershot).

out-of-the-way places on the peripheries . . . within national and increasingly global systems of buying and selling, of using natural and human resources, and of marketing images and notions about products. Some lucky few of them make high ethnic art, and sell it for good prices, and obtain a good portion of the proceeds. Others make objects classed as tourist or folk art, usually for much less money, and often through a middleperson. (268)

Errington points out the bitter irony that international demand for "exotic" objects is growing at the very moment when the makers of these objects are severely threatened by international economic policies and resource extraction projects that impoverish them and undermine the ways of life that give the objects they make their "exotic" allure. And, what counts as fashionable decoration this year may be unfashionable next year, leaving the producers with very little to fall back on.

"She's Fake": The Problem of the Authentic

Michelle Bigenho is an anthropologist and violinist whose multi-sited ethnography examines music performance in Bolivia, in part through her experiences performing with *Música de Maestros*, an ensemble that attempts to recreate performances of contemporary cultural music that ensemble members have studied in the countryside (Bigenho 2002: 4). During Bigenho's time with the ensemble, the group was made up of both classically trained and traditionally trained Bolivian musicians as well as three foreigners: a Japanese musician who played the Andean flute; a Cuban musician who played violin; and Bigenho, an American, who also played violin. Along with a dance ensemble, the musicians were invited to represent Bolivia in a folklore festival in France (Figure 9.7). As the bands were lining up, a member of the Belgian delegation walked over to Bigenho and announced in French, "She's fake." The Belgian woman then "pointed to one of the Bolivian dancers dressed in her dancing costume with her long fake braids worked into her short brown hair. As she pointed, she said 'She's real'" (88).

In this way, Bigenho raises the question of "authenticity." What is real when it comes to music, painting, sculpture, dance, or other "folk" art forms? How do the images that people in dominant

Figure 9.6 Cecil Paul, a Haisla elder, stands next to the G'psgolox totem pole, which now stands in the Kitlope Valley near Kitimat, British Columbia. The totem pole was returned from Sweden's Museum of Ethnography in 2006. Why might some people object to displaying "art by appropriation" in museums?

with alternative realities, a separation of means from ends, and the possibility of commenting on and transforming the everyday world. In today's global art market, however, the role is often more commercial. Errington observes that the people who make "primitive art" are no longer "tribal" but have become

modern-day peasants. . . . They live in rain forests and deserts and other such formerly

nations have of Indigenous peoples affect the production and circulation of art? And, finally, who gets to decide what is authentic? To address these issues, Bigenho distinguishes three different forms of authenticity:

1. *Experiential authenticity*, which exists in the sensory experience connected with a piece of art
2. *Cultural–historical authenticity*, which stems from the way in which a piece of art is represented in relation to the historical or mythical history of the art form
3. *Unique authenticity*, which is tied to the individual artist's new, innovative, and personal production of a work of art

Bigenho expands on these forms by relating them to her experience with music. In music performances, *experiential authenticity* is "connected to a shared experience with others, a fleeting moment of the groove, a listener's great night at a concert" (18). *Cultural–historical authenticity* makes a claim to a connection with the origin of the music. For example, the performances of *Música de Maestros* were authentic in the sense that the musicians sought to perform culturally and historically authentic renditions of Bolivian music. Bigenho also points out that in terms of Indigenous art, the power of cultural–historical authenticity derives from the Indigenous artist's position in relation to the nation-state. *Unique authenticity* is the creative activity of composing musicians. This form of authenticity raises the issue of who owns cultural products and whether it is possible to talk about collective creation and ownership of the music of a community, a people, or an ethnic group.

Issues surrounding ownership are particularly significant in relation to questions of who owns experiences and representations. Bigenho came face to face with such questions when she put together a recorded compilation of music from one of the villages in which she worked. She discussed with the villagers how to register the copyright on the compilation. While the villagers recognized that the music they played was composed by individuals, they felt strongly that ownership of the performed music was collective. When Bigenho went to La Paz to register the copyright, however, she found that it was impossible to register the compilation under collective authorship or ownership. In fact *she*, as the compiler, could register the work, but

Figure 9.7 *Música de Maestros* in costume performing in a folklore festival in France.

the people who created the work could not, unless they were willing to be recognized as individuals. What she discovered was that, according to Bolivian law, the music in the compilation was legally folklore:

> the set of literary and artistic works created in national territory by unknown authors or by authors who do not identify themselves and are presumed to be nationals of the country, or of its ethnic communities, and that are transmitted from generation to generation, constituting one of the fundamental elements of traditional cultural patrimony [i.e., inherited property] of the nation. (221)

As a result, the music was part of the "national patrimony" and belonged to the nation-state. But in the context of Bolivian cultural and ethnic politics, Bigenho observes, the villagers gained visibility and connections as a collective Indigenous entity, which they believed would provide them with possible economic advantages. Whether they were correct remains to be seen, but this example of the connections of art and authority is being repeated all over the world.

Sculpture and the Baule Gbagba Dance

The Baule of the Ivory Coast are renowned for their sculpture (see EthnoProfile 3.1 and Figure 9.8). Susan Vogel (1997; excerpts © Susan M. Vogel,) who has been studying Baule sculpture for several decades, identifies four forms of Baule sculpture:

1. Art that is watched (performances featuring carved masks)
2. Art that is seen without looking (sacred sculpture)
3. Art that is glimpsed (private sculptures of personal figures for hunting and sculptures for spirit spouses)
4. Art that is visible to all (everyday objects that the Baule see as beautiful trifles)

The Western concept of "art" does not exist in Baule villages. Rather, "to approach art from a Baule perspective entails speaking of experiences that are not primarily visual and of art objects that are animate presences, indistinguishable from persons, spirits, and certain prosaic things" (Vogel 1997: 108). The Baule attribute great powers to their artwork—powers that Westerners would consider incredible. The meaning of most art objects, as well as the emotional responses that these objects evoke, derives from their ability to act. For the Baule, what Western museum-goers call

© Petitgolo/Dreamstime.com

Figure 9.8 A Baule wood sculpture from the nineteenth century.

sculpture contains enormous powers of life and death, and Baule people do not consider their sculpture apart from these powers (85).

Here is one situation in which art objects are used in performance: the Gbagba dance, as described by Vogel. This event, in which sculpture and dance intersect, has deep social and cultural significance for the Baule.

The Gbagba dance is a daylong entertainment performance. It may also be performed for the funeral of an important woman. The style of mask used in the performance is called *Mblo*, and, in the past, a village may have had a dozen or more such masks: some, representations of animals; some, portraits of people. Gbagba also includes singing, and two of the songs repeated throughout the day refer to death.

The Gbagba begins with funny morality skits based on scenes from everyday life. These skits are performed by unmasked young dancers and may include older masked performers representing domestic animals (usually sheep and goats). Next come dance-based skits in which more skilled dancers don masks representing large wild animals; these dance skits always end with the successful "killing" of the portrayed animal.

When the first masks appear, so, too, does the costumed figure of the trickster Ambomon. Wearing a cloth hood rather than a mask, Ambomon dances in a rapid and acrobatic way that includes somersaults and tumbling. Ambomon is a comical figure who may or may not be a god. He displays no respect for possessions, rank, or decent behaviour. He stands in direct contrast to the orderly vision of the world, as expressed by the masks; he is the spirit of disorder. Yet, at the same time, Ambomon is the only figure in the dance that *must* appear—he can appear without any of the masked figures, but the masked figures cannot appear without him. When Gbagba is danced for a funeral, only Ambomon enters the courtyard to pay his respects to the deceased and to greet the mourners. Vogel proposes that the obligatory presence of Ambomon suggests to the Baule that the only certainty in life is the threat of disorder and death (167).

Ambomon's energetic style of dance is quite different from the more subtle dance style of the other performers. In a typical female solo dance, for example, the dancer moves forward very slowly in a curved line, with body and neck held upright, hands in front, palms up. Sometimes the dancer carries something in her hand. The dancer's facial features are impassive, her eyes are downcast, and the main movement is in her neck, shoulders, and back. A male dancer may be a bit more vigorous, but

> Baule dancing in general can be characterized as symmetrically balanced and essentially vertical (the dancer's knees may be flexed but the head and torso are held upright). As in so many other Baule creations, the dancer's body is closed in outline. These qualities are also characteristic of Baule sculpture and must be recognized as expressing an aesthetic preference with moral connotations that is deeply embedded in Baule culture and is expressed in myriad ways. (156)

At the end of the day, portrait masks appear, one by one. These portrait masks are usually of specific women, and the subject of each portrait always dances alongside the male who dances wearing the mask. Only the best dancers wear these masks. During these final performances, the finest skills in the community are on display—the best dancers, the most beautiful masks, the best drummers and singers—and the distinguished women who are represented now take their places (Figure 9.9).

The Baule use the term *double* to refer to the portrait mask and its subject. The portrait mask is considered the person's true double; the mask never performs unless the person is there to dance. The "relationships between individuals and their portrait masks are close, complex, and lifelong and become elements of their identities" (166). When the subject of a portrait mask dies or cannot dance any more, a relative becomes the new double or the mask is never danced again.

In conclusion, Vogel observes that the Gbagba dance event has deep social and cultural significance for the Baule:

> The performance teaches basic lessons about the Baule world—about hierarchies and mysteries. Each skit has a simple moral lesson, evident even to children: that humans, for example, with skill and supernatural aid, can dominate even the largest and most awesome wild animals, while the portrait masks present a model of human accomplishment and beauty. At the same time, the dance provides deeper

Reprinted by permission of Susan Vogel

Figure 9.9 Portrait mask of Moya Yanso about to enter the Gbagba dance in the Baule village of Kami in 1972. The mask—an important object—is hidden by the cloths until the last moment, when the mask, its dancer, and its subject will appear dramatically.

insights about blurred boundaries—about the interpenetration of bush and village and the complexity of gender. The subject of a portrait, most often a woman, sees herself impersonated by a man dancing "like a woman" and wearing a mask that is her double or namesake. A frequent theme of Baule art is opposite-sex doubling, meaning that two figures appear not as a pair of complementary beings but as manifestations of a single being having qualities of both sexes. The concept is too troubling to articulate openly in words, but in Gbagba it is available to wordless contemplation. (167–8)

The Mass Media: A Television Serial in Egypt

Contemporary anthropologists recognize the importance of the mass media (e.g., television, films, websites) as a venue for cultural productions. In cases where a certain amount of creativity is involved—for example, in scripted and/or heavily edited movies and television shows—these productions can be thought of as art. Anthropological study of such productions, their creators, and their viewers can often reveal their cultural significance.

In many countries, soap operas or television serials are among the most popular mass entertainments, watched by millions. In some parts of the world, these programs are seen by their creators not simply as entertainment but also as tools, useful for teaching certain people in their societies what they need to learn to be modern citizens. But what the intended audience gets from the program is not always the message the creators thought they were transmitting.

Anthropologist Lila Abu-Lughod (1995) studied an Egyptian television serial called *Hilmiyya Nights* that was broadcast during Ramadan (the Islamic holy month of fasting) over five successive years. The serial followed the fortunes and relationships of a group of characters from the traditional Cairo neighbourhood of Hilmiyya, taking them from the late 1940s, when Egypt was under the rule of King Farouk and the British, up to the early 1990s, even incorporating Egyptian reaction to the first Gulf War. The central action revolved around the rivalry, financial dealings, and love interests of two wealthy men, and the narrative tied the lives of its characters to Egyptian national political events. Above all, the show promoted the theme of national unity. With few exceptions, all the characters were shown to be basically good and patriotic.

Abu-Lughod studied two separate groups of Egyptians during the 1990s: poor working-class women in Cairo and villagers in Upper Egypt. When she asked poor women in Cairo what they liked about the show, they volunteered not the serious political or social messages but two female characters: the glamorous, aristocratic femme fatale and the arrogant belly dancer turned cabaret owner. Although these two characters were hardly respectable, they were nevertheless favourites because they defied the moral system that kept good women quiet. Indeed, Abu-Lughod found that both the urban women and the villagers accepted the moral stances presented in the program only when they resonated with their own worlds. Overall, the women ignored the aspects of the serial that were not part of their experiences.

Most interestingly, Abu-Lughod argues that television, especially for the villagers, created its own world, one that was a small part of the viewers' daily lives: "What they experienced through television added to, but did not displace, whatever else already existed. They treated the television world not as a fantasy escape but as a sphere unto itself with its familiar time slots and specific attitudes" (Abu-Lughod 1995: 203–4). Moreover, the modern views presented on *Hilmiyya Nights* were not the only voices that brought "modernity" to the villagers. Indeed, the villagers were deeply affected in a wide variety of ways by the outside world, whether through local government policies or through multinational corporations' advertisements. As Abu-Lughod observes, "television is, in this village, one part of a complex jumble of life, and the dramatic experiences and visions it offers are surprisingly easily incorporated as discrete—not overwhelming—elements in the jumble" (205).

Television in Egypt, she notes, has had measurable social effects: for example, families prefer to stay home to watch television rather than visit among households in the evenings. Television may also have increased the number of "experiences" shared across generations and genders as young and old, men and women, now spend time together watching television.

Ultimately, the intended impact of *Hilmiyya Nights* was undermined but not because nobody was watching television: both urban poor and villagers had their sets on almost constantly. Rather, the positive messages that the creators of *Hilmiyya Nights* and similar serials intended were lost because they were only part of the complex flow of programming in Egypt, which included many other kinds of information: news, entertainment, advertising, and so on. More important, viewers evaluated all these messages in terms of their own life experiences; hence, the messages were often neutralized or contradicted by the viewers' powerful everyday realities.

Myth

We have proposed that play lies at the heart of human creativity. However, because play has the potential to undermine the social order, societies tend to apply cultural rules meant to channel play in less destructive directions. Rules designed to limit artistic expression—for example, rules that prohibit artists from questioning certain social, religious, or sexual principles—are one result of this channelling process. All societies depend on the willingness of their members not to question certain assumptions about the way the world works. Because the regularity and predictability of social life might collapse altogether if people were free to imagine, and act upon, alternatives to the local version of reality, most societies find ways to persuade their members that the local version of reality is the only reality—period. The most widely accepted and respected way of doing this is through the use of myth.

Myths are stories whose truths seem self-evident because the narrative does such a good job of integrating personal experiences with a wider set of assumptions about the way society, or the world in general, must operate. Traditionally, these stories involve a teller and an audience; thus, myths are products of high verbal art. Frequently the official myth tellers are the ruling groups in society: the elders, the political leaders, the religious specialists. They may also be considered master storytellers. The content of myths usually concerns past events (usually at or near the beginning of time) or future events (usually at or near the end of time). Sometimes, myths account for the origins of a specific cultural practice. (See the "In Their Own Words" box that follows.) Myths are socially important because they tell people where they have come from, where they are going, and, thus, how they should live right now (Figure 9.10).

In some societies, myths play a relatively informal role in laying out the guidelines of social conduct. This is the case in most complex Western societies, such as Canada, where many different groups, each with its own mythic tradition, often live side by side. Because the Canadian government supports cultural diversity, or multiculturalism, it regularly prohibits one group from silencing an opposing group. Yet Canada is not without its myths. For many Canadians, the notion of multiculturalism itself is the dominant myth, and our assumption is that it makes us more tolerant. Yet, as is the case with most myths, the ideal it represents is not always reflected in reality (Dods 2010).

Myths and related beliefs that are taken to be self-evident truths are sometimes arranged into an official code, or set of rules. When these rules are extreme and deviation from the code is treated harshly, anthropologists sometimes speak of **orthodoxy**. Societies differ in the degree to which they require members to adhere to orthodox interpretations of key myths. But even societies that place little emphasis on orthodoxy are likely to exert some control over the interpretation of key myths because myths have implications for action. They may justify past action, explain present action, or generate future action. To be persuasive, myths must offer plausible explanations for our experience of human nature, human society, and human history. The power of myths comes from their ability to make life meaningful for those who accept them.

The success of Western science has led many members of Western societies to dismiss non-scientific myths as flawed attempts at science or history. Only relatively recently have some scientists come to recognize the similarities between scientific and non-scientific storytelling about events such as the origin of life on earth. Scientific stories about origin—*origin myths*—are matched against material evidence found in the *natural* world; the success of

orthodoxy "Correct doctrine"; the prohibition of deviation from certain generally accepted rules or beliefs.

Figure 9.10 A vase painting illustrating part of the *Popol Vuh*, the Mayan creation story. What can a creation story communicate to people about how they should live their lives?

In Their Own Words

The Dane-zaa Creation Story

The following is an excerpt from the creation story of the Dane-zaa First Nations, the people who were known as the Fort St. John Beaver Band until they divided into the Doig River and Blueberry River First Nations in 1977. The excerpt is from *Where Happiness Dwells: A History of the Dane-zaa First Nations* by Robin Ridington and Jillian Ridington in collaboration with the Elders of the Dane-zaa First Nations. As Ridington and Ridington note, "fur traders first recorded Dane-zaa names in a North West Company post journal in 1799, but Dane-zaa families had lived in the land east of the Rocky Mountains, where the Peace River flows through what is now northeastern BC and northwestern Alberta, for millennia" (2013: 3). Today, about 1,000 Dane-zaa reside in British Columbia and 2,000 in Alberta.

Every culture has a story that takes us back to the beginning of time. The Dane-zaa creation story has many parallels with explanations of the universe found in Western science. It describes the unfolding of time and space, but unlike the creation story told by physicists, the Dane-zaa creation story is also about people, animals, and other living things. It also bears similarities to the biblical story of creation but creation unfolds in the Dane-zaa universe as a result of conversations between the creator and conscious and sentient animal persons, rather than through the actions of a solitary creator. As in the Bible, the Dane-zaa creation story begins with an enormous body of water and a creator, but it then takes a different direction. The creator, Yaak'ih Sadę (Sky Keeper), draws a cross on the water as a way of establishing the four directions. He or she (Dane-zaa Záágé? has gender neutral pronouns, and we follow that usage in our commentaries) then sends animals down beneath the water's surface to bring back earth, from which Yaak'ih Sadę creates land. Muskrat dives way down and brings a bit of earth up under his or her fingernails. The creator tells this earth to grow, and it

eventually becomes large enough to support people and the animals whose bodies give the people life. Instead of giving man domination over other beings, the creator enters into a conversation with the animal people, who already existed in the creator's mind. Indeed, humans do not play an important part in the Dane-zaa creation story. Sky Keeper made men and women, just as he or she made him- or herself. . . .

This creation story is the basis on which Dane-zaa First Nations' understanding of the past, present, and the future has been built. The creation story is so familiar to those brought up speaking Dane-zaa Záágé? that it is seldom told from the beginning to the end. Every Dane-zaa person recognizes elements of the story that form part of other stories. References to the cross on the water and to the Muskrat come up frequently in ordinary conversation, much the same way that a literate Christian can bring up a Bible story, knowing that his or her audience of believers will understand the references. . . . When Dane-zaa children listen to elders telling stories, they hear bits and pieces of the creation story. When Robin heard segments in the mid-1960s, he realized that there was a bigger story, and he wanted to hear the whole thing from beginning to end. Only someone from outside the culture would have thought to ask for the whole story in one sitting. The obvious person to give such a special telling was the last Dreamer[*], Charlie Yahey.

[*] The Dreamers have been essential to Dane-zaa life since before white people came to their land. Dreamers are men, and sometimes women, who can follow a trail song to a place beyond the sky where they come into contact with the spirits of the people who have gone before. Prior to contact they were hunt chiefs who visualized the plans for communal hunts. Since white people came, Dreamers have dreamed about the future and told their people how to cope with the pressures of living in a changing world. (2013: 9)

this match determines whether the myths are accepted or rejected. By contrast, non-scientific origin myths get their vitality from how well they match with the *social* world.

Myth as a Charter for Social Action

Early in the twentieth century, Bronisław Malinowski introduced a new approach to myth. He believed that to understand myths, we must understand the social context in which they are embedded. Malinowski argued that myths serve as "charters" or "justifications" for present-day social arrangements. Myths contain some "self-evident" truth that explains why society is as it is and why it cannot be changed. If the social arrangements justified by the myth are challenged, the myth can be used as a weapon against the challengers.

Malinowski's (1948 [1926]) famous example is of the origin myths of the Trobriand Islanders (see EthnoProfile 8.1). Members of every significant kinship group know and retell the history of the place from which their group's ancestress and her brother emerged from the depths of the earth. These origin myths are set in the time before history began. Each ancestress–brother pair brought with them a distinct set of special objects, knowledge, skills, crafts, spells, and the like. On reaching the surface, the pair took possession of the land. That is why, today, the people on a given piece of land have rights to it. It is also why they possess a particular set of skills, crafts, and spells. Because the original sacred beings were a woman and her brother, the origin myth can also be used to endorse present-day social arrangements. Membership in a Trobriand clan depends on a person's ability to trace his or her kinship to that clan's original ancestress through matrilineage. A brother and a sister represent the prototypical members of a clan because they have both descended from the ancestress through female links. Should anyone question the wisdom of organizing society in this way, the myth can be cited as proof that this is indeed the correct way to live.

In Trobriand society, clans are ranked relative to one another in terms of prestige. In the Trobriand myth that explains rank, one clan's ancestor, the dog, emerged from the earth before another clan's ancestor, the pig, thus justifying ranking the dog clan above the pig clan in terms of prestige. To believe in this myth, Malinowski asserted, is to accept a transcendent justification for the ranking of clans. He made it clear, however, that if social arrangements change, the myth changes, too—in order to justify the new arrangements. At some point, the pig clan became more prominent than the dog clan. This social change resulted in a modification in the mythic narrative. The dog was said to have eaten food that was taboo. In doing so, the dog gave up its claim to higher rank. Thus, to understand a myth and its transformations, one must understand the social organization of the society that makes use of it.

Myth as a Conceptual Tool

Beginning in the mid-1950s, a series of books and articles by French anthropologist Claude Lévi-Strauss transformed the study of myth (see, e.g., Lévi-Strauss 1955, 1967 [1962]). Lévi-Strauss argued that myths have meaningful structures that are worth studying in their own right, quite apart from the uses to which the myths may be put. According to Lévi-Strauss, these structures can help us understand and overcome complex issues that are otherwise difficult to comprehend.

Using a linguistic metaphor, Lévi-Strauss argued that myths are composed of smaller units—phrases, sentences, words, and so on—that are arranged in ways that give both narrative as well as structural coherence. These arrangements represent and comment upon aspects of social life that are thought to oppose each other. Examples include the male and the female, the natural world and the cultural world, life and death, the spirit and the body, and so on.

The complex syntax (or structure) of myth attempts to reconcile those opposed aspects to one another in an attempt to overcome their contradictions and achieve holism. Of course, these contradictions can never be overcome completely; for example, the opposition of life to death is incapable of any earthly resolution. But myth can transform an insoluble problem into a more accessible, concrete form. Mythic narrative can then provide the concrete problem with a solution. For example, in a myth, a hero may bridge the opposition between life and death by travelling from the land of the living to the land of the dead and back. Perhaps a myth describes the journey of a bird that travels from the earth (the home of the living) to the sky (the home of the dead). Many cultures have such myths. One of the earliest recorded is the Egyptian myth of Osiris, in which Osiris dies, is brought back to life, and becomes the ruler of the underworld.

From this point of view, myths do not just talk about the world as it is; they also describe the world as it might be. To paraphrase Lévi-Strauss, myths are good to think with; mythic thinking can propose other ways to live our lives. He insists, however, that the alternatives myths proposed are ordinarily rejected as impossible. Thus, even though myths allow for play with self-evident truths, this play remains under strict control.

Is Lévi-Strauss correct? There has been a great deal of debate on this approach since Lévi-Strauss first introduced it. But even those who are most critical of his analyses of particular myths agree that mythic structures are meaningful because they display the ability of human beings to play with possibilities as they attempt to deal with basic contradictions at the heart of human experience.

For Malinowski, Lévi-Strauss, and their followers, those who believe in myths are not conscious of how their myths are structured or of the functions their myths perform for them. More recent anthropological thinking takes a more reflexive approach. This research recognizes that ordinary members of a society *are* often aware of how their myths structure meaning, allowing them to manipulate the way myths are told or interpreted in order to effect change, to prove a point, or to buttress a particular referential perspective on human nature, society, or history. Therefore, myths are the art form by which people create meaning through language (see Ridington 1998). In a myth, parts can stand for wholes, and "each story is connected to every other and to a highly contextualized discourse that assumes familiarity with biography and shared experience" (1998: 346).

Ritual

Play allows unlimited consideration of alternative referential perspectives on reality. Art permits consideration of alternative perspectives but imposes certain limitations restricting the form and the content. Myth aims to narrow the possible referential perspectives and often promotes a single, orthodox perspective presumed to be valid for everyone. It thus attempts to shape the way members of a culture think about themselves and their surroundings. But because societies aim to shape action as well as thought, art, myth, and ritual are often closely associated with one another.

A Definition

Recall the definition of *ritual* given at the beginning of this chapter:

> A repetitive social practice set off from everyday routine and composed of a sequence of symbolic activities that adhere to a culturally defined ritual schema and are closely connected to a specific set of ideas significant to the culture.

This definition of ritual has four elements:

1. Ritual is *a repetitive social practice*. This means that rituals are repeated again and again, and they involve more than one person. Rituals tend to be composed of a sequence of social, symbolic activities, such as dance, song, speech, gestures, the manipulation of certain objects, and so forth.

2. Ritual is *set off from the social routines of everyday life*. They occupy a special place in social life, a place separate from day-to-day activities and interactions.

3. Rituals *adhere to a characteristic, culturally defined ritual schema*. This means that members of a culture can tell that a certain sequence of activities is a ritual even if they have never seen that particular ritual before.

4. Ritual action is *closely connected to a specific set of ideas that are somehow significant to the culture*. These ideas are often encoded in myth. They might concern the nature of evil, the relationship of human beings to the spirit world, how people ought to interact with one another, and so forth.

The purpose for which a ritual is performed guides how these ideas are selected and symbolically enacted. What gives a ritual its power is that the people who perform it assert that the authorization for the ritual comes from outside themselves—from their state, society, God, ancestors, or "tradition." These people have not made up the ritual themselves; rather, it connects them to a source of power that they do not control but that controls them.

The Western idea of ritual includes the notion that it is "religious." However, in anthropological terms, ritual includes a much broader range of activities. According to the definition given above, a scientific experiment, a graduation ceremony, procedures in a court of law, and a child's birthday party are rituals just as much as weddings, bar mitzvahs, and Catholic Mass are.

Consider the example of a young child's birthday party in North America. Several children are formally invited to help celebrate the birthday. Each child arrives with a wrapped gift, which is handed to the birthday child and then set aside. The children often put on birthday hats. They then play group games of some kind, some of which are now played *only* at birthday parties. The games culminate with the appearance of a birthday cake, illuminated by candles (one for each year of the child's life) and accompanied by the singing of "Happy Birthday." The birthday child makes a wish and blows out the candles (Figure 9.11). Following the cake and ice cream, the birthday child opens the presents, examines each one, and thanks the guest (often with an adult's prompting). Shortly after the presents are opened, the guests' parents or guardians appear and the guests receive party favours and leave. The ritual order of these events matters. The central events of the party must occur in the order described. Additionally, if you come from a tradition in which birthday parties are celebrated, it is likely that you cannot remember *learning* how to celebrate a birthday party—it is something you have always known. It's what everyone does. It's just how it is. Its authority comes from "tradition."

In the birthday party ritual, children (both hosts and guests) learn to associate receiving gifts with important moments in life. They discover the importance of exchanging material objects (reciprocity) in defining significant social relations. They learn to defer gratification (the presents cannot be opened immediately). They live out patterns of sociability and friendship while recognizing the centrality of the individual (the child celebrating the birthday). Finally, the children participate in patterns of sharing, of celebrating the self, and of recognizing relationships with friends and kin that are important in other areas of North American life.

Figure 9.11 Part of the ritual aspect of the North American birthday party is having the birthday child blow out the candles and make a wish. Did you celebrate such parties as a child? What aspects of the dominant North American culture do such rituals reinforce?

Ritual as Action

A ritual has a particular sequential ordering of acts, utterances, and events: that is, ritual has a *text*. Because ritual is action, however, attention must be paid to the way the ritual text is performed. The *performance* cannot be separated from its text; text and performance shape each other. Through ritual performance, the ideas of a culture become tangible, take on a form, and shape participants' views on their society. At the same time, ritual performance can serve as a commentary on the text to the extent of transforming it. For example, Jewish synagogue ritual following the reading of the Torah (the Hebrew holy book) includes lifting the Torah scroll, showing it to the congregation, and then closing it and covering it. In some synagogues, a man and a woman, often a couple, are called to lift and cover the Torah: the man lifts it and, after he seats himself, the woman rolls the scroll closed, places the tie around it, and covers it with the cloth that protects it. Robert Lavenda once observed a performance of this ritual in which the woman lifted the Torah and the man wrapped it; officially, the ritual text was carried out, but the performance became a commentary on the text—on the role of women in Judaism, on the Torah as an appropriate subject of attention for women as well as for men, on the roles of men and women overall, and so on. The performance was noteworthy—indeed, many of the regular members of the congregation seemed

quite surprised—precisely because it violated people's expectations and in doing so directed people's attention toward significant social issues.

Ritual performers are not robots but active individuals whose choices are guided by, but not rigidly dictated by, previous ritual texts. After all, human behaviour is fundamentally open. Rituals highlight the fact that human understanding of the world is not just mental and not just physical; instead, it is a holistic coming together of mind and body, thought and feeling. By performing our ideas, and by feeling the implications of our myths, their truths become self-evident.

Rites of Passage

Let us examine how ritual action can reaffirm certain fundamental truths by looking at one kind of ritual performance: the **rite of passage**. At the beginning of the twentieth century, French anthropologist Arnold Van Gennep noted that certain kinds of rituals around the world had similar structures. These were rituals associated with the movement (or passage) of people from one position in the social structure to another. They included births, initiations, confirmations, weddings, and funerals (Figure 9.12).

Van Gennep (1960) found that all these rituals began with a period of *separation* from the old position. During this period, the ritual passenger left behind the symbols and practices of his or her previous position. For example, military recruits leave their families

rite of passage A ritual that serves to mark the movement and transformation of an individual from one social position to another.

Figure 9.12 This funeral procession in Kyoto, Japan, bears resemblance to North American funeral processions. Certain kinds of rituals around the world have similar structures.

behind and are moved to a new place. They are forced to cut their hair and leave behind the clothing and activities that marked who they were in civilian life.

The second stage in a rite of passage involves a period of *transition*, in which the ritual passenger is neither in the old life nor in the new one. This period is marked by rolelessness, ambiguity, and perceived danger. Van Gennep referred to this part of a rite of passage as the **liminal period**, from the Latin *limen* ("threshold"). During this period, the individual is on the threshold, betwixt and between, neither here nor there, neither in nor out. Often, the person involved is subjected to ordeal by those who have already passed through this stage. In the military service, this is the period of basic training, in which recruits (not yet soldiers but no longer civilians) are forced to dress and act alike. They are subjected to a grinding-down process, after which they are rebuilt into something new. Another example of this sort of period of transition is the wake that precedes a funeral in many cultures; the wake is a time of transition from the here and now to the timelessness of eternity.

During the final stage—*re-aggregation*—the ritual passenger is reintroduced into society in his or her new position. In the military, this involves graduating from basic training and visiting home—but this time in uniform, on leave, and as a member of the armed forces. A more familiar rite of passage in North

liminal period The ambiguous transitional state in a rite of passage in which the person or persons undergoing the ritual are outside their ordinary social positions.

communitas An unstructured or minimally structured community of equal individuals frequently found in rites of passage.

America is high school graduation, which is understood as a movement from one social position (a high school student) to another (e.g., a college or university student, a member of the workforce, or an independent adult).

Cultural anthropologist Victor Turner greatly increased our understanding of rites of passage when he concentrated on the liminal stage, which he saw as an ambiguous state. Turner notes that the symbolism accompanying this stage often expresses ambiguity and uncertainty. Liminality, he tells us, "is frequently likened to death, to being in the womb, to invisibility, to darkness, to bisexuality, to the wilderness, and to an eclipse of the sun or moon" (1969: 95). This concept may be familiar to readers from the tales recorded by the Brothers Grimm. Many of what are now called *fairy tales* were originally folk tales and have rites of passage and liminality as part of the story. Consider the original version of *Snow White*, in which a young girl is first forced to live in the woods (outside her society) and then killed before being brought back to life and back to society, at which time she is deemed ready for marriage (i.e., ready to take on the role of wife and mother). Similar themes appear in *Sleeping Beauty*, *Rapunzel*, and many other folk tales.

Turner observed that people in the liminal state tend to develop intense comradeships in which their non-liminal distinctions disappear or become irrelevant. Turner calls this form of social relationship **communitas**. Turner contends that all societies need some kind of temporary communitas as much as they need more permanent structure. Communitas gives "recognition to an essential and generic human bond, without which there could be no society" (Turner 1969: 97). However, periods of communitas are brief, generally existing only within a ritual context. Communitas is dangerous, not just because it threatens structure but because it threatens survival itself. Lost in a world of communitas, an individual is cut off from the things that structure ensures (e.g., food, social support). At some point, communitas must give way to structure. In turn, this structure generates a need for the release of communitas.

The feeling of oneness associated with communitas is also possible in play and art. Indeed, in our own societies we can find this sort of group interaction at sports games, rock concerts, or large-scale public events, such as Toronto's Caribbean Carnival (Caribana), Carnaval de Québec, or the Calgary Stampede. In each case, people are temporarily brought together as equals to share in a cultural experience that exists outside the boundaries of everyday life.

Human beings all undergo transitions, great and small, throughout their lives. Let us now consider death as an example in particular. We experience "the coming-into-being, completion, and attenuation of personhood," and through this experience "life and death are attributed, contested, and enacted" (Kaufman and Morgan 2005: 317). In this context, we can consider "two basic anthropological models of cultural representations of death":

> The first is the journey model, in which death is considered to be a long-term transformation. In many societies, death is imagined as a continuation of the journey begun in life. Death as a journey is usually contrasted with the Western model of death as "punctual" and, insofar as it is rooted in biological understandings of death, a terminal end. (Dernbach 2005: 120–1)

Anthropologist Marc-Antoine Berthod (2005) speaks of the tension that is evoked as a moment of suspended silence when the "being" of the dead or near-dead is in a state of redefinition. Our silence at such times affirms what Berthod sees as our embarrassment at asserting the radical otherness of the deceased or the nearly deceased (535). Our preoccupation with this radical otherness is emphasized by the enduring popular culture media presentation of the "near" dead: zombies. *Night of the Living Dead, Dawn of the Dead*, and *Zombieland* movies, TV's *The Walking Dead*, Michael Jackson's "Thriller" video, as well as novels such as *World War Z* provide entertainment beyond the nineteenth-century classic book of the undead by Mary Shelly, *Frankenstein*. Even with the scientific discussion of zombification by Davis (1985, 1988), we are in the realm of considering *otherness*.

We may have models of *after-life* life but we seldom confront the cultural issues of the "life of the dead" (Berthod 2005: 521) during funerary rituals and mourning. In North America, these rites may be insignificant, such as the straight and swift disposal of the corpse, or elaborate and detailed, such as a state funeral, but they are rarely drawn out in the fashion found in some other cultures. In some cultures, the end-of-life transition may move and change through time and be deeply integrated into the world of the living. Consider the case of the Trobriand Islanders:

> Trobriand mortuary rituals, which extend over a period of five to ten years, represent an effort to deconstruct the total social person by separating elements of the body, artifacts, and spiritual essence, so that each element is reinvested in the world of the living.... [D]eath ... is a process of continuity and change, a journey and an ending, mourning and memory work, an uncontrollable happening, and a complex social achievement. (Dernbach 2005: 121)

In some cases, rituals even invite the deceased to actively participate, albeit in spiritual form. Among the Chuukese people of Micronesia, for example, funerary rituals involve the spirits of the recently deceased appearing to and even possessing their living relatives (Dernbach 2005). The Chuukese believe that the spirits of the dead linger in the world of the living for a period of time before moving on to the world of the dead. The purpose of this liminal phase is believed to be twofold: it provides comfort and guidance to the living, and it gives the spirit a chance to grow accustomed to its new circumstances.

Mortuary rituals of some form are universal, if only in the fulfillment of government regulations. However, in an increasingly techno-rich culture, this can be prolonged, projecting the cellular life of a body long past the point at which the individual as a social being can be defined as actually "living." Here we have the "modern" concept of the irreversible death of the brain. In the biotechnical world, human beings face the challenge of developing rites and rituals that support the living through the process of stages of death as it is variously defined in medicine and law.

For the dying, death is about departing from everything; for the remaining, it is about contemplating the space left empty by "the departed" and the ultimate destination of "the departed." Ultimately, death is a *social event*—an occurrence that has shared meaning that humans mark through various rituals. These rituals reaffirm life by declaring that there was and perhaps remains a "beingness" of the dead. Thus, rituals, whether religious or medical, benefit the living in various ways, mainly by providing comfort in a time of loss and support in the contemplation of our finiteness. Ultimately, ritual confirms people's place in the fabric of life—the life of their family, their community, and their world.

Play and Ritual as Complementary

How does play differ from ritual? Play and ritual (like metaphorical and literal language) are complementary forms of metacommunication (Handelman 1977). Just as the movement from non-play to play is based on the premise of metaphor ("Let's make-believe"), the movement to ritual is based on the premise of literalness ("Let's believe"). The result of these contrasting premises is that play is associated with inauthenticity while ritual is associated with truth.

Because of the connection of ritual with self-evident truth, the metacommunication of the ritual frame ("This is ritual") is associated with an additional metacommunication: "All messages within this frame are true." It is ritual that asserts *what should be* to play's *what can be*. The ritual frame is more rigid than is the play frame. Consequently, ritual is the most stable liminal domain, whereas play is the most flexible. Players can move with relative ease into and out of play, but such is not the case with ritual.

Finally, play usually has little effect on the social order of ordinary life. Thus, play is allowed a wide range of commentary on the social order. Ritual is different: its role is explicitly to maintain the status quo. Societies differ in the extent to which they promote ritual behaviour. When nearly every act of everyday life is ritualized and other forms of behaviour are strongly proscribed, we sometimes speak of **orthopraxy**. Traditionally, observant Jews and Muslims, for example, lead a highly ritualized daily life, attempting from the moment they awaken until the moment they fall asleep to carry out even the humblest of activities in a manner that is ritually correct. In their view, ritual correctness is the result of God's law, and it is their duty and joy to conform their every action to God's will.

Ritual may seem overwhelming and all-powerful, but it can sometimes be manipulated to achieve non-traditional ends. This manipulation can take many forms. It might involve giving up some elements of the ritual while keeping others, as when a bride and groom have a wedding outdoors instead of in a church but still have a member of the clergy officiate at the ceremony. Or, it might involve emphasizing the importance of one ritual while downplaying another, as when Protestant Baptists downplayed the communion ritual and emphasized the baptism ritual as a way of articulating their challenge to Roman Catholicism. It might even involve exchanging one set of rituals for another, as when lone rural migrants abandoned their traditional rituals and converted to Islam shortly after their arrival in northern Cameroon.

Ethnographer Margaret Drewal (1992) argues that, at least among the Yoruba (see Map 9.1), play and ritual overlap. Yoruba rituals combine spectacle, festival, play, sacrifice, and so on. They also integrate diverse media—music, dance, poetry, theatre, and sculpture. They are spontaneous events in which the mundane order is inverted, reversed, and sometimes even subverted. For example, in everyday Yoruba life, gender roles are rigidly structured. Yoruba rituals, however, allow some cross-dressing by both men and women,

orthopraxy "Correct practice"; the prohibition of deviation from certain generally accepted forms of behaviour.

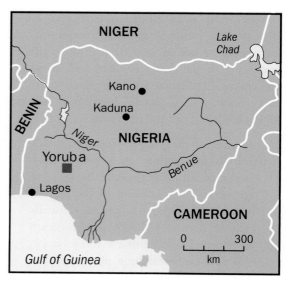

Map 9.1 Yoruba

providing institutionalized opportunities for men and women to cross gender boundaries and to express the traits that the Yoruba consider to be characteristic of the opposite sex. Sometimes these performances are parody, but sometimes they are serious and respectful (190).

Combining Play, Art, Myth, and Ritual

To reiterate, play, art, myth, and ritual are often experienced together. Consider Australian anthropologist Bruce Kapferer's (1983) study of demon exorcism among the Sinhalese Buddhist working class and peasantry in Sri Lanka (see Map 9.2). The night-long ceremony, designed to cure disease, combines ritual, comedy, music, and dance. It is "a marvellous spectacle" meant "to change the experiential condition of [the] patients and to bring patients back into a normal conception of the world" (1983: 177, 236).

At the beginning of the ceremony, the patient and the audience are in different realities. The audience is in the paramount reality of everyday life; the patient is in the alternative reality of the illness. During the first part—called the Evening Watch—the audience becomes increasingly engaged in this alternative reality through music, song, and dance. The performance culminates in the appearance of the illness demons (played by actors), which are portrayed as figures of horror.

At this point, the second part—the Midnight Watch—begins. This part of the ceremony is a comic drama that lasts until nearly 3:00 a.m. The comic content transforms the demons into figures of ridicule and begins to fragment the demonic reality. The gods appear and reassert their dominance, and the

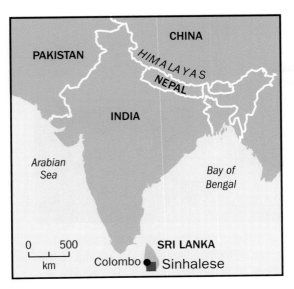

Map 9.2 Sinhalese

sick person begins to see that the demons are really subordinate to the gods, not superior to them.

The last part of the exorcism is the Morning Watch, which continues until 6:00 a.m. During this part, the patient and the audience become re-engaged in the reality of ordinary life. The final comic drama of the performance "confirms the demonic absurdity and destroys the demonic," thus reaffirming the reality of everyday life (220). Having played on the mind, body, and emotions of the patient and the audience, the performance ends. The experience is transformative for all involved.

To understand the performance as a whole, the interactions of all aspects of the performance must be grasped. Kapferer calls this the ceremony's *aesthetics*. He argues that the ceremony succeeds because it is composed of many different parts that fit together in a way that is satisfying to the Sinhalese. In the aesthetic realm—a realm in this case created by the related forces of play, art, myth, and ritual—ideas, symbolic objects, and actions come together in a deeply meaningful way.

Play, art, myth, and ritual are different facets of the holistic human capacity to view the world from a variety of perspectives. The human capacity to play is channelled in different directions in different cultures, but it is always present. When the products of this containment process come together in key cultural productions, such as the Sinhalese curing ceremony, they display both the opportunities and the dangers that result from open human creativity.

Living Anthropology

Games and a Look at the Body in Sport

by Sarah Jacobs, PhD Student, Anthropology, University of Calgary

While play reflects our shared biological and cultural heritage (after all, many animals play), games are uniquely human. People engage in games from mah-jong, to football, wind-surfing, and horse racing. There are even funerary or wake games. What does all this variety have in common? Sociologist Roger Caillois (1961) has proposed six defining characteristics of games:

1. *They are pursued for pleasure* (either the pleasure of the competitors, the spectators, or both).
2. *They require rules agreed to in advance.* Often these rules differ from the rules governing everyday life. Just think about how inappropriate it is to invade someone's personal space on a Canadian street and yet how important it is to "play the body" in hockey.
3. *They are played in a circumscribed time and place.* This might be a football pitch or race route or the sacred *akhara* that is the training place for Indian wrestling.
4. *There is a fiction to the activity.* This is not to say that the outcome of an event cannot have very real consequences but simply that games create a world apart from everyday life and provide a venue for exploration. During a sporting event, for instance, athletes and spectators can imagine or—for a brief period—even enact social identities and relationships not possible under ordinary circumstances.
5. *They are not work,* strictly speaking. While professional athletes may appear to be an exception to this idea, what Caillois is getting at is that games are non-productive in a material economic sense. We may add economic significance to games by placing bets, providing stipends to competitors, or paying for tickets to watch a match, but the gaming activity in and of itself does not make or produce anything.
6. *The outcome is uncertain.*

Although perhaps not complete, this list provides a starting place to explore games in human societies. Anthropologist Victor Turner (1982) combined his own theories about social

Continued

dramas with Caillois' ideas in order to explore the expressive and ritual aspects of games, from childhood play to Olympic sport. But perhaps the best-known analysis of the social and symbolic dimension of games is an essay written by Clifford Geertz, titled "Deep Play: Notes on the Balinese Cockfight." In it, he employs a "thick description" of cockfighting, concluding that, "in the cockfight, then, the Balinese forms and discovers his temperament and his society's temper at the same time" (Geertz 1972: 28). These studies emphasize that while games may be fun, they are no trivial matter. Moreover, games can be "played out" not only in the micro-interpretive domain, but at the macro-structural level as well. Arjun Appadurai (1995) argues that cricket was integral to contesting colonial rule in India and forging a new national identity.

Clearly, games provide an opportunity to study cultural, social, political, and historical processes. But in the case of sport, games also provide an opportunity to study the body. Sport is both material and discursive. It is embodied, experiential, and affective. And through sport, athletes can test the limits of their bodies (and the bodies of their competitors). Many anthropologists have studied how sport relates to emotion, disability, pain, gender, and the "natural" body. Because "sport 'travels' across boundaries" (Besnier and Bronwell 2012: 454), these inquiries question dichotomies that create stable categories of local/global, male/female, able/disabled, pleasure/pain, nature/culture, and mind/body.

The history of performance-enhancing substances within the Olympic Games provides an interesting case study of essentialized categories. Over the past half-century, the Olympic movement has become increasingly concerned with monitoring "doping." On the surface, this seems straightforward. According to Olympic officials, athletes shouldn't do or ingest things to gain an advantage that unnaturally alters their bodies: this

Figure 9.13 A group of boys play a game of cricket, India's most popular sport, in Mumbai. Arjun Appadurai argues that cricket was integral to contesting colonial rule in India and forging a new national identity.

disrupts a level playing field for all, is unfair, and is cheating. Yet high-performance athletes train their bodies not only to improve their abilities but to tap unrealized capacities (Beamish and Ritchie 2006). In this quest to ever-improve athletic capacities, many permissible forms of training blur the boundaries between nature/culture and body/technology. As a greater number of technologies are integrated into training regimens—and into the bodies of athletes—it becomes increasingly difficult to define what counts as training versus "doping." And, especially in the case of genetic, surgical, and cyborg-type modifications, it is difficult to demarcate where technology ends and the body begins (see Miah 2004). The quest of Olympic athletes to be "faster, higher, stronger" (the Olympic motto) places a facet of human societies that is as, seemingly, frivolous as games at the intersection of self, identity, morality, and politics.

Key Terms

Chapter Summary

1. Play is a generalized form of behavioural openness that functions as practice for the real world, increases creativity, and serves as a way of *organizing* activities. It allows us to set up a separate reality that permits reflexive consideration. Sport is a form of play that can take on a deeper significance, especially for adults.

2. Art is a kind of play that is subject to certain culturally appropriate restrictions on form and content. It aims to evoke an aesthetic response from the artist and the observer.

3. Myths are stories whose truths seem self-evident because they do such a good job of integrating personal experiences with a wider set of assumptions about the way the world works. As stories, myths are the products of high verbal art. A full understanding of a myth requires an understanding of the social context in which the myth is embedded.

4. Ritual is a repetitive social practice composed of sequences of symbolic activities, such as speech, singing, dancing, gestures, and the manipulation of certain objects. In studying ritual, attention is paid not just to the symbols but also to how the ritual is performed. Cultural ideas are made concrete through ritual action. Rites of passage are rituals in which members of a culture move from one position in the social structure to another.

5. Ritual and play are complementary. Play is based on the premise "Let's make-believe," while ritual is based on the premise "Let's believe." As a result, the ritual frame is far more rigid than the play frame. Although ritual may seem overwhelming and all-powerful, individuals and groups can sometimes manipulate ritual forms to achieve non-traditional ends.

Critical Thinking Questions

1. What adult roles do you remember learning through childhood play? Did the games you played reflect dominant cultural stereotypes within the culture (for example, that a "standard" family has both a mommy and a daddy)? In what ways did the games creatively diverge from the reality of adult life?

2. How are art and play alike in presenting alternative realities?

3. How do you think that the multiculturalism myth impacts the ways that Canadians act and interpret their place in the world? What other myths do you see at work in your society?

4. How would you describe your experience as a university or college student as a rite of passage? Have you ventured through periods of separation, transition, and re-aggregation?

Suggested Readings

Alland, Alexander. 1977. *The Artistic Animal: An Inquiry into the Biological Roots of Art* (New York: Doubleday Anchor). An introductory look at the biocultural bases for art. This work is very well written, clear, and fascinating.

Blanchard, Kendall. 1995. *The Anthropology of Sport*, rev. edn (Westport, CT: Bergin and Garvey). An excellent introduction to the topic.

Errington, Shelly. 1998. *The Death of Authentic Primitive Art and Other Tales of Progress* (Berkeley: University of California Press). A sharp and witty book about the production, distribution, interpretation, and sale of "primitive art."

King, Thomas. 1993. *Green Grass, Running Water* (Toronto: HarperCollins). This novel explores contemporary Native American culture and North American literature, juxtaposing the real and the magical to show how the magical gives essential meaning to the real. It is an engaging example of both metacommunication and transformation-representation.

Ridington, Robin. 1998. "Coyote's Canon: Sharing Stories with Thomas King," *American Indian Quarterly* 22, 3: 343–62. The counterpoint of Coyote is King as he presents a Native American perspective on the American literary and cultural canon.

Turner, Victor. 1969. *The Ritual Process* (Chicago: Aldine). An important work in the anthropological study of ritual, this text is an eloquent analysis of rites of passage.

Vogel, Susan. 1997. *Baule: African Art/Western Eyes* (New Haven: Yale University Press). A book of extraordinary photographs and beautifully clear text, this work explores both Baule and Western views of Baule expressive culture.

Wickwire, Wendy. 2001. "The Grizzly Gave Them the Song: James Teit and Franz Boas Interpret Twin Ritual in Aboriginal British Columbia, 1897–1920," *American Indian Quarterly* 25, 3: 431–52. Compares and contrasts the ethnographic information collected and interpreted by two researchers in British Columbia.

Related Websites

The Antiquity of Man
www.antiquityofman.com/Solomon_myth_ritual.html

Canadian Art
www.canadianart.ca

Illinois State Museum
www.museum.state.il.us/muslink/nat_amer/post/htmls/il_am.html

The Museum of Anthropology at the University of British Columbia
www.moa.ubc.ca

University of Pittsburgh: The Grimm Brothers' Children's and Household Tales (in English)
www.pitt.edu/~dash/grimmtales.html

Turtle Island Native Network: Culture
www.turtleisland.org/culture/culture-haisla.htm

Winnipeg Art Gallery: Inuit Art
http://wag.ca/art/collections/inuit-art

10

States of Being in Wellness and Illness

by Roberta Robin Dods

Chapter Outline

Medical Anthropology

Beyond the Science–Tradition Divide

Integrated Approaches and Holism in Medical Anthropology

Cultural Interpretations and Labels of Illness and Disease

Environments and Well-Being

Health-Care Delivery Systems

Epidemiology and Public Health

Integrated, Applied Critical Medical Anthropology: Holism in the Service of Wellness

Learning Objectives

By the end of Chapter 10, you will be able to

- understand that medical anthropology draws on many disciplines to study well-being, health, illness, and disease;
- appreciate the importance of traditional knowledge and biomedical knowledge in the management of wellness and illness;

- consider how human wellness and illness are affected by three interacting environments: the biotic (biological), the abiotic (physical), and the cultural; and
- consider the various social, cultural, personal, economic, and political factors that affect how illness is understood and how health care is provided.

In *Childhood in the Middle Ages* (1990), historian Shulamith Shahar writes about the lives and deaths of children in Europe from the twelfth through the fifteenth century. She also notes the case of one sixteenth-century Englishwoman who had given birth to 17 children, none of whom survived to adulthood. This woman was a member of the upper class and had access to the best her society could offer in terms of education, housing, food, and health care, yet her resources were not enough to save her children from diseases and medical conditions that would be treatable today. Further, considering the low life expectancy of 35 years and the high rates of maternal death related to childbirth that she faced, it is a marvel that this woman survived birthing so many children in the first place.

One might say this woman's situation is simply a product of the time in which she lived. In some sense, this is correct. After all, life expectancies have increased dramatically in many societies since the Middle Ages, and several regions of the world are seeing a decline in maternal mortality ratios. However, we must also consider the position from which this woman's situation is being viewed and whether or not this is a position of privilege. In Canada, many people have access to public and private institutions that offer cutting-edge medical technologies, including vaccines, medications, and machines. Many Canadians live in communities that provide adequate sanitation programs to regulate the quality of drinking water and the disposal of sewage and garbage. The life expectancy at birth in Canada today is over 80 years, and quality of life is generally quite high well into old age. For the most part, Canadians have relatively smaller families, and various birth control and fertility technologies allow many people to choose when and under what conditions they will have children. And while diseases such as diphtheria, polio, and measles contributed to high infant and childhood mortality rates in past centuries, they are no longer considered a general threat to the population today (Figure 10.1). Smallpox, once a major epidemic, is now unimaginable in most societies since it was eradicated worldwide by 1979. These are only a few examples of how the landscape of health and well-being has improved in ways never imagined by previous generations.

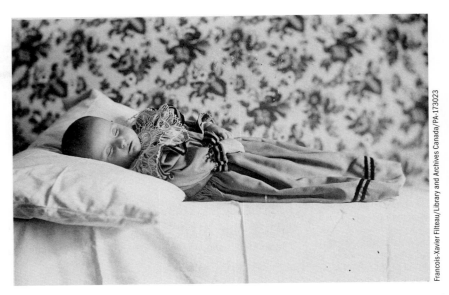

Francois-Xavier Filteau/Library and Archives Canada/PA-173023

Figure 10.1 This 1898 *memento mori* photograph of an infant from Hull, Quebec, suggests the preoccupation with high infant mortality rates at the turn of the twentieth century, which were more than 20 per 100 live births in some regions. At the time, infectious diseases were a common cause of death. What factors have kept infant mortality rates relatively low in most Western nations in recent decades?

However, conditions are different for people in less affluent regions of Canada and the world. In many areas, a high proportion of children and adults still die of diseases transmitted through unclean water. And, as Table 10.1 indicates, maternal mortality ratios continue to vary greatly across the globe. All too often, when it comes to issues of health and wellness, the divide between rich and poor is starkly evident. This division was apparent when cholera broke out in Haiti in 2010: the poorest segments of the population had the least access to uncontaminated water and life-saving resources. This division is also evident within wealthy nations, as less affluent people in all societies face greater health challenges than do their more affluent neighbours. Thus, while some may look at the world of the Englishwoman who lost 17 children so long ago as frozen in history, there are millions of people today who would recognize that world and who would understand what it is like to face the threat of deadly contagious diseases on a daily basis.

Shaman Kim Gee-Chan performs a ritual for clients at a shamanic centre in Yangju, South Korea. Many Koreans continue to consult shamans for medical reasons, divination, or personal advice. With South Korea being one of the most technologically advanced countries, many shamans in turn have adapted their services, offering counselling online and through apps.

Table 10.1 Maternal Mortality Ratios (MMRs) by Specific Regions of the World

	MMR (per 100,000 live births)					
	1990	**1995**	**2000**	**2005**	**2010**	**2015**
Africa	965	914	840	712	620	542
Americas	102	89	76	67	62	52
Southeast Asia	525	438	352	268	206	164
Europe	44	42	33	26	19	16
Eastern Mediterranean	362	340	304	250	199	166
Western Pacific	114	89	75	63	50	41
Global	385	369	341	288	246	216

Source: World Health Organization Global Health Observatory Data Repository, http://apps.who.int/gho/data/view.main.1370?lang=en. © 2015. Reproduced with permission.

health A person's general social, psychological, and physical condition.

well-being A culturally defined state (or role) of general physical and mental comfort and good health; a lack of illness.

medical anthropology An area of anthropological inquiry that focuses on issues of well-being, health, illness, and disease as they are situated in their wider cultural contexts.

biomedicine Traditionally Western forms of medical knowledge and practice based on biological science.

disease Forms of biological impairment identified and explained within the discourse of biomedicine.

suffering The forms of physical, mental, or emotional distress experienced by individuals who may or may not subscribe to biomedical understandings of disease.

sickness Classifications of physical, mental, and emotional distress recognized by members of a particular cultural community.

culture-bound syndromes Sicknesses, as well as the therapies to relieve them, that are unique to a particular cultural group.

illness A suffering person's own understanding of his or her distress.

traditional knowledge Knowledge that is culturally held and passed on from generation to generation.

Medical Anthropology

What does it mean to be healthy? What does it mean to be sick? Members of the same society who share understandings of what it means to be in good **health** are also likely to agree about what symptoms indicate poor health. In Canada, many people understand health as a state of physical, emotional, and mental **well-being**, together with an absence of disease or disability that would interfere with such well-being. Anthropologists recognize, however, that what counts as wellness or its opposite is very much shaped by people's cultural, social, and political experiences and expectations. This means that measuring health or its reverse in a straightforward way can sometimes be challenging. Increasing numbers of anthropologists now apply insights and practices from the various subfields of anthropology in efforts to understand and find solutions to health challenges faced by members of the many communities where they work. This area of specialization is generally called **medical anthropology**, where the term *medical* does not refer specifically to the field of medicine but to a wider array of concerns related more broadly to human ideas of well-being, health, illness, and disease.

Medical anthropologists have been deeply influenced by, as well as critical of, findings by Western physicians and medical scientists who claim to describe normal human biological functioning, the causes for impairment of such functioning, and the scientifically developed therapies available to cure or manage such impairment. These traditionally Western forms of knowledge and practice are often called **biomedicine**, and forms of biological impairment identified and explained within the biomedical discourse are those to which medical anthropologists often apply the term **disease**. Western exploitation, colonial expansion, and industrialization have fostered the spread and adoption of the biomedical model beyond Western societies.

The biomedical model is also contrasted with non-biomedical models. In describing systems of belief and practice that do not use the biomedical model, anthropologists have developed a technical vocabulary that does not presume the universality of biomedical understandings of health and disease. For example, many medical anthropologists prefer to use the term **suffering** to describe the forms of physical, mental, or emotional distress experienced by individuals who may or may not subscribe to biomedical understandings of disease. Medical anthropologists have often used the term **sickness** to refer to classification of physical, mental, and emotional distress recognized by members of a particular cultural community. Sometimes, such sicknesses may bear a close resemblance to disease recognized by scientific biomedicine, but other times, the sickness, as well as the therapy to relieve it, may be unique to a particular cultural group. Such sicknesses have been called **culture-bound syndromes**. Finally, some medical anthropologists contrast both the biomedical understanding of disease and the local cultural categories of sickness with a suffering person's own understanding of his or her distress, which is called **illness**.

Beyond the Science–Tradition Divide

In this complex world, there is always a dynamic tension between **traditional knowledge** and scientific modes of inquiry. This tension plays out in all lives and is increasingly intensified by concepts of modernization. Thus, it is, naturally, a central concern in medical anthropology.

In the 1970s and 1980s, many medical anthropologists saw a strong opposition between medical systems based on traditional knowledge and those based on scientific modes of inquiry. Some anthropologists even saw the characterization of these two primary categories as the "broad aims of the research" (Colson and Selby 1974: 246). In one category, there is the biomedical approach, in which a team of medical professionals, working within an institutionalized system, combat an illness with little reference to the social or cultural conditions of the patient or "client." Medical anthropologist Allan Young (1976) calls this an "internalizing system," as it focuses on what is happening *inside* the individual's body, such as a virus attacking the person's cells. Young contrasts this with "externalizing systems," which often focus on what is happening *outside* the individual's body, such as spiritual forces causing the illness. In this category, there are traditional ethnomedical systems, in which a wise, often spiritually powerful specialist fights an illness based on the knowledge and beliefs of his or her specific cultural group, generally with an awareness of the context of social relationships (Fabrega 1971: 167).

Contemporary medical anthropologists try to move beyond such "either/or" approaches for a number of reasons. First, they understand that the two systems are not mutually exclusive; indeed, many cultures in the modern world incorporate both traditional and biomedical concepts into their medical systems. Second, medical anthropologists see that they can arrive at a more holistic appreciation of all knowledges by examining the traditional in terms of the scientific; and the scientific, in terms of the traditional. Third, they perceive that biomedical knowledge is actually a form of traditional knowledge, as such knowledge is rooted in Western history, was developed as Western society developed, and was passed along within Western cultures. Fourth, they note that the lines between folk medicine and scientific medicine are not always clear. For example, Dr Irwin Ziment, of the UCLA (University of California, Los Angeles) Collaborative Centers for Integrative Medicine, observes that "chicken soup contains drug-like agents similar to those in modern cold medicines. For example, an amino acid released from chicken during cooking chemically resembles the drug acetylcysteine, prescribed for bronchitis and other respiratory problems" (quoted in Day 2010).

Finally, contemporary medical anthropologists understand that "modern" is a relative concept. Each culture defines its own modernity based on its own cultural values and its own ideas about the past and the present. Thus it is ethnocentric to see the Western version of modernity, along with its biomedical approaches, as more modern than the modernities of cultures that support ethnomedical approaches. Whether it is called "science" or "tradition," knowledge is constantly advancing as cultures are always changing. Traditional peoples are open to new concepts, and they have often incorporated elements from biomedical science into their treatment regimes. At the same time, there are ideological reasons for limiting such borrowings, for example, in order to protect identities or cultural values. As Lorenza Menegoni notes, "in some cases, reaffirmation of traditional medicine is enacted as a defence of ethnic identity" (1996: 382). (Also see the "In Their Own Words" box that follows, on Indigenous medicine and identity in Nicaragua.)

Ultimately, although biomedical approaches can be very effective when it comes to saving lives, they have their limitations. Considered on their own, biomedical approaches can, at times, stand in opposition to the anthropologist's goal of understanding individuals and their lives as situated in specific *contexts*. Medical anthropologists recognize this opposition and actively seek to remain open to non-biomedical, culturally defined ways of knowing and being. They understand the need to contextualize all situations. Thus, they consider various aspects of cultural systems, from the local through to the global. Perhaps most importantly, medical anthropologists understand that the relationship between traditional and biomedical approaches is often very complex; in practice, the two have a lot to offer one another, but these approaches successfully work together only when cultural contexts are taken into account.

This final observation is perhaps most significant when contrasted with the biomedical approaches of many foreign aid workers, particularly those operating in the mid-to-late twentieth century, who believed they could effectively introduce biomedical technologies around the globe without considering potential social, economic,

ethnomedical systems Alternative medical systems based on practices of local sociocultural groups.

In Their Own Words

Indigenous Medicine and Identity in Nicaragua

Hugo De Burgos, assistant professor of anthropology at the University of British Columbia Okanagan, discusses survival of ethnic identity and the use of traditional medical practices to reinforce concepts of identity and to mediate place in a wider community.

"Rescuing our Indigenous medicine is to recover our Indigenous identity and culture. Using our traditional medicine is expressing our Indigenous identity."

—Antonio Guzmán, Nicaraguan Indigenous leader

Medical systems are more than social schemes for healing. They are also systems of ecological adaptation; explanatory models for physical and social suffering; and mechanisms for social control. The practical and symbolic functions of a medical system are not restricted to medical concerns. Their multiple implications pervade non-medical spheres of social life, shaping in this way their initially medical purpose. Medical beliefs and practices constitute cultural configurations that inform, shape, and mediate human experience in ways that go beyond purely medical functions.

The people of Veracruz del Zapotal, or Veracruceños, are a Spanish-speaking Indigenous community of Nahua descent from Nicaragua. Currently figuring approximately 3,800, they inhabit the Veracruz del Zapotal valley and the mountain region between the rivers of El Camarón, Guachipilín, and Rio Grande in the department of Rivas, in southern Nicaragua. In their struggle to remain culturally distinct, Veracruceños have

been able to direct their medical behaviour, articulate their medical ideas, and organize their medical resources for political purposes. Since the early 1990s, they have used their Indigenous medicine as a strategy to claim and assert their precariously kept ethnic identity. In the past, these people made use of medical knowledge according to tradition, but not in a political manner. With the introduction of the "revival of Indigenous medicine," a new disposition toward their Indigenous medicine emerged.

Claiming ethnic identity through the use of medicine is informed by an elaborate discourse on how traditional medicine *is* Indigenous identity and on how Indigenous identity is conversely embedded in traditional medicine. Through the use of Indigenous medicine as both *material medica* and a symbolic system, Veracruceños promote community practices that enhance an Indigenous world view. Indigenous medicine is for Veracruceños, as anthropologist and medical psychologist W.H.R. Rivers noted so long ago, a symbolic system, and all symbolic systems are valuable sites for meaning-making, at the level of the individual as well as the community. Indigenous medicine is seen by Veracruceños as a cultural trait, a part of the repertoire of practices and knowledge that makes Veracruceños culturally distinct. This sharply contrasts with the construction of scientific biomedicine, which is, categorically, non-specific to any particular people or culture.

Source: De Burgos, Hugo. 2009. "Indigenous Medicine and Identity in Nicaragua," guest editorial in *Cultural Anthropology: A Perspective on the Human Condition*, 1st Canadian edn, Emily Schultz, Robert Lavenda, and Roberta Robin Dods, 308.

and cultural impacts on local populations. Not surprisingly, their efforts failed in many cases, resulting in ineffective, patchy distributions of medical supplies and treatments. How can cultural bias be avoided when investigating health issues? Some questions a researcher might keep in mind in order to try to minimize cultural bias include the following:

- How do cultures define what constitutes wellness?
- How do people characterize different illnesses?
- What degree of intervention is considered appropriate?

Integrated Approaches and Holism in Medical Anthropology

Medical anthropology is highly interdisciplinary. With roots in overlapping social, cultural, and medical studies of the late nineteenth and early twentieth centuries, the field has evolved into a productive melding of the biological sciences, the social sciences, and the humanities. Today, medical anthropologists draw on such diverse disciplines as biology, ecology, biochemistry, sociology, psychology, political science, economics, linguistics, ethics, and religious studies.

While not all of these disciplines are centrally concerned with health issues, they all have components that can inform a society's understanding of wellness and illness. For example, a researcher interested in linguistics might record a list of plant names that could instruct others on the medicinal uses of plants and their place in religious practices. Additionally, a medical researcher who studies the transmission of a disease from person to person might offer valuable information on the inner workings of families or larger kinship, social, or economic groups. In other cases, medical anthropologists might make useful observations on how an individual's age, sex, gender, class, geographic location, and economic status affect his or her access to treatment.

Because the approach that medical anthropologists take is so broad, applications of medical anthropology are often found in settings that are not overtly anthropological. A good example comes from journalist Ingrid Peritz's (2010) exposé on lack of equal access to abortion clinics in Canada. As Peritz notes, "While decades of court battles and debates have led Canadians to view abortion access as a given, the on-the-ground reality looks like a country carved into have and have-not communities." Peritz takes a holistic approach to the topic, considering factors such as the social stigma attached to abortion, insufficient government funding, unsupportive public policy, and low numbers and geographically patchy distributions of abortion clinics. Indeed, journalistic investigations of medical issues often take into account a wide variety of personal, social, cultural, and political factors (see, e.g., Laverdière and Ashton 2014; Röhricht et al. 2014).

Integrated approaches are equally informative when considering wider health issues on a global scale. As medical anthropologist William Dressler notes, biological disease is "socially distributed between and within societies, especially societies being transformed by their increased dependency within international capitalist market systems" (2001: 456). For example, the rate at which a disease spreads within a region can be tied to transnational decisions based on political, economic, and ideological considerations. Further, as medical anthropologist Linda Whiteford points out, decisions made in one powerful nation can have an intense impact on health and well-being around the globe: "Without doubt, global health policies reflect national priorities; the role of the UN and other international agencies, such as the World Health Organization (WHO), is shaped by funders' [i.e., wealthy nations'] priorities" (2009: 106). As Dressler and Whiteford

both suggest, an integrative anthropological perspective can contribute much-needed cultural context to the discussion of international health concerns.

Openness to Traditional Knowledge

Medical anthropologists' openness to a variety of integrated perspectives makes their approach particularly suited to examining both traditional knowledge and biomedical approaches (Dods 2004). For example, in the non-biomedical context, medical anthropologists have observed medical-religious practitioners, such as shamans, in traditional healing roles (Figure 10.2). In previous contexts, researchers had considered shamanistic practices as responses to general physical complaints (Mair 1969), as expressions of social values (Wilson 1951), or, more often, as forms of religious rituals. Yet some saw such systems as analogous to science, and medical anthropologists came to see such practices as legitimate forms of healing. Their research has advanced anthropologists' understanding of the importance of folk practitioners as Indigenous healers.

Viewing traditional knowledge as a source of wisdom has led to new and varied work in the field. Consider the work that ethnobotanist Paul Alan Cox and his team of researchers conducted in Samoa. In his discussions with local healers, Cox learned of prostratin, an antiviral chemical compound found in the bark of the mamala tree. The compound's antiviral properties had long been known to traditional Samoan healers, who use the

shaman A part-time religious practitioner who is believed to have the power through altered states of consciousness to travel to or contact supernatural forces directly on behalf of individuals or groups. Note that this term is not used specifically in the context of traditional America but is found in other cultures where such a religio-medical practitioner is found.

© Anton_Ivanov/Shutterstock.com

Figure 10.2 A Togolese local shaman sits by the table in his house. What can anthropologists learn by taking an integrated approach to understanding the sorts of healing rituals this man might use?

bark to treat hepatitis. Biomedical researchers have since found that prostratin shows potential to be effective in the treatment of the human immuno-deficiency virus (HIV). In a letter published in the journal *Science* in 2008, Cox and his colleagues recognize their debt to the Samoan healers:

> Because knowledge of prostratin's antiviral activity originated from ethnobotanical studies with Samoan healers, the AIDS Research Alliance (ARA) and the Government of Samoa agreed that 20 per cent of ARA's profit from prostratin will be returned to the Samoan people. Similarly, Samoa and the University of California, Berkeley, agreed to share equally in commercialization of the prostratin gene sequences. In the spirit of these previous agreements, we encourage future developers of prostratin analogs for antiviral therapy to negotiate fair and equitable benefits with the Samoan people. (Cox et al. 2008: 1589)

As Cox and his team demonstrate, respecting traditional knowledge also means behaving ethically toward those who share that knowledge.

Furthermore, medical anthropologists must be aware of their own biases, which they may bring to their research. As researcher George M. Foster points out,

> anthropologists filter the data of all exotic systems through the lens of belief and practice of the people they know best. Whether

etiology The study of the causes of a disease and/ or an illness.

it be causality, diagnosis, the nature and role of the curer, or the perceptions of illness within the wider supernatural and the social universe, general statements seem strongly influenced by the writers' personal experiences. (1976: 733)

In effect, Foster's words reveal the importance of remaining reflexive when considering medical approaches within the cultures being studied.

Cultural Interpretations and Labels of Illness and Disease

Interpretations of illness and disease differ across cultures. Foster (1976) suggests that there are two principal interpretations of **etiology** (Table 10.2) present when comparing traditional medical systems cross-culturally:

1. The *personalistic,* in which people believe that illness is caused by supernatural forces (e.g., magical powers, an evil spirit, or a deity)
2. The *naturalistic,* in which people believe that the causes of illness are rooted in the physical world (e.g., dampness, cold, or an imbalance in bodily substances)

In the personalistic interpretation, all misfortune is explained by referring to illness, religion, and magic as indivisible, and a cure must be brought about by

Table 10.2 Foster's Two Principal Interpretations of the Causes of Illness

	Personalistic	Naturalistic
Causation	Active (supernatural) agents	Natural forces; equilibrium loss
Illness and misfortune	An illness is a special case of misfortune that can be named from a "typology" of misfortunes	Illnesses are unrelated to misfortune, although it is unfortunate that a person is ill
Religion, magic	Ultimately tied to illness	Largely unrelated to illness
Causality	Multiple levels (e.g., a supernatural being *and* the magic this being uses)	Single level (e.g., a biological imbalance)
Prevention	Positive action (e.g., perform rituals to keep supernatural beings content)	Avoidance (i.e., avoid encountering forces that cause illnesses)
Responsibility	Beyond patient's control	Resides with patient

Source: Based on Foster 1976: 781.

an individual with access to the supernatural. The sick are victims, and death is frequently defined as unnatural. In the naturalistic interpretation, disease comes from *natural forces* or *conditions in nature*, and a cure can thus be found in nature. Foster observes that the naturalistic form was found in many prominent cultures of the past, such as in ancient Chinese civilizations. Foster's distinction between the personalistic and the naturalistic echoes Young's distinction between internalizing and externalizing systems discussed above.

Similar systems of interpretation exist in contemporary societies as well. In mainstream Canada, medical conditions are generally interpreted through the paradigms of biomedicine, which tends to focus on the *biological causes* of medical conditions, with a single classification covering a wide array of symptoms (Table 10.3). Increasingly, first as a consequence of colonization and subsequently as a result of globalization, these interpretations are being accepted as definitions of illness and disease in cultures that did not traditionally assume biomedical approaches. Yet traditional definitions still hold sway in many areas of the world (e.g., in Sri Lanka; see Table 10.4), particularly in places where patients are cared for by traditional healers. In more traditional systems of classification, the focus tends to be on the *effect* a disease has on the person who is suffering.

Of course, cultural interpretations of disease and illness change over time. With respect to the biomedical approach, evidence of such change can be found in the evolution of the words used to describe certain medical conditions. For example, in English, what was once called *apoplexy* (with connotations of being overwhelmed by a powerful state) is today called *stroke* (suggesting a physical assault from a tangible source). As historian Barbara Duden (1991) suggests, understandings of disease and illness are tied to the social reality at a particular period in time.

Under European colonialism, many Indigenous peoples developed new categories to describe disease as new bacteria and viruses invaded their world. For example, the Anishinaabe (Ojibwe) of Canada continue to divide diseases into two types:

1.   "White man's sickness"
2.   "Anishinaabe sickness"

Table 10.3 **Biomedical Systems of Disease Classification**

Broad Term	Description
Allergy	Abnormality of immune mechanisms that normally act to protect the body against foreign proteins
Developmental or congenital disease	Malfunction of an organ or system resulting from an abnormal environment within the uterus during fetal development
Functional defect	Disease for which there is no obvious anatomical explanation (e.g., a disease brought on by stress)
Genetic disease	Malfunction of an organ or system resulting from a mutation of a gene, inheritance of a harmful gene, or an alteration in the number or arrangement of chromosomes
Infection	Disease produced by viruses, prions, bacteria, or other invasive biological entities; arbitrarily distinguished from infestation with parasitic insects
Metabolic disease	Disease due to faulty biochemical processes involved with converting food to energy on a cellular level
Neoplasm	"New growth," including benign tumours and malignancies (cancers)
Psychiatric disease	Mental illness, including psychosis (a severe mental and emotional disorder, probably caused by a biochemical imbalance), neurosis (a moderate emotional disorder involving obsessive-compulsive behaviours, probably caused by learned behaviours in combination with biochemical factors), and addiction (a dependence on substances or behaviours that alter moods)
Thrombosis	Blood clot that forms in a blood vessel and blocks the flow of blood to an organ
Trauma	Injury produced by mechanical stress (e.g., fracture), a physical agent (e.g., frostbite), or a chemical agent (e.g., burn from a strong acid)

Source: Adapted from McElroy and Townsend 1996: 46.

Table 10.4 An Example of a Traditional Ethnomedical System of Disease Classification (from Sri Lanka)

Specific Demon (Sanniya)	Literal Translation	Associated Conditions
Amukku	Vomiting bouts	Vomiting and stomach diseases
Abutha	Non-spirit related	Non–spirit-related insanity
Butha	Spirit related	Spirit-related insanity
Bihiri	Deaf	Deafness
Deva	Divine	Epidemic diseases
Gedi	Lumps	Boils and skin diseases
Gini Jala	Great fire or flame	Malaria and high fevers
Golu	Dumb	Dumbness
Gulma	Worms	Parasitic worms and stomach diseases
Jala	Water or diarrhea	Cholera and chills
Kana	Blind	Blindness
Kora	Lame	Lameness and paralysis
Maru	Death	Delirium and death
Naga	Snake	Bad dreams about snakes
Pissu	Insanity	Temporary insanity
Pith	Bilious	Bilious diseases
Slesma	Phlegm	Phlegm and epilepsy
Vatha	Wind humour or rheumatic	Flatulence and rheumatism

Source: Bailey and de Silva 2006: 1327. Reproduced with permission from BMJ Publishing Group Ltd.

In the first category, they place the diseases of the colonial and neocolonial reality, which first included smallpox, measles, chickenpox, and tuberculosis (TB); now it also includes high blood pressure, diabetes, cancer, and acquired immune deficiency syndrome (AIDS). The Anishinaabe believe that these diseases are best treated by biomedical personnel and techniques. In the second category are illnesses that are caused by human action or are the result of the rules that govern relationships between people being broken (Garro 2004: 910–11). For these conditions, sufferers look to external "other-than-human persons" for help (Garro 2004: 910–11).

The boundaries between different cultural interpretations of disease and illness can become blurred in practical situations. For example, Jeffrey Ehrenreich (1996) describes the sickness and eventual treatment of an Awá woman named Rosa in Ecuador. Both Rosa and her husband, Ishmael, believed she was dying from a disease caused by the malice of a *brujo* ("witch"). Ishmael had insulted a specific man in their community, and he now believed that this man was a *brujo* who had brought

revenge illness on Rosa for Ishmael's social mistake. Initially, Rosa underwent traditional treatment in the form of shamanic curing ceremonies. When traditional approaches failed, Ishmael carried Rosa on his back for five days to reach the post at which Ehrenreich and his fellow researcher Judith Kempf were working. From a biomedical perspective, Rosa's symptoms suggested a parasitic worm infestation and resulting starvation. Biomedical approaches were unsuccessful at first, possibly because Rosa vomited up both the food and the medication she consumed. But this changed when the anthropologists adopted shamanistic methodology in addition to biomedical treatment regimes. A combination of Hebrew prayers, chicken soup, and anti-parasitic medication resulted in Rosa's becoming well again (1996: 137–9). Thus, while each culturally defined interpretation of Rosa's condition led to a different treatment, it was a combination of the two that cured Rosa, made possible by the anthropologists' openness to traditional knowledge.

Historically, conflicting cultural interpretations of an illness and its appropriate treatment have not always been reconciled so harmoniously. Consider the historical debate surrounding the **folk illness** or condition that the biomedical approach and some anthropologists once referred to as Wendigo-psychosis (Figure 10.3). In Algonquian culture, the Wendigo (*witiko*) is a malevolent cannibalistic spirit that can influence human action. The Algonquians also believe that, under certain conditions, a human can transform into such a being. When this occurs, the group recognizes that the afflicted individual is in need of treatment. The purpose of treatment is not only to alleviate the suffering of the individual but also, and more importantly, to protect the group as a whole. Traditionally, a shaman must treat the condition by defeating the Wendigo; and the only way to do so is to kill the afflicted individual. From a biomedical perspective, defeating the Wendigo might be viewed as a form of euthanasia.

In the nineteenth and early twentieth centuries, non-Indigenous authorities began hearing stories of the Wendigo condition and its treatment. According to the interpretation of those authorities, the afflicted were suffering from a form of psychosis (McGee 1972), the proper treatment of which could be found in a mental institution. They believed that the traditional treatment was a form of murder. Thus, in 1907, Jack Fiddler, an Anishinini (Severn) chief and powerful shaman known for defeating the Wendigo, was prosecuted for murder in a Canadian court. He was found guilty but later pardoned when the cultural context was considered.

More recently, scholars have recognized that it may not be possible to fully understand the Wendigo condition from a biomedical perspective (see Carlson 2009). At the very least, an understanding of the condition requires those coming from a biomedical perspective to overcome their own cultural biases of interpretation. Nadia Ferrara and Guy Lanoue (2004) suggest that rather than being a dangerous illness characterized by the *actual* consumption of human flesh, the Wendigo condition is in fact a culturally specific *concept* that helps members of the culture overcome certain fears and resolve internal psychological conflicts. Anthropologist Lou Marano also sees the Wendigo condition as more of a conceptual tool than an actual illness. In his view,

> the crucial question is not what causes a person to become a cannibalistic maniac, but under what circumstances a Northern Algonkian is *likely to be accused* of having become a cannibalistic maniac and thus

folk illness A culture-bound illness; a set of symptoms that are grouped together under a single label only within a particular culture.

Figure 10.3 Swift Runner, a Cree man from Alberta, killed and ate his family during a cold winter in 1878. He said that he was suffering from the influence of the Wendigo at the time of the murders. He later confessed, was remorseful, and was executed at Fort Saskatchewan.

> run the risk of being executed as such. It is argued that those so executed were victims of triage homicide or witch hunts, events common in societies under stress. (Marano 1982: 385)

Essentially, Marano believes that the interpretation of the Wendigo condition as a psychosis is simply an "artifact of research" conducted from a biased biomedical perspective.

As these examples suggest, anthropologists can look to a culture's interpretation of illness to find deeper insight into how members of that culture collectively interpret their world and their place in that world. As Sam Migliore (2001) notes in his examination of illness narratives surrounding a condition called "nerves" among Sicilian Canadians, "such narratives are an important means by which people, often in collaboration with one another, give meaning to various life experiences" (100). Migliore further notes that, when looking for meaning in cultural interpretations of illness, anthropologists need to

- address ambiguity, vagueness, and variability as central concerns in the anthropological quest for understanding;
- focus on how people use folk concepts, as well as discourse in general, in their everyday thoughts and actions;
- recognize that our definitions and explanations do not capture the essence of a particular folk concept but, rather, give us an insight into some of the more common or popular uses of that concept within a given group; and
- examine the decision-making processes that lead people to use or generate certain meanings rather than others (2001: 119).

An important part of this process of investigation is looking at the labels that people use to describe their experiences, as well as the meaning attached to those labels (e.g., see Table 10.4).

Medical Labels as Signifiers

Biomedical labels, like all labels, are mutually agreed-upon signifiers. They denote clusters of symptoms that biomedical professionals understand to be related to one another. As such, they facilitate medical research. For example, without labels, epidemiologists would not be able to track the spread of

a specific disease. In all cultures, medical labels help people identify and interpret illness.

Nonetheless, medical labels can be constricting on the personal level. From the perspective of the person who is unwell, the labels often reflect a position of dependence or marginalization. An afflicted individual might be defined as "the sick family member," "the supplicant," "the patient," or even "the client." Each label suggests a perceived role. More specific medical labels often carry a stigma associated with suffering, contagion, or death. As such, they can lead to stereotyping, separation, status loss, and discrimination of persons and populations who are thus labelled (Link and Phelan 2001). Consider the longstanding cross-cultural response to the term *leprosy* (Figure 10.4). For thousands of years, the name of this disease has triggered feelings of fear, not only because of the nature of the disease itself but also because of the historical treatment, which consisted of segregating individuals afflicted with the disease into "leper colonies" for the benefit of the wider population. Thus, to be labelled "a leper" was to be cast as a marginalized figure, someone to be feared as an outsider. Even after the discovery of effective treatments of leprosy in the early twentieth century, the disease still carries a social stigma. Today, leprosy is often referred to by its alternative name, "Hansen's disease" (named so after the doctor who first identified the bacterium responsible for the disease), to evoke fewer negative associations.

In a study at McMaster University in Hamilton, Ontario, researchers have shown that the label used to name a disease influences the perceived seriousness of a specific set of symptoms. They investigated synonymous terms, such as *erectile dysfunction disorder* and *impotence,* and found that participants who were presented with a newer medicalized term perceived the condition to be more severe. The researchers came to the following conclusion: "A simple switch in terminology can result in a real bias in perception" (Young et al. 2008). Such findings also suggest that simple, non-medicalized terms might be best for communicating medical information to the general public.

The act of labelling can itself have significant social outcomes for individuals and communities. Anthropologist Sarah E. Castle (1994) illustrates this in her discussion of two folk illnesses that result in the death of children in a rural village in Mali. Local peoples refer to these illnesses as *foondu* ("the bird") and *heendu* ("the wind"), and they understand both to be caused by supernatural forces and

Figure 10.4 A couple helps a man with leprosy in Chiang Rai, Thailand. Leprosy has always carried a stigma, even after effective treatments were developed. How should anthropologists approach medical labels that carry stigma?

to be "untreatable, particularly with modern medicine." As Castle observes,

> Foondu and heendu are rarely seen in living children but are frequently discussed in relation to child death. In a survey of mothers of children who had died before the age of five years . . . about half the deaths were attributed to these two illnesses. These folk illnesses act as explanatory mechanisms in this high mortality area. (314)

Labelling an illness as either *foondu or heendu* clears the child's caretakers from any fault (e.g., lack of care or effort to bring about a cure), as the label could not have been applied while the child was still alive. Here the psychotherapeutic value of the folk illness emerges: it can offer a deflection of failure (e.g., failure to keep the child alive) from the self to other sources. Additionally, when the child is ill, family members are not resigned to the death of the child as inevitable; they have hope for a positive outcome. Such hope would be destroyed if the fatal disease were labelled before death. Finally, because the post-mortem diagnoses are conferred by senior women in a patrilineage, they also reinforce hierarchical power relationships among women while encouraging "social support from affines for the woman whose child has died" (Castle 1994: 314).

Environments and Well-Being

Researchers in many disciplines are becoming increasingly aware of the impact of physical, social, and cultural environments on human well-being. Using the integrative approach that is characteristic of their discipline, medical anthropologists examine not only the influence of environments on human health but also the many human factors that shape those environments, including political, economic, social, and cultural factors. Consider the landscapes that arise with the disposal of unwanted electronic goods. Such "dead" gear does not simply disappear. Rather, it is transported to less affluent nations where it sits in vast wastelands—digital dumps of frightening contamination. These dumps are mined by the poor for recyclable resources. Case in point: the Agbogbloshie dump in Accra, Ghana (Figure 10.5). Here the electronic waste of wealthier nations is burned for the retrieval of materials such

© Andrew McConnell/Alamy Stock Photo

Figure 10.5 Agbogbloshie dump in Accra, the capital city of Ghana, is a vast wasteland of unwanted electronic equipment. What kinds of impacts might your own usage of electronics have on environments close to home and those farther away?

as copper, brass, aluminum, and zinc; in the process, the surrounding soil and water are contaminated with lead, cadmium, antimony, PCBs (polychlorinated biphenyl), beryllium, mercury, and chlorinated dioxins. Many of the scavengers of this lethal waste are boys, who labour to send money home to their impoverished families in northern Ghana. Thus are created the contentious borderlands of wellness and illness.

Integrated Worlds of the Biotic, the Abiotic, and the Cultural

The environments in which human beings live are made up of **biotic**, **abiotic**, and cultural components (Figure 10.6). Within these environments, all components are interlinked in complex, often invisible ways. Tinkering with one part could risk disrupting the entire system.

Ecologically, humans are tied to their surroundings. From a *medical-ecological* perspective, then, good health often results from living in an environment that is capable of supporting human life in all of its social, psychological, and physical needs. Conversely, bad health, including disease and illness, is often the consequence of a disruption in the life-sustaining balance of the environment. A wide variety of environmental factors can have consequences for human health, with components of the most immediate surroundings having

biotic Living; biological.

abiotic Non-living; physical.

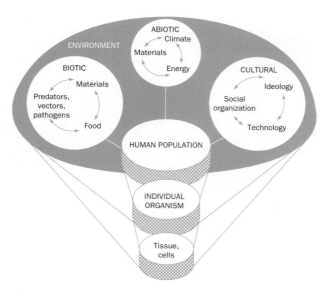

Figure 10.6 Human wellness and illness are affected by three interacting environments: the biotic (biological), the abiotic (physical), and the cultural.

Source: McElroy and Townsend 1996:25.

realized niche The portion of the habitable world that a group of people is forced to utilize and to which it becomes highly adapted.

the greatest impact on a population. In terms of physical location, a population's immediate environment is its **realized niche**.

In many cases, realized niches face pressure from large-scale political, economic, and social processes. Certainly, these processes featured in the poisoning of the Wabigoon River and the surrounding area in northwestern Ontario. Over the

course of the 1960s and early 1970s, Reed International's pulp and paper plant in Dryden, Ontario, released a dangerous amount of mercury into the Wabigoon River. The mercury was a by-product of chemical processing in the plant, and the river seemed to be the most convenient and economical place to dispose of the excess waste. In doing so, the plant's operators were not in violation of any legal restrictions. Before long, the links between the contaminated natural environment and human health became apparent. The Grassy Narrows First Nation peoples (see EthnoProfile 10.1), who relied on the Wabigoon River for their water, food (fish), and livelihood (fisheries), began showing signs of extensive mercury poisoning, including serious neurological symptoms. The community went from wellness to severe illness in less than a decade. Yet both the Canadian and Ontario governments as well as the operators of the plant ignored or downplayed the evidence for decades. Eventually, the government did step in by restricting chemical dumping. However, this was not in time to save the Grassy Narrows commercial fishery, as this too had to be closed to prevent the distribution of contaminated fish to the wider population. With the closing of the fishery, the community's problems were compounded as it went from 95 per cent employment to 95 per cent unemployment. The ramifications of this poisoning continue today, almost 60 years after the mercury began to move up the food chain.

EthnoProfile 10.1
Grassy Narrows First Nation (Asubpeeschoseewagong Netum Anishinabek)

Region: North America

Nation: Canada; the Anishinaabe Nation

Language: Traditionally Anishinaabe (Ojibwe); today, also English

Population: 1,000 (700 living on the reserve) (2014; approximate numbers)

Environment: Boreal forest, threatened by deforestation

Livelihood: Pre-contact, hunting, gathering, and trapping; today, various jobs, inside and outside the community

Political organization: Elected tribal council operating within a modern nation-state

For more information: "Grassy Narrows First Nation: Protecting Traditional Lands," www.turtleisland.org/news/news-grassy.htm; "Grassy Narrows: The Right to a Healthy Environment," www.amnesty.ca/our-work/issues/indigenous-peoples/grassy-narrows

Around 2015 more complete public discussions of this ongoing problem started to take place, with hope emerging that there would finally be an appropriate governmental response. Simon Fobister, chief of the Grassy Narrows First Nation, wrote twice to the federal government in 2016 but received no response. Fobister stated that the government was "passing the buck" when the federal government claimed, in February 2017, that cleaning up the mercury contamination was a provincial matter (Kirkup 2017). Others also voiced criticism regarding the federal government's lack of a clear commitment to cleaning up the river. Richard Pearshouse, a senior researcher with Human Rights Watch in Geneva stated, "Ottawa has an obligation under international law to respect, protect and fulfill the human rights at issue in Grassy Narrows," (quoted in Kirkup 2017). Also in 2017, the government of Ontario finally responded with a "comprehensive remediation action plan" for a clean-up and significant support for the affected people, including a promise of $85 million to ameliorate the "gross neglect" of the people and their environment (Bruser et al. 2017). Subsequently, the Canadian government announced they would build a treatment facility for Grassy Narrows. Fobister states, "The community believes the price tag for the centre will be around $4.5 million, but a feasibility study needs to be completed to determine the cost" (quoted in Kirkup and Jones, 2017). It is cases such as these where anthropologists can offer support and become active in the community to help prevent contamination to the environment, promote solutions to problems lingering from the past, and insist on the essential human right to clean air, water, and food.

For those whose diets contain a considerable amount of "country foods"—traditional foods, such as wild game and fish taken from the natural environment—**bioaccumulation** and **biomagnification** are growing concerns (Figure 10.7). When uncontaminated, a traditional, protein-rich country food diet is considerably healthier than a diet high in carbohydrates. Yet today, such traditional diets are not only high in protein and other nutrients but also high in toxic substances. Considering the pervasiveness of environmental toxins, and considering that most contaminated food looks no different from uncontaminated food, it has become nearly impossible for Indigenous peoples to maintain traditional diets without suffering severe consequences to their health. Here medical anthropologists recognize that emerging health problems can be identified and responded to only through the reconciliation of traditional knowledge and biomedical knowledge,

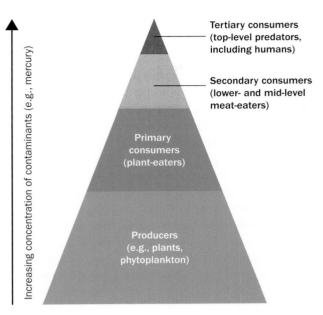

Figure 10.7 Through the process of biomagnification, a toxic substance, such as mercury, becomes more concentrated as it moves up the food chain. The result is that organisms at the top of the food chain—including human beings—have relatively high levels of the substance in their bodies. As concentrations increase, the substance becomes more and more likely to have a negative impact on the health of the organisms.

although this reconciliation has not been straightforward or in any way simple.

In nearly every case of severe contamination, the toxins come from sources beyond the affected community. Nowhere is this more distinctly the case than in the Arctic. As Indigenous and Northern Affairs Canada (INAC) (previously Aboriginal Affairs and Northern Development Canada [AANDC]) notes,

> Many sites in the North have been contaminated due to private sector mining, oil and gas, and government military activities that occurred before their environmental impact was fully understood. In addition, studies in the early 1990s found that a number of pollutants originating from sources outside the Arctic or in some cases outside Canada were reaching unexpectedly high levels in the Arctic ecosystem. (AANDC 2012)

INAC has created two programs to assist the peoples of Canada's Arctic: the Northern Contaminated Sites Program (NCSP), which "focusses on the cleanup and remediation of a number of contaminated sites in the North," and the Northern Contaminants Program (NCP), which "addresses human

bioaccumulation An accumulation of a toxic substance in a biological organism over time.

biomagnification An increase in the concentration of a toxic substance from the bottom to the top of a food chain.

exposure to contaminants in wildlife species that are important to the traditional diets of Northern Aboriginal peoples" (AANDC 2012). Of course, the success of these programs depends on the merger of tradition and science in open cross-cultural discourse.

Large-scale programs such as the NCSP and the NCP are often created in response to the findings of studies conducted by academic researchers. One such anthropological study is Sylvie Poirier and Lorraine Brooke's 2000 examination of perceptions of ecological contaminants among the Salluit, one of 16 Inuit communities in Nunavik (northern Quebec). In many ways, the traditional Inuit view of the environment is consistent with the anthropological interpretation of the environment as composed of integrated biotic, abiotic, and cultural elements:

> In Inuit ontology, the environment is seen as complex systems of interacting agencies (and variables) and they [the Inuit] appreciate well that interface with one part of the system has implications for the other part. . . As hunters they view and experience their relationship with the environment and the animal world in a particularly intimate, communicative, and reciprocal manner. Human beings, animals, and the environment are all perceived as sharing partners; their modes of becoming are intrinsically linked. . . . [E]very animal [is thought of as] a sentient being or other-than-human person . . . not simply as a representative of another wildlife species that needs to be monitored or managed. (Poirier and Brooke 2000: 81, 86)

With increasing media access in the North, the Inuit have developed an understanding of pollutants. Yet, trusting their traditional knowledge and their world view, many, at the time of this study, remained convinced of their own ability to perceive and avoid dangerously sick animals and therefore guard their own health. They had not developed a confidence in the southern biologists and their warnings of contaminants in the meat (86). Thus, Poirier and Brooke highlight the need for cross-cultural discourse. They note a distinction between **defensive research**, which is based on the interests and methodologies of southerners, and **positive research**, which gives the Inuit the chance to have input in the research process. Poirier and Brooke conclude that taking a "positive" approach would "give northern perceptions of southern people a much wider scope

and fuller understanding" and would not decrease the quality of the research (89).

Nutritional Health

A healthy diet must be based on food that is not only free from harmful contaminants but also full of nutrients. The human body requires a regular, balanced supply of carbohydrates, proteins, fats, minerals, and vitamins in order to function properly and maintain a strong immune system. Thus, nutritional health is the basis of good health.

Worldwide, the availability of sufficient amounts of nutritious food has been a growing concern for more than a century. While conducting fieldwork in Botswana in the late 1970s, Roberta Robin Dods noted that most local children had enough calories in their diet but not enough nutrition. In particular, the children were not getting enough vitamins, minerals, protein, and certain essential amino acids. Their diet was restricted to what was available, and the staple food was mielie-meal, a coarse flour ground from maize. Those who could afford to do so would add small pieces of vegetables and sometimes meat to the main mielie-meal dish. Without these additions, the diet was too heavily composed of carbohydrates, which provide energy by converting to blood sugar but do not build bones and tissue. Dods noted that a simple way to enhance this diet would be to add legumes, such as beans, which are a good source of protein and essential amino acids. Today, medical and nutritional anthropologists continue to investigate conditions that lead to inadequate nutrition; in many cases, their work is useful to doctors and health-care practitioners who work to inform local populations about the importance of good nutrition (Figure 10.8).

Anthropologists who study nutritional health tend to have very broad research interests, and their findings often contribute to national and international policies on health and nutrition, food safety and inspection, and world hunger (Mintz and Du Bois 2002: 111). In one notable study, Penny Van Esterik (2002) investigated food-safety regulations and the contamination of foods for infants, looking at both breast milk and commercially available baby formulas. Other researchers have addressed issues related to child growth and development in association with nutrition, activity, and health (Dufour 1997). The expanding interest in the role of nutrition in a population's health has led to the development of a new subdiscipline in medical

defensive research
Research that is designed and conducted by individuals outside the affected community without consulting members of the community about their interests or concerns.

positive research
Research that is designed with fair consideration of the interests and concerns of members of the affected community and conducted with consideration of cultural contexts within the community.

anthropology: nutritional anthropology. (Refer back to Chapter 8 for more on the anthropology of food and nutrition.)

The integrated, culturally aware approach characteristic of medical anthropology can also inform non-anthropologists attempting to improve nutritional health around the globe. A recent example comes from the research of Chris Charles, a graduate student at the University of Guelph (see Brown 2011). While conducting fieldwork in a small village in Cambodia, Charles became fixated on solving a problem: how to help locals to incorporate iron into their diets. A significant proportion of the local population, especially women and children, were suffering from iron deficiency anemia, a debilitating and potentially life-threatening condition. However, they could not afford to eat meat (a source of iron) or buy iron pills on a regular basis. Charles's first solution was to suggest that the local women place a piece of iron in their cooking pots, which would transfer the much-needed nutrient to the food during the cooking process. The problem was that the women did not want to place an unappealing lump of metal in with their food. After investigating the local culture, Charles arrived at the innovative solution of providing pieces of iron shaped like a fish that the locals considered to be a symbol of good luck. The resulting product, which was branded as the Lucky Iron Fish (Figure 10.9), is an example of the breakthroughs that are possible when cultural contexts are taken into account.

Structural Violence and Social Trauma

Physical, social, and cultural environments are also influenced by political and economic forces that negatively impact human well-being. You may recall that in Chapter 6 we noted that individual subjectivity and identity are heavily influenced by the processes of socialization and enculturation. But social and cultural expectations are sometimes overturned by experiences that intrude on predictable daily routines, and these experiences, too, will shape individuals' subjectivities. Among the most powerfully intrusive experiences that can have severe health consequences are those occasioned by violence and trauma. **Structural violence** is violence that results from the way that political and economic forces structure risk for various forms of suffering within a population. Paul Farmer is a physician and medical anthropologist who has worked in Haiti since 1983 (see Map 10.1; Figure 10.10). In his position, he has

Figure 10.8 A health-care worker in Rwinkwavu, Rwanda, teaches children and adults about nutrition. Aside from lack of knowledge about nutrition, what are some factors that might prevent people from eating a well-balanced diet?

witnessed extreme forms of human suffering that are a part of everyday life for those at the bottom of Haitian society. Much of this suffering is in the form of infectious and parasitic disease, but it can also include other forms of extreme suffering, such as hunger, torture, and rape (Farmer 2002 [1996]: 424). In Haiti, the operations of structural violence create spaces in which the poorest and least powerful members of society are subjected to

structural violence
Violence that results from the way that political and economic forces structure risk for various forms of suffering within a population.

Figure 10.9 The Lucky Iron Fish is part of a relatively simple health initiative to supplement iron-deficient diets in Cambodia. What have the creators of this initiative done to tailor it to the culture whose people they are trying to help?

Map 10.1 Haiti

highly intensified risks of all kinds, increasing the likelihood that sooner or later they will experience one or more varieties of social suffering. The structural aspect of this violence is important to emphasize since the attention of most Western outside observers, even those who want to alleviate suffering, is often trained on individuals and their personal experiences, with the resulting temptation to blame the victims for their own distress.

Anthropologists are interested in identifying the cause and effects of large-scale, collective violence. Incidents of warfare, genocide, ethnic cleansing, gang rape, and other such forms of mass violence have been recognizable features of the twentieth century, leading to widespread death, the disruption

Figure 10.10 Dr Paul Farmer treats a patient at Clinique Bon Sauveur in Haiti. Why is it important for anthropologists and others to investigate the structural aspects of violence and suffering in less affluent areas of the world?

of social institutions, the destruction of economic and political arrangements, and the displacement of surviving populations into unfamiliar and often hostile new settings. Anthropologist Robert M. Hayden (2000), who investigates occurrences of mass rape in times of ethnic or nationalist conflicts, argues that mass rape is likely when the state itself is in a transitional or unsettled condition, with both its territory and its governance uncertain. However, when the state is not itself threatened, there is some evidence that rape is avoided, even when murder is accepted. In approaching such topics, some have chosen to speak in terms of **social trauma**: "events in life generated by forces and agents external to the person and largely external to his or her control and . . . generated in the setting of armed conflict and war" (Apfel and Simon 2000: 103). Psychoanalysts Roberta Apfel and Bennett Simon distinguish social traumas, such as "separation and loss, imprisonment and exile, threats of annihilation, even death and mutilation," from the less devastating "ordinary traumas" or "necessary losses" that all people are likely to face, such as natural death, divorce, illness, or accidents (103).

Anthropologists investigating large-scale trauma regularly work together with other specialists because such phenomena are so complex. The causes of large-scale collective violence involve psychic, social, political, economic, and cultural factors, and this sort of violence aims to destroy not just individual psychological functioning but also the physical body and the body politic. Individual and cultural factors together bring about the trauma and are equally implicated in the ways in which survivors come to deal with trauma's aftermath (Suárez-Orozco and Robben 2000: 1).

Anthropologists Marcelo Suárez-Orozco and Antonius Robben note that societies as well as individuals need to heal. In both cases, successful healing requires the re-establishment of "basic trust": individuals need to find ways to trust other individuals, and all survivors need to be able to find ways to develop trust in the institutions of their society. Some dimensions of healing can be successfully promoted by the efforts of psychiatrists and medical specialists who focus on individuals; for example, interpreting the suffering of veterans in medical terms acknowledges that their suffering was not a consequence of their own personal defects but a consequence of the trauma they had experienced in war. At the same time, a continuing focus on individuals diverts attention away from the sociocultural dimensions of such trauma: "Combat trauma shatters the meaningfulness of the self and the world, and makes its sufferers put their bodies and minds on constant alert for any possible attack. They become distrustful of others, their own memories, and visual perceptions" (Suárez-Orozco and Robben 2000: 20). The taken-for-grantedness of everyday social life is destroyed, allowing "the uncanny" to become a recurring and unassimilable feature of their lives. As Yolanda Gampel notes, "what has been hidden becomes visible, what is familiar becomes strange and frightening" (2000: 49–50).

Survivors may exhibit a remarkable resiliency, "the capacity to survive violence and loss, and moreover, to have flexibility of response over the course of a life time," including a sense of agency that they also pass on to their children (Apfel and Simon 2000: 103). In still other cases, traumatized persons and groups turn to "hatred and violence as ways of coping with traumatic wounds" (Apfel and Simon 2000: 102). Volkan has described one way in which this can happen, in terms of what he calls a group's *"chosen trauma"* (quoted in Apfel and Simon 2000: 102). A chosen trauma arises, Volkan argues, from experiences of collective violence and loss that survivors are unable to mourn. This can lead to a collective focus on the group's past experiences of victimization, and the entire identity of the group's members may come to centre on the chosen trauma. Moreover, the chosen trauma can be passed on to subsequent generations along with the expectation that it is up to them to right past wrongs, using violence if necessary. Volkan states, "While the group does not consciously choose to feel victimized, it does choose to psychologize losses and to transform them into powerful cultural narratives which become an integral part of the social identity" (23).

The power of chosen traumas derives in large part from the fact that they remain un-mourned, thus cutting off possible forms of social and cultural healing that can rebuild trust in social institutions. Suárez-Orozco and Robben note, for example, that "institutional acknowledgement—in the form of 'truth' commissions and reparations (monetary and symbolic)—and justice—in the form of trials of perpetrators—can begin partially to restore the symbolic order that is another casualty of the work of violence" (2000: 5). These kinds of institutional acknowledgements, most often initiatives taken at the level of the nation-state, may coincide with more local actions (e.g., healing rituals) designed to aid recovery and rebuild social trust (22, 24).

The residential school trauma of Indigenous peoples in Canada is an example of a large-scale social trauma. In December 2015, the Truth and Reconciliation Commission of Canada (TRC) released its final report, which was a culmination of six years of testimonies from more than 7,000 residential school survivors (APTN News 2015). Around 150,000 Indigenous children attended the schools; many were physically and sexually abused and experimented on, and at least 6,000 children died at the schools (APTN News 2015). The summary of the final report opens with the following:

> For over a century, the central goals of Canada's Aboriginal policy were to eliminate Aboriginal governments; ignore Aboriginal rights; terminate the Treaties; and, through a process of assimilation, cause Aboriginal peoples to cease to exist as distinct legal, social, cultural, religious, and racial entities in Canada. The establishment and operation of residential schools were a central element of this policy, which can best be described as "cultural genocide." (TRC 2015: 1)

Too many Canadians, the report also notes, know little about this history, which influences policy and perceptions in the public realm (8). The final report further notes that the relationship between the federal government and Indigenous peoples is deteriorating and that conflicts over Indigenous education, child welfare, and justice are barriers to reconciliation (TRC 2015: 8). Today, the Canadian federal government is moving to various forms of reconciliation, including talks about settlement for the "Sixties Scoop," a period beginning in 1965 when Indigenous children were forcibly removed from their homes and put in foster care or placed for adoption in non-Indigenous homes. While some are hopeful that these recent moves toward reconciliation will bring action on the issues that many Indigenous communities currently face, others caution that the way these attempts at reconciliation are being handled leave much to be desired (see "In Their Own Words" box that follows), and others note that Canada still has a long way to go.

All of these examples reveal how very much the personal is political. Everything from gendered

In Their Own Words

Responding to Canada's Truth and Reconciliation Commission Report

Métis artist David Garneau responds to the final report of Canada's Truth and Reconciliation Commission that was released in December 2015.

The final report of Canada's Truth and Reconciliation Commission begins: "For over a century, the central goals of Canada's Aboriginal policy were to eliminate Aboriginal governments; ignore Aboriginal rights; terminate the Treaties; and, through a process of assimilation, cause Aboriginal peoples to cease to exist as distinct legal, social, cultural, religious, and racial entities in Canada." The rest is footnotes—sober, thorough, harrowing, insightful and moving descriptions of the mechanisms and effects of the slow, relentless genocide machine. It is essential reading. However, it is written in the past tense, written as indigenous assimilation and dispossession—of which Indian Residential Schools were just one element—are confined to history. The Report's sense of future is constrained by conclusions that precede its research: that settlers want to re-form their fundamental relationships with Indigenous people; that truth-telling will result in reconciliation; that First Nations, Inuit and Metis people identify themselves as citizens of Canada.

Without a doubt, many Indigenous people believe that "sharing their truth" has been a good thing. But many more are suffering from having themselves, or their relations, rip open these wounds in public. "Canada's Truth and Reconciliation" has benefitted the state and non-Indigenous people more than it will ever improve the lives of the First Nations, Inuit and Metis. The purpose of state-designed Reconciliation is to settle settlers, to reconcile non-Indigenous Canadians with their heinous past and to distract from their heinous present, to have settlers feel at home on stolen lands. Canada's Truth and Reconciliation project considers individual Indigenous truths and some past shared truths but not how all function in a colonial enterprise that exceeds the Indian Residential Schools and includes the present. It assumes that reconciliation is the answer to the "Indian problem;" that First Nations, Inuit and Metis peoples enjoyed a prior universal conciliation, and now just need re-conciliation. Canada is what happened to Indigenous people. Canada is the name of colonization in these territories. Reconciliation is colonialism rebranded.

While I do hope that the facts and stories condensed in the TRC Report will be foundational to recasting Indigenous-settler relations, the ideology that shapes it is counter-productive to sovereign Indigenous resurgence. The Report's concentration on Indian Residential Schools, on Indigenous pain and degradation and on reconciliation as the basis for change is incomplete and less productive (for Indigenous peoples) than is a focus on the larger mechanics of colonialism, its resistance and on the varieties of creative Indigenous resurgence.

---

violence, such as rape or honour killings, to child slavery to forced relocation due to persecution, war, or violence starts with the individual but comes to be recognized through the group. Sociologist Srila Roy (2008) would call violence that happens on the personal level "ordinary" or "everyday" violence, as opposed to the "extraordinary" violence of political terror that happens on a much broader and more public scale. Everyday violence is often widely accepted within a specific community due to cultural allowances—allowances that tend to normalize the brutalization of certain individuals on the basis of who holds the power to do so. Unfortunately, there is often little recourse as the people who are in a position to help the victims, including police, lawmakers, or elders, can tend to support the cultural values and/or the more powerful individuals

responsible for perpetuating the violence (see, e.g., Zuckerhut 2011).

Health-Care Delivery Systems

Health-care systems take a variety of forms, based in the specifics of social and physical realities (Figure 10.11). "Clinical realities"—those realities that are tied to a health-care system—vary considerably, based on factors such as the following:

- The patient's demographic factors (e.g., ethnicity, race, age, sex, gender, class)
- The patient's perceived situation in time (e.g., attitudes on age and life-cycle stages)

As a Metis artist and curator, I am heartened by the Report's inclusion of art, but dismayed by its limited vision. Art is primarily imagined in this text as serving memorial, testimonial, and therapeutic functions: "Commemorations and memorials . . . are visible reminders of Canada's shame and church complicity. They bear witness to the suffering and loss that generations of Aboriginal peoples have endured and overcome" "Sharing intercultural dialogue about history, responsibility, and transformation through the arts is potentially healing and transformative for both Aboriginal and non-Aboriginal peoples."

While there is a nod to the possibility of art as resistance, no examples are given and the concept is not developed beyond statements such as "These various projects indicate that the arts and artistic practices may serve to shape public memory in ways that are potentially transformative for individuals, communities, and national history."

The report is cautious; its authors refer to the "potential" for healing and transformation but do not make stronger claims they cannot substantiate. Art does heal and transform, but it can also embarrass and traumatize. Monuments can function as containers of disturbing narratives rather than open dialogue. Exhibitions, plays, operas, films and other public art can make a spectacle of Indigenous pain and rarely provide after-care or remediation for the troubles they stir up. But most importantly, the TRC Report's aesthetic imaginary is restricted to personal therapy and Canadian nationalism. It does not include the healing possibilities of literal Indigenous sovereignty. Its denouement

wish finds First Nations, Inuit and Metis people reconciling themselves to their fate within Canada as its citizens brought to heel.

We should, of course, provide therapeutic art opportunities and produce monuments; however, these services and things must arise from and serve the needs of Indigenous peoples rather than the Canadian state. I am of two minds regarding how we should proceed. Indian Residential School survivors were offered payment for pain on a sliding scale. The scheme was to isolate individuals, compensate them according to capitalist measures rather than engage in conciliation and restitution for whole, wounded communities, including children of survivors. So, on one hand, I wonder if it is wise to engage Indigenous artists to be similarly contracted to speak for whole communities. Perhaps monuments of this sort should be collective cultural works rather than individual artistic expressions. On the other hand, individual artists often create brilliant things that no committee could anticipate, works that do speak with and through community. We, who identify as Indigenous artists (not simply as artists who are also Indigenous), if we are also cultural workers, need to exercise our creative sovereignty, not simply by striving for individual success within the dominant art world, or by working within the Reconciliation (colonial) ideology.

Source: Excerpt from Scott Benesiinaabandan, Cathy Busby, David Garneau, and Krista Belle Stewart. 2016. "Responding to Canada's Truth and Reconciliation Commission Report." *C Magazine*, Issue 128, Winter 2016. Reprinted with permission of David Garneau.

- Cultural constructs (e.g., how open a woman is allowed to be in presenting her symptoms to a male doctor)
- Geopolitical circumstances of place (e.g., rural or urban)
- Concepts of reality (e.g., whether a disease or a symptom is perceived to be real or imagined)
- Social and physical resources available to the afflicted individual or group (e.g., access to medical treatment)
- Depth of interaction with other individuals or groups (e.g., relationships with kin, family, friends, and acquaintances)
- Curative norms, which are often defined by class, sex, and/or age (e.g., biomedical treatments of heart disease are different for men than they are for women)
- Level of institutional complexity (e.g., in complex bureaucratic medical practices, patients may face alienation or problems of access)

Out of these and many other social and cultural threads, the fabric of care is woven. For some it is a warm blanket; for others it is gossamer thin indeed.

While health-care systems take many different *forms* across the globe, medical anthropologist Arthur Kleinman (1980) notes five core clinical *functions* of a health-care system from a cross-cultural perspective:

1. The cultural construction of illness and/or disease as a psychosocial occurrence
2. The evaluation of treatment approaches based on *general* criteria, independent of the individual incidents of illness

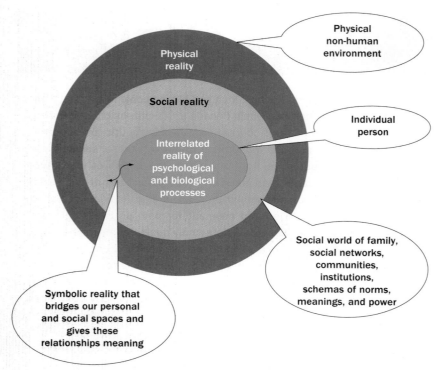

Figure 10.11 "Clinical reality" is constructed based on aspects of physical and social realities—cultural norms, schemas, beliefs, and behaviours, as well as various communication interactions surrounding disease and illness. Central are the practitioner–patient relationships, the therapeutic regimes, and the way outcomes are defined and evaluated.

Source: Adapted from Kleinman 1980: 28.

placebo effect An effect produced in response to an individual's belief that a treatment will have a desired effect, despite evidence that the treatment has no medicinal properties.

3. The management of *specific* illness incidents through communicative operations, such as labelling and explaining
4. The performance of healing activities, including supportive care, healing rituals, psychotherapy, medication, and surgery; and end-of-life palliative care, where healing is not physical but can sustain the human sense of self or "spirit" and offer closure
5. The management of outcomes, from cure, recurrence, chronic illness, and impairment to treatment failure and death (71–2)

Kleinman notes that his list is a summation and that there can be great variation in the emphasis placed on each of the five functions from culture to culture and from group to group (72). This is because, as Kleinman states, "the cultural construction of illness . . . is frequently a personally and socially adaptive response" (72), increasing the likelihood of variation. Despite such variation, Kleinman also stresses that similarities among cultures can be found regarding clinical interest and practice (83).

Variety in Curing Practices

When people are faced with a mild disease, illness, or injury, they may take care of the treatment without the help of a medical practitioner. For example, for a cold they might take over-the-counter medication; for a cut, they might use commercial bandages and antiseptics. They might also resort to home remedies or folk cures recommended by a member of their family or their community. On your grandmother's assurance that "it has always been done that way," you may swallow some vile cough syrup she has concocted or some soothing chicken soup she has prepared with care. Frequently, many Canadians find that these home remedies are effective—if only through the **placebo effect**—and they do not need to venture far beyond their home for a cure. Families can often be the front line, the fortitude, and the foundation of health care regardless of the cultures in which an individual lives.

When people feel that treatment requires more than home remedies, they will seek outside help from someone with advanced knowledge of the condition. If they are part of a culture that relies on traditional knowledge, they might appeal to a medicine woman or man or a shaman (female or male) for assistance (Figure 10.12). To an observer unfamiliar with traditional knowledge, traditional curative measures may seem no more effective than a home remedy; yet traditional cures can be highly effective for reasons not often considered in biomedicine. Marilyn Walker (2003), for example, notes that shamanistic music used in Siberia induces altered states of consciousness, allowing the shaman to access the patient's unconscious. Other cultures use similar ceremonial activities to mediate inner and outer worlds and thus rebalance the patient in these worlds.

At times even trained medical practitioners may not be able to help. For example, if you are bitten by a black mamba (neurotoxic venom) in a remote area, you may not be able to find medical assistance before it is too late. An untreated adult will generally die within an hour, but small children never survive. What can anyone then do? Merely comfort the victim as she or he dies. Similarly hopeless situations may arise after an accident or when a patient is in the final stages of an incurable disease. The only recourse is compassion.

Sometimes—all too often in some places—the treatment that patients seek may depend on their financial resources rather than the severity of the condition. Medical treatment can be very expensive, and the harsh reality is that class and geopolitical disparities affect people's access to and quality of treatment. As McGill University researchers Vinh-Kim Nguyen and Karine Peschard note,

> high levels of socioeconomic inequality correlate with worsened health outcomes across an entire society.... [A]ffliction must be understood as an embodiment of social hierarchy, a form of violence that for modern bodies [individual and group] is increasingly sublimated into differential disease rates and can be measured in terms of morbidity and mortality between social groups. (2003: 447)

The reality of such disparities is clear when examining the various statistics on HIV/AIDS generated by national and pan-national organizations. Consider that in excess of 95 per cent of all new infections of HIV/AIDS occur in countries commonly classified as "developing" and that at least 50 per cent of these infections are in women (WHO 2014a, 2014b). Consider also that the number of childhood cases being reported is increasing, not only among children born to infected mothers but also among children forced to work in the sex trade. Indeed, one may wonder what *development* can mean to communities where so many people are dead or dying

© Images & Stories/Alamy Stock Photo

Figure 10.12 A number of members of the Altai people, who live in Siberia, still practise shamanistic rituals. In what ways might such rituals be effective in treating certain types of illnesses?

of this disease. Socioeconomic disparity is also a significant factor in HIV transmission within more affluent nation-states. In Canada, rates of transmission are highest in Indigenous communities, where many people live in what could be considered "developing" conditions. Data collected by the Public Health Agency of Canada suggest that 34.3 per cent of HIV/AIDS infections occur in Indigenous people, while Indigenous people make up only 4.3 per cent of the Canadian population (PHAC 2013; Statistics Canada 2011) (Figure 10.13).

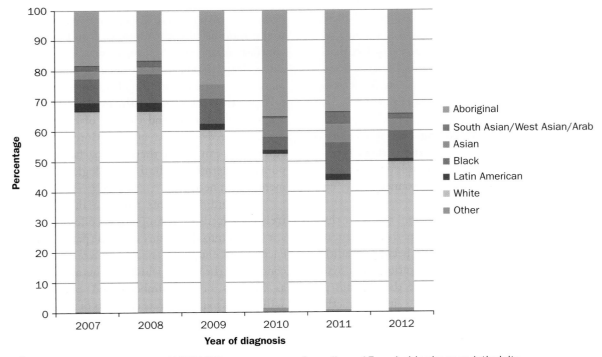

Figure 10.13 Proportion of HIV/AIDS cases among Canadians 15 and older by race/ethnicity.

Patient–Practitioner Interactions

All systems of treatment have a two-step process: (1) diagnosis and (2) treatment. Both are based on effective communication between patients and their health-care providers. To effectively interact with one another, all parties must be able to understand and use the languages of their culture's health and treatment institutions. For the patient, there is a need to develop an intersubjective space where meanings can be negotiated, much as anthropologists do in fieldwork. Not infrequently, negotiations are incomplete, and an unresolved disconnect remains between what are, essentially, two or more cultures: that of the patient and that of at least one of the medical practitioners.

Naming the illness or disease is very important in this process, as it communicates the symptoms, frames the diagnosis, and dictates the range of available treatments. Yet naming can be problematic in some instances, such as when a population considers a disease to be newly introduced from the outside world. Consider how cancer is understood among Indigenous peoples in Australia:

> Many Indigenous languages do not have a word for cancer, making it difficult to conceptualize. This emphasizes the belief that it is a "white man's disease" that only came about after colonization. Whether this is true or whether it was never labelled as cancer until colonization is unknown; however, many signs point to the fact that the change in Indigenous lifestyle from traditional to Westernized has increased the risk of cancer. (Shahid et al. 2010)

All systems begin by naming. Human beings structure and make sense of their world using schema and prototypes. The naming process is universal, but the contents are culture specific. Named is the "condition" and named is the "cure."

While all health-care systems recognize the importance of patient–practitioner communication, considerable differences exist between traditional systems and biomedical institutionalized systems in terms of how they perceive the patient's place in the system. In traditional systems, practitioners form personal relationships with their patients, investing considerable time in getting to know the patient and communicating a sense of concern. Traditional practitioners also situate treatments in an environment that is deeply familiar to the patient—in effect, their home turf. In biomedical systems, on the other hand, where time is money and the volume of patients affects the bottom line, the patient is viewed as a client. Doctors keep their distance from their patients/clients, and they administer treatment only in official medical environments. Of course, biomedical systems have their benefits: the act of "industrialization" affords a wide range of interventions supported by medical institutions, technologies, and highly trained personnel. Nevertheless, institutionalized treatment is removed from the familiar and can be very discomforting and alienating for the patient/client. Feelings of alienation can be particularly intense when the patient/client is crossing cultural and/or class boundaries and moving from traditional systems to industrialized medical systems.

Patient–practitioner relationships also differ between urban and rural locations. In the urban setting, unlike in the rural, the curer may not be a member of the community in which she or he works. Medical anthropologist Irwin Press (1978) has found that most urban curers do not become spokespersons for the communities in which they work and that they seldom know the majority of their patients on a personal level. Thus, it rests with patients to provide the symptoms and suggest the cause of the illness, while it is up to practitioners to provide a diagnosis based on their understanding of the symptoms. Rural curers, in contrast, often take the lead in searching for the cause, drawing on their knowledge of the patient's place within the community. Press also notes that folk practices associated with rural environments are actually flexible and capable of changing to meet the needs of urban clients. More traditional curers also can adjust their approaches to incorporate modern biomedical technologies and treatments when necessary.

By recording patients' narratives on illness and treatment, medical anthropologists offer us important insight into the culture clash the patient experiences when entering a system of care. Of central concern are the ways in which patients are treated—as humans or as numbers—and practitioners' willingness to incorporate elements of the patient's culture into the system of treatment. In such narratives, with embedded critique of treatment, patients are empowered to maintain or regain human identity and a sense of control over their lives.

SEARCH as an Integrative Model

Maintaining or regaining human identity and a sense of control is the objective of the Society for Education, Action, and Research in Community Health (SEARCH), a nongovernmental organization (NGO) established in 1986 by spouses Dr Abhay Bang and Dr Rani Bang in the Gadchiroli district of Maharashtra, India. Two of the NGO's stated goals are promoting the reproductive health of women and improving the health of mothers, infants, and children.

In rural India, infant and maternal mortality rates are very high; according to one statistic, one woman dies every five minutes giving birth to a child there (UNICEF 2004). Yet most of these deaths are preventable. SEARCH has addressed this problem by establishing public-health programs in 39 villages in Maharashtra, each of which combines grassroots fieldwork with sophisticated medical monitoring, research, and advocacy. The result is a community-based health system that combines the best features of folk medicine with appropriate modern medical interventions. At the village level, the system is administered by a literate woman, herself a mother, who is trained to identify problems early and provide basic care. Physicians visit the villages every two weeks to supervise the care in place but do not give additional treatments. In the years since its inception, SEARCH has been an overwhelming success. Between 1988 and 2003, the infant mortality rate dropped from 121 to 30 deaths per 1,000 live births, and policy-makers from Bangladesh, Nepal, and many African countries are currently investigating how the SEARCH approach can be implemented in their communities (Shetty 2011).

An understanding of the principles of SEARCH can help anthropologists interpret the effectiveness of different approaches to health care seen elsewhere. For example, consider medical anthropologists Carolyn Sargent and Grace Bascope's (1996) study on birthing practices in Mexico, the US (Texas), and Jamaica. In their study, the researchers focused on "ways of knowing" about birthing and technology in high- and low-technology settings. They also considered the relationship between biomedical knowledge and social status. The collaborative birthing system of the Mayan women in Mexico incorporated midwives and other adult women who used their knowledge in a low-tech response. In general,

patients felt at ease with their place in the system. By contrast, the women in Texas felt alienated from their public hospital system, although they appreciated the technology that provided needed caesarean deliveries. In Jamaica, the lack of communication between the English-speaking staff and the Spanish-speaking patients distanced patients from caregivers in a system dominated by biomedical knowledge but lacking adequate access to and use of biomedical technology. In each situation, the SEARCH model can help us reassess the relationship between biomedical knowledge and patient comfort and security. By extension, anthropologists can apply such reassessment techniques beyond birthing practices to all medicalized situations.

Political Intervention: Population Control and Management

The structure and focus of health-care delivery systems frequently reflect local or national political interests, particularly when health-care systems receive government funding. Most often, political and medical arenas intersect over issues surrounding population control and management. When the government's interests are aligned with those of its citizens, the health-care system can function smoothly and contribute to social cohesion. But a clash between national and personal health interests can result in an array of social problems.

One example of a government's attempt to regulate health-related issues for political reasons is China's controversial one-child policy. The policy was implemented in 1979 and began to be formally phased out in 2015. Its aim was to bring control of individuals' reproduction and family size under the central government in order to lower the rate of population growth. At the local level, the program was administered by community functionaries. While most citizens abided by the national policy, some families attempted to circumvent the law by hiding pregnancies and births from government administrators. The 2000 national census found that 8,052,484 people were unregistered (Zhou 2005). Without official registration, these people were left without legal rights to health care or education. Additional social issues have emerged, including the preference for male children, increased female infanticide, abandoned infant girls, forced abortions for women pregnant with their second child, and forced sterilizations. The imbalance in the sex ratio has steadily increased over the past three decades, with current estimates ranging from 111 to 131 males for every 100 females. Further, it is estimated that by 2020 China will have a "bachelor army" consisting of 30 million to 40 million single men (Ross 2010) (Figure 10.14). The effects of the policy will undoubtedly be felt for decades to come.

A number of countries, including China, are facing a very different problem: how to manage the health issues of an aging population. This problem has come to the fore in recent years for a number of reasons. One major factor is the worldwide increase in life expectancy: an increase in the mean global life expectancy from 47 years in 1950–55 to 71.4 years in 2015 (WHO 2017), and a rise to 82 years is expected by 2095–2100 (UN 2017). Additionally, the shift from rural (with traditional family structures) to urban (with smaller family units) living situations means that aging individuals have fewer family members to rely on for support. For many countries, the demographic shift brought about by the aging of the "baby boomers" is also underway.

Elderly people face increasing rates of physical as well as cognitive conditions (e.g., Alzheimer's disease). Part of the struggle is to find financial resources to support this growing sector of patients, particularly in nation-states where universal and near-universal medical interventions have been the norm. Yet the challenge is not only financial; social systems must also arrange for care that will allow the elderly to maintain their identities when they enter systems of care. Ethnographer and social scientist Joanna Latimer (1999) notes that as people age, their social status often declines, especially if they have medical conditions. Further, they are often seen as less suitable for receiving active medical care compared to their younger counterparts. Yet Latimer also finds that older patients can take steps to preserve their status and identity by actively taking part in the process of defining their place within the medical system, stating that "[i]f individuals participate in the authoring of the categories to which they are assigned, then selfhood is preserved" (1999: 205).

Farmer has investigated the intersections between politics and health care in his work with the NGO Partners in Health, in his role as UN special envoy to Haiti, in his advocacy in the Americas and Africa, and in a number of his extensive writings (see, e.g., Farmer 2005, 2006; Farmer et al. 2013; Rylko-Bauer et al. 2009). As a physician and a medical anthropologist, Farmer explores the depth and breadth of health-care issues through specific and general analysis. Additionally, with Barbara Rylko-Bauer (2002), he has discussed managed care and the inequities that are generated when market forces focus on the management of inequality rather than on the provision of the tools for delivery of care. Farmer and his colleagues direct anthropologists' attention to the urban–rural divide and to the global have–have not chasm. They do not just report on conditions but seek reasons for what they see. Arguably, the most important issue is found in the succinct epilogue of *Global Health in Times of Violence*:

> If ethics are the embodiment of beliefs that individuals, groups, and cultures use to guide their behaviours and actions then we must question the violence of these ethics. We must question and challenge the contemporary moral economies that . . . tolerate the failure to provide needed and available medical assistance, and that exacerbate social and economic inequalities. . . . Connecting global violence to health requires that our analysis shift from a structural and geopolitical scale to a place

managed care A system of care, tied to the market-based delivery of medicine, particularly in the US, in which a patient's choice of treatment and of practitioner is directed by an intermediary organization that aims to provide the most cost-effective services available while generating profits for its members.

© sandsun/iStockphoto

Figure 10.14 A family sits on the square near the Forbidden City in Beijing, China. China's one-child policy has caused a crisis in the country, with men far outnumbering women. What social problems might this situation cause for individuals at various life stages?

that is intimate and experiential. . . . Finding the intimacy in the global requires new ways to assess, analyze, and present information . . . [that connects] the global to the personal. (Rylko-Bauer et al. 2009: 224–5)

Farmer and his colleagues argue against complacency; they challenge anthropologists to act on what they have found. They also call attention to the individuals who are affected by all the sociopolitical conditions that lead to patchy health-care delivery, from the structure of political economies to the rural–urban divide to social class placement. For anthropologists, the actualities of individual lives remain as the foundation of study from which the personal is connected to the global.

Epidemiology and Public Health

Because disease spreads along social networks, and because social structures can facilitate this spread, collaboration between anthropologists and medical epidemiologists can be productive. Today, a number of anthropologists are looking at the cross-cultural distribution of diseases and the variables determining these distributions (race, class, religion, time, etc.). These researchers understand that knowledge about cultural responses can offer insight into cultural biases and how these biases play out in surveillance systems and treatment regimens for epidemics. Medical anthropologists James Trostle and Johannes Sommerfeld (1996) have suggested the term *cultural* **epidemiology** for this type of interdisciplinary research.

To prevent or at least slow the spread of a disease, medical personnel must identify the major paths of transmission. They must also try to anticipate how, where, and when people are most likely to become infected. Finally, they must try to inform the general population of the risks involved in certain activities. All of these goals can be accomplished most effectively if the medical personnel understand the habits and cultural situation of the affected people. For example, consider the response to the 2003 SARS (Severe Acute Respiratory Syndrome) epidemic. On a global scale, the WHO targeted travellers by advising against travel to sites where there were known infections, primarily Hong Kong, China, Taiwan, Singapore, and Toronto (see WHO 2003a). Within affected countries, local regulatory bodies targeted populations most

at risk. In Hong Kong, where the rate of infection was greatest, this involved shutting down schools and placing more than a thousand people under quarantine across the country (Cheng 2004: 71). In Canada, where transmission was traced to contact with recent travellers and mainly restricted to the city of Toronto, the response included selective quarantining of individuals, increased screening for symptoms at airports, and the cancellation of many nonessential conferences and conventions in Toronto (Figure 10.15). In most countries, popular radio, print, and television media spread information about the disease and how to avoid infection. While the disease ultimately killed fewer people than did influenzas in the same period, the rapid emergence of the disease and the relative youth of its victims suggested a serious threat and a potentially devastating global pandemic.

While the widespread threat from SARS turned out to be fairly short-lived, other epidemics have proven to be more persistent. In the past few years epidemic-level infections that have arisen on a global scale are Ebola, HIV/AIDS, and most recently the Zika virus. The Zika virus became a widespread epidemic through Brazil and other parts of South and North America in early 2015. In February 2016, the WHO declared the outbreak a "public health emergency of international concern" as growing evidence revealed that the Zika virus could cause birth defects

epidemiology The study of the occurrence, spread, management, and prevention of infectious diseases.

Figure 10.15 A Toronto resident dons a medical mask to protect himself from the SARS virus in 2003.

CP PHOTO/Kevin Frayer

and neurological problems. Malaria also remains of particular concern, as it leads to more than 200 million clinical cases and more than 600,000 deaths every year (WHO 2014c). There has also been a concerning resurgence of tuberculosis (TB).

A first step toward fighting a disease is to understand its ecology, namely how it affects and is affected by its environment. Such understanding led researchers to identify that malaria is spread by mosquitoes that live in tropical and subtropical regions. Also important is knowledge of the social and cultural practices of the people who have to live in regions affected by the disease. Together, medical and cultural knowledge have led to successful control of mosquitoes through water clean-ups and the use of preventative measures, such as insecticides and sleeping nets (Figure 10.16). In most cases, the ultimate goal is to develop a vaccine that can protect people from infection.

Environmental changes, whether natural or human made, can have a dramatic effect on the prevalence of certain diseases. The WHO alerts us to the need to pay attention to how diseases may spread as a result of climate change:

> Changes in infectious disease transmission patterns are a likely major consequence of climate change. We need to learn more about the underlying complex causal relationships, and apply this information to the prediction of future impacts, using more complete, better validated, integrated, models. (WHO 2003b)

Researchers have already begun to apply this sort of integrated approach to the study of malaria and other diseases commonly found in tropical and subtropical regions. Based on observations of how climate change has progressed over recent decades, scientists can predict how these diseases will spread into areas in which they were uncommon in the past. While climate change is a large-scale force, smaller human-driven changes to local environments—such as building dams and cutting down forests—can also lead to increased prevalence of a wide variety of diseases (Table 10.5).

Past successes provide hope for future breakthroughs. After all, we have managed to eradicate smallpox, the disease that was largely responsible for the depopulation of the Americas shortly after European contact. At the same time, the celebration of this success is tempered by the fear that smallpox could be used as a biological weapon. Although the disease was eradicated in the general population, samples are still held in at least two controlled medical research facilities (see Chapter 14 for more on this), and few people born after 1980 have been vaccinated against the disease.

Figure 10.16 A baby sleeps under a mosquito net in his family's home in the village of Essaout, Senegal. Mosquito nets are one of the ways to prevent the spread of diseases, such as malaria. How does this preventative measure fit within the cultural context in which it is being used? How might such a technology be adapted for use in other regions?

Table 10.5 Examples of How Environmental Changes Increase the Occurrence of Infectious Diseases in Humans

Environmental Change	Disease	Major Route of Transmission	Effect of Environmental Change
Construction of dams, canals, irrigation systems	Malaria	Bite from an infected mosquito	Increases the habitat and breeding ground of mosquitoes
	Schistosomiasis ("snail fever")	Contact with water containing parasites	Increases the habitat and breeding ground of snails that host the parasites
	Helminthiasis (parasitic worms)	Ingestion via contaminated water or food	Increased contact with larvae due to moist soil
Agricultural intensification	Malaria	Bite from an infected mosquito	Widespread use of insecticides leads to insecticide-resistant mosquitoes
	Venezuelan hemorrhagic fever	Inhalation of secretions from infected rodents	Increases the habitat and breeding ground for rodents; contact with rodents more likely
	Hantavirus diseases	Inhalation of secretions from infected rodents	Increases the habitat and breeding ground for rodents; contact with rodents more likely
Urbanization, urban crowding	Cholera	Ingestion via contaminated water or food	Increased risk of water contamination and contact with contaminated water with more people living in close proximity to one another
	Dengue fever	Bite from an infected mosquito	Increased risk associated with more people living in close proximity to one another
	Cutaneous leishmaniasis	Bite from an infected sand fly	Increased risk associated with more people living in close proximity to one another
Deforestation, new habitation	Malaria	Bite from an infected mosquito	Increases the habitat and breeding ground of mosquitoes; increased contact with infected mosquitoes
	Visceral leishmaniasis	Bite from an infected sand fly	Increased contact with infected sand flies
Reforestation	Lyme disease	Bite from an infected tick	Increased habitat and breeding ground for ticks

Source: Adapted from WHO 2003b. "Climate change and human health - risks and responses" published by WHO in collaboration with UNEP and WMO. © 2003. Reproduced with permission.

Integrated, Applied Critical Medical Anthropology: Holism in the Service of Wellness

In some sense, medical anthropology is more "applied" than many of the other areas of anthropological research. This is appropriate, as health issues affect all human beings on a personal level and are also tied to biological, environmental, economic, and political influences beyond their control. Taking an integrated approach to health issues allows anthropologists to avoid becoming too closely aligned with any one set of interests—for example, the interests of powerful biomedicine industries. This integrated approach is emphasized in particular by a growing group of anthropologists who call themselves *critical medical anthropologists*. These anthropologists draw attention to the ways in which many forms of physical, mental, and emotional suffering correlate with forms of socioeconomic and political inequality. (See the "In Their Own Words" box that follows for more on critical medical anthropology.)

In Their Own Words

Critical Medical Anthropology

Arima Mishra outlines CMA (critical medical anthropology) in her introduction to a special issue of *Indian Anthropologist* on medical anthropology and public health.

The emergence of critical medical anthropology (hereafter referred to as CMA) in the mid-1980s is a turning point in redefining the scope of medical anthropology. Its implications specifically for the field of public health can be discerned in two main contexts. The first, establishing a theoretical and analytical shift, it breaks itself free from a narrow focus on medical anthropology as mere cultural fillers/brokers for biomedicine and mainstream public health. In this role, anthropology has been expected to identify the cultural or social factors that inhibit the success of a public health program, non-compliance of the patients to a specific medical regimen or delay in seeking medical care, thus uncritically accepting the hegemonic ideologies and power relations . . .

CMA has been defined as "a theoretical and practical effort to understand and respond to issues and problems of health, illness and treatment in terms of the *interactions* between the macro level of political economy, national level of political and class structure, institutional level of health system, community level of popular and folk beliefs and actions, micro level of illness experience, behaviour and meaning . . ." (Singer 1995: 81). Offering an internal critique of traditional medical anthropological works that restrict documentation of health, illness and health care to a micro-level analysis (only), CMA argues for examining the local in relation to the national and global—thus shifting the units of analysis to interactions and interfaces at different levels. Such kinds of analysis, it is argued, could do justice to the holistic endeavor of disciplines like anthropology and sociology in addressing pertinent issues in the field of global health.

Using critical theoretical frameworks, CMA highlights the *political economy of health and health care* thus bringing the role of power to the foreground—interrogating the role of power in social relationships, production and practices of health knowledge, categories, policies and programs. CMA is consciously political as it distinctly recognizes that health itself is a political issue. It acknowledges the fundamental importance of class, racial and other forms of inequality as determining the distribution of health, disease and access to health care. It defines power as a fundamental variable in health related research, police and practice (Singer 1990, 1995; Baer, Singer and Johnsen 1986;

Anthropologists' approach must also be global in nature, as the forces of globalization connect all people and have the power to influence the well-being of every individual.

Being applied requires anthropologists to be present in the real world and aware of all of the factors that shape that world. When anthropologists approach a medical issue, care should be taken to place scientific knowledge in its sociohistorical context. Anthropologists must also try to take an unbiased approach, giving consideration to scientific principles as well as traditional knowledge. This approach can help clarify health issues that are situated in a sociopolitical colonial heritage. Consider the issues that Indigenous communities living within Canada's political boundaries continue to face. Little has been done to counter the inequality that results from the urban–rural divide. A gap remains between traditional Indigenous knowledge of medicine and biomedical practices. Environments in which many Indigenous people live continue to be invaded and polluted, and there has been a continued failure to provide adequate assistance to Indigenous individuals who live in substandard urban areas. And these conditions are not unique to Canada; they are repeated to varying degrees in post-colonial contexts around the world.

Through their health-related research, medical anthropologists can and do contribute to policy and programming at both local and international levels. Their aim is not just to understand but to work to change cultural patterns related to health care that can be seen as inappropriate, oppressive, or exploitive (Singer 1995: 81). For example, medical anthropologists have contributed

Scheper-Hughes 1990). CMA thus calls for anthropology *of* medicine/public health (critically applied anthropology) contrasted with anthropology *in* medicine/public health (clinically applied anthropology).

Anthropology of public health adopts a critical and analytical perspective turning its gaze (from the individual communities alone) to the world of practitioners, policy makers, global actors, NGOs and, in fact, to the very framework of public policy itself and its consequences (intended and unintended). The notion of culture is transformed from that of cultural "beliefs" of the lay communities to examining how medicine/public health itself is practiced, experienced and culturally constituted. CMA is committed to expanding the scope of anthropological enquiry in *breadth* (dealing with innumerable issues related to specific diseases, suffering, health of minorities, reproductive and sexual health, organ trade, health system regulations and governance and bio communicability, to offer a snapshot view) and *depth* (multi-sited ethnography, inter-disciplinary research). Inhorn and Wentzell's recently edited volume (2012) maps the present and future terrain of medical anthropology's work at the intersections of different fields including public health, techno-science and genetics/genomics . . .

The second context in which CMA deserves significant attention for the public health project is due to its conscious effort to blend theory with practice. As Singer (1990) notes CMA is a theoretical lens to inspire action and engagement. Baer (1990) defines CMA as that which seeks to merge theory and praxis in a desire to promote experiential health (wherein health is understood in a larger sense of access to and control over basic material and non-material resources to sustain and promote life). CMA thus not merely unpacks the nuances and complexities of the on-the-ground realities, but actively seeks to engage and advocate for desired change . . .

Elaborating the role of critical medical anthropology to global health from a health system perspective, Pfieffer and Nichter (2008) note that, apart from other contributions, CMA can ensure that the "evidence base that frames global public debates is inclusive and represents multiple dimensions of humane experience including the voices of those whose lives are affected by global processes" (p. 413). Critical medical anthropology thus advocates for a critical, analytical, reflexive gaze and is concerned with the world of praxis, social activism committed to equity and rights through the use of sound theoretical frameworks and grounded evidence informing public health policy development.

Source: Mishra, Arima. 2013. "Special Issue on Anthropology and Public Health: An Introduction," *Indian Anthropologist* 43, 1: 1–3.

to the global awareness of culturally situated forms of violence against women, such as female genital mutilation, sex-selective abortion and infanticide, and dowry abuse and murder. Here one of the core ethical issues in applied anthropology arises: How do anthropologists reconcile the commitment to the principle of cultural relativism with the moral obligation to preserve the well-being of the peoples with whom they work? Merrill Singer observes,

> The anthropological tradition of cultural relativism (whatever its limitations) and the discipline's enduring concern with insider understanding . . . [results in] an appreciation of and commitment to the principle of self-determination. Support of self-determination is further supported by the anthropological obligation to counter Western, colonial ethnocentrism and to create opportunities for the voices of so-called people without history (i.e., oppressed third-world populations) to be heard on the contemporary world stage. (Singer 1995: 98–9)

Certainly, self-determination and consent are taken as core rights in the UN's Universal Declaration of Human Rights (see UN 2014).

Can anthropologists help bring about change when asked? Of course! Anthropologists can effect transformations by focusing on consciousness-raising and empowering objectives directed toward "unmasking the structural roots of suffering and ill health" (Singer 1995: 99). By taking a critical approach in which anthropologists appreciate the intersubjective space of social relationships and social action, they can also foster collaborative, respectful relationships with the peoples who are the centre of their studies. Respectful interaction rests in recognizing that all human beings live in their own modernity and define their modernity through

a process of *cultural bricolage*—the creation of something new and useful from the bits and pieces of past and present cultural realities. Ultimately, a mixture of tradition and innovation may lead all human beings to new ways of solving the age-old problems of disease and illness.

Living Anthropology

States of Precarity: Wellness, Illness, and Refugees' Mental Health

by Nhi Ha Nguyen, PhD Student, Cultural Studies, Queen's University

"Oppression is a result of many conditions, not the least of which reside in consciousness," noted Paul Farmer (2004: 307) in his ethnographic account of social suffering in Haiti, "An Anthropology of Structural Violence." A medical anthropologist by training, Farmer's concept of "structural violence" refers to the invisible barriers (such as lack of knowledge, deficit medical infrastructure, etc.) that hinder successful diagnoses and continuous treatments of preventable infectious diseases and treatable illnesses. Those barriers are manifestations of systemic social inequalities embedded in consciousness, yet "consciousness" also implies a state of mind, structured as much by biological factors, as it is influenced by social forces. Addressing a form of consciousness, this contribution discusses mental health in anthropology regarding refugees—a population that has been the centre of attention in our time of heightened (in)security.

Per Vigo et al. (2016), mental illnesses contribute 5 out of 20 top causes of the global burden of disease, and their cumulative impact on the global economy is estimated to be approximately US \$16 trillion in the next 20 years (Bloom et al. 2011: 1582). Yet, the amount of public resource allocation for mental-health services composes "under 4% of overall healthcare budgets" (Prince et al. 2007: 860). This leads to a significant lack of trained professionals and alarmingly low treatment rates:

> "the availability and utilisation of outpatient facilities is dramatically different for countries of different income levels: the number of visits per 100,000 population in high-income countries (6,668) is over 50 times greater than in low-income countries (102) and 20 times greater than lower-middle income countries (320). Similar disparities are seen between Regions, with the African Region in particular having an extremely low rate of visits per 100,000 population. (WHO 2014d: 44)

Perhaps thus neglected in the policy-making arena, interest in mental health, in contrast, abounds across the social sciences. Considered fundamental to these inquiries is Foucault's *Madness and Civilization* (1964), a structuralist account on how the meaning of insanity has changed under the influence of social institutions. Exploring the effects of one such institution on individual identities, Erving Goffman focused on the depersonalization and stigmatization of mental patients in the iconic *Asylums* (1961). More broadly, Hahn (1984) offered a comprehensive perspective on illness and disease, while Conrad and Baker (2010) investigated cultural ideas of illnesses, along with their relevance to policy-making practices. Diverse as it is, mental-health research commonly relies on the *Diagnostic and Statistical Manual of Mental Disorders* (DSM–V, APA 2013). The manual aims for universality, which is extremely useful in cross-cultural diagnoses, as in the case of refugees, yet also medicalizes social problems (Kleinman 2012: 181–2): that is, Western psychiatry tends to ignore socioeconomic elements, such as the way different cultures conceptualize mental wellness, or the role of economic factors.

Even as they draw from Western biomedical models, the social sciences, and particularly anthropology, often place culture at the centre of social imaginings of mental health. Embedded in cultural ideas of stigma, mental illness is often addressed under Kleinman et al.'s concept of social suffering (1997), for it embodies everyday enactments of structural violence (Farmer 2004) and interpersonal human experience in crises. Although the recent development of "pharmaceutical anthropology" (van der Geest 2006) is promising, anthropological interest in mental health care has declined after the 1980s–90s. Aside from accounts of refugees' health issues that arise *because of* their trauma (notably Malkki 1995), there has not been a comparative study of refugees' mental health before and after their arrival, nor has there been a reliable health-care system for them in the countries of asylum.

Following Kleinman's call for a more involved anthropology of mental health (2012), refugees' experience can certainly benefit from ethnographic inquiries. In anthropological terminology, refugees are persons who, having undergone a violent rite of separation (cf. Turner 1967), are caught in a liminal, in-between state prior to resettlement in countries of asylum. Being a refugee does not automatically imply mental illnesses; nevertheless, such issues are prevalent enough that the French government, for instance, requires physicians' certificates affirming a physical and psychological basis for fleeing persecution (Fassin and d'Halluin 2005). There has indeed been an increase in refugees admitted on the basis of health problems (Fassin 2005), returning us to the humanitarian basis for resettlement in the 1951 Convention (UNHRC 2017).

The lack of psychiatric structure to accommodate refugees' mental-health needs, and social barriers surrounding mental illnesses in contemporary countries of asylum, is indeed a form of structural violence. This concern for refugees' mental health presents a valuable opportunity for anthropology to discuss two topical issues: (1) mental health-care systems in countries of origin, and (2) the many difficulties in continuing medical health care for pre-settlement refugees in countries of asylum. Is this not why anthropology exists—for its unique insight into the human condition, mediated by institutional forces and sociopolitical infrastructures?

Key Terms

abiotic   251
bioaccumulation   253
biomagnification   253
biomedicine   242
biotic   251
culture-bound syndromes   242
defensive research   254
disease   242
epidemiology   265

ethnomedical systems   243
etiology   246
folk illness   249
health   242
illness   242
managed care   264
medical anthropology   242
placebo effect   260
positive research   254

realized niche   252
shaman   245
sickness   242
social trauma   256
structural violence   255
suffering   242
traditional knowledge   242
well-being   242

Chapter Summary

1. Medical anthropology is highly interdisciplinary, drawing on and influencing such diverse fields as biology, ecology, biochemistry, sociology, psychology, political science, economics, linguistics, ethics, and religious studies. Thus, medical anthropologists value integrated approaches and holism in their work, and they are always open to a variety of perspectives.

2. Medical anthropologists recognize the tension between traditional knowledge and Western scientific knowledge, but they also recognize that the two approaches intersect in many ways. In the past, the systems were depicted as being in opposition to each other, but contemporary medical anthropologists try to move beyond "either/or" interpretations.

3. Medical anthropologists are aware that physical (biotic and abiotic), social, and cultural environments can have a dramatic impact on human well-being. Within every environment, all components are linked in complex, often indivisible ways. Thus, researchers examine the influence of environments—especially *realized niches*—on human health. Two areas of particular interest are environmental contamination and access to a balanced diet.

4. Health-care systems take many different forms around the world. Yet medical anthropologists recognize four outcomes of medical treatment that occur cross culturally, regardless of the approach to effecting a cure: (1) the treatment may cause the patient to recover;

(2) the patient may recover regardless of the interventions taken by caregivers because the disease/illness/injury was, in effect, self-correcting or self/healing; (3) the placebo effect may work to bring about a cure, simply because the patient believes that it will be effective; and (4) treatments may be ineffective, in some cases leading to the death of the patient.

Critical Thinking Questions

1. How is the medical system in Canada an externalizing system? What evidence can you find of internalizing approaches to wellness in Canada? How can these two approaches complement one another?

2. What are the links between environmental contamination and health? How important are efforts to clean up contaminated environments and prevent contamination in the future?

3. How do socioeconomic and geopolitical disparities affect treatment options? Why are wealthier nations often slow to act in response to the health crises in less affluent regions of the world? What can be done about disparities *within* relatively affluent nations?

4. Anthropologist Bruce Lincoln has observed that the human body in sickness transcends its individual psychological and physical vulnerability, becoming the "site where social pressures and tensions are experienced most acutely" and various community "contradictions and lacerations that divide a community" are played out (2001: 791). How have social pressures and tensions factored into your own experiences with disease and illness? How might Lincoln's observations relate to an epidemic within a community?

Suggested Readings

Berkes, Fikret, Peter George, Richard Preston, and John Turner. 1992. "The Cree View of Land and Resources: Indigenous Ecological Knowledge," report prepared for TASO (Technology Assessment in Subarctic Ontario), Second Series, no. 8 (Hamilton: McMaster University). An interesting paper that discusses the traditional values of the James Bay Cree with respect to their land base and the resources they use (animals, fish, and birds).

Dods, Roberta Robin. 2004. "Knowing Ways/Ways of Knowing: Reconciling Science and Tradition," *World Archaeology* 36, 4: 547–57. This paper discusses the structure of traditional ecological knowledge and Western scientific knowledge, concluding that both forms of knowledge offer access to important information and that the greatest insight can come when they are combined.

Farmer, Paul. 2005. *Pathologies of Power: Health, Human Rights, and the New War on the Poor* (Berkeley: University of California Press). A highly respected text in which Paul Farmer investigates the many intersections between politics and health care.

Mackie, Gerry. 2003. "Female Genital Cutting: A Harmless Practice?" *Medical Anthropology Quarterly*, New Series 17, 2: 135–58. This article discusses issues of self-determination and consent in the context of cultural relativism.

Mintz, Sidney W., and Christine M. Du Bois. 2002. "The Anthropology of Food and Eating," *Annual Review of Anthropology* 31: 99–119. This article links diverse areas of research, including food security and social change. The authors note that much remains to be done in examining nutritional practices in many areas of the world.

Rylko-Bauer, Barbara, and Paul Farmer. 2002. "Managed Care or Managed Inequality? A Call for Critiques of Market-Based Medication," *Medical Anthropology Quarterly* 16, 4: 476–502. This paper challenges us to consider the actual cost of care managed by corporations that base decisions on potential profits.

Stephenson, Peter H. 2001. "Expanding Notions of Culture and Ethics in Health and Medicine to Include Marginalized Groups: A Critical Perspective," *Anthropologica* 43, 1: 3–17. A nuanced and historically contextualized paper that examines the ethical challenges involved in practising medicine—both Western and traditional—in a globalizing world.

Van Esterik, Penny. 2002. "Contemporary Trends in Infant Feeding Research," *Annual Review of Anthropology* 31: 257–78. An informative investigation into health and nutrition concerns related to infant care and feeding.

Related Websites

Centre for Global Mental Health
www.centreforglobalmentalhealth.org

Health Canada: First Nations and Inuit Health
www.hc-sc.gc.ca/fniah-spnia/index-eng.php

Lucky Iron Fish
http://luckyironfish.com

Partners in Health
www.pih.org

Society for Medical Anthropology
www.medanthro.net

UNFPA's State of World Population 2016
www.unfpa.org/swp

UN's World Population Prospects 2017
http://esa.un.org/wpp

WHO's HIV/AIDS Data and Statistics
www.who.int/hiv/data/en

11 World View

Chapter Outline

The Role of Metaphor, Metonymy, and Symbol

Key Metaphors

Religion

World Views in Operation: Two Case Studies

Maintaining and Changing a World View

World Views as Instruments of Power

Religion and Secularism

Learning Objectives

By the end of Chapter 11, you will be able to

- consider the role of metaphor, metonymy, and symbol in constructing world views;
- recognize key metaphors for constructing world views;

- appreciate the role of religion and religious expression;
- understand world views as instruments of power; and
- compare and contrast the roles of religion and secularism.

What guides us as we attempt to give life meaning? How do we devise cultural forms through which we can make sense of our being and belonging? How do we frame our physical and metaphysical contexts? In this chapter we attempt to answer these very complex questions by exploring **world view**.

The Role of Metaphor, Metonymy, and Symbol

Metaphor

One way to grasp a particular world view and the cultural patterns that it contains is to "follow the metaphor." Canadians, for example, might examine the cultural metaphor of their country as a cultural mosaic to understand how Canadians interpret their place in the world. They might also contrast this metaphor with the American metaphor of the United States as a melting pot to uncover how our cultural perceptions differ from those of our neighbours to the south. Following metaphors successfully, however, requires understanding how metaphors work.

Recall from Chapter 4 that metaphor asserts the existence of a meaningful link between two expressions from different semantic domains. For example, metaphorical statements, such as "Arnold is a turkey," create an ambiguity that can be resolved only in context. If we know that Arnold is characteristically inept, ignorant, and annoying and that turkeys are thought to be stupid and clumsy, our metaphor becomes intelligible and apt. But why resort to metaphor to represent our opinion of Arnold? Why not simply say "Arnold is inept, ignorant, and annoying"? When we choose to use metaphoric language instead of literal language, it is usually because literal language is not equal to the task of expressing the depth of meaning we intend. Our experience of Arnold may be complex and difficult to pin down in literal language. That is, there is something about the image of a turkey that encompasses more of what we think about Arnold than can ever be represented by a list of adjectives. We therefore select a figurative image whose features are familiar and use this image as a tool to help us express what kind of person Arnold is. The metaphor does not demonstrate unequivocally that Arnold *is* a turkey. Rather, it simply asserts that there is a link between Arnold and a turkey.

World views aim to encompass the widest possible understanding of how the world works. In constructing world views, people tend to examine what they already know for clues that might help them make sense of what puzzles them. Metaphor is a powerful tool for constructing world views because it clarifies areas of human experience that are vague or poorly understood. Consider the Christian metaphor "The Lord is my shepherd." It links a subject we have trouble describing (the Lord) to a familiar image (a shepherd).

Metaphors tend to be structured in a typical way. The first part of a metaphor, the **metaphorical subject**, represents the domain of experience that needs to be clarified (e.g., the Lord). The second part of a metaphor, the **metaphorical predicate**, suggests the domain of experience that is familiar (e.g., shepherding) and may help us understand what the metaphorical subject is all about (Figure 11.1). To understand the metaphor, we have to list every conceivable attribute of the metaphorical predicate and then decide which ones describe the metaphorical subject. These attributes are called **metaphorical entailments** (Lakoff and Johnson 1980). They suggest what follows from, or is entailed by, linking the metaphorical subject to the metaphorical predicate (e.g., by calling the Lord a shepherd). If we were to change the metaphorical predicate—for example, by asserting that "The Lord is my friend"—an entirely different set of metaphorical entailments would follow.

Metonymy

Metonymy is the relationship that links all of the parts of a semantic domain to one another. In the metaphor "The Lord is my shepherd," the links between the metaphorical predicate *shepherd* and its metaphorical entailments are links of metonymy (see Figure 11.1). The word *shepherd* can stand for any and all attributes (e.g., protecting sheep from wild animals) connected to the semantic domain defined by shepherding. At the same time, any of

world view An encompassing picture of reality created by members of a society.

metaphor A form of thought and language that asserts a meaningful link between two expressions from different semantic domains.

metaphorical subject The first part of a metaphor, which indicates the domain of experience that needs to be clarified.

metaphorical predicate The second part of a metaphor, which suggests the familiar domain of experience that may clarify the metaphorical subject.

metaphorical entailments All the attributes of a metaphorical predicate that relate it to the metaphorical subject.

metonymy The culturally defined relationship of the parts of a semantic domain to the domain as a whole and of the whole to its parts.

Buddhist monks walking in Angkor Wat, Cambodia. Angkor Wat was originally constructed as a Hindu temple before transforming into a Buddhist temple toward the end of the twelfth century. The ancient temple remains a popular place of pilgrimage for Buddhist monks coming from around the world.

© Xavier Zimbardo/Getty Images

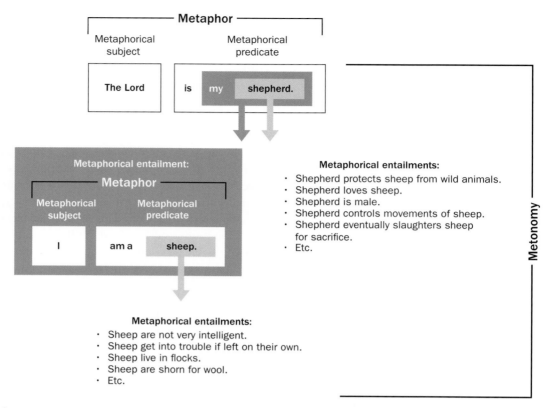

Figure 11.1 An analysis of the metaphor "The Lord is my shepherd." This metaphorical statement is an invitation to ponder what it means to be *a shepherd* and what it means to be *my shepherd*, and then to apply this knowledge to our understanding of the Lord.

these attributes may entail the word *shepherd*. Because semantic domains are culturally defined, the meaningful elements that are linked by metonymy within any semantic domain are also culturally defined. Shepherding occurs in many societies, and yet the range of meanings associated with it may vary: compare a society in which shepherds are women, sheep graze freely, and mutton is primarily for family consumption with a different society in which shepherds are men, sheep graze in enclosed fields, and most animals are sold on the market for cash. Of course, members of the first society may think that theirs is the only sensible way to herd sheep and vice versa. Put another way, in any society, semantic domains defined by links of metonymy are viewed as "natural" or "true" associations.

The links of metonymy we discover within a particular semantic domain may help us make sense of experiences that seem chaotic and meaningless. Consider what happens in the case of what some people call *religious conversion*. An individual who is troubled and confused may see his personal situation suddenly come into focus when he starts thinking of himself as a lost sheep. Further, he may reason

that a lost sheep must have been lost by someone— the shepherd to whom it belonged. This reflection, in turn, may lead him to ask who his shepherd might be. If he learns that some people believe that the Lord is their shepherd, he may be attracted to those people and want to learn more. Thus, his exploration of the links of metonymy within a particular semantic domain in the context of his own life may lead him to conclude that the metaphor "The Lord is my shepherd" resonates with the power of divine revelation. Such reflections play an important role in religious conversion, but they are equally important in other realms—for example, in the realm of science, when a new theory is adopted because it makes sense of otherwise puzzling data.

Symbol

As people increase their understanding of themselves and the wider world by creating apt metaphors, they devise *symbols* to remind themselves of their significant insights and the connections between those insights. As noted in Chapter 1, a symbol is something—be it a word, an image, or an action—that stands for something else. Symbols signal the presence and importance of given domains of experience. They are special cases of metonymy. Some symbols—what Sherry Ortner (1973) terms *summarizing symbols*—represent a whole semantic domain and invite us to consider the various elements within it. Examples include the cross representing the Christian faith or the Canadian flag representing our country and its citizens as a whole. Others—what Ortner terms *elaborating symbols*—represent only one element of a domain and invite us to place that element in its wider semantic context. (See the "In Their Own Words" box that follows on Andean house re-thatching.) A familiar example of an elaborating symbol is the image of the cultural mosaic, which represents the relationships among different cultural groups in Canada.

Key Metaphors

World views are attempts to answer the following question: What must the world be like for my experiences to be what they are? Over the ages, thoughtful people in all cultural traditions have drawn on different metaphors to suggest various answers to this question (Daugman 2001). Those suggestions

---

In Their Own Words

House Re-thatching in an Andean Annual Cycle

Canadian social anthropologist Peter Gose illustrates that Andean roofing can be very complex and, at the same time, provide meaningful insights into many areas of life.

By Andean standards, house re-thatching is only a moderately ritualized labour process. Its imagery varies considerably from locality to locality, and . . . [it] is best understood through its position in the annual cycle of agrarian labour and ritual. . . . [T]he relatively modest ritual imagery of house re-thatching means little if anything in itself and cannot stand on its own as symbolism. Rather, it is motivated and given most of its significance by the practices that surround and support it in the annual cycle. House re-thatching in the Andes takes place as the dry season is giving way to the growing season. This seasonal shift involves a corresponding change in social relations from an emphasis on private appropriation by individual households during the harvest to an extensive and institutionalized inter-household co-operation that will prevail throughout the growing season. . . . [T]hese seasonally opposed moralities overlap in the house re-thatching and each lay claim to its content. . . . [C]ontradiction animates the imagery of this act and makes it signify in a way that we would miss if we considered it in abstraction from its grounding in the annual cycle. . . . [I]t is only when the imagery of the performance is subsumed by the annual cycle that it acquires the directedness necessary to "reflect and refract" another part of reality, that is, to become properly symbolic. . . . The . . . images do not function as self-contained "semantic values" that just happen to crop up around the house re-thatching but as metaphorical vehicles that intervene in and organize the very nature of the act. Put differently, this imagery does not exist for itself, in isolation from the instrumentality of the house re-thatching as a labour process, but in order to give that labour process a cultural form. And in turn, the seasonal position of the house re-thatching gives this imagery direction and entry into a real context within which it can truly signify. An example of this sort of interaction can be found in the transportation of hay down the mountain on the first day, which at first appears entirely unremarkable but, on further consideration, is seen to be embroiled in the entire "domestication" complex, including the origins of agriculture in descent. If this theme of "domestication" were not so thoroughly developed by other aspects of the rite, there would be no justification for this interpretation of the downward movement of hay. But once such a theme is established, it becomes equally hard to deny that the apparently technical act of transporting hay contributes to it. In sum, this rite teaches not only a negative lesson, that it is impossible to separate meaning from practice, but also a positive one, that the two taken together as praxis form a whole that is greater than its parts. Yet the praxis of commoners within the annual cycle is characterized not by a vapid holism but rather by a contradictory interpenetration of opposed moralities of private appropriation and collective production. This contradiction is most evident in the seasonal position of the rite, but it also works through its spatial and sequential organization and can even be identified in each of its individual symbols. Because the source of these contradictions lies beyond the act itself, house re-thatching must be understood as a moment in a larger seasonal process, not as a self-contained "text."

Source: Gose, Peter. 1991. "House Re-thatching in an Andean Annual Cycle: Practice, Meaning, and Contradiction," *American Ethnologist* 18, 1: 38, 57. Reprinted with permission of the American Anthropological Association.

key metaphors Symbolic representations that are widely understood within a culture and central to that culture's world view.

that have become entrenched in any particular tradition are based on especially apt metaphors—**key metaphors** that make sense of experience in a variety of circumstances. Over time, as circumstances change and the established metaphors become less apt, new key metaphors replace the old, forming the basis for new world views.

Robin Horton suggests that people who construct a world view are searching for a way to bring "order, regularity, and predictability" to all aspects of their daily lives. As they search for key metaphors, therefore, they look at those areas of everyday experience that are most associated with order, regularity, and predictability (Horton 1982: 237). Thus, cross-culturally, key metaphors typically relate to three such realms of experience: the societal, the organic, and the technological.

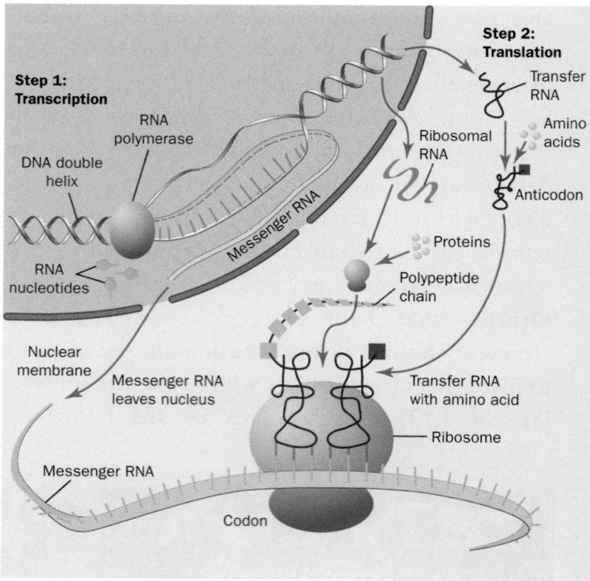

Societal Metaphors

societal metaphor A key metaphor whose predicate lies in the social order.

In societies where human social relations provide great order, regularity, and predictability, the central model for the world is the social order. People within these societies tend to use **societal metaphors** as they try to explain various aspects of their reality. For example, geneticist Richard Lewontin and his colleagues (1984) point out that biologists studying cells have used a societal metaphor almost from the very beginning. These biologists liken cells to a factory assembling the biochemical products needed to support the body's economy. This metaphor recurs in the twentieth-century work of Francis Crick, one of the discoverers of the structure of DNA (deoxyribonucleic acid). As Lewontin and colleagues suggest, "Read any introductory textbook to the new molecular biology and you will find these metaphors as a central part of the cellular description. Even the drawings of the protein synthesis sequence are often deliberately laid out in 'assembly-line' style" (1984: 59) (Figure 11.2).

organic metaphor A key metaphor whose predicate lies in the image of a living body.

Similarly, contemporary sociobiologists have borrowed certain concepts from modern economic thought and used them to describe the behaviour of genes or of living organisms. Sociobiologists describe the nurturing behaviour of parents toward their offspring as "parental investment." They talk about the cost–benefit analyses that people make before deciding whether or not to sacrifice themselves for others and even describe genes as "selfish." To some sociobiologists, the natural world is just the capitalist market on a larger scale. Indeed, Marshall

Figure 11.2 An example of a protein synthesis diagram laid out in "assembly-line" style.

Sahlins (1976) and others have argued that, from its inception in the late eighteenth century, modern biology has taken its key metaphors from the social world familiar to eighteenth-century biologists—the world of early capitalism.

Organic Metaphors

An **organic metaphor** applies the image of a living body to something else. A common organic metaphor is based on an interpretation of the body of a living organism as divisible into different systems (digestive, reproductive, respiratory, and so on), each carrying out a specialized task. When all these systems are functioning in harmony with one another, the organism is said to be healthy. If we compare society to a living organism, for example, we look for the subsystems into which society can be divided, identify the tasks each is supposed to perform, and describe a healthy society as one in which all the subsystems are functioning harmoniously. Indeed, this sort of organic metaphor is responsible for the social-scientific metaphor of society as an organism, with various interlinked components that rely on one another for survival. Alternatively, we can use an organic metaphor to analyze the life course of a society or civilization in terms of its birth, youth, maturity, old age, and death.

Personification (attributing human characteristics to non-human entities) is another form of organic metaphor. The belief that the vending machine in your lunch room has a malevolent and greedy personality or that you can persuade your car to start on a cold morning by speaking gentle and encouraging words to it both involve personification.

Technological Metaphors

A **technological metaphor** uses objects made by human beings as metaphorical predicates. Technological metaphors that use machines as metaphorical predicates have long been prominent in the world views of Western societies. For example, in the seventeenth century, philosopher René Descartes popularized the notion that the human body was a machine, albeit one inhabited by an immortal soul. Subsequently, another philosopher, Julien Offray de La Mettrie, carried this metaphor to its radical conclusion in *L'homme-machine* ("man-machine"), where he argued that the concept of the human soul was superfluous because machines do not have souls. As Western science and technology have grown in importance, machine metaphors have also become more widespread.

In the twentieth century, a major revolution in cognitive psychology was brought about by a shift in key technological metaphors. Psychologists rejected the steam engine metaphor of nineteenth-century industrial technology in favour of the computer metaphor of twentieth-century cybernetic technology. Computer jargon has become popular among scientists investigating the functions of the brain, the nervous system, and even the whole human body. Today, it seems impossible to avoid such language given the many suggestive insights into human mental functioning that the computer metaphor makes possible.

Using a computer as a model for the mind can produce varying interpretations. Everything depends on the kind of computer you choose as the metaphorical predicate and the aspects of computer operations you emphasize. For example, biological determinists might prefer to think of the mind as a "dedicated" computer whose functions are fully specified and wired into the hardware, allowing little flexibility. But if we think of the mind as a sophisticated general-purpose computer, we cannot predict the specific tasks it performs simply by knowing the design of its hardware (i.e., its physical structure). Rather, by loading different software programs, we direct the computer's hardware to perform particular tasks.

Were we to extend this kind of computer metaphor to explain the development of culture, we could argue that the co-evolution of brain and culture is the process by which a program hungry for system memory makes demands on hardware design. At a certain point, the computer's memory becomes full, and a flash drive is required to store the extra material. The human cultural equivalent of this flash drive would be oral tradition and forms of symbolic inscription, such as writing.

Religion

For many readers of this text, the most familiar form of world view is probably **religion**. The anthropological concept of religion, like many analytical terms, began as a description of a certain domain of Western culture. As a result, it has been very difficult for anthropologists to settle on a definition of *religion* that is applicable in all human societies.

Scholars have often argued that religion differs from other kinds of world views because it assumes the existence of a supernatural domain: an invisible world populated by one or more beings who are more powerful than human beings and are able to influence events in the "natural" human world. The problem is that the distinction between "natural" and "supernatural" was originally made by non-religious Western observers, where "real" was equated to the "natural" world, which was separate from their defined "imaginary" or "supernatural" world. However, as we discussed in Chapter 2, each culture has its own concept of what is "real." Thus many anthropologists who study different religious traditions believe that it is less distorting to begin with their informants' statements about what exists and what does not. In this way, they are in a better position to understand the range of forces, visible and invisible, that religious believers perceive as active in their world.

Anthropological inquiry into religious world views needs to begin with broad objectives that can move to increasing specificity as the details of a particular religious tradition are revealed by its adherents. With this approach in mind, anthropologist John Bowen defines religion as "ideas and practices that postulate reality beyond that which is immediately available to the senses" (2002: 5). These ideas and practices are not individual. Rather, they are *social*: they are shared among a group of people and shape how members of the group interact with one another and with the universe in a variety of ways (Figure 11.3).

technological metaphor
A key metaphor whose predicate lies in objects made by human beings.

religion "Ideas and practices that postulate reality beyond that which is immediately available to the senses" (Bowen 2002: 5).

Figure 11.3 Religious beliefs and practices are social. Here, a group of Muslim men learn the Quran at Al-Masjid an-Nabawi in Medina, Saudi Arabia. Have you engaged in religious practice in a large group? In what ways are social religious practices different from other types of social activity?

Bowen's definition of *religion* is significant because it emphasizes that religions involve *beliefs* as well as *actions*. Both of these components of religion can take a variety of forms. Religious beliefs may include belief in spirits and/or gods, belief in impersonal forces that affect the world, belief in the correct practice of ritual, and/or belief that ancestors continue to be active in the world of the living. Religious actions can include a wide variety of behaviours. Anthropologist Anthony Wallace (1966) has proposed a set of

"minimal categories of religious behaviour" that describe many of the practices usually associated with religions. Several of the most salient are as follows:

1. *Prayer*. Where there are personified cosmic forces, there is a customary way of addressing them, usually by speaking or chanting out loud. Often people pray in public, at a sacred location, and with special materials: incense, smoke, objects (such as rosary beads or a prayer wheel), and so on.

2. *Physiological exercise*. Many religious systems have methods for physically manipulating psychological states to induce an ecstatic spiritual state. Wallace suggests four major kinds of manipulation: drugs; sensory deprivation; mortification of the flesh by pain, sleeplessness, and fatigue; and deprivation of food, water, or air. In many societies, the experience of ecstasy, euphoria, dissociation, or hallucination seems to be a goal of religious effort (Figure 11.4).

3. *Exhortation*. In all religious systems, certain people are believed to have closer relationships with the invisible powers than others, and they are expected to use those relationships in the spiritual interests of others. These people give orders, heal, threaten, comfort, and interpret.

4. *Mana*. Mana refers to an impersonal superhuman power that is sometimes believed to be transferable; for example, by laying her or his hands on a sick person, a healer may be able to transfer healing power to that person's body to remove or destroy an illness. In Guider, Cameroon, some people believe that the ink used to copy passages from the Quran has power. Washing the ink off the board on which the words are written, and drinking the ink, transfers the power of the words into the body of the drinker. The principle here is that sacred things are to be touched so that power may be transferred.

5. *Taboo*. People or objects that may not be touched are taboo. Some people believe that if such people or objects are touched, the cosmic power they contain will "drain away" or injure the toucher. Many religious systems have taboo objects. Traditionally, Catholics were not to touch the host (the consecrated bread) during communion; Jews may not touch the handwritten text of the biblical scrolls. In ancient Polynesia, commoners could not touch the chief's body; even an accidental touch resulted in the death of the commoner. Food may also be taboo; many societies have elaborate rules concerning the

Figure 11.4 A *kavadi* bearer bestows a blessing onto a believer as he makes the pilgrimage to the Batu Caves in Kuala Lumpur, Malaysia.

foods that may or may not be eaten at different times or by different kinds of people.

6. *Feasts.* Eating and drinking in a religious context is very common. The Holy Communion of Catholics and Protestants is a meal set apart by its religious context. The Passover Seder for Jews is another religious feast (Figure 11.5). For the Huichol of Mexico, the consumption of peyote is set apart by its religious context. Even everyday meals may be seen to have a religious quality if they begin or end with prayer.

7. *Sacrifice.* Giving something of value to the invisible forces or their agents is a feature of many religious systems. This may be an offering of money, goods, or services; or the sacrificial killing of animals or, very rarely, human beings. Sacrifices may be made in thanks to the cosmic forces in hopes of influencing them to act in a certain way or simply to gain general religious merit (Figure 11.6).

Figure 11.5 Siblings read from the Haggadah at a Passover Seder in Tel Aviv, Israel.

Religion and Communication

Those who are committed to religious world views are convinced of the existence of beings or forces that are ordinarily invisible but actively involved in their lives. Indeed, some of the most highly valued religious practices, such as religious ecstasy or trance, produce outer symptoms that may be perceived by others, but their most powerful effects can be experienced only by the individual who undergoes them personally. If you had such a personal experience and wanted to tell others about it, how would you proceed?

You might well begin by searching for metaphors based on experiences already well known to your audience. One Hindu worshipper in Kuala Lumpur, Malaysia, who successfully went into trance during the festival of Thaipusam, described his experience as "floating in the air, followed by the wind" (*Floating in the Air* 1973) (Figure 11.7). And the Hebrew poet who wrote the biblical Psalm 23, which begins with the metaphor "The Lord is my shepherd," tried to express his experience of the power and love of his God by comparing this God to a shepherd and himself to a sheep. Indeed, the language human beings use to talk about omnipresent and omniscient supernatural beings is often full of metaphors. Even those religious followers who claim to have had personal experience of a supernatural reality will probably still find themselves forced to resort to poetic, metaphorical language if they want

to explain that experience to other people—and perhaps even to themselves.

When societal metaphors are used, members of the tradition are likely to conceive of the forces at work in the universe as personified beings with many of the attributes of human agents at work in their own society. As societies differ from one another, so too does the way their members characterize the universe. Thus, members of societies organized in strong groups based on kinship usually conceive of a universe peopled with the spirits of powerful ancestral figures who take an interest in the lives of their living descendants. However, members of societies run by vast and complex bureaucracies (e.g., the Roman Empire) are apt to picture the universe as being run by an army of hierarchically ordered gods and spirits, all of which may be supervised by a chief god.

Figure 11.6 Tamil women offering sacrifices during a ceremony in Albion, Mauritius.

Figure 11.7 A family prays together at Batu Caves in Kuala Lumpur, Malaysia. Why might a religious follower use metaphors rather than literal descriptions to describe feelings brought about by religious practices?

Organic metaphors may also figure in the construction of religious understanding. Anthropologist James Fernandez (1977) reports that organic metaphors are common in the Bwiti religion of the Fang (see Map 11.1). The human heart, for example, is an apt metaphor for Bwiti devotees because "(1) it is the heart which is the most alive of the bloody organs, (2) it is traditionally conceived by the Fang to be the organ of thought, and (3) in its bloodiness it is associated with the female principle. . . . Many meanings are at work in this metaphor, for that bloody organ, the heart, has a congeries of useful associations" (1977: 112).

Societies that rely on technological metaphors tend to construct a world view in which the universe is a highly complex machine put together by a skilled builder or builders. When we say that we are only *cogs in a machine,* or talk about social status

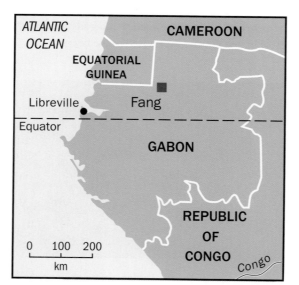

Map 11.1 Fang

priest A religious practitioner skilled in the practice of religious rituals, which he or she carries out for the benefit of the group.

and roles as interchangeable *parts*, we are using machine metaphors. In a mechanical world view, all processes are complex, orderly, predictable, and knowable; thus, it is possible for humans to effectively intervene in the world and alter the course of a process without the aid of a spiritual being or force. Therefore, while this world view is popular in Western societies today, many people question whether it can be called *religious*.

Religious Organization

In the societal metaphor, the forces in the universe are personalized, and people seeking to influence those forces must handle them as they would handle powerful human beings. Thus, communication is the central feature. When we address each other, we expect a response. The same is true when we address personalized cosmic forces. Yet communicating with supernatural forces can be a tremendously complex undertaking. Some societies, therefore, have developed complex social practices to ensure that it is done properly. In these societies, religion is institutionalized, and social positions are created for specialists who supervise or embody correct religious practice.

Anthropologists have identified two broad categories of religious specialists: (1) *shamans* and (2) *priests*. A *shaman* is a religious practitioner and healer who is believed to have the ability to contact invisible powers directly on behalf of individuals or groups. Shamans are often thought to be able to travel to the cosmic realm to communicate with the beings or forces that dwell there in order to plead with them to act in favour of their people. Shamans may then return with messages for their people. In many societies, the training that a shaman receives is long and demanding and may involve the use of powerful psychoactive substances, producing altered states of consciousness to access cosmic beings. This position can embody dangerous ambiguities: someone who can contact such beings for positive benefits may also be able to contact them to produce negative outcomes, such as disease or death. Cultural anthropologist Barbara Tedlock (2005) observes that shamanism was possibly the domain of women in its earliest forms. Certainly, it is the world's oldest form of religious and medical practice, and it remains a force for healing today.

Priests, in contrast, are skilled in the practice of religious rituals, which are carried out for the benefit of the group (Figure 11.8). Priests do not necessarily have direct contact with cosmic forces. Often their

© Shaun Cunningham/Alamy Stock Photo

Figure 11.8 Priests are experts in carrying out religious rituals. This Taoist priest wears her traditional costume as she performs a cleansing ceremony at the annual Dragon Boat Races in Victoria, British Columbia.

major role is to mediate such contact by ensuring that the required ritual activity has been performed according to the established tradition. Priests are found in hierarchical societies. Status differences separating rulers and subjects in such societies are reflected in the unequal relationship between the priest and other members of the religion.

Religion in Contemporary Society

Someplace in time we saw a world at once awesome and fearful. We came to contemplate the transcendental (i.e., things relating to a spiritual realm). How this happened is a mystery, but new research in evolutionary biology and cognitive behaviour gives us indications of the emergence of religious thought and the representation of the supernatural (Boyer and Bergstrom 2008). Were we *Homo sapiens*, or earlier forms of the genus *Homo*? Is it possible that some form of wonder is a trait of all living beings, as Buddhists would contend? From our traditional past, where document is the artifact, we can identify

categories of sacred and/or profane that tell us of our understanding of the transformational nature of the world in which we live. This message comes to us even in the "now," and it "does not just foster conformity and stability but . . . space for invention and innovation" (Dods 2007).

Anthropologists Garrett Cook and Thomas Offit (2008) give us an example of how religions can evolve by borrowing from surrounding cultures while still preserving their most essential aspects. During their fieldwork in Guatemala, Cook and Offit visited the small Maya town of Santiago Momostenango. To begin, they note an ongoing tension in this town between Catholics—followers of Catholicism, which was brought to the region by European colonizers beginning in the sixteenth century—and Costumbristas—followers of the local religion Costumbre. Over the years, Costumbre has evolved to incorporate elements of both traditional Maya practices and Christian traditions. For example, Costumbristas worship traditional earth lords and ancestors as well as saints and a figure known as Jesu Cristo (an interpretation of the Christian figure Jesus Christ). In recent years, Costumbre has continued to respond to external cultural influences, for example, by replacing traditional dance-dramas with more modernized costumed performances, and by incorporating Westernized foods in place of more traditional fare.

Cook and Offit observe that Costumbre has changed in response to pressure from a number of forces, including the emergence of new classes and new ways of making a living, increased exposure to popular media containing messages from around the world, the introduction of new religious choices, and "a growing generation gap" (2008: 46). Despite having changed, however, Costumbre continues to retain a number of its core aspects. Indeed, it seems that it is through the process of borrowing and synthesizing elements from other cultures—what Cook and Offit refer to as **transculturation**—that traditional elements can be preserved. By changing to reflect new cultural and social realities, Costumbre is able to remain vibrant and relevant to new generations.

Even as Indigenous and quasi-Indigenous religions, such as Costumbre, have devised innovative ways to keep their traditions alive, a less flexible religious practice has been gaining ground in postcolonial settings: Pentecostal Christianity. Indeed, in recent decades, Pentecostal Christianity has

transculturation
Cultural change resulting from contact between different cultures.

become increasingly popular in Latin America and Africa, often replacing forms of Christianity introduced in colonial times (e.g., Catholicism). In many forms, Pentecostal Christianity strongly rejects Indigenous practices and beliefs; often, it demonizes local gods as evil forces that must be rejected (see, e.g., Cook and Offit 2008). Yet in some regions, the Pentecostal movement has brought with it positive social developments. As anthropologist Naomi Haynes (2012) observes, for example, the Pentecostal movement in Zambia has given local followers access to resources they can use to battle economic uncertainty. In particular, membership in a Pentecostal congregation offers individuals the opportunity to form interpersonal connections that can lead to social and economic gains. Sociologist Daniel P.S. Goh (2010) notes similar outcomes in Singapore, where the Pentecostal movement has exposed young Singaporeans to a world view that helps them make sense of their post-colonial surroundings.

While religious participation is growing in some regions of the world, religious attendance is declining in many Western nations, including Canada. In part, this decline stems from an increase in the number of people who choose not to align themselves with an official religion (see Eagle 2011). Of course, religious attendance varies by region, and along urban–rural lines. In Canada, for example, surveys have found that the Atlantic provinces (New Brunswick, Prince Edward Island, Nova Scotia, and Newfoundland and Labrador) tend to have the highest

attendance rates while rates in British Columbia are traditionally low (Clark and Schellenberg 2006) (Figure 11.9). Further, small rural communities tend to have higher attendance rates than do larger cities (Clark 2000). Factors such as age, gender, and immigration status also have an impact, with older individuals, women, and recent immigrants being more likely to attend religious services (Clark 2000; Clark and Schellenberg 2006).

Anthropologists Robert V. Kemper and Julie Adkins (2006) have taken a close look at how these and other factors impact attendance at the congregational level. In their study, they examine four specific Protestant congregations in North Texas:

1. One that has been experiencing a decline in membership for decades
2. One that has been experiencing a decline in membership for a few years
3. One that had experienced a decline but is now growing in membership
4. One that is growing in membership

In their analysis, Kemper and Adkins hypothesize that the long-term decline they witnessed in the first congregation they investigated may be due to the fact that the congregation is located in an older, out-of-the-way residential area that is unlikely to attract visitors. In contrast, the more recent decline they witnessed in the second congregation may be due to Protestants leaving the area and more and more Hispanic Catholics moving in. In the case of

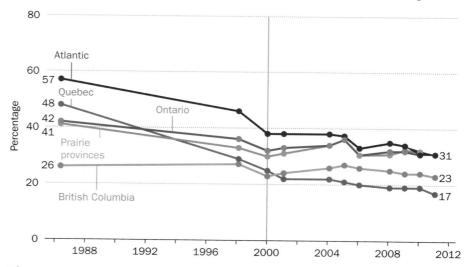

Figure 11.9 Decline in religious attendance in Canada, by region. Note that the numbers represent the percentage of Canadians 15 and older who attend religious services at least once a month.

Source: Pew Research. 2013. "Trends in Religious Attendance, by Region," *Religion & Public Life Project,* available at www.pewforum.org/2013/06/27/canadas-changing-religious-landscape/#_ftnref14.

the congregation experiencing a rebound in membership, Kemper and Adkins hypothesize that the recent growth may have resulted from (1) congregational members' efforts to reach out to the students, staff, and faculty of a college located across the street from the church and (2) the ability of the congregation's enthusiastic new pastor to connect with members of the community. Finally, the researchers attribute the growth experienced by the final congregation to a dramatic increase in population, including an increase in the number of Protestants moving to the area. As these case studies suggest, the ways in which various factors combine to contribute to the decline or growth within a specific congregation are varied and complex (333).

World Views in Operation: Two Case Studies

Anthropologists often say that people of different cultures live in different worlds. This is a metaphorical statement. It asserts that our understanding of reality depends on the particular point of view embodied in our culture. Of course, every culture contains subcultures that may draw pictures of reality that conflict with each other. The experience of juggling multiple points of view in our own society helps us to cope with unfamiliar perspectives in other societies.

As we navigate our own and other societies, we encounter world views that are fully formed. We face a rich tapestry of symbols and rituals and everyday practices linked to one another in what often appears to be a seamless web. Where do we begin to sort things out? The following examples from the field offer some valuable insights into this essential question.

Mind, Body, and Emotion in Huichol Religious Practice

Anthropologist Barbara Myerhoff (1974) discusses the world view of the Huichol in relation to their sacred peyote hunt (Figure 11.10). The Huichol are maize farmers who live in the Sierra Madre Occidental area of northwestern Mexico (see Map 11.2). Annually, they travel to a desert about 600 kilometres from their homes to hunt peyote, a small spineless cactus that contains psychoactive compounds. Because peyote is sacred to the Huichol, this journey is also sacred, representing a pilgrimage to Wirikuta, the original Huichol homeland where the First People, both deities and ancestors, once lived. The journey is hard and dangerous, both physically

Figure 11.10 A Huichol shaman's violin and arrows, together with a basket of freshly gathered peyote.

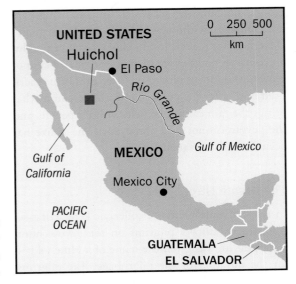

Map 11.2 Huichol

and spiritually. The pilgrims seek to restore and experience the original state of unity that existed at the beginning of the world.

This state of unity is symbolized by deer, maize, and peyote. The deer symbolizes the masculine, hunting past and thus connects the Huichol with their ancestors. In Huichol thought, the deer gave them peyote and appears every year in the hunt in Wirikuta. Blood from a sacrificed deer makes the maize grow and makes it nourishing. The deer is more powerful than human beings but not as remote as the gods. It symbolizes independence, adventure, and freedom.

Although the Huichol have only recently begun to grow maize, it is central to their present-day life. A life based on maize is tedious and precarious: the Huichol have to stay home to watch the crops, and, even if they are careful, the maize may not grow. Maize symbolizes the labour of the present: food, domesticity, sharing between the sexes, routine, and persistent diligence. It also provides the Huichol with the language of beauty. "Maize," the Huichol say, "is our life."

Peyote, when gathered in the land of its origins, is sacred. It is used to induce personal visions, which are not shared with others. It is also used ritually, in which case so little is eaten that no visions are produced. It seems that the purpose of ritual consumption is to reach communion with the deities. The Huichol think of peyote as plant and animal at once; at the climactic moments of the peyote hunt, it is hunted like the deer: "Peyote is neither mundane, like maize, nor exotic and exciting, like deer. It is that solitary, ahistorical, asocial, asexual, nonrational domain without which [human beings] are not complete, without which life is a lesser affair" (Myerhoff 1974: 227). In Huichol religious thought, deer, maize, and peyote fit together: maize cannot grow without deer blood, the deer cannot be sacrificed until after the peyote hunt, the ceremony that brings the rain cannot be held without peyote, and the peyote cannot be hunted until the maize has been cleaned and sanctified.

The Peyote Hunt

In 1966, Myerhoff and her colleague Peter Furst accompanied Huichol pilgrims on the peyote hunt. Each pilgrim was given the name of a Huichol god for the duration of the pilgrimage. The pilgrims, under the guidance of a shaman, all followed strict rules about sexual continence and other behaviours, separating themselves from their everyday routine. Once the pilgrims entered Wirikuta, many ways of speaking and acting were reversed. "Stand up" meant "sit down"; "go away" meant "come here." The van in which they travelled became a "burro" that would stop "if he ran out of tequila." The shaman who led the pilgrimage told Myerhoff that "on the peyote hunt, we change the names of things because when we cross over there, into Wirikuta, things are so sacred that all is reversed" (1974: 148):

> In the sacred land, the pilgrims became hunters, searching for peyote. Once the first peyote cactus was found, it was trapped by two arrows. The pilgrims then encircled it and presented their offerings. The shaman cut it out of the ground, sliced sections, and put one section in each pilgrim's mouth. The little group was sharply etched against the desert in the late afternoon sun—motionless, soundless, the once-bright colours of their costumes now muted under layers of dust—chewing, chewing the bitter plant. So [sixteenth-century missionary and pioneering ethnographer Bernardo de] Sahagún described the ancient Indians who wept in the desert over the plant they esteemed so greatly. The success of the undertaking was unquestionable and the faces changed from quiet wonder to rapture to exaltation, all without words, all at the same moment. . . . Their camaraderie, the completeness of their communion with one another was self-evident. The companions were radiant. Their love for life and for one another was palpable. Though they did not speak and barely moved, no one seeing them there could call the experience anything less than collective ecstasy. (155–7)

Following this moment of *communitas*, the pilgrims collected as much peyote as they would need for their community and hastened to depart. The reversals and other requirements remained in effect until they reached home.

The unification of deer, maize, and peyote gives the peyote hunt its power to provide answers to questions of the ultimate meaning of life. Myerhoff suggests that the way the Huichol's religious system answers these questions is distinctive. Some religions explain present-day moral incoherence by asserting that an original paradise was lost following an ancient sin. Other systems assert that there is an afterlife in which all the suffering of the world will be set right. The Huichol refuse to let go of their past:

> Their most precious religious heritage—their beginnings—is idealized and recovered.

Even if only for a little while, by means of the peyote hunt, Paradise may be regained. Through the deer–maize–peyote complex, the deer and a life dedicated to hunting the deer is still a fact of present-day life rather than a fading, shabby memory, chewed over by old men at the end of the day. (1974: 262)

The deer–maize–peyote complex and the peyote hunt represent the union of mind, body, and emotion. Through a holistic ritual experience that is profoundly meaningful, deeply moving, and thoroughly physical, the Huichol re-experience the correctness of their way of life.

Witchcraft, Oracles, and Magic among the Azande

Evans-Pritchard, in his classic work *Witchcraft, Oracles, and Magic among the Azande* (1976 [1937]), describes how the Azande of central Africa (see EthnoProfile 11.1) use **witchcraft** beliefs to explain unfortunate things that happen to them, and how they employ **oracles** and **magic** to exert a measure of control over the actions of other people. Evans-Pritchard was impressed by the intelligence, sophistication, and skepticism of his Azande informants. For this reason, he was all the more struck by their ability to hold a set of beliefs that many Europeans would regard as superstitious.

Azande Witchcraft Beliefs

The Azande believe that *mangu* (translated by Evans-Pritchard as "witchcraft") is a substance in the body of witches, generally located under the sternum in the chest. Being part of the body, the witchcraft substance grows as the body grows; therefore, the older the witch, the more potent his or her witchcraft. The Azande believe that children inherit witchcraft from their parents. Men and women may both be witches. Men practise witchcraft against other men; women, against other women. Witchcraft works when its "soul" removes the soul of a certain organ in the victim's body, usually at night, causing a slow, wasting disease. Suffering such a disease is therefore an indication that an individual has been bewitched.

Witchcraft is a basic concept for the Azande, one that shapes their experience of adversity. All deaths are due to witchcraft and must be avenged by magic, often with the help of a witch doctor (Figure 11.11). Other misfortunes are also commonly attributed to witchcraft, unless the victim has broken a taboo, has failed to observe a moral rule, or is believed to be responsible for his or her own problems. An incompetent potter whose pots break while firing, for example, may claim that witchcraft caused them to break, but everyone will laugh because they know that the potter lacks skill. Witchcraft is believed to be so common that the Azande are neither surprised nor awestruck when they encounter it. Their usual response is anger.

witchcraft The practice of magic, whether intentional or not.

oracles Invisible forces to which people address questions and whose responses they believe to be truthful.

magic A set of beliefs and practices designed to control the visible or invisible world for specific purposes.

EthnoProfile 11.1
Azande

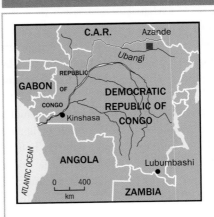

Region: Central Africa

Nations: Northeast Democratic Republic of the Congo, South Sudan, southeast Central African Republic

Language: Zande (Pazande), an Adamawa-Ubangi language of the Niger-Congo group

Population: 1 million–4 million (2000s estimates)

Environment: Sparsely wooded savannah

Livelihood: Agriculture with maize, rice, and groundnuts (peanuts); cassava and sweet potatoes as main crops; hunting, fishing, and chicken raising

Political organization: Traditionally, highly organized tribal kingdoms; today, part of modern nation-states

For more information: Evans-Pritchard, E.E. 1976 [1937]. *Witchcraft, Oracles, and Magic among the Azande*, abr. edn (Oxford: Oxford University Press).

Figure 11.11 An Azande "witch doctor."

To the Azande, witchcraft is a completely natural explanation for events. Consider the circumstances that might lead to someone's being crushed by a collapsing granary. Azande territory is hot, and people seeking shade often sit under traditional-style granaries, which are raised on logs. Termites are common in Azande territory, and sometimes they destroy the supporting logs, causing a granary to collapse. Occasionally, when a granary collapses, people sitting under it are killed. Why does this happen? The Azande are well aware that the termites chew up the wood until the supports give way, but to them that explanation is not enough. Why, after all, should that particular granary have collapsed at that particular moment? To skeptical observers, the only connection is coincidence in time and space. Western science does not provide any explanation for why these two chains of causation intersect. But the Azande do: witchcraft causes the termites to finish chewing up the wood at just that moment; thus, that witchcraft must be avenged.

Dealing with Witches

How to expose the witch? For this task, the Azande employ specific trials as oracles. Pre-eminent among these is the poison oracle. The poison is a strychnine-like substance imported by the Azande.

The oracle "speaks" through the effect the poison has on chickens. When witchcraft is suspected, a relative of the afflicted person will take some chickens into the bush along with a specialist in administering the poison oracle. This person will feed poison to one chicken, name a suspect, and ask the oracle to kill the chicken if this person is the witch. If the chicken dies, a second chicken will be fed poison, and the oracle will be asked to spare the chicken if the suspect just named is indeed the witch. Thus, the Azande double-check the oracle carefully; a witchcraft accusation is not made lightly.

People do not consult the oracle with a long list of names. They need only consider those who might wish them or their families ill: people who have quarrelled with them, who are unpleasant or anti-social, and whose behaviour is somehow out of line. Indeed, witches are always neighbours because neighbours are the only people who know you well enough to wish you and your family ill.

Once the oracle has identified the witch, the person performing the ritual removes the wing of the chicken and has it taken by messenger to the compound of the accused person. The messenger presents the accused witch with the chicken wing and says that he has been sent concerning the illness of so-and-so's relative: "Almost invariably the witch replies courteously that he is unconscious of injuring anyone, that if it is true that he has injured the man in question he is very sorry, and that if it is he alone who is troubling him then he will surely recover because from the bottom of his heart he wishes him health and happiness" (Evans-Pritchard 1976 [1937]: 42). The accused then calls for a gourd of water, takes some water in his mouth, and sprays it out over the wing. He says aloud, so the messenger can hear and repeat what he says, that if he is a witch he is not aware of it and that he is not intentionally causing the sick person to be ill. He addresses the witchcraft in him, asking it to become cool, and concludes by saying that he makes this appeal from his heart, not just from his lips.

People accused of witchcraft are usually astounded; no Azande thinks of himself or herself as a witch. However, the Azande strongly believe in witchcraft and in the oracles, and if the oracle says someone is a witch, then that person must be one. The accused witch is grateful to the family of the sick person for letting this be known. Otherwise, if the accused had been allowed to murder the victim, all the while unaware of it, the witch would surely be killed by vengeance magic. The witchcraft accusation carries a further message: the behaviour of the accused is sufficiently outside the bounds of acceptable Azande behaviour to have marked him or her as a potential witch. The accused witch, then, is being told to change his or her behaviour.

Patterns of Witchcraft Accusation

Compared with the stereotypes of Euro-American witchcraft—old women dressed in black, riding on broomsticks, casting spells, causing milk to sour or people to sicken—Azande witchcraft seems quite tame. People whose impression of witchcraft comes from Western European images may believe that witchcraft and witch-hunting tear at the very fabric of society. Yet anthropological accounts, such as Evans-Pritchard's, suggest that practices such as witchcraft accusation can sometimes keep societies together.

Anthropologist Mary Douglas looked at the range of witchcraft accusations worldwide and discovered that they fall into two basic types: (1) the witch is an evil outsider; (2) the witch is an internal enemy, either the member of a rival faction or a dangerous deviant (1970: xxvi–xxvii). These different patterns of accusation perform different functions in a society. If the witch is an outsider, witchcraft accusations can strengthen in-group ties. If the witch is an internal enemy, accusations of witchcraft can weaken in-group ties; factions may have to regroup, communities may split, and the entire social hierarchy may be reordered. If the witch is a dangerous deviant, the accusation of witchcraft can be seen as an attempt to control the deviant in defence of the wider values of the community. Douglas concludes that how people understand witchcraft is based on the social relations of their society.

Maintaining and Changing a World View

What makes a world view stable? Why is a world view rejected? These questions are related to general questions about persistence and change in human social life. Anthropologists recognize that culture change is a complex phenomenon, and they admit that they do not have all the answers even as they struggle with intersubjective negotiations.

Changes in world view must, first of all, be related to the practical everyday experiences of people in a particular society. Stable, repetitive experiences reinforce the acceptability of any traditional world view that has successfully accounted for such experiences in the past. When experiences become

unpredictable, however, thinking people in any society may become painfully aware that past experiences can no longer be trusted as guides for the future, and traditional world views may be undermined.

Coping with Change

Drastic changes in experience lead people to create new interpretations that will help them cope with those changes. Sometimes the change is an outcome of local or regional struggles. The Protestant Reformation of the sixteenth century, for example, adapted the Christian tradition to changing social circumstances in northern Europe by breaking ties to the Pope, turning Church lands over to secular authorities, allowing clergy to marry, and so forth. Protestants continued to identify themselves as Christians even though many of their religious practices had changed.

In Guider, Cameroon (see Map 11.3), lone rural migrants have frequently abandoned old religious practices and taken on urban customs and a new identity through conversion to Islam. However, the conflict between new and old need not necessarily lead to conversion. Sometimes the result is a creative synthesis of old religious practices and new ones, a process called **syncretism**. Under the pressure of Christian missionizing, Indigenous people of Central America identified some of their own pre-Christian, personalized superhuman beings with particular Catholic saints (Figure 11.12). Similarly, Africans brought to Brazil identified Catholic saints with African gods to produce the syncretistic religion Candomblé. The example of Costumbre in Guatemala, discussed earlier, is yet another example of a syncretic religion.

syncretism The synthesis of old religious practices (or an old way of life) with new religious practices (or a new way of life), introduced from outside, often by force.

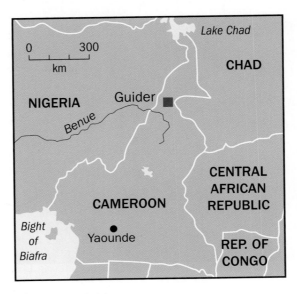

Map 11.3 Guider

Figure 11.12 The figure of Santa Muerte, seen here in Mexico City, is a personification of death blended with Roman Catholic iconography. In what ways can syncretic figures such as this one help worshippers make sense of their worlds?

revitalization A conscious, deliberate, and organized attempt by some members of a society to create a more satisfying culture in a time of crisis.

nativism An attempt to return to traditional customs.

Anthropologists have debated the nature of syncretistic practices. They note that while some such practices may be viewed as a way of resisting new ideas imposed from above, others may be introduced from above by powerful outsiders deliberately making room for local beliefs within their own world view. The Romans, for example, made room for local deities within their imperial pantheon, and today's Catholicism explicitly urges non-European Catholics to worship using local cultural forms (Stewart and Shaw 1994).

Figure 11.13 Fang women perform the Belebele dance during a Bwiti ceremony. How do revitalization movements such as this one differ from nativistic movements?

When groups defend, or refashion, their own way of life in the face of outside encroachments, anthropologists sometimes describe their activities as **revitalization**: a deliberate, organized attempt by some members of a society to create a more satisfying culture (Wallace 1972: 75). Revitalization arises in times of crisis, most often among groups who are facing oppression and radical transformation, usually at the hands of outsiders (such as colonizing powers). Revitalization movements engage in a "politics of religious synthesis" that produces a range of outcomes (Stewart and Shaw 1994). Sometimes syncretism is embraced; other times it is rejected in favour of **nativism**, a return to the old ways. Some nativistic movements expect the appearance of a messiah or a prophet who will bring back a lost golden age of peace, prosperity, and harmony, a process often called *revivalism*, *millenarianism*, or *messianism*.

A classic New World example of a millenarian movement was the Ghost Dance movement among Indigenous peoples on the Great Plains of the United States in the 1890s. When the buffalo were exterminated, Indigenous Plains dwellers lost their independence and were herded onto reservations by Euro-Americans, who were better armed and greater in number than the Indigenous people. Out of this crisis emerged Wovoka, a prophet who taught that the existing world would soon be destroyed and that a new crust would form on the earth. All settlers and Indigenous people who followed the settlers' ways would become buried. Those Indigenous people who abandoned the settlers' ways, led pure lives, and danced the Ghost Dance would be saved. As the new crust formed, the buffalo would return, as would all the ancestors of the believers. Together, all would lead lives of virtue and joy.

Because the world was going to change by itself, violence against the oppressors was not a necessary part of the Ghost Dance. Nevertheless, the movement frightened settlers and the US Army, who suspected an armed uprising. Those fears and suspicions led to the massacre at Wounded Knee, South Dakota, in which American soldiers killed almost all the members of a Lakota (Sioux) band, including women and children.

A revitalization movement that has enjoyed greater longevity is the syncretistic Bwiti religion of the Fang in Central Africa (Figure 11.13; Map 11.1). Since the late nineteenth century, the Fang have faced three important challenges to their world view. First, the reality of "the far away" represented by French colonialism came to challenge the reality of "the near" and familiar. Second, the protective traditional powers of "the below" were challenged by Christian missionaries' messages of divinity in "the above." Third, the pluralism of colonial life challenged the community's sense of cohesion by establishing a double standard in which the colonized were treated differently from the colonizers (Fernandez 1982: 571). Bwiti allows its members to cope with the first challenge by using the psychoactive drug *eboga* ("ibogaine") to go out to the far and convert it into the near. In the second case, the Christian god of "the above" and the traditional gods of "the below" are both incorporated into the Bwiti pantheon. For the third, Bwiti ritual promotes among members the communal feeling of "one-heartedness."

Bwiti has created a world view that allows many Fang to cope with the strains of exploitation. Within Bwiti, some old metaphors (the forest, the body social, the kinship system) have been reanimated, some new ones (red and white uniforms, a path of birth and death, the world as a globe or a ball) have been created, and all have been fitted together in a satisfying way. This world has, however, closed itself off from the wider society of Gabon. Bwiti represents a kind of escape from the pressures of the outside world (Fernandez 1982: 566).

Nativistic movements may, however, represent resistance to, rather than escape from, the outside world. They may attempt to actively remove or avoid any cultural practices associated with outsiders. One such "anti-syncretistic" group is the Kwaio, living on the island of Malaita in the Solomon Islands (Figure 11.14; see also Map 11.4). Almost all their neighbours have converted to Christianity, and the nation of which they are a part is militantly Christian. Members of other groups wear Western-style clothing, work on plantations or in tourist hotels, attend schools, and live in cities. The Kwaio have refused all this: "Young men carry bows and arrows; girls and women, nude except for customary ornaments, dig taro in forest gardens; valuables made of strung shell beads are exchanged at mortuary feasts; and priests sacrifice pigs to the ancestral spirits on whom prosperity and life itself depend" (Keesing 1982: 1).

Anthropologist Robert Keesing (1992), known for his work with the Kwaio people, admits that he does not know exactly why the Kwaio responded to colonial influence in this way. He suspects that pre-colonial social and political differences between the Kwaio and their coastal neighbours influenced later developments. The colonial encounter was certainly relevant. In 1927, some Kwaio attacked a British patrol, killing the district officer and 13 Solomon Islands troops. The subsequent massacre of many Kwaio by a police force of other Malaitans, and their

Figure 11.14 Although the Kwaio have recently adopted some outsider practices, such as wearing manufactured clothing, they continue to adhere to many of their traditional ways.

marginalization and persecution by the colonial government, contributed to Kwaio resistance.

The Kwaio maintain their old ways deliberately, in the face of alternatives; their traditional way of life is therefore lived in a modern context: "In the course of anti-colonial struggle, *kastomu* (custom) and commitment to ancestral ways have become symbols of identity and autonomy" (Keesing 1982: 240). In the eyes of the Kwaio, the many Solomon Islanders who became Christianized and acculturated lost their cultural ties and thereby their ties to the land and to their past, becoming outsiders in their own homeland. Thus, maintaining tradition is a form of political protest. From this perspective, many contemporary

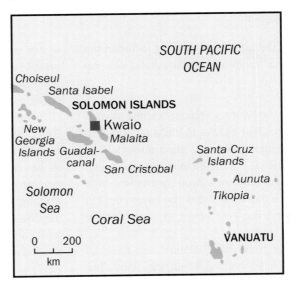

Map 11.4 Kwaio

anti-syncretistic movements in the world, from various religious fundamentalisms to movements for national identity and cultural autonomy, can be understood as having aims very similar to those of the Kwaio, sparked by many of the same forces.

World Views as Instruments of Power

We have discussed the process that people use to build their world views, and we have noted how world views vary enormously from culture to culture. But within any particular cultural tradition, there are probably always different world views.

How does a particular picture of reality become the "official" world view for a given culture? And once that position is achieved, how is it maintained? To be in the running for the official picture of reality, a world view must be able, however minimally, to make sense of some people's personal and social experiences. Sometimes, however, it may seem to some members of society that barely credible views of reality have triumphed over alternatives that seem far more plausible. Thus, something more than persuasive ability alone must be involved, and that something is power. As cognitive linguists George Lakoff and Mark Johnson put it, "People in power get to impose their metaphors" (1980: 157). Powerless people may be unable to dislodge the official world view of their society. They can, however, refuse to accept the imposition of someone else's world view and develop an unofficial world view based on metaphors that reflect their own condition of powerlessness (Scott 1990). Such unofficial world views may even suggest appropriate action for transforming that condition. (See the "In Their Own Words" box that follows on custom and confrontation.)

How can metaphors, or the symbols that represent them, be used as instruments of power and control? First, a symbol can be used to refer to a self-evident truth when people in power seek to eliminate or impose certain forms of conduct. Thus, a deceased parent, whose memory must be respected, may be invoked to block some actions or to stimulate others. Holy books, such as the Quran, may also be used in this way. For example, a legal record from Guider indicates that a son once brought suit against his father for refusing to repay him a certain amount of money. The father claimed that he had paid. Both father and son got into an increasingly heated argument in which neither would give ground. Finally, the judge in the case asked the father to take a copy of the Quran in his hand and swear that he was telling the truth. This he did. The son, however, refused to swear on the Quran and finally admitted that he had been lying. In this case, the status of the Quran as the unquestioned word of God, which implied the power of God to punish liars, controlled the son's behaviour.

Second, a symbol may be under the direct control of a person wishing to affect the behaviour of

In Their Own Words

Custom and Confrontation

In the following passage, the late Roger Keesing recorded the words of one of his Kwaio informants, Dangeabe'u, who defends Kwaio custom.

The government has brought the ways of business, the ways of money. The people at the coast believe that's what's important and tell us we should join in. Now the government is controlling the whole world. The side of the Bible is withering away. When that's finished, the government will rule, unchallenged. It will hold all the land. All the money will go to the government to feed its power. Once everything—our lands, too—are in their hands, that will be it.

I've seen the people from other islands who have all become Christians. They knew nothing about their land. The white people have gotten their hands on their lands. The whites led them to forget all the knowledge of their land, separated them from it. And when the people knew nothing about their land, the whites bought it from them and made their enterprises. . . .

That's close upon us too. If we all follow the side of the Bible, the government will become powerful here, too, and will take control of our land. We won't be attached to our land, as we are now, holding our connections to our past. If the government had control of our land, then if we wanted to do anything on it, we'd have to pay them. If we wanted to start a business—a store, say—we'd have to pay the government. We reject all that. We want to keep hold of our land, in the ways passed down to us.

Source: Keesing, Roger. 1992. *Custom and Confrontation: The Kwaio Struggle for Cultural Autonomy* (Chicago: University of Chicago Press), 184.

others. Consider the role of official interpreters of religious or political ideology, such as priests or kings. Their pronouncements define the bounds of permissible behaviour. As Keesing points out,

> [s]enior men, in Melanesia as elsewhere in the tribal world, have depended heavily on control of *sacred knowledge* to maintain their control of earthly politics. By keeping in their hands relations with ancestors and other spirits, by commanding magical knowledge, senior men could maintain a control mediated by the supernatural. Such religious ideologies served too, by defining rules in terms of ancient spirits and by defining the nature of men and women in supernatural terms, to reinforce and maintain the roles of the sexes—and again to hide their nature. (1982: 219)

Keesing's observations remind us that knowledge, like power, is not evenly distributed throughout a society. Some people possess knowledge and control symbols to which others are denied access. Furthermore, this distribution of knowledge is not random: different kinds of people know different things. In some societies, what men know about their religious system is different from what women know, and what older men know may be different from what younger men know. Such discrepancies can have important consequences. Keesing suggested that men's control over women and older men's control over younger men are based on differential access to knowledge (14). It is not just that these different kinds of people know different things; rather, the different things they know (and don't know) enable them (or force them) to remain in the positions they hold in the society.

Religion and Secularism

The European Enlightenment gave birth to a world view that has come to be called **secularism**, and the spread of this world view has had repercussions across the globe. The development of secular ideas and practices profoundly transformed the religious and political institutions that had dominated European society in the Middle Ages. Earlier generations of anthropologists took secularism for granted as the expected outcome of cultural evolution. More recently, however, anthropologists have been led to reconsider the nature of both the Enlightenment and secularism, prompted most sharply by resistance to the secular institutions of Western nation-states.

Strong resistance has come from some immigrant groups living within those states as well as some groups in non-Western nation-states who insist that citizenship and religious identity belong together.

Perhaps the most difficult struggles to adapt to life in secular Western nation-states have been those of some Muslim groups. The distinction between what the liberal democratic state expects and what some Muslims want has recently been explored by anthropologist Talal Asad. His efforts to develop an "anthropology of secularism" highlight the ways in which notions of the secular were shaped over the course of European history, particularly by the Protestant Reformation of Christianity, the subsequent wars of religion in the sixteenth and early seventeenth centuries, and the Enlightenment and the French Revolution of the eighteenth century. Secularism is usually defined as the separation of religion and state and commonly understood as the Enlightenment solution to the bloody and irresolvable wars of religion that followed the Reformation. But Asad's account shows that European secularism presupposed a specific post-Reformation concept of "religion" and a very specific post-Enlightenment concept of "the state," as well as a notion of secular citizenship that owes much to the notion of individual agency developed in Protestant theology. "The secular," he argues, "is a concept that brings together certain behaviours, knowledges, and sensibilities in modern life" (Asad 2003: 25).

The particularities of modern secularism may be clarified if we return to the distinction made in Chapter 9 between orthodoxy and orthopraxy. Religious disputes in the Reformation and the wars of religion concerned questions of *orthodoxy*—that is, correct religious beliefs. In European secularism, thus, *religion* is defined primarily in terms of the beliefs to which its adherents are committed. Similarly, the secular *state* is always understood to be the modern nation-state within a capitalist economy. It is from these understandings of *religion* and *state* that the Enlightenment concept of *citizenship* developed. Secular citizenship, Asad explains, is supposed to "transcend the different identities built on class, gender, and religion, replacing conflicting perspectives by unifying experience. In a sense, this transcendent mediation *is* secularism" (2003: 5). Secular citizens are first and foremost individuals unencumbered by ties to other social groups who possess *within themselves* the motivation to formulate goals, who have the resources to initiate action to pursue those goals, and who are responsible for the consequences of their actions. This concept of

secularism The separation of religion and state.

agency, absolutely crucial to the successful functioning of democratic government and the capitalist market, was itself the product of Protestant theology. In the religious context, independent, self-motivating individuals were responsible before God; in their role as citizens of a liberal secular state, they are individually responsible before the law.

Thus, secularism as a political doctrine clearly emerged as a response to specific religious, political, and economic developments in early modern Europe. Secularism depends, for example, on the notion that a "worldly" domain of social life exists that is distinct from a realm in which religion holds sway. In Christian Europe, this domain was recognized when proponents of what would become "science" successfully argued that the "supernatural," spiritual realm of God was separate and distinct from the "natural," material world of lifeless, inert matter (Keller 1997). This distinction between supernatural and natural worlds "signals the construction of a secular space that begins to emerge in early modernity" (Asad 2003: 27). That secular space would be the ground to which the modern nation-state would lay claim.

Religion and state remained entangled after the wars of religion, however, since "religious freedom" was left in the hands of the states themselves. In most cases, citizens were to profess the faith of their rulers, and if their rulers changed allegiance, the allegiance of citizens was to follow. But in every state, this arrangement created religious minorities of "dissenters" whose rights as citizens were regularly curtailed. Protest against these inequalities led to the French Revolution, which brought a more democratic form of secularism to Europe. Now religious affiliation was a matter of individual conscience and could not be imposed by the state. One consequence of this change was the "eventual emergence of 'minority rights.' But this consequence contained a paradox. Religious minorities in a secular state were at once equal to other citizens [and] . . . unequal to the majority, requiring special protection" (Asad 2003: 174).

Secularism is "not a simple matter of absence of 'religion' in the public life of the modern nation-state. For even in modern secular countries the place of religion varies" (Asad 2003: 5–6). But Asad's analysis suggests that adaptation to life in a liberal secular state is likely to be difficult and painful for those whose religious commitments are rooted primarily in forms of religious *orthopraxy*—correct practice. Many traditions, he notes,

> attribute to the living human body the potential to be shaped (the power to shape itself)

for good or ill. . . . The living body's materiality is regarded as an essential means for cultivating what such traditions define as virtuous conduct and for discouraging what they consider as vice. The role of fear and hope, of felicity and pain, is central to such practices. . . . [The] more one exercises a virtue, the easier it becomes; . . . the more one gives into vice, the harder it is to act virtuously. (89–90)

Islamic religious traditions are rooted in such orthopraxy, and cultivating correct practice depends upon being embedded within a community of like-minded practitioners. When successful, such orthopraxy is understood to produce "the virtue of faithfulness, [which is] an unquestioning habit of obedience." Faithfulness is "a disposition that has to be cultivated like any other and that links one to others who are faithful, through mutual trust and responsibility" (Asad 2003: 90). Religious orthopraxy of this kind can be sustained only by faithful practitioners whose entire way of life is informed by, and acts to reinforce, these unquestioning habits of obedience. If this is the case, then such forms of orthopraxy would appear to be incompatible with secularism:

> For many Muslim minorities (though by no means all) being Muslim is more than simply belonging to an individual faith whose private integrity needs to be publicly respected by the force of law, and being able to participate in the public domain as equal citizens. It is more, certainly, than a cultural identity recognized by the liberal democratic state. It is being able to live as autonomous individuals in a collective life that extends beyond national borders. (180)

It was precisely this apparent incompatibility that was made visible in the recent "affair of the headscarves" in France.

Muslim Headscarves in France: A Case Study

In recent decades, many immigrants to France have come from Muslim countries, particularly in North Africa. By the late 1980s, some French public schools had high proportions of Muslim students. As their numbers increased, controversy developed when some of the female students were denied the right to wear their traditional headcoverings in school. From the point of view of Muslim families, wearing headcoverings in public was a religiously required mode of dress necessary to protect female modesty in public. Controversy erupted when the French government insisted that the headscarves could not be worn in school.

Understanding why the French government was so adamant in its refusal depends on understanding what secularism means in the French republic. Anthropologist John Bowen (2010) describes the history of the relation between religion and state that developed in France after the French Revolution in 1789. As noted, a major consequence of the Revolution was the elimination of special privileges for the Catholic Church, which until that time had been the official religion of the French state. Since the Revolution, the French state has been resolutely secular, requiring that all French citizens, whether students or employees of the state, refrain from drawing attention in public to their religious affiliations. Although Catholic students were allowed to wear necklaces with Catholic crosses, male Jewish students wishing to wear a kippah (headcovering) and female Muslim students wishing to wear headscarves were told to remove their headcoverings or they would be prohibited from attending school.

By 1989, religious groups claiming the right to exercise their religious values in public were ready to test the French secular ideal. In October 1989, three Muslim French girls of North African descent wore headcoverings to their public school. The school insisted that they remove the scarves and dress like the other girls. The girls and their families refused, claiming that wearing the scarf was part of their religious practice. Some of the students also refused to attend biology classes—on the grounds that studying biological evolution contradicted their religious beliefs—or to attend coed physical education classes because they believed that they were immodest. Other schools around the country were challenged in the same way; and in November 1989 the government ruled that the Muslim girls' right to religious expression included wearing a headscarf. But after the French government changed from socialist to centre-right, the issue arose again in 1993; this time, the government banned the wearing of headcoverings in schools.

The government's decision to ban the headscarves was not merely a political response to the xenophobic far right in French politics, which claims that immigration has caused all of the economic problems that France faces and is opposed to "non-French" practices. Rather, the decision follows from the secular world view of the French state, and it was supported by many people on the political left, not just those on the right. Bowen observes that the French state grants full citizenship rights to the children of immigrants, but in return, the "social contract" assumes that the children will be educated to be culturally French. In the official French view, students are to see themselves as identical in all respects except for achievement in school. If certain groups within the system are allowed to argue that they are in some way fundamentally different from all other citizens, especially if the difference is defined as religious, the resolutely secular identity of the French state is called into question, raising issues that were presumed to have been properly settled long ago. Clearly, those who allied in opposition to, or in support of, the wearing of headscarves assumed very different things about the character of the state and what counted as religious toleration.

The Muslim girls were supported by some conservative Catholics and some antiracism activists, while many on the extreme right wing and many on the left opposed the decision to permit headscarves to be worn. This is one of the major arguments that has been raised: secularism is challenged by the wearing of headscarves. The French left has long seen itself as guardian of the secular, anticlerical tradition that began with the French Revolution, and public education was the means by which the power of the Church was to be combatted. Many partisans of the left also argued that the scarves were a symbol of the oppression of women: "Putting on jeans is an act of freedom; putting on the scarf is an act of submission" (Bowen 2014: 284; citing Moruzzi 1994). The political right agreed with that argument but placed it in the context of "the battle between Christianity and Islam, and the general threat to French identity posed by immigrants" (250).

Although France's highest administrative court reaffirmed the ban on headscarves in public schools in October 1999 (Gregory 1999), the controversy continued. In February and March 2004, the French national assembly and senate voted overwhelmingly to ban "conspicuous" religious symbols in the schools. Although this law is presented as necessary to protect the secular state from the divisiveness of religious particularism and prohibits the Jewish kippa and large Christian crosses as well as Muslim headscarves, many argue that the Muslim headscarf is the real target. The law, which affects 1,200 of the 250,000 Muslim students in French schools, has provoked heated debate in France. Some analysts insist that this law will prompt a hardening of positions on all sides; others argue that it will take the pressure off girls who may feel forced by others to wear the scarf against their will; still others insist that the real issue concerns the preservation of the secular French state against inroads by any form of religion. As philosopher Elizabeth Badinter explains,

Figure 11.15 Muslim women and supporters demonstrating against Islamophobia in Paris, France.

Because of the nature of the secularist state, you will never see a policeman wearing a Sikh's turban. While he represents the state's authority, he cannot express his religious affiliation. The terms multi-racial and

multi-cultural are not the same. In France, as citizens, we adhere to a social contract, and in doing so we step back from the symbols of our private affiliations. (quoted in Smith 2004)

Muslims around the world have protested the passage of the French law, and thousands of women have marched in Paris in support of it. The outcome of this struggle remains unclear (Figure 11.15). Meanwhile, the controversy continues: in 2011 it became illegal in France to wear a face-covering veil or mask (including balaclavas, niqabs, and burkas if they cover the face) in public places.

World views represent comprehensive ideas about the structure of the world and the place of one's own group, or one's own self, within that world. The ethnographic record offers a broad array of different world views, each testifying to the imaginative, meaning-making cultural capacity of humans. These models of the world, moreover, do not exist apart from everyday social practices; on the contrary, they are heavily implicated in our interactions with others. And when those interactions lead to crisis, humans respond by seeking ways to make the crisis appear meaningful and therefore manageable. We are meaning-making, meaning-using, meaning-dependent organisms, and nowhere is this clearer than when a meaningful way of life is under assault.

Living Anthropology

Space Exploration and Planetary Perspectives

by Michael P. Oman-Reagan, Vanier Scholar, Memorial University

Today astronauts live and work on the international space station, robotic rovers explore Mars, and plans are being made for settlements on the moon and Mars. While we confront global challenges of climate change, displacement, hunger, and more, private corporations and national agencies, including Canada, India, the United States, China, and Russia, are going into space. Anthropologists are also increasingly thinking about outer space.

The scientists, astronauts, and others who work in space exploration have varied and often conflicting ideas about what it means to explore space, how it relates to the challenges we face on Earth, and what human futures should look like. In my research on space science and exploration in North America,

I work with these communities to learn about their perspectives. Is space exploration just one more opportunity for resource extraction by a privileged powerful few, or is it a chance to inspire planetary co-operation? The answer depends on who you ask. On the one hand, some venture capitalists and politicians talk about space as a "frontier" to be exploited and colonized. They describe outer space by comparing it with the American mythos and using metaphors of "manifest destiny" to justify the violent histories of "settling" the "wild West." On the other hand, scientists and astronauts often discuss space science and exploration as a way humanity can overcome conflicts, develop problem-solving technologies, and build a more peaceful global society to benefit everyone.

Canadian astronaut Chris Hadfield says that looking back on our planet from space gave him a radically new perspective. This new world view experienced by astronauts has been called the "overview effect"—a shift toward a global perspective. Some astronauts say that considering conflicts and differences at a planetary scale reveals the urgent need to create a more harmonious society. Since the first photographs of our entire planet from space were released, this "whole earth" perspective has been an often-used metaphor in Euro-American culture to describe large-scale thinking about political, social, and environmental relationships.

In the 1980s American astronomer Carl Sagan popularized space science and exploration through his books and television series *Cosmos*, often discussing science through a social and political lens. Sagan promoted a "pale blue dot" perspective in which he asked us to think about the Earth as a relatively small point in space, as it appeared in photographs taken by the *Voyager 1* spacecraft from 6 billion kilometres away. Sagan's world view framed the meaning and possibilities of space exploration through a scientific, and atheistic, lens. In contrast, when American astronaut Buzz Aldrin landed on the Moon in 1969 he brought his Christian traditions with him, performing a communion ceremony just after the *Apollo 11* Lunar Module touched down. For Aldrin, the experience and accomplishment of being the first human on the moon had meaning in terms of his religious world view.

When Italian astronaut Samantha Cristoforetti went to the International Space Station in 2014, she brought a *Star Trek* uniform with her and used social media to post selfies and reference her favourite science fiction series. Cristoforetti often framed her time on the space station in terms of the secular, humanistic ideals celebrated by the series. Likewise, American astronaut Mae Jemison, the first woman of colour in space, was inspired to become an astronaut when she saw actress Nichelle Nichols in her ground-breaking role as Uhura on *Star Trek*. Today Jemison works on developing the social and technical capabilities for interstellar travel in hopes of "finding a better version of ourselves" through that process.

In my fieldwork, I've found that these different perspectives about space emerge from diverse cultural backgrounds, educational experiences, understandings of history, science fiction narratives, and more—which all influence how scientists, astronauts, and others imagine current and future possibilities for humanity in space. As people study, explore, and imagine futures in space, they bring their cultures and world views with them. One day, if we build settlements on the moon or Mars, anthropologists will have new opportunities to ask how radical changes in our environment influence world views. Which cultures and world views will we bring as we move into space? How will they change as we make a new planet into a home? If we send only astronauts trained in a military tradition or only missions to extract resources for profit, how might those ideologies shape the future? How will the symbols and metaphors we bring from Earth change on Mars? Will they influence new syncretic practices and world views or even new religions? Future generations of anthropologists will be able to study communities in space settlements to answer these and other questions. Perhaps you will be among them, as an anthropologist on another world.

Key Terms

key metaphors 278
magic 287
metaphor 275
metaphorical entailments 275
metaphorical predicate 275
metaphorical subject 275
metonymy 275

nativism 290
oracles 287
organic metaphor 278
priest 282
religion 279
revitalization 290
secularism 293

societal metaphor 278
syncretism 289
technological metaphor 279
transculturation 283
witchcraft 287
world view 275

Chapter Summary

1. Shared cultural assumptions about how the world works are called *world views*.
2. Metaphors are valuable tools for constructing world views. They can give us insight into aspects of our world that are at times difficult to understand.

Metonymy is the relationship that links the parts of a semantic domain to one another, making metaphor possible. Symbols remind us of the cultural links and insights established through metaphor and metonymy.

3. Differences in world views derive from differences in experience that people try to explain by means of metaphor. People use at least three kinds of key metaphors as foundations for particular world views: societal metaphors, organic metaphors, and technological metaphors.

4. Followers of a particular religion tend to share a world view. Over time, religious beliefs and practices change in response to external cultural forces. By evolving, religions remain vibrant and relevant to new generations, even in the face of secularism.

5. Power and knowledge are not evenly distributed throughout a society. More powerful individuals and groups often impose their preferred key metaphors on the rest of society. Those without power can resist this imposition by creating their own contrasting metaphors and constructing alternative world views.

Critical Thinking Questions

1. How do *summarizing symbols* and *elaborating symbols* differ? What do the symbols of the Canadian flag and the cultural mosaic mean to you? Can you think of any other examples of these sorts of symbols within the Canadian context?

2. Key metaphors that have served as the foundation of world views in different societies include societal, organic, and technological metaphors. What is an example of each type of key metaphor?

3. Consider the Canadian metaphor of the cultural mosaic. If we "follow the metaphor," what will we find as the Canadian world view?

4. Drastic changes in experience lead people to create new interpretations that will help them cope with the changes. How can metaphors, or the symbols that represent them, be used as instruments of power and control in such times?

Suggested Readings

Bowen, John. 2014. *Religions in Practice: An Approach to the Anthropology of Religion*, 6th edn (Boston: Pearson). A contemporary introduction to the anthropology of religion, focusing on religious practice and interpretation with a very wide range of case studies.

Boyer, Pascal, and Brian Bergstrom. 2008. "Evolutionary Perspectives on Religion," *Annual Review of Anthropology* 37: 111–30. A relatively recent article exploring perspectives on the evolutionary emergence of religious thought and the representation of the supernatural.

Evans-Pritchard, E.E. 1976 [1937]. *Witchcraft, Oracles, and Magic among the Azande*, abr. edn (Oxford: Oxford University Press). An immensely influential and very readable anthropological classic.

Frazer, James George. 2006 [1922]. *The Golden Bough* (NuVision Publications), available online in various formats. An example of the "armchair" anthropology of the nineteenth century, this book nonetheless developed the theoretical background used for the anthropological analysis of religion.

Lambek, Michael. 2008. *A Reader in the Anthropology of Religion*, 2nd edn (Malden, MA: Blackwell). An excellent collection of classic and contemporary readings in the anthropology of religion.

Malinowski, Bronisław. 1948 [1926]. *Magic, Science, and Religion, and other Essays* (New York: Doubleday Anchor), excerpt available at www.adolphus.nl/xcrpts/xcmalinow.html The essays in this book cover many aspects of Malinowski's fieldwork in the Trobriand Islands and subsequently in Africa. Malinowski's lifelong interest in the ideational life of the people he worked with is evident in this book.

Robidoux, Michael A. 2002. "Imagining a Canadian Identity through Sport: A Historical Interpretation of Lacrosse and Hockey," *Journal of American Folklore* 15, 456: 209–25. Do we have a key metaphor as a country based on the game of hockey? Here, we can examine this in a historical perspective.

Related Websites

Human Rights Watch: France: Face-Veil Ruling Undermines Rights
www.hrw.org/news/2014/07/03/
france-face-veil-ruling-undermines-rights

Pew Research: Canada's Changing Religious Landscape
www.pewforum.org/2013/06/27/
canadas-changing-religious-landscape

We Do Not Have Shamans: The Case against "Shamans" in North American Indigenous Cultures
http://www.angelfire.com/electronic/awakening101/not_
shamans.html

Wounded Knee Museum
www.woundedkneemuseum.org

PART III | Organization of Life: Local to Global

Human beings have used their cultural creativity, together with political and economic resources, to create imagined communities that now encompass the entire world. These communities have complex hierarchical forms of social organization. In the following chapters, we look at how society is organized and the power human beings have to produce, reproduce, or change that organization. We then turn to a discussion of globalization and the rise of global forms of inequality, particularly as they are associated with European colonial empires and their aftermath. Finally, we examine the work of those anthropologists who have tried to do more than record and analyze contemporary social change—anthropologists who have taken on the task of applying anthropological information to the solution of contemporary human social problems.

12

Social Organization and Power

Chapter Outline

The Search for the Laws of Social Organization

The Power to Act

Power as an Independent Entity

The Power of the Imagination

History as a Prototype of and for Political Action

Negotiating the Meaning of History

Learning Objectives

By the end of Chapter 12, you will be able to

- consider that social organization refers to the patterning of human interdependence;
- understand power as a transformative capacity that is exercised by both co-ercive and persuasive means;
- appreciate the power of the imagination for investing the world with meaning; and
- recognize how people bargain for control over interpretations of reality.

In 1992, following 12 years of civil war and two years of intensive negotiation, representatives of the government of El Salvador and of the Salvadoran guerrilla movement known as the Farabundo Martí National Liberation Front (FMLN) signed a peace accord. The civil war had cost over 75,000 lives and had turned a million Salvadorans into refugees. It was one of the bloodiest insurrections in twentieth-century Latin America. How could so many years of fierce fighting end at the negotiator's table?

The roots of the conflict go back to the nineteenth century, when a tiny elite of Salvadoran landowners managed to monopolize 60 per cent of the land in order to raise coffee for export. The result was one of the most highly polarized class structures in all of Latin America. Close to 98 per cent of the citizens were forced to survive on plots too small to support them, to live as tenant farmers or labourers on land they did not own, or to become landless migrants. When the coffee market crashed during the depression of the 1930s, the majority on the bottom rebelled against their exploitation, and the Salvadoran army crushed them in a brutal massacre known as *la matanza* ("the massacre").

During the Cold War between the United States and the Soviet Union that began in the late 1940s, even comparatively mild efforts to reform the system were repressed. After 1958, the US government interpreted challenges to the Salvadoran government as signs that El Salvador might be vulnerable to a Cuban-style communist revolution and viewed Salvadoran repression of reformers and rebels as a fight against the spread of communism, an explanation the Salvadoran government willingly endorsed. By the late 1970s, convinced that peaceful social change would never occur, political moderates in El Salvador swelled the ranks of five guerrilla groups that united to form the FMLN. The government response in the 1980s was as brutal as it had been in the 1930s and included a new *matanza* in the peasant village of El Mozote, in which over 200 men, women, and children were massacred for their supposed collaboration with the guerrillas (Danner 1994).

By 1990, Salvadoran society was still polarized, but the prospect of endless war caused Salvadorans on both sides to rethink their positions. Members of the Nationalist Republican Alliance (ARENA) party had won national elections in 1989 and seemed less hostile to democracy, and their elite supporters had become convinced that continued fighting would only hurt their business interests. The United States was also tiring of the war and could no longer ignore highly publicized human rights violations committed by the Salvadoran government. Furthermore, the notion that supporting the Salvadoran government was stemming the spread of communism lost its force following the collapse of communism in Eastern Europe. At the same time, Salvadoran guerrillas concluded that military victory offered no permanent guarantees. Led by guerrilla leaders, the FMLN eventually agreed to meet their enemies at the peace table.

What drives people to take up arms against powerful, well-armed government forces? What convinces battle-hardened fighters who believe that their cause is just to lay down their arms and negotiate when they have no certainty of success? Historian Peter Winn observes that the 1992 UN-brokered accord in El Salvador "was a political compromise that allowed both sides to claim victory while leaving the future in doubt" (1992: 535). Not all Salvadorans supported the negotiated settlement, and sporadic violence directed against some guerrillas-turned-politicians after 1992 threatened the fragile peace it brought about. In May of 1994, however, the first national elections held since the signing of the peace accord were peaceful. The ARENA presidential candidate won two-thirds of the vote against the left coalition, whose candidate won one-third of the vote. By late 1996, the FMLN was reflecting on the experiences of its first legislative session and planning on making alliances with other parties for future elections.

To be sure, the absence of violence at one moment of political crisis does not mean that violence will not be used later. The UN accord did not end economic and political inequality in El Salvador. And the damage caused by various natural disasters over the past decades have only added to

Syrian refugees arrive by dinghy on the coast of Greece from Turkey. While Turkey remains the largest host country of registered refugees, hundreds of thousands have continued on to Greece and farther into Europe. In 2016 it was estimated that at least 2,500 refugees died during a five-month period due to boat capsizing while trying to reach Europe. As the civil war in Syria continues, the United Nations estimates that 13.5 million Syrians are in need of humanitarian assistance.

© YURI CORTEZ/AFP/Getty Images

Figure 12.1 Young Salvadorans wave FMLN party flags and shout slogans outside a polling station in a non-violent show of support in San Salvador in 2009. What do you notice about how the FMLN is represented in this photo? What do you think this may say about how the status of the FMLN has changed?

social organization The patterning of human interdependence in a given society through the actions and decisions of its members.

these continuing woes. But the peace settlement of 1992 has not been broken to date (Figure 12.1), and the mere fact that violence is not automatic suggests that the exercise of power, even in a highly stratified society, is more complicated than it may appear.

There are always choices to be made about how a society is to be organized or how that organization may be changed. Who has the power to make and enforce these choices? Where does that power come from? What forms can power take? To answer these questions, this chapter focuses on social organization and the power that human beings have to produce, reproduce, or change that organization.

We have already described, in Chapter 3, the variety of forms of human society and some attempts by anthropologists to analyze that variation. The nineteenth-century social theorist Lewis Henry Morgan (1871, 1877) urged anthropologists to pay close attention to what he called the *arts of subsistence*. But he ran into difficulties when he observed significant differences in ways of life that were *not* connected with significant differences in ways of making a living. In terms of Morgan's scheme of "ethnical stages," for example, both "barbarians" and "civilized peoples" relied on farming and herding, and in many cases their technologies were quite similar. What did distinguish them were differences in who did

what, how it was done, and for whom. That is, they differed from one another in terms of **social organization**.

The Search for the Laws of Social Organization

Even before the birth of the social sciences, Western thinkers searched for the inflexible laws of society that would explain differences in social organization in a non-arbitrary way. Biological determinists look for biological processes operating deeply within human beings, forcing them to act in some ways and forbidding them to act in others. Other thinkers explain similarities and differences in social organization as adaptations to particular ecological conditions. In the nineteenth century, unilineal evolutionists, such as Lewis Henry Morgan and Karl Marx, believed that the laws of society are rooted in the dynamics of history and work themselves out over time for each human group. Although Marxist analysis still has its adherents, the use of the unilineal evolutionary approach is now seen as somewhat counterproductive to understanding the diversity of historical realities manifest in all cultures.

The Arbitrariness of Social Organization

Perhaps the most important and controversial contribution of anthropology to the debate about laws of social organization is the argument that social relations in any society are ultimately arbitrary. This does not mean that societies are free to do or be whatever they like; rather, it means that there is no way to reduce the complexities of human societies to a single underlying cause.

For example, the adaptive flexibility of the human brain and body would be impossible if our behaviour were under rigid genetic control. Environmental determinism is implausible because no society has ever been left on its own long enough for so-called "environmental pressures" to exert their forces without outside human interference. European colonial conquest vividly demonstrated how the most delicately balanced societal adaptation to a given environment can be totally disrupted, if not destroyed, when outsiders arrive with plans of their own and the power to enforce those plans. Yet even if societies could be isolated from one another and left to work out their own destinies in their own environments, it is unlikely that identical societies

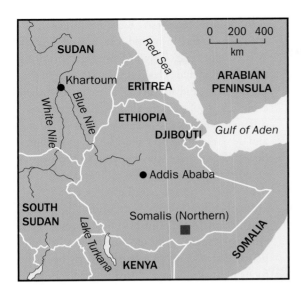

Map 12.1 Somalis (Northern)

would develop in identical step-by-step sequences as Morgan argued. Anthropologist I.M. Lewis pointed out, for example, that the northern Somalis and the various Cushitic-speaking peoples of Kenya and Ethiopia live next to each other in semi-arid scrubland (see Map 12.1) and even herd the same kinds of animals (1967: 166ff.). Despite these similarities, the Somalis and the neighbouring Cushitic-speaking peoples are quite different in social structure: the Cushitic-speaking peoples engage in much less fighting and feuding than do the Somalis; their families split up to take care of the animals, whereas Somali families do not; and lineage organization is less significant among them than it is among the Somalis.

The Power to Act

Human beings actively work to reshape the environments in which they live to suit themselves. Because the resources available in any environment can be used to sustain more than one way of life, however, human beings must choose which aspects of the material world to depend on. Human choice is equally important in the domain of social organization.

Some archaeologists suggest that population growth, for example, is a constant aspect of the human condition that determines forms of social organization. Anthropologist Marshall Sahlins (1976: 13) reminds us, however, that population pressure determines nothing more than the number of people that can be supported when the environment is used in a particular way. Members of a society can respond to that pressure in various ways: they

can try to get along on less, they can intensify food production by inventing new technologies, they can reduce their numbers by inventing new social practices (e.g., infanticide, birth control), or they can migrate. Indeed, the manner in which a group might choose to implement any of these options is equally undetermined by population pressure. Which members of the group will have to do with less? Which members will control technological innovation? Who will be expected to migrate? And will the ultimate decision be imposed by force or voluntarily adopted? Population pressure alone cannot determine the answer to any of these questions.

The ability to choose implies the ability to transform a given situation. Thus, the ability to choose implies **power**, which we can understand broadly as "transformative capacity" (Giddens 1979: 88). When the choice affects an entire social group, we speak of **social power**. In any social situation, we all have some degree of social power, although some people have more influence than others. When one group is officially recognized as having more social power than any other group has, we speak of **political power**. Social activists Lisa VeneKlasen and Valerie Miller (2002) note three levels of political power: the visible, the hidden, and the invisible. On the visible level are the "definable aspects of political power—the formal rules, structures, authorities, institutions, and procedures of decision-making" (47). Individuals who are not part of the dominant governing group can observe the operations of visible power, and they can assert their social power in support of or in resistance to visible political decisions. Hidden power is exerted when a group with a great deal of social power discreetly influences the decisions that are made on the visible level, often with negative consequences for groups and individuals with less social power (47–8). Invisible power is "the most insidious of the three": it is embedded in cultural norms and makes certain issues, interests, and problems invisible by shaping "people's beliefs, sense of self, and acceptance of their own superiority or inferiority" (48). This form of power is what keeps certain minorities from protesting when they are treated as less than equal to others.

When thinking about how political power impacts social organization, we can also consider Eric Wolf's (1999) concept of *structural power*, which is power that organizes social settings themselves and controls the allocation of social labour. Uncovering the patterns of structural power requires paying

power Transformative capacity; the ability to transform a given situation.

social power The ability to transform a situation that affects an entire social group.

political power Social power held by a group that is in a position to affect the lives of many people.

attention to (1) the large-scale and increasingly global division of labour among regions and social groups, (2) the unequal relations between these regions and groups, and (3) the way these relations are maintained or modified over time. The way in which clothing for sale in wealthy nations (e.g., Canada, the United States) is manufactured in countries with cheap labour forces (e.g., Indonesia, El Salvador, China) is an example of structural power. People are hired to work long hours for low wages in unpleasant conditions to make clothing that they cannot afford to buy; their labour disproportionately benefits the companies for which they work and the foreign consumers who will buy the clothing they produce.

The study of social and political power in human society is the domain of **political anthropology**. In an overview of the subfield, anthropologist Joan Vincent has argued that political anthropology is vital because it involves a complex interplay between ethnographic fieldwork, political theory, and critical reflection on political theory (2002: 1). Vincent divides the history of political anthropology into three phases:

- The *first phase*, from 1851 to about 1939, she considers the "formative" era in which basic orientations and some of the earliest anthropological commentaries on political matters were produced.
- The *second phase*, from 1942 to about 1971, is the "classic" era in the field; this phase developed under conditions of the post–World War II British Empire through the period of decolonization in the 1950s and 1960s. This phase is most closely associated with the flourishing of British social anthropology rooted in structural-functionalist theory, and it produced well-known works by

such eminent figures as E. E. Evans-Pritchard, Max Gluckman, Edmund Leach, and Fredrik Barth (Figure 12.2). Topics of investigation during this period include classifying pre-industrial political systems and attempting to reconstruct their evolution, displaying the characteristic features of different kinds of pre-industrial political systems and demonstrating how these functioned to produce political order, and studying local processes of political strategizing by individuals in non-Western societies (see, e.g., Lewellen 1983).

- Decolonization drew attention to emerging national-level politics in new states and the effects of "modernization" on the "traditional" political structures that had formerly been the focus of anthropological investigation. But the turbulent politics of the 1960s and early 1970s called into question not only received social forms but also received forms of anthropological scholarship. Beginning in the 1960s, political anthropologists developed new ways of thinking about political issues and new theoretical orientations to guide them, inaugurating in the 1970s and 1980s a *third phase* in which political anthropology posed broader questions about power and inequality (Vincent 2002: 3). Under conditions of globalization, anthropologists interested in studying power have joined forces with scholars in other disciplines who share their concerns, and they have adopted ideas from influential political thinkers, such as Antonio Gramsci and Michel Foucault, to help them explain how power shapes the lives of those they describe in their ethnographies.

The cross-cultural study of social power reveals a paradox of the human condition. On one hand, open cultural creativity allows humans to imagine worlds of pure possibility; on the other hand, we all live in material circumstances that make many of those possibilities profoundly unrealistic. We can imagine many different ways to organize ourselves into groups, but the situations in which we live have been firmly shaped by history, and the opportunity to restructure social organization is ordinarily quite limited. Therefore, we will look closely at the ways in which the material circumstances of everyday life generate fields of power that channel and inhibit agency and cultural creativity—and how human beings can sometimes creatively exercise power and agency in order to evade or subvert those restrictions.

political anthropology
The study of social and political power in human society.

© travelib pakistan/Alamy Stock Photo

Figure 12.2 Norwegian anthropologist Fredrik Barth conducted some of his earliest fieldwork in the Swat District of Pakistan in the 1950s. Here, a rope salesman interacts with a customer in a local market in modern-day Swat District.

The Role of the State

In the beginning, political anthropologists were strongly influenced by other Western thinkers who had investigated the same topics. Many of these earlier thinkers had assumed that the state was the prototype of "civilized" social power. The absence of a state, therefore, had to represent anarchy and disorder. Although the state often perpetrated injustice or exploitation as a side effect of its monopoly of force, this could be viewed as a necessary price for social order.

Early anthropologists, such as Lewis Henry Morgan, however, showed that kinship institutions organized social life in societies without states. A later generation of political anthropologists showed how different kinship institutions distribute power among their members and how non-kin institutions, such as secret societies, sometimes carry out important political roles. They were able to show repeatedly that societies without states can reach and carry out decisions affecting the entire social group by means of orderly traditional processes. More recently, archaeologist Gary M. Feinman and his colleagues (2000) have proposed a network–corporate/hierarchical–egalitarian matrix (see Figure 12.3 in the "In Their Own Words" box that follows) that applies to power organization and application in all societies regardless of their complexity. This approach

expands on traditional evolutionary models through the recognition that an unequal distribution and ostentatious display of wealth does not always correlate tightly with the concentration of power or proscribed inheritance rules. It also recognizes a wide range of power-wielding strategies, which in themselves have marked organizational and integrative implications. (Feinman et al. 2000: 453)

(Note Gary Feinman et al.'s discussion of political hierarchies and organization within societies in the "In Their Own Words" box that follows.)

In Their Own Words

Political Hierarchies and Organizational Strategies in the Puebloan Southwest

American archaeologist Gary M. Feinman and his colleagues have investigated alternative ways to explain organization within societies. Although this example comes from researchers investigating ancient Puebloan societies, it is informed by ethnography of several contemporary peoples of the southwestern United States. Thus, in attempting to find explanations for the past, they have given us insight for today.

The network strategy of political action is associated with heavily personalized or centralized forms of leadership [see Table 12.1]. Wealth is concentrated in the hands of a few, who use their network of personal connections to enhance and expand their individualized power and authority. The network strategy broadly corresponds to descriptions of accumulators (Hayden 1990), aggrandizers (Clark and Blake 1994), strivers (Maschner 1995), and entrepreneurial elites (Hayden 1995), which are well entrenched in Western leader-centric ideas about power and individualism. In contrast, the corporate strategy bears certain similarities to [Gregory] Johnson's sequential hierarchies and [Dean] Saitta's communal mode and adheres closely to descriptions of [Colin] Renfrew's (1974) group-oriented chiefdoms and [Edward] Lehman's (1969) concept of systemic power. In

Table 12.1 Tendencies of Corporate–Network Modes

Network	Corporate
Concentrated wealth	More even wealth distribution
Individual power	Shared power arrangements
Ostentatious consumption	More balanced accumulation
Prestige goods	Control of knowledge, cognitive codes
Patron/client factions	Corporate labour systems
Attached specialization	Emphasis on food production
Wealth finance	Staple finance
Princely burials	Monumental ritual spaces
Lineal kinship systems	Segmental organization
Power inherited through personal glorification	Power embedded in group association/affiliation
Ostentatious elite adornment	Symbols of office
Personal glorification	Broad concerns with fertility, rain

Continued

corporate organizations, economic resources are more dispersed, leadership is less personalized, and ostentatious displays and individual aggrandizement are less apt to be found. Instead, communal ritual, public construction, large co-operative labour tasks, shared power, social segments that are woven together through broad integrative ritual and ideological means, and suppressed economic differentiation are emphasized [see Table 12.1]. . . . Corporate–network strategies of political action represent a continuous comparative dimension. We stress that these strategies are not an explicit substitute for the familiar dimensions of hierarchical complexity. Instead, corporate–network strategies are an orthogonal comparative dimension to that of hierarchies [see Figure 12.3]. In other words, corporate–network tendencies may be found in political organizations with little hierarchical development or in those characterized by complex bureaucracies with multiple levels of decision-making. . . . As a consequence, we propose that there are at least two important comparative dimensions (corporate–network and hierarchical complexity) relevant to explaining long-term change and variation.

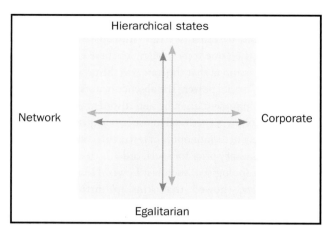

Figure 12.3 Two comparative dimensions for the examination of social organization.

Source: Feinman, Gary M., et al. 2000. "Political Hierarchies and Organization Strategies in the Puebolan Southwest," *American Antiquity* 65, 3: 453–4. © 2000 The Society for American Archaeology. Reproduced with permission.

Coercion: With and without Traditional State Institutions

The traditional Western prototype of power in human social relations is based on physical coercion. A typical "natural" manifestation might be a fist fight. This prototype represents an exceedingly pessimistic view of human nature. It suggests that co-operative social living is not natural for humans, as innate instincts drive us toward **free agency**. By extension, political activity is competition between individual free agents over political control. When free agents make decisions, no larger groups, no historical obligations, and no collective beliefs can or ought to stand in their way. In this view, cultural evolution took a giant leap forward when our ancestors first realized that sticks and stones could be used as weapons, not only against non-human predators but especially against human enemies, and human history is a chronicle of the production of better and better weapons. Thus the civilizations we are so proud of have been born and sustained in violence.

Even in many stateless societies of the past, coercion played a role in maintaining control. While there was no central political power, other institutions often functioned to punish those who deviated from cultural norms. Members of such

free agency The freedom of self-contained individuals to pursue their own interests above everything else and to challenge one another for dominance.

domination Coercive rule.

societies did not fear the king or the police but rather the ancestors, supernatural forces, or the lineage elders. Power still often involved physical coercion, with co-operation resulting largely from the fear of punishment.

In the global systems of today, pressure from power-seeking states—states bent on acquiring control over new territories and resources—impinges on the lives of those who traditionally lived in what were essentially stateless societies. (Note John Wagner's discussion in the "In Their Own Words" box that follows.) Additionally, when political and institutional coercion comes into play in an atmosphere of ethnic, racial, religious, and economic power struggles, the Darfurs of the world emerge (Figure 12.4). Nothing can focus our understanding of these power struggles more than the personal accounts of those who have lived through such violence. (See, e.g., Ari Folman's animated movie, *Waltz With Bashir* [2008], an account of his experience as a 19-year-old Israeli soldier and the 1982 Sabra and Shatila massacre in Lebanon.)

Domination and Hegemony

Our reasons for accepting social power structures are often ambiguous. Do we submit to institutionalized power because we have been coerced and fear punishment? Or do we submit because we believe that the power structures in our society are legitimate given our understandings about the way the world works? What leads people to accept coercion by others as legitimate (Figure 12.7)?

Karl Marx argued that rulers consolidate their power by successfully persuading their subjects to accept a ruling-class ideology that portrays their domination as legitimate. Thus, in his view, dominated groups suffer from *false consciousness*. However, the concept of false consciousness is problematic because it views people as passive and incapable of withstanding ideological indoctrination.

More promising was the approach taken by Italian political theorist Antonio Gramsci (1971). Writing in the 1930s, Gramsci pointed out that coercive rule—what he called **domination**—is expensive and unstable. Rulers do better if they can persuade the dominated to accept their rule as legitimate. To do so, they may provide some genuine material benefits to their subjects and also use schools and other cultural institutions to disseminate

Figure 12.4 Many people around the world suffer when power struggles erupt in violence. People displaced by armed conflicts are often forced to live in refugee camps, where they have few resources and little power to improve their situation. Here, a Syrian mother walks with her three children in one of the asylum centres near Belgrade, Serbia. In 2016, as the result of a civil war in Syria, the United Nations identified 13.5 million Syrians requiring humanitarian assistance, of which more than 6 million are internally displaced within Syria and over 4.6 million are refugees outside Syria.

In Their Own Words

Water as Commodity in the Okanagan Valley of British Columbia

John Wagner, of the University of British Columbia Okanagan, works in Papua New Guinea and the Okanagan region in Canada. His research interest could be broadly described as environmental. More specifically, he focuses on water and the consequences of its commodification.

Conflict is a normal and inevitable part of life in all societies, but wars involving the loss of thousands or even millions of human lives are not. Why do human beings go to war? Many recent and ongoing civil wars such as those in Rwanda, Sudan, or the former Yugoslavia are described in the media as either *ethnic* or *religious* in nature. In fact, the causes of war are always more complex than these simplistic explanations indicate, and *competition over resources* is almost always a significant, if not a determining, factor. An increasing number of resource conflicts today are also global in scale, an outcome of the increasingly integrated nature of the world economy. Many analysts . . . have proposed that water may well replace oil as the chief source of armed conflict in the twenty-first century.

The economic, military, and technological control of water has, in fact, been essential to the emergence of state-level human societies since they first occurred several thousands of years ago in Mesopotamia, Egypt, China, India, and the Americas. These *hydraulic societies*, as they are often called, typically acquired their economic strength through construction of large irrigation systems that facilitated greater agricultural productivity, food surpluses, and thus the capacity to maintain professional armies and bureaucracies.

As human demands on freshwater resources grow, and clean water in particular becomes an increasingly scarce resource, armed conflicts and other less immediately destructive forms of conflict are likely to become more frequent. Intensive commoditization of water under these conditions can worsen the divide between rich and poor, leaving the poor of many countries without sufficient access to clean water for even their most basic needs. Over the past few decades, bottled water has become a billion-dollar-per-year industry, water utility services are being privatized in both affluent and less

Continued

Kelowna Public Archives

Figure 12.5 A historic apple box image from the Okanagan Valley. How can the images used to depict a place influence how that place is understood?

Figure 12.6 The conversion of family-farm agricultural land in the Okanagan Valley to waterfront properties for affluent hobby-farmers fetches a high price in the real estate market.

developed nations, and bulk water transfers are occurring on a massive scale.

The Okanagan Valley of British Columbia illustrates another way in which water is being commoditized within today's global marketplace. Home originally to the *Syilx*, an Indigenous hunting/gathering society, this arid and mountainous region was settled by Europeans in the late nineteenth and early twentieth centuries. Irrigation systems were constructed by land development companies to carry water from upland reservoirs to subdivided lots on the valley bottom. Once irrigated, those lands were ideally suited to the intensive cultivation of tree fruits. A family-farm orchard industry thus emerged and became a dominant feature of Okanagan culture and landscape [Figure 12.5]. That economy is being displaced today, however, by an economy based on the region's growing popularity as a resort destination and retirement centre. Water as a commodity lies at the heart of this new form of development but in a very different sense than previously. Despite low levels of rainfall in the region, a series of large lakes stretch along the valley bottom, remnants of a glacier that covered the

area 10,000 years ago. The lakes are valued for recreational purposes: for boating, scuba diving, and swimming; and waterfront and lake-view properties fetch a high premium in today's booming real estate market [Figure 12.6]. The orchard oases that surround the lakes at lower elevations enhance the aesthetic and economic value of lake-view properties, but, ironically, the orchard industry is in decline precisely because of this new form of commoditization. As a commodity, water has much higher value in the recreational tourism and housing industries than it does in the agricultural industry. As a consequence, land prices have escalated beyond the level at which they are affordable for agricultural purposes. In the Okanagan Valley, as elsewhere in Canada, conflict over water is not likely to result in armed conflict, but it is likely to result in long-term social and economic change and a sharper divide between water haves and have-nots.

Source: Wagner, John. 2009. "Water as Commodity in the Okanagan Valley of British Columbia," guest editorial in *Cultural Anthropology: A Perspective on the Human Condition*, 1st Canadian edn, Emily Schultz, Robert Lavenda, and Roberta Robin Dods, 190–1.

hegemony A system of leadership in which rulers persuade subordinates to accept the ideology of the dominant group by offering mutual accommodations that nevertheless preserve the rulers' privileged position.

an ideology justifying their rule. If they achieve all this—while also ensuring that none of these concessions seriously undermine their privileged position—they have established what Gramsci called **hegemony**.

Hegemony is never absolute; it is always vulnerable to challenges. (For more on hegemony, see the "In Their Own Words" box that follows.) Struggles may develop between rulers trying to justify their

domination and subordinate groups who exercise agency by challenging "official" ideologies and practices that devalue or exclude them. Hegemony may be threatened if subordinate groups maintain or develop alternative, or *counter-hegemonic*, cultural practices. Successful hegemony, by contrast, involves linking the understandings of dominant and subordinate groups into what appears to be mutual accommodation.

Gaynor Macdonald discusses the "pervasive social sickness" produced by colonial hegemony for Indigenous groups, specifically focusing on the Indigenous peoples of Australia.

Aboriginal peoples throughout Australia, from one to two centuries beyond those frontier days, often refer to their contemporary social suffering as due to their colonization. This claim would have to be dismissed if colonization is understood as past event. But Aboriginal statements are not simply focused on an unjust past which has led to present discrimination. Rather, they alert us to the ways in which colonization itself continues in various guises, something anthropology has paid insufficient attention to. If colonization is to be understood as process, how should it be understood? The ongoing impact of an initial colonization in Australia is largely understood through the persistence of injustice (cf. Watson 2007) or the lack of provision of the same rights of access available to non-indigenous citizens. But these are issues of long-standing and do not of themselves account for the late 20th century and contemporary degree of social suffering.

Yet I will argue that the Aboriginal interpretation is correct. An analysis of the reasons for this escalation in social suffering requires that we understand colonization as a *cultural* process (see for example, Kelm 1998), not solely one of social control and political-legal transformation. Colonization as processual experience does not unfold in predictable ways: it is experienced differently in different times and places; it provides opportunities for some and suffering for others. Neither is it a universal story: it has had many different faces, rationales and unfoldings. It is a long, slow, often clumsy and ill-thought (if thought at all) set of intertwining and contradictory processes which engage the people involved—colonizer and colonized—over time in a variety of ways.

An important component in these historical processes is the complex composition of the invading population, something the term colonizer does not adequately capture but which can significantly impact on relations with colonized peoples who, in relative terms, are more likely to share a social and cultural world. It then becomes more apparent that colonial relations quickly become variegated, as hegemony is asserted, frustrated and reasserted and as new subjectivities emerge, are contested and transform. This is an analysis that must be grounded in the specifics of time, place and human encounters. It is already a contradiction to speak of "the colonizer" as singular, as if the power differentials between militia and convict, between wealthy and impoverished immigrant, gold digger and missionary, did not make for different views and encounters with an indigenous other who was likewise not singular, and made even less so by the differential impacts of

encroachment. However, as *persons*, there was a distinct difference between the ways in which each understood themselves vis-à-vis their own, and vis-à-vis the "other" they encountered.

Colonial subjectivity itself is a changing experience but the ontological dimensions of the variable and long-term processes of colonization have not been a focus for anthropology (but see for example, Samson 2004). What happens to "persons" when change is imposed, one after another? Personhood is not something "one can take on and off like a glove" (Douglas and Ney 1998). We know people everywhere are capable of enduring changed circumstances and yet rebuilding meaningful lives. But is there a limit—a kind of change which so violates our personhood that it renders us unable to make a creative human response? When is change so traumatic that it disables our human capacity to adjust, disintegrates ethical sensibilities or moves us beyond moral relationships?

There is no universalizing or generalizing story of colonization that can be told for the Australian continent and there are few local studies. It is widely recognized that Aboriginal peoples have had diverse colonial histories resulting, by the 1970s, in the awkward and misleading division of them into peoples of either "settled" (living in urban or rural areas, predominantly in southern Australia) or "remote" Australia (Rowley 1970). The former, which includes the Wiradjuri people of central nsw [New South Wales], were long assumed to have "lost their culture" and thus the distinctiveness of being "traditional" or "authentic."

I want to look at the changes Wiradjuri people experienced over time, looking at how different stages of the colonial project impacted on Wiradjuri subjectivities. Colonization is the experience of having one's world taken over by a hegemonic force—but this is not a totalizing experience and to understand its impacts, it is necessary to examine the intent and outcomes of the colonial project, how and why it changed over time, what parts of Wiradjuri worlds were taken over, when, how and why. This requires appreciation of the colonial project in specific historical times and places and thus the differential impacts on those rendered its subjects.

Above all, colonization is a relationship between people who begin as "other" to each other but who soon become socially and economically intertwined into a single social field. It is in the ways in which the myriad relations which arise as one people establish control over the lives of another that colonization is *experienced*. It is in these relationships, rather than in laws and policies enacted in metropoles, that colonial subjects are made and hegemony imposed. And, it is in these relationships that we can likewise see how uneven hegemonic control is—ineffective in one place and time, oppressive elsewhere.

Continued

The reach of the newly imposed state is shaped according to differential values placed on resources and local circumstances; curbed by the "tyranny of distance" (Blainey 1982); expanded as the technologies of state develop over time.

Source: Macdonald, Gaynor. 2010. "Colonizing Processes, the Reach of the State and Ontological Violence: Historicizing Aboriginal Australian Experience," *Anthropologica* 52, 1: 50–1. Reprinted with permission of University of Toronto Press.

Figure 12.7 Prior to colonial conquest by outsiders, Muslim emirs from northern Cameroon had coercive power.

Anthropologists who study the exercise of power in different types of societies have found Gramsci's contrast between domination (rule by coercive force) and hegemony (rule by persuasion) to be very useful. This contrast allows anthropologists to move beyond some of the tortuous and implausible accounts of power that depend on fear of punishment or false consciousness. In place of these determinants, researchers can examine the verbal skills and personal charisma of leaders who have limited coercive force at their disposal but who can nonetheless persuade others to follow them by skilfully aligning shared meanings, values, and goals with a particular interpretation of events or proposed courses of action.

The concept of hegemony is also attractive because it draws attention to the central role of cultural beliefs and symbols in struggles to consolidate social organization and political control. One particularly pervasive

cultural belief that has influenced how hegemonic relationships take shape is the belief that men should be dominant over women. Sociologist R.W. Connell has suggested that early societies' gendered divisions of labour, in which men occupied the dominant positions, constitutes the genesis of hegemonic class systems that later emerged. Connell observes that the structure of relationships between women and men

> operates at every level of human experience, from economic arrangements, culture, and the state to interpersonal relationships and individual emotions. . . . Moving toward a gender-equal society involves profound institutional change as well as change in everyday life and personal conduct. To move far in this direction requires widespread social support, including significant support from men and boys. (2005: 1801)

However, as historian Robert Nye points out, hegemonic masculinity remains the dominant model of identity in heteronormative societies:

> [A]llowing for variations in class, the kind of masculinity that is performed by most men in groups is usually of the hegemonic kind, no matter what the men's education, occupation, or ideological outlook. Even if men stake out and perform masculinities at odds with the hegemonic masculinity of their own society, they must know the code in order to oppose it, and so they know, in a pinch, how to enact it. (2005: 1952)

Despite women's many successful challenges to male-dominated hegemonic power structures over the past century or so, gendered power differentials continue to have a strong influence on the lives of many.

As another example, consider the Azande of central Africa (see EthnoProfile 11.1), who believe that people use witchcraft only against those they envy. This seems highly plausible to people who experience daily friction with their neighbours. At the same time, however, this belief makes it impossible to accuse Azande chiefs of using witchcraft against commoners—because, as the Azande themselves ask, why would chiefs envy their subjects? In this way, hegemonic ideology deflects challenges that might be made against those in power.

In other settings, however, hegemonic ideology may justify certain individuals' engagement in social action that would be condemned if engaged in by others. Consider the connection between witchcraft and kingship among the Beng of Ivory Coast (see Map 12.2). The Beng are organized into two regions, each ruled by a king and a queen who come from a specific matrilineal clan. The king is said to be the owner of the earth, which is the primary focus for worship among the Beng. Violations of taboos concerning the earth are believed to endanger the entire region and therefore must be dealt with by the king of the region, who is said to have the power to foresee those natural calamities that are punishment for sins committed. In general, "the king is responsible for not only the legal but also the moral and spiritual well-being of the people living in this region" (Gottlieb 1989: 249).

The legitimate power of the king is in direct contrast to the power of witches, who are considered to be utterly immoral. Using illegitimate power, working in secret, they kill and "consume" their close matrilineal kin. Nevertheless, when a man becomes king, he has one year to "bewitch: (i.e., kill) three close relatives in his matriline. If he fails to do so, he will die. Rather than destroying his power, this exercise of illegitimate power legitimates his rule. By killing three close matrilineal relatives, the king shows his commitment to the greater public "good." He is demonstrating his control over, and independence from, the narrow interests of his own kinship group. Operating on a plane beyond that of common morality, the king, who has sacrificed part of himself, will rule the kingdom fairly. From the point of view of the Beng, including members of the king's own matrilineal clan, the king's actions not only are legitimate but also make it possible for him to rule.

Gramsci was particularly interested in how hegemony is (or is not) successfully established in state societies. In a post-colonial and globalizing world, where all people are presumed to be citizens of one nation-state or another, understanding the effects of decisions and actions of state authorities becomes crucial for making sense of many events on a local level. Anthropologists have often focused on the processes by which ruling groups in former colonies attempt to build national identities. For example, the British colony of Ceylon became independent in 1948, later changing its name to Sri Lanka. The majority of residents of Ceylon belonged to two populations: the Tamils, concentrated in the northern part of the island (see

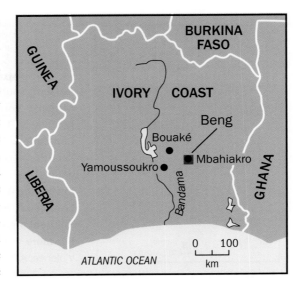

Map 12.2 Beng

EthnoProfile 12.1), and the Sinhalese, who lived elsewhere and in much greater numbers. After independence, however, new Sinhalese rulers worked to forge a national identity rooted in their version of local history, which excluded the Tamils. In 1956, Sinhala was made the only official language; in the 1960s and 1970s, the Tamils' access to education was restricted and they were barred from the civil service and the army (Daniel 1997: 316). The Tamils became a persecuted minority. In 1979, when some Tamils began to agitate for a separate state of their own, the Sri Lankan government responded with severe and violent repression, sending many of the Tamils into exile and stimulating the rise of the nationalist Liberation Tigers of Tamil Eelam (LTTE), which grew "into one of the most dreaded militant organizations in the world" (323) (see Figure 12.8). The period of the Sri Lankan Civil War (1983–2009) was marked by escalating violence, with both sides committing "gross human rights abuses, including war crimes"; today, instances of "torture and enforced disappearances" continue to be reported, but still no one is held responsible (Amnesty International 2013).

Over the years, the Sri Lankan government used violent means of coercion to force Tamil residents out of Sri Lanka. But it has also used violence against Sinhalese citizens who objected to state policies. Between 1987 and 1990, Indian troops were brought into Sri Lanka to supervise a peace agreement between Tamils and Sinhalese. These troops found themselves fighting the LTTE in the north and facing violent resistance in Sinhalese areas:

[T]he rest of the country was convulsed by a wave of terror as young members of a group called the JVP (Janata Vimukti Peramuna,

EthnoProfile 12.1
Tamils

Region: South Asia
Nations: Northeastern Sri Lanka, also southeastern India
Language: Tamil, one of the many Dravidian languages
Population: 3.1 million in Sri Lanka (several hundred thousand have fled the country), nearly 70 million in India (2012 estimates)
Environment: Low plains; tropical monsoon climate
Livelihood: Plantation agriculture; clothing manufacture
Political organization: Part of a modern nation-state
For more information: Trawick, Margaret. 2002. "Reasons for Violence: A Preliminary Ethnographic Account of the LTTE," in *Conflict and Community in Contemporary Sri Lanka*, ed. Siri Gamage and I.B. Watson (Thousand Oaks, CA: Sage); Indrapala, K. 2007. *The Evolution of Ethnic Identity: The Tamils of Sri Lanka* (Colombo: Vijitha Yapa).

or People's Liberation Front) attacked the government not only for betraying the nation by allowing the Indian presence but also for its own unjust political and economic policies.... The government responded with a wave of terror, directed at young males in particular, which reached its climax with the capture and murder of the JVP leadership in late 1989. As far as we can tell, the government won the day by concentrated terror—killing so many young people, whether JVP activists or not, that the opposition ran out of resources and leadership. (Spencer 2000: 124–5)

After 1990, violence directed by the state against Sinhalese citizens lessened, and, in 1994, a new government promised to settle the ethnic conflict by peaceful means. But even before then, Sri Lankan government efforts at nation-building had not rested entirely on violence. Leaders also tried to exercise persuasive power to convince Sinhalese citizens that the state had their welfare in mind and was prepared to take steps to improve their lives. For example, anthropologist Michael Woost (1993) has described how the government of Sri Lanka used a wide range of cultural media (television, radio, newspapers, the school system, public rituals, and even a lottery) to link the national identity to development. National development strategies were presented as attempts to restore Sinhalese village society to its former glory under the pre-colonial rule of Sinhalese kings. The ideal village, in this view, is engaged in rice-paddy cultivation carried out according to harmonious principles of Sinhala Buddhist doctrine. The villagers, Woost knew, could hardly escape this nationalist development discourse, but they did not resist it as an unwelcome imposition from the outside. On the contrary, they incorporated development goals into their own values and accepted that state-sponsored development would improve their lives.

This acceptance might suggest that the state's attempt to establish hegemony had succeeded, but collaboration with the state was undermined as

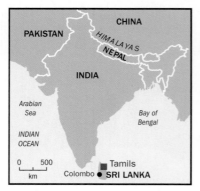

© Buddhika Weerasinghe/Getty Images

Figure 12.8 A newly resettled ethnic minority Tamil civilian walks between the fences in the land that was released back to owners in April 2015 after 25 years as a military forces high security zone in Sri Lanka. The results of the UN's Human Rights Council investigation into alleged war crimes committed by both the Sri Lankan government and the Liberation Tigers of Tamil Eelam (LTTE) during the Sri Lankan Civil War were released in October 2015, with the council adopting a consensus resolution in which Sri Lanka pledged to undertake many human rights reforms.

three different village factions selectively manipulated development discourse in their struggle to gain access to government resources. For example, nationalistic rhetoric connected development with "improvement of the land." One village faction claimed it had "improved the land" first by building houses or planting tree crops. A second faction claimed it had "improved the land" first by introducing paddy cultivation in the village. A third faction claimed it had "improved the land" first since its members had intermarried with early settlers who had planted a large mango tree, a sign of permanent residence. Each faction made what the other factions interpreted as unjust claims, and each blamed the lack of village unity on the un-Buddhist greed of its opponents. These disagreements eventually led the state to withdraw its offer of resources, ultimately preventing the implementation of a village development scheme that all factions wanted!

Woost argues that the outcome of this political wrangling demonstrated the contradictory and fragile nature of the hegemonic process: paradoxically, the villagers' active appropriation of nationalist ideology undermined efforts to establish the very social order it was supposed to create. Gramsci himself was well aware that establishing successful hegemony in a nation-state was a difficult process whose outcome was not assured; indeed, it was the very inability of Italians to achieve this goal that stimulated many of his reflections on domination and hegemony.

Biopower and Governmentality

Is there a set of skills that would bring into existence—and sustain—a peaceful, prosperous nation-state in places like Sri Lanka? This question was addressed by French philosopher Michel Foucault, who looked at the way European thinkers from the end of the Middle Ages onward had posed (and attempted to answer) similar questions. Together with colleagues, he identified the emergence of a new form of power in the nineteenth century. He called this form of power **biopower**, or *biopolitics*. Biopower is preoccupied with managing bodies—both the bodies of individual citizens and the "body" of the population as a whole.

According to Foucault, a state based on biopolitics is very different from states in the Middle Ages, which were based on the rule of law, or administrative states of the fifteenth and sixteenth centuries, which were based on regulation and discipline. Of prime concern in those states was making sure that the ruler maintained *control* of the state. It was generally thought that a ruler should preserve

control by any means necessary, even if those means harmed the ruler's subjects. But by the seventeenth century, this approach to state rule was proving increasingly inadequate. Political thinkers began to speak instead about *governing* a state, likening such government to the practices that preserved and perpetuated other social institutions, such as family households and religious orders (Foucault 1991: 90). The example of household management, at that time called *economy*, was a preferred model of government, and debate concerned how to incorporate "the correct manner of managing individuals, goods, and wealth within the family ... into the management of the state" (92). Thus, the concept of *political economy* was born. But running the state in terms of political economy—managing citizens and their relations with goods and resources, with the territory, and with customs, and coping with misfortunes, such as famines, epidemics, and death—could not be undertaken effectively until rulers possessed adequate knowledge about such things. In the eighteenth century, such knowledge was produced by state bureaucracies that began to count and measure people and things subject to state control, giving birth to the discipline of *statistics*. Statistics suggested that populations had unique attributes, and rulers concluded that management of the population through the use of statistics was the proper task of government.

The art of governing appropriate to biopolitics—what Foucault calls **governmentality**—requires rulers to anticipate calamities and intervene to prevent such calamities from harming the state or its population. In this arrangement, statistics were powerful tools that could identify a series of possible and probable events, calculate their potential cost, and prescribe a form of intervention that would render such events tolerable, such that they would not undermine the security of the state. For example, such interventions include forms of insurance that protect economic activities in the event of a catastrophe that would otherwise curtail or destroy them (Gordon 1991: 18–20).

To an extent, governmentality is a form of power at work in the contemporary world, and institutions that rely on it count and measure their members in a variety of ways (Figure 12.9). Although, as Canadian philosopher Ian Hacking insists, not all bureaucratic applications of such statistical knowledge are evil (1991: 183), the fact remains that providing the government (or any bureaucratic institution) with detailed vital statistics can be very threatening, especially in cases where people are concerned that the state does not have their best interests at heart. After

governmentality The art of governing appropriate to promoting the welfare of populations within a state.

biopower Power held by a modern government over the bodies of its individual citizens and over the "body" of all its citizens.

all, states want to tax citizens, vaccinate and educate their children, restrict their activities to those that benefit the state, control their movements beyond (and sometimes within) state borders, and otherwise manage what citizens do. In a globalizing world full of nation-states, anthropologists are increasingly likely to encounter in their fieldwork both the pressures of governmentality and attempts to evade or manipulate governmentality.

The Ambiguity of Power

The contrasts between domination and hegemony and Foucault's explorations of the machinery of governmentality demonstrate that the exercise of power cannot be equated with physical violence alone. Moreover, the occasional violent outburst of one member of a foraging society against another is not the same thing as the organized violence of one army against another in a conflict between modern nation-states. No one

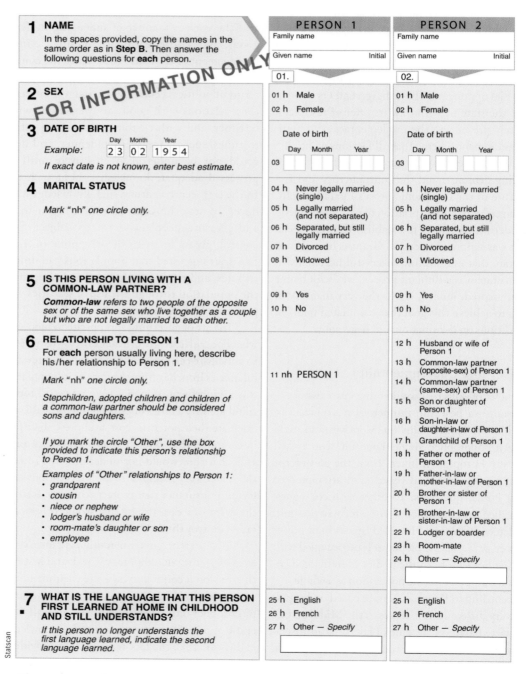

Figure 12.9 Censuses are one way in which a state collects information in order to govern effectively. What is the census form pictured above measuring about the Canadians who are answering it? How does this census define kinship and marriage?

can deny that human beings can be violent with one another. But is this the whole story?

"It is useful to accept the proposition that while men have in some sense always been equal (i.e., in that each always has some independent power), they have in another sense never been equal (in that some always have more power than others)" (Adams 1979: 409). Some political anthropologists who think of power as coercion have traditionally emphasized the universality of human inequality. Some have concentrated on power in societies without states, whereas others have taken a more Gramscian approach and reconsidered the nature of independent power available to individuals living in societies with states. The first focus involves looking at power as an independent entity. The second looks at the power of the human imagination to define the nature of social interactions and to persuade other actors to accept these definitions of the situation.

Power as an Independent Entity

In some of the traditionally stateless societies of Indigenous peoples in North and South America, power is understood to be an entity existing in the universe independent of human beings. As such, it cannot be produced and accumulated through the interactions of human beings. Strictly speaking, power does not belong to human beings at all. At most, people can hope to *gain access* to power, usually through ritual means. From this point of view, "control over resources is evidence of power rather than the source of power" (Colson 1977: 382).

Societies that see power as an independent force usually embed this understanding within a larger world view in which the universe consists of a balance of different forces. Individuals may seek to manipulate those natural forces to their own ends, but only if they can do so without upsetting the universal balance. As a consequence, coercive means of tapping power sources are ruled out in such societies. Violence threatens to undo the universal balance. Thus, in many Indigenous North and South American societies, a person approached power through prayer and supplication. The vision quest (as among the Lakota) is a good example of such an approach: through fasting and self-induced suffering, individuals hoped to move the source of power to pity so that the source might then freely bestow on them the power they sought in the form of a vision or a song or a set of ritual formulas. Power freely bestowed would not disrupt the balance of the universe. (Power mobilized through suffering is a theme that arises in

other cultural contexts as well. Consider the use of hunger strikes as political tools, most memorably employed by Mahatma Gandhi in his decades-long struggle for political reform in India.)

In a world view that sees power as an independent force, violence and access to power are mutually contradictory. Cultures that conceive of cosmic power in this way also tend to view individual human beings as independent entities who cannot be coerced but must be supplicated. Individuals in such societies are not free agents in the Western sense (i.e., free of social ties and responsibilities); rather, they are free in the sense that they can refuse to be forced against their will to conform to someone else's wishes. They exercise the power of **resistance**. The power of individuals to resist emphasizes the importance of **consensus** as the appropriate means to decide issues affecting the group. In seeking consensus, proponents of a particular course of action must use **persuasion** rather than coercion to get other members of the group to support their cause. They resort to verbal argument, not physical intimidation. As a result, the most respected members of stateless societies, those generally regarded as leaders, are persuasive speakers. Indeed, as anthropologist Pierre Clastres (1977) points out, such respected individuals are often referred to by other members of their society as "those who speak for us." The shamans (or *mara'akate*) of the Huichol people of northern Mexico serve this function. By virtue of their verbal ability, they see themselves (and are seen by their fellows) as especially well suited to negotiate with outsiders on behalf of all the Huichol.

Clastres suggests that stateless forms of social organization are strongly resistant to the emergence of hierarchy (1977: 35) (Figure 12.10). Indeed, he argues that members of stateless societies struggle to prevent such authority from emerging. They sense that the rise of state power spells the end of individual autonomy and disrupts beyond repair the harmonious balance between human beings and the forces of the wider world. Canadian anthropologist Richard Lee agrees, arguing that band societies, and some farmers and herders, have found ways to limit "the accumulation of wealth and power":

> Such societies operate within the confines of a metaphorical ceiling and floor: a ceiling above which one may not accumulate wealth and a floor below which one may not sink. These limits . . . are maintained by powerful social mechanisms known as levelling devices. . . . Such societies therefore have social and political resources of

resistance The power to refuse being forced against one's will to conform to someone else's wishes.

consensus An agreement to which all parties collectively give their assent.

persuasion Power based on verbal argument.

© Terry Whittaker

Figure 12.10 The Aché people of Paraguay were a central example in Pierre Clastres's studies of stateless societies. Formerly nomadic, the Aché now reside in permanent settlements but continue to make hunting trips, as shown here.

anomie A pervasive sense of rootlessness and normlessness.

alienation The deep separation that individuals experience between their innermost sense of identity and the labour they are forced to perform in order to survive.

their own and are not just sitting ducks waiting to adopt the first hierarchical model that comes along. (1992: 39–40)

Here, you may recall our discussion of *institutionalized sharing*, a common levelling device, in Chapter 8.

The Power of the Imagination

Gramsci's discussion of the interplay between coercion and persuasion and Foucault's discussions of governmentality and biopolitics offer more nuanced understandings of the different levels on which social power can operate. Many anthropologists feel that a discussion of social power is incomplete if it does not also pay attention to the way individuals make sense of and use the constraints and opportunities for action open to them, however limited they may be.

All people have the power to interpret their experiences, regardless of the complexity of a social system and whether or not the power of coercion is monopolized by a central authority. People retain this power even under totalitarian dictatorship. It is notoriously difficult to erase the sense of self from human consciousness, even in the face of degradation and imminent death, as can be seen in the art and writings of inmates of the concentration camps of Nazi Germany. Anthropologist Hoyt

Alverson argues that "a belief in one's power to invest the world with meaning (the 'will to believe') and a belief in the adequacy of one's knowledge for understanding and acting on personal experience are essential features of all human self-identity" (1978: 7). This is the power to resist outside influences, to reject alternative choices that others want to impose. This does not mean that individuals work out the meanings of their experiences in isolation. All human activities, including the growth and development of self-identity, take place in a social, cultural, and historical context. Still, each individual retains the power to interpret that context from his or her unique vantage point, in terms of his or her unique experiences. Cynics might argue that the power of the imagination must, in the real world, be restricted to private opinions; the mind can resist, but the body must conform. From this perspective, for example, the actions of a miner who labours underground daily for a meagre wage are clear-cut and unmistakable: he works for money to buy food for his family. However, ethnographic data suggest that this may not be the whole story.

The modern prototype of the downtrodden and exploited human being is the industrial labourer, the sufferer of the dislocations of the Industrial Revolution. Social scientists in the early twentieth century attempted to describe these changes. Émile Durkheim coined the term **anomie** to refer to the pervasive feelings of rootlessness and normlessness that people were experiencing. Karl Marx used the term **alienation** to describe the deep separation workers seemed to experience between their innermost sense of identity and the labour they were forced to do in order to earn enough money to live.

Do industrial workers in what used to be called "the Third World" similarly suffer from anomie and alienation? The issue has been hotly debated. Some argue that their condition could well be far worse than that of Western workers, at least in part because of the lingering effects of colonialism in these regions. This argument is rooted in what has been called "the scars of bondage" thesis. This thesis predicts that the more complete the political domination and exploitation of a people, the more deeply they will be scarred, brutalized, and dehumanized by the experience. For people suffering the twin exploitations of colonialism and industrialism, the outcome could only be the most bitter, unrelieved tragedy. However, as Alverson (1977) showed, the "scars of bondage" thesis was not confirmed by his ethnographic research among Tswana migrants who worked in South African mines in the 1960s. When these miners later described their experiences in South Africa, instead of seeing themselves as victims, they drew on their own cultural traditions, identifying themselves with resilient culture heroes.

Similarly, anthropologist June Nash (1979), working among Bolivian tin miners (see Map 12.3), has made interesting observations about the power of the human imagination to transform experiences by investing them with meaning. At the time of her fieldwork, the labour force in Bolivian mines was drawn from local Indigenous populations who had been effectively separated from their involvement in traditional Indigenous communities. Nonetheless, the Bolivian tin miners she knew were able to combine elements of the dominant industrial culture with elements drawn from Indigenous traditions. These Bolivian miners had created new, cohesive cultural patterns; far from being dissonant and alienating, the miners' culture provides an intact sense of self and belonging and an ability to celebrate life as meaningful (Figure 12.11).

How can we explain, in the lives of these Bolivian miners, the combination of what appears to be both genuine suffering and genuine celebration? Exploitation certainly leaves its mark on its victims: poor health, high infant mortality rates, shattered hopes. Yet many of these Bolivian miners were not irrevocably brutalized by these experiences. Their powers to invest their experiences with meaning remained intact, despite crushing conditions of exploitation. Nash notes, "My experience living in mining communities taught me, more than anything else, how a people totally involved in the most exploitative, dehumanizing form of industrialization managed to resist alienation" (1979: 319–20). She argues that the events people experience are less important than how they interpret those events. Nash concludes that the ethnocentrism of Western observers has kept them from recognizing the creative, revolutionary potential embodied in hybrid cultures like that of the Bolivian tin miners.

Bargaining for Reality

The power that people have to invest their experiences with meanings of their own choosing suggests that a ruler's power of coercion is limited, which was Gramsci's key insight. Thought alone may be unable to alter the material circumstances of coercion, yet it has the power to transform the meaning of those material circumstances.

Any hegemonic establishment runs the risk that the dominated may create new, plausible accounts of their experiences of domination. American anthropologist and political scientist James Scott (1990) refers to these unofficial accounts as "hidden transcripts." Occasionally, those who are dominated may be able to organize themselves socially in order to transform their hidden transcripts into a counter-hegemonic discourse aimed at discrediting the political establishment and may be able to persuade some or all of those around them that their interpretation of social experience is better or truer than that of the current rulers. Such challenges to incumbent political power are frequently too strong to be ignored and too widespread to be simply obliterated by force. When coercion no longer works, what remains is a struggle between alternative accounts of experience.

Anthropologist Lawrence Rosen (1984) worked in the Moroccan city of Sefrou (see Map 12.4). As he listened to the local people discussing and defining their relationships with one another, he realized that none of the traditional concepts they used could be said to have a fixed meaning. Any definition offered by

Map 12.3 Bolivian Tin Miners

© Paolo Arsie Pelanda/Shutterstock.com

Figure 12.11 Miners resting in an underground mine in Potosí, Bolivia, praying in front of the patron saint "El Diablo," a guardian of the government-run Bolivian tin mine complex. The offerings of cigarettes and coca leaves that the miners have placed in front of the statue are an example of how Bolivian miners have created new, cohesive cultural patterns. The roots of this custom date from much earlier times. How is this process of cultural adaptation political?

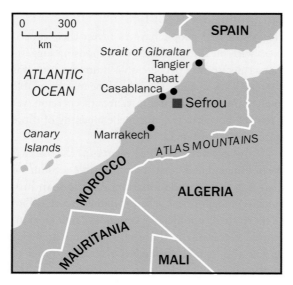

Map 12.4 Sefrou

one person would be verbally challenged by another. Rosen concluded that political and social life in Sefrou could not be understood unless one accepted that, for the locals, negotiation was the norm. Rosen calls this sociopolitical negotiation "bargaining for reality."

The reality bargained for is not an impersonal, unchangeable set of truths about the world. Moroccans aim to persuade one another to accept alternative ways of understanding a particular situation. Persuasive accounts must be *coherent*: they must explain events and processes central to the experiences of those to whom they are addressed, they must be expressed in language that other members of society can understand, and they must hang together in a way that is not blatantly contradictory.

The power relationship between men and women in Sefrou illustrates this process. In his fieldwork, Rosen found that men viewed women as less intelligent, less self-controlled, and less altruistic, and they expected women to obey them. Although women often assented to the male account of this relationship, they did not accept it in all circumstances. Women had developed an alternative account that explained elements in their lives that the male account either overlooked or interpreted differently.

Women in Sefrou depended on men—first their fathers, later their husbands, and perhaps eventually their sons—for material support. But marriages were fragile, and women often had to rely on males of their patriline when their husbands divorced them (a wife could not legally divorce her husband). Consequently, security for women depended on women strengthening their positions within their families. In particular, women attempted to influence marriage negotiations because marriage automatically rearranges social relationships within the family. Women were

eager to protect themselves and their daughters from oppressive demands by a husband and his kin. They viewed their actions as sensible and compassionate, not as misplaced interference. Nor did they accept the view that men are intellectually and morally superior to women. Indeed, they often viewed men as self-centred and childish.

In effect, Moroccan men and women lived side by side in different worlds. They shared experiences but interpreted those experiences differently. In everyday life, women had little direct contact with men, so these different interpretations of experience did not constantly come into conflict. But marriage negotiations inevitably brought these different perspectives into contention. The outcome was reality bargaining, as several different actors attempted to make their definitions of the situation prevail.

Rosen described one marriage negotiation that he encountered in Sefrou (1984: 40–7). A girl refused to marry the suitor her family had chosen, and her continued resistance had disrupted the harmony of her father's household. Rosen visited the household in the company of a respected male informant who was an old friend of the family. During their visit, both parties interpreted the girl's refusal differently. The family friend described the girl's behaviour as a typical case of female selfishness and immorality. He spoke harshly of her and repeatedly asserted that when her father returned they would force her to come to her senses and make the marriage. Her mother never openly contradicted these assertions. All the while, however, she quietly and insistently continued to make counter-assertions of her own. She reported her daughter's reason for rejecting the match: her intended husband came from a distant city. If she married him, she would have to leave her family behind and go live among strangers. It was not that she objected to an arranged marriage; rather, she did not want to marry this particular man because to do so would take her so far away from home. From a woman's perspective, the daughter's anxieties were entirely rational given the powerlessness and isolation that she would endure as a result of the marriage.

As it turned out, after a year-and-a-half of successful resistance, the young girl was eventually persuaded to marry the suitor. She changed her mind when she became convinced that consenting to the marriage was an economically sound move, not a submission to patriarchal authority. So, women may agree with the male position in general terms and yet successfully dispute its relevance in a particular situation. Men may get women to comply with their wishes, and yet the women's reasons for doing so may have nothing to do with the reasons men offer to justify their demands.

Map 12.5 Sedaka

James Scott carried out two years of ethnographic research among peasant rice farmers in a Malaysian village he called Sedaka (a pseudonym) (see Map 12.5). He found that poor Malaysian peasants were at the bottom of a social hierarchy, dominated locally by rich farmers and nationally by a powerful state apparatus. These peasants were not kept in line by some form of state-sponsored terrorism; rather, the context of their lives was shaped by what Scott calls *routine repression*: "occasional arrests, warnings, diligent police work, legal restrictions, and an Internal Security Act that allows for indefinite preventive detention and proscribes much political activity" (1985: 274).

Scott wanted to find out how this highly restrictive environment affected political relations between members of dominant and subordinate classes in the village. He quickly realized that the peasants were not about to rise up against their oppressors, not because they accepted their poverty and low status as natural and proper but because organized overt defence of their interests would have been difficult given the conflicting loyalties generated by local economic, political, and kinship ties. As well, the peasants knew that overt political action in the context of routine repression would be foolhardy. And they had to feed their families. Their solution was to engage in what Scott calls *everyday forms of peasant resistance*: this included "foot dragging, dissimulation, desertion, false compliance, pilfering, feigned ignorance, slander, arson, sabotage, and so forth" (1985: xvi). These actions may have done little to alter the peasants' situation in the short run; however, Scott argues, in the long run they may have been more effective than overt rebellion in undercutting state repression.

What we find in everyday forms of peasant resistance are indirect attempts to challenge local hegemony.

Scott says, "The struggle between rich and poor in Sedaka is not merely a struggle over work, property rights, grain, and cash. It is also a struggle over the appropriation of symbols, a struggle over how the past and present shall be understood and labelled, a struggle to identify causes and assess blame" (1985: xvii). When peasants criticize rich landowners or rich landowners find fault with peasants, the parties involved are not just venting emotion. According to Scott, each side is simultaneously constructing a world view. Rich and poor alike are offering "a critique of things as they are as well as a vision of things as they should be.... [They are writing] a kind of social text on the subject of human decency" (23).

Scott described the dynamics of this struggle during the introduction of mechanized rice harvesting in Sedaka. Traditionally, rice harvesting was manual labour (Figure 12.12). In the late 1970s, however, the introduction of combine harvesters eliminated the rich farmers' need for hired labour, a loss that dealt poor families a severe economic blow. When the rich and poor talked about the harvesters, each side offered a different account of their effect on economic life in the village.

While both sides agreed that using the machines hurt the poor and helped the rich, consensus evaporated when each side was asked whether the benefits of the machines outweighed their costs. The poor offered practical reasons against the use of combine harvesters: the heavy machines were inefficient and their operation destroyed rice paddies. They also offered moral reasons: they accused the rich of being "stingy," of ignoring the traditional obligation of rich people to help

Figure 12.12 Until recently, rice harvesting in rural Malaysia was manual labour that regularly allowed poor peasants to earn cash and receive grain from their employers as a traditional form of charitable gift. The peasants worked against routine repression not by revolting, but by resisting in the everyday. Do you witness everyday forms of resistance in your own life? What do they look like?

the poor by providing them with work and charity. The rich denied both the practical and the moral objections of the poor. They insisted that using harvesters increased their yield. They accused the poor people of bad faith, claiming that the poor suffered because they were bad farmers or lazy, and they attributed their own success to hard work and prudent farm management.

Rich rice farmers would never have been able to begin using combine harvesters without the outside assistance of both the national government and the business groups who rented the machines to them at harvest time. Poor peasants were aware of this, yet they directed their critique at the local farmers and not at the government or outside business organizations. After all, the rich farmers "are a part of the community and therefore *ought* not to be indifferent to the consequences of their acts for their neighbours" (Scott 1985: 161). The stinginess of the rich did not just bring economic loss. It also attacked the social identity of the poor, who vigorously resisted being turned into non-persons and insisted on being accorded the "minimal cultural decencies in this small community" (xviii). The only weapon they controlled in this struggle was their ability, by word and deed, to undercut the prestige and reputation of the rich.

This strategy worked in Sedaka because rich local farmers were not ready to abandon the traditional morality that had regulated relations between rich and poor. They had not yet become so Westernized that they no longer cared what other villagers thought of them. A shrewd campaign of character assassination may have caused at least some of the rich to hesitate before ignoring their traditional obligations. The improvement might have been minor, strictly in economic terms, but it would have been major in terms of the ability of the poor to defend their claims to citizenship in the local community. In addition, the wider political arena could always change in the future. Scott was convinced that many of the poor peasants he knew might well engage in open, active rebellion if routine repression disappeared.

When disputes are settled in this manner, experience is transformed, as Scott observed:

> The key symbols animating class relations in Sedaka—generosity, stinginess, arrogance, humility, help, assistance, wealth, and poverty—do not constitute a set of given rules or principles that actors simply follow. They are instead the normative raw material that is created, maintained, changed, and above all manipulated by daily human activity. (1985: 309)

In a similar way, Rosen referred to central Moroccan values, such as intelligence, self-control, and generosity, as **essentially negotiable concepts**: "There is an element of uncertainty inherent in these terms such that their application to any situation by one person can be contested by another" (1984: 43). Bargaining for reality involves just this sort of manoeuvre: "What is negotiable, then, is less one's view of reality as such than its scope, its impact, and its differential importance" (47). In articulating their particular world views, social groups aim "not just to convince but to control; better stated, they aim to control by convincing" (Scott 1985: 23).

The issues arising from the post-colonial environment also extend into basic definitions and negotiations of rights of citizenship and who controls these definitions and negotiations. This is of concern to anthropologists as well as scholars working in other disciplines, such as political science. (Note Joyce Green's discussion in the "In Their Own Words" box that follows.) The rights of those designated by a society as *the least amongst us* are essentially the only rights existing under law for all. What can be granted by authorities to the "least" can become the reality for the "most" in any regime of subjugation. This point moves beyond contested world views to contested human rights.

essentially negotiable concepts Culturally recognized concepts that evoke a wide range of meanings and whose relevance in any particular context must be negotiated.

In Their Own Words

Canaries in the Mines of Citizenship

Joyce Green, a political scientist from the University of Regina, discusses the issues of citizenship and membership for First Nations women in Canada.

So what is an excluded Indian woman to do? The standard responses to citizen dissatisfaction with an aspect of the political regime include legal challenge, political activism, partisan activity, and building new social consensus. Indian women concerned about citizenship and membership issues have tried all of these but have not yet found the political leverage to have their concerns ranked high by predominantly white or Aboriginal male politicians, mainstream political parties, and colonial courts.

Law, democratic mainstream politics, and Indigenous politics seem unable or unwilling to contend with the issues raised by this problematic minority. Denied band membership, meaningful exercise of Aboriginal and treaty rights, and, perhaps most importantly, denied the right to practise identity by living and raising children in their own communities, the affected women and their children are exiled to the dominant society where, thanks to racism, they are seen forever as "Indian."

Nor will the state apply its emerging view of rights in a way that works to the advantage of these women. Rather, the federal government retreats behind its self-serving rhetoric of respect for "self" government, washing its hands of any responsibility to guarantee these women's rights. Meanwhile, Indian Act band governments claim to be governments of First Nations, practising a constitutionally recognized Aboriginal and treaty right which includes control of membership or citizenship.

The Sawridge pleadings suggest some of these invoke colonial sexist practices as constitutionally protected "tradition." In sum, neither the state nor band governments defended these women with rights discourse, though both use it when it suits them. Neither has affirmed their value as human resources to society. Neither guarantees equality of citizenship by taking the steps needed to permit these women to live in a way that honours their identity and values their participation.

Democracy fails these women. Premised on majority rule, and on the theoretical cultural-neutral and gender-neutral citizen and politician, it is unable to ensure their representation in a political system implicitly premised on their sex and ethnic inferiority. Privileging mythical notions of undifferentiated equality, the ideology grounding Canadian democracy is inherently hostile to affirming rights-bearing specificity, especially where Aboriginal rights may result in constitutional and public policy measures that benefit Aboriginal people in ways not available to non-Aboriginal Canadians; that is, where differing kinds of citizenship result. This hostility has been evident in non-Aboriginal

opposition to treaty fishing rights and to land and governance rights sustained by the Supreme Court of Canada.

To date, Canadian law has failed these women, even with rights discourse foregrounded. The Lavell case of 1974, eight years prior to the entrenchment of the Canadian Charter of Rights and Freedoms, is infamous for dignifying sex discrimination as non-discrimination in law. The Sawridge case 21 years later sought to define Indian women's sexual equality rights out of existence. Lawmakers fail to see that any law affirming these women's rights must affirm them in their specificity as Indigenous women, part of colonized societies, to whom the state is historically an oppressor and only potentially an ally. While the Charter protections from discrimination on the basis of gender have motivated the federal government to eliminate the most egregious forms of legislative discrimination against Indian women, the measures are inadequate and stem from incomplete analyses that ignore the centrality to these women of their Aboriginal identities and rights, and their right to be fully acknowledged as part of their communities.

Yet citizenship may have the capacity to transcend the contradictions and pitfalls of decolonization in conditions defined by liberal and neo-liberal ideology and by the realpolitik of contemporary Canada. Even though Aboriginal rights constitute a different kind of right belonging only to members of Aboriginal nations, in addition to other citizenship rights enjoyed by all citizens of Canada, in the final analysis, people are not so incommensurable as to not share fundamental and inalienable human rights. All governments are impositions of authority upon those they govern, no matter how democratic or culturally authentic their processes. Authority must be held accountable for protecting the conditions fundamental to our humanity. In addition to human rights, which may be expressed and practised in different culturally specific fashions, Aboriginal rights must also be protected for all Aboriginal women and men.

Source: Green, Joyce. 2001. "Canaries in the Mines of Citizenship: Indian Women in Canada," *Canadian Journal of Political Science* 34, 4: 736–8. Reproduced with permission.

History as a Prototype of and for Political Action

When individual actors within a particular cultural and situational context attempt to impose their definition of the situation on those with whom they interact, they draw on elements of a shared tradition of values and beliefs. This shared tradition, however, does not consist of values and beliefs divorced from experience and history. To some degree, people in all cultures continue to reshape—to bargain over—not merely which part of an agreed-on tradition is relevant in a particular situation but also which version

of the tradition ought to be agreed on. The combinations they come up with are sometimes surprising.

Consider the development of rural justice groups called *rondas campesinas* ("peasants who make the rounds") in the northern Peruvian highlands (see Map 12.6). Rondas consist of armed groups of peasants who walk the paths around their hamlets at night keeping an eye out for animal rustlers (Figure 12.13). The rondas began in one small hamlet in the northern Peruvian department of Cajamarca in 1976. During the 1980s, they spread hundreds of miles within Cajamarca and surrounding departments. At the same time, their functions

Map 12.6 Northern Peruvian Highlands

were radically expanded: they became an alternative justice system with open peasant assemblies to resolve problems ranging from wife-beating to land disputes. By the early 1990s, rondas operated in 3,400 hamlets in the northern Peruvian Andes.

Anthropologist Orin Starn (1992) notes that at least five forces spurred *campesinas* to establish their alternative justice system:

1. The theft of animals shot up dramatically with the onset of the Peruvian economic crisis of the mid-1970s. The rise in theft was extremely serious for the poor farmers of the northern Andes, most of whom had small flocks and earned less than $2,000 per year.

2. Peasants got no relief from the official justice system. As the economy worsened, many government authorities tried to enlarge their shrinking salaries through bribery, kickbacks, and extortion, and poorer peasants were increasingly unable to pay.

3. The government had a weak presence in the mountains, providing an opportunity for peasants to develop a new form of community organization.

4. Country people in northern Peru value toughness and bravery in the face of violence and were able to channel their aggressiveness into the service of order and discipline in the rondas.

5. Local organizers had outside supporters. In the province where the rondas began, these were activists from the Maoist Red Homeland (Communist) party. In a neighbouring province, peasant teachers of Christianity became early ronda leaders and were defended by priests and nuns as well as the local bishop.

During the 1980s, rondas were transformed from vigilante groups to dispute-resolution groups. Compared to the expensive, time-consuming, humiliating, and ineffective official justice system, the rondas were inexpensive, efficient, effective, and local. By the late 1980s, rustling was virtually eliminated and rondas in some communities were adjudicating over 100 cases a month. The rondas also involve the elaboration of political identity and culture. Songs and poems celebrate the rondas, and festivals commemorate their anniversaries.

To create the rondas, peasants drew on national and local cultural patterns. Peasants had served on patrols to stop thieves on haciendas (expansive estates) before the haciendas were broken up in the late 1960s. Men in the hamlets who had served in the Peruvian military incorporated military strategies and forms into the rondas. The peasants also employed local patterns, keeping the ronda patrols under the collective authority of the community. Likewise, when the rondas took on adjudication roles, they adopted some forms from the state bureaucracy, using a table like a judge's bench, rubber stamps, a recording secretary with notarized minutes, and so on. But the openness of the ronda system is very different from the state bureaucracy, for the final decision rests on the ronda president's evaluation of the response of the people attending. Assemblies of rondas are often held outside, where the event occurred, such as a farmyard. All attending have detailed knowledge of some kind that may be brought into play, and everyone jumps in to attempt to settle the dispute.

But the rondas, for all their effective innovation, are sometimes still enmeshed in old practices:

© Orin Starn

Figure 12.13 *Rondas campesinas* have become an alternative justice system in highland Peru. Here, a group of *ronderos* pose with a stolen donkey recovered from rustlers in 1986.

- They are connected with political parties in Peru, and squabbles involving the parties have weakened the ronda movement.
- They see themselves as the genuine upholders of the law and the Peruvian constitution. Thus, even though they have challenged the government's monopoly on the administration of justice, they are not working to overthrow the state.
- In some rondas, the leaders stay on for many years, hoard power, and begin to show favouritism. (More often, communities encourage constant rotation of leaders to avoid this problem.)
- The rondas perpetuate patriarchy. Although the rondas have given women a place in order to censure wife-beating, and a number of offenders have received a stern warning or whipping, only men patrol; female participation in assemblies is limited and mostly passive, and women are never ronda officers.
- The rondas sometimes use violent measures to bring about justice. While their ultimate aim is to create peace and order in a violent environment, the ronderos employ some of the techniques of the Peruvian police—for example, whipping with barbed wire and hanging accused rustlers by their arms—to achieve their goal.

Starn concludes that, on the whole, the rondas have given Peruvian peasants the vision of an alternative modernity and have renewed among them a powerful sense of independent identity.

Negotiating the Meaning of History

The meanings of the central symbols of any cultural tradition are essentially negotiable. That is, each symbol evokes a wide range of meanings among those who accept it. But what that symbol means in any particular situation, as well as the appropriateness of applying that symbol to the situation, is never obvious. Such matters are cultural dilemmas that people struggle to resolve. Consider the Moroccan and Peruvian examples discussed in this chapter, and consider the power to invest experience with one's own meanings. This is a very real power. And yet many anthropologists are divided about the effectiveness of resistance as a solution to the problems of those at the very bottom of society. While some individuals and groups have been able to successfully assert themselves and their view of the world in the face of tremendous oppression, others have been destroyed by such oppression. Political theorist John Gledhill observes that it would be "dangerous to be over-optimistic"; after all, "counter-hegemonic movements exist, but much of the world's population is not participating in them" (1994: 198). He is particularly skeptical about the power of everyday forms of peasant resistance: the ability of such practices to undermine the local elite, he warns, may "merely provide the scenario for the replacement of one elite by another, more effective, dominant group" (92). At the beginning of the twenty-first century, with no utopian solutions in sight, the most that anthropologists may be able to do is agree with historian A.R. Tawney, who wrote about the agrarian disturbances in sixteenth-century England: "Such movements are a proof of blood and sinew and of a high and gallant spirit. . . . Happy the nation whose people has not forgotten how to rebel" (quoted in Wallerstein 1974: 357).

Living Anthropology

Biometrics and the Quest for Secure Identities

by Stephanie Ketterer Hobbis, Postdoctoral Research and Teaching Fellow, Anthropology, University of British Columbia (Okanagan)

Expected to triple in size by the early 2020s, the biometric industry is globally on the rise. When crossing borders we are increasingly required to provide biometric proof of our identity. Fingerprints and pictures are taken and compared to the biometric data stored on our passports. Soon biometrics may replace password and PIN (personal identification number) technologies and even render credit and debit cards unnecessary for authorizing payments. An increasing number of countries are implementing biometric technologies as ways to administer social security payments, to improve trust in the integrity of elections, and even to create first ever (nearly) comprehensive registries of a given population.

Continued

Biometric technologies promise certainty. They offer a way, so it seems, to secure identities, to verify people are who they claim to be by linking individual bodies to unique physiological features. Thus, biometric technologies also promise to improve and securitize governance, for example by providing more reliable data on the health of individual bodies—biometrics allow for medical records to be more easily and securely linked across institutions and to individual patients. In developing countries like the Solomon Islands, where I completed fieldwork in 2014 and 2015, biometric technologies are promoted as a pathway to development, as a way to combat corruption and the mismanagement of funds more broadly. Political systems are believed to be more stable as a result of "cleaner" elections based on biometrically secured voters' rolls. Aid money is thought to be less likely to be wasted if the recipients are better known, more transparent, and, therefore, possibly more accountable.

Anthropology, drawing on its difficult history with human (racial) classification based on particular physical attributes and the colonial usages of biometrics as means of control (see Maguire 2009), is well situated to critically examine the consequences of this rapid proliferation of biometric technologies, the complexities of their political promise, and the unequal, global power relations that these technologies often represent. In the Solomon Islands case, biometric voter registration was primarily pushed for by international state builders and development partners who praised the system as increasing citizens' trust and confidence in the state and its representatives. The system itself was provided by a Canadian company. Government officials also supported biometric voter registration, catering to funder requests but also to their own interests: biometric voter registration provided a useful distraction from more contested domestic issues, such as the ways candidates obtain and manage campaign funds. Voters, on the other hand, were by and large left in the dark about the particularities of the technology, the scope of its potential usages beyond the election, and broader ethical debates about the global securitization of identities. Biometrics were promoted as an objective rather than a political technology within a context that is marked by a continuing distrust in law enforcement after the involvement of police officials in a civil conflict between 1998 and 2003, and the subsequent international classification of the Solomon Islands as a "failed state."

While few of my local respondents were aware of how exactly state authorities could use, or maybe abuse, biometric information for classification, profiling, and exclusions, many were suspicious of the biometric system, or at least of those implementing it. Rumours were circulating about politicians' manipulation of the system through computer viruses or, more simply, through electoral clerks whose decision-making may hinge on the candidates they were supporting. Some of my respondents also voiced broader, culturally situated suspicions about the integrity of the system. Among the Lau-speakers of Malaita Province with whom I worked, the sharing of bodily identifiers and the recording of one's "true name," both a necessity for biometric voter registration, increase an individual's vulnerability to malevolent sorcery. The *Solomon Star,* Solomon Islands' primary newspaper, reported that in Makira Province voters worried that the biometric system is "666 technology," a way for the devil to take stock before the apocalypse.

In comparison to international and state-based supporters of the new system, few voters were confident that the technology would effectively deal with any of the perceived root causes of political instability. Instead of providing a sense of security, narratives about biometric voter registration re-revealed political vulnerabilities. Solomon Islander narratives questioned the proposed objectivity of technological solutions to broader sociopolitical challenges. At the same time, international praise of the system reminds us of disconnects and zones of conflict between global aspirations and contextually situated desires, fears, and uncertainties in encounters with the global state-based political-economic system.

Key Terms

alienation 316
anomie 316
biopower 313
consensus 315
domination 306
essentially negotiable concepts 320

free agency 306
governmentality 313
hegemony 308
persuasion 315
political anthropology 304
political power 303

power 303
resistance 315
social organization 302
social power 303

Chapter Summary

1. Social organization refers to the patterning of human interdependence in a given society through the actions and decisions of its members. Anthropologists understand that the complexities of human social organizations can

never be reduced to a single cause. The power that human beings have to reproduce or to change their social organization is an important focus of anthropological study.

2. The ability to act implies power. Power operates according to principles that are culturally constructed. Anthropologists interested in how power is exercised in states have been influenced by the works of Antonio Gramsci and Michel Foucault. Gramsci distinguished coercive domination from hegemony, arguing that coercion alone is rarely sufficient for social control. Foucault's concept of governmentality emphasizes the importance of practices that create and sustain peaceful and prosperous social life. These sorts of practices can be tailored to specific populations through the use of statistics.

3. Anthropological research in societies without states has shown how social obligations can restrict individuals from pursuing their own self-interests. In those societies, power is usually seen to be an independent entity to which one may gain access by supplication, not coercion. Likewise, individuals cannot be coerced but must be persuaded to co-operate. They are not free agents in the modern Western sense, but they are empowered to resist conforming to another's wishes.

4. All human beings possess the "power to invest the world with meaning." Rulers always face the risk that those they dominate may create new, persuasive accounts of their experience of being dominated, organize themselves to defend and disseminate their account, acquire a following, and unseat their rulers. When people bargain for reality, they draw on elements of a shared culture and shared history in order to persuade others of the validity of their position. Much political debate concerns which lessons from the past are relevant to the present. When disputes are settled in this manner, experience is transformed.

Critical Thinking Questions

1. Why would the anthropological contention that social relations in any society are ultimately arbitrary be a controversial idea?

2. What are the similarities and differences between domination and hegemony?

3. What was the initial bureaucratic role of statistics, and why were (are) they considered important?

4. If power is part of the natural order of things yet independent of direct human control, what are the consequences that follow? Consider personal access to power, social constructs and relationships related to power, and the individual's ability to change the balance in a power relationship.

Suggested Readings

Arens, W., and Ivan Karp, eds. 1989. *Creativity of Power: Cosmology and Action in African Societies* (Washington, DC: Smithsonian Institution Press). Contains 13 essays exploring the relationship among power, action, and human agency in African social systems and cosmologies.

Barrett, Stanley R., Sean Stokholm, and Jeanette Burke. 2001. "The Idea of Power and the Power of Ideas: A Review Essay," *American Anthropologist*, New Series, 103, 2: 468–80. A critique of Eric Wolf's *Envisioning Power: Ideologies of Dominance and Crisis* (1999). The authors argue that the concept of structural power is redundant and expendable as it is presented by Wolf.

Bashir, Halima. 2008. *Tears of the Desert: A Memoir of Survival in Darfur* (New York: One World). One woman's description of her survival of torture and gang rape, inflicted for speaking out about an attack on primary school children.

Fogelson, Raymond, and Richard N. Adams, eds. 1977. *The Anthropology of Power* (New York: Academic Press). A classic collection of 28 ethnographic essays on power all over the world.

Vincent, Joan, ed. 2002. *The Anthropology of Politics: A Reader in Ethnography, Theory, and Critique* (Malden, MA: Blackwell Publishers). A challenging but worthwhile collection of key texts in political anthropology, ranging from the eighteenth-century Enlightenment to twenty-first-century critique.

Related Websites

Wikipedia: Ronda Campesinas
https://en.wikipedia.org/wiki/Rondas_campesinas
Council on Hemispheric Affairs (COHA): A New Face to Salvadoran Politics?
www.coha.org/a-new-face-to-salvadoran-politics

Pueblo Indian History and Resources
www.indianpueblo.org
Constitutional Law of Canada: *Sawridge Band v. Canada*
http://web5.uottawa.ca/www5/jmagnet/index. php?option=com_mtree&task=viewlink&link_id=217&Itemid=9

13

A Global World

Chapter Outline

Views of the Political Economy

Cultural Processes in a Global World

Globalization and the Nation-State

Human Rights, Globalization, and the Language of Social Justice

Cultural Imperialism, Cultural Hybridization, and Cosmopolitanism

Learning Objectives

By the end of Chapter 13, you will be able to

- understand various theories that explain how different cultures and nations have related to one another;
- consider globalization and the pressures on the nation-state;

- recognize the challenges of human rights in a "globalized world"; and
- compare and contrast cultural imperialism, cultural hybridization, and cosmopolitanism.

In March 1989, anthropologist Terence Turner published a report describing how Indigenous Amazonians had organized themselves to resist outside encroachment on their traditional lands. These peoples had long been affected by the destruction of the Amazonian rainforest, and anthropologists and other observers had often feared that they were destined for extinction. No one imagined that they would become leaders in defence of the environment, working successfully with national and international allies.

Yet this is exactly what happened. Some 28 Indigenous nations came together to prevent the construction of a hydroelectric dam complex in the state of Pará in northern Brazil. Instrumental to this movement were the Kayapó (see EthnoProfile 13.1). The Kayapó leader Payakan combined traditional Indigenous political skills with a keen understanding of the international media. He and other Kayapó chiefs toured Europe and appeared publicly with well-known celebrities, including the musician Sting, who supported their cause. As Turner observes, "The boldness and global vision of this project are breathtaking; nothing like such a concerted action by even a few, let alone 28 unrelated Indian societies, has ever taken place in the Amazon. The Indians are trying to tell us something important; we should listen" (1989: 21–2).

Unfortunately, in 2010, the government of Brazil signed a contract renewing plans for a hydroelectric dam complex in Pará. Despite continued protests from the Kayapó, from other Indigenous peoples, and from activist groups around the globe, the dam complex—now known as the Belo Monte Dam—is currently under construction. Upon completion, it is expected to be the world's third-largest hydroelectric dam complex. It is estimated that the Belo Monte Dam will displace 20,000 to 40,000 Indigenous people and devastate approximately 1,500 square kilometers of Amazonian rainforest (see Amazon Watch 2014).

This example is but one of many that illustrate how Indigenous peoples continue to struggle in neocolonial environments. In the discussions that follow, we explore just how closely the Western world and the societies where anthropologists have traditionally worked are interrelated. We also explore how those interrelationships have changed over the years. We look at ourselves as much as we look at the peoples on which anthropological research traditionally focused. Through this reflexive exercise, we try to establish a context for contemplating the common fate of humankind.

EthnoProfile 13.1
Kayapó

Region: South America

Nation: Brazil

Language: Kayapó, part of the Gê language family

Population: 7,000 (2012 estimate)

Environment: Rainforest and savannah; wet and dry seasons

Livelihood: Extensive agriculture, hunting and gathering

Political organization: Headmen with no formal power; age grades

For more information: Rabben, Linda. 1999. *Unnatural Selection: The Yanomami, the Kayapó and the Onslaught of Civilization* (London: Pluto Press); "About the Kayapó," available at www.kayapo.org.

A herder walks with cows among wind turbines in Nairobi, Kenya. Around the world, modern technologies are reshaping traditional ways of life.

Views of the Political Economy

Looking back, we can distinguish two important phases of anthropological theorizing in the last 70 years or so. The first phase corresponds to the period of the Cold War—from the end of World War II to the break-up of the Soviet Union in 1991—which was also the period in which European colonial empires were dismantled. The struggle was between the Western capitalist-style nations (collectively known as the First World) and the "communist world" (the Second World). Control of the "non-aligned world" (the Third World) was the objective. This struggle affected anthropologists who were engaged in major debates about the efficacy of, first, **modernization theory** and then **dependency theory**.

The second phase began in the late 1980s, with the dismantling of economic and political barriers that had separated the first, second, and third worlds from one another. These events unleashed new patterns of movement and exchange that have come to be called globalization. Issues connected to globalization now dominate anthropological discussions of local, regional, and international issues.

Even today, the three-world analysis structure developed during the Cold War still has some currency. The First World continues to consist of powerful, wealthy nations, and the Third World consists of less powerful, less wealthy nations. While the Second World is no longer strictly represented by states that fit the "communist" mould, perhaps here we could now place those states and societies in conflict with First World aspirations of "development" and "democratization"—for example, Islamic societies whose ideologies oppose those of the West. To this structure, we can add a fourth category—the Fourth World—to describe the world of Indigenous peoples living in neocolonial areas of the world. Examples of Fourth World societies include those of the First Nations and Inuit peoples of Canada. Major concerns for peoples of the Fourth World include issues of Indigenous identity and the pressures of globalization.

Before we can begin to understand the complex forces of globalization, however, we must look more closely at earlier perspectives on global relationships.

modernization theory
A theory that argues that the social change occurring in non-Western societies under colonial rule was a necessary and inevitable prelude to higher levels of social development that had been reached by the more "modern" nations.

dependency theory
A theory that argues that the success of "independent" capitalist nations has required the failure of "dependent" colonies or nations whose economies have been distorted to serve the needs of dominant capitalist outsiders.

Decolonization: Modernization versus Dependency

In the early days of decolonization, many Western leaders and scholars interpreted the meaning of colonialism and its consequences through modernization theory. As colonial empires were reframed as newly independent states, Western thinkers postulated that these states would become prosperous, self-sustaining countries so long as they imitated the policies and practices believed to have been responsible for the successes of "modern" Western nation-states. Colonization was viewed as a positive process. Former colonies were viewed as "young" nation-states in need of paternal guidance from more "mature" modern states. Modernization theory became a road map that promised self-sustaining prosperity.

Yet many observers, particularly those living in former colonies, rejected modernization theory. Some criticized it for promoting a form of unilineal evolutionism in which tradition and modernity were seen as polar opposites. Others criticized it for failing to recognize that the prosperity of Western nations had *depended on* the exploitation of cheap raw materials, cheap labour, and the captive markets that colonies provided. This observation led to the development of dependency theory.

Dependency theory, developed in the 1960s by Latin American economists and social scientists, explained why most of the former colonies remained poor and weak long after they had obtained independence from colonial domination. Challenged was the assumption that nations are naturally autonomous and independently responsible for their own success or failure at modernizing. Indeed, it became clear that the West would never have prospered if colonial powers had not exploited other peoples' resources to fuel their own development. As anthropologist James Peoples puts it, "capitalistic economic relations that have produced development for a few countries are also responsible for the underdevelopment of the many. People in the less developed countries [have been] robbed of their economic surplus by the economic agents of the rich nations" (1978: 535). Without the ability to similarly exploit foreign resources, the former colonies could never hope to achieve the levels of economic prosperity experienced by the former colonizers.

Although more widely accepted than modernization theory, dependency theory was not without its critics. Primarily, the theory was criticized for assuming a simple exploitative relationship between rich nations and poor nations. As such, it failed to recognize and investigate the economic strategies of peoples in areas categorized as dependent. Moreover, it treated formerly colonized peoples as passive rather than active agents, thus dismissing their efforts in shaping their own modernity (see Peoples 1978: 536).

Despite its shortcomings, however, dependency theory resonated in the post-colonial world. It drew attention to the way that dependent nations endure the reshaping of their economic structures to meet demands generated outside their borders. For example, land that could be used to raise food crops for local consumption is used to grow export goods, such as flowers, bananas, sugar, coffee, and even illegal drugs (Figure 13.1). In such cases, local needs are often neglected in order to satisfy the wants of rich nations. The international capitalist economic order was accused of distorting the economies of dependent nations. Analysis suggested that "underdevelopment" would persist until dependent countries took control of their own destinies and restructured their economies and their societies to meet local needs. Thus, anti-capitalist revolutionary movements arose in various Third World countries, such as Cuba.

World-System Theory

An extension of dependency theory is Immanuel Wallerstein's (1974) **world-system theory**, which describes how societies across the globe are linked together through a large-scale economic system. Thoroughly rejecting modernization theory, Wallerstein set forth a global framework for understanding development and underdevelopment. He traced exploitative relations between First World and Third World countries to the late fifteenth and early sixteenth centuries, when emerging European capitalism began incorporating other regions and peoples into a world economy based on the capitalist mode of production. The Hudson's Bay Company, established in 1670, is a Canadian example of an organization that profited from this arrangement.

Originally, the European world economy was not the only world economy in existence; perhaps its most important competitor was China. Nevertheless, the European mode was able to surpass other forms because of capitalism: "The secret of capitalism was in the establishment of the division of labour within the framework of a world economy that was *not* an empire" (Wallerstein 1974: 127). Banking,

Figure 13.1 A farmer picks coffee berries on a plantation in Chiang Rai, Thailand. Because of its low nutritional value and high resource requirements, coffee is considered a luxury good. Why do farmers in "dependent" nations grow luxury crops? How might using land to grow luxury crops for export rather than nutritional crops for domestic consumption impact local populations?

finance, and highly skilled industrial production became central, and nations with these specialties became the **core** of the European world economy. The core (i.e., powerful Western nations) exploited the **periphery** to support its own high standard of living. The periphery, in contrast, practised various forms of coerced labour to produce goods to support core industries, and the standard of living for coerced workers was generally low. There also existed a **semi-periphery**, which consisted of states such as Mexico and Brazil that initially played peripheral roles but eventually accumulated sufficient industrial capacity and other resources to possibly achieve core status in the future.

The main critique of Wallerstein's model is that it offers only two possibilities for change:

1. Units within the system may change roles (e.g., a semi-peripheral state may move to the core, or vice versa).
2. The system as a whole may be transformed into something else as the result of a system-wide socialist revolution.

In its abstraction, the model misses the actual vibrancy of local activity.

world-system theory A theory that argues that capitalism incorporates various regions and peoples into a world system whose parts are linked economically but not politically.

core In world-system theory, the nations specializing in banking, finance, and highly skilled industrial production.

periphery In world-system theory, those exploited former colonies that supply the core with inexpensive food, goods, and raw materials.

semi-periphery In world-system theory, states that have played peripheral roles in the past but that now have sufficient industrial capacity and other resources to possibly achieve core status in the future.

Globalization: Developments and Debates

By the end of the twentieth century, no part of the world was unaffected by capitalist economic practices. For some individuals and groups, the emerging era of globalization seemed to present an opportunity to challenge the previously unquestioned truths about development and underdevelopment. Such challenges often came in the form of new social movements (Figure 13.2). Examples include vigilante movements (such as the *rondas campesinas* of Peru; see Chapter 12), squatter movements in cities, movements defending the rights of women and of minorities, and movements protecting fragile

neoliberalism A political perspective that promotes individual freedom, open markets, and free trade while opposing strong state involvement in personal and economic affairs.

©ZUMA Press, Inc./Alamy Stock Photo

Figure 13.2 In the last decades of the twentieth century, a number of new social movements developed around the world, including the Green Belt Movement, a tree-planting project in Kenya, run mostly by women. Pictured here is the movement's founder, environmental activist Wangari Maathai (1940–2011), who won the Nobel Peace Prize in 2004. In what ways do movements like the Green Belt Movement challenge capitalist economic practices?

environments. Through these movements, people were attempting to construct cultural institutions that met their needs in ways that often bypassed national governments or development agencies. Observing these widespread social changes, anthropologists began pointing out that many of the new social movements—especially those arising in formerly colonized nations—involved struggles over meanings as well as material conditions (see, e.g., Escobar 1992).

The apparent triumph of capitalism over communism at the end of the Cold War re-animated the defenders of modernization theory, now repackaged as **neoliberalism**, as Marxian analysis was dismissed. States were encouraged by international institutions, such as the World Bank and the International Monetary Fund, to accept that prosperity depended on their finding a niche in the growing global capitalist market. The widely held belief was that market discipline would allow state officials to support economic enterprises that would earn income in the market; as a result, individuals' personal income would increase, thus eliminating the need for state-supported safety nets for the poor. Western leaders enthusiastically embraced the beckoning opportunity to bring the entire world within the encompassing capitalist economy.

At the same time, many anthropologists and others attacked the notion of "development" promoted by Western governments and international aid agencies. They argued that the source of the problems in "underdeveloped" countries was misidentified as a simple lack of wealth or resources (see, e.g., Ferguson 2002). Rather, the problems of these countries were rooted in complex political, economic, social, and cultural forces. In the more than 25 years since the end of the Cold War, the truth of these arguments has become clear. Forces unleashed on a global scale have reconstructed the global political economy in unprecedented ways, with outcomes that no one could have predicted. Today, an event that occurs in one nation can easily have an impact—whether obvious or subtle—on people living on the other side of the world. (See the "In Their Own Words" box that follows. Anthropologists have found that the best way to begin understanding the intricacies of global interconnections is through a holistic approach.

In Their Own Words

Global Fractures

Carolyn Nordstrom is a professor of anthropology at the University of Notre Dame. Her specialties include political and economic anthropology, anthropology of war and peace, globalization, and culture theory. In the reading that follows, Nordstrom introduces the concept of "fracture zones" as she challenges us to see the depth of the danger we face when the local becomes global in the world of war.

This article introduces the idea of "fracture zones"—lines of instability that radiate out from specific and discernible crises. Fractures constitute vulnerabilities in trade networks, financial systems, economic enterprises, and socio-political services so great that the very viability of these institutions (as they define the modern state) is undermined. I followed these pathways ethnographically for over three years between 2001 and 2006—from the frontlines of political violence in Southern Africa into global supply chains and the complex relationships of extra/legal and extra/state networks passing through Europe, the US, and parts of Southern Asia. . . . Fracture zones are often hidden in the shadows of analysis of global power relations, and thus their impact on the economic and political realities of the world often goes unrecognized. There is a logical reason for this. Fracture lines run internationally and follow power abuses, pathological-profiteering, institutional inequalities, and human rights violations—actions that fill the pockets and secure the dominance of some while damaging the lives of others. . . . [W]hat are taken to be commonplace international acts of power surrounding political violence are neither logical nor innocent. They set in motion lethal instabilities that can topple political and economic systems in peacetime locales around the globe that are far removed from

the site of crisis.... All that is needed is a slight pressure—an economic downturn, a political conflagration, a natural disaster, an armed attack—and the lines of instability splinter, no longer able to support the society's basic service institutions. Peacetime nations that are instrumental in creating these fractures can crumble along these lines if fractures are sufficiently widespread and institutionalized.

The irony is that people often take these actions as pathways to achieving and maintaining power when the truth is far different. . . .

But what, exactly, constitutes a crisis? What are the boundaries we draw around it? Perhaps more accurately, what boundaries are we taught to see and not see, and what politics defines these? This is situated in [Ernesto] Laclau's (2000) fundamental question: "What is inherent in the hegemonic relationship?"

Taken as multiplicity, the ways in which these fractures are inculcated into the defining dynamics of the world's econo-political systems, plus the ways in which they cause dangerous vulnerabilities to the very foundations of governing and market systems, can be seen and perhaps changed. But these realities are not transparent: those who benefit from exploiting them work hard to render these processes invisible. Fractures are etched as undetectably as possible into the institutions grounding political and economic relations worldwide. The tendency in research analysis to focus on a single issue (economics, political studies, criminal investigations) helps hide the very realities that it purports to explain.

Source: Nordstrom, Carolyn. 2008. "Global Fractures," *Social Analysis: The International Journal of Social and Cultural Practice* 52, 2: 71–86. Reproduced by permission of Berghahn Books Inc.

Cultural Processes in a Global World

Most theories that were developed before the final decades of the twentieth century presupposed a world of relatively clear-cut geographic and cultural boundaries. In our globalized world, however, these boundaries are not nearly as well defined as they once were. Consider how various advances in communications technologies have made it relatively easy to stretch social relationships of all kinds over huge distances that previously would have been unbridgeable. Indeed, globalization is essentially an "intensification of . . . interconnectedness" on a global scale, and it involves "a world full of movement and mixture, contacts and linkages, and persistent cultural interaction and exchange" (Inda and Rosaldo 2002: 2). Yet this "interconnectedness" requires that "globalizing processes . . . come to terms with the realities of particular societies" (Inda and Rosaldo 2002: 4).

Under globalization, cultural practices have the opportunity to stretch far beyond the societies in which they first developed. Along the way, they may change form and take on new meaning, but this doesn't necessarily mean that they will lose their original significance. As anthropologist Theodore Bestor tells us, "globalization doesn't necessarily homogenize cultural differences nor erase the salience of cultural labels. Quite the contrary, it grows the franchise" (2005:18). The example Bestor uses to illustrate his point is the relatively recent popularity of sushi—specifically, bluefin tuna—in many Western nations:

> The tuna trade is a prime example of the globalization of a regional industry, with intense international competition and thorny environmental regulations; centuries-old practices combined with high technology; realignments of labour and capital in response to international regulation; shifting markets; and the diffusion of culinary culture as tastes for sushi, and bluefin tuna, spread worldwide. (Bestor 2005: 14)

In Japan, sushi remains, despite its global spread, a continuation of traditional, local food customs. For us in the West, it is a mark of the global economy.

However, not all reactions to globalization's impact on local cultural practices are positive. Anthropologist Susan J. Terrio (1996) observes how traditional French chocolatiers have faced intense international competition that threatens their livelihood as well as their cultural identity. She notes that in France there exists a strong desire to preserve the "authenticity" of the French culture:

> A universalist notion of civilization still survives in France and is strongly linked to the view that French culture itself best embodies it (Rigby 1991). Many French people see their achievements in literature, philosophy, and the arts, both high and popular, as evidence of this. Moreover, the French state and its representatives take seriously the protection of their language and culture forms from intrusive foreign influences. Current debates on the ubiquitous spread of English and the effect of European norms on traditional foods . . . illustrate this. (Terrio 1996: 68)

To the French in general, "the area of culture remains highly charged and contested" (68). This is particularly true today, as the European Union continues to strengthen the political, cultural, and other ties among European nations.

Perhaps not surprisingly, globalization does not affect all individuals and all cultures equally. Consequently, different groups and actors interpret and experience global processes in different—often very personal and unique—ways. One factor that impacts how a particular group experiences globalization is location. Even today, there exist "large expanses of the planet" that are, due to their geographical remoteness, "only tangentially tied to the webs of interconnection that encompass the globe" (Inda and Rosaldo 2002: 4). Another factor is the sort of "temporal conflict" that arises when interactions such as business meetings occur between individuals in different time zones (Birth 2007). While the meeting might fall in the middle of the day for some of the individuals involved, it might force others to lose sleep or miss out on important social events. Yet other factors involve different cultural interpretations—of everything from commodities, wealth, and consumption to "the nature of sociality and the politics of democratic empowerment" (Mukhopadhyay 2005: 59).

Anthropologists Faye Ginsburg and Rayna Rapp (1995) identify one particularly troublesome consequence of unequal experiences of globalization: *stratified reproduction*. Whereas some categories of people (Westerners, the wealthy) are empowered to nurture and reproduce, others (non-Westerners, the poor) are not. Consider, for example, how members of the elite in some nations "import" child-care workers. These workers then send their earnings home to support their own children, who are raised by parent surrogates, frequently grandmothers. Anthropologist Faye Harrison presents an analysis of feminist political ecology, noting that "the most problematic effects of globalization are engendering gross disparities in wealth, health, and life expectancy that disproportionately compromise the well-being of women and the families and communities that depend on their knowledge and labour" (2004: 1).

Undoubtedly, the forces of globalization are transforming the world in which we live. We have seen this transformation at work in the growth of transnational corporations that relocate their manufacturing operations from core to periphery, and in the transformation of locally significant cultural products (e.g., tribal masks, ceremonial costumes) into commodities to be marketed throughout the world. We have seen it in tourism, which has grown into the world's largest industry (Figure 13.3; see the "In Their Own Words" box on slumdog tourism that follows), and in migration patterns that have brought people from very different cultures closer together.

In Their Own Words

Slumdog Tourism

In August 2010, *The New York Times* published an op-ed essay by Kennedy Odede, then in his third year at Wesleyan University and the executive director of Shining Hope for Communities, a social services organization he co-founded to work in the Kibera slum. Shining Hope for Communities can be found at http://www.shofco.org/.

Nairobi, Kenya

Slum tourism has a long history—during the late 1800s, lines of wealthy New Yorkers snaked along the Bowery and through the Lower East Side to see "how the other half lives."

But with urban populations in the developing world expanding rapidly, the opportunity and demand to observe poverty firsthand have never been greater. The hot spots are Rio de Janeiro, Mumbai—thanks to "Slumdog Millionaire," the film that started a thousand tours—and my home, Kibera, a Nairobi slum that is perhaps the largest in Africa.

Slum tourism has its advocates, who say it prompts social awareness. And it's good money, which helps the local economy.

But it's not worth it. Slum tourism turns poverty into entertainment, something that can be momentarily experienced and then escaped from. People think they've really "seen" something—and then go back to their lives and leave me, my family and my community right where we were before.

I was 16 when I first saw a slum tour. I was outside my 100-square-foot house washing dishes, looking at the utensils with longing because I hadn't eaten in two days. Suddenly a white woman was taking my picture. I felt like a tiger in a cage. Before I could say anything, she had moved on.

When I was 18, I founded an organization that provides education, health and economic services for Kibera residents. A documentary filmmaker from Greece was interviewing me about my work. As we made our way through the streets, we passed an old man defecating in public. The woman took out her video camera and said to her assistant, "Oh, look at that."

For a moment I saw my home through her eyes: feces, rats, starvation, houses so close together that no one can breathe. I realized I didn't want her to see it, didn't want to give her the opportunity to judge my community for its poverty—a condition that few tourists, no matter how well intentioned, could ever understand.

Other Kibera residents have taken a different path. A former schoolmate of mine started a tourism business. I once saw him take a group into the home of a young woman giving birth. They stood and watched as she screamed. Eventually the group continued on its tour, cameras loaded with images of the woman in pain. What did they learn? And did the woman gain anything from the experience?

To be fair, many foreigners come to the slums wanting to understand poverty, and they leave with what they believe is a better grasp of our desperately poor conditions. The expectation, among the visitors and the tour organizers, is that the experience may lead the tourists to action once they get home.

But it's just as likely that a tour will come to nothing. After all, looking at conditions like those in Kibera is overwhelming, and I imagine many visitors think that merely bearing witness to such poverty is enough.

Nor do the visitors really interact with us. Aside from the occasional comment, there is no dialogue established, no conversation begun. Slum tourism is a one-way street: They get photos; we lose a piece of our dignity.

Slums will not go away because a few dozen Americans or Europeans spent a morning walking around them. There are solutions to our problems—but they won't come about through tours.

Source: Odede, Kennedy. 2010. "Slumdog Tourism," *New York Times* (9 Aug.).

Figure 13.3 A group of women shopping at a market in Delhi, India. Tourism has grown into the world's largest industry, and tourists have begun to encroach on people and cultures all over the world.

In many areas of the world, migration now happens on such a massive scale that observers speak of the "de-territorialization" of peoples and cultures that, in the past, were presumed to be firmly attached to specific geographical locations. When de-territorialized peoples re-territorialize in a new location, social conflicts may arise. Re-territorialization also generates new forms of cultural identity, as relocated populations struggle for recognition in their new surroundings while also trying to preserve connections to their culture of origin. Globalization has drawn the attention of many anthropologists to areas where people from different cultures have found themselves forced to interact with one another. Such contexts exhibit a "diffusion of culture traits gone wild, far beyond that imagined by the Boasians" (Kearney 1995: 557). Since this sort of cultural mixing is now happening worldwide, it undermines views of culture that depend upon settled peoples with distinct cultural attributes.

Where does Wallerstein's portrayal of the global processes as part of a world *system* fit now? Anthropologist Arjun Appadurai (1990) points out that ever-intensifying global flows of people, technology, wealth, images, and ideologies are highly contradictory, generating global processes that are fundamentally disorganized and unpredictable. Meanwhile, anthropologist Jonathan Friedman (1994) argues that the disorder may be real, but it is also a predictable consequence of the breakdown of Western global hegemony. In his view, these developments exemplify a pattern of commercial expansion and contraction that began at least 5,000 years ago with the rise of the first commercial civilizations, each of which was characterized by its own form of "modernity." Thus, the capitalist world system of the West "tends, as in previous mercantile civilizations, to become decentralized and more competitive. Weakened and crisis-ridden, the centre is likely to decline and lose its hegemonic power to new rising centres of imperialist accumulation" (1994: 2–3). As a result, "modernity in this sense is just another tradition, labile and fragile, that has emerged, however partially, and disappeared numerous times on the stage of human history"—for example, in ancient Greece, Rome, China, and India, and in the Arab Middle Ages (229–30). Awareness of this oscillating pattern reveals that "the variety of social structures documented in the anthropological literature can be understood as transformations of one or two basic types of organization in changing conditions of marginality in larger systems," based on whether they occur as a new commercial civilization begins to spread or as that civilization begins to decline (40).

Recognizing this pattern makes Friedman even more pessimistic than Wallerstein about possibilities for the future. He sees current changes in the capitalist world system as simply the latest example of "a more cyclically sinister history of civilizational systems" that have risen and fallen repeatedly throughout history (1994: 99). Friedman remains unmoved by those who suggest that anything new or hopeful might emerge from the current state of the world: "The capacity to even conceive of consciously changing the world for the better lies, perhaps, in changing the system as a whole, a system whose more general properties have eluded the storms of innumerable revolutions and cataclysm" (41). Not all anthropologists accept Friedman's arguments, as his conclusions cannot account for the "local structures" and "autonomous cultural schemes" that appear at any point in the cycle. It is this historically specific local detail—what Inda and Rosaldo (2002: 27) call "the conjectural and situated character of globalization"—that anthropologists aim to document and analyze.

Consider this: we have always lived in a world where elements of culture—ideas and material things—have made their way from culture area to culture area and across time, down through the ages. What may be challenging in the modern world, however, are (1) the speed at which this cultural transmission takes place and (2) the complexity of the range of cultural elements and other factors involved in this process.

Cultural Process and Visual Anthropology

Globalization, shifting environmental conditions, and various forms of warfare and displacement affect aspects of social stratification beyond classical categories of band, tribe, chiefdom, and state discussed earlier in this text. Many now fall into categories of sufficiency in a world where poverty statistics define lives ordered by stratified "states." Additionally, within states there are many people considered to be *stateless*, non-citizens even though they are residents of (or even born within) formal state systems. These people are even more vulnerable and approach 10 million in number (Abrahamian 2015).

In such stratified societies, higher-ranking groups have a disproportionate access to wealth, power, and prestige. The term for these people is "the 1%," and they are disproportionally represented in the Global North and in "Western" countries. It was reported in 2015 that the richest 1 per cent now have more wealth than the rest of the world combined (Oxfam 2016). In a world with resource stress, access to *resources of necessity*, such as food, clean water, medical care, safety, and in effect anything that can be classified as a "need," can become a serious pressure point.

Anthropologists are increasingly turning their analytical- and action-directed gaze to specific factors that impinge on the well-being of people facing concerns regarding safety and sufficiency of food, water, and medical care. An expanding area of research confronting various issues of inequity has been **visual anthropology**, which could be better characterized as "digital anthropology" because it captures not only images but sound as a database from which action anthropology can start. It is from such data that analysis becomes witness to diverse assaults on human survival and human dignity, and witness turns to activism (Richardson and Habib: 2013). Further, the digital is providing connectivity that supports cross-cultural/pan-cultural communication for mutual support and the development of strategies of adaptation or resistance in a world of radical change.

Use of Visual/Digital Data

The use of images is not new to anthropology. For example, Boas turned to the use of various recording devices as soon as they were available. He recorded music and language and photographed many people, even taking pictures of himself for illustrative purposes (Figure 13.4).

visual anthropology The anthropological contribution to visual culture of ethnographic photography, film, and digital media representations of cultural data.

National Anthropological Archives, Smithsonian, OPPS NEG MNH 8298

Figure 13.4 Franz Boas demonstrates a position in the Kwakiutl (Kwakwaka'wakw) Hamatsa dance ritual, as he observed it at Fort Rupert, British Columbia, in 1894.

Anthropologists, other social science researchers, and artists are also revisiting early photographs with a critical eye. For example, Edward Sheriff Curtis's famous photographs of Indigenous people that comprised his body of work known as *The North American Indian,* depicting an "idealized representation of Native culture," are now being showcased alongside contemporary Indigenous artists' work in order to ask audiences to "think critically about the portrayal of Native experience through photography" (Portland Museum 2016).

With emerging concepts of agency there arose serious concerns on the recording of participants through various devices (photographs, movies, sound recordings) and the form that participant permission would take. "The question of technology is primarily a social, cultural, and political one" (Frosh 2003: 185), and for academics in Canada this means working within the framework of specific REB (Research Ethics Board) requirements and the regulations set out by the Tri-Council of Canada for research with human subjects. A team from Australia (Cox et al. 2014) presented researchers with six categories of ethical issues for visual research that provide guidance for visual research methods (Figure 13.5). In particular, the section on "fuzzy boundaries" notes that the potential for boundaries between the roles of researchers, participants, artists, and others is

intensified in projects using visual research methods because researchers may spend significant periods of time engaged in fieldwork, researchers and participants may co-create products, participants may be peer researchers, or participants may share or create images in a process that requires great personal investment beyond the normal role of a research participant. This blurring of boundaries creates ethical challenges, such as how to best exit from the project when participants have invested deeply in building new relationships and contributing to the research. (Cox et al. 2014: 15)

The guidelines also note that appropriate acknowledgement of authorship of visual material is important for a variety of reasons, including the following:

- ensuring the integrity of research processes and maximising the benefits of participation for individuals who agree to be involved in research;
- supporting the development and maintenance of strong research relationships between participants and researchers;
- maximising the richness of insights and contributions that participants might be willing to share as part of the research process; and
- pre-empting possible future resentment or disappointment if participants or contributing artists/practitioners later feel their contributions have been inadequately acknowledged within reporting and dissemination activities, or that their visual materials have been inappropriately publicly displayed. (Cox et al. 2014: 17)

Lastly, the guidelines emphasize the importance of how visual material is displayed and in what context, noting "issues of representation and audience/s are central to all types of dissemination activities in visual research" (Cox et al. 2014). Much of the information in these guidelines is echoed in Canadian governmental documents on research with humans that can be found online (see Tri-Council

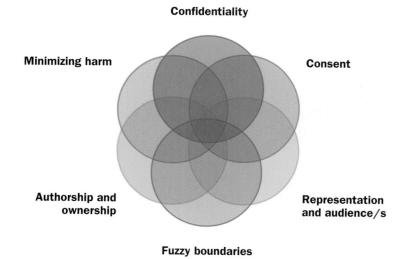

Figure 13.5 Six categories for ethical research using visual research methods.

Source: Cox et al. 2014: 8. Reproduced with permission of Dr Marilys Guillemin. Reproduced with permission of Dr Marilys Guillemin.

In Their Own Words

Embodied Ways of Listening: Oral History, Genocide and the Audio Tour

In this excerpt Steven High looks at the Montréal Life Stories project, a project that has been recording the life stories of Montréalais displaced by war, genocide, and other human rights violations. High examines how the project has been integrated into online digital stories, and how sound artists and audio tours can form the basis for research.

A significant proportion of Montréal's diverse immigrant population is composed of people displaced by mass violence, ranging from the Holocaust to war and atrocity crime in Rwanda, Cambodia, the Congo, Latin America, and Haiti. Quite naturally, these communities developed "their own occasions, rituals, archives, and practices of remembering" (Smith and Watson 2010: 25). For almost two decades, Page-Rwanda, formed by the relatives and friends of those who died during the 1994 genocide, has organized an annual commemorative walk to the St. Lawrence River. Hundreds of Rwandan *Montréalais* attend a special mass before walking in a procession behind a banner reading "Commemoration du Genocide contre les Tutsis du Rwanda." This formal commemorative ceremony ends at the base of the sailors' memorial tower, where community members throw flowers of remembrance into the river. Rivers have great ritualistic and symbolic importance in Rwandan history and culture, first under the Tutsi Monarchy and then during the genocide. In a massive ritual of purification of the body politic, Hutu génocidaires attempted to annihilate Rwanda's Tutsi minority, throwing some of the dead and dying into the Nyabarongo and Akagera Rivers. Thousands of bodies washed up downstream on the shores of Lake Victoria.

For the past seven years, the Montréal Life Stories project has been recording the life stories of Montréalais displaced by war, genocide and other human rights violations. Funded by the Community-University Research Alliance (CURA) program of the Social Sciences and Humanities Research Council, the Montréal Life Stories project brought together over 300 faculty members, students, interns, artists, and community members as well as eighteen organizational partners from the city's Rwandan, Cambodian, Haitian, and Jewish communities as well as educational, heritage, new media and human rights groups. In all, 450 people were interviewed in multi-session life story interviews lasting as long as 20 hours. We endeavoured to understand the violence within the context of the remembered life, what Daniel James calls the "foundational myth of the self" (2000: 186). At its core, observes Alessandro Portelli, oral history is a "dialogic discourse" that searches for connection between "biography and history; between individual experience and societal transformation" (1997: 4–5). We find significance not only in the words spoken but in the form structure of oral narratives. Even "wrong tales" tell us something important, "errors, inventions, and myths lead us through and beyond facts to their meanings" (Portelli 1990: 2).

What happens after the interview is increasingly important in oral history. The life stories recorded by our project were integrated into online digital stories, live performances, art installations, animated and documentary film, museum exhibitions, pedagogical materials, an immersive bus tour, audio portraits, audio walks and a searchable research database. Who controls the process is vitally important. Interviewees were therefore invited to participate in subsequent stages of the research-creation process, co-producing online digital stories, participating in workshops, and so on. Community members authored many of the project's public outcomes. The CURA program is unusual in so far as communities become partners in research and not simply objects of study, learning with rather than simply learning about (Greenspan 2010). The intensity of the academic gaze remains undiminished . . . Community involvement in the project was real and sustained. Interpretative power was thus shared broadly.

Building on the work of sound artists Graeme Miller and Janet Cardiff, oral historian Tony Butler, as well as the broader insights gleaned from the Montréal Life Stories project, this paper considers the notion of space-time dissonance in the making of *Une Fleur dans le Fleuve/A Flower in the River*, a 53-minute audio walk that follows the same commemorative path taken by the Rwandan community. The tour explores the personal meaning and legacy of mass violence through the personal narratives of six Rwandan exiles and survivors. There is a tendency in Montréal, like elsewhere in North America, to view Rwanda 1994 as a distant place and time. But it is here and now. There are thousands of Rwandan genocide survivors living in Canada today. Their personal stories are now part of our collective story . . . But how might we tell stories of violence? . . . [E]mbodied listening is the necessary first step in this direction—but the bridge analogy fails to capture the spatial and temporal dissonance experienced by audio walkers as these two worlds uncomfortably rub up against each other.

Source: High, Steven. 2013. "Embodied Ways of Listening: Oral History, Genocide and the Audio Tour," *Anthropologica* 55, 1: 73–85. Reprinted with permission of University of Toronto Press.

at www.pre.ethics.gc.ca/pdf/eng/tcps2/TCPS_2_FINAL_Web.pdf, and Social Sciences and Humanities Research Council of Canada [SSHRC] at www.sshrc-crsh.gc.ca/home-accueil-eng.aspx).

There is no doubt that people's interest is captured by the image. Images can be critically important research tools and excellent and nuanced records of an instant in time—an instant that may be fleeting in a world of change in a way that the word on the written page may not be. An image may be a moment held against a new reality for analytical comparison or contrast. We may be recording daily life and occasions, as well as terrible things in varying degrees. In this context, Susan Sontag, in *Regarding the Pain of Others* (2003), notes that there is a "vast repository" of "atrocious images." These images are reminders that "depravity exists" and that people cannot forget or ignore as "[n]o one after a certain age has the right to this kind of innocence, of superficiality, to this degree of ignorance, or amnesia" (8).

Visual representations can be static, in the one "shot," or they can show us an entire sequence of events, as in a video clip. They can also be found in the form of audio files. (Read more in the "In Their Own Words" box that on the previous page.) Regardless of the medium, all visual and audio representations call us to pay attention—to be in the now and to be engaged. This is what anthropology is attempting to do, as seen in emerging innovative forms of ethnography (Culhane 2011). Such research methods will continue to become increasingly important as technology and digital connections across the globe become all the more prevalent in everyday human life.

Globalization and the Nation-State

Are Global Flows Undermining Nation-States?

In the recent past, one of the fundamental suppositions about global social organization was that the world was a mosaic of independent nation-states. The flow of people, technology, wealth, images, and ideologies unleashed by globalization, however, has seemed to suggest that the conventional ideas about nation-states require revision. Further, many nation-states are actually composed of disparate ethnic groups with diverging self-interests. National governments are virtually powerless to

control what their citizens read or watch in the media. Nation-states allow migrants, businesspeople, students, and tourists to cross their borders because they need their labour or expertise or tuition or vacation dollars, but in doing so states must contend with the political values or religious commitments or families that these outsiders bring with them. Is the weakening of boundaries between states a good thing?

Massive global displacements of people have characterized the modern world. In the nineteenth century, developing capitalist markets pushed and pulled waves of emigrants out of their homelands and installed them in different parts of the globe. When immigration volumes were fairly low and jobs were plentiful, newcomers could often assimilate into their new homes with relative ease. But globalization has changed all that. Today, desperate economic and political situations in migrants' home territories, plus ease of transportation, have increased the volume and speed of migration; at the same time, market crises in the countries where migrants have settled have sharply reduced the economic opportunities available to them. Thus, migrants often find themselves caught between the hope for better opportunities and the threat of failure. Additionally, their visibility in enclaves of settlement, often in the poorer areas of cities, and the hostility sometimes directed against them by locals promotes the sense that hopes of assimilation are unrealistic. In such an atmosphere, many migrants have strong reasons for maintaining ties to their homeland.

Migration, Transborder Identities, and Long-Distance Nationalism

The term **diaspora** is commonly used to refer to migrant populations with a shared identity who live in a variety of different locales around the world. However, anthropologists Nina Glick Schiller and Georges Fouron (2002) point out that not all such populations see themselves in the same way. In their work, they describe different types of *transborder identities*, and they prefer to use the term *diaspora* to identify a form of transborder identity that does not focus on nation-building. (See the "In Their Own Words" box that follows.) Should members of a diaspora begin to organize in support of nationalist struggles in their homeland, or to agitate for a state of their own, they become **long-distance nationalists** (2002: 360–1).

diaspora Migrant populations with a shared identity who live in a variety of different locales around the world; a form of transborder identity that does not focus on nation-building.

long-distance nationalists Members of a diaspora who begin to organize in support of nationalist struggles in their homeland or to agitate for a state of their own.

In Their Own Words

Diaspora and Identity

One of the authors, Roberta Robin Dods, examines the relationship between diaspora and identity, focusing in particular on Italian Canadian communities.

If we consider culture as a performance art, we can see why it must be that culture is in a constant state of change. The performance is by nature unscripted and unbounded, shaped not only by what the performers bring to the performance—their knowledge, experiences, perspectives, beliefs, and so on—but also by the context in which it takes place. Changing the context changes the performance.

When people leave their homeland to re-establish themselves in a new place, they bring with them elements of their culture. Once they reach their destination, however, they must adapt what they have brought with them to their new context. For immigrants to Canada, this new context is often a major city made up of people from many different cultural backgrounds. In many cases, the most comfortable place for immigrants to settle is in ethnic enclaves where they can be close to people whose cultural backgrounds are similar to their own and who are likewise negotiating a hybridized cultural identity in a new homeland. As they draw on experiences from their old and new worlds, these people develop complex cultural identities based on their uniquely transnational world views.

Nicholas Harney has made some general observations on migrants' experiences with diaspora and identity:

> First, the experience of dispersal is to more than one place. Second, there is active communication, both institutional and kin, between different locations within the diaspora and also with the homeland. Third, a collective sentiment of groupness is cultivated and distinct from the host society. Fourth, there is a collective memory about the past, real or imagined. Fifth, diasporas are also disciplined, structured, and influenced by their location within the political, bureaucratic, and cultural sphere of a host society which may adopt strategies for managing diversity. (2002: 44)

These features remain central and salient regardless of the origins or destinations of migrants.

In his field research, Harney has taken a more specific look at how processes of identity formation operate among Italian Canadians living in Toronto. As he observes, "Italian immigrants and their descendants negotiate identity in locally specific circumstances . . . within the context of state-sponsored multiculturalism in Canada and multiple diasporic discourses linking peoples in Italy and Canada" (2002: 43). Central to this identity is the family as the "pragmatic transnational link" (Levin 2002: 8). For example, in the home, family members generally speak Italian but with English words and phrases incorporated into the discussion. Such language environments not only maintain Italian-ness, they mark regional dialectical differences of the homeland.

Family dinners also contribute to identity formation. In Italian Canadian households, dinners often feature regional dishes from the homeland. Food of *home* is more than nutrition. It is a metaphor for identity, and it marks boundaries of distinctiveness within and between culture areas. Food touches us on so many levels—smell, taste, visual appeal. It becomes "embodied forms of memory" (Holtzman 2006: 361)—memories of family meals and special occasions, memories of other times and places.

As Harney observes, modern technologies make it easier for immigrants to stay in touch with people "back home" and to learn about cultural developments in the homeland:

> In an accelerated fashion, Italian immigrants and their children can interact with and expend emotional energy on ties with their "homeland" in every sphere of social life. Magazines arrive from regions of origin in Italy, and hometown websites seek out rite-of-passage life histories, photographs, and social activities of co-villagers dispersed around the world. (2002: 48)

These sorts of close connections help Italian Canadians feel connected to their homeland despite the great physical distance that separates them from it (Figure 13.6).

In many cases, migrants leave their homeland for better opportunities elsewhere. In some cases, these opportunities materialize into success and security; in others, the result is disappointment. Either way, immigrants often imagine an "idealized return" to the homeland (Levin 2002). In the past, this return often remained imagined, but the relative ease of international travel today has made it a possibility for many. Indeed, "travel allows frequent and well-timed returns, for example, on ritual occasions marking life-cycle events and to socialize children in the homeland, which

Continued

Figure 13.6 A crowd gathers in front of the CHIN Radio building in Toronto's Little Italy to watch the Good Friday procession. CHIN Radio was the first multicultural, multilingual radio station to be established in Ontario and now hosts over 30 different diaspora communities with programs on local activities, news, music, interviews, and discussions on being an immigrant in Canada.

express relationships more concretely than does verbal or written contact alone" (Levin 2002: 4). While these sorts of brief visits can be refreshing and identity affirming, more permanent migrations back to the homeland can be difficult.

Recently, in a northern Italian city, I met an elderly woman who had returned to the region after having lived in Ottawa for 45 years. This woman was a widow without children, now living with relatives "back home" in Italy. Yet her return was not what she had hoped it would be. She was lonely, living with a family she barely knew, and missing her Italian Canadian friends in Ottawa. Here was a painful reversal—a woman seeing herself as foreign in her country of origin. "Home" remained elsewhere, in the place where she had made a life with her husband even while she maintained the almost mythic idea of "back home." Her story of Canada had the nostalgia often found in immigrants' "back home" memories. Her life was book-ended by two places, each calling to her through their defining metaphors of identity.

Note: Nicholas Harney quotes reprinted with permission of University of Toronto Press.

transborder state A state in which it is claimed that those people who left the country and their descendants remain part of their ancestral state, even if they are citizens of another state.

transborder citizenry A group made up of citizens of a country who continue to live in the homeland plus the people who have emigrated from the country and their descendants, regardless of their current citizenship.

The term *long-distance nationalism* was coined by political scientist Benedict Anderson to describe the efforts of émigrés to offer moral, economic, and political support to the nationalist struggles of their countries of origin. Anderson emphasizes the dangerous irresponsibility of the "citizenship-less participation" of long-distance nationalists: "while technically a citizen of the state in which he comfortably lives, but to which he may feel little attachment, he finds it tempting to play identity politics by participating (via propaganda, money, weapons, any way but voting) in the conflicts of his imagined *Heimat* [homeland]" (2002 [1992]: 269–70). Schiller and Fouron argue, however, that the conditions of globalization have led to new forms of long-distance nationalism that do not correspond to Anderson's original description. They point to the emergence of the **transborder state**: a form of state "claiming that its emigrants and their descendants remain an integral and intimate part of their ancestral homeland, even if they are legal citizens of another state" (2002: 357). This form of long-distance nationalism creates what Schiller and Fouron call a **transborder citizenry**: a group of people—some living in the homeland, some living abroad—who maintain strong ties to a shared homeland (Figure 13.7).

Transborder states and transborder citizenries are more than symbolic concepts: they have become formalized in law. Canada and many other nations allow their citizens to hold dual citizenship. Some countries go so far as to set up special government ministries to address the needs of citizens living abroad. This situation is very different from Anderson's notion of "citizenshipless participation." Schiller and Fouron stress that transborder states and citizenries "cannot be seen as top-down fostering of elite beliefs"; rather, they spring "from the life experiences of migrants of different classes" and are "rooted in the day-to-day efforts of people in the homeland to live lives of dignity and self-respect that compel them to include those who have migrated" (2002: 359).

But some transborder citizens face difficulties. In some cases, their efforts at nation-building may be blocked by political forces in the homeland who do not welcome their contributions. In other cases, the state in which they have settled may not welcome their continued involvement in the affairs of their homeland. Often, the severity of these difficulties depends on the tone of the relationship between the country of settlement and the country of origin.

The globalizing forces that produce long-distance nationalism and transborder states and citizens have undermined previous understandings of what nation-states should look like. In addition, they have revealed unacknowledged problems and weaknesses within certain nation-states. For example, the existence and strength of transborder states and citizenries show that some nation-states—especially those sending migrants—are actually what Schiller and Fouron call *apparent states*: they have all the outward attributes of nation-states—government bureaucracies, armies, a seat at the United Nations, and so on—but in fact they are unable to meet the needs of their people (2002: 363).

The strength of long-distance nationalism and transborder citizenries also exposes inconsistencies and paradoxes in the meaning of *citizenship*. Schiller and Fouron contrast **legal citizenship** with **substantive citizenship**. They point out that, for transborder citizens, these two types of citizenship do not necessarily coincide. *Legal citizenship* is granted by state laws and can be difficult for migrants to obtain. But even those transborder citizens who obtain legal citizenship often experience a gap between what legal citizenship promises and the way they are treated by the state. For example, a state may treat its citizens who have lived their entire lives within its borders more favourably than it treats its recently naturalized citizens. *Substantive citizenship*, in contrast, is defined by the actions people take to assert their membership in a state and to bring about political changes to improve their lives. Some transborder citizenries call for the establishment of fully fledged **transnational nation-states**. That is, "they challenge the notion that relationships between citizens and their state are confined within that territory," and they work for the recognition of a new political form that reflects the realities of their experiences of national identity (Schiller and Fouron 2002: 359).

The contrast between formal and substantive citizenship illustrates that traditional, seemingly straightforward notions of citizenship have begun to break down in the context of globalization. While such developments may provide new opportunities for some, they create difficulties for others. For example, individuals with complicated or ambiguous citizenship status may have a hard time accessing state-supported social programs (see Clarke 2004; Gledhill 2001). Too often, globalization can have a marginalizing effect on the powerless. As our world continues to globalize, we must ensure that those in need are not left behind.

©James Heatlie Photography/iStockphoto

Figure 13.7 Canada Day celebrations from abroad in Trafalgar Square, London, England on 1 July 2017. Hundreds of people came out to celebrate Canada's 150th birthday. Here a crowd enjoys snacks and refreshments at the Canada Day Bar, including "Nanaimo Bars: The Original," "La Petite Cabane à Sucre de Québec," "Fresh Cooked Waffles and Maple Syrup," and "Canadian Wild Blueberries." Would you view the celebration as a form of transborder citizenry? Have you seen or experienced other forms of transborder citizenry?

Flexible Citizenship among Diasporic Chinese Families

In her research on diasporic communities of elite Chinese families, anthropologist Aihwa Ong (2002 [1999]) has examined the concept of **flexible citizenship**, defined by "the strategies and effects of mobile managers, technocrats, and professionals seeking both to circumvent *and* [to] benefit from different nation-state regimes by selecting different sites for investment, work, and family relocation" (174). This form of citizenship has clear benefits for individuals working in business or commerce.

Although the successes of Chinese business-people are often attributed by outsiders to "Chinese culture," Ong's research challenges this simplistic explanation. Many Chinese businesspeople have responded creatively to opportunities and challenges they have encountered since the end of the nineteenth century, when Chinese merchants first became involved in the capitalist economic centres of European colonial empires in East and Southeast Asia. They succeeded because they were able to cultivate values and practices that allowed them to evade or exploit the rules governing three different kinds of institutions: (1) Chinese kinship and family, (2) the nation-state, and (3) the marketplace.

legal citizenship The rights and obligations of citizenship granted by the laws of a state.

substantive citizenship The actions people take, regardless of their legal citizenship status, to assert their membership in a state and to bring about political changes that will improve their lives.

transnational nation-states Nation-states in which the relationships between citizens and their states extend to wherever citizens reside.

flexible citizenship Strategies employed by individuals who regularly move across state boundaries in order to circumvent and benefit from different nation-state regimes.

The break from mainland Chinese ideas of kinship and Confucian filial piety came when Chinese merchants first moved into the capitalist commercial circuits of European empires. Money could be made in these settings, but success required Chinese merchant families to cut themselves off from ties to mainland China and to reinforce bonds among family members and business partners in terms of *guanxi*: "relationships of social connections built primarily upon shared identities such as native place, kinship, or attending the same school" (Smart 1999: 120).

Diasporic Chinese merchant and industrial families developed a set of values and practices that centred on the well-being of the family:

> An individual's sense of moral worth is based on endurance and diligence in income-making activities, compliance with parental wishes, and the making of sacrifices and deferral of gratification, especially on the part of women and children.... Children, especially sons, are expected to collect symbolic capital in the form of educational certificates and well-paying jobs that help raise the family class position and prestige. (Ong 2002 [1999]: 178)

Having managed to evade the discipline of mainland Chinese kinship and family practices, the family discipline of overseas Chinese individuals enabled them to become wealthy and provided the resources to subvert the control of the nation-state. The orientation of these wealthy families toward national identity and citizenship, Ong explains, is "market-driven." In Hong Kong, for example, in the years leading up to its return to mainland China in 1997, many wealthy Chinese thought of citizenship "not as the right to demand full democratic representation but as the right to promote familial interests apart from the well-being of society" (178). None of the overseas Chinese people she knew expressed any commitment to nationalism, either local or long-distance.

Rather, overseas Chinese families actively worked to evade the regulations of nation-states. For example, Chinese from Hong Kong who wanted to migrate to Britain in the 1960s were able to evade racial barriers that blocked other "coloured" immigrants because of their experience with capitalism and their reputation for peaceful acquiescence to British rule. When the British decided to award citizenship to some Hong Kong residents in the 1990s, they used a point system that favoured applicants with education, fluency in English, and training in professions of value to the economy, such as accountancy and law. Wealthy applicants were also highly favoured, in Britain and elsewhere (Figure 13.8). In many countries, citizenship, or at least a passport, could be purchased by those who had the money.

Although they had managed to evade or subvert both the traditional principles governing Chinese kinship and family and the regulations of nation-states, these overseas Chinese families remained vulnerable to the discipline of the market. This was a very different market from the one that had existed before the development of the transportation, communication, and manufacturing technologies that enabled people to move money and factories around the world with ease. Making money in the context of globalization required the flexibility to take advantage of economic opportunities wherever and whenever they appeared; accordingly, overseas Chinese families took steps to position family members in different settings. Ong describes one family in which the eldest son remained in Hong Kong to run part of the family hotel chain located in the Pacific region while his brother lived in San Francisco and managed the hotels located in North America and Europe. Sometimes even younger children are separated from their parents for business-related

Figure 13.8 Chinese shoppers flock to the luxury French department store Galeries Lafayettes in Paris, France. Historically, some Chinese families have been able to use their money, along with their business experience, to succeed in Western society.

©Directphoto Collection/Alamy Stock Photo

reasons—for example, they might be sent away to attend a good school while their parents manage businesses in other countries on different continents. Yet these flexible business arrangements are not without costs. "Familial regimes of dispersal and localization . . . discipline family members to make do with very little emotional support; disrupted parental responsibility, strained marital relations, and abandoned children are . . . common circumstances." At the same time, individual family members truly do seem to live comfortably as citizens of the world. A Chinese banker in San Francisco told Ong: "I can live anywhere in the world, but it must be near an airport" (2002: 190).

The values and practices to which overseas Chinese families adhere, and which seem responsible for their tremendous achievements in a globalized capitalist economy, suggest to Ong that, for these elite Chinese, the concept of nationalism has lost its meaning. Instead, she says, they seem to subscribe to a **post-national ethos** in which they submit to the regulations of the capitalist market while trying to evade the regulations of nation-states, ultimately because their only true loyalty is to the family business (2002: 190). Ong notes, however, that flexible citizenship informed by a post-national ethos is not an option for non-elite migrants: "whereas for bankers, boundaries are always flexible, for migrant workers, boat people, persecuted intellectuals and artists, and other kinds of less well-heeled refugees, this . . . is a harder act to follow" (190).

Ong also points out that, on the way to their success, contemporary Chinese merchants "have also revived pre-modern forms of child, gender, and class oppression" (2002: 190). Yet neither the positives nor the negatives should, she insists, be attributed to any "Chinese" essence; instead, she thinks these strategies are better understood as "the expressions of a habitus [i.e., a general constitution created by lifestyle, values, interests, etc.] that is finely tuned to the turbulence of late capitalism" (191).

Human Rights, Globalization, and the Language of Social Justice

The original UN Declaration on Human Rights in 1948 and numerous subsequent declarations, accompanied by the intensification of processes of globalization, have created conditions for growing discussions of **human rights**. The challenge has been the emerging, different understandings about what it means to be human, or what kinds of rights people may be entitled to under radically changed conditions of everyday life. Questions of human rights become most salient in settings defined by **multiculturalism**, a situation found almost everywhere in today's globalized world but of particular interest to Canadians. Multicultural settings combine different cultural understandings of what it means to be human.

For the past few decades, rights discourses have also extended to gender politics. For example, in 1992, the Committee on the Elimination of Discrimination against Women (CEDAW) declared that violence against women was a form of gender discrimination that violated the human rights of women. This declaration was adopted by the UN General Assembly in 1993. According to anthropologist Sally Engle Merry, this declaration "demonstrates the creation of new rights—rights which depend on the state's failure to protect women rather than its active violation of rights"; further, "the emergence of violence against women as a distinct human rights violation depends on redefining the family so that it is no longer shielded from legal scrutiny" (2001: 36–7). Although CEDAW has proven contentious over the years, other human rights documents have been signed without controversy by many national governments.

Signing on to a human rights declaration ostensibly binds governments to take official action to implement changes in local practices that might be seen to violate the rights asserted in the declarations. Human rights discourses are common currency in all societies, at all levels. After all, it is "no use imagining a 'primitive' tribe which has not yet heard of human rights," since "what it means to be 'Indigenous' is itself transformed through interaction with human rights discourses and institutions" (Cowan et al. 2001: 5).

Because of the wide adoption of human rights discourses throughout the world, some people have come to speak of an emerging "culture of human rights" that has now become "the pre-eminent global language of social justice" (Merry 2001: 38). These developments mean that anthropologists need to take note of the important influence this human rights discourse is having in the various settings where they do their research. What counts as "human rights" has changed over time, in part due to the efforts of an increasing number of nongovernmental organizations (NGOs) that have

post-national ethos An attitude toward the world in which people submit to the regulations of the capitalist market while trying to evade the regulations of nation-states. A set of rights that should be accorded to all human beings everywhere in the world.

multiculturalism A situation in which people of various cultural backgrounds live in close proximity to one another.

become involved in various countries of the world. Many of these organizations are deeply committed to projects designed to improve people's lives and protect their rights. As Merry says, these developments "have created a new legal order" that has given birth to new possibilities throughout the world for the elaboration and discussion of what human rights are all about (2001: 35). In addition, because the "culture of human rights" is increasingly regarded as the "culture of globalization," it would seem to be a topic well suited to anthropological analysis.

On the face of things, defending human rights for all people seems unproblematic. Few people who are aware of the devastation wrought by colonial exploitation, for example, would want to suggest that the victims of that exploitation did not have rights that needed to be protected at all costs. And yet, when we look closely at particular disputes about human rights, the concept no longer seems so simple. Anthropologist Jane Cowan and her colleagues (2001) have noted that there are two major arguments that have developed for talking about the way human rights and culture are related:

1. That *human rights are opposed to culture* (and cannot be reconciled with each other)
2. That a key universal human right is precisely one's *right to culture*

Next, we will consider each in turn. We will also consider two ways in which anthropologists have been able to contribute something new to the discussion:

1. By exploring the concept of "human rights as culture"
2. By examining some of the ways the concept of culture has been mobilized in the discussion of human rights

Rights versus Culture

Arguments that pit human rights against culture depend on the assumption that (1) "cultures" are homogeneous, bounded, and unchanging sets of ideas and practices and (2) each society has only one culture, which its members are obligated to follow. As we saw in Chapter 1, this view of culture has been severely criticized by cultural anthropologists. But it is a view of culture that is very much alive in many human rights disputes. Adherents of this view consider interference with customs of any sort—even customs that

appear to outsiders to violate human rights—to constitute a human rights violation. They see such interference as disrupting a supposedly harmonious way of life and preventing those who are committed to such a way of life from observing their own culturally specific understandings about rights. Ultimately, they believe that cultures should be allowed to enjoy absolute, inviolable protection from interference by outsiders. This has been the position adopted, for example, by some national governments that have refused to sign the CEDAW declaration that violence against women violates women's human rights.

Some people defend cultural practices against international human rights discourse because they feel that such discourse echoes back to the colonial period, when colonialists blindly imposed their ethnocentric views and practices on those they dominated. However, such a dismissal of human rights discourse needs to be closely examined. In the case of the right of women to protection from violence, for example, Merry (2001) points out that although some forms of violence against women may be culturally sanctioned in some societies, violence against women can take many forms even in those societies, and not all of these are accorded the same amount of cultural support. Even practices such as wife-beating or female genital cutting (Figure 13.9), which in the past could be justified in some circumstances as culturally appropriate actions, are now being questioned and even outlawed in the societies where they were practised. Thus "culture values" cannot be held responsible for everything, and members of the same society can disagree about these matters and sometimes change their minds.

As talk about human rights has become incorporated into local cultural discussions in recent decades, anthropologists are not surprised to discover that the notion undergoes transformation as people try to make sense of what it means in their own local contexts (Cowan et al. 2001: 8). Being forced to choose between rights *or* culture, however, seems increasingly unviable in a global, multicultural world, especially when the rights-versus-culture debate often *exaggerates* cultural differences. Finally, it is worth asking if "culture" is sometimes used as a scapegoat to mask a government's unwillingness to extend certain rights to its citizens. Indeed, a government's appeal to "culture" or "traditional values" is often a weak excuse for condoning the violation of its citizens' human rights. Anthropologists must be awake to the use of specific "traditions" as tools for political ends.

Rights to Culture

A second popular argument about the relationship between rights and culture begins from very different premises. Far from viewing universal "human rights" as alien and opposed to "cultures," this argument states that all peoples have a universal human right to maintain their own distinct cultures. This right has been made explicit in a number of international rights documents, and it draws strength from the ideas, popularized by earlier generations of anthropologists, that cultural diversity is intrinsically valuable and that people should be free to observe their own cultural practices without outside interference. The right-to-culture argument seems to involve conceding that such things as universal human rights actually do exist. The right-to-culture position therefore shows exactly the kind of transformation that the ideas of rights and culture undergo when caught in global–local struggles provoked by globalization.

One of the key issues in the struggle to protect the right to culture—as well as any human rights deemed worthy of protection—concerns the kinds of legal mechanisms needed to ensure such protection. The great promise of international documents like the UN Declaration on Human Rights seems to be that people are now free to bring allegations of human rights abuses to an international forum to seek redress. But, in fact, this is not the case.

- First, as human rights activists have discovered, human rights are legally interpreted as *individual* rights, not group rights.
- Second, the way in which people are to seek protection of their individual human rights is to demand that the *governments of the nation-states in which they are citizens* recognize and enforce the individual rights defended in international documents.

This second point has proven particularly problematic. International institutions, such as the UN, have been unwilling to challenge the sovereignty of individual nation-states. Making the defence of all human rights, including a right to culture, dependent on the policies of particular national governments has been viewed by activists and others as a serious contradiction in human rights discourse that undermines its effectiveness. (See the letter from the Assembly of First Nations to the Canadian government in the "In Their Own Words" box that follows.)

Figure 13.9 Among many East African people, including the Maasai, female genital cutting is an important part of the transformation of girls into women. Do you think this practice constitutes a human rights violation? Why, or why not?

Rights as Culture

As with all cultures, the "culture of human rights" is based on certain ideas about human beings, their needs, their ability to exercise agency, and the kinds of social connections between human beings that are considered legitimate or illegitimate. The entire question of "legitimacy" in human rights discourse points to the central role played by *law*, both as a way of articulating specific human rights and as a tool for defending those rights. Under the rights-as-culture interpretation, *law* is understood to be the "world view" or "structuring discourse" that shapes the culture of human rights (Cowan et al. 2001: 11). Further, the "facts" upon which this culture depends "are socially constructed through rules of evidence, legal conventions, and the rhetoric of legal actors" (11).

Analysts who talk about a "culture of human rights" as the new culture of a globalizing world note that it focuses on the rights of *individuals*. Additionally, they note that it proposes to relieve human suffering through *technical* rather than *ethical* solutions, and it emphasizes *rights* over *duties* or *needs* (Cowan et al. 2001: 12). As such, it may have the power to de-politicize conflicts that are caused and/or shaped by cultural differences. In our contemporary world, where state structures are under stress and the dynamics of transnational and multicultural living sometimes provoke

In Their Own Words

Open Letter to All Political Parties

Living with the contradictions between international policy and governmental implementation, the Assembly of First Nations, with their significant allies, wrote an open letter to all political parties on the one-year anniversary of the UN's adoption of its Declaration on the Rights of Indigenous Peoples. Following the release of this letter in 2008, it took the Canadian government another two years to formally endorse the UN's Declaration.

Tomorrow, 13 September 2008, we celebrate the one-year anniversary of the United Nations Declaration on the Rights of Indigenous Peoples. The Declaration was adopted by the UN General Assembly on 13 September 2007 after more than two decades of negotiation and debate.

Despite having previously played a positive role in building international support for this human rights instrument, Canada was one of only four states to oppose the Declaration.

There are over 370 million Indigenous people worldwide. Indigenous peoples urgently require international affirmation and protection of their human rights. Their rights are routinely ignored and trampled by national governments, even when these rights are entrenched in domestic laws.

The Declaration affirms minimum human rights standards necessary for the "survival, dignity, and well-being of the Indigenous peoples of the world." These include the right of self-determination, protections from discrimination and genocide, and recognition of rights to lands, territories, and resources that are essential to the identity, health, and livelihood of Indigenous peoples.

The Declaration also explicitly requires that all provisions are to be balanced with the rights of others and interpreted in accordance with principles of justice, democracy, non-discrimination, good governance, and respect for the human rights of all.

On 8 April 2008, the Canadian House of Commons passed a resolution to endorse the UN Declaration, calling on Parliament and the Government of Canada to "fully implement the standards contained therein." Unfortunately, the minority Conservative government has persisted with its unfounded claims that the Declaration cannot be applied in Canada and should not be used as a standard of human rights protection in countries that voted against it.

Human rights declarations become universally applicable upon their adoption by the UN General Assembly, regardless of how individual states vote. To claim that countries should be exempt from principles and standards they vote against flies in the face of six decades of Canadian human rights advocacy at the United Nations and sets a dangerous example for other countries of the world.

Indigenous peoples and human rights organizations urge Canada to join the global community in implementing this long overdue and much needed universal human rights instrument. To continue in any other manner undermines Canada's commitment to human rights at both the domestic and international levels.

In June, a private members bill was introduced in the House of Commons, calling for concrete measures to advance the Declaration in Canada. This includes requiring the Minister of Indian Affairs and Northern Development to report regularly to Parliament on implementation. Regretfully, Parliament will not have the opportunity to vote on this bill before the 14 October election. We recommend that this worthy initiative be re-introduced and embraced by all political parties in the new Parliament.

In February 2009, Canada's human rights record will be examined as part of the UN Human Rights Council's Universal Periodic Review process. As a sign of its commitment to respecting the human rights of all, Canada should endorse the Declaration.

Our organizations take the occasion of the anniversary of the adoption to call on all political parties to affirm their support for the UN Declaration on the Rights of Indigenous Peoples. In accordance with the 8 April 2008 Motion, all parties should commit themselves to take action to ensure effective implementation of the Declaration when the new Parliament begins its work.

Source: Union of BC Indian Chiefs. 2008. "First Nations Pressure Canada to Endorse the UN Declaration on the Rights of Indigenous Peoples" (12 Sept.), available at http://www.turtleisland.org/discussion/viewtopic.php?f=11&t=6286. Reprinted with permission of Union of British Columbia Indian Chiefs.

violent and bloody political confrontations, a human rights discourse capable of de-politicizing such confrontations could very well have an important role to play.

Some anthropologists see the development of such de-politicizing discourses as a vital necessity and a key challenge in a globalized world. In the meantime, to the extent that human rights discourse is conceived to be a "culture," most anthropologists would probably agree that this culture concept would be more illuminating if it reflected current anthropological understandings of culture as open, heterogeneous, and flexible (Cowan et al. 2001: 13). This understanding of culture can become an effective tool to help us understand how human rights processes work.

Culture as a Way of Thinking about Rights

To use the culture concept as a tool for analyzing human rights processes means looking for "patterns and relationships of meaning and practice" that are related to the culture of human rights (Cowan et al. 2001: 13). Since human rights are articulated in legal documents and litigated in courts, one of the most important emergent patterns is the way these rights are shaped to accommodate the law. Groups and individuals who assert that their human rights have been violated regularly take their cases to courts of law. But this means that in order to get the courts to take them seriously, they need to understand how the law operates. They must have a realistic awareness of the kinds of claims that the law considers admissible. Further, they must know how to craft cases that will fit the laws.

Many groups among whom anthropologists work have engaged in political struggles with national governments in which they argue for protection of their rights to practise their culture freely. These kinds of political struggles regularly involve claims about protecting the culture's distinct and unchanging values and practices from state policies. These kinds of arguments for a right to culture are often cases of "*strategic essentialism*" in which the unity and unchanging homogeneity of a particular "culture" is deliberately constructed in order to build group solidarity and to engage the state in a focused and disciplined way. Such "essentialism" often comes to dominate discussions of group rights, since the law tends to take an essentialist view of culture (Cowan et al. 2001: 11).

Because human rights law recognizes only certain kinds of rights violations, groups with grievances must tailor their claims to fit the violations that human rights law recognizes. For example, groups involved in the Hawaiian sovereignty movement have successfully achieved some of their political goals by making claims based on the requirements of their "traditional culture"

Figure 13.10 A Hawaiian protest sign at Iolani Palace, Honolulu, Hawaii.

(Merry 2001) (Figure 13.10). Their approach is effective because they live in a society that is "willing to recognize claims on the basis of cultural authenticity and tradition but not reparations based on acts of conquest and violation" (Merry 2001: 42–3).

Outside the courtroom, many members of Indigenous groups think of their culture the way contemporary anthropologists think about culture: there are some common patterns, but culture is basically unbounded, heterogeneous, and open to change. But human rights law is ordinarily written in such a way that claims for cultural rights will be considered only if the culture in question is presented as bounded, homogenous, and unchanging. As a result, Indigenous peoples are often forced to portray themselves and their cultures in ways that are very different from their own everyday understandings of who they are. While doing so may enable them to win legal judgments in their favour, it can also reshape their ideas about what their culture is. Groups that enter into the human rights process, thus, are entering into ethically ambiguous territory that is "both enabling and constraining" (Cowan et al. 2001: 11).

Human Rights in Thailand: Child Prostitution

Reaching successful accommodations between human rights discourse and local cultural practices is not always easy. A particularly difficult set of issues must be confronted when attempting to enforce

Map 13.1 Thailand

the rights of children. Anthropologist Heather Montgomery (2001) did field research in a slum settlement in Thailand (Map 13.1). The settlement, known as Baan Nua, was located near a prosperous seaside resort catering to foreign tourists. Those who lived in this settlement had broken all ties to other kin and other places from which they had migrated, which meant that the bonds linking parents and children in the settlement had become especially strong. Of over-riding importance among these families was the duty of children to work to help support their families. Children did their best to fulfill this duty as soon as they were able, trying many different jobs, including begging. But none of these options earned very much. And so, sooner or later, children began working as prostitutes for wealthy foreign tourists who visited the resort. At the time of Montgomery's research, 65 children in the community were working as prostitutes in the local sex tourism industry.

Children could earn five times as much money working as prostitutes as they could get from begging; plus they were able to visit fancy hotels and were well fed. Many of the clients, moreover, developed long-term relationships with the families of the child prostitutes, often lending them large sums of money—in one case, enough to rebuild the family home. It was friends and neighbours of the children, not their mothers, who recruited them into prostitution. When faced with the reality of the nature of their children's employment, mothers were able to claim that they had not found out until it was too late, and they interpreted the children's acts as evidence of their strong sense of filial duty in fulfilling obligations to help support the family: "Both

adult and child were aware of the child's duties, but there was a degree of unease about how far a child had to go to fulfill them" (Montgomery 2001: 90). The children claimed not to hate the men whom they worked for, especially those who kept in touch even when not in Thailand and who continued to send them money. Because of the financial generosity and long-term involvement of these men with their children, mothers said they felt the men were trustworthy. The actual sexual acts for which the children were paid took place outside the settlement and were never publicly discussed.

Commercial sex and even child prostitution are not new in Thailand, and the situation in Baan Nua is not unique. On the basis of estimates from UNICEF, between 60,000 and 200,000 Thai children are prostitutes, and HIV/AIDS is a serious and continuing issue. In recent years, many Thais, especially those working in the media and for NGOs, have denounced child sex tourism and tried to force the national government to put a stop to it (Figure 13.11). Human rights discourse—particularly discourse about the rights of the child—have played a prominent role in this campaign.

Children's rights are based on Western ideas about what constitutes an acceptable human childhood and about when childhood begins and ends. For example, the 1989 Convention on the Rights of the Child defines a child as anyone less than 18 years of age, and Anti-Slavery International has claimed that child-marriage is a form of slavery and therefore violates human rights. But as Montgomery observes, "it does not take an anthropologist to recognize that a child marrying at 15 in full accordance with traditional norms and local custom in India is very different from a child marrying at 15 in the UK" (2001: 82). In common with other forms of human rights discourse, declarations on the rights of the child normally emphasize the importance of *rights* over *duties*. As Montgomery notes, this issue is particularly significant when it comes to the rights of children working as prostitutes.

The model of ideal Western childhood contained in the UN Convention on the Rights of the Child includes the idea that "every child has a right to a childhood that is free from the responsibilities of work, money, and sex" (Montgomery 2001: 83). The problem with this standard is that it fits so poorly with understandings of childhood in which, for example, children are expected (or needed) to work for money to support the family, and it seems unable to imagine situations in which the entire support of a family depends on a child's earnings from prostitution. Yet that is an accurate description for many families and children in Baan Nua.

Local Thai activists have been particularly interested in enforcing Article 34 of the UN Convention, which aims to protect children "from all forms of sexual exploitation and sexual abuse" (Montgomery 2001: 86). But the Convention also recognizes many other children's rights, including the notion that the child's best interests must always be kept uppermost and that children have a right to live with their families. The problem is that "the assurance of one right often occurs at the expense of others. How these rights are prioritized is not culturally neutral" (85). "Too often . . . Article 34 is quoted in isolation, decontextualizing sexual abuse and presenting it as the paramount difficulty that poor children face without linking it to global issues of poverty, cultural background, and discrimination" (86–7). The child's best interests are certainly compromised through prostitution, but they are also compromised when children are removed from their families and communities or when they have nothing to eat. This is particularly poignant in the case of the children of Baan Nua, many of whom claimed that they were not exploited, and all of whom were strongly motivated to engage in prostitution based on the cultural belief that children are obliged to support their parents. Montgomery concludes:

> By ensuring that their families could stay together and have a sustainable income, it would be possible to eradicate child prostitution without enforcing punitive measures against their parents. . . . Thailand's positions in globalized political and economic relations are as important as cultural specificities in perpetuating that sexual exploitation. . . . Article 34 would be redundant if the other rights enshrined in the convention . . . could be reliably enforced. (97–8)

This example suggests two important conclusions, which are also relevant to broader discussions of human rights:

1. It is possible to find ways of accommodating the universal discourse of human rights to the particularities of local conditions.
2. No single model of the relationship between rights and culture will fit all cases.

Moreover, as the culture of human rights becomes better established, it increasingly becomes enmeshed in political and legal institutions that go beyond the local level. As activists become more experienced

©Jon Arnold Images Ltd/Alamy Stock Photo

Figure 13.11 This sign, attached to the back of a trishaw taxi in Chiang Mai, Thailand, encourages bystanders to help fight child sex tourism by reporting offenders. To whom do you think the sign's message is directed? How might the effect be different if the message were written in the local Thai language?

operating in globalized circumstances, they are likely to become more sophisticated about making use of these different settings as they plan their human rights strategies (Cowan et al. 2001: 21). Struggles over human rights are hardly likely to go away; indeed, along with struggles over global citizenship, they can be seen as the prime struggles of our time (Mignolo 2002). Anthropologists are well positioned to help make sense of these complex developments as they unfold.

Cultural Imperialism, Cultural Hybridization, and Cosmopolitanism

Cultural Imperialism or Cultural Hybridization?

The global spread of people, technology, wealth, images, and ideologies has clearly had a profound impact on local social settings. But how should anthropologists characterize the processes by which these changes have come about? One explanation, formulated during the Cold War debates about modernization and dependency, was found in the concept of **cultural imperialism**, which is based on two notions:

1. That some cultures dominate other cultures (In recent history, it is the culture(s) of "the West" that are seen to have come to dominate all other cultures of the world, due to the spread of colonialism and capitalism.)
2. That cultural domination by one culture leads inevitably to the destruction of subordinated cultures and their replacement by the culture of those in power

Thus, Western cultural imperialism is seen as responsible for destroying, for example, local music, technologies, dress, and food traditions and replacing them with Western popular music, mp3 players, flashlights, cellphones, smartphones, T-shirts, blue jeans, McDonald's hamburgers, and Coca-Cola. The inevitable outcome of Western cultural imperialism is seen to be "the cultural homogenization of the world," with the unwelcome consequence of "dooming the world to uniformity" (Inda and Rosaldo 2002: 13–14).

The discourse of cultural imperialism developed primarily outside anthropology, but anthropologists could not ignore it. After all, it purported to describe what was happening to the people they studied. Anthropologists, too, were aware that Western music, fashion, food, and technology had spread among those they worked with. But cultural imperialism did not seem to be a satisfactory explanation for this spread for at least three reasons:

1. Cultural imperialism denies *agency* to non-Western peoples who make use of Western cultural forms. It assumes that they are passive and without the resources to resist anything of Western origin that is marketed to them.
2. Cultural imperialism assumes that non-Western cultural forms never move "from the rest to the West." Yet non-Western music, food, and material culture have large and eager followings in Western nations.
3. Cultural imperialism ignores the fact that cultural forms and practices sometimes move from one part of the non-Western world to other parts of the non-Western world, bypassing the West entirely. For examples, Indian movies have been popular for decades in northern Nigeria, Mexican soap operas have large followings in the Philippines, and karaoke is popular all over the world (Inda and Rosaldo 2002: 22–4) (Figure 13.12).

Thus, anthropologists began to search for alternative ways of understanding global cultural flows.

From the days of Boas and his students, anthropologists have not only recognized the significance of cultural borrowing but also emphasized that borrowing cultural forms or practices from elsewhere always involves *borrowing-with-modification*. Indeed, people never adopt blindly; they always adapt what they borrow for local purposes. Importantly, and put another way, people rarely accept ideas or practices or objects from elsewhere without **indigenizing** them—that is, finding a way of reconciling them with local practices in order to serve local purposes.

cultural imperialism
The idea that some cultures dominate other cultures and that cultural domination by one culture leads inevitably to the destruction of subordinated cultures and their replacement by the culture of those in power.

indigenization
The process of bringing something foreign under the control of local people or of adapting something foreign to serve local purposes.

Figure 13.12 Over 1,000 people gather at Bearpit Karaoke at the Mauerpark Flea Market in Berlin, Germany. Karaoke machines were first patented in Japan in the 1970s; now, karaoke is enjoyed all over the world. What does the international popularity of karaoke suggest about cultural borrowing in the contemporary globalized world?

In the 1980s, for example, a number of weavers in Otavalo, Ecuador, organized small production firms and purchased television sets to entertain their employees while they worked at their looms. In addition, some men had so much business that they encouraged their wives to take up weaving, even though women were not traditionally weavers. In order to spend more time weaving, women started to use indoor cookstoves, which relieved them from the time-consuming labour of traditional meal preparation over an open fire (Colloredo-Mansfeld 1999). From the perspective of anthropologist Rudi Colloredo-Mansfeld (1999), these adoptions of items of Western technology could not be understood as the consequences of Western cultural imperialism because they had nothing to do with trying to imitate a Western lifestyle. It made more sense to interpret these changes as Otavalan *indigenization* of televisions and cookstoves, since these items from elsewhere were adopted precisely in order to promote Indigenous Otavalan weaving. Thus, borrowing-with-modification involves *customizing* that which is borrowed to meet the purposes of the borrowers, which may be quite remote from the purposes of those among whom the form or practice originated (Inda and Rosaldo 2002: 16). This form of cultural change is very different from having something from elsewhere forced upon you against your will.

At the same time, it is necessary to recognize that the consequences of borrowing-with-modification can never be fully controlled. Thus, Otavalan weavers may start watching television because local reruns of old American television series relieve the tedium of weaving, but once television-watching becomes a habitual practice, it also exposes them to advertising and news broadcasts that may stimulate unpredictable local changes. The indigenization of cultural forms from elsewhere makes it possible *both* to do old things in new ways *and* to do new things as well (Figure 13.13). Cultural borrowing is double-edged; borrowed cultural practices are both amenable to indigenization and yet able to escape it. The challenges are particularly acute in globalizing conditions—colonial or post-colonial—where borrowed ideas, objects, or practices remain entangled in relationships with donors even as they are made to serve new goals by recipients. It is not surprising, therefore, that people in multicultural settings who must deal with tempting cultural alternatives emanating from more powerful groups regularly struggle to control processes of cultural borrowing and to contain indigenized cultural practices within certain contexts.

When discussing this sort of complex globalized cultural exchange, anthropologists often speak of **cultural hybridization**, or *cultural hybridity*. Cultural hybridization is more than simple cultural borrowing: it is a form of *cultural mixing* that produces something new, something that cannot be collapsed or subsumed either within the culture of the donor or within the culture of the recipient. Further, it is a highly positive form of cultural mixing: rather

cultural hybridization Cultural mixing that produces a new cultural form.

©Lynn Meisch

Figure 13.13 Musical performance has become an important part of the Otavalo economy, as musicians from Otavalo travel throughout the world performing and selling woven goods. They have indigenized CD production as well and have been quite successful in selling CDs of their music to tourists in Otavalo and to listeners abroad.

than indicating a regrettable loss of original "purity," cultural hybridization draws attention to positive processes of cultural creativity.

The move from talk of dependency and cultural imperialism to talk about globalization and cultural hybridization is widely seen as a move from *modernist* discourse to *postmodernist* discourse. Modernist discourse embodies Enlightenment assumptions about rationality, science, progress, capitalism, and democracy. Postmodernist discourse calls all of these Enlightenment assumptions into question. While modernists tend to portray non-Western societies and cultures as bounded, orderly, and unchanging, postmodernists argue that all social and cultural borders have always been porous and thus open to people, ideas, and practices from elsewhere. This postmodern position is not confined to academic contexts; it has had important implications for everyday cultural choices. If hybridity is a normal part of human social experience, social groups can legitimately challenge the idea that "authentic" traditions never change. Thus, they can feel free to revise or discard cultural practices as they see fit. Possessing this sort of freedom means that they possess agency—the capacity to exercise at least some control over their lives. And exercising agency calls into question charges that a group is succumbing to cultural imperialism or losing cultural "authenticity."

However, close examination of talk about cultural hybridization reveals at least three problems.

First, it is not clear that the concept actually frees anthropologists from the modernist commitment to the existence of bounded, homogeneous, unchanging "cultures." That is, the idea of cultural hybridity is based on the notion of cultural mixing. But what is it that is mixed? Two or more non-hybridized, original, "pure" cultures! But such "pure," homogeneous, bounded, unchanging cultures are not supposed to exist. Thus we are caught in a paradox. For this reason anthropologist Jonathan Friedman, among others, is highly critical of discussions of cultural hybridity; in his view, cultures have *always* been hybrid, and it is the existence of *boundaries*, not cultural borrowing, that anthropologists need to explain. Besides, hybrid cultural mixtures often get transformed into new, unitary cultural identities. This process can be seen, Friedman argues, in the way in which the "mixed race" category in the US has been transformed into a "new, unitary group of mixtures for those who feel 'disenfranchised' by the current single-race categories" (1997: 83). Friedman also points out that hybrid identities are

not liberating when they are thrust upon people rather than being adopted freely. He draws attention to cases in Latin America where the *mestizo* (mixed European–Indigenous) identity has been used "as a middle-/upper-class tool" against Indigenous groups by hybridizing them "from above": that is, criticizing their claims to a common Indigenous identity in order to undermine their sense of solidarity as members of a single group: "We are all part-Indian, say members of the elite who have much to lose in the face of minority claims" (81–2).

These examples highlight a second difficulty with hybridity talk: those who celebrate cultural hybridization often ignore the fact that its effects are experienced differently by those with power and those without power. As Friedman says, "the question of class becomes crucial" (1997: 81). The complexity of this issue is seen in many popular discussions of "multiculturalism" that celebrate cultural hybridization and that, in the context of globalizing capitalism, turn hybridity into a marketable commodity. The commodification of hybridity is problematic because it glosses over differences in the experience of cultural hybridization, offering multiculturalism as an array of tempting consumables for outsiders. "Multiculturalism is aimed at nourishing and perpetuating the kind of differences which do not [threaten]," writes cultural theorist Nira Yuval-Davis (1997: 197). International folk festivals, festivals of nations, and the like—events that emphasize costume, cuisine, music, and dance—spring to mind (Figure 13.14). But the troubling fact is that cultural hybridity is experienced as both non-threatening and very threatening, depending on the terms on which it is available. Because of power differences among groups challenged by cultural hybridization, any globalized "multicultural" setting reveals active processes of cultural hybridization *together with* the defence of discrete cultural identities that seem to *resist* hybridization (Werbner 1997: 3). Cultural hybridization is unobjectionable when actors perceive it to be under their own control, but it is resisted when it is "perceived by actors themselves to be potentially threatening to their sense of moral integrity" (Werbner 1997: 12). The threat is greatest for those with the least power who feel unable to control forms of cultural hybridization that threaten to undermine the fragile survival structures on which they depend in an unwelcoming multicultural setting.

Examinations of class and power also lead us to a third problem with the concept of cultural hybridization. Discussion of hybridity can actually *hide* the differences between elite and non-elite experiences of multiculturalism, potentially diverting attention away from social problems that exist in multicultural or culturally hybridized environments. Anthropologist John Hutnyk, for example, deplores the way "world music" (see https://en.wikipedia.org/wiki/World_music) is marketed to middle-class consumers, noting that such sales strategies divert attention "from the urgency of anti-racist politics" (1997: 122). When cultural hybridization becomes fashionable, it easily turns the experiences of hybridized elites into a hegemonic standard, suggesting that class exploitation and racial oppression are easily overcome or no longer exist. In Brazil, for example, a country with a long history of tensions along racial and class lines, the hybridization of local and Western ideals of physical attractiveness has resulted in a new "culture of beauty" that overshadows discussions of social inequality (Edmonds 2007). Rather than focusing on the social problems that promote inequality, lower- and middle-class Brazilians—particularly Brazilian women—blame their lack of opportunity on their lack of "beauty." To remedy the perceived problem, they turn to surgeons to perform cosmetic procedures that are common among the more affluent members of societies. Many believe that fixing their physical "flaws" through cosmetic surgery will lead to upward social mobility as well as "First World modernity and glamour" (370). While cosmetic surgery has led to improved self-esteem for some, it rarely brings about a great degree of economic or social change.

In some cases, dismissing or ignoring differences in how elites and non-elites experience cultural hybridization can spark dangerous confrontations. Anthropologist Peter van der Veer (1997) argues that such a dynamic ignited the furor in Britain that followed the publication of Salman Rushdie's novel *The Satanic Verses* (1988). Rushdie is an elite, highly educated South Asian migrant to Britain who experienced cultural hybridity as a form of emancipation from oppressive religious and cultural restrictions. His novel contained passages describing Islam and the Prophet Muhammad that, from his elite point of view, embodied "transgression" that was liberating. But migrants from South Asia in Britain are not all members of the elite. Most South Asian Muslim immigrants in Britain are part of the working class, and they saw *The Satanic Verses* not as a work of artistic liberation but as a deliberate attempt to mock their beliefs and practices: "These immigrants, who

Figure 13.14 A group of students perform their Irish step-dancing routines at a St Patrick's Day parade in Queens, New York. How should we understand this cultural performance? Is it Irish, American, or a hybrid of many cultures?

are already socially and culturally marginalized, are thus double marginalized in the name of an attack on 'purity' and Islamic 'fundamentalism'" (van der Veer 1997: 101–2). Even more important, however, may be the way popular interpretations of their objections in the press and among Western intellectuals ignored these immigrants' own, very different but very real, *non-elite* experiences of cultural hybridization. Van der Veer stresses that British Muslims who objected to the novel were

> not necessarily fundamentalists at all; their religious ideas are just as hybrid and syncretic as those of the author. They, too, are migrants, but the sources of their identity are authenticated not by profane literary texts but by what are to them sacred religious traditions. (1997: 102)

Put simply, elites experience cultural hybridization in ways that are often very different from the ways non-elites experience cultural hybridization. We all ignore this fact at our peril.

From Cultural Hybridity to Cosmopolitanism

The era of globalization in which we live is exciting and offers opportunities for some. But it is also an era of uncertainty and insecurity. Possibilities for new and liberating ways of life are undercut by sharpening economic and political differences and looming threats of violence. Is it possible, in the midst of all this confusion and conflict, to devise productive ways of coping with our changing circumstances and addressing cultural differences? No one expects such efforts to be easy. But anthropologists and other concerned scholars are currently struggling to come up with concepts and practices that might be helpful.

Our era is not the first to have faced such challenges. Cultural theorist Walter Mignolo (2002) argues that multiculturalism was born in the sixteenth century when European conquest in the New World first raised troubling issues among Western thinkers about the kinds of relationships that were possible and desirable between the conquerors and the Indigenous peoples whom they had conquered. During the ensuing centuries, the challenges posed by a multicultural world did not disappear.

In the late eighteenth century, in an attempt to identify the proper way for human beings to live in the world, German philosopher Immanuel Kant revived a concept that was first coined by the Stoic philosophers of ancient Rome: **cosmopolitanism** (Mignolo 2002). Kant's cosmopolitanism was firmly embedded within the values and practices of Enlightenment civilization, which meant that it was embedded in Western elite forms of cultural hybridization. That is, Kantian cosmopolitanism "by and large meant being versed in Western ways, and the vision of 'one world' culture was only a sometimes unconscious, sometimes unconscionable, euphemism for 'First World' culture" (Abbas 2002: 210). To the extent that discussions of cosmopolitanism continue to focus on Western elites only, they would seem to offer little to anthropologists and others who are interested in finding a place for non-elite and non-Western experiences of cultural hybridization.

Nevertheless, is it possible to rework our understandings of cultural hybridity to stretch the notion of cosmopolitanism beyond its traditional association with privileged Western elites? Many anthropologists have become comfortable talking about "alternative" or "minority" modernities that depart from the Western norm. In a similar fashion, any new anthropological understanding of cosmopolitanism would have to be plural, not singular, and it would have to include non-elite experiences of cultural hybridization that reflect the experiences of those who have been the victims of modernity (see Breckenridge et al. 2002). The goal would be to develop new, broader ways of understanding peoples' lived experiences from multiple perspectives at once.

cosmopolitanism Being at ease in more than one cultural setting.

Does anthropological talk about a world of "cosmopolitanisms" offer any advantage over earlier anthropological talk about a world of "cultures"? It might, if anthropologists can find a way to think about cultural hybridization (and resistance to hybridization) that overcomes the problems discussed above. Anthropologist Pnina Werbner (1997) suggests that this might be possible if we can think about cultural hybridization as a *process* rather than as a series of momentary, shocking, "transgressive" challenges that periodically disrupt the ongoing, tense standoff among defenders of different cultural positions. Rather than assuming that all hybridity (or all resistance to hybridity) is the same—either all "good" or all "bad"—Werbner's approach would make it possible to distinguish *different processes* of cultural hybridization and cultural resistance. To illustrate, Werbner distinguishes between cultural processes that lead to *ethnicity* and cultural processes that lead to *racism* (see Chapter 6). In her view, a process-oriented theory of cultural hybridization "must differentiate . . . between a politics that proceeds from the legitimacy of difference [ethnicity] and a politics that rests on coercive unity [racism]," and it "must explain how and why cultural hybrids are still able to disturb and 'shock' . . . in a postmodern world that celebrates difference" (Werbner 1997: 21). To arrive at such a theory, anthropologists would need to examine "the way discourses interact to create bridges or precipitate polarizing processes" (21).

For example, Catherine Bryan (2012), in a study conducting interviews with migrants to Nova Scotia, found that "the cosmopolitanism that facilitated migration through the NSNP [Nova Scotia Nominee Program] did not help the migrants interviewed resettle or integrate in Nova Scotia as planned" (141). For many of the interviewees, migration to Canada was "very much understood as an expansion of their cosmopolitanism," and many cited as their objectives for immigration increased security, political stability, and social opportunities, particularly for female children. However, upon arrival in Nova Scotia, many migrants faced downward class mobility that in itself was "highly gendered," due to lack of opportunities for male migrants to find work and inabilities for female migrants to return to their country of origin to find work, thereby "effectively undermin[ing] the gendered objectives of migration" (141) and revealing the complexity that arises when examining the processes of cultural hybridization and cultural resistance.

Werbner's approach to cultural hybridization as a process has much in common with what Walter Mignolo calls *border thinking*. That is, in a globalized world, concepts like "democracy" and "justice" can no longer be defined within a single Western logic—or, for that matter, from the perspective of the political left or the political right. *Border thinking* involves detaching these concepts from their hegemonic "Western" meanings and practices and using them as "connectors"—tools for imagining and negotiating new, cosmopolitan forms of democracy or justice informed by the ethical and political judgments of non-elites (Mignolo 2002: 179, 181).

Finally, in re-imagining what cosmopolitanism might mean, it is important not only to go beyond Kantian limitations but also to go beyond standard anthropological orientations to other ways of life. An understanding of cosmopolitanism that is limited to being open to other cultures or to being inclusive—the traditional orientation of cultural relativism—is insufficient to cope with the challenges presented by a globalizing world. For one thing, "Otherness has lost its innocence as a result of the colonial experience" (Abbas 2002: 226). And for another, "silenced and marginalized voices are

bringing themselves into the conversation of cosmopolitan projects rather than waiting to be included" (Mignolo 2002: 174).

The hope is that border thinking can produce a *critical cosmopolitanism* capable of negotiating new understandings of human rights and global citizenship in ways that can dismantle barriers of gender and "race" that are the historical legacies of colonialism (Mignolo 2002: 161, 180). In many cases, this will require creative new ways of understanding and interacting with others. It will also require overcoming power differentials and giving equal attention to non-elites.

Many of the cases in this chapter demonstrate the human ability to cope creatively with changed life circumstances. They remind us that human beings are not passive in the face of the new, that they actively and resiliently respond to life's challenges. Changing circumstances that may benefit some human groups can overwhelm and destroy others. Western capitalism and modern technology have exploded into a vortex of global forces that resist control. A critical cosmopolitanism involving concerted practical action to lessen violence and exploitation may be all that can prevent these forces from destroying us all.

Living Anthropology

The Anthropological Cellphone

by Geoffrey Hobbis, Associated Postdoctoral Fellow, Centre de Recherche et de Documentation sur l'Océanie (Marseille), and Sessional Instructor, Anthropology, University of British Columbia (Okanagan)

Cellphones have been an object of interest for anthropologists working in the Global South for over a decade. Due to a confluence of factors, such as swift technological development and increasing affordability, cellphones started to rapidly proliferate around the globe in the 2000s and smartphones quickly followed in the 2010s. So omnipresent in daily life, cellphones could not escape the attention of anthropologists. They have been key to maintaining kinship networks across international boundaries for diasporic communities, to creating spaces where previously marginalized voices may be heard, and, more broadly, they have been integrated in everyday social life, into gender relations, child-rearing, mortuary rituals, language formation, conflict resolution, and much more.

The most famous anthropological work on this subject is Heather Horst and Daniel Miller's (2006) *The Cell Phone: An Anthropology of Communication*. Based on ethnographic research

in Jamaica, they charted the call history and contact list of users' handsets as digital records of a person's social networks. Horst and Miller showed how cellphones play a critical role in continued negotiations of social relationships and how cellphones were integrated into the global remittance economy to leverage transfers of money, typically from relatives working in the Global North in cities such as Toronto and Montreal.

Things have gotten more complex in the decade since Horst and Miller's work. Now there are smartphones. In addition to telephony, they allow for surfing the Web and for the production and consumption of multimedia. Even people living in the remotest parts of the globe are making their own music, pictures, and movies, and they listen, view, and watch media files from around the world. In the small village of Gwou'ulu in the Lau Lagoon, Malaita Province, Solomon Islands, where I did ethnographic fieldwork in 2014–2015,

Continued

some 250 adults owned approximately 100 cellphones, filled to the brim with local and foreign songs, pictures, and movies. Each foreign file, often downloaded from the Internet at urban Internet cafés and circulated offline through Bluetooth and the exchange of microSD cards, contains new ideas reflected, and challenged, in local approaches to digital media.

A great example is a music video posted to YouTube on 22 December 2015: Rosie Delmah's cover of Adele's "Hello." In only 15 months the music video was viewed over 55 million times. Featuring Conkarah, a well-known Solomon Islands musician, the video reimagines Adele's song in Solomon Islands reggae. The video switches between the singers and scenes of contemporary daily village life, such as kids playing on the beach or kicking a soccer ball around. The popularity of reggae in the Global South itself speaks to the globalizing influence of mass media, and yet, Solomon Islanders have effectively remade that style in their own way. The entire clip is rich with anthropological data on globalization and what anthropologists have studied as the cultural logic of globalization, as hybridization, creolization, localization, or glocalization—in this case, the blending of music styles digitally rematerialized in a music video that is itself globally circulated.

Global-local encounters are often also filled with the potential for friction, conflict, and more broadly a sense of uncertainty. The Solomon Islands has long boasted a popular music industry with fans across the Pacific, but with its digitization many think something has been lost. Tape-based audio recording captured something digital techniques cannot, something of place, of *ples* in Solomon Islands Pijin, which, despite increasing global connections, remains an important source of Solomon Islanders' identities. I was told that even if a person heard a song for a first time, the listener of an audio tape would be able to pin down the region where it was made based on the tinny-ness of the recording, cracks in the singing, and idiosyncratic flaws in the instrumentation. Now that all music recordings sound the same, a sense of place is missing in the partial homogenization of digital video and audio production.

Cellphones, as connections between the global and the local, as communication and multimedia technologies, are a significant site for anthropological investigations. They offer insights into the complex continuations, transformations, and ruptures brought about by the global circulation of peoples, goods, and ideas and the ways they interact with local particularities. Cellphones materialize these connections, and they reveal individuals' choices in their engagements with new technologies and global cultural flows.

Key Terms

core 329
cosmopolitanism 354
cultural hybridization 351
cultural imperialism 350
dependency theory 328
diaspora 338
flexible citizenship 341
human rights 343

indigenization 350
legal citizenship 341
long-distance nationalists 338
modernization theory 328
multiculturalism 343
neoliberalism 330
periphery 329
post-national ethos 343

semi-periphery 329
substantive citizenship 341
transborder citizenry 340
transborder state 340
transnational nation-states 341
visual anthropology 335
world-system theory 329

Chapter Summary

1. Anthropologists have made use of a variety of theoretical perspectives to explain the relationship between the West and the rest of the world. Three significant examples from the twentieth century are *modernization theory*, *dependency theory*, and *world-system theory*. Today, most theorists see the situation through the lens of globalization. Most anthropologists agree that the effects of globalization are uneven—some groups in some parts of the world benefit, whereas others do not.

2. The contrasts between formal and substantive citizenship suggest that conventional notions of citizenship are breaking down. People who migrate across national borders often develop transborder identities, which in some cases allow them to both circumvent and benefit from different nation-state regimes by investing, working, and living in different places.

3. Discussions of human rights have intensified in recent decades. Some arguments about human rights include the right to one's culture. Some anthropologists have identified a relatively new "culture of human rights"—an international culture that emphasizes individual rights over duties or needs and that proposes technical rather than ethical solutions to human suffering.

4. Some anthropologists discussing globalization prefer to speak about borrowing-with-modification or indigenization of practices or objects imported from elsewhere. Many anthropologists describe these processes as examples of cultural hybridization or hybridity. At the same time, some criticize talk of cultural hybridization for assuming that "pure" cultures existed prior to mixing or for failing to recognize differences between how the powerful and the powerless experience cultural change.

Others would like to revive the notion of cosmopolitanism and rework it in order to be able to speak about alternative cosmopolitanisms that reflect the experiences of those who have been the victims of modernity. The ideal end result would be a critical cosmopolitanism capable of negotiating new understandings of human rights and global citizenship in ways that can dismantle barriers of gender and "race" that are the historical legacies of colonialism.

Critical Thinking Questions

1. What would you consider to be the main factor(s) in the emergence of globalization?
2. What would you consider to be the key factor(s) in local variations on the acceptance of globalization?
3. Are national boundaries being challenged by the Internet? How, and to what possible ends?
4. What are some of the ways elites and non-elites experience cultural hybridization differently? Why do you suppose these differences occur?

Suggested Readings

Barber, Benjamin R. 1995. *Jihad versus McWorld: How Globalism and Tribalism Are Reshaping the World* (New York: Times Books). This book examines the basis for the misunderstanding between the Muslim world and the capitalist Western world.

Dyck, Noel, and James B. Waldram. 1993. *Anthropology, Public Policy, and Native Peoples in Canada* (Montreal and Kingston: McGill-Queen's University Press). A comprehensive review of governmental policy issues and the conditions experienced by First Nations peoples up to the beginning of the 1990s.

Harney, Nicholas. 2002. "Building Italian Regional Identity in Toronto: Using Space to Make Culture Material," *Anthropologica* 44, 1: 43–54. This paper is a close and highly nuanced examination of the ways in which Italian Canadians create meaningful spaces and identities in the city of Toronto.

Inda, Jonathan Xavier, and Renato Rosaldo, eds. 2007. *The Anthropology of Globalization: A Reader*, 2nd edn (Malden, MA: Blackwell). A comprehensive collection of articles by anthropologists who address the process of globalization from varied points of view and different ethnographic situations.

Lewellen, Ted C. 2002. *The Anthropology of Globalization: Cultural Anthropology Enters the Twenty-First Century* (Westport, CT: Greenwood). A relatively recent anthropological look at the ways in which the forces of globalization are shaping our world.

Murray, David A.B. 2000. "Between a Rock and a Hard Place: The Power and Powerlessness of Transnational Narratives among Gay Martinican Men," *American Anthropologist* 102, 2: 261–70. Murray explores the narratives gay men tell each other in Martinique, arguing that these stories often depict life in Quebec as utopic in comparison to life in either France or Martinique.

No'eau Warner, Sam L. 1999. "'Kuleana': The Right, Responsibility, and Authority of Indigenous Peoples to Speak and Make Decisions for Themselves in Language and Cultural Revitalization," *Anthropology and Education Quarterly* 30, 1: 68–93. This paper addresses the issue of the politicization of Hawaiian language and cultural revitalization by non-Indigenous Hawaiian language educators.

Sylvain, Renée. 2005. "Disorderly Development: Globalization and the Idea of Culture in the Kalahari," *American Ethnologist* 32, 3: 354–70. This article discusses issues of identity, struggles for rights, and other challenges facing the San of southern Africa.

Related Websites

Conservation International
www.conservation.org
Fairtrade Canada
http://fairtrade.ca
Global Affairs Canada: Development
www.international.gc.ca/international/index.aspx?lang=eng

International Bureau for Children's Rights
www.ibcr.org
International Women's Rights Project (IWRP), CEDAW
http://iwrp.org/projects/cedaw
Women Activities and Social Services Association
http://wassa.org.af/

14 Applying Anthropology in Everyday Life

Chapter Outline

Anthropology in the World at Large

Practical Applications

Anthropology and Policy

Anthropology and the Challenges of Global Citizenship

Awareness and Uncertainty

Freedom and Constraint

Going Somewhere?

Learning Objectives

By the end of Chapter 14, you will be able to

- understand the value of applied or "action" anthropology;
- appreciate anthropology's value in addressing the challenges of global citizenship;
- consider the world of uncertainty and the awareness

needed to confront this world (reflexivity);
- challenge views on freedom; and constraint; and
- contemplate what our technological advancements might mean for the future of humanity.

Anthropology in the World at Large

Why study anthropology? Perhaps the best initial answer comes from French anthropologist Maurice Godelier:

> [A]nthropology . . . is one of the social science disciplines that is best able to help us understand the complexity of our now globalized world and the nature of the conflicts and the crisis we are experiencing. In such a world, it would be irresponsible and indecent for anthropologists to stop trying to understand others—and themselves at the same time—and making their results known. (2010: 217)

Here Godelier highlights the power of anthropology to help us understand our world. It can help us make sense of a wide variety of issues that impact human beings' lived experiences. Certainly, it can teach us about others, but it can also teach us about ourselves (Figure 14.1).

Many anthropologists now work in the area called *applied anthropology*. While the term *applied* has become somewhat the defining appellation for *engagement*, researchers, such as Joshua J. Smith, ask us to consider the nuances found in contrasting *applied* with the term *action*, as articulated by anthropologist Sol Tax many years ago. As Smith states, "The distinction is largely to do with the locus of power, that is, acknowledging and divesting oneself of it, so as to not have power over others and to be better able to avoid denying or impeding peoples' or persons' abilities to determine their own destinies" (2015: 446). Central here is the alignment of the anthropologist to or with the authority through which she or he is "hired" for specific objectives. Of course, this is a serious issue in extinguishing **coloniality** in the discipline since coloniality has

> the tendency of a "self" in an encounter to impose boundary coordinates . . . [and] move to rationalize the dominant presence of this self within these coordinates and to make the presence of the other subordinate to it . . . [and further it] operates as an apparatus of modernity, a workaday containment field

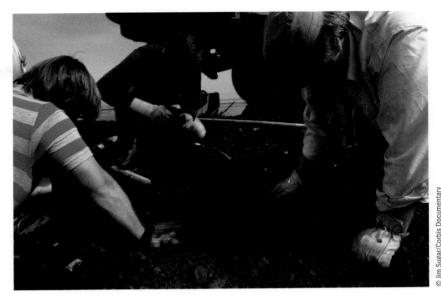

Figure 14.1 Studying anthropology can help us understand our own culture. Here, anthropology graduate students help Professor Bill Rathje examine the dirt at a landfill in San Francisco in an effort to understand local human behaviour through waste habits.

© Jim Sugar/Corbis Documentary

> for defining, constraining and incorporating persons, as well as delimitated populations and polities. (Noble 2015: 429, 430)

Thus, there are, to begin, two questions anthropologists should ask and turn to their reflexivity to consider:

1. What is the moral core we bring to our work, indeed to our lives?
2. How does our concept of "self" affect the lives of "others"?

This extends outward to understandings of global citizenship, as we will discuss further in this chapter.

Therefore, when participating in "action" or "advocacy-oriented" work, anthropologists must remain acutely aware of the "potential ramifications of [their] engagement" (Johnston 2010: 235). And, as a mother once observed to her adult daughter (Dods), "You get to go home, we have to live here"—so the mess you make impacts the lives of "others." Indeed, anthropologists must constantly examine

coloniality Identified and described as the present legacy of colonialism in the societies of today; manifest as the social discrimination from Eurocentrism yet also from the outlived formal colonialism integrated in succeeding social orders (Quijano 2000).

View of the Battery, St John's, Newfoundland and Labrador. When viewed through the anthropological perspective, even familiar settings that we encounter here in Canada can be a source of new insight into the many ways in which everyday beliefs and behaviours are shaped by culture.

the ethical implications of their work and consider how actions might have unintended consequences (see Mullins 2010). Furthermore, anthropologists must be aware that their work is by nature *collaborative*. This collaboration involves not only anthropologists and other advocates but also the people they are engaged in helping (see Lassiter 2005).

It is also important to consider that many, if not most, anthropologists are employed within the academy. Thus, they set parameters for the discipline that have far-reaching consequences. They do so in an institutional atmosphere of publish or perish while the academy is perhaps engaged in neoliberal governmentality based on "establishing ever-greater numbers of 'quantitative' metrics, which are frequently based on 'knowledge economy' approaches hybridized with biomedical standards in order to audit 'qualitative' forms of research" (Krautwurst 2014: 267). Here is a disconnect that needs to be acknowledged and investigated.

As we saw in Chapter 1, applied anthropology involves the practical application of information provided by the four main anthropological specialties (cultural anthropology, linguistic anthropology, archaeology, and biological anthropology). Medical anthropology, discussed in detail in Chapter 10, is one important area of work that falls under the umbrella of applied anthropology. Medical anthropologists often engage in practical research with significant applied results—for example, research that explores issues of aging and can lead to the development of programs that assist the elderly in culturally appropriate ways. Additionally, medical anthropologists draw attention to practical issues of medical ethics. As Canadian medical anthropologist Margaret Lock notes in her discussion of medicalization and resistance,

> [e]thnography makes it possible to examine the way in which scientific knowledge is selectively deployed in different global contexts by drawing on morals and value systems that are historically, politically, and culturally informed. . . . I find culture (used reflexively and in conjunction with a political/economy framework) a necessary concept for most research projects, especially when culture is explicitly made to do work by the particular people or institutions that one is studying. (2001: 488)

Of particular interest are the health and well-being of women and children in a world where access to prenatal care, adequate nutrition, clean water, immunization programs, and treatment is patchy, while diseases such as malaria and HIV are rampant (Figure 14.2). Indeed, many applied anthropologists work on HIV-related projects. One example is medical anthropologist Holly Wardlow's work on HIV infections in rural Papua New Guinea. Through her work, Wardlow demonstrates how a researcher's site-specific observations often point to broader cultural concerns. She notes that "married women are at risk for HIV primarily because of their husbands' extramarital sexual liaisons, and wives have little control over this risk, which is not lessened by their own fidelity. . . . [T]he dynamics of marital HIV transmission [are embedded in] economic, social, and cultural factors that propel and structure men's extramarital sexuality" (2007: 1006). Thus, the intimacies of their lives and the structures of their social worlds create a dangerous space for women in many parts of the world.

Anthropologists have gone into public policy and planning as interpreters, mediators, civil servants, and urban planners. A few are psychotherapists, employing the insights of anthropologist Gregory Bateson and others on family systems and family therapy, while some are cross-cultural social workers. Some have taken on activist roles, working with Indigenous peoples' organizations or human rights organizations, such as Survival International and Cultural Survival. Others have become involved in international development, working with various agencies on projects such as devising appropriate technologies, resolving fuel shortages, locating potable water, arranging financial assistance, conducting feasibility studies for dams and other enterprises, implementing bilingual education programs, and improving and managing livestock and crops. In looking at how anthropologists have contributed to meaningful change, anthropologist Melissa Checker lists six core themes in this sort of "action" anthropological work:

1. War and peace
2. Climate change
3. Natural, industrial, and development-induced disaster recovery
4. Human rights
5. Health disparities
6. Racial understanding, politics, and equity (2009)

To this list, we could add a seventh: alienation and resettlement, which are often the outcomes of issues that arise in these six core areas (especially the first, second, third, and sixth).

Practical Applications

The case studies that follow reveal in greater detail the value of applied anthropology.

Doing Business in Japan

Doing business in a cultural setting that is very different from your own requires you to be aware of and sensitive to local customs and cultural norms. When working in such a setting, we can learn a great deal from the work of Edward T. Hall, the father of intercultural communication. Hall's work in diverse cultures and understanding of cultural perceptions of space and time constraints allowed us to start to see through the eyes of others. What popped into view were the dynamics of intersubjective space in intercultural (and intracultural) contexts, as well as ways to understand in order to be sensitive to these dynamics. (For more on this topic, see Hall 1959, 1966, 1976, 1983, Hall and Hall 1987.)

Anthropologist Richard Reeves-Ellington (1993) has built on this earlier work in the field of intercultural dynamics. In the early 1990s, he designed and implemented a cross-cultural training program for a North American company doing business in Japan (see Map 14.1). He found that many of the traditional methods of anthropology—cultural understanding, ethnographic data, and participant-observation—helped managers conduct business in Japan. Reeves-Ellington began the training program by having employees gather general *cultural information artifacts*. To complete this task, he asked them to focus on questions such as the following:

- "How are things classified?"
- "What are the artifacts of an agreed classification system?"

He also had them gather *social knowledge* by asking questions such as the following:

- "What are proper principles for behaviour?"
- "What are the values that drive the categories and artifacts?"

Finally, he had them investigate *cultural logic*. This task centred on answering the following question:

- "What is the world view?"

Social knowledge or values are based on an underlying, taken-for-granted cultural logic. Coming to

Figure 14.2 Medical anthropologist Andrea Wiley (left) in the Himalayas of Ladakh, India, where she studied maternal and child health. Think back to the example of SEARCH used in Chapter 10. How can anthropologists use their skills to contribute to grassroots efforts and community-based health initiatives?

understand Japanese cultural logic is of great importance to foreigners wishing to live and work in Japan.

The managers at the company decided to learn how to carry out introductions, meetings, leave-taking, dinner, and drinking in Japan. Each practice was analyzed according to the framework of artifacts, social knowledge, and cultural logic, and each was taught by a combination of methods that included collecting observations while visiting Japanese museums, theatres, shrines, baseball games,

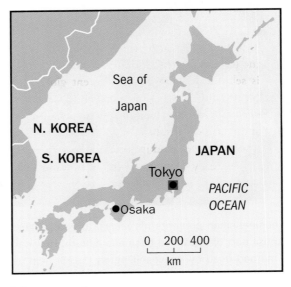

Map 14.1 Japan

and business meetings. The managers analyzed these observations and discussed stories that show how badly things can go when cultural knowledge is insufficient.

One thing the managers needed to learn about introductions involved the presentation of the business card (*meishi*). In Japan, the proper presentation and use of the *meishi* is the central element in the practice of making introductions at business meetings (Figure 14.3). Reeves-Ellington explained that, to a Japanese businessperson, the *meishi* is an extension of the self. Damage to the card, then, is damage to the individual. Therefore, mistreatment of a *meishi* will ruin a relationship. Reeves-Ellington notes that his students did not fully appreciate the consequences of these beliefs until he told them a story:

A major US company was having problems with one of its distributors, and the parties seemed unable to resolve their differences. The president of the US company decided to visit Japan, meet with his counterpart in the wholesaler organization, and attempt to resolve their differences. The two had not met previously and, upon meeting, each followed proper *meishi* ritual. The American, however, did not put the

Japanese counterpart's *meishi* on the table; instead he held on to it. As the conversation became heated, the American rolled up the *meishi* in his hand. Horror was recorded on the face of the Japanese businessman. The American then tore the *meishi* into bits. This was more than the Japanese could stand; he excused himself from the meeting. Shortly afterward the two companies stopped doing business with each other. (1993: 209)

Table 14.1 shows the information regarding introductions and the use of the *meishi* that Reeves-Ellington's students derived from their work based on their analytic framework of artifacts, social knowledge, and cultural logic.

On three critical measures—effective working relationships with Japanese executives, shortened project times, and improved financial returns—the anthropologically based training program that Reeves-Ellington designed was a success. Both employees and their Japanese counterparts felt more comfortable working with each other. Prior to the program, joint projects required an average of 15 months to complete; projects run by executives applying the methodologies of the program cut completion time to an average of 8 months. Financial returns based on contracts negotiated by personnel who had not participated in the program averaged a gross income of 6 per cent of sales, whereas those negotiated by personnel applying the anthropological techniques averaged a gross income equal to 18 per cent of sales.

As this example illustrates, cross-cultural understanding—a major focus of anthropological research—is important to work in disciplines other than anthropology. (For more examples of lessons that are central to anthropology and also useful in other areas, see the "In Their Own Words" box that follows. Also see Niemeier et al. [1998] and Reeves-Ellington [2009] for more examples specific to business and organizational leadership.)

Urban Social Planning and Restructuring in Canada

Alexander Ervin is an anthropologist in Saskatoon, Saskatchewan, who has had considerable experience participating in collaborative, community-based research that involves social service and health agencies (see EthnoProfile 14.1). In his view, anthropologists seem to be particularly well suited for

© iStop Images GmbH/Alamy Stock Photo

Figure 14.3 A Japanese businessman presents his *meishi* to a colleague. The *meishi* exchange is a central part of Japanese business culture. How can the applied anthropological method used by Reeves-Ellington (1993) help us understand the significance of this exchange? In what other situations might a similar methodological framework be useful?

Table 14.1 Introductions at Business Meetings

Artifacts	Social Knowledge	Cultural Logic
Technology		Human relations
• Business cards (*meishi*).	• Once given, a card is kept—not discarded. • *Meishi* are not exchanged a second time unless there is a position change.	• *Meishi* provide understanding of appropriate relations between parties. • *Meishi* take uncertainty out of relationships.
Visual behaviour		Environment
• Presentation of *meishi* by presenting card, facing recipient. • Senior people present *meishi* first. • Guest presents first, giving name, company affiliation, and bowing. • Host presents *meishi* in same sequence. • Upon sitting at conference table, all *meishi* are placed in front of recipient to assure name use.	• Before the next meeting between parties, the *meishi* are reviewed for familiarization with the people attending the meeting. • The *meishi* provide status for the owner.	• *Meishi* help establish insider/outsider environment. • *Meishi* help establish possible obligations to environment. Human activity • *Meishi* help to establish human activities.

Source: Reeves-Ellington 1993: 203–16. Reprinted by permission of Human Organization.

this kind of applied work because they "have been trained conceptually and methodologically to seek linkages among behaviours, institutions, and values, and to attempt to construct integrated overviews of whatever is the phenomenon under investigation" (1996: 324). As government policy-makers move to cut costs by downsizing, few policy disciplines are able to provide information about how the different social-service providers and their services fit together, and few are able to listen effectively to grassroots perceptions of issues, needs, and solutions. Anthropologists, however, are trained to do precisely these things.

To illustrate, Ervin discusses his work with the Saskatoon Social Planning Council, which was established in 1992 with a push from activists working with organizations that specialize in the delivery of human services in Saskatoon. The council was created to investigate and work toward resolving local social issues. As with other social planning councils in Canada, it is involved in an extremely wide range of policies and issues, and it carries out policy research to assess local needs and problems and to evaluate local programs. Ervin's main task has been

to design a plan for investigating issues that fall under the council's domain. The goal of the research is to provide information that the human service organizations can use to help solve some of the problems the research identifies.

The council's first investigation project was a multi-dimensional study of the well-being of children in the city. The investigation took a wide variety of issues into account, including poverty, hunger, recreation, education, family, Aboriginal and immigrant issues, substance abuse, and general health concerns. Several organizations collaborated on the project, including the regional health board, the Catholic and public school boards, and the social services district office. A working group of representatives from each organization was formed to analyze the data, much of which was collected by anthropology students at the University of Saskatchewan. When the group released its report, the council called together the organizations that had collaborated on the project, as well as other organizations and individuals involved with children's issues in Saskatoon, to consider the results and discuss possible solutions.

In Their Own Words

What Can You Learn from an Anthropology Major?

The Career Development Centre at SUNY Plattsburgh developed a document that highlights what students typically learn from a major in anthropology. Note that the skills listed below are valuable not only in anthropological settings but also in other situations—especially those commonly encountered in the business world.

1. Social agility

In an unfamiliar social or career-related setting, you learn to quickly size up the rules of the game. You can become accepted more quickly than you could without this anthropological skill.

2. Observation

You must often learn about a culture from within it, so you learn how to interview and observe as a participant.

3. Analysis and planning

You learn how to find patterns in the behaviour of a cultural group. This awareness of patterns allows you to generalize about the group's behaviour and predict what they might do in a given situation.

4. Social sensitivity

Although other people's ways of doing things may be different from your own, you learn the importance of events and conditions that have contributed to this difference. You also recognize that other cultures view your ways as strange. You learn the value of behaving toward others with appropriate preparation, care, and understanding.

5. Accuracy in interpreting behaviour

You become familiar with the range of behaviour in different cultures. You learn how to look at cultural causes of behaviour before assigning causes yourself.

6. Ability to *appropriately challenge* conclusions

You learn that analyses of human behaviour are open to challenge. You learn how to use new knowledge to test past conclusions.

7. Insightful interpretation of information

You learn how to use data collected by others, reorganizing or interpreting the data to reach original conclusions.

8. Simplification of information

Because anthropology is conducted among publics as well as about them, you learn how to simplify technical information for communication to non-technical people.

9. Contextualization

Although attention to details is a trait of anthropology, you learn that any given detail might not be as important as its context and can even be misleading when the context is ignored.

10. Problem solving

Because you often function within a cultural group or act on culturally sensitive issues, you learn to approach problems with care. Before acting, you identify the problem, set your goals, decide on the actions you will take, and calculate possible effects on other people.

11. Persuasive writing

Anthropologists strive to represent the behaviour of one group to another group and continually need to engage in interpretation. You learn the value of bringing someone else to share—or at least understand—your view through written argument.

12. Assumption of a social perspective

You learn how to perceive the acts of individuals and local groups as both shaping and being shaped by larger socio-cultural systems. The perception enables you to "act locally and think globally."

Source: Omohundro, John. 2000. "What Can You Learn from an Anthropology Major?" in *Careers in Anthropology* (New York: McGraw-Hill).

EthnoProfile 14.1
Saskatoon

Region: North America
Nation: Canada
Language: English is the official language, but Cree is also spoken, as there is a large population of First Nations peoples, mostly from Plains Cree communities.
Population: 253,000 (2014 estimate)
Environment: Northern plains
Livelihood: Industrial, commercial, agricultural, educational centre
Political organization: City in contemporary nation-state
For more information: "City of Saskatoon," www.saskatoon.ca

Ervin believes that anthropologists can make important contributions in urban policy contexts, especially in needs assessment, through "the process of identifying and seeking solutions to problems of particular populations, irrespective of whether programs have already been designed to address them" (1996: 330). Anthropologists seem particularly well suited for participating in these projects, given their commitment to participatory research and holism. Indeed, from Ervin's point of view, there is a major need in urban policy research for anthropologists who are *flexible* in their approach—that is, who can move from one policy domain to another and construct integrated overviews of the phenomenon under investigation.

Anthropology and Policy

Central to applied anthropology is, as illustrated throughout this text, the use of holism, comparison, and cultural relativism. Because anthropologists contextualize their work and consider alternative perspectives, they are frequently hesitant to make policy recommendations that are as detailed as those often made by individuals working in other professional disciplines. This may be because anthropologists are particularly aware of the problems in applied work, the problems in trying to make people, or systems, change. Anthropologists are trained to analyze social and cultural systems, and when they are asked how to change these systems, they begin to ask questions. These questions are based on an awareness of the enormous complexity of human life when it is viewed from ground level.

Anthropologists have developed a keen awareness that not everyone makes the same basic assumptions about the world that planners and officials make. They know that sometimes technical experts providing help in other cultures know less about the issues they are investigating than do the people they are advising; further, they know that these "experts" are not always qualified to give culturally appropriate advice (Figure 14.4). Anthropologists realize that changes do not benefit everyone equally

Figure 14.4 A Palestinian widow in Gaza confers with a fieldworker in the greenhouse she built, with the help of an international humanitarian aid organization, on ground that she cleared herself. She uses the garden to grow seasonal food to feed her six children.

© David Silverman/Getty Images

and that some people gain as others lose. They also understand that even if they get involved in planning a program, implementing that program depends on diverse external factors over which they have no control. And they know that they get to go home while others remain to deal with the outcomes of policy-makers' decisions. Anthropologists believe they have much to contribute in helping to build a better world, yet they are also highly sensitive to the kinds of issues that arise when dealing with complex human systems. Applied anthropologists are well aware of the ambiguities of the human experience.

Anthropology and the Challenges of Global Citizenship

One of the challenges faced by people everywhere in the world today is that of defining citizenship in a complex, diverse, and difficult world. Can anthropologists provide ways for people to understand the issues involved?

Anthropology and Democracy

In the decades since the end of the Cold War, the capitalist market has spread into nearly all parts of the globe; as a result, many observers have assumed that other Western institutions will also eventually spread into all regions. The fall or mutation of dictatorial political regimes in a number of Latin American and European countries, for example, was viewed as an opportunity to introduce Western political practices, including political parties and formal elections. Many members of the Western political and economic elite eagerly proclaimed the arrival of democracy as soon as the first elections were held, and they have often been very suspicious of political movements that challenge formal electoral institutions "in the name of democracy."

But anthropologists and other social scientists working in these same countries are often able to present a different perspective on the "transition" to democracy. Fieldwork brings them into close, regular contact with citizens who have their own ideas about what kinds of social institutions do or do not operate in a democratic fashion. Taking these observations seriously has drawn anthropologists into a growing debate about what democracy is, what it has been, and what it can be. In particular, their work has helped to show that formal Western electoral

politics may produce less democratic outcomes than other, traditional institutions could produce.

For example, anthropologist Serge Tcherkézoff (1998) has followed debates about the shape democracy ought to take in the independent nation of Samoa (see EthnoProfile 4.1). Traditionally, Samoa was a land of villages, each of which was governed by a council of *matai*, or "sacred chiefs." This system survived Christian missionaries, German colonization, and decades of foreign administration (during the time that the area was a protectorate of New Zealand). A referendum sponsored by the UN in 1962 led to independence, and the people then voted to set up a parliamentary system of national government. However, their constitution specified that only *matai* could vote and run for office. In 1990, the law was changed to allow all citizens to vote, but even today *matai* remain the only ones allowed to run for office (Figure 14.5).

Does this hybrid of a Western parliamentary system and the Samoan *faamatai*, or "chief-system," represent an undemocratic attempt by chiefly "aristocrats" to maintain power within formally democratic political institutions? In Tcherkézoff's opinion, the question is deeply misleading because it rests on a fundamental misunderstanding of how the Samoan chief-system functions. He points out that if outsiders insist on thinking of *matai* as aristocrats, then there are no families in Samoa who are not aristocratic. This is because each *matai* is actually the head of an extended family. Each extended family is held together by kinship connections, joint ownership of land, and joint participation in rituals directed to their founding ancestor. *Matai*, in fact, means "the one who bears the family name," and members of each extended family choose the person who will be ritually invested with this title. It is the job of each *matai* to serve his family and his *matai* name by leading worship directed to the ancestor and engaging in other activities designed to elevate the reputation of his extended family. If a *matai* fails to live up to these expectations, his extended family can strip him of his title and give it to someone else. Every family has a *matai*, which is why Tcherkézoff says that there are no families that are not chiefly families. Further, *matais* serve at the will of the kin who choose them, which is why, he tells us, "when Samoans heard about 'democracy,' they said that they 'already have it'" (1998: 423).

So why are Samoans arguing about the connection between the *matai* system and democracy? As Tcherkézoff explains, this debate involves a variety of different ideas about what *democracy* means and which kinds of institutional arrangements are most likely to ensure it. Some Samoans favour a view of democracy in which the emphasis is on individual freedom: anyone can run for office and anyone can vote. They point out, for example, that traditionally nobody becomes a *matai* until he has served his family for many years and his predecessor has died, which limits the field of possible parliamentary candidates to one relatively old man per extended family. How can it be democratic to restrict the opportunities of younger people to run for office? These sorts of arguments fit well with traditional Western arguments that speak of democracy in connection with individual freedom from arbitrary restrictions.

But those Samoans who want the *matai* system to continue stress that it is more democratic than typical Western-style stems of democracy because it creates representatives who can never forget that they are responsible to those who elected them— the other members of their extended family. In thinking about democracy in this way, these Samoans are refusing to reduce democratic citizenship to the right to vote. Rather, they take the view that democracy involves not just being treated as an equal by others but also the obligation of those who make political decisions for others to remain accountable and accessible to those whom they represent. Thus, the *matai* system can be viewed as highly democratic because it ensures that every extended family will be represented in some form in the electoral process and that any *matais* elected to parliament will not be able to ignore the wishes of those who put them in office.

Politics in Samoa also has a regional dimension. Tcherkézoff points out that Samoa was primarily a nation of villages in the past, but the capital city has been growing in size in recent years. Many of those who live in the growing urban area depend more on wage labour and less on agriculture and fishing, the activities central to life in villages, where *matais* traditionally exercised their authority. Thus, those who want to preserve the *matai* system also defend it as a way of maintaining equality between those who live in the city and those who still live in rural areas. They fear that if any citizen were allowed to run for office, Samoa would be fractured into two societies: an urban sector with a Western political system, which would have no way to hold their parliamentary representatives accountable, and a rural sector in which *matais* still exist but only as

Figure 14.5 The parliament building in Samoa. Today, Samoans continue to take part in a debate that involves a variety of ideas about what *democracy* means and what kinds of institutional arrangements are most likely to ensure it. What does democracy mean to you?

powerless guardians of local folklore. Should this happen, "then some Samoans say that 'democracy' will not be achieved and will even go backwards" (Tcherkézoff 1998: 427).

As Tcherkézoff makes clear, the debate about democracy in Samoa is complex and nuanced: Samoans have a sophisticated understanding of the advantages and drawbacks of different democratic political forms, some of which are indigenous to Samoa and some of which came from elsewhere:

> The problem is that Samoa has the chance to build its future on ideas and experiences that come both from the *faamatai* tradition and from the Western tradition of democracy, and to maybe create a new synthesis where the advent of democracy will not just be the replacement of hierarchy (in the *faamatai*) by inequality (in the Western-style politics). There lies the real question of the future of the country. (Tcherkézoff 1998: 430)

Anthropology and Multicultural Politics in the New Europe

One of the more interesting things about the late twentieth and early twenty-first centuries is that Europe—the continent that gave birth to the

Enlightenment and colonial empires, and to anthropology itself—has now become a key setting for the anthropological study of social and cultural changes. Europeans are struggling with the concept of multiculturalism in ways we in Canada can recognize. Indeed, we are the people with the Canadian Multiculturalism Act, passed in Parliament in 1988, which recognizes "the diversity of Canadians as regards race, national or ethnic origin, colour, and religion as a fundamental characteristic of Canadian society . . . while working to achieve the equality of all Canadians in the economic, social, cultural, and political life of Canada" (Preamble). How are European nations dealing with the influx of people they consider non-European?

Let us look at an example from Italy. In 1999, British anthropologist Michael Herzfeld (2003) moved into Rione Monti, a working-class Roman neighbourhood close to the Coliseum (see Map 14.2), to do fieldwork exploring social change in the way people use the concept of the past. Long-time residents of Monti share a common local culture, which includes use of the *romanesco* dialect rather than standard Italian, and a strong sense of local identity that distinguishes them from "foreigners," including diplomats and non-Roman Italians. Their identity survived fascist dictator Benito Mussolini's demolition of part of the neighbourhood in the early twentieth century. They also successfully dealt with a local criminal underworld by mastering a refined code of politeness. The underworld had faded away by the 1970s, but beginning in the 1980s, residents began to face two new challenges to their community:

1. Historic Roman neighbourhoods became fashionable, and well-to-do Italians began to move into Rione Monti, pushing many workers into cheaper housing elsewhere.
2. In the 1990s, another group of newcomers arrived: immigrants from eastern Europe.

Italy is one of the more recent destinations of immigration into Europe, reversing the country's historical experience as a source, rather than a target, of immigration. After Germany, France, and Britain passed laws curtailing immigration in the 1970s, Italy became an increasingly popular destination for immigrants from Africa, Asia, Latin America, and, after the Cold War, other European nations, particularly those of Eastern Europe. Until relatively recently, laws regulating immigration were few, and the country appeared welcoming. But this is changing (Figure 14.6): "Italy has not historically been a racist country, but intolerant attitudes toward immigrants have increased. To a large extent, this seems to be the result of a longstanding underestimation of the magnitude of the changes and thus poor policy implementation for a lengthy period, in spite of the best intentions officially proclaimed" (Melotti 1997: 91).

Italian anthropologist and political sociologist Umberto Melotti (1997) contrasts the distinctive ways in which immigration is understood by the governments of France, Britain, and Germany. According to him, the French project is *ethnocentric assimilationism*: since the early nineteenth century, when French society experienced a falling birth rate, immigration was encouraged and immigrants were promised all the rights and privileges of native-born citizens as long as they adopted French culture completely, dropping other ethnic or cultural attachments and assimilating the French language, culture, and character (75). The British project, in contrast, is *uneven pluralism*: that is, the pragmatic British expect immigrants to be loyal and law-abiding citizens, but they do not expect immigrants to "become British," and they tolerate private cultivation of cultural differences as long as these do not threaten the British way of life (79–80). Finally, Melotti describes the German project as *the institutionalization of precariousness*, by which he means that despite the fact that Germany has within its borders more immigrants than any other European country, and began receiving immigrants at the end of the nineteenth century, its government continues to insist that Germany is not a country of

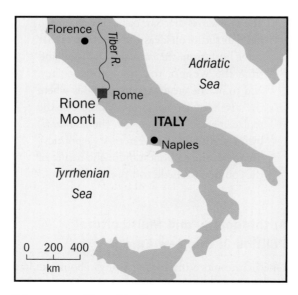

Map 14.2 Rione Monti

immigrants. Immigrants were generally considered "guest workers," and even today it remains somewhat difficult for immigrants to obtain German citizenship.

Some European countries face issues of multiculturalism that are rooted in longstanding tensions between two or more ethnic groups that are equally established within the same country. This is the case in Belgium, for example, where there has been historic conflict between the Dutch-speaking Flemings in the north and the French-speaking Walloons in the south. The country has found a partial solution to cultural tension by allowing both groups to enjoy considerable autonomy, and the state's role is to protect the rights of each community in the public sphere.

Coming to terms with increasing numbers of Muslims living in countries where Christianity has historically been dominant is a central theme in multicultural debates within Europe. Although almost all European states consider themselves secular in orientation, the relation between religion and state is far from uniform. France is unusual because of its strict legal separation between religion and state. In Britain, the combination of a secular outlook with state funding of the established Anglican Church has allowed citizens to support forms of religious inclusion, such as state funding of "faith schools" (i.e., schools that combine religious and secular content) for non-Protestant immigrants. Today, there are over a dozen state-funded Muslim schools in England (AMS 2014). In Germany, where a secular outlook also combines with state-subsidized religious institutions, the state has devised curricula for elementary schools designed to teach all students about different religious traditions, including Islam, in ways that emphasize the possibility of harmonizing one's religious faith with one's obligations as a citizen. Although this approach may be seen as presumptuous or paternalistic, its supporters counter that its advantages outweigh its costs. Perhaps as a result of their country's history, many contemporary Germans have less faith than the British that a civic culture of religious tolerance will automatically lead to harmony without state intervention, and less faith than the French in the existence of a separate secular sphere of society from which religion can be safely excluded (Schiffauer 1997).

These are, of course, thumbnail sketches of more complex attitudes and practices. But they illustrate the fact that there is no single "European" approach to the challenges posed by immigration and

Figure 14.6 In recent years, intolerance toward immigrants has increased in Italy. As part of a 2015 protest in Turin, men and women marched barefoot in defence of the rights of migrants. These young immigrants hold a sign that reads "Racism! No, thank you." How would you use your anthropological skills to look at this situation? What questions would you ask?

multiculturalism. In a way, each European state, with its own history and institutions, is experimenting with different ways of coping, and their failures and successes will influence the kinds of multicultural relations and institutions that develop in the future. This experimentation is particularly significant in light of the fact that European nation-states have joined together in the European Union (EU), a superstate with 28 members in 2017 (though the United Kingdom, as of June 2017, has begun negotiations on the terms to withdraw from the EU in the process known as "Brexit" after a referendum was held in 2016. The long-term effects of Brexit remain to be seen). Reconciling the diverse, culturally informed interests and needs of member states poses enormous challenges for the EU as a whole.

Many scholars and activists hope that solutions can be found that will involve extensions of social justice throughout the EU. But there is still a lot of work to be done, and there are no guarantees about the outcome. British Pakistani professor of public policy Tariq Modood points out, for example, that European multiculturalism requires supporting conceptions of citizenship that allow the "right to assimilate" as well as the "right to have one's 'difference' . . . recognized and supported in the public and the private spheres" (1997: 20). Further, in Modood's view, European multiculturalism must recognize that "participation in the public or national culture is necessary for the effective exercise of citizenship" while at the same time defending the "right to widen and adapt the national culture" (20). The potential and actual contradictions among some of these goals are apparent, but insofar as they are seen as necessary, the challenge becomes finding ways to move forward. And here, with no blueprint to follow, all parties find themselves involved in creating new cultural practices. Based on her experience in France, anthropologist Marie-Bénédicte Dembour is convinced that "we need to accept the discomfort of moving in-between, as a pendulum" (2001: 71–2). Modood earlier noted: "There is indeed a tension here, and perhaps it can only be resolved in practice through finding and cultivating points of common ground between dominant and subordinate cultures, as well as new syntheses and hybridities. The important thing is that the burdens of change . . . are not all dependent on one party to this encounter" (1997: 364).

Anthropologists are inevitably drawn into these discussions, not only because they carry out research in the communities struggling for resolution but also because many of them are citizens of the societies whose future depends on the solutions that are implemented. As a result, theoretical debates in the field are intertwined with political debates in society, and scholars can disagree with one another just as political activists do. For example, Norwegian anthropologist Thomas Eriksen (2001) reports on the outcome of a formal debate organized by the

Department of Anthropology at the University of Oslo in 1997, in which the thesis to be contested was the assertion that cultural freedom protects not only a group but also the rights of every individual within a group. Eriksen notes that those supporting the thesis and those arguing against it "not only reached opposite conclusions but also failed to engage in a proper dialogue: they tended to depict each other . . . as hopeless Romantics and cynical modernists, respectively" (144). In the end, Eriksen observes, the debate raised the same kinds of issues and provoked the same kinds of responses and standoffs that can be found in the wider society. After the debate, the audience was invited to vote for the side they thought had made the best case. The results were 78 in favour of the motion, 75 against. This almost perfect standoff, Eriksen points out, is very different from what the outcome would likely have been 10 or 15 years earlier, when there would have been "almost certainly a massive 'yes' vote" (145). As Eriksen speculates, "perhaps the tide will turn again" (145).

Thus, the struggles and dilemmas facing residents of Rione Monti are widespread across the new Europe. But the specifics of the situation in Rione Monti, and the cultural resources available to longstanding residents, have their own particularity. For the most part, the traditionally left-wing Monti residents have resisted turning against immigrant families in the neighbourhood. Still, they are unhappy with many of the ways in which immigration has impacted their lives (Figure 14.7). For example, they do not like the location of the Ukrainian church in a building that overlooks the neighbourhood's central square because churchgoers gather there twice a week, invading "their" space (Herzfeld 2003: 4). Herzfeld reports that the residents of Monti, like other Romans, claim not to be racist (which accords with Melotti's views of Italians in general) and that they seem less hostile to immigrants of colour than to Ukrainians. Ukrainians are more numerous in Monti and more threatening because they look like local people and compete with local people for work and space in the neighbourhood (5). At the same time, the Monti code of politeness "underlies the facility with which democratically inclined residents today construct a popular street democracy, a system of neighbourhood associations" (2). At the beginning of the twenty-first century, immigrants were not able to deploy this code, a fact that signalled their outsider status and could lead to misunderstandings and bad feelings. If they could learn to use the code, however, fresh opportunities for political

Figure 14.7 In the neighbourhood of Rione Monti in central Rome, long-time residents and new immigrants are negotiating new forms of relationships.

© ASK Images/Alamy Stock Photo

co-operation might be forged. This arrangement could be decisive, for the code of politeness is the foundation of local democratic processes.

More recently, Herzfeld has made the following observations on the situation in Rione Monti:

> People are being kicked out of their homes by a variety of implacable forces ranging from the underworld and the banks to religious institutions claiming a charitable identity. Loansharking is rife; so are prostitution, racism against immigrant populations, police intolerance, political extremism. The economic pressures that these facts indicate are being exacerbated by the current problems of the country as a whole and of the European Union, but in some form they have always been part of Roman life, and Romans know how to deal with them—not always successfully, but usually with aplomb and dignity. (2013)

As these observations suggest, codes can mutate, indeed disintegrate, with changing economic conditions and demography. Tolerance can be eroded in tough and/or changing times and be shown to be merely skin deep—and not an integrated component of our definition of self.

Anthropology and Human Rights

Anthropologists have long been involved in an intensifying understanding of human rights, and they have contributed to the recognition by human rights legal advocates that the collective rights of groups deserve as much attention as do the rights of individuals. Anthropologist Ellen Messer observes that anthropologists have examined, and continue to examine,

> the contexts of human rights abuses to understand how the political economic conditions that create cultural customs such as infanticide, underfeeding of women and children, and other abuses of women might be improved and make the customs of less evident utility. They also continue to work with interpreters of local traditions, so that through persuasion and contextualization, and by drawing on the authority of multiple traditions, people might be empowered to improve human rights in their own lives. (1993: 241)

Perhaps one of the foremost anthropologically oriented organizations involved with human rights is

Cultural Survival, founded in 1972 by anthropologists Pia Maybury-Lewis and David Maybury-Lewis. The organization is dedicated to helping Indigenous people and ethnic minorities deal as equals in their encounters with industrial society (Figure 14.8). Over the years, many Canadian anthropologists have contributed to projects with similar aims across the globe. Indeed, in this and other contexts, "Canadian anthropology has been on the leading edge of engaged anthropology for decades," essentially avoiding the energy-sapping debate on the merits of theoretical versus applied anthropology that often dominates anthropological discussions in the United States and elsewhere (Waldram 2010: 225).

Biological anthropologists have also contributed in an important way to the defence of human rights in the world. Until his death in 2014, forensic anthropologist Clyde Snow was at the forefront of such efforts (Figure 14.9). Snow was often called on by police departments, medical examiners, and other law-enforcement officials to try to identify human remains and to determine the cause of death, and he was involved in a number of international human rights cases. Beginning in 1984, he worked with the American Association for the Advancement of Science to help the Argentinian National Commission on Disappeared Persons to determine the fate of some of the more than 10,000 people who had vanished during the "dirty war" waged by the Argentine military government against supposed subversives. Snow began his work in Argentina by training a team of medical and anthropology

Figure 14.8 Kuna women work with Cultural Survival radio producer Rosy Sul González on grassroots Kuna language maintenance efforts in Panama. What sorts of things can organizations and anthropologists do to ensure that Indigenous peoples are actively involved in their projects?

© Jess Cherofsky/Cultural Survival

© ORLANDO SIERRA/AFP/Getty Images

Figure 14.9 Some applied anthropologists, like the late Clyde Snow (shown here), use their knowledge and skills in skeletal identification to defend human rights around the world.

students in the techniques of forensic investigation, both skeletal and archaeological, and then helped them exhume and examine the remains of many *desaparecidos* ("those who have disappeared"). Their efforts helped convict a number of leaders, including high-ranking military and police officers, responsible for the deaths (Huyghe 1988). Snow has commented on the importance of this sort of work: "There are human rights violations going on all around the world. But to me murder is murder, regardless of the motive. I hope that we are sending a message to governments who murder in the name of politics that they can be held to account" (55).

See the "In Their Own Words" box that follows for a discussion of how anthropology's traditional task has become more complicated.

Social anthropologists Paul Oldham and Miriam Frank (2008) have considered the adoption of the UN's 2007 Declaration on the Rights of Indigenous Peoples. Declarations are important, but only insofar as they become the road map for action. They challenge us to consider the role that anthropology might play in promoting human rights. In Canada, for example, we might ask what anthropologists can do to help ease the suffering of Aboriginal peoples who continue to struggle with the after-effects of the residential school system.

In Their Own Words

Into the Warp and Woof of Multicultural Worlds

Changes in the contemporary world are producing what anthropologist George Marcus calls "transcultural 'traditional' peoples," whose members live in many different places and whose sense of cultural identity involves a mix of many cultural elements.

The power of global cultural homogenization in the late twentieth century challenges the conventions and rationales by which anthropology has so far produced its knowledge of other cultures. The reorganization of the world economy through technological advances in communication, production processes, and marketing has thoroughly de-territorialized culture. For example, the Tongan Islanders of Polynesia that I studied in the early 1970s now constitute a diaspora of communities in locales around the Pacific Rim. As many, if not more, Tongans now live permanently in Australia, New Zealand, and the United States as in the islands themselves. One might fairly ponder where both the cultural and geographical centre of the Tongan people resides.

Their identity is produced in many locales and through the mix of many cultural elements. And their conditions are similar to those of numerous other peoples that anthropologists have traditionally studied. It is no longer just the most powerful, large-scale, and most modern societies, such as the United States and Japan, that exist in international, transcultural science.

Among such transcultural "traditional" peoples, levels of cultural self-consciousness and alternatives increase. The authenticity of performances, rituals, or apparently deep-seated norms like those of kinship cannot be merely assumed, either by locals or by visitors such as anthropologists. To some extent, media documentaries have absorbed anthropology's function of presenting vividly the life-ways of other cultures to Euro-American publics that themselves can no longer be considered as homogeneous or mainstream. And, finally, the subjects of anthropological study independently and articulately translate their own perspectives with sensitivity to the effects of different media.

Awareness and Uncertainty

At this point, let us return to the question we posed at the beginning of this chapter: Why study anthropology? The second part of our answer is more personal.

Anthropology brings all of us into contact with different ways of life—past and present. It makes us aware of just how arbitrary our own understanding of the world is as we learn how other people have developed satisfying but different ways of living. In addition, if we are from Western countries that were responsible for colonialism and its consequences, it makes us painfully aware of just how much our own tradition has contributed to the form of the modern world. Further, it makes us aware of just how much our well-being is situated in the wealth and resources generated elsewhere in the world.

Knowing and experiencing cultural variety gives rise, perhaps inevitably, to doubt. We come to doubt the ultimate validity of the central truths of our own cultural tradition, which have been ratified and sanctified by the generations who preceded us. We doubt because a familiarity with alternative ways of living makes the ultimate meaning of any action, of any object, a highly ambiguous matter. Ambiguity is part and parcel of the human condition.

Human beings have coped with ambiguity from time immemorial by means of culture, which places objects and actions in contexts and thereby makes their meanings plain. This doubt can lead to anxiety, but it can also be liberating.

Such liberation leads to a recognition of themes of central concern for informed global citizens—freedom, health, divisions of wealth, environment, personhood, governance, transnationalism, and the like. An excellent example is how these themes combine in the context of the debate about who should control the remaining samples of the "eradicated" disease smallpox (see the "In Their Own Words" box on this topic that follows). Western scientists and politicians argue that the samples are necessary for research purposes. Yet other people—especially people living in Africa, where the disease was most devastating during the twentieth century—argue that all samples should be destroyed to prevent them from leaking out into the public. Between these two positions, other individuals and groups have developed their own unique perspectives based on their own unique situations. By employing the anthropological perspective, anthropology allows us to understand the many sides of the debate and respect the validity of the many perspectives involved in seeking a positive outcome.

Peoples who in particular have become classic anthropological subjects, such as the Samoans, the Trobriand Islanders, the Hopi of the Southwest USA, and the Todas of India, know their status well, and have, with some ambivalence, assimilated anthropological knowledge about them as part of their sense of themselves. A recent example was the visit of a Toda woman to Houston, Texas. A trained nurse among her people, as well as a cultural broker, she was on tour in the United States giving talks about the Todas, of the sort that anthropologists might have given in past decades. By chance, she was visiting the home of a colleague just as a British documentary about the Todas appeared on the television—a documentary in which the visitor was featured prominently as the filmmaker's prime source of information. The visitor's comments as she watched the program along with my colleague did not much concern the details of Toda culture but rather dealt with the ironies of the multiple representations of her people—by herself, by anthropologists, and by the British Broadcasting Corporation.

The lesson of this story is compelling. The penetrations of a world economy, communications, and the effects of multiple, fragmented identities on cultural authenticity, once thought restricted to advanced modernity, have increased markedly among most local and regional cultures worldwide. They have thus engendered an ethnography in reverse among many peoples who not only can assimilate the professional idioms of anthropology but can relativize them among other alternatives and ways of knowledge. This does not mean that the traditional task of anthropology to represent distinctive and systematic cultural forms of life has been fundamentally subverted by its own subjects. Rather, anthropology's traditional task is now much more complicated, requiring new sensibilities in undertaking fieldwork and different strategies for writing about it.

Republished with permission of West Publishing Company, from Marcus, George. 1990. "Into the Warp and Woof of Multicultural Worlds," guest editorial in *Cultural Anthropology: A Perspective on the Human Condition* 2e, eds Emily Schultz and Robert Lavenda (St Paul, MN: West), 1990; permission conveyed through Copyright Clearance Center, Inc.

In Their Own Words

Homes for the Smallpox Virus

This editorial article considers the efficacy of keeping samples of the smallpox virus—one of the deadliest viruses known to humans—decades after its eradication from human populations. Similar ethical discussions will arise in other world-health situations (e.g., in efforts to reconstruct the virus that caused the 1918 "Spanish flu" pandemic, or to study the Ebola virus in laboratories across the globe).

19 January 2011

At a May meeting of the World Health Assembly—a gathering of delegates from all WHO member states—the United States and Russia will once again face a clamour, led by African countries, to eliminate the last known live samples of the smallpox virus—thirty years after the WHO declared it eradicated. Unfortunately, humanity cannot dispense with this destroyer of life so easily.

The scourge is believed to have killed more people over the millennia than any other, its victims running into the hundreds of millions. Legions more were blinded and permanently disfigured. The last natural outbreaks occurred in Africa as late as the 1970s, within living memory, and it is understandable that African countries are pushing most vehemently to bring about its extinction.

The fact of smallpox's survival three decades after its eradication through a global program of vaccination, even in maximum-containment, "biosafety level 4" laboratories at the US Centers for Disease Control and at a research institution in Russia, constitutes a real and constant danger. But the elimination of the live virus would not remove that threat. On the contrary, it might serve in a perverse way to exacerbate it.

Live viruses might well persist in unknown laboratories, or even, it has been theorized, lie in wait in permafrost cemeteries. It is also possible that the virus could be artificially reconstructed and used in a bioterrorism attack. For that reason, the US ordered the emergency production of 168 million doses of smallpox vaccine after 11 September 2001 and continues to add to its stocks.

This is not bioterror hysteria. It is a sensible precaution. Such a threat is much greater than any risk posed by the collections maintained at two WHO-authorized high-security laboratories. These samples, frozen in liquid nitrogen, are the source of anxiety for those who want to declare total victory in the war against smallpox. But such chest-thumping would harm research into the human immune system and undermine the capacity of science to identify and research antiviral agents and next-generation vaccines. Surely this is a case of its being better to know thy enemy.

Source: "Homes for the Smallpox Virus." Editorial in *The Globe and Mail* (19 Jan. 2011), © The Globe and Mail Inc. All Rights Reserved. Reprinted by permission.

Freedom and Constraint

So why study anthropology? The third part of our answer is humanistic—it relates to our interest in our fellow human beings and our desire to learn about and from the diversity of humanity.

All human beings live in culturally shaped worlds, enmeshed in webs of interpretation and meaning. Anthropologists have been tasked to go out to bear witness to and record the vast creative diversity in *world-making* that has been the history of our species. In our lifetimes, we will witness the end of many of those ways of life. This loss can be tragic, for as these worlds disappear so too does something special about humanity: variety, creativity, and awareness of alternatives. We are also witness to change—a loss also but also a gain—as we face the challenge of moving into an unknown, unknowable future. Our survival as a species, and our viability as individuals, depend on the possibility of choice, of perceiving and being able to act on alternatives in the various situations we encounter during our lives. If we think of human life as a minefield, then the more paths we can see and imagine through that minefield, the more likely we are to make it through. As alternatives are destroyed, wantonly smashed, or thoughtlessly crushed, our own human possibilities are reduced.

Anthropologists have, for the last century or so, gone out into the world to write the record of human accomplishment, learn from it, and teach its meaning to others. Surely our greatest human accomplishment is the creation of the sometimes-beautiful worlds in which we all live. Anthropologists have rarely given in to the romantic notion that these other worlds are all good, all life-enhancing, all fine or beautiful. They are not. Ambiguity and ambivalence are, as we have seen, hallmarks of the human experience. There are no guarantees that human cultures will be compassionate rather than cruel or that people will agree they are one or the other. There are not even any guarantees that our species will survive. But all anthropologists have believed that these are *human* worlds that have given those who have lived in them the ability to make sense out of their experiences and to derive meaning for their lives, and that we are a species at once bound by our culture and free to change it.

Going Somewhere?

Concluding Remarks from Roberta Robin Dods

And so we arrive at the end of this book and my contribution to the four editions where I have brought you a Canadian perspective. In a sense, we are all on a metaphorical road to *somewhere,* and this has been emphasized for me from my decades of engagement in anthropology and archaeology: essentially the story of us—all of us.

From our human beginnings in the Paleolithic we have some indicators of material culture altering our relationship to the natural world we were and remain a part of. First indications came from the invention of tools from stone that became more complex over time. Then came fire. Without fire, we would have remained in the long-running and deeply stable Paleolithic, chipping away and staying near to what warmth we could find.

Fire came to us first in its wild form from a brilliant light show in the sky, through a bolt of lightning striking the ground, essentially a gift from above. Once found, this gift had to be cherished, fed, and protected. Who was our first ancestor to understand that stone struck on stone could make fire? That fire could be "domesticated"? With this domestication, we became the keepers of a crucial technology, one that must have seemed magical. Fire allowed us to alter our relationship with our world. It turned cold to warmth, night to day. It altered what and how we ate, and it provided a circle of protective light from the predators and scavengers of the night. It gave us a cozy, intimate place for gathering and a way to communicate over great distances. Its heat altered materials, allowing us to shape malleable metals and create pottery. It allowed us to fashion diverse forms of weapons. As we studied the light and the heat of fire, and its ability to transform our world, we became chemists and physicists. Much later, fire gave us the Industrial Revolution—the steam engine to drive us into a different cultural world. It also gave us a fearsome power as Oppenheimer observed when it came to atomic applications: "I am become death, the destroyer of worlds." There were other "great" inventions and innovations—the domestication of plants and animals (food economies) and the wheel (transportation), to name only two—but fire was transformative in a foundational way.

Today, with the dawn of the digital age, technology lights our minds, sparks our imagination in new ways! There were a number of forward-thinking individuals who anticipated the ways in which such technologies might change our lives. Think science fiction, perhaps most notably Arthur C. Clarke, whose mid-twentieth-century works explore such contemporary concepts as artificial intelligence, nanotechnology, and gene mapping. In the realm of anthropology, Edward T. Hall was a similarly forward-thinking individual. In his 1976 book *Beyond Culture*, he discussed *extension transference,* a term he coined for the relationship between our biology and our technology. Hall understood that technological change could lead to biological change, although our human culture (both ideational and material) is capable of immediate and widespread change, adapting much more quickly than our genetic makeup.

And the future? We can speculate, and holism offers us entrée to wider fields of knowledge such as that offered by theoretical physicist Michio Kaku. He gives us, in accessible form, some insight into what might be possible in the world of the future. One troubling question that Kaku poses is: "Can consciousness exist by itself, free from the constraints of the physical body?" (2014: 266) This question speaks to our deep desire to not be transient. Kaku explores a number of new and evolving technologies that may one day make it possible for us to separate our consciousness from our body: cloning and mind transfer, and computer-based "backups" of the human mind, suggesting the possibility of our consciousnesses existing as beams of light, pure energy able to roam free through the universe—our fire set free! While such developments may seem fanciful to some, they represent the unlimited possibilities available through human creativity and agency. How much of what makes us *us* have we given over to technology? Can digital connections ever replace the sensation of sharing the same physical space with another person, perhaps sitting around a nice warm fire on a cool evening? As anthropologists, we cannot help but ask such questions as we contemplate what our technological advancements might mean for the future of humanity.

Key Term

coloniality 359

Chapter Summary

1. Anthropological research can be challenging to conduct in today's world, but it is also very rewarding. Applied anthropology can contribute to contemporary solutions of various social issues. Applied anthropologists do their work using holism, comparison, relativism, and a concern for particular cases.

2. Anthropology teaches many lessons that are relevant to a wide variety of situations. Even if you do not go on to work as an anthropologist, you can refer to your knowledge of anthropology as a guide for a way of living in the world in a state of reflexivity—a state of constant engagement and growth.

3. Anthropologists involved in expanding the understanding of human rights have participated in organizations for the defence of human rights. In particular, they have contributed to the recognition by human rights legal advocates that the collective rights of groups (such as Indigenous peoples) deserve as much attention as the rights of individuals.

4. Cultural anthropology brings us into contact with different ways of life and challenges our awareness of just how arbitrary our own understanding of the world is as we learn how other people have developed satisfying but different ways of living.

Critical Thinking Questions

1. How would you describe the potential of applied anthropology to address various issues of concern in today's world? Give at least three specific examples.

2. Review the list of the 12 main skills you can learn from a major in anthropology (p. 364). Which have been the greatest challenges for you?

3. Why do you suppose anthropologists are particularly aware of the problems in applied work—the problems in trying to make people, or systems, change? What is it about anthropology that engenders such sensitivity?

4. How would you describe the ambiguity and ambivalence of the human experience in the sometimes-beautiful worlds in which we all live?

Suggested Readings

Oldham, Paul, and Miriam Anne Frank. 2008. "'We the People . . .': The United Nations Declaration on the Rights of Indigenous Peoples," *Anthropology Today* 24, 2: 5–9. A report on the adoption of the UN document on the rights of Indigenous peoples worldwide. Note that not all states have signed on.

Rylko-Bauer, Barbara, Merrill Singer, and John Van Willigen. 2006. "Reclaiming Applied Anthropology: Its Past, Present, and Future," *American Anthropologist,* New Series, 108, 1: 178–90. An examination of the central role that application has played throughout anthropology's evolution, as well as the role of advocacy in relation to greater engagement, and the relationship of theory to practice.

Smith, Susan E., Dennis G. Willms, and Nancy A. Johnson, eds. 1997. *Nurtured by Knowledge: Learning to Do Participatory Action Research* (New York: Apex Press). A discussion of PAR (participatory action research), a methodology that enables people to take control of their lives through the integration of formal and informal knowledge and by using this integrated knowledge in a transformative way to challenge their assumed realities.

Wardlow, Holly. 2007. "Men's Extramarital Sexuality in Rural Papua New Guinea," *American Journal of Public Health* 97, 6: 1006–14. A consideration of the role of extramarital activity in the spread of HIV/AIDS.

Related Websites

Justice Laws Website: Canadian Multiculturalism
http://laws-lois.justice.gc.ca/eng/acts/C-18.7/

Government of Canada: International Youth Internship Program (IYIP)
http://www.international.gc.ca/world-monde/study_work_travel-etude_travail_voyage/youth_internship-stages_jeunes.aspx?lang=eng

Cultural Survival
www.culturalsurvival.org

Truth and Reconciliation Commission of Canada
http://www.trc.ca/websites/trcinstitution/index.php?p=890

Society for Applied Anthropology
www.sfaa.net

Survival International
www.survivalinternational.org

USAID
www.usaid.gov

Glossary

abiotic Non-living; physical.

achieved statuses Social positions people may attain later in life, often as the result of their own (or other people's) effort.

affinal Related through marriage.

affluence The condition of having more than enough of whatever is required to satisfy consumption needs.

age sets Non-kin social groups composed of young men born within a specified time span.

agency An individual's ability to make choices and to effect change through her or his actions.

alienation The deep separation that individuals experience between their innermost sense of identity and the labour they are forced to perform in order to survive.

anomie A pervasive sense of rootlessness and normlessness.

anthropological perspective An approach to the human condition that is holistic, comparative, and evolutionary.

anthropology The integrated study of human nature, human society, and human history.

applied anthropology The use of information gathered from the other anthropological specialties to solve practical problems within and between cultures.

archaeology The specialty of anthropology interested in what human beings can learn from material remains left behind by earlier human societies.

art A representation that relates to an object, an experience, or some other component of the world and that evokes a felt response.

articulated style A field-independent way of viewing the world that breaks it up into small pieces, which can then be organized into larger chunks.

ascribed statuses Social positions people are assigned at birth.

band A form of social organization that consists of a small group of foragers (usually fewer than 50 people), in which labour is divided according to age and sex, and social relations are highly egalitarian.

bilateral descent A pattern of descent in which a descent group is formed based on connections of relatedness made through both a mother and a father.

binary opposition A pair of opposites used as an organizing principle (e.g., body–soul; yin–yang; male–female).

bioaccumulation An accumulation of a toxic substance in a biological organism over time.

biocultural organisms Organisms whose defining features are co-determined by biological and cultural factors.

biological (or physical) anthropology The specialty of anthropology that looks at humans as biological organisms and tries to discover what characteristics make humans different from and/or similar to other living things.

biological evolution Change (through mutation) in the genetic makeup (the DNA/RNA) of a population that is passed on through the generations.

biomagnification An increase in the concentration of a toxic substance from the bottom to the top of a food chain.

biomedicine Traditionally Western forms of medical knowledge and practice based on biological science.

biopower Power held by a modern government over the bodies of its individual citizens and over the "body" of all its citizens.

biotic Living; biological.

bisexuality Sexual attraction to both males and females.

blended family A family created when previously divorced or widowed people marry, bringing with them children from their previous marriages.

bridewealth The transfer of certain symbolically important goods from the family of the groom to the family of the bride, representing compensation to the wife's lineage for the loss of her labour and for child-bearing capacities.

capitalism An economic system dominated by a supply and demand market designed to create capital and profit.

caste A ranked group within a socially stratified society that is closed, prohibiting individuals from moving from one caste into another.

chiefdom A form of social organization in which the leader (a chief) and the leader's close relatives are set apart from the rest of society and allowed privileged access to wealth, power, and prestige.

clan A descent group formed by members who believe they have a common ancestor, even if they cannot specify the genealogical links.

class A ranked group within a hierarchically stratified society whose membership is defined primarily in terms of wealth, occupation, and/or access to power.

client The party of lower status in a clientage.

clientage Institution linking individuals from upper and lower levels in a stratified society.

cline The gradual intergradation of genetic variation from population to population.

cognition (1) The mental process by which human beings gain knowledge, and (2) the "nexus of relations between the mind at work and the world in which it works" (Lave 1988: 1).

cognitive style Recurring patterns of cognitive activity that characterize an individual's perceptual and intellectual activities.

colonialism The cultural domination of a people by larger, wealthier powers.

coloniality Identified and described as the present legacy of colonialism in the societies of today; manifest as the social discrimination from Eurocentrism yet also from the outlived formal colonialism integrated in succeeding social orders.

colourism A system of social identities negotiated, based on the situation, along a continuum of skin colours between white and black.

communicative competence Mastery of adult rules for socially and culturally appropriate speech.

communitas An unstructured or minimally structured community of equal individuals frequently found in rites of passage.

comparative A characteristic of the anthropological perspective that requires anthropologists to consider similarities and differences in a wide range of human societies before generalizing about human nature, human society, or human history.

conjugal family A family based on marriage; at minimum, a spousal pair and their children.

connotative meaning Additional meanings of a word that derive from the typical contexts in which they are used and rely on personal and cultural associations.

consanguineal Relationships of descent, regardless of whether the child is related by birth, adoption, sperm/ovum donation, or surrogacy, therefore based on "blood" either genetically or socially defined.

consensus An agreement to which all parties collectively give their assent.

consumption Using up material goods necessary for human survival.

core In world-system theory, the nations specializing in banking, finance, and highly skilled industrial production.

cosmopolitanism Being at ease in more than one cultural setting.

creole A complex language with native speakers that has developed over one or more past generations from two or more distinct languages.

cultural anthropology The specialty of anthropology that studies how variation in beliefs and behaviours is shaped by culture and learned by different members of human groups.

cultural ecology The study of the ways in which human beings relate to one another and to their natural environment.

cultural evolution Evolution of the beliefs and behaviours incorporated into human development through the experiences of teaching and learning.

cultural hybridization Cultural mixing that produces a new cultural form.

cultural imperialism The idea that some cultures dominate other cultures and that cultural domination by one culture leads inevitably to the destruction of subordinated cultures and their replacement by the culture of those in power.

cultural pattern A behaviour or idea that members of a specific society repeatedly pass on to one another, across generations, and that is thus recognizable to all members of that society.

cultural persona The presentation of self in compliance with specific cultural models (patterns) of values and meanings.

cultural relativism Approaching the cultures of other peoples with a sympathy such that applying your own beliefs, values, and practices does not become the standard for the basis of understanding.

cultural synaesthesia A culturally shared response to a sense other than the one being stimulated (e.g., hearing a sound and seeing it as a colour).

culture Sets of learned behaviours and ideas that humans acquire as members of a society.

culture area A geographical region in which cultural traditions share similar culture traits.

culture shock The feeling of physical and mental dislocation/discomfort a person experiences when in a new or strange cultural setting.

culture traits Particular features or parts of a cultural tradition, such as a dance, ritual, or style of pottery.

culture-bound syndromes Sicknesses, as well as the therapies to relieve them, that are unique to a particular cultural group.

cyborg anthropology A form of anthropological analysis based on the notion of organism–machine hybrids, or cyborgs; it offers a new model for challenging rigid social, political, and economic boundaries that have been used to separate people by gender, sexuality, class, and "race," boundaries proclaimed by their defenders as "natural."

decolonization The withdrawal of a colonial power from a territory that had been under its control.

defensive research Research that is designed and conducted by individuals outside the affected community without consulting members of the community about their interests or concerns.

denotative meaning The formal meaning(s) of a word, as given in a dictionary.

dependency theory A theory that argues that the success of "independent" capitalist nations has required the failure of "dependent" colonies or nations whose economies have been distorted to serve the needs of dominant capitalist outsiders.

design features of language The characteristics of language that, when taken together, differentiate it from other known animal communication systems.

determinism The philosophical view that one simple force (or a few simple forces) causes (or determines) complex events.

diachronic Considering one entity through its timeline.

dialectic of fieldwork The process of building a bridge of understanding between anthropologist and participant so that each can begin to understand the other.

diaspora Migrant populations with a shared identity who live in a variety of different locales around the world; a form of transborder identity that does not focus on nation-building.

discourse In speech, a meaningful utterance or series of utterances united by a common theme.

disease Forms of biological impairment identified and explained within the discourse of biomedicine.

distribution The allocation of goods and services.

domination Coercive rule.

dowry The transfer of wealth from parents to their child (usually a daughter) at the time of the child's marriage.

dualism The philosophical view that reality consists of two equal and irreducible forces.

ecology The study of the ways in which living species relate to one another and to their natural environment.

econiche The sum total of relations between a species and the plants and animals on which it relies for survival; these relations define those places where a species is "at home."

economic anthropology "The part of the discipline [of anthropology] that debates issues of *human nature* that relate directly to the decisions of daily life and making a living" (Wilk 1996: xv).

economy The culturally specific processes used by members of a society to provide themselves with material resources.

ecotone A transition area between two different ecozones that displays characteristics of both ecozones.

ecozone The particular mixture of plant and animal species occupying any particular region of the earth.

ego The person from whose perspective the kinship associations are being mapped and/or discussed. (Note that the term is capitalized when used to designate real, specific people.)

elementary cognitive processes Mental tasks common to all humans without cognitive impairment.

emotion The product of entanglements connecting bodily arousal and cognitive interpretation.

enculturation The process by which human beings living with one another must learn to come to terms with the ways of thinking and feeling that are considered appropriate in their respective cultures.

endogamy Marriage within a defined social group.

epidemiology The study of the occurrence, spread, management, and prevention of infectious diseases.

essence An unchanging core of features unique to things of the same kind, making them what they are.

essentially negotiable concepts Culturally recognized concepts that evoke a wide range of meanings and whose relevance in any particular context must be negotiated.

ethnic groups Social groups that are distinguished from one another on the basis of ethnicity.

ethnicity A social classification based on a common cultural heritage and selected cultural features, such as language, religion, or dress.

ethnocentrism The opinion that one's own way of life is the most natural, correct, or fully human way of life.

ethnography An anthropologist's recorded description of a particular group of people's way of life.

ethnology The comparative study of two or more cultures.

ethnomedical systems Alternative medical systems based on practices of local sociocultural groups.

ethnopragmatics The study of language use in a specific culture, grounded in an ethnographic approach, with close attention to the relationships among language, communication, and social interaction.

etiology The study of the causes of a disease and/or an illness.

evolutionary A characteristic of the anthropological perspective that requires anthropologists to place their observations about human nature, human society, or human history in a flexible framework that takes into consideration change over time.

exogamy Marriage outside a defined social group.

extended family A family pattern made up of three generations living together: parents, married children, and grandchildren.

extensive agriculture A form of cultivation that depends on slash-and-burn (swidden) techniques, rainwater, human muscle power, and a few simple tools, such as digging sticks, hoes, and/or machetes.

fact A widely accepted observation that becomes intelligible only when it is interpreted and placed in a context of meaning.

family At minimum, a woman or a man and her or his dependent children.

family of choice A family created over time by new kin ties as friends and lovers demonstrate their genuine commitment to one another.

fieldwork An extended period of close involvement with the people in whose way of life anthropologists are interested, during which anthropologists ordinarily collect most of their data.

flexible citizenship Strategies employed by individuals who regularly move across state boundaries in order to circumvent and benefit from different nation-state regimes.

folk illness A culture-bound illness; a set of symptoms that are grouped together under a single label only within a particular culture.

food collectors People who gather wild plant materials, fish, and/or hunt for food.

food producers People who depend on domesticated plants and/or animals for food.

framing An understood boundary that marks certain behaviours as "play" or as "ordinary life."

free agency The freedom of self-contained individuals to pursue their own interests above everything else and to challenge one another for dominance.

friendship The relatively unofficial bonds that people construct with one another that tend to be personal, affective, and a matter of choice.

functional cognitive systems Culturally linked sets of cognitive processes that guide perception, conception, reason, and emotion.

gay An affirmative and empowering self-designation for individuals medically classified as homosexual, which became widespread over the course of the twentieth century.

gender The culturally constructed beliefs and behaviours considered appropriate for each sex.

gender roles Sets of behaviours that are commonly perceived as masculine or feminine within a specific culture.

global style A field-dependent way of viewing the world that first sees it as a bundle of relationships and only later sees the smaller pieces involved in these relationships.

globalization Reshaping of local conditions by powerful global forces on an ever-intensifying scale.

governmentality The art of governing appropriate to promoting the welfare of populations within a state.

grammar A set of rules that describe the patterns of linguistic usage observed by members of a particular speech community.

habitus Everyday, routine social activity rooted in habitual behaviour.

health A person's general social, psychological, and physical condition.

hegemony A system of leadership in which rulers persuade subordinates to accept the ideology of the dominant group by offering mutual accommodations that nevertheless preserve the rulers' privileged position.

heteroglossia The coexistence of multiple varieties of a specific language.

heteronormativity An ideology that promotes heterosexuality as the social ideal, supported by the cultural definition of "appropriate" behaviour based on culturally defined categories of "male" and "female," "masculine" and "feminine."

historical particularism The study of cultures in their own historical contexts.

holism A perspective on the human condition that assumes that mind and body, individual and society, and individual and environment interpenetrate and even define one another.

homosexuality The heteronormative opposite of heterosexuality; that is sexual relations involving two men or two women (i.e., same-sex sexuality).

human agency Human beings' ability to exercise at least some control over their lives.

human rights A set of rights that should be accorded to all human beings everywhere in the world.

humanism ". . . A philosophical and ethical stance that emphasizes the value and agency of human beings, individually and collectively, and generally prefers critical thinking and evidence (rationalism and empiricism) over acceptance of dogma or superstition" (Wikipedia).

idealism The philosophical view that pure, incorruptible ideas—or the mind that produces such ideas—constitute the essence of human nature.

ideology Those products of consciousness—such as morality, religion, and metaphysics—that purport to explain to people who they are and to justify the kinds of lives they lead.

illness A suffering person's own understanding of his or her distress.

imperialism A system in which one country controls other, less powerful territories through colonization, often augmented by military force.

indigenization The process of bringing something foreign under the control of local people or of adapting something foreign to serve local purposes.

informants People in a particular culture who work with anthropologists and provide them with insights about local ways of life.

institutions Stable and enduring cultural practices that organize social life.

intensive agriculture A form of cultivation that employs plows, draft animals, irrigation, and fertilizer to bring a large amount of land under cultivation at one time.

intersubjective meaning Meaning rooted in the symbolic systems of a culture and shared by participants in that culture.

jāti A localized, named, endogamous group.

joint family A family pattern made up of brothers and their wives (or sisters and their husbands) along with their children and sometimes their parents living together.

key metaphors Symbolic representations that are widely understood within a culture and central to that culture's world view.

kinship Social relationships that are prototypically derived from the universal human experiences of mating, birth, and nurturance.

labour The activity linking human social groups to the material world around them.

language The system of symbols we use to encode our experiences of the world and of one another.

language ideology A system of beliefs about how language features relate to social features and what they reveal about the people who use them.

language revitalization Attempts by linguists and activists to preserve or revive languages with few native speakers that appear to be on the verge of extinction.

legal citizenship The rights and obligations of citizenship granted by the laws of a state.

lesbian A term used around the turn of the twentieth century to describe female same-sex sexuality; based on the name of the Greek island of Lesbos, the home of the female poet Sappho, who was reputed to love women rather than men.

liminal period The ambiguous transitional state in a rite of passage in which the person or persons undergoing the ritual are outside their ordinary social positions.

lineage A descent group composed of blood relatives who believe they can trace their descent from known ancestors.

linguistic anthropology The specialty of anthropology concerned with the study of human languages.

linguistic competence Mastery of adult grammar.

linguistic relativity principle The assertion that language has the power to shape the way people see the world.

linguistics The scientific study of language.

long-distance nationalists Members of a diaspora who begin to organize in support of nationalist struggles in their homeland or to agitate for a state of their own.

magic A set of beliefs and practices designed to control the visible or invisible world for specific purposes.

mana From Austronesian languages; it denotes a supernatural power or force that can be embodied in a person or an object (e.g., "May the force be with you").

managed care A system of care, tied to the market-based delivery of medicine, particularly in the US, in which a patient's choice of treatment and of practitioner is directed by an intermediary organization that aims to provide the most cost-effective services available while generating profits for its members.

market exchange A mode of exchange in which the exchange of goods (trade) is calculated in terms of a multi-purpose medium of exchange and standard of value (money) and carried on by means of a supply–demand–price mechanism (the market).

marriage An institution that prototypically (1) involves a man and a woman, (2) transforms the status of the participants, (3) carries implications about sexual access, (4) gives offspring a position in society, and (5) establishes connections between the kin of a husband and the kin of a wife.

material culture Objects created or shaped by human beings and given meaning by cultural practices.

material world The physical world in all its manifestations. We experience this world through our senses of sight, hearing, smell, taste, touch, and movement.

materialism The philosophical view that the activities of our physical bodies in the material world constitute the essence of human nature.

means of production The tools, skills, organization, and knowledge used to extract energy from nature.

mechanized industrial agriculture Large-scale farming that is highly dependent on industrial methods of technology and production.

medical anthropology An area of anthropological inquiry that focuses on issues of well-being, health, illness, and disease as they are situated in their wider cultural contexts.

metacommunication Communicating about the process of communication.

metalanguage Language used to talk about language.

metanarrative A grand-scale story or theme that members of a given culture recognize and that often drives ideas and actions within that culture.

metaphor A form of thought and language that asserts a meaningful link between two expressions from different semantic domains.

metaphorical entailments All the attributes of a metaphorical predicate that relate it to the metaphorical subject.

metaphorical predicate The second part of a metaphor, which suggests the familiar domain of experience that may clarify the metaphorical subject.

metaphorical subject The first part of a metaphor, which indicates the domain of experience that needs to be clarified.

metonymy The culturally defined relationship of the parts of a semantic domain to the domain as a whole and of the whole to its parts.

mode of production "A specific, historically occurring set of social relations through which labour is deployed to wrest energy from nature by means of tools, skills, organization, and knowledge" (Wolf 1982: 75)

modernization theory A theory that argues that the social change occurring in non-Western societies under colonial rule was a necessary and inevitable prelude to higher levels of social development that had been reached by the more "modern" nations.

modes of exchange Patterns according to which distribution takes place: reciprocity, redistribution, and market exchange.

monogamy A marriage pattern in which a person may be married to only one person at a time.

morphemes The shortest meaning-bearing units in any language (e.g., /bɔɪ/ refers to a young male).

morphology The study of the smallest units of meaning (morphemes) in a language.

motivation The inner impulse to set (or accept) and accomplish goals.

multiculturalism A situation in which people of various cultural backgrounds live in close proximity to one another.

multi-sited ethnography A method of anthropological research focused on a specific topic followed through different field situations. These field situations can be within one culture but socially distinct (social class and caste, for example) or in different geographical locations (different cultures). Data collection relies on detailed methods of survey (objective) and interviews (subjective).

myth A representative story that embodies a culture's assumptions about the way that society, or the world in general, must operate.

nation A group of people believed to share the same history, culture, language, and even physical substance.

nationalism The attempt made by government officials to instill a sense of nationality into the citizens of a state.

nationality A sense of identification with and loyalty to a nation-state; membership, defined by citizenship, in a geopolitical sovereign state.

nation-state An ideal political unit in which national identity and political territory coincide.

native speaker A person who has spoken a particular language since early childhood.

nativism An attempt to return to traditional customs.

naturalizing discourses The deliberate representation of particular identities (e.g., caste, class, race, ethnicity, and nationality) as if they were a result of biology or nature rather than history or culture, making them appear eternal and unchanging.

neoclassical economic theory A formal attempt to explain the workings of capitalist enterprise, with particular attention to distribution.

neocolonialism The persistence of profound social and economic ties linking former colonial territories to their former colonial rulers despite political sovereignty.

neoliberalism A political perspective that promotes individual freedom, open markets, and free trade while opposing strong state involvement in personal and economic affairs.

non-conjugal family A woman (or, less commonly, a man) and her (or his) children, with or without a second parent.

norms Rules (usually unwritten) for behaviour assumed to be typical within a specific social or cultural group.

nuclear family A family made up of two generations: parents and their unmarried children.

objectification The intentional construction of a collective public identity; the process that produces what we commonly think of as ethnicity.

objective knowledge Knowledge about reality that is absolute and true for all people, in all times and places.

oracles Invisible forces to which people address questions and whose responses they believe to be truthful.

organic metaphor A key metaphor whose predicate lies in the image of a living body.

orthodoxy "Correct doctrine"; the prohibition of deviation from certain generally accepted rules or beliefs.

orthopraxy "Correct practice"; the prohibition of deviation from certain generally accepted forms of behaviour.

paleoanthropology The study of the fossilized remains of human beings' earliest ancestors.

participant-observation The method anthropologists use to gather information by living and working with the people whose culture they are studying while participating in their lives as much as possible.

patron The party of higher status in a clientage.

perception The act of becoming aware of the world through what we have termed the five traditional senses: taste, touch, sight, hearing, smell. To this could be added the sensing of movement, balance, gravity, temperature, and pain.

periphery In world-system theory, those exploited former colonies that supply the core with inexpensive food, goods, and raw materials.

personality The relative integration of an individual's perceptions, motives, cognitions, and behaviour within a sociocultural matrix.

persuasion Power based on verbal argument.

phenomenology The study of first-person experience of consciousness in the material world, which is based on the conscious (intentional) framing of the meaning or content of the observed. In different conditions or situations, people come to recognize their responses to different conditions of intentionality. These include "embodiment, bodily skills, cultural context, language and other social practices, social background, and contextual aspects of intentional activities." (https://plato.stanford.edu/entries/phenomenology/#WhatPhen).

phenotype Observable, measurable outward characteristics of an organism.

phonemes Basic units of distinct sound that are characteristic of a language and that come together to form words (e.g., /b/ and /ɔɪ/ in boy).

phonology The study of the sounds (phones and phonemes) of a language.

pidgin A fairly simple language with no native speakers that develops in a single generation between members of communities that possess distinct native languages.

placebo effect An effect produced in response to an individual's belief that a treatment will have a desired effect, despite evidence that the treatment has no medicinal properties.

play A framing (or orienting) context that (1) is consciously adopted by the players; (2) is pleasurable; and (3) alludes to the non-play world by transforming the objects, roles, actions, and relations of ends and means characteristic of the non-play world.

political anthropology The study of social and political power in human society.

political economy A social structure that is organized around material (economic) interests, in which these interests are protected and enhanced through the use of power (politics).

political power Social power held by a group that is in a position to affect the lives of many people.

polygamy A marriage pattern in which a person may be married to more than one person at a time.

positionality A person's uniquely situated social position, which reflects his or her gender, nationality, political views, previous experiences, and so on. See *situated knowledge*.

positive research Research that is designed with fair consideration of the interests and concerns of members of the affected community and conducted with consideration of cultural contexts within the community.

positivism The view that there is a single reality "out there" that can be detected through the senses and that there is a single, appropriate scientific method for investigating that reality.

post-national ethos An attitude toward the world in which people submit to the regulations of the capitalist market while trying to evade the regulations of nation-states.

power Transformative capacity; the ability to transform a given situation.

pragmatics The study of language in the context of its use.

priest A religious practitioner skilled in the practice of religious rituals, which he or she carries out for the benefit of the group.

primatology The study of non-human primates, the closest living relatives of human beings.

production The transformation of nature's raw materials into a form suitable for human use.

prototypes Examples of a typical instance, element, relation, or experience within a culture.

queer A self-identification claimed by some persons whose gender identities or sexual practices fall outside the range defined by "the heterosexual–homosexual continuum."

race A broad human population category that allegedly corresponds to distinct, heritable sets of biological attributes and often conflates geographic ancestry and physical type.

racialism Belief in the existence of biologically distinct races.

racism The systemic oppression of members of one or more socially defined "races" by members of another socially defined "race" that is justified within the ruling society by the rulers' faulty belief in their own biological superiority.

realized niche The portion of the habitable world that a group of people is forced to utilize and to which it becomes highly adapted.

reasoning style Culture- and context-dependent ways in which we appraise, come to understand, and think about a cognitive task.

reciprocity A mode of exchange in which individuals exchange goods and/or services (1) under the assumption that the exchanges will eventually balance out, (2) with the expectation of immediate balance, or (3) in the hope that at least one party will get something for nothing.

redistribution A mode of exchange in which a centralized social organization receives contributions from all members of the group and redistributes them in a way that provides for every member.

reflexivity Critically thinking about the way one thinks; reflecting on one's own experience.

reification A form of negative racial or ethnic absolutism that encourages the violent elimination of targeted groups and is central to the practice of racism.

relatedness The socially recognized ties that connect people in a variety of ways.

relations of production The social relations linking the people who use a given means of production within a particular mode of production.

religion "Ideas and practices that postulate reality beyond that which is immediately available to the senses" (Bowen 2002: 5).

resistance The power to refuse being forced against one's will to conform to someone else's wishes.

revitalization A conscious, deliberate, and organized attempt by some members of a society to create a more satisfying culture in a time of crisis.

rite of passage A ritual that serves to mark the movement and transformation of an individual from one social position to another.

ritual A repetitive social practice set off from everyday routine and composed of a sequence of symbolic activities that adhere to a culturally defined ritual schema and are closely connected to a specific set of ideas significant to the culture.

scarcity A condition under which it is assumed that resources (e.g., money) will never be plentiful enough for people to obtain all the goods or services they desire.

schemas Patterned, repetitive experiences that are shared and easily understood by members of a particular culture.

science studies Research that explores the interconnections among the sociocultural, political, economic, and historic conditions that make scientific research both possible and successful.

secret societies Non-kin social groups that initiate young men or women into social adulthood and reveal "secret" knowledge to initiated members.

secularism The separation of religion and state.

segmentary opposition An approach to dispute resolution and social organization in which groups beyond the most basic emerge only in opposition to other groups on the same hierarchical level.

self The result of the process of socialization and enculturation for an individual.

semantics The study of meaning.

semi-periphery In world-system theory, states that have played peripheral roles in the past but that now have sufficient industrial capacity and other resources to possibly achieve core status in the future.

sex The conventional biological distinction between male and female based on morphological sex (observable sex characteristics), gonadal sex (ovaries in females; testes in males), and chromosomal sex (XX or XY chromosomes).

sexuality An individual's sense of his or her own sexual desires, orientation, and preferences.

shaman A part-time religious practitioner who is believed to have the power through altered states of consciousness to travel to or contact supernatural forces directly on behalf of individuals or groups. Note that this term is not used specifically in the context of traditional America but is found in other cultures where such a religio-medical practitioner is found.

sickness Classifications of physical, mental, and emotional distress recognized by members of a particular cultural community.

situated knowledge Knowledge that is set within or specific to a precise context or situation.

small-scale society A community of several dozen to several hundred people usually held together by family (kinship) ties and often engaged in traditional subsistence activities.

social forms Culturally conforming collective ways of interacting with our surroundings and the people we encounter; these forms of interaction, often taken for granted, are encoded forms of behaviour that are enforced by the group.

social organization The patterning of human interdependence in a given society through the actions and decisions of its members.

social power The ability to transform a situation that affects an entire social group.

social race An achieved status with a racial label in a system of stratification that is composed of open, class-like categories to which racial labels are assigned.

social structure The enduring aspects of the social forms in a society, including its political and kinship systems.

social trauma Individual and group experience of negative physical, mental, and emotional effects resulting from powerfully disturbing occurrences caused by forces and agents external to the person or group.

socialization The process by which human beings learn to become members of a group, both by interacting appropriately with others and by coping with the behavioural rules established by the group.

societal metaphor A key metaphor whose predicate lies in the social order.

sodalities Non-kin social groups that may be organized on the basis of age, sex, economic role, and/or personal interest.

species A reproductive community of populations (reproductively isolated from others) that occupies a specific niche in nature.

sport An aggressively competitive, often physically exertive activity governed by game-like rules that are ritually patterned and agreed upon by all participants.

state A stratified society, controlled by a formal government, that possesses a territory that is defended from outside enemies with an army and from internal disorder with police.

strategic essentialism The use of essentialist rhetoric as a conscious political strategy to create a temporary solidarity to facilitate a specific social action.

stratified societies Societies in which there is a permanent hierarchy that accords some members privileged access to wealth, power, and prestige.

structural violence Violence that results from the way that political and economic forces structure risk for various forms of suffering within a population.

structural-functional theory A position that explores how particular social forms function from day-to-day in order to reproduce the traditional structure of the society.

structured interviews A method for gathering information whereby an anthropologist (or another researcher) asks a set of predetermined questions and records participants' responses.

subject position An individual's unique position in the world, which is shaped by social variables, such as class, gender, and socioeconomic status.

subjective meaning Meaning that seems true to a particular person, based on his or her personal values, beliefs, opinions, and assumptions.

subjectivity An individual's awareness of his or her own agency and position as a subject.

subsistence strategies The patterns of production, distribution, and consumption that members of a society use to meet their basic material survival needs.

substantive citizenship The actions people take, regardless of their legal citizenship status, to assert their membership in a state and to bring about political changes that will improve their lives.

suffering The forms of physical, mental, or emotional distress experienced by individuals who may or may not subscribe to biomedical understandings of disease.

syllogism A series of three statements in which the final statement (the conclusion) must follow logically from the first two statements (the premises).

syllogistic reasoning A form of reasoning based on the syllogism.

symbol Something that stands for something else.

synchronic Considering a number of entities in the same timeframe.

syncretism The synthesis of old religious practices (or an old way of life) with new religious practices (or a new way of life), introduced from outside, often by force.

syntax The study of sentence structure.

taxonomies Hierarchical systems that sort groups of things that share at least one quality (e.g., dogs) into subgroups that share a greater number of qualities (e.g., poodles, collies, boxers).

technological metaphor A key metaphor whose predicate lies in objects made by human beings.

thinking The active cognitive process of "going beyond the information given" (Bruner 1957).

traditional knowledge Knowledge that is culturally held and passed on from generation to generation.

transborder citizenry A group made up of citizens of a country who continue to live in the homeland plus the people who have emigrated from the country and their descendants, regardless of their current citizenship.

transborder state A state in which it is claimed that those people who left the country and their descendants remain part of their ancestral state, even if they are citizens of another state.

transculturation Cultural change resulting from contact between different cultures.

transformation-representation The process in which experience is transformed as it is represented symbolically in a different medium.

transformist hegemony A nationalist program to define nationality in a way that preserves the cultural domination of the ruling group while including enough cultural features from subordinated groups to ensure their loyalty.

transgender A term proposed in the 1960s by medical researchers to classify individuals who, in one way or another, seemed dissatisfied with the sex and gender assignments they had received at birth.

transnational nation-states Nation-states in which the relationships between citizens and their states extend to wherever citizens reside.

tribe A form of social organization generally larger than a band, in which members usually farm or herd for a living; social relations are relatively egalitarian, although there may be a chief who speaks for the group.

typology A classification system based on systematic organization into types on the basis of shared qualities.

unfree labour An all-encompassing term for the formalized coercion of men, women, and children (through need or violence) to provide their labour. Such labour can range from migrant farm work to sex slavery to the use of children as soldiers.

unilineal cultural evolutionism A nineteenth-century theory that proposed a series of stages through which all societies must go (or had gone) in order to reach civilization.

unilineal descent A pattern of descent in which a descent group is formed based on connections of relatedness made through *either* a father (patrilineal descent) *or* a mother (matrilineal descent).

values Specific culturally defined principles of behaviour.

varna Traditional social ranks that divide Indian society into four functional subdivisions: priests, nobility (rulers and warriors), commoners (farmers and merchants), and labourers or servants.

visual anthropology The anthropological contribution to visual culture of ethnographic photography, film, and digital media representations of cultural data.

visuality The ways that individuals from different societies learn to interpret what they see and to construct mental pictures using the visual practices that their own cultural system favours.

vocabulary The words used in a particular language or by members of a particular speech community.

well-being A culturally defined state (or role) of general physical and mental comfort and good health; a lack of illness.

"white man's burden" Europeans' sense that it was their duty to colonize, rule, and "civilize" all peoples they viewed as "savage."

witchcraft The practice of magic, whether intentional or not.

world view An encompassing picture of reality created by members of a society.

world-system theory A theory that argues that capitalism incorporates various regions and peoples into a world system whose parts are linked economically but not politically.

zone of proximal development (ZPD) The difference between what individuals can achieve on their own and what they can achieve under the guidance of more experienced individuals.

References

Chapter 1

Abu-Lughod, Lila. 1991. "Writing against Culture," in *Recapturing Anthropology*, ed. Richard Fox (Santa Fe, NM: SAR), 137–62.

Anderson, Benedict R. O'G. 1991. *Imagined Communities: Reflections on the Origin and Spread of Nationalism* (London; New York: Verso).

Baer, Hans, Merrill Singer, and Ida Susser. 2003. *Medical Anthropology and the World System*, 4th edn (Westport, CT: Praeger).

Benedict, Ruth. 1934. *Patterns of Culture* (New York: Houghton Mifflin).

Bernhardt, Barbara, Jessica Ball, and Jeff Deby. 2007. "Cross-cultural Interaction and Children's Speech Acquisition," in *The International Guide to Speech Acquisition*, ed. S. McLeod (Clifton Park, NY: Delmar).

Bierschenk, Thomas. 2014. "From the Anthropology of Development to the Anthropology of Global Social Engineering," *Zeitschrift für Ethnologie*, Bd. 139, Special Issue: Current Debates in Anthropology: 73–97.

Chrisjohn, Roland, Sherri Young, and Michael Maraun. 1997. *The Circle Game: Shadows and Substance in the Indian Residential School Experience in Canada* (Penticton: Theytus Books Limited).

Darnell, Regna. 2001. *Invisible Genealogies: A History of Americanist Anthropology* (Lincoln: University of Nebraska Press).

Deacon, Terrence W. 1997. *The Symbolic Species: The Co-evolution of Language and the Brain* (New York: Norton).

Dods, Roberta Robin. 2004. "Knowing Ways/Ways of Knowing: Reconciling Science and Tradition," *World Archaeology* 36, 4: 547–57.

Duchêne, Alexandre, and Monica Heller, eds. 2012. *Language in Late Capitalism: Pride and Profit* (New York: Routledge).

Ferguson, Nelson. 2011. "From Coal Pits to Tar Sands: Labour Migration between an Atlantic Canadian Region and the Athabasca Oil Sands," *Just Labour: Canadian Journal of Work and Society* 17: 106–18.

Geertz, Clifford. 1973. *The Interpretation of Cultures* (New York: Basic Books).

Goodale, Mark. 2006. "Ethical Theory as Social Practice," *American Anthropologist* 108, 1: 25–37.

Goodwin-Hawkins, Bryonny. 2012. "Weaving Time in the Textile Valley," *Etnofoor* 24, 1: 13–28.

Government of Canada, Social Development Canada. 2006. "Social Participation—Sense of Belonging/Indicators of Well-Being in Canada," 12 September.

Greenwood, Davydd, and William Stini. 1977. *Nature, Culture, and Human History* (New York: Harper and Row).

Hedican, Edward J. 2008. *Applied Anthropology in Canada: Understanding Aboriginal Issues*, 2nd edn (Toronto: University of Toronto Press).

Heller, Monica, and Lindsay Bell. 2012. "Frontiers and Frenchness: Pride and Profit in the Production of Canada," in *Language in Late Capitalism: Pride and Profit*, ed. Alexandre Duchêne and Monica Heller (New York: Routledge).

Herskovits, Melville. 1973. *Cultural Relativism*, ed. Frances Herskovits (New York: Vintage).

Herzfeld, Michael. 2001. *Anthropology: Theoretical Practice in Culture and Society* (Malden, MA: Blackwell Publishers).

Hinton, Alexander Laban. 2002. "The Dark Side of Modernity: Toward an Anthropology of Genocide," in *Annihilating Difference: The Anthropology of Genocide*, ed. Alexander Laban Hinton (Berkeley: University of California Press), 1–40.

Hobsbawm, Eric, and Terence Ranger, eds. 1992. *The Invention of Tradition* (Cambridge: Cambridge University Press).

Ignace, Ron, George Speck, and Renee Taylor. 1993. "Some Native Perspectives on Anthropology and Public Policy," in *Anthropology, Public Policy and Native Peoples in Canada*, ed. Noel Dyck and James B. Walram (Montreal and Kingston: McGill-Queen's University Press), 166–91.

Low, Setha M., and Denise Lawrence-Zúñiga, eds. 2003. *The Anthropology of Space and Place: Locating Culture*, 1st edn (Malden, MA: Wiley-Blackwell).

Lyotard, Jean-François 1987. "The Postmodern Condition," in *After Philosophy: End or Transformation?* ed. K. Baynes, J. Bohman, and T. McCarthy (Cambridge: MIT Press), 73–94.

Marks, Jonathan. 1995. *Human Biodiversity* (New York: Aldine).

Marx, Karl. 1963 [1852]. *The 18th Brumaire of Louis Bonaparte* (New York: International Publishers).

Miller, Daniel. 2010. *Stuff* (Cambridge: Polity Press).

Mills, Anthony J. 2013. "Dakhleh Oasis Project," Monash University Arts, available at http://artsonline.monash.edu.au/ ancient-cultures/excavations-in-dakhleh-oasis-egypt

Ortner, Sherry, ed. 1999. *The Fate of "Culture": Geertz and Beyond* (Berkeley: University of California Press).

Potts, Richard. 1996. *Humanity's Descent* (New York: Morrow).

Rodriguez, Jeanette, and Ted Fortier. 2009. *Cultural Memory: Resistance, Faith, and Identity* (Austin: University of Texas Press).

Rosaldo, Renato. 2008. "Of Headhunters and Soldiers: Separating Cultural and Ethical Relativism," *Markkula Center for Applied Ethics*, available at www.scu.edu/ethics/publications/iie/v1n1/relativism.html

Rosen, David M. 2007. "Child Soldiers, International Humanitarian Law, and the Globalization of Childhood," *American Anthropologist* 109, 2: 296–306.

Rylko-Bauer, Barbara, Merrill Singer, and John Van Willigen. 2006. "Reclaiming Applied Anthropology: Its Past, Present, and Future," *American Anthropologist* 108, 1: 178–90.

Sabloff, Jeremy A. 2008. *Archaeology Matters: Action Archaeology in the Modern World* (Walnut Creek, CA: Left Coast Press, Inc.).

Singer, Merrill. 1998. "The Development of Critical Medical Anthropology: Implications for Biological Anthropology," in *Building a New Biocultural Synthesis*, ed. Alan H. Goodman and Thomas L. Leatherman (Ann Arbor: University of Michigan Press), 93–123.

Smith, Gavin A., and R. Brooke Thomas. 1998. "What Could Be: Biocultural Anthropology for the Next Generation," in *Building a New Biocultural Synthesis*, ed. Alan H. Goodman and Thomas L. Leatherman (Ann Arbor: University of Michigan Press), 451–73.

Tylor, Edward B. 1958 [1871]. *Primitive Culture* (New York: Harper and Row).

Chapter 2

AAA (American Anthropological Association). 2009. *Code of Ethics of the American Anthropological Association*, available at www.aaanet.org/issues/policy-advocacy/upload/AAA-Ethics-Code-2009.pdf

Agar, Michael. 1996. *The Professional Stranger: An Informal Introduction to Ethnography*, 2nd edn (San Diego: Academic Press).

Allen, Timothy F.H., and Thomas W. Hoekstra. 1991. "Role of Heterogeneity in Scaling of Ecological Systems under Analysis," *Ecological Heterogeneity (Ecological Studies)*, vol. 86, ed. Jurek. Kolasa and Steward. Pickett (New York: Springer Verlag), 47–68.

Appadurai, Arjun. 2002. "Grassroots Globalization and the Research Imagination," in *The Anthropology of Politics*, ed. Joan Vincent (Malden, MA: Blackwell), 271–84.

Barber, Benjamin R. 1992. "Jihad vs. McWorld," *Atlantic Monthly* 269, 3: 53–65, available at www.theatlantic.com/magazine/archive/1992/03/jihad-vs-mcworld/303882

Bernard, H. Russell. 2011. *Research Methods in Anthropology*, 5th edn (Lanham, MD: AltaMira Press).

Boellstorff, Tom. 2008. *Coming of Age in Second Life. An Anthropologist Explores the Virtually Human* (Princeton, NJ: Princeton University Press).

Bradburd, Daniel. 1998. *Being There: The Necessity of Fieldwork* (Washington, DC: Smithsonian Institution Press).

Briggs, Charles L. 2007. "Anthropology, Inter-viewing, and Communicability in Contemporary Society," *Current Anthropology* 48, 4: 551–80.

Briggs, Jean. 1980. "Kapluna Daughter: Adopted by the Eskimo," in *Conformity and Conflict: Readings in Cultural Anthropology*, 4th edn, ed. James Spradley and David McCurdy (Glenview, IL: Scott Foresman), 44–62.

Carrithers, Michael. 2005. "Anthropology as a Moral Science of Possibilities," *Current Anthropology* 46, 3: 433–56.

CIHR, NSERC, SSHRC (Canadian Institutes of Health Research, Natural Sciences and Engineering Research Council of Canada, Social Sciences and Humanities Research Council of Canada). 2010. *Tri-Council Policy Statement: Ethical Conduct for Research Involving Humans*, available at www.pre.ethics.gc.ca/pdf/eng/tcps2/TCPS_2_FINAL_Web.pdf

Côté, James E. 2000. "The Mead–Freeman Controversy in Review," *Journal of Youth and Adolescence* 29, 5: 525–38.

Cruikshank, Julie. 2006. *Do Glaciers Listen? Local Knowledge, Colonial Encounters, and Social Imagination* (Vancouver: UBC Press).

Darnell, Regna. 2009. "Anthropological Approaches to Human Nature, Cultural Relativism, and Ethnocentrism," *Anthropologica* 51: 187–94.

Desjarlais, Robert, and C. Jason Throop. 2011. "Phenomenological Approaches in Anthropology," *Annual Review of Anthropology* 40: 87–102.

DeWalt, Kathleen, and Billie DeWalt. 2011. *Participant Observation*, 2nd edn (Walnut Creek, CA: AltaMira Press).

Dods, Roberta Robin. 2004. "Knowing Ways/Ways of Knowing: Reconciling Science and Tradition," *World Archaeology* 36, 4: 547–57.

Evans, Mike. 2004. "Ethics, Anonymity, and Authorship in Community Centred Research, or Anonymity and the Island Cache," *Pimatisiwin: A Journal of Aboriginal and Indigenous Community Health* 2, 1: 60–75.

Freeman, Derek. 1983. *Margaret Mead and Samoa: The Making and Unmaking of an Anthropological Myth* (Cambridge: Harvard University Press).

Gravel, Pierre Bettez. (1976). "'And Sometimes All for Nought' or Reflections of an Anthropologist upon His Return from the Field," *Western Canadian Journal of Anthropology* 6, 4: 103–23.

Greenwood, Davydd, and William Stini. 1977. *Nature, Culture, and Human History* (New York: Harper and Row).

Gupta, Akhil, and James Ferguson. 1997. "Discipline and Practice: 'The Field' as Site, Method, and Location in Anthropology," in *Anthropological Locations: Boundaries and Grounds of a Field Science*, ed. Akhil Gupta and James Ferguson (Berkeley: University of California Press), 1–46.

Haraway, Donna. 1991. *Simians, Cyborgs, and Women: The Reinvention of Nature* (New York: Routledge).

Hastrup, Kirsten, and Peter Elsass. 1990. "Anthropological Advocacy: A Contradiction in Terms?" *Current Anthropology* 31, 3: 301–11.

Hess, David J. 1997. *Science Studies: An Advanced Introduction* (New York: New York University Press).

Howell, Nancy. 1988. "Health and Safety in the Fieldwork of North American Anthropologists," *Current Anthropology* 29, 5: 780–7.

Knorr Cetina, Karin. 2000. *Epistemic Cultures* (Cambridge, MA: Harvard University Press).

Kumar, Nita. 1992. *Friends, Brothers, and Informants: Fieldwork Memoirs of Banaras* (Berkeley: University of California Press).

Liebersohn, Harry. 1994. "Discovering Indigenous Nobility: Tocqueville, Chamisso, and Romantic Travel Writing," *American Historical Review* 99, 3: 746–66.

Marcus, George. 1995. "Ethnography in/of the World System: The Emergence of Multi-sited Ethnography," *Annual Review of Anthropology* 24: 95–117.

Matthiasson, John S. 1992. "The Emergence of a New Political Paradigm," *Living on the Land: Change Among the Inuit of Northern Baffin Island* (Peterborough, ON: Broadview Press).

Nayar, Mahima. 2012. "Identifying Informants or Labeling: Methodological Concerns," *Indian Anthropologist*, 42, 1: 27–38.

Pack, Sam. 2006. "How They See Me vs How I See Them: The Ethnographic Self and the Personal Self," *Anthropological Quarterly* 79, 1: 105–122.

Rabinow, Paul. 1977. *Reflections on Fieldwork in Morocco* (Berkeley: University of California Press).

Salzman, Philip Carl. 2002. "On Reflexivity," *American Anthropologist* 104, 3: 805–13.

Seeger, Anthony. 2004. *Why Suyá Sing: A Musical Ethnography of an Amazonian People* (Urbana, IL: University of Illinois Press).

Shankman, Paul. 2009. *The Trashing of Margaret Mead: Anatomy of an Anthropological Controversy* (Madison: University of Wisconsin Press).

Smith, Wilfred Cantwell. 1982. *Towards a World Theology* (Philadelphia: Westminster).

Stoller, Paul. 2007. "Ethnography/Memoir/Imagination/Story," *Anthropology and Humanism* 32, 2: 178–91.

Taussig, Michael. 2011. *I Swear I Saw This: Drawings in Fieldwork Notebooks, Namely My Own* (Chicago: The University of Chicago Press).

Theodossopoulos, Dimitrios. 2013. "Introduction: Laying Claim to Authenticity: Five Anthropological Dilemmas," *Anthropological Quarterly* 86, 2: 337–60.

Turgeon, Laurier, and Madeleine Pastinelli. 2002. "'Eat the World': Postcolonial Encounters in Quebec City's Ethnic Restaurants," *Journal of American Folklore* 115, 456: 247–68.

Undie, Chi-Chi. 2007. "My Father's Daughter: Becoming a 'Real' Anthropologist among the Ubang of Southeast Nigeria," *Dialectical Anthropology* 31: 293–305.

Valentine, Bettylou. 1978. *Hustling and Other Hard Work: Life Styles in the Ghetto* (New York: Free Press).

Wallerstein, Immanuel. 1974. *The Modern World System* (New York: Academic Press).

Wardle, Huon, and Paloma Gay y Blasco. 2011. "Ethnography and An Ethnography in the Human Conversation," *Anthropologica* 53, 1: 117–27.

Weiner, Annette. 1976. *Women of Value, Men of Renown* (Austin: University of Texas Press).

———. 1988. *The Trobrianders of Papua New Guinea* (New York: Holt, Rinehart, and Winston).

Wolcott, Harry F. 1999. *Ethnography: A Way of Seeing* (Walnut Creek, CA: AltaMira Press).

Wolf, Eric. 1982. *Europe and the People without History* (Berkeley: University of California Press).

Chapter 3

Appadurai, Arjun. 1990. "Disjuncture and Difference in the Global Cultural Economy," in *Global Culture*, ed. Mike Featherstone (London: Sage), 295–310.

Asad, Talal. 2002. "From the History of Colonial Anthropology to the Anthropology of Western Hegemony," in *The Anthropology of Politics*, ed. Joan Vincent (Malden, MA: Blackwell), 133–42.

Bailey, A.G. 1969 [1937]. *The Conflict of European and Eastern Algonquian Cultures, 1504–1700*, 2nd edn (Toronto: University of Toronto Press).

Berger, Carl. 1990. "Wilson, Sir Daniel," in *Dictionary of Canadian Biography*, vol. 12, available at www.biographi.ca/en/bio/wilson_daniel_12E.html

———. 1970. "The Emergence of Hunting Territories among the Northern Ojibwa," *Ethnology* (Jan.) 9, 1: 1–15.

———. 1973. "Ojibwa Cannibalism," paper presented at the IX International Congress of Anthropological and Ethnological Sciences (Chicago).

Bishop, Charles A. 1981. "Northeastern Indian Concepts of Conservation and the Fur Trade: A Critique of Calvin Martin's Thesis," in *Indians, Animals, and the Fur Trade*, ed. S. Krech III (Athens: University of Georgia Press), 39–58.

Cheyfitz, Eric. 1991. *The Poetics of Imperialism: Translation and Colonization from the Tempest to Tarzan* (New York: Oxford University Press).

Chrisjohn, Roland, Sherri Young, and Michael Maraun. 1997. *The Circle Game: Shadows and Substance in the Indian Residential School Experience in Canada* (Penticton: Theytus Books Limited).

Comaroff, John L., and Jean Comaroff. 1992. *Ethnography and the Historical Imagination* (Boulder CO: Westview Press).

Darnell, Regna. 2011. "The Paradoxical Legacy of Postmodernism," *Anthropologica* 53, 2: 328–30.

de Gobineau, Arthur. 1967 [1915]. *The Inequality of Human Races*, trans. Adrian. Collins, with Introduction by Oscar. Levy (New York: Howard Fertig).

Dods, Roberta Robin. 1998. "Prehistoric Exploitation of Wetland Habitats in North American Boreal Forests." Thesis, Doctor of Philosophy (PhD) (London: Institute of Archaeology, University College London, University of London).

———. 2003. "Wondering the Wetland: Archaeology through the Lens of Myth and Metaphor in Northern Boreal Canada," *Journal of Wetland Archaeology* 3: 17–36 (Oxbow Books).

———. 2007. "Pyrotechnology and Landscapes of Plenty in the Northern Boreal," in *The Archaeology of Fire: Understanding Fire as Material Culture*, ed. Dragos Gheorghiu and George Nash (Budapest: Archaeolingua).

Epprecht, Marc. "'Bisexuality' and the Politics of Normal in African Ethnography," *Anthropologica* 48, 2: 187–201.

Etienne, Mona. 1980. "Women and Men, Cloth and Colonization: The Transformation of Production–Distribution Relations among the Baule (Ivory Coast)," in *Women and Colonization: Anthropological Perspectives*, ed. Mona Etienne and Eleanor Leacock (New York: Praeger), 270–93.

Fortes, Meyer. 1950. "Kinship and Marriage among the Ashanti," in *African Systems of Kinship and Marriage*, ed. A.R. Radcliffe-Brown and Daryll Forde (Oxford: Oxford University Press).

———, and E.E. Evans-Pritchard. 1940. *African Political Systems* (Oxford: Oxford University Press for the International African Institute).

Frank, Andre Gunder. 1967. *Capitalism and Underdevelopment in Latin America; Historical Studies of Chile and Brazil* (New York: Monthly Review Press).

Gledhill, John. 1994. *Power and Its Disguises* (London: Pluto Press).

Gray, Chris Hables, Steven Mentor, and Heidi J. Figueroa-Sarriera. 1995. "Introduction," in *The Cyborg Handbook*, ed. Chris Hables Gray (New York: Routledge).

Haraway, Donna. "A Cyborg Manifesto: Science, Technology, and Socialist-Feminism in the Late Twentieth Century," in *Simians, Cyborgs and Women: The Reinvention of Nature* (New York; Routledge, 1991), 149–81.

Herring, D. Ann. 1994. "'There Were Young People and Old People and Babies Dying Every Week': The 1918–1919 Influenza Pandemic at Norway House," *Ethnohistory* 41, 1: 73–105.

Hitchcock, Robert. 2012. "The Contributions of Richard B. Lee to Anthropology, Ethnoarchaeology, and Indigenous Peoples' Studies," *Journal of Archaeological, Ethnographic and Experimental Studies* 4, 2: 226–60.

Høygaard, Arne. 1941. *Studies on the Nutrition and Physiopathology of Eskimos*. [Skrifter utgitt av Det Norske Videnskaps-Akademi i Oslo. I. Mat.-Naturv. Klasse 1940, No. 9.] (Oslo: I Kommisjon Hos Jacob Dybwad).

Humanism. (2017). In *Wikipedia, The Free Encyclopedia*, 5 September, available from https://en.wikipedia.org/w/index.php?title=Humanism&oldid =799111651

Inda, Jonathan Xavier, and Renato Rosaldo. 2002. "Introduction: A World in Motion," in *The Anthropology of Globalization*, ed. Jonathan Xavier Inda and Renato Rosaldo (Malden, MA: Blackwell), 1–34.

Kearney, Michael. 1995. "The Local and the Global: The Anthropology of Globalization and Transnationalism," *Annual Review of Anthropology* 24: 547–65.

Kesterton, Michael. 2007. "Stone Age Campaign," in *Social Studies column, The Globe and Mail*, sec. L6 (18 July).

Kroeber, Alfred L. 1939. "Cultural and Natural Areas of Native North America," *University of California Publications in American Archaeology and Ethnology* 38: xii.

Latour, Bruno, and Steve Woolgar. 1986. *Laboratory Life: The Construction of Scientific Facts* (Princeton, NJ: Princeton University Press).

Lewellen, Ted. 1983. *Political Anthropology: An Introduction* (South Hadley, MA: Bergin and Garvey).

Mafeje, Archie. 1976. "The Problem of Anthropology in Historical Perspective: An Inquiry into the Growth of the Social Sciences," *Canadian Journal of African Studies* 10, 2: 307–33.

McGregor, Gaile. 1985. *The Wacousta Syndrome* (Toronto: University of Toronto Press).

Miller, Daniel. 2005. *Materiality* (Durham, NC: Duke University Press).

Morgan, Lewis Henry. 1871. *Systems of Consanguinity and Affinity of the Human Family* (Washington: Smithsonian Institute).

———. 1877. *Ancient Society: Or, Researches in the Lines of Human Progress from Savagery through Barbarism to Civilization* (New York: Holt).

Morris, A. 1877. *The Treaties of Canada with the Indians of Manitoba and the North-West Territories, including the Negotiations on Which They Were Based, and Other Information Relating Thereto* (Toronto: Belford, Clarke, and Co.).

Nader, Laura. 1972. "Up the Anthropologist—Perspectives Gained from Studying Up," in *Reinventing Anthropology*, ed. Dell H. Hymes (New York, Pantheon Books), 284–311.

Naiman, Robert J., Jerry M. Melillo, and John E. Hobbie. 1986. "Ecosystem Alteration of Boreal Forest Streams by Beaver (Castor Canadensis)," *Ecology* 67, 5: 1254–69.

Niezen, Ronald. 2003. *The Origins of Indigenism: Human Rights and the Politics of Identity* (Berkeley: University of California Press).

Overholt, Thomas W., and J. Baird Callicott. 1982. *Clothed-in-Fur and Other Tales: An Introduction to an Ojibwa World View* (Washington: University Press of America).

Painter, Nell Irvin. 2010. *The History of White People* (New York: W.W. Norton & Company).

Rich, E.E. 1961. *The Hudson's Bay Company, 1670–1870: Vol. I, 1670–1763* (New York: Macmillan).

Rodney, Walter. 1972. *How Europe Underdeveloped Africa* (London: Bogle-L'Ouverture Publications).

Rogers, Edward S., and Mary B. Black. 1976. "Subsistence Strategy in the Fish and Hare Period, Northern Ontario: The Weagamow Ojibwa, 1880–1920," *Journal of Anthropological Research (SWJA)* 32, 1: 1–43.

Ronan, Colin A., and Joseph Needham. 1978. *The Shorter Science and Civilisation in China* (Cambridge: Cambridge University Press).

Steinbeck, John. 2006 [1939]. *The Grapes of Wrath* (London: Penguin Classics).

Survival International. 2014. "Stamp It Out," available at www .survivalinternational.org/stampitout

Thomsen, Christian Jürgensen. 1936 [1836]. *Ledetraad til Nordisk Oldkyndighed [A Guide to Northern Antiquities]* (Copenhagen).

Trigger, B.G. 1975. "Review of Culture and Nationality by A.G. Bailey," *American Anthropologist* 77, 3: 636–7.

Waldram, James B. 2010. "Engaging Engagement: Critical Reflections on a Canadian Tradition," *Anthropologica* 52, 2: 225–32.

Waubageshig, ed. 1970. *The Only Good Indian: Essays by Canadian Indians* (Toronto: New Press).

Wolf, Eric. 1969. *Peasant Wars of the Twentieth Century* (New York: Harper and Row).

———. 1982. *Europe and the People without History* (Berkeley: University of California Press).

Chapter 4

Adesope, Olusoa O., Tracy Lavin, Terri Thompson, and Charles Ungerleider. 2010. "A Systematic Review and Meta-analysis of the Cognitive Correlates of Bilingualism," *Review of Educational Research* 80, 2: 207–45.

American Philosophical Association. 1990. *Critical Thinking: A Statement of Expert Consensus for Purposes of Educational Assessment and Instruction.* ERIC document ED 315–423.

Bakhtin, Mikhail. 1981 [1975]. *The Dialogical Imagination* (Austin: University of Texas Press).

Barron, Lee. 2013. "The Sound of Street Corner Society: UK Grime Music as Ethnography," *European Journal of Cultural Studies* 15, 5: 531–47.

Bickerton, Derek. 1981. *Roots of Language* (Ann Arbor, MI: Karoma).

Brenneis, Donald, and Ronald K.S. Macauley, ed. 1996. *The Matrix of Language* (Boulder, CO: Westview Press).

Childs, Becky, and Mallinson, Christine. 2004. "African American English in Appalachia: Dialect Accommodation and Substrate Influence," *English World-Wide* 25: 27–50.

Chomsky, Noam. 1957. *Syntactic Structures* (The Hague: Mouton).

——. 1965. *Aspects of the Theory of Syntax* (Cambridge, MA: MIT Press).

Croom, Adam M. 2013. "How to Do Things with Slurs: Studies in the Way of Derogatory Words," *Language and Communication* 33, 3: 177–204.

Crystal, David. 1987. *The Cambridge Encyclopedia of Language* (Cambridge: Cambridge University Press).

Daly, Mary. 1978. *Gyn/ecology: The Metaethics of Radical Feminism* (Boston: Beacon Press).

——. 1984. *Pure Lust: Elemental Feminist Philosophy* (Boston: Beacon Press).

——. 2001. Interview, in *Philosophy Now* 33, available at http://philosophynow.org/issues/33/Mary_Daly

Deacon, Terrence W. 1997. *The Symbolic Species: The Co-evolution of Language and the Brain* (New York: Norton).

Dods, Roberta Robin. 2002. "The Death of Smokey Bear: The Ecodisaster Myth and Forest Management Practices in Prehistoric North America," *World Archaeology* 33, 3: 475–87.

Duranti, Alessandro. 1994. *From Grammar to Politics: Linguistic Anthropology in a Western Samoan Village* (Berkeley: University of California Press).

Ekman, Paul. 1965. Communication Through Nonverbal Behaviour: A Source of Information about an Interpersonal Relationship," in *Affect, Cognition, and Personality: Empirical Studies*, ed. Silvan Solomon Tomkins and Carroll Ellis Izard (Oxford, England: Springer), 390–442.

Elliot, Alison. 1981. *Child Language* (Cambridge: Cambridge University Press).

Evans-Pritchard, E.E. 1963. *Social Anthropology and Other Essays* (New York: Free Press).

Fitch, W. Tecumseh. 2011. "Genes, Language, Cognition, and Culture: Towards Productive Inquiry," *Human Biology: Special Issue on Integrating Genetic and Cultural Evolutionary Approaches to Language* 83, 2: 323–9.

Gentner, Dedre, and Susan Goldin-Meadow. 2003. "Whither Whorf," in *Language in Mind: Advances in the Study of Language and Thought*, ed. Dedre Gentner and Susan Goldin-Meadow (Cambridge, MA: MIT Press).

Gilster, Paul. 1997. *Digital Literacy* (New York: John Wiley).

Hall, Edward T. 1959. *The Silent Language* (New York: Doubleday).

Hanks, William. 1996. *Language and Communicative Practices* (Boulder, CO: Westview Press).

Haraway, Donna. 1988. "Situated Knowledges: The Science Question in Feminism and the Privilege of Partial Perspective," *Feminist Studies* 14, 3: 575–99.

Herring, Susan C., and Sharon Stoerger. 2014. "Gender and (A)nonymity in Computer-Mediated Communication," in *The Handbook of Language, Gender, and Sexuality*, 2nd edn, ed. Susan Ehrlich, Miriam Meyerhoff, and Janet Holmes. (Oxford, UK: Wiley Blackwell), 567–86.

Hill, Jane, and Judith Irvine. 1992. *Responsibility and Evidence in Oral Discourse* (Cambridge: Cambridge University Press).

Hockett, Charles F. 1966. "The Problems of Universals in Language," in *Universals of Language*, ed. J.H. Greenberg (Cambridge, MA: MIT Press), 1–29.

Hoenes del Pinal, Eric. 2011. "Towards an Ideology of Gesture: Gesture, Body Movement, and Language Ideology Among Q'eqchi'-Maya Catholics," *Anthropological Quarterly* 84, 3: 595–630.

Holme, John A. 1988. *Pidgins and Creoles: Volume 1, Theory and Structure* (Cambridge: Cambridge University Press).

Hymes, Dell. 1972. "On Communicative Competence," in *Sociolinguistics: Selected Readings*, ed. J.B. Pride and J. Holmes (Baltimore: Penguin), 269–93.

Jourdan, Christine. 1991. "Pidgins and Creoles: The Blurring of Categories," *Annual Review of Anthropology* 20: 187–209.

Kenny, Michael G. 1999. "A Place for Memory: The Interface between Individual and Collective History," *Comparative Studies in Society and History* 41, 3: 420–37.

Knapp, Mark L., Judith A. Hall, and Terrence G. Horgan. 2013. *Nonverbal Communication in Human Interaction*, 8th edn (Boston: Wadsworth).

Labov, William. 1972. *Language in the Inner City: Studies in the Black English Vernacular* (Philadelphia: University of Pennsylvania Press).

Lanehart, Sonja L., ed. 2009. *African American Women's Language: Discourse, Education, and Identity* (Newcastle, UK: Cambridge Scholars Publishing).

Lee, Jamie Shinhee. 2006. "Linguistic Constructions of Modernity: English Mixing in Korean Television Commercials," *Language in Society* 35, 1: 59–91.

Leikin, Mark. 2012. "The Effect of Bilingualism on Creativity: Developmental and Educational Perspectives," *International Journal of Bilingualism* 17, 4: 431–47.

Mertz, Elizabeth, and Jonathan Yovel. 2010. *Handbook of Pragmatics Highlights*, ed. Jef Verschueren and Jan-Ola Östman (Dordrecht, Netherlands: Kluwer).

Mills, Kathy A. 2015. *Literacy Theories for the Digital Age: Social, Critical, Multimodal, Spatial, Material and Sensory Lenses* (Vol. 45). (Bristol, UK: Multilingual Matters).

Morgan, Marcyliena. 1995. "Theories and Politics in African American English," *Annual Review of Anthropology* 23: 325–45.

Petchauer, Emery. 2011. *Hip-Hop Culture in College Students' Lives: Elements, Embodiment, and Higher Edutainment* (New York: Routledge).

Sapir, Edward. 1966 [1933]. *Culture, Language, and Personality*, ed. David Mandelbaum (Berkeley: University of California Press).

Sims, Christine P. 2005. "Tribal Languages and the Challenges of Revitalization," *Anthropology and Education Quarterly* 36, 1: 104–6.

Slobin, Dan. 1987. "Thinking for Speaking," *Proceedings of the Annual Meeting of the Berkeley Linguistics Society* 13: 435–44.

Sommer, Iris E.C., et al. 2004. "Do Women Really Have More Bilateral Language Representation than Men? A Meta-analysis of Functional Imaging Studies," *Brain* 127, 8: 1845–52.

Sussman, Nan M., and Dianne H. Tyson. 2000. "Sex and Power: Gender Differences in Computer-Mediated Interactions," *Computers in Human Behaviour* 16: 381–94.

Tannen, Deborah. 1990. *You Just Don't Understand: Women and Men in Conversation* (New York: Ballantine).

Usborne, Esther, Josephine Peck, Donna-Lee Smith, and Donald M. Taylor. 2011. "Learning through an Aboriginal Language: The Impact on Students' English and Aboriginal Language Skills," *Canadian Journal of Education* 34, 4: 200–15.

Valverde, Sergi, and Ricard V. Solé. 2015. "A Cultural Diffusion Model for the Rise and Fall of Programming Languages," *Human Biology* 87, 3: 224–34.

Voloshinov, Valentin N. 1986 [1929]. *Marxism and the Philosophy of Language*, trans. Ladislav Matejka and I.R. Titunik (Cambridge, MA: Harvard University Press).

Walsh, Michael. 2005. "Will Indigenous Languages Survive?" *Annual Review of Anthropology* 34: 293–315.

Washington, Julie A. and Craig, Holly K. 1998. "Socioeconomic Status and Gender Influences on Children's Dialectal Variations," *Journal of Speech, Language, and Hearing Research* 41: 618–26.

Whorf, Benjamin. 1956. *Language, Thought, and Reality*, ed. John B. Carroll (Cambridge, MA: MIT Press).

Woodbury, Anthony. 2012. "Endangered Languages." Linguistic Society of America, available at www.linguisticsociety.org/content/endangered-languages

Woolard, Kathryn A. 1998. "Introduction: Language Ideology as a Field of Inquiry," in *Language Ideologies: Practice and Theory*, ed. Bambi Schieffelin, Kathryn Woolard, and Paul V. Kroskrity (New York: Oxford University Press), 3–47.

Chapter 5

Aikhenvald, Alexandra Y. 2012. "Round Women and Long Men: Shape, Size, and the Meanings of Gender in New Guinea and Beyond," *Anthropological Linguistics* 54, 1: 33–86.

Bacigalupo, Ana Mariella. 2004. "The Mapuche Man Who became a Woman Shaman: Selfhood, Gender Transgression, and Competing Cultural Norms," *American Ethnologist* 31, 3: 440–57.

Blackwood, Evelyn, and Saskia E. Wieringa, eds. 1999. "Preface," in *Female Desires: Same-Sex Relations and Transgender Practices across Cultures* (New York: Columbia University Press), ix–xiii.

Bock, Philip K., ed. 1994. *Psychological Anthropology* (Westport, CT: Praeger).

Boellstorff, Tom. 2007. "Queer Studies in the House of Anthropology," *Annual Review of Anthropology* 36: 17–35.

Bruner, Jerome S. 1957. "Going beyond the Information Given," in *Contemporary Approaches to Cognition*, ed. Jerome S. Bruner, Egon Brunswik, Leon Festinger, Fritz Heider, Karl F. Muenzinger, Charles E. Osgood, and David Rapaport (Cambridge, MA: Harvard University Press), 41–69.

Cole, Michael, and Sylvia Scribner. 1974. *Culture and Thought: A Psychological Introduction* (New York: Wiley).

D'Andrade, Roy G. 1992. "Cognitive Anthropology," in *New Directions in Psychological Anthropology*, ed. Theodore Schwartz, Geoffrey M. White, and Catherine A. Lutz (Cambridge: Cambridge University Press), 47–58.

Dalsgaard, Steffen. 2008. "Facework on Facebook: The Presentation of Self in Virtual Life and Its Role in the US Elections," *Anthropology Today* 24, 6: 8–12.

Das, Veena, and Arthur Kleinman. 2000. "Introduction," in *Violence and Subjectivity*, ed. Veena Das et al. (Berkeley: University of California Press), 1–18.

Davies, Bronwyn., and Rom Harré. 1990. "Positioning: The Discursive Production of Selves," *Journal for the Theory of Social Behaviour* 20, 1: 44–63.

Edberg, Mark. 2004. "The Narcotrafficker in Representation and Practice: A Cultural Persona from the US–Mexican Border," *Ethos* 32, 2: 257–77.

Ejorh, Theophilus. 2012. "The African Diasporic Community in Contemporary Ireland: Intersection of Ascriptive and Circumstantial Identities," *Ethnicities* 12, 1: 67–85.

Ellen, Roy. (2010). "Theories in Anthropology and 'Anthropological Theory.'" *Journal of the Royal Anthropological Institute* 16, 387–404.

Epprecht, Marc. 2006. "'Bisexuality' and the Politics of Normal in African Ethnography," *Anthropologica* 48: 187–201.

Fernandez, James W. 1980. "Edification by Puzzlement," in *Explorations in African Systems of Thought*, ed. Ivan Karp and Charles Bird (Bloomington: Indiana University Press), 44–69.

Geller, Pamela L. 2009. "Bodyscapes, Biology, and Heteronormativity," *American Anthropologist, New Series* 111, 4: 504–16.

Gelman, Susan A., and Cristine U. Legare. 2011. "Concepts and Folk Theories," *Annual Review of Anthropology* 40: 379–86.

Gilligan, Carol. 1982. *In a Different Voice* (Cambridge, MA: Harvard University Press).

Gilsenan, Michael. 1982. *Recognizing Islam: Religion and Society in the Modern Arab World* (New York: Pantheon).

Goffman, Erving. 1973. *The Presentation of Self in Everyday Life* (New York: Woodstock).

Goulet, Jean-Guy A. 1996. "The 'Berdache'/'Two-Spirit': A Comparison of Anthropological and Native Constructions of Gendered Identities among the Northern Athapaskans," *Journal of the Royal Anthropological Institute* 2, 4: 683–701 (published by Royal Anthropological Institute of Great Britain and Ireland).

Gregory, Richard. 1983. "Visual Perception and Illusions: Dialogue with Richard Gregory," in *States of Mind*, ed. Jonathan Miller (New York: Pantheon), 42–64.

Halperin, David M. 2014. "Sex/Sexuality/Sexual Classification," in *Critical Terms for the Study of Gender*, ed. Catherine R. Stimpson and Gilbert Herdt (Chicago: University of Chicago Press), 449–86.

Hatzfeldt, Sophie. 2011. "Queer Deconstruction of Heteronormative Identity," *Imponderabilia: The International Student Anthropology Journal*, available at http://imponderabilia.socanth.cam.ac.uk/articles/article.php?articleid=30

Heider, Karl. 1979. *Grand Valley Dani* (New York: Holt, Rinehart, and Winston).

Herdt, Gilbert. 1994. "Mistaken Sex: Culture, Biology, and the Third Sex in New Guinea," in *Third Sex, Third Gender*, ed. Gilbert Herdt (New York: Zone Books), 419–45.

Himani, Bannerji. 2000. *The Dark Side of the Nation: Essay on Multiculturalism, Nationalism, and Gender* (Toronto: Canadian Scholars' Press).

Hudson, R.A. 1980. *Sociolinguistics* (Cambridge: Cambridge University Press).

James, Clifford. 1997. *Routes: Travel and Translation in the Late Twentieth Century* (Cambridge, MA: Harvard University Press).

Kinsey, Alfred C., Wardell B. Pomeroy, and Clyde E. Martin. 1948. *Sexual Behaviour in the Human Male* (Philadelphia: Saunders).

——, ——, ——, and Paul H. Gebhard. 1953. *Sexual Behaviour in the Human Female* (Philadelphia: Saunders).

Kinsey Institute. 2014. "Kinsey's Heterosexual–Homosexual Rating Scale," *The Kinsey Institute*, available at www.kinseyinstitute.org/research/ak-hhscale.html

Klein, Fritz. 1978. *The Bisexual Option* (New York: Arbor House).

Lancaster, Roger. 1992. *Life Is Hard: Machismo, Danger, and the Intimacy of Power in Nicaragua* (Berkeley: University of California Press).

Laqueur, Thomas. 1990. *Making Sex* (Cambridge, MA: Harvard University Press).

Lave, Jean. 1988. *Cognition in Practice: Mind, Mathematics and Culture in Everyday Life* (Cambridge: Cambridge University Press).

Lee, Richard B. 1992. *The Dobe Ju/'hoansi*, 2nd edn (New York: Holt, Rinehart, and Winston).

——. 2013. *The Dobe Ju/'hoansi*, 4th edn (Belmont, CA: Cengage).

Levinson, S.C. 1998. "Studying Spatial Conceptualization across Cultures," *Ethos: Journal of the Society for Psychological Anthropology* 26, 1: 7–24.

Li, Peter S. 1998. *The Chinese in Canada* (Toronto: Oxford University Press).

Lutz, Catherine. 1988. *Unnatural Emotions: Everyday Sentiments on a Micronesian Atoll and Their Challenge to Western Theory* (Chicago: University of Chicago Press).

Mandler, George. 1975. *Mind and Emotion* (New York: Wiley).

Marchand, Trevor H. J. 2010. "Making Knowledge: Explorations of the Indissoluble Relation between Minds, Bodies, and Environment," *The Journal of the Royal Anthropological Institute* 16: S1–S21.

Mead, George Herbert. 1934. *Mind, Self, and Society*, ed. Charles W. Morris (Chicago: University of Chicago Press).

Miller, Claire Cain. 2015. "The Search for the Best Estimate of the Transgender Population," *New York Times*, 3.

Moll, Luis, ed. 1990. *Vygotsky and Education* (Cambridge: Cambridge University Press).

Murphy, Robert, and Yolanda Murphy. 1974. *Women of the Forest* (New York: Columbia University Press).

Mushquash, Christopher J., and Dana Bova. 2007. "Cross-cultural Measurement and Assessment Issues," *Journal on Developmental Disabilities* 12: 53–66.

Najmabadi, Afsaneh. 2014. *Professing Selves: Transsexuality and Same-Sex Desire in Contemporary Iran* (Durham, NC: Duke University Press).

Nanda, Serena. 1994. "Hijras: An Alternative Sex and Gender Role," in *Third Sex, Third Gender*, ed. Gilbert Herdt (New York: Zone Books), 373–417.

Nwoye, Augustine. 2006. "Remapping the Fabric of the African Self: A Synoptic Theory," *Dialectical Anthropology* 30: 119–46.

Olwig, Karen Fog. 2011. "Children's Sociality: The Civilizing Project in the Danish Kindergarten," *Social Analysis: The International Journal of Social and Cultural Practice* 55, 2: 121–41.

Oyama, Susan, Paul E. Griffiths, and Russell D. Gray, eds. 2001. *Cycles of Contingency: Developmental Systems and Evolution* (Cambridge, MA: MIT Press).

Parkin, David. 1984. "Mind, Body, and Emotion among the Giriama," paper presented at Humanity as Creator lecture series (St Cloud State University).

Peletz, Michael. 2006. "Transgenderism and Gender Pluralism in Southeast Asia since Early Modern Times," *Current Anthropology* 47, 2: 309–40.

Rasmussen, Kim, and Søren Smidt. 2001. *Spor af børns institutionsliv: Unges beretninger og erindringer om livet i børnehaven*. Copenhagen: Hans Reitzels Forlag.

Richardson, Sarah S. 2012. "Sexing the X: How the X became the 'Female Chromosome,'" *Signs* 34, 4: 909–33.

Ringrose, Kathryn M. 1994. "Living in the Shadows: Eunuchs and Gender in Byzantium," in *Third Sex, Third Gender*, ed. Gilbert Herdt (New York: Zone Books), 85–109.

Roscoe, Will. 1994. "How to Become a Berdache: Toward a Unified Analysis of Gender Diversity," in *Third Sex, Third Gender*, ed. Gilbert Herdt (New York: Zone Books), 329–72.

Rosenblatt, Daniel. 2004. "An Anthropology Made Safe for Culture: Patterns of Practice and the Politics of Difference in Ruth Benedict," *American Anthropologist* 106, 3: 459–72.

Sahlins, Marshall. 2011. "What Kinship Is (Part Two)," *The Journal of the Royal Anthropological Institute* 17 2: 227–42.

Sidoroff-Dorso, Anton. 2014. "Synaesthesia, Culture, and Neuroimaging," presentation given to the Department of Medical Electronics (BMS College of Engineering, Karnataka, India), slides available at www.academia.edu/2556437/Synesthesia_Culture_and_Neuroimaging

Sullivan, Nikki. 2003. *A Critical Introduction to Queer Theory* (Melbourne, Australia: Circa Books).

Sullivan-Blum, Constance R. 2006. "Discourses in the Christian Same-Sex Marriage Debate," *Anthropologica* 48: 203–15.

Turnbull, Colin. 1961. *The Forest People* (New York: Simon and Schuster).

———.1983. *The Mbuti Pygmies: Change and Adaptation* (New York: CBS College Publishing).

Van Wolputte, Steven. 2004. "Hang on to Your Self: Of Bodies, Embodiment, and Selves," *Annual Review of Anthropology* 33: 251–69.

Vogel, Susan M. 1997. *Baule: African Art, Western Eyes* (New Haven: Yale University Press).

Vygotsky, Lev. 1978. *Mind in Society: The Development of Higher Psychological Processes* (Cambridge, MA: Harvard University Press).

Wang, Xinyuan. 2016. *Social Media in Industrial China* (London: UCL Press).

Young, Diana. 2005. "The Smell of Greenness: Cultural Synaesthesia in the Western Desert (Australia)," *Etnofoor* 18, 1: 61–77.

———. 2011. "Mutable Things: Colours as Material Practice in the Northwest of South Australia," *The Journal of the Royal Anthropological Institute* 17, 2: 356–76.

Chapter 6

Allen, Theodore. 1994–7. *The Invention of the White Race*, 2 vols (London: Verso).

Alonso, Ana María. 1994. "The Politics of Space, Time, and Substance: State Formation, Nationalism, and Ethnicity," *Annual Review of Anthropology* 23: 379–405.

Bauman, Zygmunt. 1989. *Modernity and the Holocaust* (Ithaca, NY: Cornell University Press).

Berreman, Gerald D. 1962. *Hindus of the Himalayas: Ethnography & Change.* Oakland, CA: University of California Press.

Beals, Alan. 1962. *Gopalpur, A South Indian Village* (New York: Holt, Rinehart, and Winston).

Béteille, André. 2010. *Caste, Class, and Power: Changing Patterns of Stratification in a Tanjore Village* (Oxford: Oxford University Press).

Chance, John K. 1978. *Race and Class in Colonial Oaxaca* (Stanford: Stanford University Press).

Comaroff, John, and Jean Comaroff. 1992. *Ethnography and the Historical Imagination* (Boulder, CO: Westview Press).

Cox, Oliver Cromwell. 1948. *Caste, Class, and Race: A Study in Social Dynamics* (Garden City, NY: Doubleday).

De Vos, George, and Hiroshi Wagatsuma. 1966. *Japan's Invisible Race* (Berkeley: University of California Press).

Dourish, Paul. 2008. "Points of Persuasion: Strategic Essentialism and Environmental Sustainability," *The Economist. 2014.* "Bill Gates on poverty: Three myths debunked." Available at: https://www.economist.com/blogs/feastandfamine/2014/01/bill-gates-poverty Pervasive 2008 Workshops.

Gray, Janice. 1997. "The Mabo Case: Radical Decision?" *Canadian Native Studies Journal* 17, 1: 33– 74.

Hale, Charles. 1997. "Cultural Politics of Identity in Latin America," *Annual Review of Anthropology* 26: 567–90.

Harrison, Faye. 1995. "The Persistent Power of 'Race' in the Cultural and Political Economy of Racism," *Annual Review of Anthropology* 24: 47–74.

Hardoon, Deborah, et al. 2017. "An Economy for the 99%." OXFAM Briefing Paper. Available at: https://www.oxfam.ca/sites/default/files/file_attachments/bp-economy-for-99-percent-160117-summ-embargo-en.pdf

———. 1998. "Introduction: Expanding the Discourse on 'Race'," *American Anthropologist* 100, 3: 609–31.

Hartigan Jr, John. 1997. "Establishing the Fact of Whiteness," *American Anthropologist* 99, 3: 495–504.

Harvey, David. 2005. *A Brief History of Neo-liberalism.* Oxford, UK: Oxford University Press.

Jones, J.S. 1986. "The Origin of *Homo Sapiens*: The Genetic Evidence," in *Modern Trends in Primate and Human Evolution*, ed. B. Wood, L. Martin, and P. Andrews (Cambridge: Cambridge University Press), 317–30.

Kelly, John D., and Martha Kaplan. 2001. *Represented Communities: Fiji and World Decolonization* (Chicago: University of Chicago Press).

Lancaster, Roger. 1992. *Life Is Hard: Machismo, Danger, and the Intimacy of Power in Nicaragua* (Berkeley: University of California Press).

Lindgren, Björn. 2005. "The Politics of Ethnicity as an Extended Case: Thoughts on a Chiefly Succession Crisis," *Social Analysis* 1 (Dec. 2005): 234–53.

Livingstone, Frank B. 1964. "On the Nonexistence of Human Races," in *The Concept of Race*, ed. M. F. Ashley-Montagu (New York: Collier), 46–60.

Malkki, Liisa. 1992. "National Geographic: The Rooting of Peoples and the Territorialization of National Identity among Scholars and Refugees," *Cultural Anthropology* 7, 1: 24–44.

Maquet, Jacques. 1970. "Rwanda Castes," in *Social Stratification in Africa*, ed. Arthur Tuden and Leonard Plotnicov (New York: Free Press).

Marks, Jonathan. 1995. *Human Biodiversity* (New York: Aldine).

Matthiasson, John S. 1992. "The Emergence of a New Political Paradigm," in *Living on the Land: Northern Baffin Inuit Respond to Change* (Peterborough, ON: Broadview Press), 161–2.

Max-Neef, Manfred. 2010. "The World on a Collision Course and the Need for a New Economy." *AMBIO* 39: 200-210.

Mayr, Ernst. 1982. *The Growth of Biological Thought* (Cambridge, MA: Harvard University Press).

Mitra, Subrata. 1994. "Caste, Democracy, and the Politics of Community Formation in India," in *Contextualizing Caste: Post-Dumontian Approaches*, ed. Mary Searle-Chatterjee and Ursula Sharma (Oxford: Blackwell Publishers/The Sociological Review), 49–71.

Mosse, David. 2010. "A Relational Approach to Durable Poverty, Inequality and Power." *Journal of Development Studies* 46(7):1156 -78.

OECD 2015. "Glossary of Statistical Terms." Accessed 9 January, 2015. http://stats.oecd. org/glossary/detail.asp?ID=1163

Painter, Nell Irvin. 2010. *The History of White People* (New York: W.W. Norton and Company).

Patriquin, Martin. 2014. "The Epic Collapse of Quebec Separatism, *Maclean's* (11 Apr.), available at www.macleans.ca/politics/the-epic-collapse-of-separatism

Polanyi, Karl. 1964. *The Great Transformation:* The Political and Economic Origins of Our Time. Boston, MA: Beacon Press.

Rasmussen, Susan J. 1999. "The Slave Narrative in Life History and Myth, and Problems of Ethnographic Representation of the Tuareg Cultural Predicament," *Ethnohistory* 46, 1: 67–108.

Reddy, Deepa S. 2005. "The Ethnicity of Caste," *Anthropological Quarterly* 78, 3: 543–84.

Schultz, Emily. 1984. "From Pagan to Pullo: Ethnic Identity Change in Northern Cameroon," *Africa* 54, 1: 46–64.

Sen, Amartya. 1982. *Poverty and Famines.* New York, NY: Oxford University Press.

Sharma, Ursula. 1999. *Caste* (Buckingham: Open University Press).

Smedley, Audrey. 1998. "'Race' and the Construction of Human Identity," *American Anthropologist* 100, 3: 690–702.

Spivak, Gayatri Chakravorty. 1987. *In Other Worlds: Essays in Cultural Politics.* (New York: Taylor and Francis).

Tonkinson, Robert. 1998. "National Identity: Australia after Mabo," in *Pacific Answers to Western Hegemony: Cultural Practices of Identity Construction*, ed. Jürg Wassmann (Oxford: Berg), 287–310.

van den Berghe, Pierre. 1970. "Race, Class, and Ethnicity in South Africa," in *Social Stratification in Africa*, ed. Arthur Tuden and Leonard Plotnicov (New York: Free Press), 345–71.

Warner, W. Lloyd. 1936. "American Caste and Class," *American Sociological Review* 42, 2: 234–7.

Werbner, Pnina. 1997. "Afterword: Writing Multiculturalism and Politics in the New Europe," in *The Politics of Multiculturalism in the New Europe: Racism, Identity, and Community*, ed. Tariq Modood and Pnina Werbner (London: Zed Books), 261–7.

Williams, Brackette. 1989. "A Class Act: Anthropology and the Race to Nation across Ethnic Terrain," *Annual Review of Anthropology* 18: 401–44.

World Bank. 2016. "Poverty." Accessed 11 July, 2016, at: http://www.worldbank.org/en/topic/poverty

Yunus, Muhammad. 2011. Sacrificing Microcredit for Megaprofits. Accessed at: http://www.nytimes.com/2011/01/15/opinion/15yunus.html

Chapter 7

Allen, Catherine J. 1988. *The Hold Life Has: Coca and Cultural Identity in an Andean Community* (Washington, DC: Smithsonian Institution Press).

Anderson, Benedict. 1983. *Imagined Communities* (London: Verson).

Archambault, Caroline S. 2010. "Women Left Behind? Migration, Spousal Separation, and the Autonomy of Rural Women in Ugweno Tanzania," *Signs* 35, 4: 919–42.

———, and Jennifer Glassco. Forthcoming. "Landless, Waterless and Wireless": How the Youth Use Social Media to Protect Their Land in Southern Kenya.

Bauman, Zygmunt. 1989. *Modernity and the Holocaust* (Ithaca, NY: Cornell University Press).

———. 1990. "Modernity and Ambivalence," in *Global Culture*, ed. Mike Featherstone (London: Sage), 143–69.

Baxter, P.T.W. 1978. "Boran Age Sets and Generation Sets: Gada, a Puzzle or a Maze?" in *Age, Generation, and Time*, ed. P.T.W. Baxter and Uri Almagor (New York: St Martin's Press), 151–82.

———, and Uri Almagor, eds. 1978. *Age, Generation, and Time* (New York: St Martin's Press).

Bell, Sandra, and Simon Coleman, eds. 1999. "The Anthropology of Friendship: Enduring Themes and Future Possibilities," in *The Anthropology of Friendship* (Oxford: Berg), 1–19.

Bellman, Beryl. 1984. *The Language of Secrecy* (New Brunswick, NJ: Rutgers University Press).

Berkowitz, Dana. 2013. "Gay Men and Surrogacy," in *LGBT-Parent Families: Innovations in Research and Implications for Practice*, ed. Abbie E. Goldberg and Katherine R. Allen (New York: Springer), 71–85.

Bledsoe, Caroline. 1993. "The Politics of Polygyny in Mende Education and Child Fosterage Transactions," in *Sex and Gender Hierarchies*, ed. Barbara Diane Miller (Cambridge: Cambridge University Press), 170–92.

Bodenhorn, Barbara. 2000. "'He Used to Be My Relative': Exploring the Bases of Relatedness among Iñupiat of Northern Alaska," in *Cultures of Relatedness: New Approaches to the Study of Kinship*, ed. Janet Carsten (Cambridge: Cambridge University Press), 128–48.

Brain, Robert. 1976. *Friends and Lovers* (New York: Basic Books).

Brooke, James. 2003. "Dowry Too High: Lose Bridge and Go to Jail," *New York Times*, May 17.

Brown, Wayne. 2003. "Mary Two-Axe Earley: Crusader for Equal Rights for Aboriginal Women," *Electoral Insight*, November, available from www.elections.ca/content.aspx?section=res&dir=eim/issue9&document=p10&lang=e

Burch Jr, Ernest S. 1970. "Marriage and Divorce among the North Alaskan Eskimos," in *Divorce and After*, ed. Paul Bohannan (Garden City, NY: Doubleday), 152–81.

Clark, Gracia. 1994. *Onions Are My Husband* (Chicago: University of Chicago Press).

Connolly, Jennifer. 2009. "Forbidden Intimacies: Christian–Muslim Intermarriage in East Kalimantan, Indonesia," *American Ethnologist* 36, 3: 492–506.

Daly, Martin., and Margo. Wilson. 1985. "Child Abuse and Other Risks of Not Living with Both Parents," *Ethology and Sociobiology* 6, 4: 197–210.

Danet, Brenda, and Susan B. Herring, eds. 2007. *The Multilingual Internet: Language, Culture and Communication Online* (New York: Oxford University Press).

de Bruijn, Mirjam, and Rijk van Dijk. 2012. "Examples of 'Ethnographies of Linking' in Anthropology," *Anthropologica* 54, 1: 45–59.

Dolgin, Janet. 1995. "Family Law and the Facts of Family," in *Naturalizing Power*, ed. Sylvia Yanagisako and Carol Delaney (New York: Routledge), 47–67.

Evans-Pritchard, E.E. 1951. *Kinship and Marriage among the Nuer* (Oxford: Oxford University Press).

Fortes, Meyer. 1950. "Kinship and Marriage among the Ashanti," in *African Systems of Kinship and Marriage*, ed. A.R. Radcliffe-Brown and Daryll Forde (Oxford: Oxford University Press).

———. 1953. "The Structure of Unilineal Descent Groups," *American Anthropologist* 55: 25–39.

Gardner, Katy. 2008. "Keeping Connected: Security, Place, and Social Capital in a 'Londoni' Village in Sylhet," *Journal of the Royal Anthropological Institute* 14 3: 477–95.

Georges, Eugenia. 1990. *The Making of a Transnational Community: Migration, Development, and Cultural Change in the Dominican Republic* (New York: Columbia University Press).

Greenwood, Davydd, and William Stini. 1977. *Nature, Culture, and Human History* (New York: Harper and Row).

Goody, Jack, and S. J. Tambiah. 1973. *Bridewealth and Dowry* (Cambridge: Cambridge University Press).

Hillewaert, Sarah. 2015. "Writing with an Accent: Orthographic Practice, Emblems, and Traces on Facebook," *Journal of Linguistic Anthropology* 25: 195–214.

Hitchcock, Robert K. 2003. "Land, Livestock, and Leadership among the Ju/'hoansi San of North Western Botswana," *Anthropologica* 45, 1: 89 -94.

Horst, Heather A. 2011. "Reclaiming Place: The Architecture of Home, Family, and Migration," *Canadian Anthropology Society* 53, 1: 29–39.

———. 2012. "Chapter 3: New Media Technologies in Everyday Life," in *Digital Anthropology*, ed. Heather Horst and Daniel Miller (New York: Berg).

Huber, Brad R., William F. Danaher, and William L. Breedlove. 2011. "Material Resource Investments at Marriage: Evolutionary, Social, and Ecological Perspectives," *Ethnology* 50, 4: 281–304.

Hunter, David, and Phillip Whitten, eds. 1976. *Encyclopedia of Anthropology* (New York: Harper and Row).

Jankowiak, William, and Helen Gerth. 2012. "Can You Love More Than One Person at the Same Time? A Research Project," *Anthropologica* 54, 1: 95–105.

Karp, Ivan. 1978. *Fields of Change among the Iteso of Kenya* (London: Routledge and Kegan Paul).

Koenig, Boris. 2014. "Les économies occultes du « broutage » des jeunes Abidjanais: Une dialectique culturelle du changement générationnel" *Autrepart* 71, 3: 195–215.

Kozinets, Robert V. 2015. *Netnography Redefined*, 2nd edn (London: Sage).

Kuper, Adam. 1982. *Wives for Cattle: Bridewealth and Marriage in Southern Africa* (London: Routledge and Kegan Paul).

Lamphere, Louise. 2005. "Replacing Heteronormative Views of Kinship and Marriage," *American Ethnologist* 32, 1: 34–6.

Lee, Richard B.

1992. *The Dobe Ju/'hoansi*, 2nd edn (New York: Holt, Rinehart, and Winston).

———. 2013. *The Dobe Ju/'hoansi*, 4th edn (Belmont, CA: Cengage).

Levine, Nancy. 1980. "Nyinba Polyandry and the Allocation of Paternity," *Journal of Comparative Family Studies* 11, 3: 283–8.

———. 1988. *The Dynamics of Polyandry: Kinship, Domesticity, and Population on the Tibetan Border* (Chicago: University of Chicago Press).

———, and Walter Sangree. 1980. "Women with Many Husbands," *Journal of Comparative Family Studies* 11, 3: 283.

MacCormack, Carol P. 1980. "Proto-social to Adult: A Sherbro Transformation," in *Nature, Culture, and Gender*, ed. Carol MacCormack and Marilyn Strathern (Cambridge: Cambridge University Press), 95–118.

McPherson, Naomi. 2007. "Myth Primogeniture and Long-Distance Trade-Friends in Northwest New Britain, Papua New Guinea," *Oceania* 77, 2: 129–57.

Miller, Daniel, and Don Slater. 2000. *The Internet: An Ethnographic Approach* (Oxford: Berg).

Minturn, Leigh. 1993. *Sita's Daughters* (New York: Oxford University Press).

Mishra, Charudutt, Herbert H.T. Prins, and Sipke E. Van Wieren. 2003. "Diversity, Risk Mediation, and Change in a Trans-Himalayan Agropastoral System," *Human Ecology* 31, 4: 595–609.

Nardi, Bonnie. 2015. "Virtuality," *Annual Review of Anthropology* 44: 15–31.

Pedersen, Marianne Holm. 2011. "Revisiting Iraq: Change and Continuity in Familial Relations of Iraqi Refugees in Copenhagen

Philips, Amali. 2011. "Sharia and Shah Bano: Multiculturalism and Women's Rights," *Anthropologica* 53, 2: 275–90.

Rezende, Claudia Barcellos. 1999. "Building Affinity through Friendship," in *The Anthropology of Friendship*, ed. Sandra Bell and Simon Coleman (Oxford: Berg), 79–97.

Richards, Audrey. 1954. *Chisungu* (London: Methuen).

Ryan, Jenny. 2012. "The Digital Graveyard: Online Social Networking Sites as Vehicles of Remembrance," in *Human No More*, ed. Neil Whitehead (Boulder: University Press of Colorado).

Schneider, David M. 1968. *American Kinship: A Cultural Account* (Englewood Cliffs, NJ: Prentice-Hall).

Segalen, Martine. 1986. *Historical Anthropology of the Family* (Cambridge: Cambridge University Press).

Shostak, Marjorie. 1981. *Nisa: The Life and Words of a !Kung Woman* (New York: Vintage Books).

Soysal, Levent. 2010. "Intimate Engagements of the Public Kind," *Anthropological Quarterly* 83, 2: 373–99.

Spronk, Rachel. 2011. "'Intimacy Is the Name of the Game': Media and the Praxis of Sexual Knowledge in Nairobi," *Anthropologica* 53, 1: 145–58.

Van Willigen, John, and V.C. Channa. 1991. "Law, Custom, and Crimes against Women," *Human Organization* 50, 4: 369–77.

Statistics Canada, 2016 Census of Population, Statistics Canada Catalogue no. 98-400- X2016031. Data retrieved from www12.statcan.gc.ca/census-recensement/2016/dp-pd/dt-td/Rp-eng.cfm?LANG=E&APATH=3&DETAIL=0&DIM=0&FL=A&FREE=0&GC=0&GID=0&GK=0&GRP=1&PID=109650&PRID=10&PTYPE=10944 5&S=0&SHOWALL=0&SUB=0&Temporal=2016&THEME=117&VID=0&VNAMEE=&VNAMEF=

Vonnegut Jr, Kurt. 1976. *Slapstick, or Lonesome No More!* (New York: Dell Publishing).

Weiner, Annette. 1980. "Stability in Banana Leaves: Colonization and Women in Kiriwina, Trobriand Islands," in *Women and Colonization: Anthropological Perspectives*, ed. Mona Etienne and Eleanor Leacock (New York: Praeger), 270–93.

———. 1988. *The Trobrianders of Papua New Guinea* (New York: Holt, Rinehart, and Winston).

Weston, Kath. 1991. *Families We Choose* (New York: Columbia University Press).

———. 1998. *Long Slow Burn: Sexuality and Social Science* (New York: Routledge).

Whitehead, Neil L., and Michael Wesch. 2012. "Introduction," in *Human No More*, ed. Neil Whitehead (Boulder: University Press of Colorado).

Wilson, Monica. 1951. "Witch Beliefs and Social Structure," *American Journal of Sociology LVI*, 4: 307–13 (Oxford: Oxford University Press).

Witherspoon, Gary. 1975. *Navajo Kinship and Marriage* (Chicago: University of Chicago Press).

Chapter 8

Barlett, Peggy F. 1987. "Industrial Agriculture in Evolutionary Perspective," *Cultural Anthropology* 2, 1: 137–54.

Berlan, Amanda. 2013. "Social Sustainability in Agriculture: An Anthropological Perspective on Child Labour in Cocoa Production in Ghana," *The Journal of Development Studies* 49, 8: 1088–100.

Braroe, Niels. 1975. *Indian and White* (Stanford: Stanford University Press).

Brodt, Sonja. 2001. "A Systems Perspective on the Conservation and Erosion of Indigenous Agricultural Knowledge in Central India," *Human Ecology* 29, 1: 99–120.

Counihan, Carole. 2004. *Around the Tuscan Table* (London: Routledge).

Crate, Susan A. 2011. "Climate and Culture: Anthropology in the Era of Contemporary Climate Change," *Annual Review of Anthropology* 40: 175–94.

Dods, Roberta Robin. 1998. "Prehistoric Exploitation of Wetland Habitats in North American Boreal Forests." Thesis, Doctor of Philosophy (PhD) (London: Institute of Archaeology, University College London, University of London).

Douglas, Mary. 1966. *Purity and Danger* (London: Routledge and Kegan Paul).

———, and Baron Isherwood. 1979. *The World of Goods: Towards an Anthropology of Consumption* (New York: Norton).

Ferguson, Thomas John, Richard E. Hart, Ronald Stauber, and Troy Lucio. 1985. *A Zuni Atlas* (Norman, OK: University of Oklahoma).

Fratkin, Elliot. 1997. "Pastoralism: Governance and Development Issues," *Annual Review of Anthropology* 26: 235–61.

Halperin, Rhoda. 1994. *Cultural Economics: Past and Present* (Austin: University of Texas Press).

Hitchcock, Robert K. 2003. "Land, Livestock and Leadership among the Ju/'hoansi San of North Western Botswana," *Anthropologica* 45: 89–94.

Ingold, Tim. 1983. "The Significance of Storage in Hunting Societies," *Man* 18: 553–71.

Lee, Richard B. 1992a. "Art, Science, or Politics? The Crisis in Hunter-Gatherer Studies," *American Anthropologist* 94: 31–54.

———. 1992b. *The Dobe Ju/'hoansi*, 2nd edn (New York: Holt, Rinehart, and Winston).

Malinowski, Bronisław. 1944. *A Scientific Theory of Culture and Other Essays* (New York: Oxford University Press).

Mauss, Marcel. 2000 [1950]. *The Gift: The Form and Reason for Exchange in Archaic Societies* (New York: W.W. Norton).

McLain, Rebecca, et al. 2013. "Making Sense of Human Ecology Mapping: An Overview of Approaches to Integrating Socio-Spatial Data into Environmental Planning," *Human Ecology* 41, 5: 651–65.

Milgram, B. Lynne. 2008. "Activating Frontier Livelihoods: Women and the Transnational Second-Hand Clothing Trade between Hong Kong and the Philippines," *Urban Anthropology and Studies of Cultural Systems and World Economic Development* 37, 1: 5–47.

Miller, Daniel, ed. 1995. *Acknowledging Consumption: A Review of New Studies* (New York: Routledge).

Phillips, Lynne. 2006. "Food and Globalization," *Annual Review of Anthropology* 35: 37–57.

Sahlins, Marshall. 1972. *Stone Age Economics* (Chicago: Aldine).

Schmook, Birgit, Nathalie van Vliet, Claudia Radel, María de Jesús Manzón-Che, and Susannah Candless. 2013. "Persistence of Swidden Cultivation in the Face of Globalization: A Case Study from Communities in Calakmul, Mexico," *Human Ecology* 41, 1: 93–107.

Sewid-Smith, Daisy. 1997. "The Continuing Reshaping of Our Ritual World by Academic Adjuncts," *Anthropology and Education Quarterly* 28, 4: 594–602.

Solway, Jacqueline, and Richard Lee. 1990. "Foragers, Genuine or Spurious: Situating the Kalahari San in History," *Current Anthropology* 31: 109–46.

Steward, Julian H. 1972. *Theory of Culture Change: The Methodology of Multilinear Evolution* (Urbana: University of Illinois Press).

Tollefson, Kenneth D. 1995. "Potlatching and Political Organization among the Northwest Coast Indians," *Ethnology* 34, 1: 53–73.

von Glasenapp, Markus, and Thomas F. Thornton. 2011. "Traditional Ecological Knowledge of Swiss Alpine Farmers and their Resilience to Socio-ecological Change," *Human Ecology* 39, 6: 769–81.

Weiner, Annette. 1980. "Stability in Banana Leaves: Colonization and Women in Kiriwina, Trobriand Islands," in *Women and Colonization: Anthropological Perspectives*, ed. Mona Etienne and Eleanor Leacock (New York: Praeger), 270–93.

Wilk, Richard. 1996. *Economies and Cultures* (Boulder, CO: Westview Press).

——— and Lisa Cliggett. 2007. *Economies and Cultures: Foundations of Economic Anthropology* (Boulder, CO: Westview Press).

Wolf, Eric. 1982. *Europe and the People without History* (Berkeley: University of California Press).

Chapter 9

Abu-Lughod, Lila. 1995. "The Objects of Soap Opera: Egyptian Television and the Cultural Politics of Modernity," in *Worlds Apart: Modernity through the Prism of the Local*, ed. Daniel Miller (London: Routledge), 109–210.

Adler, Ronald B., Lawrence B. Rosenfeld, Russell F. Proctor, and Constance Winder. 2016. *Interplay: The Process of Interpersonal Communication* (Toronto: Oxford University Press).

Alland, Alexander. 1977. *The Artistic Animal* (New York: Doubleday Anchor).

Appadurai, Arjun. 1995. "Playing with Modernity: The Decolonization of Indian Cricket," in *Consuming Modernity: Public Culture in a South Asian World*, ed. Carol A. Breckenridge (Minneapolis: University of Minnesota Press), 23–48.

Bateson, Gregory. 1972. "A Theory of Play and Fantasy," in *Steps to an Ecology of Mind*, ed. Gregory Bateson (New York: Ballentine Books), 177–93.

Beamish, Rob, and Ian Ritchie. 2006. *Fastest, Highest, Strongest: A Critique of High-Performance Sport* (New York: Routledge).

Berthod, Marc-Antoine. 2005. "La Vie des Morts dans le Regard des Anthropologues," *Anthropos* 100, 2: 521–36.

Besnier, Niko, and Susan Bronwell. 2012. "Sport, Modernity, and the Body," *Annual Review of Anthropology* 41: 443–59.

Bigenho, Michelle. 2002. *Sounding Indigenous: Authenticity in Bolivian Music Performance* (New York: Palgrave).

Blanchard, Kendall, and Alyce Cheska. 1985. *The Anthropology of Sport* (South Hadley, MA: Bergin and Garvey).

Bromberger, Christian. 1995. *Le match de football: Etnologie d'une passion partisane à Marseille, Naples et Turin* (Paris: Éditions de la maison des sciences de l'homme).

Caillois, Roger. 1961. *Man, Play, and Games* (Champaign: University of Illinois Press).

CBC. 2013. "Most Families with Kids Have Gaming Consoles," *CBC News* (11 Apr.), available at www.cbc.ca/news/technology/most-families-with-kids-have-a-gaming-console-1.1325831

Csikszentmihalyi, Mihaly. 1981. "Some Paradoxes in the Definition of Play," in *Play and Context*, ed. Alyce Cheska (West Point: Leisure Press), 14–25.

Davis, Wade. 1985. *The Serpent and the Rainbow* (New York: Simon and Schuster).

——. 1988. *Passage of Darkness: The Ethnobiology of the Haitian Zombie* (Chapel Hill: University of North Carolina Press).

Dernbach, Katherine Boris. 2005. "Spirits of the Hereafter: Death, Funerary Possession, and the Afterlife in Chuuk, Micronesia," *Ethnology* 44, 2: 99–123.

Dods, Roberta Robin. 2010. "Nation/First Nations: Conflicts in Identity and the Role of Archaeology," in *Unquiet Pasts: Risk Society, Lived Cultural Heritage, Re-designing Reflexivity*, ed. Stephanie Koerner and Ian. Russell (Ashgate: Aldershot).

Drewal, Margaret. 1992. *Yoruba Ritual* (Bloomington: Indiana University Press).

Errington, Shelly. 1998. *The Death of Authentic Primitive Art and Other Tales of Progress* (Berkeley: University of California Press).

Fagen, Robert. 1981. *Animal Play Behavior* (New York: Oxford University Press).

——. 1992. "Play, Fun, and Communication of Well-being," *Play and Culture* 5, 1: 40–58.

Geertz, Clifford. 1972. "Deep Play: Notes on the Balinese Cockfight," *Dædalus* 101, 1: 1–37.

Hall, Edward T. 1966. *The Hidden Dimension* (New York: Doubleday).

Handelman, Don. 1977. "Play and Ritual: Complementary Frames of Metacommunication," in *It's a Funny Thing, Humour*, ed. A.J. Chapman and H. Foot (London: Pergamon), 185–92.

Kapferer, Bruce. 1983. *A Celebration of Demons* (Bloomington: Indiana University Press).

Kaufman, Sharon R., and Lynn M. Morgan. 2005. "The Anthropology of the Beginnings and Ends of Life," *Annual Review of Anthropology* 34: 317–41.

Lever, Janet. 1995. *Soccer Madness*, rev. edn (Prospect Heights, IL: Waverland Press).

Lévi-Strauss, Claude. 1955. "The Structural Study of Myth," *Journal of American Folklore* 68, 270: 428–44.

——. 1967 [1962]. *L'antropologie structurale* (Paris: Plon), trans. under the title *Structural Anthropology*, ed. Claire Jacobson and Brooke Grundfest Schoepf (New York: Doubleday Anchor).

Malinowski, Bronisław. 1948 [1926]. *Magic, Science, and Religion, and Other Essays* (New York: Doubleday Anchor).

Miah, Andy. 2004. *Genetically Modified Athletes: Biomedical Ethics, Gene Doping and Sport* (New York: Routledge).

Miracle, Andrew. 1991. "Aymara Joking Behaviour," *Play and Culture* 4, 2: 144–52.

Ridington, Robin. 1998. "Coyote's Canon: Sharing Stories with Thomas King," *American Indian Quarterly* 22, 3: 343–62.

——, and Jillian Ridington. 2013. *Where Happiness Dwells: A History of the Dane-zaa First Nations* (Vancouver: UBC Press).

Robidoux, Michael A. 2002. "Imagining a Canadian Identity through Sport: A Historical Interpretation of Lacrosse and Hockey," *Journal of American Folklore* 115, 456: 209–25.

Rideout, Victoria J., Ulla G. Foehr, and Donald F. Roberts. 2010. *Generation M2: Media in the Lives of 8- to 18-Year-Olds*. The Henry J. Kaiser Family Foundation, available at http://kaiserfamilyfoundation.files.wordpress.com/2013/04/8010.pdf

Schwartzman, Helen. 1978. *Transformations: The Anthropology of Children's Play* (New York: Plenum).

Turner, Victor. 1969. *The Ritual Process* (Chicago: Aldine).

——. 1982. *From Ritual to Theatre: The Human Seriousness of Play* (New York: Performing Arts Journal Publications).

Van Gennep, Arnold. 1960. *The Rites of Passage* (Chicago: University of Chicago Press).

Van Rheenen, Derek. 2012. "A Century of Historical Change in the Game Preferences of American Children," *Journal of American Folklore* 125, 498: 411–43.

Vogel, Susan M. 1997. *Baule: African Art, Western Eyes* (New Haven: Yale University Press).

Voloshinov, Valentin N. 1986 [1929]. *Marxism and the Philosophy of Language*, trans. Ladislav Matejka and I.R. Titunik (Cambridge, MA: Harvard University Press).

Chapter 10

AANDC (Aboriginal Affairs and Northern Development Canada). 2012. "Contaminants in the North," available at www.aadnc-aandc.gc.ca/eng/1100100035295/1100100035299.

APA (American Psychological Association), eds. (2013). *DSM-V: Diagnostic and Statistical Manual of Mental Disorders*, 5th edn, available at http://dsm.psychiatryonline.org/doi/book/10.1176/appi.books.9780890425596.

Apfel, Roberta J., and Bennett Simon. 2000. "Mitigating Discontents with Children in War: An Ongoing Psychoanalytic Inquiry," in *Cultures under Siege: Collective Violence and Trauma*, ed. Antonius C.G.M. Robben and Marcelo M. Suárez-Orozco (Cambridge: Cambridge University Press), 102–30.

APTN News. 2015. "A Prime Minister Gives His Word as TRC Unveils Final Report on Dark Legacy of Residential Schools," *APTN National News* (15 Dec.).

Bailey, Mark S., and H. Janaka de Silva. 2006. "Cultural Studies: Sri Lankan *sanni* Masks: An Ancient Classification of Disease," *BMJ* 333: 1327–8.

Bloom, D.E. et al. 2011. *The Global Economic Burden of Noncommunicable Disease* (Geneva: World Economic Forum).

Brown, Louise. 2011. "Canadian's Lucky Iron Fish Saves Lives in Cambodia," *The Toronto Star* (12 Nov.), available at www.thestar.com/news/gta/2011/11/12/canadians_lucky_iron_fish_saves_lives_in_cambodia.html.

Bruser, David, Robert Benzie, and Jayme Poisson. 2017. "Ontario Commits $85 Million to Clean Up 'Gross Neglect' at Grassy Narrows," *The Toronto Star* (27 June).

Carlson, Nathan D. 2009. "Reviving Witiko (Windigo): An Ethnohistory of 'Cannibal Monsters'" in the Athabasca District of Northern Alberta, 1878–1910," *Ethnohistory* 56, 3: 355–94.

Castle, Sarah E. 1994. "The (Re)negotiation of Illness Diagnoses and Responsibility for Child Death in Rural Mali," *Medical Anthropology Quarterly* 8, 3: 314–35.

Cheng, Cecilia. 2004. "To Be Paranoid Is the Standard? Panic Responses to SARS Outbreak in the Hong Kong Special Administrative Region," *Asian Perspective* 28, 1: 67–98.

Colson, Anthony C., and Karen E. Selby. 1974. "Medical Anthropology," *Annual Review of Anthropology* 3: 245–63.

Conrad, Peter, and Kristin K. Baker. 2010. "The Social Construction of Illness: Key Insights and Policy Implications," *Journal of Health and Social Behavior* 51, Suppl: S67–79.

Cox, Paul Alan, Holly E. Johnson, and Gaugau Tavana. 2008. "Giving Samoan Healers Credit for Prostratin," *Science, New Series* 320, 5883: 1589.

Day, Chet. 2010. "Chicken Soup: Nature's Best Cold and Flu Remedy," available at http://-chetday.com/coldfluremedy.htm

De Burgos, Hugo. 2009. "Indigenous Medicine and Identity in Nicaragua," guest editorial.

Dods, Roberta Robin. 2004. "Knowing Ways/Ways of Knowing: Reconciling Science and Tradition," *World Archaeology* 36, 4: 547–57.

Dressler, William W. 2001. "Medical Anthropology: Toward a Third Moment in Social Science?" *Medical Anthropology Quarterly* 15: 455–65.

Duden, B. 1991. *The Woman beneath the Skin: A Doctor's Patients in Eighteenth-Century Germany* (Cambridge, MA: Harvard University Press).

Dufour, Darna L. 1997. "Nutrition, Activity, and Health in Children," *Annual Review of Anthropology* 26: 541–65.

Ehrenreich, Jeffrey David. 1996. "Worms, Witchcraft, and Wild Incantations: The Case of the Chicken Soup Cure," *Anthropological Quarterly* 69, 3: 137–41.

Fabrega, Horacio. 1971. "Medical Anthropology," in *Biennial Review of Anthropology*, ed. J. Siegel (Stanford, CA: Stanford University Press), 167–229.

Farmer, Paul. 2002 [1996]. "On Suffering and Structural Violence: A View from Below," in *The Anthropology of Politics*, ed. Joan Vincent (Malden, MA: Blackwell), 424–37.

———. 2004. "An Anthropology of Structural Violence," *Current Anthropology* 45, 3: 305–25.

———. 2005. *Pathologies of Power: Health, Human Rights, and the New War on the Poor* (Berkeley: University of California Press).

———. 2006. *AIDS and Accusation: Haiti and the Geography of Blame*, 2nd edn (Berkeley: University of California Press).

———, Arthur Kleinman, Jim Kim, and Matthew Basilico, eds. 2013. *Reimaging Global Health: An Introduction* (Berkeley: University of California Press).

Fassin, D. 2005. "Compassion and Repression: The Moral Economy of Immigration Policies in France," *Cultural Anthropology* 20, 3: 362–87.

———, and E. d'Halluin. 2005. "The Truth from the Body: Medical Certificates as Ultimate Evidence for Asylum Seekers," *American Anthropologist* 107, 4: 597–608.

Ferrara, Nadia, and Guy Lanoue. 2004. "The Self in Northern Canadian Hunting Societies: 'Cannibals' and Other 'Monsters' as Agents of Healing," *Anthropologica* 46, 1: 69–83.

Foster, George M. 1976. "Disease Etiologies in Non-Western Systems," *American Anthropologist* 78, 4: 773–82.

Foucault, Michel. 1964. *Madness and Civilization: A History of Insanity in the Age of Reason*, trans. Richard Howard, abridged version, Antonius C.G.M. Robben and Marcelo M. Suárez-Orozco (New York: Routledge).

Gampel, Yolanda. 2000. "Reflections on the Prevalence of the Uncanny in Social Violence," in *Cultures under Siege* (New York: Cambridge University Press), 48–69.

Garneau, David. 2016. "Responding to Canada's Truth and Reconciliation Commission Report," *International Contemporary Art* Winter: 22.

Garro, Linda C. 2004. "Overview of Culture: Ojibwa," in *Encyclopaedia of Medical Anthropology: Health and Illness in the World's Cultures*, vol. 2, ed. Carol R. Ember and Melvin Ember (New York: Springer Science + Business Media, Inc.), 903–15.

Goffman, Erving. 1961. *Asylums: Essays on the Social Situation of Mental Patients and Other Inmates* (New York: Anchor Books).

Hahn, Robert A. 1984. "Rethinking 'Illness' and 'Disease,'" *Contributions to Asian Studies* 18: 1–23.

Hayden, Robert M. 2000. "Rape and Rape Avoidance in Ethno-National Conflicts: Sexual Violence in Liminalized States," *American Anthropologist*, New Series, 102, 1: 27–41.

Kirkup, Kristy. 2017. "Trudeau under Fire for Saying Grassy Narrows Is Ontario's Responsibility," *The Globe and Mail* (2 Mar.), available from https://beta.theglobeandmail.com/news/national/trudeau-under-fire-for-saying-grassy-narrows-very-much-ontarios-responsibility/article34195382/?ref=http://www.theglobeandmail.com&.

Kleinman, Arthur. 1980. *Patients and Healers in the Context of Culture* (Berkeley: University of California Press).

———. 2012. "Medical Anthropology and Mental Health: Five Questions for the Next Fifty Years," in *Medical Anthropology at the Intersections: Histories, Activisms, and Futures*, ed. Marcia C. Inhorn and Emily A. Wentzell (Durham, NC: Duke University Press), 116–28.

———, Veena Das, and Margaret M. Lock. 1997. *Social Suffering* (Berkeley: University of California Press).

Latimer, Joanna. 1999. "The Dark at the Bottom of the Stairs: Performance and Participation of Hospitalized Older People," in *Medical Anthropology Quarterly* 13, 2: 186–213.

Laverdière, Hélène, and Niki Ashton, Niki. 2014. "Canada Must Do More to Prevent Unsafe Abortions," *The Globe and Mail* (28 May), available at www.theglobeandmail.com/news/politics/canada-must-do-more-to-prevent-unsafe-abortions/article18883298

Lincoln, Bruce. 2001. "Revisiting 'Magical Fright,'" *American Ethnologist* 28: 778–802.

Link, Bruce G., and Jo C. Phelan. 2001. "Conceptualizing Stigma," *Annual Review of Sociology* 27: 363–85.

Mair, Lucy Philip. 1969. *Witchcraft* (New York: McGraw-Hill).

Malkki, Liisa. 1995. *Purity and Exile: Violence, Memory, and National Cosmology among Hutu Refugees in Tanzania* (Chicago: University of Chicago Press).

Marano, Lou. 1982. "Windigo Psychosis: The Anatomy of an Emic-Etic Confusion," *Current Anthropology* 23, 4: 385–412.

McElroy, Ann, and Patricia K. Townsend. 1996. *Medical Anthropology in Ecological Perspective Boulder* (Colorado: Westview Press).

McGee Jr, Harold Franklin. 1972. "Windigo Psychosis," *American Anthropologist*, New Series, 74, 1–2: 244–6.

Menegoni, Lorenza. 1996. "Conceptions of Tuberculosis and Therapeutic Choices in Highland Chiapas, Mexico," *Medical Anthropology Quarterly* 10: 381–401.

Migliore, Sam. 2001. "From Illness Narratives to Social Commentary: A Pirandellian Approach to 'Nerves,'" *Medical Anthropology Quarterly* 15, 1: 100–25.

Mintz, Sidney W., and Christine M. Du Bois. 2002. "The Anthropology of Food and Eating," *Annual Review of Anthropology* 31: 99–119.

Mishra, Arima. 2013. "Special Issue on Anthropology and Public Health: An Introduction," *Indian Anthropologist* 43, 1: 1–15.

Nguyen, Vinh-Kim, and Karine Peschard. 2003. "Anthropology, Inequality, and Disease: A Review," *Annual Review of Anthropology* 32: 447–74.

Peritz, Ingrid. 2010. "Despite Being Legal, Abortions Still Not Accessible for All Canadians," *The Globe and Mail* (18 Jun.), available at www.theglobeandmail.com/news/national/despite-being-legal-abortions-still-not-accessible-for-all-canadians/-article1610254

PHAC (Public Health Agency of Canada). 2013. "At a Glance: HIV and AIDS in Canada: Surveillance Report to December 31st, 2012," available at www.phac-aspc.gc.ca/aids-sida/publication/survreport/2012/dec/index-eng.php.

Poirier, Sylvie, and Lorraine Brooke. 2000. "Inuit Perceptions of Contaminants and Environmental Knowledge in Salluit, Nunavik," *Arctic Anthropology* 37, 2: 78–91.

Press, Irwin. 1978. "Urban Folk Medicine: A Functional Overview," *American Anthropologist* 80, 1: 71–84.

Prince, Martin, Vikram Patel, Shekhar Saxena, Mario Maj, Joanna Maselko, Micheal R. Phillips, and Atif Rahman. 2007. "Global Mental Health 1: No Health without Mental Health," *The Lancet* 370, 9590: 859–77.

Röhricht, Frank, Sheila Butler, Herbert Grassmann, Joop Valstar, and Courtenay Young. 2014. "Clinical Roundup: Selected Treatment Options for Depression," Mary Ann Liebert, Inc., 20, 1, available from http://online.liebertpub.com/doi/pdf/10.1089/act.2014.20110

Ross, Kaz. 2010. "An 'Army of Bachelors'? China's Male Population as a World Threat," *Journal of Asia Pacific Studies* 1, 2: 338–63.

Roy, Srila. 2008. "The Grey Zone: The 'Ordinary' Violence of Extraordinary Times," *Journal of the Royal Anthropological Institute* 14, 2: 316–33.

Rylko-Bauer, Barbara, and Paul Farmer. 2002. "Managed Care or Managed Inequality? A Call for Critiques of Market-Based Medication," *Medical Anthropology Quarterly* 16, 4: 476–502.

———, Linda Whiteford, and Paul Farmer, eds. 2009. *Global Health in Times of Violence* (Santa Fe, NM: School for Advanced Research Press).

Sargent, Carolyn, and Grace Bascope. 1996. "Ways of Knowing about Birth in Three Cultures," *Medical Anthropology Quarterly* 10, 2: 213–36.

Shahar, Shulamith. 1990. *Childhood in the Middle Ages* (New York: Routledge).

Shahid, Shaouli, Ryan Bleam, Dawn Bessarab, and Sandra C. Thompson. 2010. "'If You Don't Believe It, It Won't Help You': Use of Bush Medicine in Treating Cancer among Aboriginal People in Western Australia," *Journal of Ethnobiological Medicine* 6: 18.

Shetty, Priya. 2011. "Rani and Abhay Bang—Pioneers of Health Care in Rural India," *The Lancet* 377: 9761. doi:10.1016/S0140-6736(11)60034-2

Singer, Merrill. 1995. "Beyond the Ivory Tower: Critical Praxis in Medical Anthropology," *Medical Anthropology Quarterly* 9, 1: 80–106.

Statistics Canada. 2011. *Aboriginal Peoples in Canada: First Nations People, Métis, and Inuit* (National Household Survey, 2011), available at www12.statcan.gc.ca/nhs-enm/2011/as-sa/99-011-x/99-011-x2011001-eng.pdf.

Suárez-Orozco, Marcelo M., and Antonius C.G.M. Robben, eds. 2000. "Interdisciplinary Perspectives on Violence and Trauma," in *Cultures under Siege: Collective Violence and Trauma* (Cambridge: Cambridge University Press), 1–41.

TRC (Truth and Reconciling Commission of Canada). 2015. *Honouring the Truth, Reconciling for the Future: Summary of the Final Report of the Truth and Reconciliation Commission of Canada.*

Trostle, James A., and Johannes Sommerfeld. 1996. "Medical Anthropology and Epidemiology," *Annual Review of Anthropology* 25: 253–74.

Turner, Victor. 1967. "Betwixt and Between: The Liminal Period in Rites de Passage," in *The Forest of Symbols* (Ithaca NY: Cornell University Press), 46–55.

UN (United Nations). 2014. *The Universal Declaration of Human Rights,* available at www.un.org/en/documents/udhr

———. 2017. *World Population Prospects: Key Findings and Advance Tables (2017 Revisions).* Department of Economic and Social Affairs, Population Division (New York: United Nations), available at https://esa.un.org/unpd/wpp/Publications/Files/WPP2017_KeyFindings.pdf.

UNHRC (The UN High Commissioner for Refugees). 2017. *The 1951 Refugee Convention,* available at www.unhcr.org/1951-refugee-convention.html.

UNICEF (United Nations Children's Fund). 2004. "Building Health and Hope for Soon-to-Be Mothers in Rural India," available at www.unicef.org/infobycountry/india_fight_mortality.html.

van der Geest, Sjaak. 2006. "New Release: Anthropology and the Pharmaceutical Nexus," *Anthropological Quarterly* 79, 2: 303–14.

van Esterik, Penny. 1985. "Confronting Advocacy Confronting Anthropology," in *Advocacy and Anthropology,* ed. Robert Paine (St John's: Institute of Social and Economic Research).

———. 2002. "Contemporary Trends in Infant Feeding Research," *Annual Review of Anthropology* 31: 257–78.

Walker, Marilyn. 2003. "Music as Knowledge in Shamanism and Other Healing Traditions of Siberia," *Arctic Anthropology* 40, 2: 40–8.

Whiteford, Linda. 2009. "Failure to Protect, Failure to Provide: Refugee Reproduction Rights," in *Global Health in Times of Violence,* ed. Barbara Rylko-Bauer, Linda Whiteford, and Paul Farmer (Santa Fe, NM: School for Advanced Research Press), 89–112.

WHO (World Health Organization). 2003a. "Summary Table of SARS Cases by Country, 1 November 2002–7 August 2003," available at www.who.int/csr/sars/-country/2003_08_15/en/index.html.

———. 2003b. "Climate Change and Human Health," in *Climate Change and Human Health,* available at www.who.int/globalchange/climate/summary/en/index5.html

———. 2014a. "WHO–UN AIDS HIV Vaccine Initiative," available at www.who.int/immunization/research/forums_and_initiatives/HIV_vaccine_initiative/en

———. 2014b. "Women's Health," available at www.who.int/mediacentre/factsheets/fs334/en

———. 2014c. "Malaria," available at www.who.int/mediacentre/factsheets/fs094/en.

———. 2014d. *Mental Health Atlas, 2014* (Geneva: WHO Press), available at http://apps.who.int/iris/bitstream/10665/178879/1/9789241565011_eng.pdf

WHO. 2017. Global Health Observatory (GHO) data on Life Expectancy. Accessed at: http://www.who.int/gho/mortality_burden_disease/life_tables/situation_trends/en/

Wilson, Monica. 1951. "Witch Beliefs and Social Structure," *American Journal of Sociology* LVI, 4: 307–13 (Oxford: Oxford University Press).

Young, Allan. 1976. "Some Implications of Medical Beliefs and Practices for Social Anthropology," *American Anthropologist* 78, 1: 5–24.

Young, Meredith E., Geoffrey R. Norman, and Karin R. Humphreys. 2008. "The Role of Medical Language in Changing Public Perception of Illness," *PLoS One.* doi:10.1371/journal.pone.0003875

Zhou, Yingying. 2005. "Uncovering Children in Marginalization: Explaining Unregistered Children in China," paper prepared for the International Union for the Scientific Study of Population's General Conference (Tours, France), available at http://iussp2005.princeton.edu/download.aspx?submissionId=50479.

Zuckerhut, Patricia. 2011. "Feminist Anthropological Perspectives on Violence," *Gender and Violence in the Middle East,* ed. Moha Ennaji and Fatima Sadiqi (New York: Routledge): 13–25.

Chapter 11

Asad, Talal. 2003. *Formations of the Secular: Christianity, Islam, Modernity* (Palo Alto, CA: Stanford University Press).

Bowen, John. 2002. *Religions in Practice: An Approach to the Anthropology of Religion,* 2nd edn (Needham Heights, MA: Allyn and Bacon).

———. 2010. *Can Islam be French? Pluralism and Pragmatism in a Secularist State* (Princeton, NJ: Princeton University Press).

———. 2014. *Religions in Practice: An Approach to the Anthropology of Religion,* 6th edn (Needham Heights, MA: Allyn & Bacon).

Boyer, Pascal, and Brian Bergstrom. 2008. "Evolutionary Perspectives on Religion," *Annual Review of Anthropology* 37: 111–30.

Clark, Warren. 2000. "Patterns of Religious Attendance," *Canadian Social Trends,* available at www.statcan.gc.ca/pub/11-008-x/2000003/article/5389-eng.pdf.

——— and Grant Schellenberg. 2006. "Who's Religious?" *Canadian Social Trends,* available at www.statcan.gc.ca/pub/11-008-x/2006001/pdf/9181-eng.pdf.

Cook, Garrett, and Thomas Offit. 2008. "Pluralism and Transculturation in Indigenous Maya Religion," *Ethnology* 47, 1: 45–59.

Daugman, John. 2001. "Brain Metaphor and Brain Theory," in *Philosophy and the Neurosciences,* ed. William Bechtel et al. (Oxford: Blackwell Publishers).

Dods, Roberta Robin.

———. 2007. "Intersubjectivity and the Meaning of Things," *International Journal of the Humanities* 4, 9: 99.

Eagle, David E. 2011. "Changing Patterns of Attendance at Religious Services in Canada, 1986–2008," *Journal for the Scientific Study of Religion* 50: 187–200.

Evans-Pritchard, E.E. 1976 [1937]. *Witchcraft, Oracles, and Magic among the Azande,* abr. edn (Oxford: Oxford University Press).

Fernandez, James W. 1977. "The Performance of Ritual Metaphors," in *The Social Use of Metaphors,* ed. J.D. Sapir and J.C. Crocker (Philadelphia: University of Pennsylvania Press).

———. 1982. *Bwiti: An Ethnography of the Religious Imagination in Africa* (Princeton: Princeton University Press).

Floating in the Air, Followed by the Wind. 1973. Film distributed by Indiana University Instructional Support Services. Produced by Michigan State University.

Goh, Daniel P.S. 2010. "State and Social Christianity in Post-colonial Singapore," *Sojourn: Journal of Social Issues in Southeast Asia* 25, 1: 54–89.

Gose, Peter. 1991. "House Re-thatching in an Andean Annual Cycle: Practice, Meaning, and Contradiction," *American Ethnologist* 18, 1: 38, 57.

Gregory, Joseph, compiler. 1999. "World Briefing," *New York Times* (22 Oct.).

Haynes, Naomi. 2012. "Pentecostalism and the Morality of Money: Prosperity, Inequality, and Religious Sociality on the Zambian Copperbelt," *Journal of the Royal Anthropological Institute* 18, 1: 123–39.

Horton, Robin. 1982. "Tradition and Modernity Revisited," in *Rationality and Relativism*, ed. M. Hollis and Steven Lukes (Cambridge, MA: MIT Press), 201–60.

Keesing, Roger. 1982. *Kwaio Religion* (New York: Columbia University Press).

———. 1992. *Custom and Confrontation: The Kwaio Struggle for Cultural Autonomy* (Chicago: University of Chicago Press).

Keller, Evelyn Fox. 1997. "Secrets of God, Nature, and Life," in *The Gender/Sexuality Reader*, ed. Roger Lancaster and Micaela di Leonardo (New York: Routledge), 209–18.

Kemper, Robert V., and Julie Adkins. 2006. "Who Are My Neighbours? Congregation and Community in North Texas," *Urban Anthropology* 35, 2–3: 295–339.

Lakoff, George, and Mark Johnson. 1980. *Metaphors We Live By* (Berkeley: University of California Press).

Lewontin, Richard, Steven Rose, and Leon J. Kamin. 1984. *Not in Our Genes* (New York: Pantheon).

Myerhoff, Barbara. 1974. *Peyote Hunt* (Ithaca, NY: Cornell University Press).

Ortner, Sherry. 1973. "On Key Symbols," *American Anthropologist* 75, 5: 1338–46.

Sahlins, Marshall. 1976. *The Use and Abuse of Biology* (Ann Arbor: University of Michigan Press).

———. 1990. *Domination and the Arts of Resistance: Hidden Transcripts* (New Haven: Yale University Press).

Smith, Alex Duval. 2004. "France Divided as Headscarf Ban Is Set to Become Law," *The Observer* (1 Feb.).

Stewart, Charles, and Rosalind Shaw. 1994. *Syncretism/Anti-syncretism* (London: Routledge).

Tedlock, Barbara. 2005. *The Woman in the Shaman's Body: Reclaiming the Feminine in Religion and Medicine* (New York: Random House).

Wallace, Anthony F.C. 1966. *Religion: An Anthropological View* (New York: Random House).

———. 1972. *The Death and Rebirth of the Seneca* (New York: Vintage).

Chapter 12

Alverson, Hoyt. 1977. "Peace Corps Volunteers in Rural Botswana," *Human Organization* 36, 3: 274–81.

———. 1978. *Mind in the Heart of Darkness* (New Haven: Yale University Press).

Adams, Richard Newbold. 1979. *Energy and Structure: A Theory of Social Power* (Austin: University of Texas Press).

Amnesty International. 2013. "Sri Lanka Human Rights," available at www.amnestyusa.org/our-work/countries/asia-and-the-pacific/sri-lanka.

Clastres, Pierre. 1977. *Society against the State*, trans. Robert Hurley (New York: Urizen Books).

Colson, Elizabeth. 1977. "Power at Large: Meditation on 'The Symposium on Power,'" in *The Anthropology of Power: Ethnographic Studies from Asia, Oceania, and the New World*, ed. R. Fogelson and R.N. Adams (New York: Academic Press), 375–86.

Connell, R.W. 2005. "Change among the Gatekeepers: Men, Masculinities, and Gender Equality in the Global Arena," *Signs* 30, 3: 1801–25.

Daniel, E. Valentine. 1997. "Suffering Nation and Alienation," in *Social Suffering*, ed. Arthur Kleinman, Veena Das, and Margaret Lock (Berkeley: University of California Press), 309–58.

Danner, Mark. 1994. *The Massacre at El Mozote* (New York: Vintage).

Feinman, Gary M., Kent G. Lightfoot, and Steadman Upham. 2000. "Political Hierarchies and Organizational Strategies in the Puebloan Southwest," *American Antiquity* 65, 3: 449–70.

Folman, Ari. 2008. *Waltz with Bashir* (Culver City, CA: Sony Pictures Classics).

Foucault, Michel. 1991. "Governmentality," in *The Foucault Effect: Studies in Governmentality*, ed. Graham Burchell, Colin Gordon, and Peter Miller (Chicago: University of Chicago Press), 87–104.

Giddens, Anthony. 1979. *Central Problems in Social Theory* (Berkeley: University of California Press).

Gledhill, John. 1994. *Power and Its Disguises* (London: Pluto Press).

Gordon, Colin. 1991. "Governmental Rationality: An Introduction," in *The Foucault Effect: Studies in Governmentality*, ed. Graham Burchell, Colin Gordon, and Peter Miller (Chicago: University of Chicago Press), 1–52.

Gottlieb, Alma. 1989. "Witches, Kings, and the Sacrifice of Identity, or the Power of Paradox and the Paradox of Power among the Beng of Ivory Coast," in *Creativity of Power: Cosmology and Action in African Societies*, ed. W. Arens and Ivan Karp (Washington, DC: Smithsonian Institution Press), 245–72.

Gramsci, Antonio. (1971). *Selections from the Prison Notebooks* (New York: International Publishers).

Green, Joyce. 2001. "Canaries in the Mines of Citizenship: Indian Women in Canada," *Canadian Journal of Political Science* 34, 4: 736–8.

Hacking, Ian. 1991. "How Should We Do the History of Statistics?" in *The Foucault Effect: Studies in Governmentality*, ed. Graham Burchell, Colin Gordon, and Peter Miller (Chicago: University of Chicago Press), 181–96.

Indrapala, K. 2007. *The Evolution of Ethnic Identity: The Tamils of Sri Lanka* (Colombo: Vijitha Yapa).

Lee, Richard B. 1992a. "Art, Science, or Politics? The Crisis in Hunter-Gatherer Studies," *American Anthropologist* 94: 31–54.

Lewellen, Ted. 1983. *Political Anthropology: An Introduction.* (South Hadley, MA: Bergin and Garvey).

Lewis, I.M. 1967. *A Pastoral Democracy: A Study of Pastoralism and Politics among the Northern Somali of the Horn of Africa* (London: Oxford University Press).

Macdonald, Gaynor. 2010. "Colonizing Processes, the Reach of the State and Ontological Violence: Historicizing Aboriginal Australian Experience," *Anthropologica* 52, 1: 49–66.

Maguire, Mark. 2009. "The Birth of Biometric Security," *Anthropology Today* 25, 2: 9–15.

Morgan, Lewis Henry. 1871. *Systems of Consanguinity and Affinity of the Human Family* (Washington: Smithsonian Institution).

———. 1877. *Ancient Society.* (New York: Henry Holt and Company).

Nash, June. 1979. *We Eat the Mines, and the Mines Eat Us* (New York: Columbia University Press).

Nye, Robert A. 2005. "Locating Masculinity: Some Recent Work on Men," *Signs* 30, 3: 1937–62.

Rosen, Lawrence. 1984. *Bargaining for Reality: The Constructions of Social Relations in a Muslim Community* (Chicago: University of Chicago Press).

Sahlins, Marshall. 1976. *Culture and Practical Reason* (Chicago: University of Chicago Press).

Scott, James C. 1985. *Weapons of the Weak* (New Haven: Yale University Press).

———. 1990. *Domination and the Arts of Resistance: Hidden Transcripts* (New Haven: Yale University Press).

Spencer, Jonathan. 2000. "On Not Becoming a 'Terrorist': Problems of Memory, Agency, and Community in the Sri Lankan Conflict," in *Violence and Subjectivity*, ed. Veena Das, Arthur Kleinman, Mamphela Ramphele, and Pamela Reynolds (Berkeley: University of California Press), 120–40.

Starn, Orin. 1992. "'I Dreamed of Foxes and Hawks': Reflections on Peasant Protest, New Social Movements, and the Rondas Campesinas of Northern Peru," in *The Making of Social Movements in Latin America: Identity, Strategy, and Democracy*, ed. Arturo Escobar and Sonia E. Alvarez, Series in Political Economy and Economic Development in Latin America (Boulder, CO: Westview Press), 89–111.

Trawick, Margaret. 2002. "Reasons for Violence: A Preliminary Ethnographic Account of the LTTE," in *Conflict and Community in Contemporary Sri Lanka*, ed. Siri Gamage and I.B. Watson (Thousand Oaks, CA: Sage).

VeneKlasen, Lisa, and Valerie Miller. 2002. *A New Weave of Power, People, and Politics: The Action Guide for Advocacy and Citizen Participation* (Oklahoma: World Neighbors).

Vincent, Joan, ed. 2002. "Introduction," in *The Anthropology of Politics* (Malden, MA: Blackwell), 1–13.

Wagner, John. 2009. "Water as Commodity in the Okanagan Valley of British Columbia," guest editorial in *Cultural Anthropology: A Perspective on the Human Condition,* 1st Canadian edn, Emily Schultz, Robert Lavenda, and Roberta Robin Dods, 190 -1.

Wallerstein, Immanuel. 1974. *The Modern World System* (New York: Academic Press).

Winn, Peter. 1992. *Americas* (New York: Pantheon).

Wolf, Eric. 1999. *Envisioning Power: Ideologies of Dominance and Crisis* (Berkeley: University of California Press).

Woost, Micheal D. 1993. "Nationalizing the Local Past in Sri Lanka: Histories of Nation and Development in a Sinhalese Village," *American Ethnologist* 20, 3: 502–21.

Chapter 13

Abbas, Ackbar. 2002. "Cosmopolitan Description: Shanghai and Hong Kong," in *Cosmopolitanism*, ed. Carol A. Breckenridge et al. (Durham, NC: Duke University Press), 209–28.

Abrahamian, Atossa Araxia. 2015. "The Cosmopolites: The Coming of the Global Citizen," *Columbia Global Reports.*

Amazon Watch. 2014. "Brazil's Belo Monte Dam: Sacrificing the Amazon and Its Peoples for Dirty Energy," available at http://amazonwatch.org/work/belo-monte-dam.

Anderson, Benedict. 2002 [1992]. "The New World Disorder," in *The Anthropology of Politics*, ed. Joan Vincent (Malden, MA: Blackwell), 261–70.

Appadurai, Arjun. 1990. "Disjuncture and Difference in the Global Cultural Economy," in *Global Culture,* ed. Mike Featherstone (London: Sage), 295–310.

Bestor, Theodore. 2005. "How Sushi Went Global," in *The Cultural Politics of Food and Eating: A Reader*, ed. James L. Watson and Melissa L. Caldwell (Malden, MA: Blackwell), 13–20.

Birth, Kevin. 2007. "Time and the Biological Consequences of Globalization," *Current Anthropology* 48, 2: 215–36.

Breckenridge, Carol A., et al. 2002. "Cosmopolitanisms," in *Cosmopolitanism* (Durham, NC: Duke University Press), 1–14.

Bryan, Catherine. 2012. "Gendered Returns, Ambivalent Transnationals: Situating Transnationalism in Local Asymmetry," *Anthropologica* 54, 1: 133–42.

Clarke, John. 2004. *Changing Welfare, Changing States: New Directions in Social Policy* (London: Sage).

Colloredo-Mansfeld, Rudi. 1999. *The Native Leisure Class: Consumption and Cultural Creativity in the Andes* (Chicago: University of Chicago Press).

Cowan, Jane, Marie-Bénédicte Dembour, and Richard A. Wilson, eds. 2001. "Introduction," in *Culture and Rights: Anthropological Perspectives* (Cambridge: Cambridge University Press), 1–26.

Cox, Susan., Sarah. Drew, Marilys. Guillemin, Catherine. Howell, Deborah. Warr, and Jenny. Waycott. (2014). *Guidelines for Ethical Visual Research Methods* (Melbourne: The University of Melbourne), available at https://artshealthnetwork.ca/resources/guidelines-ethical-visual-research-methods

Culhane, Dara. 2011. "Stories and Plays: Ethnography, Performance, and Ethical Engagements," *Anthropologica* 53, 2: 257–74.

Edmonds, Alexander. 2007. "The Poor Have the Right to Be Beautiful: Cosmetic Surgery in Neoliberal Brazil," *Journal of the Royal Anthropological Institute* 13, 2: 363–81.

Escobar, Arturo. 1992. "Culture, Economics, and Politics in Latin American Social Movements Theory and Research," in *The Making of Social Movements in Latin America*, ed. Arturo Escobar and Sonia Alvarez (Boulder, CO: Westview Press), 62–85.

Ferguson, James. 2002. "The Anti-Politics Machine," in *The Anthropology of Politics*, ed. Joan Vincent (Malden, MA: Blackwell), 399–408.

Friedman, Jonathon. 1994. *Cultural Identity and Global Process* (London: Sage).

———. 1997. "Global Crises, the Struggle for Cultural Identity, and Intellectual Porkbarrelling: Cosmopolitans versus Locals, Ethnics, and Nationals in an Era of Dehegemonisation," in *Debating Cultural Hybridity: Multicultural Identities and the Politics of Anti-racism,* ed. Pnina Werbner and Tariq Modood (London: Zed Books), 70–89.

Frosh, Raul. 2003. "Digital Technology and Stock Photography: And God Created Photoshop," in *Image Ethics in the Digital Age*, ed. Larry Gross, John Stuart Katz, and Jay Ruby (Minneapolis, MN: University of Minnesota Press).

Ginsburg, Faye D., and Rayna Rapp, eds. 1995. *Conceiving the New World Order: The Global Politics of Reproduction* (Berkeley: University of California Press).

Gledhill, John. 2001. "'Disappearing the Poor?': A Critique of the New Wisdoms of Social Democracy in an Age of Globalization," *Urban Anthropology and Studies of Cultural Systems and World Economic Development* 30, 2–3: 123–56.

Harney, Nicholas. 2002. "Building Italian Regional Identity in Toronto: Using Space to Make Culture Material," *Anthropologica* 44, 1: 43–54.

Harrison, Faye. 2004. "Global Apartheid, Environmental Degradation, and Women's Activism for Sustainable Well-Being: A Conceptual and Theoretical Overview," *Urban Anthropology* 33, 1: 1–35.

High, Steven. 2013. "Embodied Ways of Listening: Oral History, Genocide and the Audio Tour," *Anthropologica* 55, 1: 73–85.

Holtzman, Jon D. 2006. "Food and Memory," *Annual Review of Anthropology* 35: 361–78.

Horst, Heather A., and Daniel Miller. 2006. *The Cell Phone: An Anthropology of Communication* (Oxford: Berg).

Hutnyk, John. 1997. "Adorno at Womad: South Asian Crossovers and the Limits of Hybridity-talk," in *Debating Cultural Hybridity: Multicultural Identities and the Politics of Anti-racism*, ed. Pnina Werbner and Tariq Modood (London: Zed Books), 106–36.

Inda, Jonathan Xavier, and Renato Rosaldo, eds. 2002. "Introduction: A World in Motion," in *The Anthropology of Globalization* (Malden, MA: Blackwell).

Kearney, M. 1995. "The Local and the Global: The Anthropology of Globalization and Transnationalism," *Annual Review of Anthropology* 24: 547–65.

Levin, Michael D. 2002. "Flow and Place: Transnationalism in Four Cases," *Anthropologica* 44, 1: 3–12.

Merry, Sally Engle. 2001. "Changing Rights, Changing Culture," in *Culture and Rights: Anthropological Perspectives*, ed. Jane Cowan, Marie-Bénédicte Dembour, and Richard A. Wilson (Cambridge: Cambridge University Press), 31–55.

Mignolo, Walter D. 2002. "The Many Faces of Cosmopolis: Border Thinking and Critical Cosmopolitanism," in *Cosmopolitanism*, ed. Carol A. Breckenridge et al. (Durham, NC: Duke University Press), 157–87.

Montgomery, Heather. 2001. "Imposing Rights? A Case Study of Child Prostitution in Thailand," in *Culture and Rights: Anthropological Perspectives*, ed. Jane Cowan, Marie-Bénédicte Dembour, and Richard A. Wilson (Cambridge: Cambridge University Press), 80–101.

Mukhopadhyay, Bhaskar. 2005. "The Rumour of Globalization: Globalism, Counterworks, and the Location of Commodity," *Dialectical Anthropology* 29, 1: 35–60.

Nordstrom, Carolyn. 2008. "Global Fractures," *Social Analysis: The International Journal of Social and Cultural Practice* 52, 2: 71–86.

Odede, Kennedy. 2010. "Slumdog Tourism," *New York Times* (9 Aug.).

Ong, Aihwa. 2002 [1999]. "The Pacific Shuttle: Family, Citizenship, and Capital Circuits," in *The Anthropology of Globalization*, ed. Jonathan Xavier Inda and Renato Rosaldo (Malden, MA: Blackwell), 172–97.

Oxfam. 2016. "An Economy for the 1%," available at www.oxfam.org/sites/www.oxfam.org/files/file_attachments/bp210-economy-one-percent-tax-havens-180116-en_0.pdf.

Peoples, James. 1978. "Dependence in a Micronesian Economy," *American Ethnologist* 5, 3: 535–52.

Portland Museum. 2016. "Contemporary Native Photographers and the Edward Curtis Legacy," available at https://portlandartmuseum.org/exhibitions/contemporary-native-photographers/.

Rabben, Linda. 1999. *Unnatural Selection: The Yanomami, the Kayapó and the Onslaught of Civilization* (London: Pluto Press).

Richardson, Boyce, and Jasmin Habib. 2013. "Boyce Richardson: Reflections on Journalism, Activism and Filmmaking among the Crees of Northern Quebec," *Anthropologica* 55, 1: 211–18.

Schiller, Nina Glick, and Georges Fouron. 2002. "Long-distance Nationalism Defined," in *The Anthropology of Politics,* ed. Joan Vincent (Malden, MA: Blackwell), 356–65.

Smart, Alan. 1999. "Expressions of Interest: Friendship and Guanzi in Chinese Societies," in *The Anthropology of Friendship*, ed. Sandra Bell and Simon Coleman (Oxford: Berg), 119–36.

Sontag, Susan. 2003. *Regarding the Pain of Others* (New York: Farrar, Straus & Giroux).

Terrio, Susan J. 1996. "Crafting Grand Cra Chocolates in Contemporary France," *American Anthropologist* 98, 1: 67–79.

Turner, Terence. 1989. "Amazonian Indians Fight to Save Their Forest," *Anthropology Newsletter* 30, 3: 21–2.

Union of BC Indian Chiefs. 2008. "First Nations Pressure Canada to Endorse the UN Declaration on the Rights of Indigenous Peoples" (12 Sept.), available at www.ubcic.bc.ca/News_Releases/UBCICNews09120801.htm.

van der Veer, Peter. 1997. "'The Enigma of Arrival': Hybridity and Authenticity in the Global Space," in *Debating Cultural Hybridity: Multicultural Identities and the Politics of Anti-racism*, ed. Pnina Werbner and Tariq Modood (London: Zed Books), 90–195.

Wallerstein, Immanuel. 1974. *The Modern World System* (New York: Academic Press).

Werbner, Pnina. 1997. "Afterword: Writing Multiculturalism and Politics in the New Europe," in *The Politics of Multiculturalism in the New Europe: Racism, Identity, and Community*, ed. Tariq Modood and Pnina Werbner (London: Zed Books), 261–7.

Yuval-Davis, Nira. 1997. "Ethnicity, Gender Relations, and Multiculturalism," in *Debating Cultural Hybridity: Multicultural Identities and the Politics of Anti-racism*, ed. Pnina Werbner and Tariq Modood (London: Zed Books), 193–208.

Chapter 14

AMS (Association of Muslim Schools). 2014. "FAQ," available at http://ams-uk.org/faq.

Canadian Multiculturalism Act (R.S.C., 1985, c. 24 (4th Supp.)), Preamble. Accessed at: http://laws-lois.justice.gc.ca/PDF/C-18.7.pdf

Checker, Melissa. 2009. "Anthropology in the Public Sphere, 2008: Emerging Trends and Significant Impacts," *American Anthropologist, New Series*, 111, 2: 162–9.

Dembour, Marie. 2001. "Following the Movement of a Pendulum: Between Universalism and Relativism," in *Culture and Rights: Anthropological Perspectives* (Cambridge: Cambridge University Press), 56–79.

Eriksen, Thomas Hylland. 2001. "Between Universalism and Relativism: A Critique of the UNESCO Concept of Culture," in *Culture and Rights: Anthropological Perspectives*, ed. Jane Cowan, Marie-Bénédicte Dembour, and Richard A. Wilson (Cambridge: Cambridge University Press), 127–48.

Ervin, Alexander M. 1996. "Collaborative and Participatory Research in Urban Social Planning and Restructuring: Anthropological Experiences from a Medium-sized Canadian City," *Human Organization* 55, 3: 324–33.

Godelier, Maurice. 2010. "In Today's World, Anthropology Is More Important than Ever," *Paideuma* 56: 205–20.

Hall, Edward T. 1959. *The Silent Language* (New York: Doubleday).

———. 1966. *The Hidden Dimension* (New York: Doubleday).

———. 1976. *Beyond Culture* (New York: Anchor Press).

———. 1983. *The Dance of Life: The Other Dimensions of Time* (New York: Doubleday).

———, and Mildred Reed Hall. 1987. *Hidden Differences: Doing Business with the Japanese* (New York: Anchor Press).

Herzfeld, Michael. 2003. "Competing Diversities: Ethnography in the Heart of Rome," *Plurimundi* 3, 5: 147–54.

———. 2013. "Interview with Michael Herzfeld," *Romeing* (16 Apr.), available at www.romeing.it/interview-with-michael-herzfeld-author-of-evicted-from-eternity-the-restructuring-of-modern-rome.

"Homes for the Smallpox Virus." 2011. Editorial in *The Globe and Mail* (19 Jan.), available at www.theglobeandmail.com/news/opinions/editorials/homes-for-the-smallpox-virus/article1876412/.

Huyghe, Patrick. 1988. "Profile of an Anthropologist: No Bone Unturned," *Discover* (Dec.), 51–6.

Johnston, Barbara Rose. 2010. "Social Responsibility and the Anthropological Citizen," *Current Anthropology* 51, S2 (Volume Supplement).

Kaku, Michio. 2014. *The Future of the Mind* (New York: Doubleday).

Krautwurst, Udo. 2014. *Culturing Bioscience: A Case Study in the Anthropology of Science* (Toronto: University of Toronto Press).

Lassiter, Luke Eric. 2005. "Collaborative Ethnography and Public Anthropology," *Current Anthropology* 46, 1: 83–106.

Lock, Margaret, Veena Das, Arthur Kleinman, Mamphela Ramphele, and Pamela Reynolds, eds. 2001. *Remaking a World: Violence, Social Suffering, and Recovery* (Berkeley: University of California Press).

Marcus, George. 1990. "Into the Warp and Woof of Multicultural Worlds," guest editorial in *Cultural Anthropology: A Perspective on the Human Condition*, 2nd edn, ed. Emily Schultz and Robert Lavenda (St Paul: West), 254–5.

Melotti, Umberto. 1997. "International Migration in Europe: Social Projects and Political Cultures," in *The Politics of Multiculturalism in the New Europe: Racism, Identity and Community*, ed. Tariq Modood and Pnina Werbner (London: Zed Books), 73–92.

Messer, Ellen. 1993. "Anthropology and Human Rights," *Annual Review of Anthropology* 22: 221–49.

Modood, Tariq., 1997. "10 Conclusions: Ethnic Diversity and Disadvantage, in *The Fourth National Survey of Ethnic Minorities: Ethnic Minorities in Britain, Diversity and Disadvantage* (London: Policy Studies Institute), 339–59.

Mullins, Paul R. 2010. "Practising Anthropology: Practising Anthropology and the Politics of Engagements: 2010 Year in Review," *American Anthropologist, New Series*, 113, 2: 235–45.

Niemeier, Susanne, Charles P. Campbell, and Rene Dirven, eds. 1998. *The Cultural Context in Business Communication* (Philadelphia: John Benjamin Publishing).

Noble, Brian. 2015. "Tripped up by Coloniality: Anthropologists as Instruments or Agents in Indigenous–Settler Political Relations?" *Anthropologica* 57, 2: 427–43.

Oldham, Paul, and Miriam Anne Frank. 2008. "'We the peoples…': The United Nations Declaration on the Rights of Indigenous Peoples," *Anthropology Today* 24, 2: 5–9.

Omohundro, John. 2000. "What Can You Learn from an Anthropology Major?" in *Careers in Anthropology* (New York: McGraw-Hill).

Quijano, Anibal. 2000. "Coloniality of Power, Eurocentrism, and Latin America," in *Nepantla: Views from the South* 1.3: 533–80.

Reeves-Ellington, Richard H. 1993. "Using Cultural Skills for Co-operative Advantage in Japan," *Human Organization* 52, 2: 203–16.

———. 2009. "Enviroscapes: A Multi-level Contextual Approach to Organizational Leader-ship," in *Multi-Level Issues in Organizational Behavior and Leadership (Research in Multi-level Issues*, Volume 8), ed. Francis J. Yammarino and Fred Dansereau (Bringley, UK: Emerald Group Publishing Limited), 337–420.

Schiffauer, Werner. 1997. "Islam as a Civil Religion: Political Culture and the Organization of Diversity in Germany," in *The Politics of Multiculturalism in the New Europe: Racism, Identity, and Community*, ed. Tariq Modood and Pnina Werbner (London: Zed Books), 147–66.

Smith, J.J. (2015). "Standing with Sol: The spirit and intent of action anthropology," *Anthropologica* 57: 445–56.

Tcherkézoff, Serge. 1998. "Is Aristocracy Good for Democracy? A Contemporary Debate in Western Samoa," in *Pacific Answers to Western Hegemony: Cultural Practices of Identity Construction*, ed. Jürg Wassmann (Oxford: Berg), 417–34.

Waldram, James B. 2010. "Engaging Engagement: Critical Reflections on a Canadian Tradition," *Anthropologica* 52, 2: 225–32.

Wardlow, Holly. 2007. "Men's Extramarital Sexuality in Rural Papua New Guinea," *American Journal of Public Health* 97, 6: 1006–14.

Credits

Index